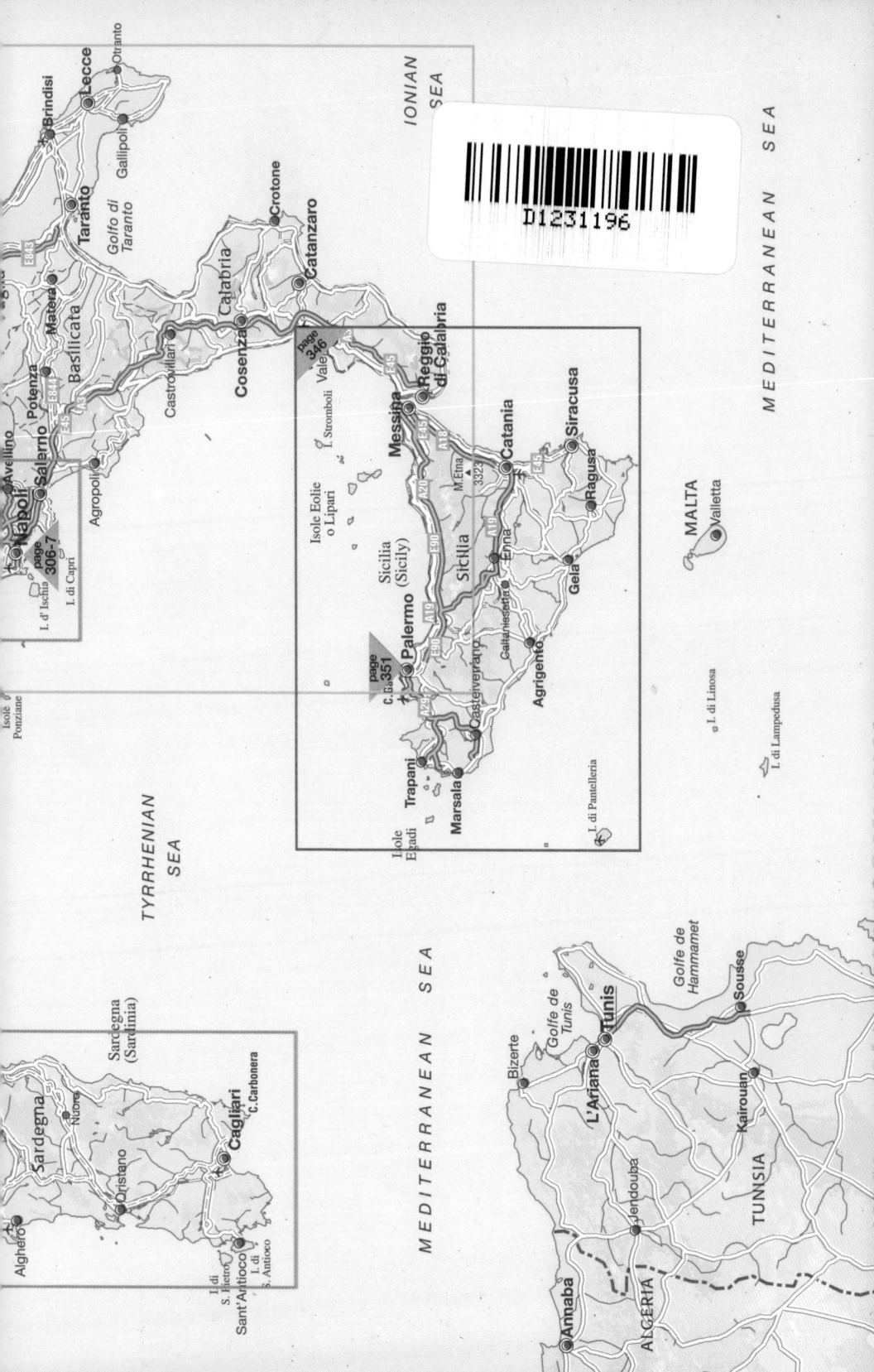

INSIGHT GUIDE

ITALY

Discovery CHANNEL

APA PUBLICATIONS

Part of the Langenscheidt Publishing Group

INSIGHT GUIDE

ITALY

ABOUT THIS BOOK

Editorial
Project Editor
Emily Hatchwell
Series Editor
Dorothy Stannardl

Distribution
UK & Ireland
GeoCenter International Ltd
Meridian House, Churchill Way West
Basingstoke, Hampshire RG21 6YR
Fax: (44) 1256 817988

United States
Langenscheidt Publishers, Inc.
36–36 33rd Street, 4th Floor
Long Island City, NY 11106
Fax: 1 (718) 784 0640

Australia
Universal Publishers
1 Waterloo Road
Macquarie Park, NSW 2113
Fax: (61) 2 9888 9074

New Zealand
Hema Maps New Zealand Ltd (HNZ)
Unit D, 24 Ra ORA Drive
East Tamaki, Auckland
Fax: (64) 9 273 6479

Worldwide
Apa Publications GmbH & Co.
Verlag KG (Singapore branch)
38 Joo Koon Road, Singapore 628990
Tel: (65) 6865 1600. Fax: (65) 6861 6438

Printing
Insight Print Services (Pte) Ltd
38 Joo Koon Road, Singapore 628990
Tel: (65) 6865 1600. Fax: (65) 6861 6438

©2009 Apa Publications GmbH & Co.
Verlag KG (Singapore branch)
All Rights Reserved
First Edition 1985
Fifth Edition 2007
Revised 2008

CONTACTING THE EDITORS
We would appreciate it if readers
would alert us to errors or outdated
information by writing to:
**Insight Guides, P.O. Box 7910,
London SE1 1WE, England.
Fax: (44) 20 7403 0290.
insight@apaguide.co.uk**
NO part of this book may be reproduced,
stored in a retrieval system or transmitted
in any form or means electronic, mechanical, photocopying, recording or otherwise, without prior written permission of
Apa Publications. Brief text quotations
with use of photographs are exempted
for book review purposes only. Information has been obtained from sources
believed to be reliable, but its accuracy
and completeness, and the opinions
based thereon, are not guaranteed.

www.insightguides.com

The first Insight Guide pioneered the use of creative full-colour photography in travel guides in 1970. Since then, we have expanded our range to cater for our readers' need not only for reliable information about what to see and what to do in their chosen destination but also for a real understanding of the culture and workings of that destination.

Now, when the internet can supply inexhaustible (but not always reliable) facts, our books carefully marry text and pictures to provide those much more elusive qualities: knowledge and discernment. To achieve this, they rely heavily on the authority and experience of a team of locally based writers and photographers.

How to use this book

Insight Guides has a proven formula of informative and well-written text paired with a fresh photojournalistic approach. The books are carefully structured, both to convey a good understanding of each place and its culture, and to guide readers through its myriad attractions:

◆ The first section, headed by a yellow colour bar, covers Italy's rich **history** and its colourful modern **culture** in authoritative **features** written by established experts.

Above: Venice's Piazza San Marco

◆ The main **Places** section, with a blue bar, provides a run-down of all the places worth seeing. Places of major interest are cross-referenced by numbers or letters to specially drawn maps.

◆ The **Travel Tips** section at the back of the book provides recommendations on hotels and restaurants, as well as an Italian phrasebook, with a menu reader. Information may be located quickly by using the index on the back cover flap.

The contributors

This is the fifth edition of *Insight Guide: Italy*. To help make a good book even better, managing editor **Cathy Muscat** enlisted the expertise of Italy specialist and Insight regular **Lisa Gerard-Sharp** who contributed many new features covering all aspects of Italy and Italian life. She paints a candid portrait of the country in *Contemporary Italy* and gets beneath the skin of its people in *The Italians*. An overview of the country's great natural beauty is given in *Wild Places* while *The Italian Look* gives the lowdown on fashion and design.

On the ground, **Adele Evans** revised the chapters on Northern and Central Italy, Rome was covered by **Natasha Foges** and Southern Italy and Sicily by **Marc Zakian**.

This current edition builds on the work of contributors to previous editions, including all-round Italian experts **Christopher Catling** and **Lisa Gerard-Sharp**, wine writers **James Ainsworth** and **Margaret Rand**. The original essay on the Mafia, penned by **Bruce Johnston**, was revised for this edition by Lisa Gerard-Sharp. **Susie Boulton** contributed the sections on Venice and **Fred Mawer** authored the Sardinia chapter. Other contributors to the original guide included **Claudia Angeletti, Katherine Barrett, Kathleen Beckett, Melanie Menagh, Clare McHugh, George Prochnik, Alberto Rossatti, Peter Spiro, Nicky Swallow, Benjamin Swett, Jacob Young**.

Like all Insight Guides, this book also owes a lot to its photographs, many of which are by **John Heseltine**, **Bill Wassman**, **Anna Mockford** and **Nick Bonetti**.

Insight editor, **Paula Soper,** put this edition together and it was proofread by **Neil Titman** and indexed by **Helen Peters**.

Map Legend

— ·· —	International Boundary
— — —	Region Boundary
⊖	Border Crossing
— · — · —	National Park/Reserve
— — —	Ferry Route
Ⓜ	Metro
✈	Airport
🚌	Bus Station
Ⓟ	Parking
❶	Tourist Information
✉	Post Office
†	Church/Ruins
	Mosque
✡	Synagogue
	Castle/Ruins
∴	Archaeological Site
∩	Cave
𝟙	Statue/Monument
★	Place of Interest

Places of interest in the **Places** section are cross-referenced to maps by number (e.g. ❶). A symbol at the top of each right-hand page tells you where to find the relevant map.

INSIGHT GUIDE
ITALY

CONTENTS

Portofino
in Liguria,
once a
humble
fishing
village and
now an
exclusive
resort

Places

THE BEST OF ITALY

*Unique attractions, festivals and events, piazzas and parks, art and culture...
here, at a glance, are our recommendations,
plus some tips that even Italians won't always know.*

BEST PIAZZAS

● **Piazza Navona, Rome** A baroque extravaganza of fountains and churches. *Page 146*
● **Piazza San Marco, Venice** The city's ceremonial stage-set of a square. *Page 169*
● **Piazza della Signoria, Florence** Outdoor sculpture gallery, dominated by *David. Page 256*
● **Campo dei Miracoli, Pisa** The aptly named "Field of Miracles" is home to the iconic Leaning Tower of Pisa. *Page 275*
● **Piazza del Campo, Siena** Fan-shaped medieval square, the stage for a thrilling annual bareback race. *Page 267*
● **Piazza Pretoria, Palermo** Its centrepiece is a legendary fountain with a sensuous abundance of near-naked nymphs, tritons and gods. *Page 352*
● **Piazza IV Novembre, Perugia** The hub of Umbria's dynamic capital. *Page 283*

ABOVE: the magnificent Colosseum.
RIGHT: faun at Pompeii.
BELOW: Siena's Campo.

BEST ANCIENT SITES

● **The Colosseum, Forum and the Palatino** Majestic ruins of the power centre of Ancient Rome and its most enduring symbol. *Pages 127, 130, 134*
● **Pompeii and Herculaneum** Remains of two thriving Roman towns set against the backdrop of Vesuvius, their slayer. *Pages 316–17*
● **Paestum** Magnificent standing temples of an ancient Greek settlement. *Page 321*
● **Selinunte** The scattered remains of a once powerful and rich Greek colony in Sicily. *Page 350*
● **Valle dei Templi** Classical temples and tombs in Agrigento, Sicily. *Page 350*
● **Ostia Antica** Once the commercial port of Rome, two-thirds of the excavated Roman town can now be seen. *Page 159*

BEST LANDSCAPES

- **The Abruzzo** One of Italy's last untamed wildernesses, where bears and wolves still roam. *Page 292*
- **The Maremma** A mixture of marshland, mountains and virgin coast. Lots of trails and riding opportunities in this wonderful Tuscan park. *Page 274*
- **Chianti country** and the **Val d'Orcia** The landscape of gentle hills, stately cypresses, vineyards and olive groves is the Tuscany of postcards. *Page 267 and 280*
- **Parco Nazionale del Gran Paradiso** An area of outstanding natural beauty, this alpine park is fabulous trekking country. *Page 230*
- **Parco Nazionale del Pollino** Italy's largest national park straddles Basilicata and Calabria and is rich in wildlife. *Page 343*
- **Monti Sibillini** and the **Nera Valley** Umbria's south-eastern corner is a wild landscape of deep gorges, rugged mountains and vertiginous views . *Page 287*

BEST ISLANDS

- **Capri** A capsule of Mediterranean beauty, with legendary status. *Page 318*
- **Ischia** The volcanic "green island" is renowned for its spas. *Page 318–19*
- **Procida** The unique charm of Procida is a magnet to film-makers. *Page 319*
- **Tremiti** A trio of rocky islands in the limpid waters of the Adriatic. *Page 298*
- **Giglio** Popular with weekending Romans and daytrippers alike. *Page 274*
- **Elba** Dramatic scenery and lots of small beaches make this ideal for families. *Page 273*
- **Aeolian Islands** Seven volcanic islands off Sicily; some offer luxury, others a back-to-nature experience. *Page 353*
- **Sardinia** For a sun-worshipper's beach holiday in a ritzy resort. *Page 356*

TOP: classic Tuscany.
LEFT: heading for the Blue Grotto in Capri.
BELOW: authentic pizza, cooked to perfection.

GOURMET ITALY

From an early-morning coffee to an after-dinner *grappa*, eating and drinking in Italy is always a memorable experience, if not an art form.

- **Emilia Romagna** The culinary region par excellence produces balsamic vinegar from Modena, Parma ham and Parmesan cheese.
- **Pizza in Naples** Birthplace of the authentic thin crust pizza cooked in a wood-fired oven.
- **Norcia** Umbria's gastronomic centre is renowned for its pork butchers and black truffles.
- **Tuscany** For wine, olive oil, tagliatelle and Chianina cattle that provide meat for the classic *bistecca alla fiorentina*.
- **Milan** Risotto, *osso bucco* (stewed veal shank), polenta and salami are all local specialities.

BEST BUYS

- **Murano glass** Exquisite glass made on a Venetian island. *Page 181*
- **Designer clothes** Milan is shopping heaven. *Page 210*
- **Ceramics** Important centres of majolica production are Faenza, Tuscany and Umbria.
- **Leather goods** From beautiful handmade bags and shoes to the cheap and cheerful.
- **Textiles** Umbria for hand-woven fabrics and lace. Como for luxury silk.
- **Marbled paper** Fine patterned paper made in Florence.

COASTAL ITALY

- **The Amalfi Coast** A vertiginous coast road, with the three landmark towns of Positano, Amalfi and Ravello. *Page 320*
- **Cinque Terre, Liguria** A cluster of five fishing villages clinging to a steep rocky coast, described by Byron as "paradise on earth". *Page 235*
- **Costa Smeralda, Sardinia** Beautiful emerald waters that draw a moneyed crowd. *Page 357*
- **Cefalu, Sicily** Clean, picturesque and an ideal family-friendly resort. *Page 353*
- **The Gargano Peninsula, Puglia** The most attractive stretch of coastline on Italy's eastern seaboard. *Page 326*
- **The Calabrian Coast**. Tropea, known as "the Capri of Calabria", is the most picturesque of a string of resorts with some fine beaches. *Page 333*

ABOVE: Portovenere on the Ligurian Coast.
LEFT: bags and belts for sale at Fratelli Rossetti, Rome. **BELOW:** the Basilica di San Marco, Venice.

BEST CATHEDRALS

- **Duomo, Siena** Perched on one of the three hills of Siena, the Duomo is a dazzling mix of styles. *Page 269*
- **Duomo, Milan** This is the most grandiose of Italy's Gothic cathedrals. *Page 205*
- **Basilica San Marco, Venice** The onion-domed and mosaic-covered cathedral dominates the square. *Page 172*
- **Basilica di San Pietro, Rome** Its giant cupola is a Roman landmark. *Page 154*
- **Duomo, Monreale** Glittering mosaics adorn Sicily's finest cathedral. *Page 351*
- **Duomo, Orvieto** Hilltop cathedral with a stunning façade. *Page 288*

TOP HILLTOWNS

- **Assisi** Birthplace of St Francis whose life is portrayed in Giotto's frescoes that decorate the great Basilica. *Page 284*
- **Bergamo** Rising out of the plain of the Po valley on a steep hill, not far from Milan. *Page 219*
- **Gubbio** The best preserved of Umbria's many medieval hilltowns. *Page 290*
- **Matera** Hilltown in deepest Basilicata, famous for its cave-dwellings. *Page 339*
- **Montalcino** and **Montepulciano** Quintessential Tuscan hilltowns, both famed for their wines. *Pages 270 and 272*
- **Ostuni** White-washed Puglian town with a distinctly Middle-Eastern feel. *Page 330*
- **Urbino** A remarkably well-preserved Renaissance town set amid spectacular mountains. *Page 291*
- **San Gimignano** Medieval Manhattan in Tuscany. *Page 274*
- **San Marino and San Leo** Medieval citadels in Rimini's rugged hinterland. *Page 291*
- **Santo Stefano** An ancient hamlet in the wilds of Abruzzo, transformed into a model for rural tourism. *Page 296*

ABOVE: Assisi and the Basilica di San Francesco.
RIGHT: Venetian carnival mask.

BEST FESTIVALS

- **Palio, Siena** A climactic bareback horse race round the Campo.
- **Carnevale, Venice** A 10-day extravaganza of masked balls, pantomime and music.
- **Giostra del Saracino, Arezzo** Mounted knights attack a wooden effigy of a Turk simulating events of the Crusades .
- **Festival dei Due Mondi, Spoleto** Prestigious festival of international music, theatre and dance.
- **Scoppio del Carro, Florence** Colourful music processions and fireworks from a golden carriage.
- **Estate Romana, Rome** A huge programme of cultural events across the city. *For all festivals, see Pages 410–11*

CULTURAL ITALY

Accademia, Florence Originally the world's first school of art, the gallery is now home to Michelangelo's most famous work, *David. Page 262*

Cenacolo Vinciano, Milan Make an advance booking to see Leonardo's *Last Supper. Page 208*

Uffizi, Florence Countless rooms and corridors in this palace hold Italy's highest concentration of Renaissance masterpieces. *Page 257*

Capitoline Museums, Rome A rich collection of ancient sculpture. The Etruscan statue of the she-wolf nursing Romulus and Remus can be seen here. *Page 134*

Guggenheim (Palazzo Venier), Venice A superb modern art collection representing most major art movements, housed in a palazzo along the Grand Canal. *Page 175*

Vatican Museums, Rome The glorious Sistine chapel is the inner sanctum of the papal treasure house. *Page 155*

Archaeological Museum, Naples Rich repository of Roman and Greek antiquities, including treasures from Pompeii and Herculaneum and the colossal Farnese sculptures. *Page 309*

Santa Giulia Museo della Città, Brescia Over 3,000 years of history covered in a Benedictine monastery, itself a major monument. *Page 225*

Cinema Museum, Turin Star-studded museum set in a cavernous former synagogue. *Page 229*

Etruscan Museum, Volterra Some of the best Etruscan art to be found outside Rome housed in a papal villa. *Page 275*

Archeological Museum, Palermo Great classical finds excavated from all over Sicily and displayed in a late-Renaissance monastery. *Page 353*

Pinacoteca di Brera, Milan Contained within a handsome 17th-century Jesuit palace, Pinacoteca di Brera houses one of Italy's finest art collections, with works by Mantegna, Raphael and Piero della Francesca. *Page 207*

Bargello, Florence This renowned museum holds Florence's most important sculptures. Donatello's bronze *David* is on display. *Page 261*

THE ETERNAL SEDUCTRESS

Italy, with her unrivalled beauty and baffling contradictions,
continues to seduce and enchant those who are drawn to her

Italy, like the sorceress Circe, tantalisingly beautiful and at the same time treacherous, has attracted kings, scholars, saints, poets and curious travellers for centuries. The spell of the "Eternal Seductress", as men have dubbed her, which once drew people across stormy mountains and seas, now leads them into hardly less turbulent airports and train stations.

Italy has always seemed somewhat removed from the rest of Europe: physically by mountains and sea, spiritually by virtue of the Pope. In the eyes of outsiders, the Italians themselves are characterised by extremes: at one end of the spectrum, the gentle unworldliness of St Francis, and, at the other, the amoral brilliance of Machiavelli; on the one hand, the curiosity of Galileo or the genius of Michelangelo, on the other, the repressive dogmatism of Counter Reformation Jesuits. There have been those who thought the Italians were unworthy of Italy, and others, such as the English novelist E.M. Forster, who considered them "more marvellous than the land".

This book believes that Italy and the Italians are equally worthy of attention. It explores the land and its people, from Calabrian villagers to Milanese sophisticates and delves into their justly famous treasures, from Etruscan statues to Botticelli's radiant *Birth of Venus*. Special features celebrate Italian passions – films, fashion, opera and food – while the history section threads its way through a tumultuous past, from the legendary founding of Rome by Romulus and Remus to the Renaissance, reunification, Mussolini and the Mafia.

In Italy the past is always present: a housing development rises above a crumbling Roman wall; ultra-modern museums display pre-Roman artefacts; old people in tiny mountain villages preserve customs which are centuries old while their grandchildren roar into the future on shiny new Vespas.

This is the country that inspires imagination in the dull, passion in the cold-hearted, rebellion in the conventional. Whether you spend your sojourn in Italy under a brightly coloured beach umbrella on the Riviera, shopping in Milan or diligently examining churches and museums, you cannot be unchanged by Italy. At the very least, you will receive a highly pleasurable lesson in living. Whether you are struck by the beauty of a church facade rising from a perfectly proportioned piazza, the aroma of freshly carved *prosciutto*, or the sight of a stylish passer-by spied over the foam of your cappuccino, there is the same superb sensation: nowhere else on earth does just living seem so extraordinary. ❏

PRECEDING PAGES: St Peter, Rome; welcome to Venice.
LEFT: St Mark's Basilica in Venice.

WILD PLACES

Italy is more than a glorified art museum. Exploring its diverse landscapes can be as rewarding as the Renaissance art

Italy is full of Leonardo da Vinci landscapes and Piero della Francesca views. The secret is to choose an area that is off the beaten track, but well mapped, well marked and not too remote. If this sounds obvious, bear in mind that Italian maps are notoriously unreliable outside the most popular walking areas, meaning the Dolomites, Lombardy and parts of Tuscany and Umbria, with the south uncharted. The majority of Italy is mapped with old Military Institute maps, designed for aligning an artillery bombardment rather than lining up a pretty view. If footpaths are marked, there is no indication as to whether they are private or public. With this in mind, companies that organise walking holidays tend to produce their own maps or take their own guides.

On the upside, there is little risk of being outnumbered by Italians on most trails: the locals generally only see walking as an adjunct to eating, with family expeditions focused on finding the best *funghi porcini* rather than the best view. The countryside is a larder rather than a living landscape. Farmers, hunters and most locals may look suspiciously at non-foraging foreigners on foot, when the journey could more easily be made by car. Curiously, as far as independent walking is concerned, serious hikers are better served than "Sunday walkers": long-distance trails in the Dolomites are generally better marked and mapped than meanders around Tuscany's hilltop hamlets. By the same token, Italian hikers, where they exist, tend to be found in "sporty" regions, especially in the north. The rest can be found following the local *strada dei sapori*, the food and wine trail – by car.

Charting the country

Before heading for the hills, lakes or coastal marshes, get to grips with the geography. The boot-shaped Italian peninsula spans 1,000 km (620 miles) from the Alps to the Mediterranean and is bordered by the Ligurian and Tyrrhenian

seas to the west, the Ionian to the south and the Adriatic to the east. If the Alps represent the top of the boot, the jagged seam is formed by the Apennines, while the toe, heel and spur are represented by the Calabrian, Salento and Gargano peninsulas. Much of Italy is covered by peaks, notably the Dolomites, which form part of the Alps, the country's northern boundary. These Alpine borders are shared with France, Austria, Switzerland and Slovenia, with Mont Blanc (4,810 metres/15,780 ft) marking the highest point in Italy. The Dolomites are the defining feature of Italy's Tyrolean Trentino-Alto Adige region, and neighbouring Veneto, with the peaks forming part of the world's largest integrated ski network, the Dolomiti Superski. Instead, the Apennines, the spine of Italy, stretch from north to south, dividing the east and west coasts, and bring a rugged climate to part of central Italy.

For lovers of seductive scenery, Italy dazzles: the north's national parks, true Alpine wilderness areas, give way to Piedmont's undu-

LEFT: Le Cinque Terre on the Ligurian Coast.
RIGHT: the rolling slopes of Tuscany.

lating farmland and patchwork of wine estates. The glittering lake district, framed by the jagged pinkish peaks of the Dolomites, creates the illusion of the Mediterranean meeting the mountains. Emilia's mundane farmland, coastal wetland and mountains lose out to Tuscany's Chiantishire, a gentle vision of olive groves, cypresses, vineyards and Medicean villa gardens. The rolling slopes are planted with olive groves that shimmer dark green and dusty silver. Domesticated Tuscany melds with the hazy spirituality of Umbria's green hills, the serenity only frayed at the edges by wild stretches of the Apennines where wolves still roam.

Further south, Campania's natural wonders are as wild as Italy gets, from a smouldering volcano to belching, sulfurous springs and eerie lakes that ancient myths refer to as the gateway to Hades.

The north

The Valle d'Aosta, concertinaed against the French border, is a patchwork of towering peaks and valleys in the northwestern corridor. Abutting it, Piedmont's craggy peaks loom over the region, which mellows into fertile foothills and feasts of truffles, nuts, fruit and powerful Barolo and Barbaresco wines. South of Turin,

RIVERS AND ISLANDS

The Po, Italy's principal river, flows from the Alps near the French border, through Turin and then crosses the Lombard plain to the Adriatic Sea, while the Arno famously runs through Florence from the Apennines before making its way to the Adriatic beyond Pisa. The third in the trilogy of rivers is the Tiber, which flows from the Apennines, south through Rome and into the Tyrrhenian Sea. The Italian peninsula is surrounded by over 70 islands, including Sicily, the largest in the Mediterranean, associated with volcanoes and earthquakes, and Sardinia, characterised by a remote, craggy interior, an emerald-green sea and superb beaches.

the Po Valley rises into the rolling Langhe and Roero hills, creating a carpet of vineyards and orchards. Further north lies metropolitan Milan, the gateway to Lombardy's lake district, watched over by the peaks and Alpine resorts beyond. Close to Lake Iseo, Franciacorta represents a chequerboard of prestigious vineyards while, to the south, Lombardy's fertile farmland comes into its own. Even if the Po Valley is synonymous with uninspiring vistas and oppressive summer humidity, the landscape has its oddities, such as the paddy fields around Pavia, a rare rice-growing belt.

Bounded by Lombardy and the Veneto, Trentino-Alto Adige is serrated by soaring mountain ranges. The towering peaks of the Alps and the Dolomites preside over forested wilderness, Alpine pastures, meadows carpeted by wild flowers, vineyards in the foothills and orchards in the valleys. Alto Adige, the northernmost province, is Italy's South Tyrol, which belonged to Austria until the end of World War I. The area still resembles the Austrian Tyrol, while Trentino, the southern province, prides itself on looking more Italian, though the subtle distinction is often lost on visitors.

East of Trentino, the Veneto stretches up into the apricot-tinged Dolomites and Cortina d'Ampezzo, the country's premier ski resort,

would probably be part of Slovenia today. Beyond Trieste, the foothills produce the county's finest white wines.

Framed by the Alps, and stretching from Piedmont across northern Lombardy to the Veneto, the lake district offers stunning scenery. West of Bergamo, the most appealing lakes are Como, Maggiore and Orta, matched by Iseo and Garda to the east. In terms of scenery, cognoscenti consider Como the most beguiling lake, Maggiore the most stately and Orta the most mystical. With its snow-clad peaks, romantic scenery and sluggish steamers, Como still stirs visitors, while on the Borromean

but is bordered by the Adriatic to the east, Lake Garda to the west and the River Po to the south. Orchards, river valleys and vineyards dot the region, which is noted for sparkling Prosecco, Valpolicella and Merlot. The bucolic Brenta Canal winds languidly through the noble countryside, with Palladian villas, formal gardens and farms lining the banks.

Italy's easternmost region, Friuli-Venezia Giulia, is a sliver of coastline across the Adriatic Sea from Venice. Were it not for the border-juggling that followed World War I, the region

Islands, Lake Maggiore boasts the grandest gardens. Pocket-sized Iseo possesses the biggest lake island in Europe but is Alpine in character, with olives and horse chestnuts rather than lemon groves and palm trees. Lake Garda remains a Mediterranean hothouse in northern climes. The old charm lingers on in the avenues lined by palms, oleanders and camellias, as well as in the profusion of lemon groves, vineyards and Italy's most northerly olive groves.

Protected by the Alps and perched on a crescent-shaped sliver of coast, Ligurian resorts enjoy balmy weather, with the Riviera di Levante, east of Genoa, the rockier, wilder stretch, especially around Le Cinque Terre.

LEFT: Odle Mountains and Val di Funes, South Tyrol.
ABOVE: Villa Balbianello, Lake Como.

The centre

Just east, Emilia-Romagna embraces the Po Valley, from coastal marshes to vineyards, as well as farmland dedicated to the production of Parmesan cheese and Parma ham. Its neighbour, Tuscany, has been landscaped since time immemorial, with the Val d'Orcia, south of Siena, representing quintessential Tuscany: clusters of cypresses, ribbons of plane trees, vineyards on the slopes, farms perched on limestone ridges. Towards the Emilian border, Tuscany becomes more rugged, dramatised by deep forests, Michelangelo's marble quarries and the Apuan Alps around Garfagnana.

the south, via volcanic lakes, vineyards and misty, undulating hills reminiscent of Umbria, which it borders.

The south

In Campania, south of Rome, the crescent-shaped Bay of Naples contains unspoilt Capri and volcanic Ischia, two of Italy's loveliest islands. On the Amalfi Coast, buildings are cantilevered above rock-studded cliffs and overlook the country's most romantic coastal drive. Campania's Cilento national park is a patchwork of wheatfields and olive groves, though wolves and wild cats survive in remote corners.

Umbria, "the green heart of Italy" (and the only landlocked region of the Italian peninsula) lives up to its name in densely forested slopes, misty valleys, tufa-stone outcrops and its sense of remoteness.

Italy's wildlife has been decimated by hunting, but this trend is being fought fiercely in Abruzzo's three national reserves. In the Parco d'Abruzzo bears have been successfully re-introduced, as have chamois in Gran Sasso, while wolves are protected in the Majella park.

Compared with the brooding, dramatic landscape of Abruzzo, one of Italy's last wildernesses, Lazio is less homogeneous, from the Apennine peaks in the north to marshland in

Further east, Puglia, the "heel" of the Italian boot, is the gateway to Greece, and is washed by both the Ionian and Adriatic Seas. Puglia produces more wine and olive oil than any other region yet is also a riot of carob trees and rosemary, with marine grottoes and turquoise seas framed by sun-bleached beaches and wind-twisted pines.

Forming the toe of the Italian peninsula, sparsely populated Calabria is crushed between the mountains and the sea, and significant for the Pollino park, the richest repository of wildlife in the south, all in a wilderness setting ranging from canyons to rivers, high plains to soaring peaks.

Just over the Straits awaits Sicily, as mountainous as it is mysterious. Partly thanks to its volcanic soil, the island is a major wine producer, with superb regional wines appreciated by connoisseurs, including around Etna, where singer Mick Hucknall owns vineyards. The Mount Etna volcanic park presents myriad safe and accessible options for exploring this most haunting of sites. Volcanic activity is the earth's indigestion, with deep rumblings producing sudden eruptions, emitting sulphurous gases and scalding vapours through cracks in the earth's surface. Further along the Tyrrhenian Coast, the compact Zingaro reserve, west of Palermo, is a gentle introduction to Sicily's charms.

Hitting the trail

Foremost among Italy's long-distance trails is the Via Alpina, which links Trieste and the Adriatic to the Mediterranean. This great transalpine trail crosses eight countries but, in the Italian Dolomites, touches upon Europe's shared Alpine heritage. It runs through the legendary landscape of the Fassa Dolomites, linked to the Ladin people, who speak an archaic version of Latin. Beyond is the land of Oetzi the Iceman, taking us back to prehistoric times, a reminder that this path traces a common Alpine heritage. Just north of Canazei, the trail crosses Passo Pordoi, the majestic Alpine pass that marks Trentino's borders with the Veneto, revealing vestiges of World War I fortifications and views over the Sella group. Rewards come in the form of rosy-hued sunsets, the striking Marmolada glacier and the lunar landscape of the Catinaccio group. Fortunately, this Alpine area is blessed with exceptional lodges and cable-car networks – the answer to your prayers when your bed is at the top of the next peak.

In Liguria, the best-known trails lie in the rugged Cinque Terre, the Unesco-protected stretch of coast that encompasses olive-growing terraces and quaint fishing villages. The "Blue Trail" (Sentiero Azzurro) clings to the coast for 13 km (8 miles) from Riomaggiore to Monterosso. Its popularity means that it is best not undertaken in the height of the summer.

Further down the coast, in Tuscany, the drained marshes of the Maremma include an

unspoilt coastal park with deep Etruscan roots, and white cattle watched over by the *butteri*, Tuscan cowboys. Umbria's Sibillini park, which marks the watershed between the Adriatic and the Tyrrhenian, is home to wild boar, wolves and peregrine falcons, though botanists are keener on the orchids and Alpine anemone. Both parks have waymarked trails.

On the Adriatic Coast, the Po Delta coastal wetlands, studded with nature reserves and abbeys, form a Unesco heritage site and one of the wildest areas in central Italy. This mosaic of marshes, dunes, mudflats and islands is dubbed the Italian Camargue: sturdy white ponies

THE PEACE PATH

The urge to head for the hills is irrepressible in a country where diversity in landscape is matched by the drama of the human story. The most poignant long-distance trail has to be the Peace Path, a 350-km (217-mile) trail that hugs the former Austro-Italian frontline during World War I. The rural landscape runs from jagged rocks to cool lakes and meadows, passing lofty forts with gun emplacements built into the rock. For information on the Dolomites trails and "The Legendary Trails" (one of the country's best series of mountain hikes), contact the Trentino region: www.trentino.to. For information on all Italian long-distance trails, contact the CAI, the Italian Alpine Club.

LEFT: Umbrian shepherd and his flock. **RIGHT:** black-winged stilt bird in wetlands of Comacchio.

contentedly share the marshes with migratory birds and waterfowl. Birdlife abounds on the mudflats, from cormorants, coots and reed warblers to white egrets and purple herons. Scenic trails criss-cross the park between Ferrara and Comacchio, passing bird sanctuaries, water defences and drainage schemes, from locks and flood plains to the raised canal banks which serve as cycle trails. The salt pans are flanked by windmills, a reminder of the time before pumpkins, peaches and strawberries took over. Since this is farming and wine-growing country, walkers will spot asparagus beds, rice paddies, hemp-growing and even vineyards.

In the south, the best trail is the Sentiero Italia, which begins in Montalto, in Calabria's Parco dell'Aspromonte, and runs along the spine of the Apennines until Umbria and even Trieste.

In terms of gentle walks though coastal scenery, chic Capri is, paradoxically, one of the wildest trails, embracing *macchia mediterranea* shrubland, as well as ocean views, glimpsed through exotic agave and bougainvillea. For wildness, walking and pure waters, Sicily's offshore islands, especially Marettimo off the west coast, and the Aeolian archipelago, appeal to adventurous visitors, while the marine reserve of Ustica, off Palermo, is the best diving spot.

The peaks, forests and lakes of the Parco d'Abruzzo, dominated by the Apennines and laced with trails, are home to 40 species of mammal and 300 types of bird, from Apennine wolves to golden eagles.

Further south, in Puglia's Gargano promontory, the northern salt lakes provide a haven for wildfowl. The Gargano – a thickly wooded peninsula that juts out into the Adriatic to form the spur of Italy's boot – was an island until river sediment formed a "bridge" linking it to the mainland. Reached via an old pilgrimage route, the wilder parts of the peninsula have a timeless quality, from the pine groves to the coastline of cliffs, rocks and caves.

Volcano-watching

Italy's volcanic parks make fascinating places to explore, from the eerie lunar landscape of Etna to the mud baths on the gorgeous Aeolian archipelago. Although Vulcano is set in one of the most beautiful archipelagos in the Mediterranean, visitors are assailed by a sulphurous, rotten-egg stench. Ignoring the limpid seas, bathers squat in a stinking mud hole and smear foul-smelling gloop over their bodies. This yellow volcanic soup and foul-smelling mud are common to many volcanic areas. As for Naples,

ABOVE: the impossibly blue Tyrrhenian Sea.
RIGHT: steaming Mount Etna.

Vesuvius may be an active volcano, but you can still visit the rim of the crater's mouth and gaze down into its smoldering core. The approach is dramatic, passing vineyards that produce the amber-hued Lacrimae Christi (Tears of Christ), a wine favoured by the ancient Etruscans. The puce-tinged summit induces a feeling of foreboding, but when gazing into the volcano's core, spare a thought for Spartacus, who, a century before the eruption that buried Pompeii, hid in the hollow of the crater, which was then covered with vines.

Set off the north coast of Sicily, the seven Aeolian Islands have a stark volcanic allure and a striking natural beauty safeguarded by the ban on new building. The archipelago's appeal lies in the marine life and underwater lava formations, as well as sulphurous Vulcano and Stromboli, "the lighthouse of the Mediterranean", which glows incandescently at night and shoots fireballs. Locals refer to Stromboli as "Iddu, a good friend with a volcanic temper; he sleeps just like us, he lives just like us." Iddu's intoxicating explosions have occurred every 15 minutes for the past 2,500 years. Few crater-seekers can resist testing his fiery wrath.

• For more information on hiking and trekking through Italy, see page 411. ❑

VOLCANOES AND EARTHQUAKES

Italy's huge volcanic chain stretches, mostly submerged, from Sicily to the Pontine Islands in Lazio along the western side of the peninsula. Although most volcanoes are extinct, active volcanoes include Vesuvius (the only active volcano on the European mainland) and Etna on Sicily, as well as Stromboli and Vulcano, in the Aeolian Archipelago north of Sicily. Pitch-black Vesuvius looms menacingly over the Bay of Naples, but the last spectacular eruption occurred in 1944. Even more tragically, the volcano burst forth on 24 August, AD 79, when it buried Pompeii and Herculaneum under molten lava. Sicily's Mount Etna is one of the world's largest volcanoes, and has been fairly active in recent years.

As for earthquakes, Umbria was hit by a devastating quake in 1997, damaging Assisi. In Sicily, earthquakes have destroyed Messina, Ragusa and Noto in the past, and more recently the Valle del Belice in 1968. Ragusa and Noto were rebuilt as baroque stage sets, but the Belice fared less well. A combination of public inertia and corrupt Mafia contractors siphoning off funds left 80,000 citizens homeless. Naples was mired in similar murky issues in 1980, when it suffered the most dramatic Italian earthquake in living memory. It struck Irpinia, west of the city, and left 6,000 dead, 10,000 injured and 300,000 homeless. In the south, natural calamities are sadly compounded by man-made blunders.

CARTA GEOGRAFICA GENERALE DELL' ITALIA

Decisive Dates

From Origins to the Roman Empire

2000–1200 BC Tribes from Central Europe and Asia, the Villanovans, settle in northern Italy.

circa **900 BC** Etruscans arrive in Italy.

753 BC Legendary date of Rome's founding.

750 BC Greeks start to colonise southern Italy.

509 BC Rome becomes a republic.

390 BC Gauls sack Rome, but are expelled.

343–264 BC Rome gains ascendancy in Italy.

264–146 BC Punic Wars; Rome extends conquests abroad; destruction of Carthage.

58–51 BC Caesar conquers Gaul.

50–49 BC Caesar crosses Rubicon, occupies Rome and is made dictator.

44 BC Caesar assassinated.

27 BC Octavius proclaimed Princeps, as Augustus Caesar; the start of Pax Romana.

AD 96–192 Golden century of peace; empire reaches its greatest extent.

303 Persecution of Christians under Diocletian.

306–337 Constantine makes Christianity the state religion and Constantinople the capital.

393 The empire is divided into eastern and western halves.

5th century Invasions by Visigoths, Huns, Vandals, and Ostrogoths.

410 Sack of Rome by Alaric the Goth.

476 End of Western Roman Empire. Ostrogoth general Odoacer deposes Emperor Romulus Augustus and assumes the title King of Italy.

Medieval Italy

535–553 Justinian brings all Italy within rule of eastern emperor.

568 Lombards overrun much of Italy; peninsula divided into Lombard state ruled from Pavia and Byzantine province centred at Ravenna.

752 The pope asks Frankish king, Pepin the Short, to join fight against the Lombards.

774 Charlemagne, son of Pepin the Short, is made King of the Lombards.

800 Charlemagne is crowned Holy Roman Emperor by Pope Leo III and establishes Carolingian Empire.

827 Saracens capture Sicily.

9th century Carolingian Empire disbands, leaving behind rival Italian states.

951 Saxon King Otto I becomes King of the Lombards; the following year he is crowned Holy Roman Emperor.

11th century Normans colonise Sicily and southern Italy.

1076 Pope Gregory VII and Emperor Henry IV become embroiled in a power struggle that marks the beginning of a 200-year conflict between the papacy and imperial powers.

1155 Guelphs, who take the side of the pope, clash with the Ghibellines, who follow the new emperor, Frederick Barbarossa.

1167 Lombard League of cities formed, to oppose the emperor.

1176 Pope Alexander III and Barbarossa reconciled.

1227–50 The power struggle resumes, and the papacy is, finally, the victor.

Late Middle Ages and Renaissance

1265 Charles of Anjou becomes King of Sicily.

1282 French settlers in Sicily are massacred.

1302 Anjou dynasty established in Naples.

1348 Black Death kills one third of Italians.

1309 Papacy established at Avignon.

1377 Papacy moves back to Rome.

1442 Alfonso V, King of Aragon, is crowned King of the "Two Sicilies" (Naples and Sicily).

1447 Francesco Sforza replaces the Visconti in Milan.

1469–92 Lorenzo de' Medici leads Florence; apogee of Renaissance.

1494 Wars of Italy begin with invasion by French King Charles VIII; Medici driven from Florence.

Centuries of Foreign Despotism

1503–13 Julius II is pope; Rome is now centre of the Renaissance.
1525 Battle of Pavia. Spain captures French king.
1527 Rome sacked by Charles V's imperial troops; Venice is now the centre of artistic activity.
1559 Treaty of Cateau-Cambrésis confirms Spanish control of Italy.
1700–13 War of the Spanish Succession ends Spanish domination; Austria becomes main foreign power on peninsula.
1796 Napoleon invades Italy, brings ideals of French Revolution and founds several republics.
1808 French capture Rome for second time, and exile the pope.
1814 Overthrow of French rule.

Towards Italian Unity

1815 Congress of Vienna; Venice given to Austria, who once again dominates Italy.
1831 Mazzini founds Young Italy movement.
1848 Uprisings across Italy against Austria led by Charles Albert, King of Piedmont.
1852 Cavour is made prime minister of Piedmont.
1854 Piedmont enters the Crimean War.
1859–60 With the help of France, Piedmont annexes most of northern Italy. Garibaldi's "Thousand" conquer Sicily and Naples.
1861 Victor Emmanuel II of Piedmont proclaimed King of Italy.
1870 Italian troops enter Rome; unification completed; Rome becomes capital.

Modern Italy

1882 Triple Alliance agreed between Italy, Germany and Austria.
1896 Italians defeated at Adowa, Ethiopia.
1900 Anarchist assassinates King Umberto I. Victor Emmanuel III is crowned king.
1915 Italy joins Allies in World War I.
1919 Rise of Fascism.
1922 Mussolini's march on Rome.
1935 War against Ethiopia.
1939 Seizure of Albania.
1940 Italy joins Germany in World War II.
1943 Allies land in Sicily. Mussolini deposed, later rescued by Germans to found puppet government in the north. In September, provisional government in the south surrenders.
1944 Liberation of Rome; abdication of King

LEFT: Francesco Petrarch, Renaissance poet.
RIGHT: Prodi celebrates 2006 general election victory.

Victor Emmanuel III.
1945 Mussolini killed by partisans.
1946 Italy declared a republic.
1957 Treaty of Rome: Italy joins Common Market as one of six founder members.
1950s–60s Italy's "economic miracle".
1966 Floods in Venice and Florence.
1978 Former premier Aldo Moro is kidnapped and killed. Period of political instability.
1980 Earthquake strikes Campania.
1990 Rise of the secessionist Northern League.
Early 1990s Corruption scandals rock Italy.
Late 1990s Extensive privatisation as part of the preparation for European Monetary Union.

2000 Millions flock to Rome, where over 700 historic sites are restored for the Holy Year.
2001 Silvio Berlusconi elected Prime Minister. His Forza Italia party governs in coalition with the National Alliance and the Northern League.
2002 The euro becomes the official currency in Italy; first general strike for 20 years.
2004 Genoa is designated European Cultural Capital.
2005 Pope John Paul II dies and is succeeded by Cardinal Joseph Ratzinger, Benedict XVI.
2006 Berlusconi ousted from power by Romano Prodi and his centre-left coalition.
2008 Berlusconi re-elected to serve a third term as Prime Minister. ❑

BEGINNINGS

Many primitive tribes settled in Italy, but under the Greeks
and the Etruscans it became the centre of the ancient world

As schoolchildren have noticed for years, Italy looks like a boot. The long, narrow peninsula sticking out of Europe's underbelly is perpetually poised to kick Sicily westward. This peculiar shape made Italy a natural site for early civilisation. The Alps, which cut across the only land link with the rest of Europe, protected the peninsula from the barbarians who roamed northern Europe, while the Mediterranean, which surrounds the three remaining sides, served as a highway, first to bring civilisation to the peninsula and later to export it.

The land itself contains two separate regions: the northern continental, and the southern peninsular. Together the two parts cover an area of about 250,000 sq. km (97,000 sq. miles). The northern section is a plain, bordered on the north and northwest by the Alps and on the south by the Apennines. Once a vast bay of the Adriatic, this plain was gradually filled with nitrate-rich silt from the Po, the Adige and other rivers, and became the most fertile region in Italy.

Mountainous spine

The Apennine range, the so-called backbone of Italy, dominates the peninsular section of the country. These mountains zig-zag down from the French Alps and the coast of Liguria in the northwest, through northern Tuscany and southeast to the Adriatic coast, and veer west again to the Strait of Messina, between Sicily and the toe of the boot. In the central region of Abruzzo, the peaks of the Gran Sasso d'Italia soar as high as 2,912 metres (9,700 ft).

It is no coincidence that the early inhabitants of Italy flourished in the west, on the lowland plains north and south of Rome. Here there are a few natural harbours and long rivers. The Tiber, Arno, Livi and Volturno are easily navigated by small craft, and their valleys provide easy communication between the coast and the interior. What is more, the plains of Tuscany, Latium and Campania comprise fertile farmland, thanks to a thick layer of ash and weathered lava from the many once-active volcanoes.

Around 200,000 years before the founding of Rome, only cave-dwelling hunter-gatherers lived on the Italian peninsula. However, with the Indo-European migrations (2000–1200 BC), tribes of primitive peoples poured into Italy

from Central Europe and Asia. These tribes lived in round huts clustered in small villages. The Villanovans, as the tribesmen are called, were farmers who could make and use iron tools. They cremated their dead and placed the ashes in tall, clay or bronze urns.

Villanovan culture spread from its original centre around Bologna south to Tuscany and Latium. Nowhere, however, did settlements grow to the size of towns, and Villanovans are not known for any great artistic achievements.

The transformation of Italy from a primitive backwater to the centre of the ancient world was due to the Greeks and the Etruscans. Both sailed across the sea in search of rich new

LEFT: an Etruscan statue of Apollo. **RIGHT:** a Greek temple at Selinunte in Sicily.

land. They sowed the first seeds of civilisation on the peninsula in the early 8th century BC.

Greek colonists settled in Sicily and on the west coast near modern-day Naples. Most came in search of land to farm, for Greece had insufficient arable land to feed the entire population. Others were political refugees: whenever a Greek king was overthrown, all his followers were forced to flee.

On arriving in Italy, Greek settlers formed independent cities, each loosely linked to their city of origin on the Greek mainland. One of the

MASTERS OF THE VINE

The Greeks were the first to bring both the vine and the olive under cultivation.

soldiers. But after years of inconclusive fighting the Greek leaders gave up the struggle.

The colonists still argued among themselves, and therefore failed to become a dominant political power in Italy. They did, however, become the major cultural and artistic force. Italian natives were eager to trade for Greek luxury goods, the like of which they had never seen. Soon Greek bronze and ceramic ware was dispersed throughout Italy and provided natives with new and sophisticated art patterns to imitate; the architecture and sculpture in the Greek

earliest colonies was at Cumae, by the Bay of Naples. Greeks from Euboea, an island northeast of Athens, settled there in about 770 BC. Other Euboeans founded Rhegion (modern Reggio di Calabria), at the tip of the boot, a few years later. The Corinthian city of Syracuse on Sicily ultimately became the most powerful of the Greek colonies. The colonists farmed the land around their cities, and traded with mainland Greece. They soon prospered and made important contributions to Italian agriculture.

During the 5th century, both Syracuse and Athens tried to establish rival empires out of the Greek colonies in Italy. Numerous battles were fought and many Italian natives were drafted as

cities also served as models. The civilising influence of the Greeks went beyond the visual arts. The natives adapted the Greek alphabet for their own Indo-European tongues and each native group soon had its own letters. By example, the Greeks also taught the Italian natives about modern warfare, lessons that they later used against their Greek teachers. The Italians learnt how to fortify towns with high walls of smooth masonry, and discovered the value of shock troop tactics with armoured spearmen.

But exceptional wealth and knowledge did not enable the Greeks to control Italy, and failure to unify the natives under Greek leadership left great political opportunities wide open.

In about 800 BC, Etruscans settled on the west coast where Tuscany (Etruscany) and Lazio are today. The origins of the Etruscans still puzzle scholars. The Greek historian Herodotus claimed that they came from Asia Minor, driven by revolution and famine at home to seek new lands. However, recent archaeological evidence suggests that Etruscan culture derives from a small group of Phoenicians from Palestine who landed in Italy and imparted to the natives the knowledge they had brought from the East.

Wherever they came from, the Etruscans were a highly civilised people who had a hearty appetite for life. Hundreds of Etruscan tombs

but they were grouped in a loose confederation for religious purposes. Representatives of the cities would gather regularly to worship the 12 Etruscan gods, but that was the extent of their political unity. Their fascination with religion far surpassed their desire for political power.

Vital trade routes

Each Etruscan city supported itself by trade. Eager to obtain luxury goods from the Greek colonists, the Etruscans developed overland routes to reach the Greek cities. These cut straight through Latium, the plain south of the Tiber occupied by Italian natives called Latins.

have survived, many with wall paintings depicting dancing, dinner parties and music-making. Other paintings show battle and hunting scenes.

The Etruscans were also extremely skilled craftsmen. Their speciality was metal working. Italy was rich in minerals, and trade in metal goods soon became the basis of an active urban society. Cities sprang up where previously there had been only simple villages. Each of the Etruscan cities (there were 12 in all) was independent,

LEFT: an ancient Greek dives gracefully into the unknown in a fresco from a tomb at Paestum.
ABOVE: the she-wolf suckling Romulus and Remus, the mythical founders of Rome.

One of their trading posts on the route south was a Latin village called Rome, originally only a cluster of mud huts. Under the influence of the Etruscans, the settlement flourished. They drained the swamp that became the Roman Forum and built grand palaces and roads.

For 300 years from the late 8th century BC, Etruscan kings ruled Rome. But, by the 5th century BC, their power was fading. In the north, Gauls overran Etruscan settlements in the Po Valley. Next, Italic tribesmen from Abruzzo threatened the main Etruscan cities. Then, in the south, the Etruscans went to war against the Greeks. The Romans chose this moment to rebel against their Etruscan masters. ❏

ROME RULES THE WORLD

Between its legendary founding by Romulus and its sacking by barbarians,
Rome presided over one of our greatest civilisations

The historians of Ancient Rome wrote their own version of events leading to the overthrow of the Etruscan kings. They drew upon legends about Rome's past and claimed that the city had only temporarily fallen under Etruscan rule. According to legend, Rome was founded by the descendants of gods and heroes.

In his epic, the *Aeneid*, Virgil tells how Aeneas, a hero of Homeric Troy, journeyed west after the sack of Troy to live and rule in Latium. In the 8th century one of his descendants, the Latin princess Rhea Silvia, bore twin sons, Romulus and Remus, fathered by the god Mars. Her uncle, King Amulius, angry because the princess had broken her vow of chastity as a Vestal Virgin, locked her up and abandoned the boys on the river bank to die. They were found there by a she-wolf who raised them. As young men, the brothers led a band of rebel Latin youths to find a new home. As they approached the hills of Rome, a flight of eagles passed overhead – a sign from the gods that this was an auspicious site for their new city.

Rape and revolt

Rome was ruled by Etruscan kings until 509 BC when the son of King Tarquinius Superbus raped a Roman noblewoman, Lucretia. She killed herself in shame and Roman noblemen rose in revolt against the Etruscans.

The leader of the Roman revolt, Lucius Junius Brutus, may have been an actual historical figure. In Roman legend he is the founder of a republic, a vigorous leader, and a puritanical ruler. The historian Tacitus wrote that he was so loyal to Rome that he watched without flinching as his two sons were executed for treason.

In the war against the Etruscans, Rome was also aided by Cincinnatus, a simple Roman farmer who left his plough to help his city. He was so able that he rose quickly to the rank of general. But once the fight was won, he surrendered his position of power and returned to his life as an ordinary citizen.

These stories of Rome's early heroes reveal a lot about the Roman character. For the Romans, *pietas* – dutiful respect to one's gods, city, parents and comrades – was all-important.

Because of this, the heroes of legend were very useful propaganda tools within the empire.

Upon the overthrow of the Etruscans, Rome's leaders founded a republic based on the Greek model, and the Senate, a group of Rome's leading citizens who previously had advisory roles in government, took control of the city.

Roman conquests

During the next 200 years Rome conquered most of the Italian peninsula. But Carthage, a city in North Africa founded by the Phoenicians, controlled the western Mediterranean. If Rome was ever to expand its borders across the Mediterranean, Carthage had to be defeated.

LEFT: the *Augustus of Prima Porta* shows a youthful emperor looking to Rome's future of *Imperium sine fine* (rule without end). **RIGHT:** Hannibal's Carthaginian forces cross the Alps during the Second Punic War.

The initial clash between the two cities, the First Punic War (264 BC), began as a struggle for the Greek city of Messina on Sicily. By the time it was over, in 241 BC, the Romans had driven the Carthaginians out of Sicily completely. The island became Rome's first province. Three years later Rome annexed Sardinia and Corsica, and further military triumphs followed. When Rome conquered Cisalpine Gaul (northern Italy) and extended its borders to the Alps, it alleviated the threat of invasion by the Gauls.

War broke out again in 218 BC when the brilliant Carthaginian general Hannibal embarked on an ambitious plan to attack Rome from the

north via Spain, the Pyrenees and the Alps. Rome eventually counterattacked Carthage, and Hannibal was forced to return and defend his homeland. He was defeated in 202 BC at the battle of Zama, southwest of Carthage.

Final defeat of Carthage

The Third Punic War was almost an afterthought. Carthage, stripped of many of its possessions 50 years earlier, had regained much of its commercial power. When the Carthaginians challenged Rome indirectly, the Romans razed the city of Carthage and ploughed salt into the soil. The Carthaginians were sold into slavery.

The blessings of peace were mixed. Rome was now more prosperous than ever before, but only the middle class and the rich benefited. For the common people, many of whom had served their city faithfully during the wars, peace meant greater poverty as the menial jobs on which they had depended were now filled by slaves. Independent farmers, who traditionally formed the backbone of the Roman state, sold their land to the owners of great estates, who used slaves to work it. These displaced farmers joined the Roman mob or wandered through Italy seeking work.

The Senate's usual way of dealing with potentially explosive situations was to feed the masses bread and entertain them with circuses. But eventually a patrician, Tiberius Gracchus, challenged the exploitative system. Elected tribune in 133 BC, he campaigned to reintroduce a law limiting the size of the great estates, and proposed redistributing state-owned farming and grazing land among the poor. The Senators, many of them wealthy landowners, blocked Tiberius's plan, and when he persisted and ran for re-election as tribune they engaged assassins to murder him and his supporters.

Gaius the populist

Tiberius's spirit did not die with him. Eleven years later, his brother Gaius was elected tribune. An effective speaker, he was popular with the Roman masses. Once in office, he called for sweeping land reform. Again the Senate struck back viciously. The Roman people were incited to riot, and Gaius was blamed. He was killed or forced to kill himself (the records are not clear), and his followers were imprisoned.

The power of the army commanders now became the determining factor in Roman politics. The general Gaius Marius, son of a farmer, returned to Rome from triumphant campaigns in Africa determined to smash the power of the despised Senate. To the Roman people, Gaius Marius was a god-like figure who had transformed the Roman citizen legions into a professional army. He and his supporters butchered the senatorial leaders and thousands of aristocratic Romans.

This fateful action, taken in the name of liberty, opened the way to dictatorship. The Senate turned to Silla, a rival general and a patrician by birth, who answered Marius's violence with a blood bath of his own. After Marius's death in 86 BC, Silla posted daily lists of people to be executed by his henchmen. He then conducted equally bloody campaigns abroad.

Silla returned to Rome and ruled as absolute dictator. The Senate could put no check on him for it had opened the door for him to take power. The Republic was dead, the victim of three centuries of empire building.

Enter Pompey the Great

For two years the streets of Rome ran with blood. But in 79 BC Silla grew tired of ruling and retired to his estate near Naples. Civil war broke out again. Silla's successor was another general, Gnaeus Pompeius, called Pompey the Great. He army across the flooded Rubicon river (the border between Cisalpine Gaul and Italy), against the orders of the Senate. With Caesar heading towards the capital, Pompey quickly left for Greece, taking his own small army and most of the Senate with him. Pompey had planned to strike back at Caesar from Greece, having secured an adequate army, but Caesar moved first. He attacked Pompey's allies in Spain, then in Greece, forcing Pompey to flee to Egypt, where he was eventually killed in 48 BC.

Caesar returned to Rome in triumph. The masses believed that his victories proved he was divinely appointed to rule Rome. For the first

restored many liberties suspended by Silla, but failed to go far enough for the rioting masses.

Pompey's solution was to join forces with two other military men, Crassus and Julius Caesar, and form the Triumvirate, a ruling body of considerable power and influence. This arrangement was successful at first but when Crassus died in 53 BC, the two remaining leaders quarrelled. For several years Pompey and Caesar eyed each other warily. Then, in 49 BC, Caesar, after his successful campaign in Gaul, led his

LEFT: Julius Caesar raised patrician eyebrows when he put his face on a coin. **ABOVE:** Emperor Augustus built the monumental *Ara Pacis* to celebrate peace.

BEWARE THE IDES OF MARCH

An Etruscan soothsayer had warned Caesar to beware of misfortune that would strike no later than 15 March 44 BC. On that day – the Ides of March – Caesar was scheduled to address the Senate. On his way to the Senate chamber he passed the soothsayer. Caesar remarked that the Ides had come safely. The Etruscan replied that the day was not yet over. In the chamber, Caesar was surrounded by conspirators and stabbed 23 times. When he saw that Marcus Junius Brutus, a patrician he had treated like a son, was among his murderers, he murmured "Et tu, Brute?" ("You too, Brutus?") and died.

time in decades there were no riots in the capital. But the upper classes were wary of Caesar's autocratic tendencies. While factions within the Senate heaped honours on the new ruler, hoping for favours in return, many patricians watched suspiciously as Caesar had statues of himself raised in public places and his image put on coins. A conspiracy formed against him.

After Caesar's death, Mark Antony, Caesar's co-consul, and Octavian, his grand-nephew, joined forces to pursue and murder the conspirators. Despite their cooperation,

one", but in fact he was the first emperor of Rome. Unlike his grand-uncle before him, he took care not to offend the republican sentiments of the Romans, and therein lay the key to his success. He allowed the Senate the outward trappings of power and influence, but little of the reality. Uninterested in status symbols or ostentation, he lived and dressed simply.

The competence and sensitivity with which Augustus reigned made for an unprecedented period of peace, order and prosperity; for some 200 years after Augustan

the two were never good friends. Initially they collaborated with an army leader, Lepidus, to form an uneasy Second Triumvirate, but the arrangement faltered when Antony fell in love with the Egyptian queen Cleopatra and rejected his wife, Octavian's sister, to marry her. In revenge, Octavian turned the Senate against Mark Antony, then declared war on his former partner. When defeat was imminent, Antony and Cleopatra committed suicide.

Augustus and the Pax Romana

Octavian's triumphant return to Rome marked the beginning of a new era. He called himself simply "Augustus", meaning "the revered

reform, the Mediterranean world basked in a *Pax Romana*, a Roman peace.

Before Augustus assumed power, the republican institutions had been unable to administer the vast territories Rome now controlled. Military dictatorship had been the result. To meet this challenge Augustus created a personal bureaucracy within his household. In addition to footmen and maids, he also had tax collectors, governors, census takers and administrators as his "servants". He allowed this personal civil service to grow to a size sufficient to run the empire, but kept it under tight control. At first, many members of the nobility refused to join: they believed that any office in the household, however influential, was too close to personal service. But poor men of talent joined Augustus readily, and throughout his reign the empire ran smoothly.

With peace, art and literature flourished. The poet Virgil, who had lived through the civil wars and military dictatorships, paid tribute to Augustus's achievements in the *Aeneid*; the poet Horace likened the emperor to a helmsman who had steered the ship of state into a safe port. Augustus himself took part in the artistic resurgence and set about rebuilding the capital. He claimed that he had found Rome a city of brick and left it a city of marble.

Augustus reigned for 41 years and set the tone of Roman leadership for the next 150. None of his successors had his ability, but his institutional and personal legacy did much to preserve peace in the flourishing Roman world.

The mad and the bad

The Emperor Tiberius had none of his stepfather's sense of proportion, nor his steadiness. He began his reign with good intentions, but he mismanaged many early problems. He spent the last 11 years of his reign at his villa on Capri, from where he issued a volley of execution orders. The historian Suetonius wrote (in the translation by Robert Graves), "Not a day, however holy, passed without an execution; he even desecrated New Year's Day. Many of his victims were accused and punished with their children – some actually by their children – and the relatives forbidden to go into mourning."

Rome was relieved when Tiberius died, only to find that there was worse to come. Caligula, his successor, ruled ably for three years, then ran wild. His derangement may have been due to illness, or simply the pressures of high office. He insisted that he was a god, formed his own priesthood and erected a temple to himself. He proposed his horse be made consul. Finally a group of his own officers assassinated Caligula, and Rome was rid of its most hated ruler.

The officers took it upon themselves to name the next emperor. Their choice was Claudius, grandson of Augustus, whom they found hiding behind a curtain in the palace after the assassination. Many thought Claudius a fool, for he stuttered and was slightly crippled, but he

proved a good and steady ruler. He oversaw the reform of the civil service, and the expansion of the Roman Empire to include Britain.

Claudius was poisoned by his ambitious wife Agrippina, who pushed Nero, her son by a previous marriage, on to the throne. Like Tiberius before him, Nero started out with good intentions. He was well-educated, an accomplished musician, and showed respect for the advice of others, especially senators. But the violent side of his nature soon became apparent. He poisoned Brittanicus, Claudius's natural son, and tried to do the same to his mother, but she had taken the precaution of building up an immu-

nity to the poison. In the end Nero accused her of plotting against him, and had her executed.

Nero's excesses caused alarm among Rome's citizens. When a fire destroyed the city in AD 64, he was accused of starting it. In fact, he was away from the city at the time and stories of him fiddling while Rome burned are probably untrue.

Nero lost his throne after the Roman commanders in Gaul, Africa and Spain rebelled. When the news reached the capital riots broke out and the Senate condemned him to death as a public enemy. With no hope left, Nero killed himself in AD 68. His suicide threw the empire into greater turmoil. He left no heir and therefore the rebellious commanders fought amongst

LEFT: a reconstruction of the Colosseum.

RIGHT: Emperor Nero with his tigress, Phoebe.

themselves for a year until a legion commander, Vespasian Flavius, emerged as emperor.

Vespasian proved a wise emperor, and his rule ushered in a period of peace. There was a short time of troubles when his son, Domitian, became emperor but, by the time he died, the Senate was powerful enough to appoint its own emperor, Nerva, a respected lawyer from Rome.

Nerva was the first of the "five good emperors" who reigned from AD 96 to 180. He was followed by Trajan, Hadrian, Antoninus Pius and Marcus Aurelius – all educated men, interested in philosophy and devoted to their duties. They were loved by the people of Rome

for administering their vast empire well and successfully defending its borders.

Decline and fall

During the period between the death of Marcus Aurelius and the sack of Rome in the 5th century, it became increasingly difficult to defend the empire from barbarians. Between AD 180 and 285, Rome was threatened in both the east and the west by barbarian tribes. The empire doubled the size of the army. The drain on manpower and resources caused an economic crisis, and the powerful army could place emperors on the throne and remove them at will. Most of these "barracks emperors" served for less than

three years and never even lived in the capital. Plague also struck Rome, which weakened the empire and made it more vulnerable to enemy attack. On all sides wars raged. In the east, the revived Persian Empire threatened Syria, Egypt and all of Asia Minor. In the west, Franks invaded France and Spain.

Major political reform was undertaken by Emperor Diocletian in 286. He believed the empire could no longer be ruled by one man, so he divided it into eastern and western regions. He chose Nicomedia in Asia Minor as his capital and appointed a soldier named Maximinus to rule the west from Milan.

Unfortunately this arrangement did not end quarrels about the succession. Constantine marched on Rome in 311 to assert his right to the throne. While on the road, however, he claimed that he had a vision. The sign of the cross appeared in the sky with the words: "By this sign win your victory." As a result, when Constantine defeated his rival, Maxentius, and emerged as the sole emperor, he ruled as a Christian and granted religious freedom to existing Christians.

In 324, he took a step further and confirmed Christianity as the state religion. Not all citizens followed the new faith; some notable families remained true to their pagan beliefs. But Constantine's conversion established Christianity, which had been spreading through the empire since the time of Nero, as the religion of the Roman state and thus of the Western world. Under his auspices, or in the decades which followed his reign, the first Christian churches of Rome were built. These included the earliest constructions of the five patriarchal churches of which the pope himself was the priest: San Pietro (St Peter's), San Giovanni in Laterano, San Paolo fuori le Mura, San Lorenzo fuori le Mura and Santa Maria Maggiore. Together with the catacomb churches of San Sebastiano and Santa Croce in Gerusalemme, along the Via Appia, these soon became centres of pilgrimage.

Despite the conversion to Christianity, the empire continued to decline. In 330, Constantine decided to move the capital east, and make a fresh start in his new city of Constantinople. Back in Italy, the barbarians gradually moved closer. The city of Rome was sacked in 410. ❏

LEFT: one of the "barracks emperors", probably Valerian.

Life in the Empire

In more than 60 treatises on morality, Plutarch (AD 46–126) laid down what was expected of a Roman gentleman. It was a damnable luxury to strain wine or to use snow to cool drinks. It was "democratic and polite" to be punctual for dinner; "oligarchical and offensive" to be late. Conversation over dinner ought to be philosophical, like debating which came first, the chicken or the egg. Salt fish was scooped up with a single finger, but two could be used if the fish was fresh. There was only one permissible way for a Roman gentleman to scratch himself, and so on.

It would be naive to think that all Romans obeyed Plutarch's strictures. Life was as diverse as in any modern capital, with an elegant high society at one end of the scale, vicious louts at the other, and every permutation in between. The one common factor was probably a passion for bathing. With underground furnaces heating the water, the baths got bigger and bigger. The well-preserved Caracalla baths could disgorge 1,600 glowing Romans per day.

In the early days, relations between patricians and plebeians were codified, as were family matters. Patricians were the source of "tranquillity", mainly by lending an ear to plebeians' problems and dispensing advice. In return, plebeians had to stump up money when the patrician was held to ransom or could not settle his debts. Money made available in such circumstances was not a loan but a plebeian's privilege, for which he was supposed to be grateful. On the other hand, plebeians were not enslaved and could switch allegiance from an unsatisfactory patrician to one more suitable.

Divorce was introduced relatively late. At first, marriage was permanent and wives automatically acquired half the conjugal property. However, husbands exercised the ultimate sanction in that they were legally entitled to murder wives for serious offences, such as poisoning the children or making duplicates of their private keys. Fathers were prevented from selling sons into slavery once the boys had married.

Citizens bombarded bureaucrats with complaints about the quality of life in Rome: disgraceful traffic congestion and refuse collection; preposterous fashions like men experimenting with trousers; escalating inflation; homosexuals getting too big for their boots; the filthy habit of smoking dried cow

dung, and so forth. The most castigated men in Rome were unscrupulous property developers who set fire to a building they wanted and then, as the flames went up, offered the uninsured owner a pittance. As soon as the deal was struck, the developer summoned a private fire brigade parked around the corner.

In a spiritual context, the lives of the Romans were wrapped up in astrology and mysticism. The spread of Bacchic rites in republican Rome alarmed the government, which called them "this pestilential evil ... this contagious disease". Senators "were seized by a panic of fear, both for the public safety, lest these secret conspiracies and noctur-

nal gatherings contain some hidden harm or danger, and for themselves individually, lest some relatives be involved in this vice".

The social decadence supposedly behind the downfall of Rome had its own decorum. Petronius Arbiter, author of the *Satyricon*, orchestrated Nero's orgies. He later fell out with Nero and was ordered to take his own life. Petronius invited friends to a farewell banquet where he sat with bandages wrapped around wrists which he discreetly slashed as the evening progressed. The controlled bleeding enabled him to sustain repartee up to the moment his head slumped. It is not known whether he expressed a parting thought on the interesting question of the chicken and the egg. ❏

RIGHT: a fresco in the Casa dei Vettii in Pompeii.

THE MIDDLE AGES

A period that saw Lombard, Saracen and Norman invasions
and clashes between emperor and pope

For four centuries after the sack of Rome in AD 410, barbarian invaders, including the Goths and the Lombards, battled with local military leaders and the Byzantine emperors for control of Italy. Under these conditions, the culture and prosperity that had characterised ancient times faded. The Roman Empire had unified Italy and made it the centre of the world, but after its demise Italy became a provincial battlefield. Since none of the rival powers could control the whole of Italy, the land was divided, and it remained so until the 19th century.

The Dark Ages began with a series of Visigoth invasions from northern and eastern Europe. The emperors in Constantinople were still in theory the rulers of Italy, but for decades they accepted first the Visigoth and later the Ostrogoth leaders as *de facto* kings. Justinian I, who became emperor in Constantinople in 527, longed to revive the splendour of the empire and sent the brilliant general Belisarius to regain direct control of Italy. But, although he met with initial success – he captured Ravenna from the Goths in 540 – a new group of barbarians soon appeared on Italy's borders: the Lombards.

Invaders from the north

The Lombards were German tribesmen from the Danube Valley. They swiftly conquered most of what is now Lombardy, the Veneto and Tuscany, causing the inhabitants of the northern Italian cities to flee to eastern coastal regions where they were protected by the Byzantines, who still controlled the seas. Many settled around the lagoon of Venice.

Meanwhile, the Lombards altered the system of government. They replaced the centralised Roman political system with local administrative units called "duchies", after the Lombard army generals who were known as *duces*. Within each duchy a *duce* ruled as king. The land was distributed to groups of related Lombard families, each headed by a free warrior, who owed limited feudal allegiance to his king but had a free hand on his own land. This, along with the Byzantines' continuing control of many provinces, meant Italy was effectively divided.

The radical changes that the Lombards brought to Italy's administration did not affect the Church. Indeed, in Rome the bishopric rose to new prominence because the emperors in Constantinople were too distant to exert any temporal or spiritual authority.

Greatest among the early popes was Gregory I (589–603), a Roman by birth, a scholar by instinct and training, and a great statesman. He persuaded the Lombards to abandon the siege of Rome, and helped achieve peace in Italy. He sent missionaries to northern Europe to spread the word of God and the influence of Rome, and sent the first missionaries to the British Isles.

Gregory's successors reorganised the municipal government of Rome, and effectively became rulers of the city. It was inevitable that the popes would eventually clash with the emperor in Constantinople. In 726, Emperor Leo decreed that veneration of images of Christ and the saints was forbidden and that all images were to be destroyed. The pope opposed his decree on the grounds that the Church in Rome should have the final say on all spiritual matters, and organised an Italian revolt against the emperor. The Lombards joined the revolt on the side of the popes and used the opportunity to chase the Byzantines out of Italy.

After the imperial capital, Ravenna, fell to the Lombard army in 751, the popes, feeling more directly threatened by the powerful Lombards than by an absent emperor, sought a new ally and turned to the Franks for help.

Pepin, king of the Franks, invaded Italy in 754. He reconquered the imperial lands but

crown him Holy Roman Emperor at St Peter's in Rome on Christmas Day 800.

Charlemagne lived only 14 years after his coronation, and none of his successors matched him in ability; authority fell into the hands of Frankish counts, Charlemagne's vassals who had accompanied him south and been granted land of their own. As representatives of the crown, they were required to raise troops, but they used these forces to fight each other for land and power.

This period of feudal anarchy was also marked by invasions. In the south the Saracens invaded Sicily in 827, and for the next 250

ceded control to the pope. Twenty years later, Pepin's son, Charlemagne, finished his father's work by defeating and capturing the Lombard king, confirming his father's grant to the papacy, and assuming the crown of the Lombards.

Charlemagne then returned to the north and campaigned against the Saxons, Bavarians and Avars, making himself ruler of a large part of western Europe. To unify his vast territories under Christian auspices, he had Pope Leo

LEFT: the 6th-century Pope Gregory the Great.
ABOVE: mosaics, such as this one of the Emperor Justinian, are glittering reminders that Ravenna was once the capital of Byzantium.

years Sicily was an Arab state. Sicily also became a base for raids on the Italian mainland, and Charlemagne's great-grandson, Louis II, who was emperor for 25 years, failed to raise an organised defence against them. The Lombard dukes in the south, whom Charlemagne had not conquered completely, allied themselves with these invaders against the Carolingian emperor. What success Louis had was overshadowed by Pope Leo IV's defence of Rome and the naval victory against the Saracens at Ostia.

The Normans in the south

In the early 11th century, small groups of Normans arrived in southern Italy. Adventurers and skilled soldiers, they would fight for anyone who would pay, Greek, Lombard and Saracen alike. In return they asked for land.

Soon landless men from Normandy arrived to fight, settle and conquer for themselves. The papacy lost no time in allying itself with this powerful group of Christians. In the 1050s, the Norman chief, Robert Guiscard, conquered Calabria in the toe of Italy. Pope Nicholas II "legitimised" Norman rule of the area by calling it a papal fief, then investing Guiscard as its king.

GREGORY THE GREAT

The pope who made peace with the Lombards to save Rome also gave his name to the Gregorian chant, and sent St Augustine to England.

and Norman control of southern Italy end.

During the 9th and 10th centuries, the papacy was controlled by Roman nobles. The men they picked for office were often corrupt. After Emperor Otto I arrived in Rome in 962, he insisted that no pope could be elected until the emperor had named a candidate. But, by reforming the papacy, the emperors started a trend that would have far-reaching consequences.

In the 11th century, the popes strove to reform the church further by imposing a strict clerical

Robert's nephew, Roger, conquered Sicily. He was crowned king in Palermo in 1130 and ruled over the island and his uncle's mainland possessions. He was a tolerant ruler, and his court became a magnet for Jewish, Greek and Arab scholars. Still visible today are the architectural achievements of this sophisticated culture. Brilliant examples of Arab-Norman architecture can be seen in Palermo and at the cathedrals of Monreale and Cefalù.

Despite external opposition (from the eastern and western emperors) and occasional domestic rebellions, Roger's son and grandson were able to preserve the regime. Only when William II died in 1189, leaving no heir, did civil war break out

hierarchy. Throughout the Holy Roman Empire, bishops were to be answerable to the pope, and priests to bishops. A single legal and administrative system would bind all members of the clergy together. These reforms immediately angered all lay rulers from the emperor down.

The struggle reached a climax when Emperor Henry IV invested an anti-reform candidate as archbishop of Milan in 1072. As a result, Pope Gregory VII decreed that an investiture by a non-cleric was forbidden and excommunicated Henry. For three days in the cold winter of 1077, the humbled emperor stood in the courtyard of a Tuscan castle where Gregory was staying, and pleaded for a reconciliation with the pope.

Henry was forgiven. However, he failed to keep his promise to recognise the claims of the papacy, and a new civil war broke out. Gregory's supporters were defeated initially and he was carried off to Salerno and death, but his successors worked to ensure the triumph of Gregory's cause, and the emperors were forced to concede their rights of investiture in 1122.

During the years of the investiture controversy and the ensuing civil wars, the cities of northern and central Italy grew rich and powerful. The emperors were too distracted to administer them directly. Around the same time, Mediterranean commerce was revived. With new wealth at their disposal, the cities forced the nobles in the countryside to acknowledge their supremacy. The Italian city-states were born. The strong and separate identity of the city-states is one of the leitmotifs of Italian history, influencing the pattern of future political affiliations, fostering separate schools of art, architecture and music, and largely determining regional attitudes today.

The maritime republics of Venice, Genoa and Pisa were foremost among the Italian cities, but inland cities that were situated on rich trade routes also prospered. Milan and Verona lay at the entrance to the Alpine passes, Bologna was the chief city on the Via Emilia, and Florence had sea access via the river Arno and controlled two roads to Rome.

The growing political power of the city-states was an important factor in renewed conflict between emperor and pope during the 13th century. Emperor Frederick II (1197–1250) tried to build a strong, centralised state in Italy. The cities that supported him kept their rights of self-government, but were forced to join an imperial federation. The cities that opposed him, wanting complete political autonomy, found an ally in Pope Gregory IX who secretly had imperial designs of his own. Northern Italy became a battlefield for civil war between the Guelfs, supporters of the pope, and the Ghibellines, allies of the emperor.

By the time Frederick died in 1250, without instituting his reforms, the Guelf cause was

won. The alliance of pope and the city-states had ruined imperial plans for a unified Italy.

The age of Dante

The Guelfs beat the Ghibellines decisively, but a feud broke out between two Guelf factions: the Blacks and the Whites. This split was especially severe in Florence where the Blacks defended the nobles' feudal tradition against the Whites, rich magnates who were willing to give merchants a voice in government.

Pope Boniface VIII sided with the Blacks and worked to have all prominent Whites exiled from Florence in 1302. Among the exiles was

Dante Alighieri, who went on to write *La Divina Commedia* (*The Divine Comedy*), a literary masterpiece that promoted Tuscan Italian to the status of a national tongue and also reveals much about the politics of the period.

Dante put his faith in the Holy Roman Empire, convinced that it could and should usher in a new period of cultural and political prominence for Italy. When Henry VII became Holy Roman Emperor in 1308, he wanted to revive imperial power in Italy and set up a government that was neither Guelf nor Ghibelline. But the cities refused to support him. Dante's home town, Florence, was the centre of the resistance to imperial plans. ❏

LEFT: *Effects of Good Government*, fresco by Lorenzetti 1338–40, in the Palazzo Pubblico, Siena
RIGHT: Dante Alighieri, as painted by Andrea del Castagno.

THE RENAISSANCE

Free from foreign interference, the city-states flourished and witnessed
an unprecedented cultural awakening

The constant fighting in northern Italy subsided in the early 14th century when both the popes and the emperors withdrew from Italian affairs. After Henry VII's demise, the emperors turned their attention to Germany. Meanwhile, the influence of the papacy declined after a quarrel between Pope Boniface and King Philip of France in 1302. The pope insisted that Philip had no right to tax the French clergy; the king's response was to send his troops to capture the pope. French pressure ensured that the next pope was a Frenchman, Clement V, and he moved the papacy from Rome to Avignon, where it stayed until 1377.

The people of Italy were thus free from outside interference during the 14th century and the Italian cities grew stronger, richer and bigger than any in Europe. Against the political background of the supremacy of the city-state, a new culture bloomed and new ideas flourished. Rulers tried new methods of administration. Scholars were allowed to rediscover the pagan past. Wealthy merchants became lavish patrons of the arts. Through their commissions, artists experimented with a new, more realistic style.

Plague and depression

Not even the Black Death – the terrible outbreak of bubonic plague that ravaged Europe in the 14th century – could smother the new cultural awakening. But the plague did cause great human suffering and a prolonged economic depression. During several months of 1347 the death rate was 60 percent in some Italian cities. The merchants' solution to the declining profits of the period was to change the way they did business. Their innovations included marine insurance, credit transfers, double-entry bookkeeping and holding companies – all of which eventually became standard business practice.

To be a good businessman in the early Renaissance required a basic education: read-

ing, writing and arithmetic. But the more complicated business became, the more knowledge was needed, including an understanding of law and diplomacy, and of the ways of the world. Thus the traditional theological studies of the Middle Ages were replaced by the study of ancient authors and of grammar, rhetoric, his-

tory and moral philosophy. This education became known as *studia humanitatis*, or the humanities.

Humanism grew partly out of the need for greater legal expertise in the expanding world of Mediterranean commerce. To learn how to administer their new, complex societies, lawyers looked back at the great tenets of Roman law. As they studied the codes of the ancients, they grew to appreciate the cultural riches of that long-buried civilisation. All aspects of Italian life were re-examined in the light of this new humanism. One way of life was thought to be ideal – that of the all-round man based on classical models. The Renais-

---

LEFT: Titian's portrait of Pope Julius II, a great patron of the arts. **RIGHT:** relief by Ghiberti from the "Gates of Paradise" of the Baptistry of St John in Florence.

sance man was a reincarnation of rich, talented Roman philosophers.

Despots and republics

Italians of the 14th century were citizens of particular cities, not members of a national unit. They revered local saints, believed myths that explained the origin and uniqueness of their city, and feuded with other cities. Rulers encouraged artists and writers to glorify their towns.

There were a few experiences and conditions that many cities shared. As the authority of the popes and emperors declined, life in the cities became increasingly violent. Leading families

would extend his powers until he controlled the entire city. Then he was in a strong enough position to make his office hereditary. This was how the della Scala family in Verona, the Carrara in Padua, the Gonzaga in Mantua and the Visconti in Milan came to power.

Once established, a despot would centralise all agencies of the government under his supervision. His power would be threatened only if he overstepped what his subjects could tolerate.

Some cities, including Venice, Florence, Siena, Lucca and Pisa, did not succumb to despotism until quite late in their history: the merchants were so powerful that rulers such as

fought each other constantly, and often came into conflict with groups lower on the social ladder that wanted a role in the political life of the city. The remedy to this bloody civil strife was the rule of one strong man. The pattern was repeated over and over again in northern Italy. Traditional republican rule which could not keep order was replaced by a dictatorship. Sometimes a leading faction would bring in an outsider, known as a *podestà*, to end the chaos – for example, the lordship of the d'Este family in Ferrara was established in this way. More often, the future despot was originally a *capitano del popolo* – the head of the local police force and citizens' army. Over time, this captain

the Medici only survived by winning their support. In these cities republicanism flourished briefly, but even so the merchants dominated the organs of the republican government.

During the 14th and 15th centuries, northern and central Italy changed from an area speckled with tiny political units to one dominated by a few large states. Both republics and despots were expansionist in outlook. They would conquer their smaller neighbours and construct out of the lands they gained a new regional state with increased economic resources.

Of the Italian city states, the most successful and the most powerful was Milan. During the 14th century, the authoritarian Visconti family dominated Milan, and led the city to innumerable military and political victories until it was the largest state in northern Italy.

The Visconti regime may have been, in its efficiency, unlike anything Europe had seen for centuries, but for the Milanese people it had great drawbacks. The personal brutality of the Visconti controlled Milan. The regime could not rely on the loyalty of the populace for its survival. When the Visconti line died out in 1447, the Milanese declared a republic, but it was not strong enough to rule over all the restive towns Milan now controlled. When, in 1450, Francesco Sforza, a famous general who had served the Visconti, overthrew the republic and became the new duke, ruling with his wife Bianca Visconti, many Milanese were relieved.

THE VISCONTI TOUCH

The eminent Renaissance historian Jacob Burckhardt admired the "strict rationalism" of Visconti's Milan and called its government a work of art.

The Republic of Florence

The spectacular transformation of Florence from a small town in the 1100s to the commercial and financial centre it had become by the end of the 14th century was based on the profitable wool trade. The wool guild of Florence, the Arte della Lana, imported wool from northern Europe and dyes from the Middle East. Using the city's secret weaving and colouring techniques, guild members produced a heavy red cloth that was sold all over the Mediterranean area. Wool trade profits had provided the initial capital for the banking industry of Florence. Since the 13th century, Florentine merchants had lent money to their allies, the pope and powerful Guelf nobles. This early experience led to the founding of formal banking houses, and made Florence the financial capital of Europe.

The leading merchant guilds of Florence spent their wealth on art. The city was a showcase of the best of Renaissance sculpture, painting and architecture. In the second half of the 13th century a building boom began with the construction of the Bargello, the Franciscan church of Santa Croce, and the Dominican church of Santa Maria Novella. Arnolfo di Cambio designed the cathedral and the Palazzo Vecchio. The Arte della Lana paid for the construction and decoration of the cathedral. The city hired Giotto to design the Campanile which is named after him, and in 1434 they had Brunelleschi finish the great dome.

The rich men of Florence controlled the city government through the Parte Guelfa. With membership came the right to find and persecute anyone with "Ghibellistic tendencies". Other political non-conformities were also not tolerated. Members of lesser guilds who demanded a greater share of power, or joined with the lower classes to fight the Parte Guelfa,

were annihilated. However, in the early 15th century the violence of class war escalated. The disenfranchised artisans struck back repeatedly. At this point the rich merchants allowed Cosimo de' Medici to rise to the leadership of Florence.

The 15th century was the golden age of the Renaissance. All the economic, political and cultural developments of the previous century had set the stage for a period of unprecedented artistic and intellectual achievement. To live in Italy at this time was to live in a new world of cultural and commercial riches. Italy was truly the centre of the world.

The political history of the century divides into two parts. Until 1454 the five chief states

---

LEFT: *The Battle of San Romano* by Paolo Uccello, showing the victory of Florence over Siena in 1432.
RIGHT: Cosimo the Elder, the Medici patriarch.

of Italy were busy expanding their borders, or strengthening their hold on territories, which meant fighting many small wars. The soldiers who fought them were mostly *condottieri* (mercenaries). After 1454 came a period of relative peace, when the states pursued their interests through alliances. These years saw the greatest artistic achievement, when Italian states of all sizes became cultural centres.

Italian wars of the Late Middle Ages and Early Renaissance had traditionally been fought by foreign mercenaries, but by the 15th century the mercenaries were more likely to be Italian. Men of all classes and from all parts of Italy joined the ranks of the purely Italian companies to fight northern wars for rival nobles. The *condottieri* looked upon war as a professional, technical skill. In battle, the object was to lose as few men as possible but still be victorious. Soldiers were too valuable to be sacrificed unnecessarily. The countryside, however, suffered heavily as village after village was plundered. The *condottieri* did not hesitate to take what they could even though they were very well paid. They were bound by no patriotic ties, only by a monetary arrangement, so an important captain could always be bought by the enemy.

One of the greatest *condottieri* was Francesco Sforza. Sforza had inherited the command of an army upon his father's death in 1424. He fought first for Milan and then for Venice in the northern wars until Filippo Visconti sought to attach him permanently to Milan by marrying him to his illegitimate daughter, Bianca.

Visconti died in 1447 leaving no heir, and Milan declared itself a republic. Sforza was expected to captain the new republican forces. Instead he went into exile. But when the republican government proved incompetent he turned his forces on the city and starved Milan into surrender. The chief assembly of the republic invited him to be the new duke of the city.

Peace and the Italian League

Sforza, the great soldier, was instrumental in bringing peace to northern Italy. He signed, and encouraged others to sign, the Treaty of Lodi, which led to the Italian League of 1455. This was a defensive league between Milan, Florence and Venice that the King of Naples and the pope also respected. It was set up to prevent any one of the great states from increasing its powers at

the expense of its weaker neighbours, and to present a common national front against attack.

The smaller states of Italy benefited most from the new league. Previously, they had spent vast resources on defence against the larger states. "This most holy League upon which depends the welfare of all Italy", wrote Giovanni Bentivoglio, a citizen of Bologna, in 1460.

During the decades of peace in Italy, Florence experienced its own Golden Age under the rule of the Medici family. The historian Guicciardini described the Florence of Lorenzo de' Medici as follows: "The city was in perfect peace, the leading citizens were united, and their author-

ity was so great that none dared to oppose them. The people were entertained daily with pageants and festivals; the food supply was abundant and all trades flourished. Talented and able men were assisted in their careers by the recognition given to arts and letters. While tranquillity reigned within her walls, externally the city enjoyed high honours and renown."

In part, the success of the Medici was a public relations coup. They allowed the Florentines to believe that the city government was still a great democracy. Only after Lorenzo's death, when Florence was briefly ruled by his arrogant son, did the citizens realise that their state, for all its republican forms, had drifted into the control of one family. They then quickly exiled the Medici and drafted a new constitution. Until then, both Cosimo and Lorenzo de' Medici had dominated Florence while shrewdly never appearing to be more than prominent citizens. They did this partly by manipulating the elections for the *Signoria*, Florence's city council, but the real base of their power lay in their acceptance by the city's leading citizens.

The Medici did more than simply rule and successfully keep the peace. They promoted art

LEFT: Francesco Sforza married Bianca (**ABOVE**), natural daughter of the last of the Visconti rulers, to become despot of Milan.

PRINCELY ADVICE

Macchiavelli was inspired by Lorenzo de' Medici when he wrote in *The Prince*: "A ruler must emulate the fox and the lion, for the lion cannot avoid traps and the fox cannot fight wolves."

and culture in Florentine life. When the famous humanist Niccolò Niccoli died, Cosimo acquired his book collection and attached it to the convent of San Marco, creating the first public library in Florence. Cosimo also had Marsilio Ficino trained to become head of the new Platonic Academy and make Florence a centre of Platonic studies. He supplied Donatello with classical works to inspire his sculpture. Lorenzo de' Medici grew up in the atmosphere his grandfather had created and when he became leader of Florence he also was a great patron of the arts. For his employees he was a peer as well as a patron. His poetry was widely admired.

An end to the peace

When Lorenzo de' Medici died in 1492, the fragile Italian League that had kept Italy at peace and safe from any foreign attacks died with him. Ludovico il Moro, the lord of Milan, immediately quarrelled with the Neapolitan king and proposed to the King of France that he, Charles VIII, conquer Naples and the surrounding states. Ludovico offered finance and safe passage through the north of Italy. Charles readily accepted and so began a truly demoralising chapter of Italian history.

The internal disarray in Italy at the time was so great that the French troops faced no organised resistance. The new leader of Florence, a Dominican friar named Girolamo Savonarola, preached that Charles was sent by God to regenerate the Church and purify spiritual life. Other Italians also welcomed the French. They believed that the invaders would rid Italy of decadence and set up governments with natives in key posts. Only when these ideas proved illusory could Italian patriots recruit an army and challenge the French.

The French and Italians met near the village of Fornovo on 6 July 1495. The Italians, led by General Francesco Gonzaga, looked certain of victory: they outnumbered the French two-to-one, and they could launch a surprise attack against their enemy. But the Italian strategy fell apart. Crucial troops could not cross the river to the French position. General Gonzaga entered the fiercest fighting and did not direct the battle as a whole, and some Italian soldiers left the battle to capture the French king's booty. When the battle ended, four thousand men had died – the majority of them Italian.

"If the Italians had won at Fornovo, they would probably have discovered then the pride of being a united people … Italy would have emerged as a respectable nation … a country which adventurous foreigners would think twice before attacking", wrote Luigi Barzini in *The Italians*. Instead, the defeat at Fornovo broke the Italian spirit and led to 30 years of foreign interventions, bloody conflicts, civil wars and revolts. ❑

RENAISSANCE ART

The revolution in art and architecture which began in Florence gave us our
greatest treasures. It also set the stage for Mannerism

Italian art shone brightest during the Renaissance when, as in most disciplines, a revolution took place. The Early Renaissance (1400–1500), the *Quattrocento*, introduced new themes that altered the future of art. Ancient Greece and Rome were rediscovered and with them the importance of man in the here and now. The human body surfaced as a new focal point in painting and sculpture. The discovery of perspective changed architecture.

The Early Renaissance centred on Florence. The city wanted to be seen as "the new Rome" and public works flourished. First was Lorenzo Ghiberti's commission for sculpting the gilded bronze north doors (1403–24) of the Baptistry, won in a competition with Filippo Brunelleschi in 1401. Ghiberti's more famous east doors (1424–52) are so dazzling that Michelangelo called them "the Gates of Paradise".

Classical architecture

It was Filippo Brunelleschi (1377–1466) who championed the new classically inspired architecture. After losing the Baptistry door competition, he went to Rome to study the proportions of ancient buildings. His studies led him to design such masterpieces as the dome of Florence cathedral, the arcade fronting the Innocenti orphanage, the church of San Lorenzo (1421–69), the Pazzi Chapel of Santa Croce (begun 1430–33), and Santo Spirito, all in Florence. You need no yardstick to appreciate the use of mathematical proportions. The overriding impression is of harmony, balance and calm.

If Brunelleschi was the most noted architect, Donatello (1386–1466) excelled in sculpture. His work expresses a new attitude to the human body. The figure of St George, made for the church of Orsanmichele and now in the Museo del Bargello, is not only a realistic depiction of the human form, but also a work of psychological insight. His *Gattamelata* (1445–50) in Padua was the first equestrian statue cast in bronze since Roman times, and his bronze *David* (1430–32), in the Bargello, was the first free-standing nude statue since antiquity.

The groundwork for the revolution in painting was laid a century earlier by Giotto (1267–1337). His frescoes – in Florence's Santa Croce, in Padua's Cappella degli Scrovegni, and Assisi's Basilica di San Francesco – depart from the flat Byzantine style and invest the human form with solidity and volume, and the

setting with a sense of space and depth. His breakthrough was carried further by the Early Renaissance's most noted painter, Masaccio (1401–28). His Florentine frescoes of *The Holy Trinity with Virgin and St John* in Santa Maria Novella (1425), and *The Life of St Peter* in the Brancacci Chapel of Santa Maria del Carmine (1427), display all the traits characteristic of the Renaissance: the importance of the human form, distinct under its clothing, human emotion and the use of perspective.

Domenico Veneziano moved to Florence in 1439 and introduced pastel greens and pinks awash in cool light. The palette was picked up by his assistant, Piero della Francesca (1416–

92), for his frescoes at San Francesco in Arezzo (1466). These are marvels of pale tone as well as mathematics – heads and limbs are variations of geometric shapes: spheres, cones and cylinders.

The artistic revolution in Florence soon spread to other parts of Italy. Leon Battista Alberti (1404–72), an author of noted treatises on sculpture, painting and architecture, introduced the tracing of classic motifs (columns, arches) on the exteriors of buildings, such as on the Palazzo Rucellai in Florence (1446–51) and the Malatesta Temple in Rimini (1450).

Giovanni Bellini (1430/1–1516) triumphed in Venice. In his *Madonna and Saints* in San

Michelangelo, Bramante, Raphael and Titian. Unlike their predecessors, who were thought of as craftsmen, they were considered to be creative geniuses capable of works of superhuman scale, grandeur and effort. Their extravaganzas were made possible by a new source of patronage – the papacy. Having returned to Rome from exile in Avignon, the popes turned the Eternal City into a centre of culture. The art of the High Renaissance is marked by a move beyond rules of mathematical ratios or anatomical geometrics to a new emphasis on emotional impact. The increasing use of oil paints, introduced to the Italians in the late 1400s, began to

Zaccaria (1505), the grandeur of Masaccio's influence is tempered by Flemish detail.

Detail most delicately expressed is the hallmark of Sandro Botticelli (1444/5–1510). The Uffizi Gallery houses the allegorical *Primavera* (1480) and the lovely *Birth of Venus* (1489).

The High Renaissance

The High Renaissance (1500–1600) was the heyday of some of the most celebrated artists in the entire history of art: Leonardo da Vinci,

replace egg tempera and opened new possibilities for richness of colour and delicacy of light.

Leonardo da Vinci (1452–1519) was born near Florence but left the city to work for the Duke of Milan, primarily as an engineer and only secondarily as a sculptor, architect and painter. In Milan, Leonardo painted the *Last Supper* (1495–98), in Santa Maria delle Grazie. The mural – an unsuccessful experiment in oil tempera, which accounts for its poor condition – is a masterpiece of psychological drama.

Leonardo also exploited new techniques in painting. *Chiaroscuro* (literally, light and dark) – the use of light to bring out and highlight three-dimensional bodies – is vividly seen in

LEFT: the anguish of Adam and Eve, from Masaccio's *Expulsion from Paradise*.
RIGHT: Botticelli's *Primavera* in the Uffizi in Florence.

the whirl of bodies in the *Adoration of the Magi* (1481–82) in the Uffizi. Another invention was *sfumato*, a fine haze that lends a dreamy quality to paintings, enhancing their poetic potential.

In 1503, Pope Julius II, a great patron of the arts, commissioned the most prominent architect of the day, Donato Bramante (1444–1514), to design the new St Peter's. Bramante had earlier made his mark with the classically inspired gem, *The Tempietto* (1502), in the courtyard of Rome's San Pietro in Montorio. The pope's directive for the new project was to create a monument which would surpass any of Ancient Rome. Working with a stock of classic forms

Michelangelo sought to liberate the form of the human body from a prison of marble: an allegory for the struggle of the soul, imprisoned in an earthly body, and a condition ripe for themes of triumph and tragedy. The tension imbues his best-known works: *David* (1501–04) in Florence's Accademia; *Moses* (1513–15) in Rome's San Pietro in Vincoli, and the beloved *Pietà* in St Peter's.

Julius II commissioned Michelangelo to paint the Sistine Chapel ceiling. The result, which was completed in only four years (1508–12), is a triumph of human emotions unleashed by the human condition: man's creation, his fall, and

(domes, colonnades, pediments) Bramante revolutionised architecture with his revival of another classic technique, concrete, which enables greater flexibility and monumental size.

Bramante died before his design was realised. In 1546, Michelangelo was put in charge of the project, and St Peter's gained its present form.

Michelangelo and Raphael

Michelangelo Buonarroti (1475–1564) first astounded the world with his sculpture: human figures with a dignity, volume and beauty inspired by Hellenistic precedents, yet given new emotional impact. It has been said that

his reconciliation with the Lord. Michelangelo returned to the Sistine Chapel in 1534 to paint the spectacular *Last Judgement*. In the intervening years he went to Florence to complete the Medici Chapel of San Lorenzo (1524–34) and the Laurentian Library (begun 1524) where the drama of the design outweighs many functional considerations. Michelangelo's architectural genius culminates in his redesign of Rome's Campidoglio (1537–39). This open piazza, flanked by three facades, became the model for modern civic centres.

While Michelangelo was busy on the Sistine Chapel ceiling, a young artist from Urbino was working nearby, decorating a series of rooms in the Vatican Palace. This artist, soon to be known as the foremost painter of the High Renaissance, was Raffaello Sanzio, or Raphael (1483–1520), who produced a vast body of work during his short life. His masterpiece in this series is the *School of Athens* (1510–11). The dramatic grouping of philosophers around Plato and Aristotle suggests the influence of Michelangelo; the individualised intention of each recalls Leonardo's *Last Supper*.

Venetian masters

In Venice, the paintings of Giorgione da Castelfranco (1476/8–1510) have all the charm and

delicacy of Bellini's; they also favour poetic mood over subject matter (*The Tempest* [1505] in Venice's Galleria dell'Accademia is a perfect example), prefiguring the Romantic movement.

Also looking ahead to the freer brushwork and shimmering colours of the Impressionists is the Venetian Titian (1488/90–1576). He mastered the technique of oil painting, and left a legacy of richly coloured, joyously spirited religious and mythological pictures as well as masterful portraits. ❏

ABOVE: *The Young Bacchus*, by Caravaggio, master of *chiaroscuro*, in the Uffizi, Florence. **LEFT:** Raphael's *Entombment*, in the Borghese Gallery, Rome.

THE MANNERISTS

The drama of Leonardo, the theatricality of Michelangelo, the poetic moodiness of Giorgione: all set the stage for the Mannerist phase of High Renaissance art, when the serenity and calm classicism that characterised the works of Raphael were abandoned. In Mannerism the human form is paramount, yet it is usually depicted in strained, disturbing poses and violent colours.

Mannerist artists include Angelo Bronzino, Jacopo Pontorno and Rosso Fiorentino, who revelled in the use of bold colours, dramatic poses and heightened emotions. This unnatural look grew out of the work of artists such as Michelangelo, who had begun to exaggerate human features to create tension and drama – in the over-large head and hands of *David*, for example, or the contorted pose of the Virgin in his *Doni Tondo*, in the Uffizi Gallery.

Expression of an "inner vision" at the expense of reality was vital to Mannerism. In Fiorentino's *The Descent from the Cross* (1521) in Volterra's Pinacoteca, the angularly draped figures bathed in an unreal light stir feelings of anxiety and tension. His friend Pontormo (1494–1557) is also known for works of unexpected colour, unnaturally elongated figures and disquieting mood.

Bronzino (1503–72), Pontormo's pupil and adopted son, epitomises Mannerism's achievements in his psychological portraits of Cosimo I, his wife, Eleanor of Toledo, and her son, Giovanni de' Medici (1550), in the Uffizi Gallery.

Parmigianino (1503–40) used distortion merely for effect. In his *Madonna with the Long Neck* (1535), in the Uffizi, the figures are extremely elongated, the setting is fantastical, and the inspiration for the work – Raphael's fluid grace – is exaggerated beyond recognition.

In Venice, Tintoretto (1518–94) combined the bold style, rich colours and glowing light inspired by Titian with a mystical inclination. His attempt to depict religion's great mystery – the transubstantiation of bread into the body of Christ – results in the haunting *Last Supper* (1592–94) in San Giorgio Maggiore, Venice, with its swirling angels created out of vapours.

In architecture, Andrea Palladio (1518–80), like his predecessor Alberti, wrote theoretical studies of ancient architecture. His own designs – including the Villa Rotonda, Vicenza (1567–70) and San Giorgio Maggiore, Venice (1565) – are based on classical concepts, and have influenced architects from Inigo Jones to Thomas Jefferson, and even architects today.

BIRTH OF A NATION

*After centuries of foreign domination and a prolonged struggle,
Italy emerged in 1870 as a united independent kingdom*

The seeds of Italian patriotism, crushed by the battle of Fornovo in 1495, lay virtually dormant for three centuries. After Fornovo, all the armies of Europe came to Italy and fought among themselves for a share of the spoils. Spain, the most powerful nation in Europe at the time, eventually emerged as the clear master of Italy. The pope crowned King Charles 1 of Spain Holy Roman Emperor in 1530, and Charles and his descendants ruled Italy for more than 150 years. The country was burdened by heavy taxation, and under Spanish influence liberty and native energy and initiative declined. The papacy was no less oppressive; the rules of the Inquisition, the Index and the Jesuit Orders forced many Italians to flee.

Under the Spaniards and later (after the 1713 Treaty of Utrecht) under the equally oppressive Austrians, Italy lost its reputation as a cultural centre. But the 1789 French Revolution inspired many Italians, and the ideals of republicanism spread rapidly. Patriots dreamt of an independent Italian republic modelled on France.

When Napoleon invaded Italy in 1796, the people rose against the Austrians and a series of republics was founded. For three years the whole peninsula was republican and under French rule. But in March 1799, an Austro-Russian army expelled the French from northern Italy and restored many of the local princes. In Naples, the republicans held out for a few months before they, too, had to surrender.

To work against the foreign oppressors and their local sycophants, Italian patriots joined secret societies, such as the Carbonari. In their love of ritual they resembled the Freemasons, but they had a serious goal: to liberate Italy.

The Risorgimento

In 1800 Napoleon won back most of Italy. The kingdom that he founded lasted only briefly but, by proving that the country could be a single

unit, it gave Italian patriots new inspiration. From the Congress of Vienna in 1815, which reinstated Italian political divisions, until Rome was taken in 1870 by the troops of King Victor Emmanuel II of Savoy (who also ruled over Piedmont and Sardinia), the history of Italy was one continuous struggle for reunification.

The period is a complex one. Many northern and southern Italians wanted the peninsula to become one nation but there was no agreement as to who would rule or how it should be achieved. Some believed in peaceful evolution. Others, like Giuseppe Mazzini, wanted to revive the Roman republic. Some were for a kingdom of Italy under the House of Savoy.

In 1848, a year of revolt all over Europe, the first Italian war for independence was fought. First, rebellions in Sicily, Tuscany and the Papal States forced local rulers to grant constitutions to their citizens. In Milan, news of Parisian and Viennese uprisings sparked the famous "five days" when the occupying Austrian army was

LEFT: Giuseppe Garibaldi, a prominent leader of the Risorgimento. **RIGHT:** Camillo Benso, Count of Cavour, Italy's first great statesman.

driven from the city. A few days later, Charles Albert of Savoy sent his army to pursue the Austrians, and the revolution began in earnest.

Charles Albert was soon supported by troops from other Italian states; however, the tide turned when the pope refused to declare war on Catholic Austria. The newly confident Austrians drove Charles Albert's army back into Piedmont. He abdicated months later, and the House of Savoy signed a peace treaty.

Garibaldi and Cavour

Venice and the Roman Republic continued the fight. In Rome, Mazzini led a triumvirate that

it was now the only Italian state with a free press, an elected parliament, and a liberal constitution. Piedmont-Savoy was also blessed, from 1852, with a brilliant prime minister, Count Camillo di Cavour, who was devoted to the cause of Italian unity. Cavour went to England and France to raise support for the Italian cause. He contributed Piedmontese troops to the Crimean War, and thus won a seat at the peace conference, where he brought the Italian question to the attention of Europe's most important statesmen. Although Cavour made no tangible gains at this meeting, he won moral support.

Europe was thus not surprised when France

governed the city with a true democratic spirit despite the siege conditions. The commander of the city's armed forces was Giuseppe Garibaldi, a life-long Italian patriot who had honed his fighting skills as a mercenary in the revolutions of South America, where he had fled after being convicted of subversion in Piedmont. Now he and his men faced the combined strength of the Neapolitans, the Austrians and the French. It was French forces that entered the city on 3 July 1849, the day after Garibaldi escaped into the mountains. The following month the Venetians succumbed to an Austrian siege.

The treaty the Austrians had signed with the House of Savoy kept them out of that region, so

and Piedmont went to war with Austria three years later. The French king, Napoleon III, and Cavour had agreed that, after the expected victory, an Italian kingdom would be formed for the Piedmontese king, Victor Emmanuel, and Nice and French Savoy would be returned to France. The people of the Italian dukedoms rushed to proclaim their allegiance to Victor Emmanuel.

Unfortunately, the French soon tired of fighting and decided to make a quick peace with Austria. The Austrians agreed to let Lombardy become part of an Italian Federation (with Austrian troops still in its garrisons), but the Veneto region went back to Austria and the dukes of Modena and Tuscany were reinstated.

In Italy, there was general outrage. Cavour resigned in protest, but first he arranged plebiscites in Tuscany and Modena. Citizens refused to have their dukes back and voted to become part of Piedmont.

Garibaldi and 1,000 red-shirted volunteers sailed for Sicily from Genoa on 5 May 1860. His arrival was a signal for the overthrow of Bourbon rule on the island. Garibaldi quickly declared himself dictator in the name of Victor Emmanuel. After fierce fighting, with the aid of Sicilian rebels Garibaldi entered Palermo

PATRIOT AND DEMOCRAT

Giuseppe Mazzini founded the Young Italy movement and agitated frenetically for unification from 1830–70.

divided over whether to take Rome by force or to negotiate a settlement with the Romans.

Finally, in 1870, after the French were weakened by a defeat in the Sudan, Italian troops fought their way into the city through Porta Pia. The pope barricaded himself in the Vatican. For half a century, no pope emerged to participate in the life of the new Italy.

The new government of all Italy was a parliamentary democracy with the king as executive. The most powerful men in the early days of the Italian state were the loyal

in triumph. Inspired by his success, men from all over Italy now came to help him and, on 7 September, Naples fell to the patriots.

Meanwhile, Victor Emmanuel gathered troops and marched south to link up with Garibaldi and his men. The two groups met at Teano, and the Kingdom of Italy was declared. The new kingdom did not include Rome, however: the pope preached against the patriots, and the French had garrisoned troops there to protect the city. The victorious nationalists were

LEFT: Garibaldi and Victor Emmanuel II of Savoy join forces at Teano.
ABOVE: celebration of Italian unity in Turin.

Piedmontese parliamentarians who were largely responsible for its creation and for designing the administration of the whole peninsula.

However, once the government moved down to Rome, this group began to splinter. The left came to power under a new prime minister, Agostino Depretis. In parliament, Depretis had shown great skill as a legislator and manipulator, but as prime minister he could not organise his party or set forth a coherent national policy. His rivals on the right had done no better, but their opposition made it hard for him to accomplish much. This was the start of the breakdown of the party system in Italy, the effects of which are discernible even today. ❑

THE MAKING OF MODERN ITALY

Wars, Fascism, corruption scandals ... with remarkable resilience,
Italy survived every challenge the 20th century presented to it

As governments so often do during times of rapid change and relative instability at home, Italy's began to look abroad for confirmation of its hard-won independence. Relations with France had cooled during the final fight for unification; when France occupied Tunisia, a traditional area of Italian influence, they became positively chilly. Italy's response was to sign the Triple Alliance with Germany and Austro-Hungary, providing mutual defence in the event of war.

Under the conservative governments of Francesco Crispi (1887–91, 1893–6), Italy also joined the scramble for colonies in North Africa. Crispi successfully colonised Eritrea, but when he tried to subdue Ethiopia (Abyssinia), the Italian army suffered a humiliating defeat at Adwa which led to Crispi's resignation. A later colonising attempt during the Italo-Turkish War (1911–12) ended in victory and the Italian occupation of Libya and the Dodecanese Islands.

North–south divide

At home, the years leading up to World War I were marked by the division that still plagues the country today: relative wealth in the north and extreme poverty in the south. The economy was overwhelmingly agricultural, and the government's protectionist policies left Italy increasingly isolated from other European markets. The industrial boom of the late 1800s, mostly in textiles and refining, was confined to the north. The crushing economic conditions in the south fuelled a wave of emigration. In the last years of the 19th century, nearly half a million people a year set out for the New World.

When World War I began with Austria's attack on Serbia in July 1914, Italy had not been consulted, in breach of the terms of the Triple Alliance. In consequence, on 2 August, Prime Minister Antonio Salandra declared Italy's neutrality. Public opinion began to swing in the direction of the Allies. To help win Italy over, the

LEFT: Benito Mussolini in 1928.
RIGHT: statue of Victor Emmanuel II in Venice.

Allied governments dangled the possibility of territorial gains: Rome was offered the chance to gain the "unrecovered" provinces of Trieste and Trentino, long held by the Austro-Hungarian Habsburg Empire. In addition, Italy would receive the Alto Adige, plus North African and Turkish enclaves. Finally swayed, in April 1915

Italy signed the secret Treaty of London and, a month later, broke the Triple Alliance and entered the war on the Allied side.

Seldom had a country been so ill-prepared for war. Italy's army was poorly equipped, and Austrian troops had already dug into defensive positions in Alpine strongholds along the 480-km (300-mile) shared border. For Italy the war was a costly stalemate; of the 5.5 million men mobilised, 39 percent were killed or wounded.

At the post-war conference table, the Treaty of St Germain (10 September 1919) gave Italy Trentino, the Alto Adige (South Tyrol) and Trieste. But Fiume, Dalmatia and the other promised territories were negotiated away by the Allies.

Disappointment in the peace talks, combined with the social and economic toll of the war, produced chaotic domestic conditions. Soon there was talk that Italy had won only a "mutilated victory", despite its wartime sacrifice. Inflation soared. Factory workers took to the streets, and peasants clamoured for land reform.

Into this power vacuum marched Benito Mussolini and his Fascist Party. When he founded the party in 1919, Mussolini played on the worst fears of all Italians. To those who fretted over the "mutilated victory", he was a chest-thumping nationalist. To placate the rich he denounced Bolshevism. To the middle classes he pledged a

return to law and order, and a corporate state in which workers and management would pull together for the good of the country.

By mid-1922, Fascism had become a major political force. When workers called for a general strike, Mussolini made his move. On 28 October, 50,000 members of the Fascist militia converged on Rome. Although Mussolini's supporters held only a small minority in parliament, the sight of thousands of menacing Fascists flooding the streets of the capital was enough to topple the tottering government of Prime Minister Luigi Facta. Refusing to sanction a state of siege, King Victor Emmanuel III instead handed the reins of government to Mussolini.

Once in control, Mussolini quickly pushed through an act assuring the Fascists a permanent majority in the parliament. After questionable elections in 1924, he dropped all pretence of collaborative government. Italy was now a dictatorship. In Christmas of that year, he declared himself head of the government, answerable only to the king. Fascist fronts took over all the rights once held by unions, and management organisations and national corporations were set up to supervise every phase of the economy.

Within two years all parties except the Fascists were banned, and opposition activists were jailed or forced into exile or underground. Anyone Mussolini could not subject by will or law was crushed by force.

Fascist rule

Despite its ugly underbelly, on the surface Fascism seemed to work. Weary of inflation, strikes and street disturbances, Italians eagerly embraced their severe new government and its charismatic *Duce*, or leader. This spontaneous response to Fascist rule was reinforced by a strong propaganda campaign. Mussolini promised to restore to Italy the glories of Ancient Rome, and for a time promises were enough. Soon, however, the government could show results. The economy stabilised, huge public works projects were launched, and Mussolini even made peace with the Vatican, hammering out the Lateran Treaty (1929), which ended the 50-year rift between Rome and the Catholic Church. He also set out on an imperial campaign, restoring control over Libya, which had been ignored during and after World War I. In October 1935, Italian troops crossed the border of Eritrea and headed for the Ethiopian capital of Addis Ababa. The League of Nations protested, but took no action. Six months later, *Il Duce* announced to a hysterical Piazza Venezia crowd that, finally, Rome had begun to reclaim its empire.

The international outcry over the Ethiopian occupation left Rome isolated. The one government willing to overlook Mussolini's expansionism was in Berlin, where Adolf Hitler's Nazis had held power since January 1933. Both Germany and Italy had supported General Francisco Franco's nationalist troops in the Spanish Civil War (1936–9), and this cooperation led eventually to the signing of the Pact of Steel between Berlin and Rome in May 1939.

Three months later, Hitler invaded Poland. Within days, Britain and France declared war on Germany. At first the Rome government remained neutral, as it had in 1914, arguing that Berlin's surprise attack on Poland did not require an automatic military response. In any case, most Italians opposed intervention, and the army was ill-prepared for war. But as Hitler claimed victory after victory – in Denmark, Norway and Belgium, and with France on the verge of collapse – the lure

BLACKSHIRTS

This name was originally given to supporters of Mussolini's Fascist Party, who wore distinctive black shirts in the 1920s; it was later linked with the Nazi SS and with Oswald Mosley's British Union of Fascists.

prevent the collapse. In 1943 US and British troops captured Sicily.

The beginning of the end was in sight. From their base in Sicily, the Allied forces began to bomb the Italian mainland, and Italian public morale sank to a new low. On 25 July 1943, the Grand Council of Fascism voted to strip *Il Duce* of his powers. Mussolini refused to step down, but the next day, King Victor Emmanuel ordered his arrest. Mussolini was detained in the Abruzzo Mountains,

of sharing the spoils of war proved irresistible. On 10 June 1940, Italy entered the war, just before the fall of France.

Eager to pull off his own battlefield coup, in the autumn of 1940 Mussolini set his sights on taking Greece. But the Greeks fought back fiercely. The Italians suffered many casualties, and only Nazi intervention prevented a likely Italian defeat. The war was also going badly for the Axis Powers in North Africa, and eventually even the Nazi General Rommel could not

LEFT: the Palazzo della Civiltà del Lavoro in Rome's EUR district, a prime example of Fascist architecture.
ABOVE: Axis allies – Mussolini and Hitler.

but in September, German air commandos airlifted him to Munich.

Chaos broke out in the final days of the war. To placate the Germans, who would otherwise have occupied the entire country, Prime Minister Marshal Badoglio publicly declared that Italy would fight on. In secret, however, he entered negotiations with the Allies, who by then had fought their way as far north as Naples. Above that line was the hastily organised *Repubblica Sociale Italiana*, headed by the liberated *Duce*. Better known as the Republic of Salo, based on Lake Garda, this was a puppet regime of Berlin, and Mussolini spent most of his time brooding on the judgement history would pass on him.

As the Allies fought northwards, the Italian Resistance felt safe enough to begin widespread activities. Combined, the forces managed to liberate Rome on 4 June 1944; the liberation of Florence followed not long after, on 12 August. The Germans and Mussolini lasted out the winter behind the so-called "Gothic line" in the Apennines, but by spring 1945 that effort, too, had collapsed.

Mussolini tried to escape into Switzerland disguised as a German soldier, but Italian partisans found him, and the next morning he was shot. His body was hauled into Milan and hung by a rope for the public to see.

Recovery and resiliency

In the immediate postwar period, Italy suffered greatly. The Italian colonies, won at such cost, were taken away and reparations had to be paid to the Soviet Union and Ethiopia. The political system needed a complete overhaul. In the 1946 elections, voters decided in favour of making the country a republic, thus formally ending the days of the monarchy. The economy was in disarray, but US aid in the form of the Marshall Plan helped to ease the burden.

For over a decade after the war, centrist coalitions ran the country. Then, in the early 1960s, the Christian Democrats, Socialists, Social

A MARXIST PARTY WITHOUT MARX

A distinctive feature of Italian politics has been the influence of the Italian Communist Party (PCI). In the post-war years, the party cleaved to the Soviet Union's political line, and Rome's centrist government kept the communists at arm's length.

Under Enrico Berlinguer, PCI secretary 1972–84, the party's orientation changed. It often led the so-called Eurocommunism movement, in favour of more independence from Moscow; it scolded the Soviets for human rights abuses and the Russian invasion of Afghanistan; on economic issues it grew ever more centrist, prompting some to dub it a "Marxist party without Marx". By

1981 the PCI could count on about a third of the popular vote, and it was second only to the Christian Democrats (DC) in size. Catholicism and communism were the two dominant political cultures of the post-war years, with the communist heartland in central Italy. The collapse of communism in Eastern Europe led to the PCI splitting into the mainstream Democratic Party of the Left (DS) and a hardline splinter group. After the upheavals of the 1990s, the DC was dissolved and the DS came to power as part of a left-wing coalition. But now the political scene is awash with new parties, even if many old faces remain.

Democrats and Republicans formed a coalition and ruled, in various combinations, until 1968.

Fuelled by cheap labour, the economy developed rapidly. The 1950s witnessed a steady migration from rural areas to the cities and from south to north. Heavy industry such as chemicals, iron, steel and cars took off. In 1957, Italy became a founding member of the European Community. By the mid-1960s, manufacturing overtook agriculture as the main source of GNP, and observers hailed Italy's "economic miracle".

Terrorism and scandals

A few years later, however, the boom had gone bust, Italy was dubbed the "sick man of Europe", and social ills set in. By far the worst was terrorism. From the late 1970s, kidnappings, knee-cappings and murders were a fact of life. The murder, in 1978, of former Christian Democrat prime minister Aldo Moro by the left-wing *Brigate Rosse* (Red Brigades) spurred new anti-terrorist measures, and eventually 32 Red Brigade members were imprisoned for the deaths of Moro and 16 others. Neo-Fascist terrorism also plagued the country, culminating, in 1980, in a bomb blast at Bologna station, killing 84 people.

In the 1980s the economy grew, and Italy briefly overtook France and Britain in the economic league. Troubles were in store, however. In the 1990s a wave of corruption scandals rocked the state. In 1992, it was alleged that some £67 million (US$100 million) had been shared out among the leaders of the five coalition parties governing Italy in 1990. Two former premiers were convicted of being chief recipients, while veteran prime minister Giulio Andreotti was charged with Mafia links *(see page 66)*, as were other leading figures, from fashion designers to industrialists. The short-lived first premiership of media magnate Silvio Berlusconi, in 1994, also stumbled over accusations of corruption. These scandals unleashed a volley of reforms spearheaded by the first left-wing government in Italy's post-war history. In order to create stronger, more durable governments, the system of proportional representation was changed to a largely first-past-the-post system. Measures were taken to prune the public sector, reform the welfare state, tackle organised crime and meet the requirements of European Monetary Union.

Into the new millennium

In a landslide victory in 2001, Silvio Berlusconi's centre-right government came to power on a tide of populism, nationalism and reforming zeal, but the country then sank into recession and floundered in protectionist measures. Perceived as a free-marketeer, the media mogul was elected to slash red tape and reform labour laws and the tax system. However, by 2006, when he left office, he had singularly failed to resolve the conflict of interest between his public and business roles,

and, as a convicted fraudster, evoked the tainted world of the Italian kickback culture. Commentator John Carlin likened the Milanese mogul to a megalomaniac Roman ruler: "The Roman emperors knew that the secret to exercising peaceful rule over the people was to provide them with bread and circus. Berlusconi owns the circus, pretty much all of it – the TV, the football, the magazines, the books. And as a head of government, who also happens to own Italy's biggest supermarket chain, he also controls, in the widest sense of the word, the bread."

Berlusconi always considered himself to be the victim of a left-wing conspiracy, while his critics were convinced that he saw himself as above

LEFT: the liberation of Rome. **RIGHT:** 10.25am, on the day in 1980 when a terrorist bomb ripped through Bologna train station.

the law, even introducing laws to favour his business interests. Both in and out of office, the former premier has appealed against charges of fraud, false accounting and corruption, and although censured, has been successful in escaping conviction. Despite a suspended sentence for fraud in 1997, Berlusconi maintains his media empire, high political profile and chairmanship of AC Milan football club. The former cruise-ship singer and showman may yet have the last laugh.

It is too early to assess Berlusconi's legacy, particularly when his status as Italy's richest man still makes him a player in most political scenarios. Detractors point to Berlusconi's ruthless pursuit of self-interest, his lack of probity and unstatesmanlike behaviour. However, while Berlusconi's gaffes regularly made him a laughing stock on the world stage, fans claim that he at least raised the Italian profile, proved a loyal ally to the United States and Britain, not least over the Iraq war, and tried to reform the fossilised state of Italian bureaucracy and liberalise the economy and health system.

An uncertain future

Italy, traditionally characterised as unstable, is facing an even more unstable future than usual. In 2006, the election of a left-wing coalition

GRAND DESIGNS

During his first premiership, Berlusconi was drawn to "grand projects" which would leave a mark and solve intractable problems with a flourish. One of the most pharaonic of *"grandi progetti"* was the plan to build the world's longest single-span suspension bridge across the Straits of Messina. The scheme, to connect Sicily with the mainland, proved costly and was unpopular with environmentalists, so was shelved by the centre-left administration. At the other end of the country, the high-speed rail link between Turin and Lyon is a controversial scheme involving the creation of a 53-km (33-mile) tunnel, to be part of a trans-European goods route to move freight off the roads. As the first huge tunnel built in an Alpine valley, its environmental effect is unquantifiable. The project divides opinion and is currently awaiting further "consultation".

In Venice, debate rages about the virtues of the Mose dam. Work on this long-delayed mobile flood barrier has been stalled by the new mayor of Venice, who has dismissed it as folly and requested further research. The project has won support from the present government and Venice in Peril, but critics, including some environmentalists, fear that the barrier is not reversible and could affect the delicate ecological balance in the lagoon, turning it into a stagnant pond. Big projects, big problems.

under Romano Prodi spelt the end of a turbulent administration in which Italy underperformed. However, the left's tiny majority provides a weak mandate at a time when the economy is in the doldrums. Prodi, the former EU president, heads a coalition of 10 parties with different agendas, including Catholics, former communists and the Greens, so an ideological roller-coaster ride cannot be ruled out. In fact, after just nine months in power, Prodi was temporarily brought down by the far left on a foreign policy issue, to be reinstated 7 days later by a senate vote of confidence.

The country faces a spiralling budget deficit and towering national debt. Industrial output has

influx of cheap Chinese imports. Recently, however, the foremost textile and clothing companies have been cultivating joint ventures with China, led by the market leader, Ermenegildo Zegna. The family firm showed great foresight as the first fashion house to set up independently in China, where Zegna now has 50 stores.

The government's plan is to reach across the divide, and also to inject greater flexibility into the job market without provoking massive protests, as has happened in France. Its hope is to liberalise the economy and weaken the straitjacket of guild-like rules that have their origins in the Middle Ages. So far, the government's

fallen, and unemployment has risen sharply. The country's experience of the euro has been unpromising, with the currency blamed for price rises and seen as the cause of the Italian malaise rather than as a symptom.

Italy is highly exposed to the challenges of globalisation as a disproportionate share of its manufacturing is concentrated in clothing, footwear and white goods, where it cannot compete with the Asian Tiger economies. The northern textile firms have been left reeling by the

LEFT: a demonstrator in Rome during the closing electoral rally of the "Ulive tree" coalition.
ABOVE: peacekeepers in Lebanon.

belt-tightening measures have found favour with Brussels but proved unwelcome with the far left. Curbing government spending and raising new taxes are hardly popularity-enhancing moves.

In a reversal of Berlusconi's administration's policy, Prodi sought to strengthen relations with the European Union and to weaken links with the United States. While the government is firmly against intervention in conflicts such as Iraq, it took the leadership for peacekeeping in Lebanon, with a 3,000-strong force. Now, after two years in opposition, Berlusconi has been re-elected. Pacific or not, Italy finds itself in unchartered waters once more – but without a Marco Polo or Christopher Columbus in sight. ❑

The Mafia

With its tradition of private justice and its code of silence, or omertà, *the Mafia remains Italy's biggest blight*

To many, the Mafia conjures up images of the *lupara,* or sawn-off shotgun used by the Sicilian underworld; corpses dripping with blood and helpless onlookers standing by. The Mafia may still colour Sicilian life, but local attitudes are changing profoundly. Not that the Mafia is a unified entity confined to Sicily, where it is known as

the "Cosa Nostra"; in Naples it mutates into the "Camorra", and in Calabria the "'Ndrangheta".

The revulsion of Sicilians to the 1992 murders of the anti-Mafia judges Giovanni Falcone and Paolo Borsellino helped weaken the Mafia's grip on public opinion, its greatest weapon, and dented the age-old code of silence, or *omertà. Pentiti* ("the penitents"), as Mafia turncoats are called, grew from a handful in 1992, when Falcone was killed, to 500 a year later. As a result dozens of Dons, including Salvatore "Toto" Riina, the Godfather of Corleone, and his successor, Bernardo Provenzano, have been jailed, and the Sicilian Mafia has gone underground.

The Mafia, once obsessed with tradition, is changing. As the old Mafia guard languishes in jail, the women have stepped into the breach, and, unlike their husbands, few have turned informer or state's evidence. Now that women have entered the wars, the last Mafia taboo has been broken. To fill the power vacuum, a "criminal mastermind" is thought to be reforming the Mafia, with the help of Cosa Nostra in the US, into a more secretive and sophisticated entity, based on "old Mafia values". The new generation of gangster is as ruthless on the stock exchange as on the streets of Palermo, and likely to be Internet-savvy – the favoured medium for money-laundering. Along with drugs, extortion and property speculation, Mafia activities now include international investment and arms-trading between Eastern Europe and the Middle East. The Mafia also exploits the phenomenon of *pentitismo,* infiltrating bogus turncoats, and weaving in false evidence to stall cases, discredit witnesses and sow uncertainty.

The good old days

The Mafia took shape in the early 19th century, in the guise of brotherhoods formed to protect Sicilians from corruption, foreign oppression and feudalism, but which thrived on human misery. Between 1872 and World War I, poverty forced 1.5 million Sicilians to emigrate to the Americas, where many joined brotherhoods, and the foundations of Cosa Nostra were laid. During Prohibition, US bootlegging marked the Mafia's graduation from rural bands to a sophisticated urban gangsterism.

In 1925, Mussolini, appalled at the Mafia's importance as a surrogate state, set out to bring it to its knees and almost succeeded. But the Mafia won a reprieve in 1943, when the Allied invasion essentially reinstated the Mob. Fearing the effects that war between the US and Italy would have on their interests, Italian and American mobsters such as Lucky Luciano struck a deal with US authorities in 1940. In return for helping to clear the way for the invasion, the Dons were to be left alone. Local mafiosi – such as Don Calogero Vizzini (39 murders) – were installed by the Allies as mayors of key towns.

Changing fortunes brought Sicilian and US Mafia elements to cities such as Milan and Naples; Naples, ruled by the Camorra, became a fiefdom of Cosa Nostra, and was chosen by US gangsters as the site of Italy's first heroin refinery. Sicily's "Americanised" Mafia achieved its quantum leap in the late 1950s with the introduction of drugs. In 1957, after a crackdown in the US against organised crime, American bosses entrusted their Sicilian counterparts with the importation of heroin, linked to Lucky Luciano and Luciano Liggio.

Clan warfare

Liggio, a wartime marketeer, elevated his Corleonese family to the pinnacle of the Cosa Nostra. After being jailed in 1974, he was eclipsed by "Wild Beast" Toto Riina. The tactics of the Corleonesi were simple: the removal of mafiosi who coveted power or caused trouble. The 1980 clan wars left Palermo's streets bathed in blood, the Corleonesi undisputed victors, and Riina linked to 1,000 murders. In response to the carnage provoked by the drugs trade, the new parliamentary anti-Mafia committee was itself targeted. The list of "illustrious corpses" included Palermo's prefect, dalla Chiesa, thought to have stumbled on the discovery of the "Third Level," a top politician who protected the Mafia. Supergrass Tommaso Buscetta claimed that former premier Giulio Andreotti ordered the Mob to kill dalla Chiesa and a journalist, because they knew too much. His evidence led to "maxi-trials" in the 1980s, where hundreds of mafiosi sat in the dock, and launched magistrate Giovanni Falcone's fight against the Mafia.

In 1992, the murder of Salvo Lima, the Sicilian leader of a party faction led by Andreotti, provoked a terror campaign that saw the assassination of the public prosecutors, Falcone and Borsellino. Even if their "heroic" deaths marked a turning point, the terror continued in 1993 with bombs in Milan and Rome which killed bystanders and devastated churches, and an explosion at Florence's Uffizi Gallery. The assassinations and attempt to destroy the nation's cultural treasures only served to strengthen Italian resolve against the Mafia.

In 2006, the fugitive Mafia Godfather, Bernardo Provenzano, was captured after 43 years on the run. The capture of the "Phantom of Corleone," also nicknamed "The Tractor" due to his propensity for mowing people down, provoked nationwide celebrations, even if cynics suspected the mobster had long been protected in his Corleone power base. After the arrest of Godfather Toto Riina in 1993, Provenzano had led the Mafia underground, consolidating its financial crime syndicate and abandoning overt violence.

Unlike the more centrally controlled Sicilian Mafia, the Neapolitan Camorra, with its 20 rival clans, has always been volatile. Since 2004, hundreds have died in continuing drugs-related turf wars. With control of an annual £11 billion (US$20 billion) drugs trade at stake, Naples' poverty-stricken northern suburbs have become a battleground, with protection rackets endemic. Drug dealers have been executed, while homes and businesses have been torched, leaving children to play truant because their parents are on the run. As Amato Lamberti, a Camorra expert, comments: "The real problem is the Camorra's roots in Neapolitan society. People hope that with time, economic development will eliminate the Camorra, but it doesn't work that way."

The Sicilian Mafia's rougher cousin, the Calabrian 'Ndrangheta, is equally fearsome. In 2004,

Italy's biggest anti-Mafia operation for a decade discovered that the drug-running 'Ndrangheta had built a complete underground village below Plati. A year later, the vice-president of Calabria's regional council was gunned down by gangsters.

As for society's relationship with the Mafia, despite a shift in attitudes, criminal practices remain entrenched, from illegal building in beauty spots to protection rackets. Even given public pressure, many doubt that the Mafia is marginalised. Infamous Corleone, Mafia heartland, pondered a name change to make a fresh start, even opening a Mafia Museum. Yet ironically, it was in a Corleone farmhouse that the Godfather was caught in 2006. ❑

LEFT: a threatening gesture is made during one of the maxi-trials. **RIGHT:** after years in hiding, Mafia godfather Bernardo Provenzano is arrested in Corleone.

THE CONTEMPORARY SCENE

Tradition and rebellion, conformity and individuality, chaos and over-regulation ... Italian life is riddled with paradoxes

According to Sergio Romano, a political journalist on *La Stampa*, "Italy is a constellation of large families, whether ideological, political, professional or criminal – the Church, the business community, the trade unions, the professions, state bureaucracies and the Mafia." He observes that "each family strives for sovereignty", acting as a fierce lobby group and dooming most national reforms to failure.

Curiously, Italian society combines anarchy and cosiness in equal measure, making it both chaotic and stultifying. At the simplest level, Italians create a cosy little world of "their" baker, dressmaker and picture-framer, conveying the social status of a patron rather than of a mere consumer. Personal recommendation is everything. Yet beyond lies the arbitrary world of bureaucracy, in which citizens feel powerless in the face of state indifference. Many commentators conclude that Italy would be a paradise if it could only reinvent the relationship between citizen and state. Yet without political chaos and conflicting social groups, the Italians would cease to be Italians and become Swiss.

The political picture

"It is not impossible to govern Italians, it is pointless." Mussolini's judgement has been borne out by the country's perpetual sense of teetering on the edge. The Italian mindset precludes a modern democracy, seeming to favour an abyss between the state and its citizens. The people swing between political disaffection and an obsession with politics. Fortunately, however, they also have an innate talent for brinkmanship, coupled with an ability to conjure compromise out of conflict. But if Italy totters along in an amiable state of chaos, it may be because Italians like it that way. "Controllers and controlled have an unspoken agreement," notes columnist Beppe Severgnini. "You don't change, we don't change, and Italy doesn't change, but we all complain that we can't go on like this."

LEFT: Via dei Condotti, Rome's most famous shopping district. **RIGHT:** keeping up with the news.

The country positions itself as the new Italy, turning its back on a baroque political structure steeped in *clientelismo* (nepotism). Even so, one in three people finds a job through a relative. Italy remains deeply old-fashioned, despite its faddism. Italians pride themselves on their free spirit, yet society remains static,

while protectionism has preserved many monopolies, including limiting the growth of supermarkets, even if shopping malls are slowly moving in. Despite their sense of tradition, Italians have a mania for modernity, novelty and new-fangled gadgetry, from the latest mobile phones to designer sinks and now shopping malls.

Milan is the business capital, a sophisticated metropolis dedicated to moneymaking and pleasure. Most wealth is still created in northern and central regions, such as Lombardy, the Veneto and Emilia-Romagna. However, although the Ferragamo, Prada and Armani fiefdoms are well known abroad, most Italian companies are family-run.

Specialised small companies provide more than two-thirds of industrial employment, from textiles in Tuscany to designer sunglasses in the Veneto. Even so, economic patterns are complex, and high unemployment and low consumer demand mask a thriving black economy. In the workplace, industrial action is commonplace. The art of conjuring compromise out of conflict in industrial relations is rooted in the social contract, a corporatist pact between government, unions and industry that has historically dominated labour relations, and is only being gradually eroded.

The impact of the euro, privatisation and the country's uncompetitiveness are major concerns. Privatisation of the public utilities did not end state interference. Given the traditional monopoly of top jobs in state companies by the political parties, politicians remain reluctant to give up their power. By the same token, the family dynasties who dominate the economy still hold sway. With his patrician charm and playboy reputation, the late Gianni Agnelli epitomised the closed, dynastic style of Italian capitalism. After his death in 2003, the Turin football stadium was renamed in his honour, and the family empire survives, even if the fate of Fiat seems to be inextricably linked with that of General Motors. Still, after a long time in the doldrums, Fiat announced positive forecasts until the end of the decade, linked to the launch of over 20 new models.

Despite a rash of mergers, power remains in the same hands: in 2001, the telecommunications industry witnessed the takeover of Olivetti and Telecom Italia by Pirelli and Benetton, the latter responsible for the clothing empire, a Formula One team, all the Italian motorways and service stations. After much debate, the decision was taken to privatise the ailing Alitalia, Italian-style – on condition that it remains the official national carrier.

A complex but coherent society

The social system is a rich landscape, not calibrated on class, success or wealth but on subtle distinctions. In conventional terms, a class system exists but has different connotations. The aristocracy thrives, thanks to its adaptability. Many *marchesi* (marquis) are entrepreneurs, carving niches in the fashion, art, wine and food industries. The Strozzi are big in banking, the Tuscan Frescobaldi and Sicilian Tasca are wine dynasties, while the Pucci and Ferragamo fashion empires thrive in Florence.

While class consciousness and accent are essentially immaterial, the *borghesi* (middle classes) form a cohesive group, as do the *agricoltori* (encompassing peasants and farmers). The ranks of the middle classes are swelling, even among the criminal caste. A recent Mafia round-up revealed that many new-generation Dons are doctors or laywers, in sharp contrast to the Cosa Nostra's agrarian roots, and even to recent Godfathers, who were barely literate. Whatever one's profession, honorific titles count, especially in the south: an engineer is addressed as "*ingegnere*"; *dottore* (doctor) is a mark of respect bestowed on

IN GOOD FAITH?

Curiously, the phrase often used to bemoan declining standards is: "There's no religion left any more." Jonathan Keates describes the Italian attitude to religion as "a lackadaisical Catholicism taken out of mothballs at christenings, first communions, weddings and funerals; the religion of photo-opportunity."

Increasingly, Italy's practising Catholics prefer to take their cue not from the Pope but from personal conscience or the liberal wing of the Church. To some, the Church symbolises temporal power. Strive as the Church might, civic culture, regional pride and fierce individualism form the real Italian faith today.

anyone with gravitas. Politics rarely impinge on social divisions: a member of the DS, the former Communist Party, may be a Catholic, wear Armani and have a Filipina maid.

Apart from the north–south divide, the key distinction is between *statali*, civil servants, and non-*statali*, the rest. Civil servants are seen as cosseted, with a protected pension and a job for life. Ranged against them are the *dipendenti* (company employees), *autonomi* (self-employed), *imprenditori* (entrepreneurs) and, lastly, the *liberi professionisti* (professionals). The employees claim the moral high ground, charging civil servants with exploiting the sys-

A new pressure group are the *precari*, workers on temporary contracts who crave security. Around 3 million people, mostly young, fall into this category, from language teachers to hotel workers. Without holiday pay, overtime or job security, many resort to "cocooning", concentrating on their private lives and opting out of the rat race. Sometimes dubbed the "IKEA generation", this group are "constrained" to buy flat-pack Swedish furniture – implying limited aspirations and prospects. In response, the state is striving to open up the public, retail, legal and transport sectors to shake up the sluggish economy and generate better jobs for the young.

tem and accusing the self-employed and professionals of tax evasion. This is a strange Italian stalemate in which private-sector workers (non-*statali*) justify tax evasion on the grounds that their taxes would only perpetuate the bloated state bureaucracy and southern incompetence. Tax evasion is a sport and a duty. If he were to cheat on his taxes in Italy, remarks Beppe Severgnini, "Two neighbours would come round to ask me how I did it, and two more would loathe me in silence."

LEFT: commercial artist at work in Trastevere, Rome.
RIGHT: the Frescobaldi dynasty, wine producers since the 16th century.

Popular culture and the arts

Both in the art world and in the broader cultural arena, Italian genius thrives on dissension, diversity and unbridled rivalry. However, music and the performing arts are more dynamic than the literary scene: Italy has always been a musical, visual and verbal culture more than a literary one. Contemporary fiction is an acquired taste, with writers often engaged in navel-gazing, esoteric concerns or petty politicking. The classical music scene is thriving and not restricted to the great opera houses: Italy boasts some of the best musical festivals in Europe, from the operatic masterpieces performed in Verona's lovely Roman amphitheatre, the Arena

Heritage Industry

Italy's share of Unesco World Heritage Sites is second to none, but there is a price to pay to sustain such riches, one that a country in perennial political turmoil can rarely afford. Air pollution, illegal building and sewage-laden water are endangering a third of Italy's Unesco sites, including such treasures as Pompeii's ancient ruins. Burdened by its costly heritage, Italy often resembles a cultural building site, with many buildings and monuments under wraps while undergoing painstaking and lengthy restoration. Vandalism is another problem. In Rome and other cities, recent damage to famous

artworks has reignited the debate about how best to protect Italy's huge sculptural heritage, much of it on open display and vulnerable to abuse. Vandals recently lopped off part of a Bernini fountain on Via Veneto, followed by damage to another celebrated fountain, the Fontana della Navicella, near the Colosseum. Vandalism in Florence's Piazza della Signoria resulted in damage to Ammanati's towering statue of Neptune, with the severing of the sea deity's right hand. This prompted calls for the removal of all Florentine public sculpture from city squares. As the despairing head of the Carabinieri's art-theft unit says: "Italy is an open-air museum, with many of its most celebrated works of art standing on streets and squares, and nowhere is this more true than in Florence."

Despite the threats to the nation's heritage, unqualified success stories abound. Amid the frantic fire-and-ice effects of the 2006 Winter Olympics, Turin was rebranded as a cinematic capital, baroque stage and cutting-edge design centre. Key galleries underwent makeovers, from the Egyptian Museum to the star-studded Cinema Museum. The Olympic legacy includes the remodelled stadium, where Juventus reign, and the new Palavela, a sweeping sail of a building, as well as bold exhibition spaces. Turin's renaissance continues, marked by the opening of Palazzo Madama after a decade under wraps, now home to the Museum of Ancient Art.

In the meantime, the country continues to open major museums and stage dazzling art extravaganzas. All over Italy, seemingly mundane restoration work ensures that masterpieces survive. In Tuscany alone, recent intervention has saved Lippi's frescos in Prato Cathedral and Vasari's Florentine frescos in the Palazzo Vecchio. Elsewhere, archaeologists are constantly unearthing Etruscan or Roman treasures, most recently in Tuscany, Naples and Brescia. Widely unacknowledged, even in Italy, Brescia boasts the greatest concentration of Roman remains north of Rome. The recent discoveries of frescoed Pompeian-style villas have propelled the city into the limelight, helped by its nomination as a Unesco heritage site.

Given the heavyweight nature of Italian heritage, stately homes tend to be treated as a burden, with little incentive for owners to turn their properties into public attractions. Italy may lag behind its French and British counterparts in the heritage industry but local landowners are increasingly taking the initiative. Tuscan aristocrats have long been entrepreneurial, with their country seats reborn as wine estates or rural resorts, but even the Sicilians are showing enterprise: princesses in Palermo are opening their homes to the public, staging cookery courses and masked balls to save the ancestral seat.

Near Trieste, Duino Castle, home of the princes Torre and Tasso, inventors of the modern postal service, is a model of entrepreneurial flair. The family, who trace their lineage back to Bonaparte, still live in the medieval castle yet welcome visitors, happily throwing their towers open to wedding banquets or corporate retreats. Few can resist celebrating an event on Roman ruins, overlooking a Druidic site dedicated to the sun god, or on a medieval terrace overlooking the Gulf of Trieste. The Italian heritage industry looks safe for some time to come. ❏

LEFT: ancestral home Duino Castle welcomes visitors.

di Verona, to the Puccini Festival at the composer's lakeside home in Tuscany's Torre del Lago. The Macerata festival, an operatic feast of Puccini and Verdi, hit the headlines in 1995 when the firing squad in Tosca used real bullets and accidentally shot the tenor. But the director of the Rossini Festival at Pesaro, the great composer's birthplace, bemoans Italian conservatism: "The public has no desire for opera to become theatre but only wants it to be about singing and tradition."

Italian high culture tends to be buffeted by perennial funding crises. The Berlusconi government's response was to stress the need for

The media moguls

Popular culture is dominated by television and by the power of monopolies. American-style anti-trust laws do not exist in Italy: telecommunications, publishing and the mass media are aces held in a few family hands. Berlusconi dominates the airwaves by owning the three most popular national television channels and influences RAI TV's three "public" channels. Mediaset, his media arm, controls channels that draw 60 percent of the audience share to "trashy TV". With a few exceptions, the output is devoted to political propaganda, poor-quality American imports and platitudinous game shows.

Italians to take more responsibility for their heritage. A shock advertising campaign showed images of mutilated artistic icons, such as Leonardo da Vinci's *Last Supper* with the disciples scratched out. The provocative slogan was: "Without your help, Italy could lose something," which singularly failed to elicit mass donations to save the country's treasures. Fortunately, local businesses and banks see themselves as stakeholders in their city's cultural identity, so pride and political pressure usually prompt a timely rescue bid.

Above: the annual Miss Italy contest, broadcast on Berlusconi-owned Rai Uno, draws millions of viewers.

The left-wing government that came to power in 2006 intended to move one of Berlusconi's channels to satellite, signalling the dismantling of his empire. However, the switch to digital terrestrial broadcasting has been postponed until 2012 to leave enough time to resolve the complex issues raised by Berlusconi's media monopoly and to rewrite the flawed legislation which favoured Italy's richest man.

Tobias Jones, author of the polemical *The Dark Heart of Italy*, is acutely aware of the country's Faustian pact: "When the medium became the message, the mogul became the prime minister." In one sense, having a head of state linked to the lowest form of culture epitomises the paradoxical nature of the country. In a society where aesthetics takes precedence over ethics, style triumphs over content, and stylish corruption triumphs over lacklustre probity. At best, it is partisan broadcasting; at worst it is a "videocracy", in which citizens wake up to a Berlusconi-designed world of vulgar television, political propaganda and venal advertising. In addition, the premier controls 60 percent of television advertising revenue, as well as the national daily, *Il Giornale*, and the Mondadori publishing empire that produces a quarter of all Italian books – and has huge interests in new media.

Not that Berlusconi is entirely without a counterweight: Carlo De Benedetti, once synonymous with Olivetti, has transmuted into another media magnate and owner of *La Repubblica*, the leading left-wing daily, and *L'Espresso*, the most influential news weekly, while the Turin-based Agnelli group owns one quarter of all national and provincial newspapers, as well as the Fiat car company and the Juventus football club.

The turbulent state of the game reflects the cynical ethos in which a top player sees his premier engineer a law under which false accounting is no longer a crime. Still, if in doubt, the Italians would rather look good than be good.

The country has a flexible moral code, except on drugs. Italy now operates a zero-tolerance policy, with anyone found in possession of hard or soft drugs open to prosecution for dealing. Not that the political class feels so constrained: a recent media sting operation tricked 50 politicians into being tested for drug use, and revealed that a third were guilty. Second only to drug-trafficking, the control of public and private contracting is the most lucrative activity for organised crime, with a turnover of £11.8 billion (US$23 billion).

A health scandal in 2007 revealed that while wealthy Lombardy possessed 150 private health clinics, Sicily had 1,800, places often linked to crime syndicates and substandard services. Investigating the illicit provision of healthcare in Calabria and Sicily is now a government priority. Fortunately, the Mafia also cares about its own members' health and happiness: criminal gangs have resorted to cheese raids, hijacking lorries containing wheels of Parmesan cheese. The love of the good life is not restricted to the virtuous.

Spectacle, sociability, conformity

Foremost among the reassuring rituals of modern Italian life is the love of spectacle. During the opera season, La Scala's newly restored marbled and mirrored lobby is awash with Milanese matrons in furs, and rivalled by the Venetians in the faithfully restored Teatro La Fenice. The love of display cuts across regional and social divides, from the chic Venice Carnival to the smallest Sardinian festival. At a deeper level, the death of Pope John Paul II in 2005 entwined several strands of Italian life: the sense of occasion and spectacle, softened by a poignant sense of solidarity.

Tellingly, there is no Italian term for privacy. The emphasis is on the everyday values of sociability, simplicity and pleasure. The essence of Italian sociability is the *passeggiata*, the evening parade, with pauses for preening, flirting and gossiping. Social life is neatly ordered, even underpinned by excessive planning. Commenting on the cloying social packaging of Italian life, novelist and long-term Italian resident Tim Parks says: "Cappuccino until ten, then espresso; aperitivo after twelve; your pasta, your meat, your dolce in bright packaging; light white wine, strong red wine, prosecco; baptism, first communion, marriage, funeral." ❏

Football fever

Football, like fashion, is at the heart of Italian life. As if to prove it, Dolce & Gabbana declare: "We have always been football fans and footballers are, for us, the new male icons." The design duo not only dressed the winning national team in the 2006 World Cup but featured the stars in steamy locker-room scenes for recent collections. They also dress AC Milan, the last Italian team to win the Champions League – even if Stefano Gabbana supports rivals Inter Milan, much to the despair of Domenico Dolce, a stalwart AC Milan fan. Still, given recent scandals, Italian football needs all the support it can get.

The 2006 World Cup victory came during the Calciopoli ("Footballgate") match-fixing furore, which continues to have repercussions. Phone taps revealed sporting fraud perpetrated by managers and referees, although the players were blameless. As a result, Juventus were stripped of their Championship titles and relegated to Serie B, while AC Milan, Fiorentina, Lazio, Arezzo and Reggina were all docked points. Yet despite the sacking of managers and the prosecution of match officials, there is little sense that probity has dribbled down the wings of the Italian game. Referees face a struggle to regain their credibility, but there are glimmers of hope. Recalling the Rolex scandal of several seasons ago, when the watches found their way onto the wrists of key referees, courtesy of Roma football club, lavish gifts are now considered bribes, a first for Italian football.

Subversively, football often lobs an own goal at its political masters, unsurprising in a country where the beautiful game is a common metaphor for political success. This is a nation whose premier, Silvio Berlusconi, rose to prominence on the back of his ownership of AC Milan, and named his political party after a football chant. Italy's top teams have always been the ultimate boy's toys for the country's power-brokers. While AC Milan still belongs to media mogul Berlusconi, Juventus remains a symbolic plaything for the Agnelli car dynasty. Fiorentina is the fiefdom of Andrea and Diego della Valle, the brothers behind Tod's, the luxury loafers, and Cinecittà film studios, even though both were implicated in match-fixing in 2006 and banned from football for four years. On the other side of the Apennines, Parma is still reeling from the loss of its princely backers, the Tanzi family, whose dynastic control of the club dribbled away during the Parmalat milk industry scandal.

LEFT: mourners at the funeral of Pope John Paul II.
RIGHT: World Cup victory celebrations.

Not that controversy is ever far from Italian football, especially in home derbies. Given the sectarian nature of society, rival teams in the same city are commonplace. In the case of bitter rivals Roma and Lazio, the clash is underscored by a polarised fan base: Roma supporters see themselves as liberal-minded urbanites and, slightly unfairly, dismiss Lazio fans as country bumpkins or Fascistic thugs.

Italian football is not the success story it once was. In the 1980s these stadia drew Europe's largest crowds, with averages of nearly 40,000 a match. Since then, gates have fallen as the fixtures and results are deemed predictable, with the same clubs predominating. Whether the Calciopoli scandal

ranks as a massive spur to reform remains to be seen. Cynics suspect that the boardroom chairs will simply be reshuffled. Sweeping aside the old order may have to wait until the glorious memories of the World Cup have faded.

The core issue of endemic corruption needs to be tackled, but more pressing now is the issue of football violence, which appears to be on the rise. In early 2007, the death of a policeman during violent clashes following a Sicilian derby led to the temporary closure of stadiums (league matches were played in eerily silent arenas). The government are looking to England for inspiration on how to deal with the rising tide of football hooliganism through such measures as the creation of fully seated stadiums and harsher punishments for offenders. ❏

THE ITALIANS

Individualism, a sense of survival and natural ebullience are qualities
almost all Italians share – but there the similarities end

It has been said that Italians do not exist, that those who are thought of as Italian regard themselves as Piedmontese, Tuscan, Venetian, Sicilian, Calabrian and so on. No one has ever classified the Italians convincingly: to be born in Palermo, Sicily, or in Turin, Piedmont, is a classification in itself. Sometimes even fellow-countrymen feel like foreigners. In Pietro Germi's film *Il Cammino della Speranza (The Path of Hope)*, a peasant says: "There's bad people in Milan, they eat rice."

According to the writer Ennio Flaiano, being Italian is a profession – except that it doesn't require much studying: one just inherits it. Generations have learned the art of *arrangiarsi*, of getting along in difficult situations. Adjusting to political change and foreign conquest has generated a flexible mentality and a detached attitude towards political regimes, all of which are considered ephemeral. The forest of rules, statutes, norms and regulations has engendered distrust of the state. The popular saying, *fatta la legge trovato l'inganno* (a law is passed, a way past it is found) is almost a national motto.

North versus south

"Southerners tend to make money in order to rule, northerners to rule in order to make money," declared the writer Luigi Barzini. The conflicting values of north and south reflect different cultures and history. Compared with the industrialised, progressive north, the agrarian, conservative south experienced feudalism, oppression, corruption, poverty and neglect. Known as the Mezzogiorno, the region has suffered grandiose white elephants, called "cathedrals in the desert": steelworks sited in remote places with no proper infrastructure. Cut off from the progress and markets of Northern Europe, southerners left for their own survival. Before 1914, more than 5 million emigrated to North America alone.

Although emigration is on the wane, the south

LEFT AND RIGHT: effortless elegance and a love of "il mare" – two very Italian traits.

still suffers from depopulation, perceived backwardness and a great gap between rich and poor. Southerners, known as *meridionali*, often encounter prejudice, with northerners resenting "subsidising" the south through taxation. Indeed, some northerners see such aid as pouring their hard-earned money into the pockets of

the Camorra in Naples or the Mafia in Sicily. The north–south divide, in all its tragicomic aspects, remains at the heart of Italian life.

Politics and individualism

The average person in the street expresses a revulsion for politics: *la politica è una cosa sporca* (politics are a dirty thing) is a typical view. This is based on a belief that all parties are the same, and that politics work only for politicians. The Italians remain sceptical of the state, and cannot conceive of abstract solutions or trust in ideologies. Behind such opinions lurks an unrestrained individualism that denies civic responsibility. Yet hand in hand with individualistic entrepreneurship, there is a nostalgic yearning for "the strong man" whose power and will is stamped on his face, whose voice captures the nation's mood. It was a wave of such nostalgia for authoritarian answers that swept Alessandra Mussolini, grand-daughter of Benito, into parliament in 1992, and, more recently, helped media magnate Silvio Berlusconi to his third term as premier.

The strong sense that Italians have of their own self-importance is evident in their dislike of queuing or of respecting rules. "We think it's an insult to our intelligence to comply with a regulation," writes commentator Beppe Sev-

ergnini. "Obedience is boring. We want to think about it. We want to decide whether a particular law applies to our specific case. In that place, at that time." Hence red traffic lights rarely mean stop. A pedestrian crossing at 6am might count as a "negotiable red", a "weak orange" at a busy traffic junction might be a "*rosso pieno*", a full red. It all depends. Only a cappuccino after 10am is non-negotiable.

Italians are far more conformist than they would wish, whether with regard to drinking coffee at set times, obeying non-smoking laws or wearing orange, if deemed the season's colour. Self-regard is reflected in the way Ital-

THE LANGUAGE

The Italian language is the closest to Latin of any of the so-called Romance languages. Modern Italian owes much to writers such as Dante and Manzoni, who assumed as their standard the educated language of Tuscany. Today the finest form of speech is said to be *la lingua toscana in bocca romana* (the Tuscan tongue in the Roman mouth).

Italian is considered the most musical language in the world: in the 16th century, the Holy Roman Emperor, Charles V, is said to have spoken Spanish with God, French with men, German with his horse, but Italian with women since it can express many subtleties of thought

and feeling. Italian can be as precise as any other language, yet the style of newspaper editorials, art criticism and political speeches, in particular, is often pompous, pretentious and wilfully obscure.

Until recently, more than 1,500 dialects existed alongside the official Italian language, most of them virtually incomprehensible outside their own village. Many contained a large number of foreign words imported by foreign occupiers. Dialect is still spoken among old people in the countryside, and in some cities, but is fading away among younger generations. The advent of television has done much for linguistic unification.

ians dress. Shoes, ties, lovely fabrics and liberty of the imagination all contribute to the *costume*. Fastidious care is lavished on cars, seen as extensions of their owners' personalities. Yet beyond the surface gloss, there is a sense of humanity that transcends differences. As Severgnini wrily points out, Italian air hostesses are hopeless at serving you coffee but good at cleaning it up and sympathising when you spill it. Giulio Andreotti, the machiavellian seven-times premier, also singles out this sense of common humanity: "In Italy there are no angels nor devils, only average sinners." This tolerant Roman Catholic society is nurtured on the con-

According to a recent survey, more than 85 percent of Italians claim to be Catholics, but only a quarter attend Mass regularly. Nonetheless Catholicism still plays an important role in rituals, from first holy communion to the marriage ceremony and Christian burial.

Sex and the family

While the family remains the bedrock of traditional Italian society, *mammismo*, the cult of the mother, is its cornerstone. The iconic image of the mother pervades the male approach to courtship and his choice of bride. Once married, however, male infidelity is often quietly con-

cept of original sin, universal temptation and redemption, so penitence can erase sins, even crimes.

Despite an authoritarian pope, abortion and divorce are legal while contraception is widely accepted. Indeed, much to the chagrin of the Vatican, Italy has the lowest birth rate in Europe. Catholicism has a stronger hold in the south and in the Veneto than in the former "red belt" of Emilia-Romagna, Umbria and Tuscany.

LEFT: market day in Dogliani, Piedmont.
ABOVE: garrulous Italians are the biggest mobile phone users in Europe. **RIGHT:** a monk in an increasingly secular society.

doned, provided that the family is supported and appearances preserved.

A recent report reveals that divorce happens every four minutes in a country once regarded as a bastion of marriage. The latest statistics record over 50,000 divorces, a 45 percent increase from 2000. Although money squabbles, marrying young and meeting new partners are cited for the rising divorce rate, three out of 10 marriages fail because of the unhealthily close attachment of Italian men to their mothers. The concept of *mammoni*, sons who cling to apron strings, is common, with boys over-indulged well into adulthood. An intrusive mother-in-law may expect her adult offspring to eat with her every Sunday, or may deal with her married son's domestic chores. Moreover, disillusioned daughters-in-law help account for the popularity of the therapist's couch, a trend exacerbated by the "superwoman" syndrome, which is, in turn, linked to the low birth rate, the lowest in Europe: if so much is now expected of working women, having one child is challenging enough.

In terms of morality, a north–south divide prevails, with southern values more traditional and northern mores similar to those of Northern Europe. Even here, appearances are more important than reality. A slick young Milanese banker attaches as much importance to family ties as does the humblest Calabrian peasant, and neither would dare miss Sunday lunch with their parents.

As for sex, discretion counts for much, and provided premarital relationships are not flaunted under the family roof, honour is maintained. Since students tend to live at home, and offspring are reluctant to flee the nest until marriage, romantic assignments can take on the complexity of a Pirandello farce. High rents are a deterrent to leaving home; male offspring may also rely on a doting mother to act as a domestic drudge. But feminism is beginning to seep into

PUTTANOPOLI ("TARTGATE")

The exploits of the House of Savoy, Italy's disgraced royal dynasty, regularly fill the gossip columns for all the wrong reasons. Prince Victor Emmanuel, head of the household, only returned to Italy in 2003 after the repeal of laws forbidding male members of the dynasty from setting foot on home soil. In Italian eyes, the prince wasted little time in courting controversy. The dynastic head became embroiled in corruption and sex scandals involving the procurement of prostitutes and gaming permits at a casino in Campione d'Italia, an Italian enclave in Switerland. Dubbed Puttanopoli ("Tartgate") by the media, the sleazy affair resulted in the jailing of the son of the last king of Italy. The experience of prison food in Potenza jail failed to demoralise the prince: "It really is true what they say – in Italy, you can eat well everywhere," he declared.

This was not Victor Emmanuel's first brush with the law: being an avowed member of the infamous P2 Masonic lodge and accidentally killing a German tourist are just two of his previous misdemeanours. In the case of "Tartgate", the prince denies any wrongdoing and, after house arrest, has recently had his travel ban lifted. But the last word lies with his outraged sister, Princess Maria Gabriella of Savoy, who disowned him as a royal: "As of today, for me, he is Mr Savoy."

family life, and mothers increasingly expect a career outside the family business. The stereotype of the roly-poly Italian mamma, with one eye on the baby and the other on the pasta, is losing its appeal.

A style of life

The Italian style of life is beset by intractable problems, from officialdom to a barely functioning legal system and dysfunctional governments. In the workplace, fear of failure stymies innovation, as does the Italians' reluctance to relocate, should a better job beckon. At the deepest level, Italians seem unable to believe in

Italy. Life is enjoyed to the fullest, with a flair gained over centuries of practice.

The new Italians

For a country with its roots in so many races, Italy is far from being a multiracial society, and Italian culture predominates. Settlers linked to Carthage, Constantinople, Normandy, North Africa and Moorish Spain have all made their mark in Italy, whether as colonisers or plunderers. But given Italy's lack of significant empire since Roman times, many of the colonial lessons have been lost. Modern Italians have been slow to accept that someone can be visi-

the possibility of constructive change. But merely listing the ills is missing the point. Italian life is not about work and progress, but about survival and individualism, family and friends, roots and relaxation. Italian life sparkles with a brilliance unmatched anywhere else in Europe. The Italians have perfected a lifestyle that may be short on efficiency but is long on enjoyment. Simple things, such as eating a meal, taking a walk, having an ice cream, watching the world go by, become special in

bly non-European yet fully assimilated, or even an Italian citizen.

But in the last decade or so, the influx of newcomers has begun to make an impact, both in the northern cities and in the southern countryside. Cosy assumptions have been shattered by the existence of ethnic-looking children, born in Italy, who speak Italian with a Roman accent, or by Romanian therapists who have taken Italian citizenship and integrated perfectly. More usually, the different ethnic groups lead parallel lives in their own communities, and there are few mixed marriages and little assimilation.

Italy's historic ethnic groups comprise the Greek, Jewish, Armenian and Albanian com-

LEFT: children are cosseted and *la famiglia* remains sacred, yet Italy has the lowest birth rate in Europe.
ABOVE: mealtimes are a family occasion.

munities who have had footholds in Italian towns since medieval times. In many cases, local traditions are retained, as happens with the Greeks and Albanians in Sicily and Calabria. Though far more recent, the Chinese community in Florence is well established, as is the African population in Brescia.

Officially, immigrants and foreign residents make up less than 5 percent of the population, with no reliable statistics on the numbers who actually take up Italian citizenship. Albanians, Romanians, Moroccans, Ukrainians and Chinese are the biggest ethnic minority groups, along with the French and South Americans, but

prising that we need to work in mainland Europe but we were shocked by the conditions. Italy is not a victim of this migration. The migrants are needed by the agriculture in an area which wants cheap labour to produce cheap food. There is poverty in Africa, but what is different here is the desperation. It is shocking that it has taken a non-governmental organisation to get the law applied in a European country."

As a key EU entry point for illegal immigration, Italy has struggled to cope with the influx of boat people, especially from Albania and Africa. First it was Puglia, caught in the eye of the "Albanian Hurricane", where political upheaval

recent waves of migrants have been from Africa and Eastern Europe.

There is no escaping the fact that most immigrants remain second-class citizens, unable to vote and unlikely to gain Italian citizenship. Moreover, the economic reality is still that immigrants do the jobs that Italians shun. Most work on production lines in northern factories or in the tomato fields in the south, especially in the heel of Italy, where virtually all Italian tomatoes are produced. Recently, the international charity Médecins sans Frontières reported on conditions among migrants in Calabria and found that most were worse off than refugees in African camps. As MSF said: "It may seem sur-

prompted thousands to commandeer ferries and tugboats to cross the narrow Strait of Otranto into safety in Italy. In the second wave, it was Sicily's turn, with the remote island of Lampedusa, sandwiched between Sicily and Libya, becoming one of the gateways for refugees and illegal immigrants from North Africa. In most cases, the goal was simply to enter the European Union rather than to settle in Italy, but many stay nonetheless, particularly given the magnetic pull of the wealthy northern cities, notably Milan and Brescia. In 2005, 23,000 illegal immigrants reached Italy, 8,000 more than the previous year, while in 2006 over 10,000 washed up on Lampedusa's shores alone, with hundreds often drowning in their bid for a new life. While many desperadoes are intercepted at sea, others reach Italy and, if not deported, start at the bottom of the economic ladder.

Integration and segregation

With little recent history of empire, the Italians veer between demonising and fetishising foreigners, particularly non-EU citizens. The typical professional workplace is still closed to ethnic minorities, but to dub the Italian majority racist would be to miss the point: Italians are most racist about their fellow-countrymen from "rival" regions, with the north–south divide as

the political agenda of separatist groups like the Northern League has exploited the resentment of the wealthy north towards the poorer south, attributing economic ills to "foreigners". The perception of immigrants as potential criminals further fuels resentment against the urban ethnic communities. People-trafficking, prostitution and gangsterism are generally attributed to "foreigners", even if the natives have proved perfectly competent at drug-running and Mafia murder themselves.

On a positive note, even in cities where racial tensions are most felt, such as Brescia and Milan, there is nothing resembling a ghetto, and none of

entrenched as ever. A *straniero* can be a foreigner or someone from the next village, so ingrained is the sense of belonging to one's own village, town or region.

On an individual basis, Italians are often welcoming. However, there is an implicit racism in the term *extracomunitari*, common parlance for non-white immigrants, and the *vu compra*, the pejorative term for African street vendors, who traipse tourist haunts such as Venice, Florence and Rome, selling fake designer bags. Moreover,

the race riots that have scarred France recently. Brescia now has an ethnic population of around 25 percent in the city centre, but even would-be racists admit that the multiethnic atmosphere is appealing, as are the ethnic shops and bohemian bars. Even if Italy is far from being a fully fledged multiracial society, there are the occasional beacons that owe less to tokenism and political correctness (not Italian notions) than to individual talent. Idris Sanneh, from Senegal, went from nowhere to stardom as a television sports commentator, and is happy to be considered a role model: "They look at me and say, if this man, coming from the deep jungle of Africa, can come to this point, I can do that too." ❏

LEFT: a Chinese stoneworker at the Luserna caves.
ABOVE: a group of young Romany tailors present their gypsy couture collection during Rome fashion week.

THE ITALIAN LOOK

*Supreme visual sense, a feeling for fashion and a creative twist
on classic lines form the essence of the Italian look*

Only an Italian fashion editor could be so sweeping: "The Versaces and Armanis are our modern-day Michelangelos, helping dress our dreams. Anything else isn't *moda* – it simply serves to cover us." In other words, from the Renaissance to Romeo Gigli is but a small step, preferably taken in Ferragamo footwear, La Perla lingerie, a Missoni scarf and a Fendi fur coat. In a country where appearances are all, even the Mafia is not immune. According to a recent survey, the successful mafioso teams an Armani suit with a Moschino waistcoat and Pollini shoes; while in prison, he insists on Fila and Tacchini sportswear.

Secret conformists

Italians pride themselves on their individuality and exhibitionism. However, dressing appropriately for the season and occasion is more important than dressing to please oneself or one's mood. To be accidentally overdressed for a visit to a park or pizzeria can be a cardinal sin; equally, a mere "stroll" can be code for parading in one's finery. If in doubt, the look of de luxe anonymity is the safe sartorial badge. Not that designer labels, hip fashion accessories and superior models of car pass unnoticed in the social stakes.

Instinctive grace and elegance are insufficient protection against conformity. In a country that worships visual display, conformity is inevitable, yet so too is competitiveness and creativity. This is the paradox of the irrepressible Italian spirit. Style is therefore an emblem of high seriousness, with great attention accorded to the simple purchase of a picture or a place mat. Design is an all-inclusive philosophy involving creative alchemy and a crafts-based aesthetic, allied to a talent for interpreting mass culture. The world remains in awe of Italian taste, inviting native talent to style American furniture, Japanese cameras, German limousines and French family cars. As a result, the inimitable character of *la linea italiana*, Italian style, has a continuing impact on international design.

Milan: fashion mecca

The contribution of fashion to Italy's balance of payments is second only to tourism. Commercially, the industry is more successful than its French counterpart, with the Milan collections considered more wearable and contemporary than those of Paris. Italian fashion thrives

on a long craft tradition, a ready supply of home-grown talent and a contemporary feel, essentially a creative twist on classic lines. Its deep design roots lie in medieval craftsmanship, traditional skills which are prized in haute couture (*alta moda*) as well as in the making of quality fabrics, jewellery, bags and shoes. Native designers also have a highly developed aesthetic sense dating back to the Renaissance.

For fashion and design cognoscenti, Milan has a monopoly on "the Italian look". As the design capital, Milan is a well-tailored, cosmopolitan city that knows how to put on a show. During fashion week, the *modelari*, the louche men who chase models, are encased in leather trousers and regulation shades. At a Dolce & Gabbana party, foreign stars gather by fountains overflowing with rose petals and pick from silver platters piled with pomegranates. Yet this picture of the city at its most hedonistic is only a party snapshot.

Milan's worldwide reputation for fashion has developed not by chance but by design. An innovative industrial culture and sound mass-production techniques set the city on its present successful course, particularly after World War II, when the burgeoning design industry came into its own. The Triennale, the prestigious design institute and Italian "temple" of design,

between the Brera and Piazza San Babila in the Quadrilatero, Milan's chic-est shopping district. Here, the Japanese buy swathes of Gucci belts or 10 Prada bags apiece to offer friends back home.

Cutting edge

Yet Turin also sees itself as a vibrant, visionary city, proud of its cutting-edge design. As the centre of the car industry and Capital of Design in 2008, the city is positioning itself as a rival to Milan, boosted by the Winter Olympics in 2006. Fittingly, the Olympic torch was designed by Pininfarina, the greatest car-design studios on the planet. During the opening cere-

is now in the 1940s premises that pioneered mass production of household objects; it also boasts an exhibition of Italian design, from vintage scooters to early Olivetti computers.

Today, Milan still dominates the fashion and design calendar, from international trade fairs to the spring and summer couture and ready-to-wear collections. The city hosts fairs dedicated to furniture, lighting, home and office design. The fashion and design showrooms are located

LEFT: Prada designs paraded at Milan fashion week.
ABOVE: a pit crew prepares a Ferrari Formula One race car before it enters the stadium for the opening ceremony of the 2006 Winter Olympic Games in Turin.

mony, the sight of a red Ferrari doing tight spins on the ice reminded the world that the Italian car industry was born here. Futurism thrived in Turin, and at its core was the cult of speed. "Italian design has become a universal language of car design," says Lorenzo Ramaciotti, general manager of Pininfarina: "An American car is expected to be solid and a little flamboyant. An Italian car is expected to be aggressive, sporty and very sexy."

A sense of style

A sense of style and design is in the Italian genes. In 1946, the Italian architect Ernesto Nathan Rogers stated that design should be all-embracing, "from the spoon to the city". Italian designers dutifully filled our world with high-tech telephones and computers, office furniture in fluid shapes, sleek chrome kitchen appliances and twirly pasta quills. Giandomenico Belotti's Spaghetti Chair was literally inspired by pasta.

Italian design encompasses the austere, the provocative, the classically restrained and the kitsch. The roll-call of honour includes the Olivetti typewriter and the Artemide lamp, as well as the Ferrari, a symbol of national pride. Italy has a reputation for inspired car and motorbike design, from exclusive Ferraris to basic Vespa scooters (*see page 87*). In reply, Designers confidently switch fields, from interior to industrial or graphic design.

Design diversity

The design field has traditionally cultivated cross-fertilisation between the craftsman and architect, designer and artist. Giò Ponti, the 20th century's greatest Modernist, believed that Italy had been created half by God and half by architects. He detested the superfluous and favoured practical, perfect forms such as his Superleggera, the consummate chair, a sculpted lightweight piece. Ponti designed Milan's Pirelli Tower (1956) as well as creating the espresso machine.

the fashion world fields designers with the aspirations of Renaissance princelings: Armani's fluid lines clash with Versace's glamour, Roberto Cavalli's camp eroticism, Romeo Gigli's romantic fantasies and Dolce & Gabbana's Sicilian kitsch.

Aesthetically, Italy is known for its smooth, streamlined objects, from washing machines to motorbikes and coffee machines – designed in 1938, the Gaggia was the first modern steamless coffee machine, and swiftly became recognised as a design icon thanks to its sleek lines and sheer functionality. Creatively, however, the country moves with the times: designs can be functional or futuristic, elitist or democratic.

The highlights of Italian design history reveal both its readiness to innovate and its essential classicism. In the 1950s, the Modernists abhorred meretricious designs, but eclectic designers were eager to experiment. The 1960s avant-garde relished visual disorder and inflatable fantasies. Yet even during the Pop Art period and Swinging Sixties, designers did not abandon their love of craftsmanship or use of high-quality materials such as leather. The 1970s represented the high point of Italian minimalism, with austere tubular steel chairs. Even so,

RIGHT: Piaggio's classic Vespa was introduced in 1946.
ABOVE: Dolce and Gabbana, masters of Sicilian kitsch.

minimalism remains a Milanese default mechanism, even in the new millennium.

The belief in *bellezza*, beauty for its own sake, means that even high-tech must be aesthetically pleasing. Olivetti is one of many high-profile companies that have always treated their designers as creative artists. The Olivetti typewriter is a design classic, its shape emblazoned over the company headquarters near Turin. Olivetti launched Italy's first portable typewriter in 1950, with Marcello Nizzoli's Lettera 22. Nizzoli's successors, Ettore Sottsass and Mario Bellini, pioneered ergonomic keyboards and the use of colourful, textured plastics.

The Milanese apartment might be a temple of minimalism, decorated with white tubular sofas, stainless-steel shelving and glass-topped dining tables with an unusual number of legs; however, domesticity *all'italiana* comes in a range of styles. Just as few Postmodernist architects choose to live in their own houses, so few Italian designers practise what they preach. Versace was the high priest of vulgarity yet filled his opulent mansions with antiques. In a grand *salotto* (living room), the clinical effect of Modernist design may be offset by rich Venetian velvets or Florentine brocades. Even in a modern setting, there is a place for family heirlooms, with

VESPA VERSUS LAMBRETTA

The Vespa scooter was created immediately after World War II by Piaggio, which turned its back on warplane production after the company factory had been destroyed by American bombers. Amid the wreckage, the workers found a German scooter that had been used by paratroopers, and it became the prototype for the first Vespa. The thinking behind the brand was to create a form of transport that was practical, cheap, easy to handle and simple to repair. The Vespa ("Wasp") was a runaway success from its first launch. Today, vintage Vespas are the height of retro-chic, sought out by avid enthusiasts.

The Lambretta, another design classic, was the rival to the Vespa, and produced in the same period, in 1947, the year after the Vespa. The wartime engineer Pierluigi Torre was commissioned to design a scooter boasting a tubular steel frame construction. The new scooter was named after the factory location, in Milan's Lambrate district. The Lambretta A 125cc scooter came with a three-speed gear box and foot-operated gear changer, but had no body panels to cover the frame or engine.

Lambrettas and Vespas are as popular as ever, both as an efficient form of transport in car-clogged cities and with hobbyists – there are owners' clubs all over the world.

regional rustic chests or walnut dressers dotted with Venetian vases. Climate, tradition and taste reject carpets in favour of tiles, terracotta or marble flooring dotted with loose rugs. As for stylish furniture, Poltrona Frau makes hand-crafted designs for private homes and public spaces, including the seating for the British Museum and the European Parliament in Strasbourg. Its comfortable Art Deco leather armchair, Vanity Fair, has been in production since 1930.

High-tech in the home also has a distinguished pedigree, with cult objects by Aldo Rossi, Ettore Sottsass and Robert Venturi, including coffee pots, chairs and trays in severe

cated consumerism. Even in poorer southern cities, rampant consumerism is common. If the authentic article is too costly, then dedicated shoppers will settle for a fake: appearances are everything. Naples is the capital of counterfeit culture, where painted marzipan fruit looks finer than real peaches.

Conspicuous consumption is only part of the public picture. An Italian city is a stage for preening and posturing. Whether dressed in Como silks and Armani suits or in shades and designer jeans, Italians make immaculate fashion victims.

It is invidious to single out the most prestigious designers, but Armani, the master of

metallic designs. Particularly prized are stainless-steel kettles by Alessi, or Achille Castiglioni cutlery and his elegant, curiously shaped lamps. The Italians broke the mould of lighting design: "Light does not simply illuminate, it tells a story," says Sottsass. The modern lighting heyday was the 1970s, but certain lamps, from 18th-century Murano chandeliers to Pietro Chiesa's Art Deco funnel lamps, stand the test of time.

Temples of consumerism

Milan may be the design showcase, but most cities are citadels of good taste, with smart shops and shiny people committed to sophisti-

deconstruction, wins accolades for his sleek, sophisticated look and minimalist colours. Armani's polar opposite was Versace, at least under Gianni's reign, which opted for vulgarity, glamour and sex appeal. Despite the loss of the creative genius in 1997, the house thrives under his sister, Donatella, who, after a spell in rehab, is reaching her prime, with a less-is-more aesthetic. The coolly intellectual approach of Prada chimes with jaded fashionistas, while supremely sexy designers such as Dolce & Gabbana are currently enamoured of red-carpet glamour. As always, Italians are beguiled by *la bella figura*, a fatal weakness for beauty and surface gloss. ❑

Who's Who in Italian Design

Alberta Ferretti

Alberta Ferretti made her name with ultra-feminine styles, often evoking past eras. Given the label's love of wafty fabrics, Alberta Ferretti generally attracts romantics rather than adventurous fashionistas. If the main label spells grown-up romance, Philosophy, the diffusion line, is its flirty younger sister.

Alessi

Based by Lake Orta, this family-run design house is known for its playful products, ranging from quirky cutlery to colourful kettles, corkscrews and plastic salt cellars. Alessi has always drawn on the skills of top designers of the calibre of Castiglione, Sottsass and Philippe Starck. The firm has recently rebranded all its products into three ranges: accessible, exclusive and the core collection.

Armani

With its sleek yet understated look, Armani is the epitome of Italian chic. Despite its neutral colour tones, Giorgio Armani's alluring womenswear transcends boring beige. The look works for rock royalty and real royalty. "Women want to be more grown up," claims Giorgio. The brand also embraces the Emporio Armani diffusion line, Armani Prive couture and Armani Casa. (Amusingly, Armani complains that everyone thinks Emporio is simply the name of his younger brother.) The designer is a supporter of Red, his ethical clothing line, with a percentage of profits donated to good causes.

B&B Italia

The market leader in luxury furniture design was founded in 1966 on the innovative principle of streamlining research, manufacture and marketing into a seamless whole. The company continues to attract leading international designers, from Gaetano Pesce to Afra and Tobia Scarpa, Mario Bellini and Patricia Urquiola. As well as contemporary furniture, B&B Italia designs hotels, stores, golf clubs and even cruise ships.

Benetton

Luciano Benetton is dubbed "the prince of pullovers", yet the company's real success was to introduce mass production to the small-scale structure of the Italian textile industry. This close-knit Veneto-based firm is now a global casual-clothing brand, boosted by innovative and controversial advertising campaigns. The firm has sponsored everything from Formula One to Fabrica, its creative think-tank near Treviso. In 2006 Benetton celebrated its 40th anniversary with an event in aid of the World Food Programme.

Bottega Veneta

Once a Venetian family accessories business, the brand is now part of the Gucci Group. It was a moribund label until it was revitalised by Giles Dea-

con and stylist Katie Grand. Even if the German designer, Tomas Maier, is now at the helm, Bottega Veneta still feels Italian. Classic rather than trend-driven, it offers pared-down clothes that sell on fabric and cut alone. Menswear favours the Milanese gentleman look, while womenswear is timeless, reflecting the lavish lifestyle embodied by the brand's home collection.

Dolce & Gabbana

Sicilian Domenico Dolce and Venetian Stefano Gabbana may no longer be a couple, but the creative partnership survives. Dolce & Gabbana have overtaken Versace as the glitziest of Italian fashion labels. Yet even when the catwalk models flaunt

LEFT: Giorgio Armani. **RIGHT:** sofa by B&B Italia.

perspex-moulded corsets and sexed-up suits of armour, the design duo are savvy enough to stock their stores with tailored denim separates or gold chain-handle iPod holders. Their strengths are sharp tailoring, cutting-edge styling and a Latino sensibility, part peasant, part Sicilian gigolo. *"Molto sexy"* is their only instruction to the D&G catwalk models.

Ermenegildo Zegna

Steeped in fashion history, this family firm are the fashion designers with their roots most deeply in fabric production and design. Based in Biella's "textile valley," Zegna is both *the* luxury menswear

brand and a supplier of fabrics to its rivals. Heirs to old-fashioned Piedmontese paternalism, the family has provided the local community with a nature reserve as well as scholarships, and also sponsors the Portofino Regatta.

Fendi

Under Karl Lagerfeld, Fendi has had a resurgence and produces refined collections that appeal to city sophisticates. As a leading label, it vies with the best in terms of luxury and quality. Fendi's legendary love of fur can make the label controversial abroad, but to Italians, the Fendi femme fatale, swathed in mink and black pearls, is still a seductive fashion icon.

Ferragamo

Also branded Salvatore Ferragamo, this Florence-based fashion dynasty started with Salvatore, a Neapolitan shoemaker to the stars, who invented the wedge. Leatherware and accessories are no longer the essence of the brand: the family-run firm has been given a fresher look by Scottish designer Graeme Black, who favours a sexy but not trashy look, with glamour-puss cocktail dresses. In 2006 Ferragamo was presented with the Walk of Style plaque on Hollywood's Rodeo Drive for sartorial services to cinema. Ferragamo also owns hotels, boat companies and wine estates.

Gucci

Gucci began as humble Florentine saddle-makers but its leather range, made from honey-cured hides, was a stepping stone to stardom. Family feuds led to the collapse of the family dynasty, and the firm is now a mega-brand, part of the Gucci Group, and embracing everything from cosmetics to watches. Chief designer Frida Giannini has brought a return to its glam-rock style, which appeals to footballers' wives and celebrities alike. Under designer John Ray, successor to the fêted Tom Ford, Gucci menswear is more romantic.

Lagostina

For generations of Italian mammas, Lagostina is synonymous with the best Italian kitchenware. The premium stainless steel cookware combines inspirational design with a dash of engineering flair to ensure superior culinary performance. Known as the "Michelangelo of stockpots", it is still on most Italians' wedding lists.

Marcolin

Founded by Giovanni Marcolin in the 1960s, this Veneto-based firm is one of the major producers of eyewear, both spectacles and sunglasses, and is owned by both the family and the Florentine designers behind Tods, Diego and Andrea della Valle. The firm also designs eyewear for Roberto Cavalli, Miss Sixty and other brands.

Missoni

Missoni are the knitwear masters, and produce more intricate, imaginative and eye-catching designs than any other fashion house. This family-run firm is now headed by Angela Missoni, who has reworked her parents' hippy-chick knitwear and offers equally vibrant, swirly designs, even if the collections are far broader, and include homeware.

Moschino

Founded by the late Franco Moschino, the chief designer is his former assistant, Rossella Jardini. Noted for its visual tricks and bold spirit rather than its tailoring, Moschino boasts a sexy yet daring look and bucks many fashion trends. Moschino's biggest fan is the burlesque striptease artiste, Dita Von Teese, who embodies the label's Forties silhouette and retro glamour.

Pininfarina

As the world's pre-eminent car designers, this Turin-based company dates back to the 1930s, when car chassis and bodywork were assembled separately. Coachbuilder turned designer "Pinin" Farina (succeeded by his son) has created car concepts for Alfa Romeo, Lancia and Ferrari (including the Testarossa in 1984), as well as branching out into the design of coffee machines, aircraft and even the Turin Olympic Torch (2006).

Prada

The husband and wife partnership of Miuccia Prada and Patrizio Bertelli has propelled the brand to fame. Prada is an intellectual yet classless brand with a "less is more" ethos. Arguably the coolest, most sought-after brand of recent years, Prada prides itself on its contemporary styling and well-cut designs. If Prada aims to be fuss-free, with the focus on crisp, demure shapes, **Miu Miu** is the cheeky, sporty-chic diffusion line. The fashion-fixated film, *The Devil Wears Prada*, only served to boost the brand.

Pucci

Founded by the eccentric Florentine aristocrat Emilio Pucci, the brand is traditionally associated with swirling, Sixties-inspired silk prints. Pucci still champions a spirited hippy-deluxe style, with technicolor purples and pinks, reinterpreted by London designer Matthew Williamson. However, it remains true to its fun-loving founder, who pronounced, from his Medici throne: "The aim of fashion is to produce happiness."

Roberto Cavalli

The Cavalli attitude is associated with man-eating sexiness and red-carpet glamour. The Cavalli dress is always a show-stop and the natural choice of movie stars. But the Florentine fashion house is slowly shifting away from thigh-high splits and cleavage towards glamorous brocade and embroidery. "The Cavalli woman is more graceful and doesn't want to make men afraid any more," says Roberto Cavalli's wife, Eva. Even so, it is still associated with the would-be glamorous, such as Victoria Beckham.

Valentino

The Rome-based couturier caters for a sleekly sophisticated and ultra-groomed clientele. Valentino is rarely a trendsetter, yet excels at eveningwear, from prom dresses to crimson gowns and wedding dresses for the Hollywood set. As he says, "I am a

romantic designer – I like women seducing men." Despite selling the company, he has stayed on as designer, and is also an active campaigner for AIDS charities.

Versace

Founded by Gianni Versace, the most flamboyant fashion house is finally back on track after the years following the superstar's death. Since Donatella Versace's spell in rehab, Gianni's sister has toned down her designs and the old vulgarity has given way to wearable, pared-down, well-cut collections for both men and women. Even so, menswear remains the sexiest and most figure-hugging of any top Italian brand. ❏

LEFT: couture shoe design by Salvatore Ferragamo.
RIGHT: a Matthew Williamson design in the Pucci spirit.

DESIGN CLASSICS

Furniture, clothes, cars, typewriters, even kitchen appliances – the influence of Italian design has permeated the way we live and work today

Italian designers bask in their reputation for refinement, innate good taste and eye for colour and line. "Quite simply, we are the best" boasts architect and cultural commentator, Luigi Caccia. "We have more imagination, more culture, and are better mediators between the past and the future. That is why our design is more attractive and more in tune with the times than in other countries." Italian design is nothing if not inclusive. The traditional distinction between architect and industrial designer is blurred, with practitioners dabbling in fields as diverse as factory building and furniture design, office lighting and graphics. In the words of Ettore Sottsass, one of the most influential designers: "Design should be a discussion of life, society, politics, food and the design itself."

MODERNISM TO POP ART

Since the beginning of the 20th century, Milan has led industrial design, reaching its apogee in the 1970s and 1980s. The Italians produced seminal designs for cars and lamps in the 1930s, matched by radios and motorbikes in the 1940s. Milan also pioneered innovative design in the 1950s, with the mass production of household appliances, from cookers and washing machines to kitchen utensils. Italian modernism supplanted the post-war European taste for the safe, hand-crafted homeliness of Scandinavian design. Stylish kettles and coffee percolators became cult objects in the 1960s, followed by quirky Pop Art furniture and the fashion designer chic of subsequent decades, from cool Armani to pared-down Prada. The inimitable character of *la linea italiana*, Italian style, still sets the standard for international design values.

△ **FERRARI FORMULA**
The Ferrari Spider (1993 model) is in a long line of fabulous cars from the most admired Italian manufacturer. Enzo Ferrari (1898–1988), the firm's founder, was also a noted racing-car designer.

▽ **WINDOW SHOPPING**
A highly structured Prada suit adorns Milan's fashion district. Prada is the fashion company that best captures the *Zeitgeist* of the new millennium. Its designs have made it the most copied (faked) label on the city streets.

▷ **WASHED OUT**
Zanussi's rigorous designs, streamlined look and user-friendly features have long made it a European market leader in the field of washing machines, refrigerators and other "white goods".

CLASSIC CAR STYLE

△ **PLASTIC FANTASTIC**
Post-modernist bookcase in laminated plastic, a bold design for the Memphis studio by Sottsass (1981). Memphis was the design event of the 1980s, a playful and much-imitated school inspired by Bob Dylan's song, *Memphis Blues.*

◁ **TALKING POINT**
Italian design often takes ideas to their extreme, as in these eye-catching New Tone sculptural sofas by Atrium. This is subversive, unconventional, avant-garde living.

Ever since the 1930s, Italian car design has been characterised by stylistic restraint, versatility and timeless elegance. At one end of the scale, the Italians still produce some of the greatest status symbols in the world. In the 1950s, the beautiful Alfa Romeo convertibles spelt playboy raffishness; Ferrari's Spider, the ultimate in glamour, was produced from 1966 to 1992, making it the only sports car to have a longer production run than Germany's Porsche 911.

Yet the Italians have also had great success with Fiat's bland but eminently practical models. Topolino ("the little mouse") was launched to great acclaim in 1939, and continued into the 1950s. Giovanni Agnelli studied North American mass production techniques and from the 1950s the family dynasty had a captive market, with customers eager for the inexpensive Fiat 500. The car industry is based in the north, with Fiat in Turin, Alfa Romeo in Milan and Ferrari in Modena. The huge Fiat Lingotto plant was set up near Turin in the 1920s. Today, the city's fortunes are still inextricably linked to Fiat. The Italians also design for foreign manufacturers, including Mercedes and Rolls Royce.

DESIGN CLASSIC
e Piaggio Vespa ("wasp"),
st produced in 1946,
came the symbol of
edom for the post-
r generation. The
spa Lifestyle bag
bove), part of a trend
brand recognition
d product
ersification, is an
stere, minimalist
ering from the
ggio stable.

ITALIAN CUISINE

*Each region has its own cuisine, from the rich dishes of Emilia-Romagna
to the sparse, intensely flavoured diet of the south*

For Italians, a meal is a celebration of life itself – less of man's art than of nature's wondrously bountiful providence. A deep respect and admiration for ingredients is found throughout the country, although both history and geography have played their part in making the cooking of Italy so strongly regional.

One of the secrets of Italian cuisine, impossible to replicate elsewhere, lies in Italy's soil. After making pulp of Mexico, the Spanish conquistador Hernando Cortés returned to the Old World laden with strange new fruits and vegetables, among them a humble, fleshy yellow sphere smaller than a ping-pong ball which, in 1554, the Italians dubbed the *pomo d'oro* (golden apple). Two hundred years on, thanks to the rich Italian soil, these jaundiced cherries had become huge, lush tomatoes in deep ruby hues; moreover, their relatively demure taste (the contemporary writer Felici had described the original fruit as "more good-looking than good") had been transformed into a piquant yet tantalisingly sweet sensation.

These days, as well as being a key ingredient in many more elaborate Italian dishes, tomatoes are stuffed with beans or rice, offered as an antipasto with alternating slices of fresh mozzarella cheese, or simply served lightly dressed in olive oil and topped with sprigs of basil.

A savoury past

Until the Renaissance, the history of Italian cooking largely corresponded with Italy's military fortunes. In the 9th century, the Arabs invaded Italy, introducing Eastern sherbets and sorbets, originally served between courses to refresh the palate. Sicily, where Arab influence was most entrenched, is still noted for its sorbets and sumptuous sweets, including *cassata siciliana*, sweet sponge filled with ricotta cheese or pistachio cream and decorated with almond paste and candied fruit. Two hundred years after the Arabs left mainland Italy, the Italians set off on their own holy wars. Their return was sweetened by the presentation of sugar cane which they had discovered in Tripoli. They called it "Indian salt", and for almost a century used it as a condiment for meat and vegetables, not suspecting its natural affinity with dessert.

Sometime in the late Middle Ages, pasta appeared. Nobody knows exactly how it was invented, but the legend of Marco Polo bringing it back from Cathay is firmly refuted by Italians. The Roman gastronome Apicius, writing in the 1st century AD, describes a *timballo* (a sweet or savoury pie made with pasta). Later, in the Middle Ages, Boccaccio recommended the combination of macaroni and cheese.

It was during the Renaissance that cooking became a fine art and evolved along the lines familiar to us today. Bartolomeo Sacchi, a Vatican librarian also known as Platina, composed a highly sophisticated cookbook entitled *De Honesta Voluptate ac Valetudine* (Concerning

LEFT: ingredients for a perfect holiday.
RIGHT: preparing *bistecca alla fiorentina* – steak Florentine made from Tuscany's Chianina cattle.

Honest Pleasures and Well-Being); within three decades the volume had seen six editions. Florentine merchants spent huge sums on establishing schools for the promotion of culinary knowledge.

Consolidation of the Venetian Spice Route led to fragrant innovations. New pastry cooks invented macaroons, *frangipane* (filled with cream and flavoured with almonds) and *panettone* (a spicy celebration brioche incorporating sultanas). Conquistadors bombarded the Old World with its first potatoes, pimentos and, of course, tomatoes. When Catherine de' Medici, a keen gourmet, married Henry II of France, she took with her to France her Italian cooks, thus laying the foundations for French cuisine. Until then, France had no cuisine of its own. Even *Larousse Gastronomique* honours Italy as the "mother" cuisine.

The north–south divide

The concept of an Italian national cuisine is highly treacherous. Italy offers the world 23 regional cuisines, a diversity reflecting the country's pre-unification history and the importance of locally available produce (for example, hare, boar, rabbit and chestnuts in Tuscany; pork and truffles in Umbria; buffalo mozzarella, squid and *polpo* – octopus – in Naples). Distinctive culinary identities evolved as naturally as particular painting styles or costumes. Even more influential than political boundaries were natural variations in soil type, climate and proximity to the sea.

But the single inescapable territorial distinction is that between the north and the south. There are two important culinary differences between the regions. Firstly, northerners eat flat pasta shaped like a ribbon while southerners eat round pasta shaped like a tube. Northern pasta is usually prepared at home with eggs and eaten almost immediately, often *alla bolognese*, the classic pasta sauce made with lean veal and tomatoes and seasoned with carrot, celery, *prosciutto* (air-cured ham), lemon zest and nutmeg. Southern pasta, on the other hand, is manufactured in factories (the first factories opened in the 19th century), does not contain eggs and is purchased dry, a tradition stemming from the days when it was dried in the warm sea breezes around Naples. The classic sauce in the south is *napoletana*, based on pork.

The second difference between north and south concerns the lubrication used for cooking. North of Emilia-Romagna, Italians often line pots and pans with butter when making a meal, whereas south of Bologna it is olive oil which sets the pans sizzling.

A feast of fish

Situated between the Adriatic and the Tyrrhenian seas, Italy hauls in well over 320 million kg (700 million lb) of fish a year. Wonderful fish abound in Emilia-Romagna. Alpine streams make the Adriatic significantly less salty than most oceans, and it is therefore an ideal habitat for *rombo* (turbot), "the pheasant of the sea", and

gobies, derived from the Latin *gobius pagenellus* (little pagans). It is said that when St Anthony of Padua went to Rimini in 1221, he preached a sermon for which all the fish, save the gobie, lifted themselves from the water.

Zuppa di pesce, which is more of a stew than a soup, is a stalwart of many menus and usually served in an enormous tureen. Luxury versions include *buridda alla Genovese*, incorporating octopus, squid, mussels, shrimps and clams.

ABOVE: fresh pasta and fresh pesto, with a sprinkling of pine nuts and parmesan – the simpler the better.
RIGHT: *The Fruit Vendor*, a 16th-century still life by Vicenzo Campi.

Anchovies and sardines are classic Mediterranean fish. *Pasta con sarde*, a speciality of Palermo, is pasta with a sauce of wild fennel, pine nuts, raisins and fried sardines. A more intricate dish, often found as an antipasto, is sardines stuffed with capers, pine nuts, pecorino cheese (often from Sardinia), bread and eggs.

Meat and game

Italy also produces some of the finest meats in the world, which may explain why the Italians don't find it necessary to add sauce to their national specialities. Tuscany's Chianina cattle are alabaster in colour and grow to weigh 1,800 kg (4,000 lb). Chianina beef is used to best advantage in *bistecca alla fiorentina* – a recipe in which the steak is marinated in a little olive oil, wine vinegar and garlic, then rapidly grilled. Lamb and kid are popular in hilly regions.

Game birds are also used extensively (Italians are said to eat anything which flies, however small), and warbler, bunting, lark, quail and pheasant are favourites on regional menus. Thrushes and larks are eaten whole, bones as well. *Piccioni* (wild pigeon), served fresh rather than hung, attain new gustatory heights in Italy. Look out for *piccioni alle olive*, pigeons wrapped in bacon, roasted and served with green olives.

SLOW FOOD

The 20th anniversary of the Slow Food movement was celebrated in 2006. The founding of this movement in Piedmont was to counter junk-food culture, and its manifesto declared: "Let us rediscover the flavours and savours of regional cooking and banish the degrading effects of fast movement." The movement has been so popular that it now has more than 60,000 members spread across five continents. Carlo Petrini, the founder, explains: "The goal of this movement is the propogation of leisurely, more epicurean eating habits, and a more enlightened and patient approach to life." As befits the founder of the Slow Food movement, Italy remains one of the leaders in food and wine tourism, leaving the country riddled with *strade dei sapori* (food trails) and *strade del vino* (wine trails). The bewildering choice runs from Parmesan cheese and Parma ham trails to routes dedicated to Calabrian leeks, Puglian olive oil, Barolo wine or Asti truffles. Whether it's Tuscany's Chianti country, the Amalfi Coast wine route or Treviso's radicchio trail, there is ample fodder for travelling gastronomes. Depending on the region, the trails may be nothing more than a list of restaurants, growers and wine estates, or a well-trodden path through gorgeous scenery, with a good mix of welcoming food and wine outlets en route.

Regional differences

Of all Italy's provinces, Rome has the most festivals, and Rome's cuisine comes nearest to that associated with feasting. Suckling pigs and suckling lambs are mouth-watering specialities. The justly famous *saltimbocca alla romana* (a thin slice of veal wrapped around a slice of *prosciutto* and a sage leaf, browned in butter and simmered in white wine) lives up to its name – "jump into the mouth". Romans also thrive on gnocchi – feathery dumplings incorporating butter, eggs, nutmeg and Parmesan – while their poor relation, polenta, a pudding or cake of yellow maize flour, is popular in Lombardy.

Emilia-Romagna, long celebrated for its gastronomy, has splendid natural resources. Moreover, the entire province has always had one of the world's best road systems, ensuring rapid distribution of ingredients. *Prosciutto* is synonymous with Parma, though Tuscany and Umbria also produce a good *prosciutto* rubbed with a garlic and pepper mixture before curing; it is often served with sliced melon or fresh figs. Emilia-Romagna is also the place for sausage. Bologna, the capital of Italian cuisine, lies in the heart of Emilia-Romagna. It is from here that *mortadella*, described by one connoisseur as "the noblest of pork products", originates. *Mortadella* is made from finely

hashed pork, generously spiced and forced into a casing made from suckling pig skin.

Bologna is also the home of tortellini, rosebud-shaped pasta filled with spinach and ricotta cheese. "If the first father of the human race was lost for an apple, what would he not have done for a plate of tortellini?", goes a local saying. Legends as to tortellini's origins abound. One version gives credit to a young cook of a wealthy Bolognese merchant who modelled the curiously shaped pasta on the navel of his master's wife, whom he had seen sleeping naked.

As well as being polenta country, Lombardy also boasts the most modern methods of food production in Italy. It produces more rice than any other European region, and the famous *risotto alla milanese*, seasoned with saffron, does justice to the native grain, which, as the great cookery writer Elizabeth David pointed out, is ideally suited to slow cooking. Variations on the risotto theme, in which rice is cooked in a broth to absorb its flavour, include *risotto nero*, in which the rice is coloured black by cuttlefish ink.

One way to transform a plain risotto into a dish fit for a king is to shave a little truffle over the top. The truffle, a fragrant mushroom which grows beneath the soil around tree trunks, is prized for its unique flavour and texture. White truffles are found in Piedmont, where they are sniffed out by specially trained dogs; the world's best come from the Astiarca. Black truffles are associated with Umbria.

Bread and pizza

Naples is the place to eat pizza baked over wood in a brick-lined oven – traditionally, *pizza napoletana* (tomatoes, mozzarella, anchovies and oregano), *pizza Margherita* (topped with mozzarella, tomatoes and basil leaves) and *pizza marinara* (topped with tomatoes, garlic, clams, mussels and oregano). A good pizza should be moist and fragrant with a raised rim known as *il cornicione* (large frame).

Bread, eaten without butter, accompanies every meal and is used to mop up juices and olive oil. Every region, even every town, in Italy has its own varieties, and the different shapes alone are said to number 1,000. In Tuscany, bread (rough, white and with a floury top) is saltless to counteract the saltiness of the food; in the south bread comes in large crusty wheels. Favourite speciality breads include *pane alle olive* (a Genoese bread incorporating olives) and focaccia, a flat bread drizzled with olive oil and sprinkled with salt, or, in a more elaborate version similar to pizza, topped with olives or onions. Sardinia is noted for its *carta da musica* (music-paper bread), a wafer-thin unleavened bread, which is crunchy and long-lasting. Shepherds traditionally took it with them on long expeditions into the hills with their flocks. It was the perfect provision on their long wanderings.

BIG CHEESE

The only authentic Parmesan cheese is Parmigiano-Reggiano, produced around Parma, Reggio nell'Emilia and Modena.

ably similar order. The first course *(il primo)* invariably consists of a pasta or rice dish (especially in the north) or soup. (Antipasti, such as toasted bread with olive oil and garlic, seafood salad or grilled vegetables, are generally served only in restaurants or at banquets.) The second course *(il secondo)*, comprising meat or sometimes (especially on Friday) fish, complements or elaborates the theme begun by the first. For example, if the first course was tortellini filled with parsley and ricotta, the second would probably be some-

The ritual of the meal

Wherever you are in Italy, the rituals surrounding food and eating remain the same. Devotion to any repast, however humble, is evident in the time Italians spend at the table. In many regions work still stops for a full two hours at midday, and everyone, from the poorest to the richest, is expected to go home and eat. Often the midday meal is the most important event of the day, the time when families swap stories and adventures.

Though their specialities differ greatly, all regions eat their particular dishes in a remark-

thing light – such as a sautéed chicken dish with lemon and a little more parsley, echoing the first course. The second course is usually enhanced by at least one, often two or three vegetable dishes, such as *funghi trifolati* (mushrooms sautéed with garlic and parsley), *fave in salsa di limone* (broad beans in lemon sauce) and *cicoria all'aglio* (chicory with garlic sauce).

Afterwards, a light green salad is generally served to cleanse the palate, and to prepare the tastebuds for the grand finale – anything from an exotic pastry *(dolce)* to one of Italy's many cheeses, perhaps served with fruit. Needless to say, each course is washed down with ample quantities of wine.   ❑

LEFT: bakery and cake shop, Turin.
ABOVE: making pizza in Naples, where it all started.

WINE IN ITALY

*In Italy, wine exists primarily to turn everyday meals
and family get-togethers into hugely pleasurable social occasions*

Wine is part of the cultural furniture in Italy. It goes on the table along with salt, pepper and olive oil – and it is made to be drunk with food. This means that the flavours of Italian wine are often both more subtle and more demanding than those of wines from countries where the link is less strong.

Just as there is hardly any such thing as Italian cooking, so the wines of Italy, too, are intensely regional. Vine-growing echoes the north–south divide, largely for climatic reasons. Wines from a delimited region are designated Denominazione di Origine Controllata (DOC). Most DOC wine (which accounts for one in every eight bottles) is produced north of Rome; as one travels south, the grape varieties, and the tastes, become increasingly exotic. Italy grows more grape varieties and makes more wine (nearly a fifth of the world's total) than any other country. Not all of it is good, but much of it is exciting. Be prepared to take a risk: you will usually be amply rewarded.

Light but quaffable

Soave and Valpolicella illustrate a useful principle. These light white and red wines are produced on a vast industrial scale. The Veneto region – from Venice to Lake Garda, from the Yugoslavian Alps to the flat Po Valley – is the largest producer of DOC wine. Soave, by far the country's biggest-selling dry white DOC, can be as memorable as muzak or waiting-room wallpaper. But for those who are prepared to pay a little more, for Soave Classico made on a small scale by first-rate producers, it can be very good indeed. Any Valpolicella billed as *ripasso* will have more character than straight Valpolicella. Recioto Amarone and Recioto Amabile (made from dried grapes) have extra depth and flavour: the former is dry, the latter sweet and reminiscent of port. Recioto Soave is the white equivalent, a golden, gently honeyed wine.

To the north and east of Venice, Friuli-Venezia Giulia is a source of much crisp, fresh

white wine from a long list of grape varieties.

Up above Lake Garda, in the mountain air of Trentino-Alto Adige, the vineyards cling to precipitous slopes under peaks that are snow-covered until well into the spring. The Alto Adige, or South Tyrol, was once part of Austria, and many growers have distinctly un-Italian

names. Reds from here can be chewy and plummy, or strawberry-fresh; whites are as crisp as the mountain air, light and ethereal.

Piedmont, Italy's other sub-Alpine wine region, is a wonderful place to visit in autumn, when the early morning fog that hangs over the vineyards clears slowly, and the streets of Alba smell of white truffles. The fog, or *nebbia*, gives its name to the main red grape variety, Nebbiolo, which ripens very late; its thick skin enables it to survive the humidity and rot that would threaten thinner-skinned varieties.

The thick skin is also responsible for the wine's deep colour, and for mouth-puckering tannins that make Barolo and Barbaresco such

LEFT: grapes drying in the Marches.
RIGHT: vineyards in Tuscany.

big, powerful, long-lived wines. They are both DOCG, a step up from DOC. These wines are to be taken seriously: wines for long, companiable dinners that stretch well into the night, not wines for an *alfresco* lunch. A glass of sweet, sparkling Asti, aromatic and irresistably quaffable, is more welcome at lunchtime, followed by one of the lighter local reds, such as Nebbiolo d'Alba.

Chianti country

Tuscany challenges Piedmont as producer of the country's most aristocratic wines. Some of the families in the business today (Antinori and Frescobaldi, for example) have been making

wine since before the Renaissance. Chianti is the staple, Italy's best-known red wine, made mostly from the Sangiovese grape. The "blood of Jove" manifests itself in varying forms, from light and fruity to capable of ageing in the bottle. Standards of winemaking in the region have improved so that most Chianti is gratifyingly better than it used to be, even a decade ago.

Brunello di Montalcino and Vino Nobile di Montepulciano, both Sangiovese-based, both expensive, have traditionally represented the heights to which Tuscan reds could aspire. But Super-Tuscans, a loose-knit family of brilliant but quirkily named *vini da tavola* that burgeoned in the 1980s, are now some of Tuscany's greatest stars. Each has its individual style: they sprang from the desire of certain winemakers to produce their dream wine outside the often stultifying law of the time. They have snappy names like Sassicaia or Solaia, and are pricey, but with inimitable richness and complexity.

Dry white wines from Tuscany are less exalted. Galestro is a brave attempt to show that Italy's high-yielding Trebbiano grape can turn into something tasty, especially when blended with Sauvignon blanc, Chardonnay and others. Vernaccia, from the medieval town of San Gimignano, is made in more traditional style. Tuscany's classiest whites, however, are sweet, made from dried grapes and called Vin Santo.

In Emilia-Romagna, where dishes are gloriously rich and sticky, Lambrusco is the natural partner. Most of it is red, some is dry, and the bubbles vary from a mere prickle to a full-blown sparkle. Much of it, too, is an improvement on the coloured sweet fizz that floods the

---

HOW TO READ AN ITALIAN WINE LABEL

Denominazione di Origine Controllata (DOC) is a delimited wine region, the equivalent of the French Appellation Contrôlée. Not all DOC wines are very good, and some top wines are in fact not DOC; the producer's name is often a surer guide. DOCG (the G standing for *e garantita*) is meant to be a better wine than a straight DOC. Indicazione Geografiche Tipici (IGT) is a classification between DOC and *vino da tavola*, which embraces the two ends of the scale – cheap everyday wine and some high-quality, expensive wines made by producers dissatisfied with DOC restrictions. *Classico* refers to the heartland of a wine region, often producing the best wine. Other words

to look for are *abboccato* (semi-sweet), *amabile* (sweet, usually in reference to sparkling wine), *secco* (dry), *frizzante* (pétillant) and *spumante* (sparkling), which may be made by the *metodo classico* (Champagne method). *Passito* is sweet wine made from semi-dried grapes to concentrate the flavours, *recioto* a sweet or dry wine made from dried grapes, and *ripasso* a rich red wine fermented in the barrels previously used for a *recioto*. In Valpolicella, *amarone* is a dry wine of great character made from dried grapes. It is fermented for a longer period to produce a full-bodied wine. *Riserva* is wine given extra ageing in the barrel.

export market. Look for Lambrusco di Sorbara to get a taste of the real thing.

Further south

Most of the best wines of central and southern Italy are red. Those from the south tend to be cheaper, but don't be fooled: a winemaking revolution has taken place in these sun-baked villages, and wines such as Apulia's Copertino and Umbria's Sagrantino offer tremendous flavours of spices, earth and dried fruit. Montepulciano d'Abruzzo, too, is a good, juicy red.

The whites of the centre and south have their virtues, but character is not always among them.

Sweet wines

Sweet, sometimes fortified whites, however, are another matter. The southern half of the country abounds in these, as do the islands, and very good they are too – although calling them whites seems perverse when most age to a rich tawny colour. Look for the names of the Malvasia or Moscato grapes on the label.

In Tuscany, try the Vin Santo ("holy wine") made from grapes which have been hung to dry for months or even years. Traditionally, this was offered to favoured guests as refreshment, along with little sweet almond biscuits, but it can equally well be drunk after dinner. ❑

All too many are clean, fresh, well made, but bland; often because they are designed for washing down food without drawing attention to themselves.

Exceptions are Orvieto Classico, from Umbria, which can have good nutty fruit, and Frascati, which at its best has an attractive sourcream tang. But if Frascati did not have Rome on its doorstep it would probably not have achieved the fame it has. Most of it is Trebbiano-based and quaffable, but the better producers use Malvasia.

LEFT: traditional wine-maker, Giampiero Bea.
ABOVE: Chianti is stored in oak barrels.

TOP WINE PRODUCERS

You can always rely on **Allegrini** for serious Valpolicella, **Anselmi** for starry Soave (go for the *cru* and *recioto*), and **Antinori** for quality Chianti, *vino da tavola* Tignanello and stupendous white Castello della Sala. **Paolo Bea** produces a unique organic Sagrantino in Umbria. For wonderful Barolo, try **Clerico**, both **Conterno** brothers or **Bruno Giacosa** (also recommended for Barbaresco). **Angelo Gaja** has great Barbaresco at great prices. **Isole e Olena** produce elegant Chianti. **Pieropan's** Recioto di Soave is rich beyond the dreams of avarice (as you'll have to be, too), and **Regaleali** and **Donnafugata** use local grape varieties to produce quality Sicilians with wacky flavours.

Italian Cinema

*As windows of the nation's soul, Italian films showed
a vital resurgence once freed from the fictions of Fascism*

Italian cinema has always flickered between epic spectacles and unabashedly intimate emotions. Before the outbreak of World War I, Italian directors had already filmed *The Romance of a Poor Young Man* and several versions of Bulwer-Lytton's monumental novel *The Last Days of Pompeii*.

When the Alberini-Santoni production company released *La Presa di Roma* in 1905 the Italian feature film was born. The subject is the 1870 rout of the Pope by Garibaldi's troops. In its most famous scene, Bersaglieri rallies his forces to breach the wall at Rome's Porta Pia. Because so much of it was shot on location, the film anticipates two dominant currents in Italian film history: realism and historical spectacle.

However, Italian cinema skipped several steps in the development of international cinema. In Britain, the United States and France, early directors associated themselves with vaudeville and music halls, and so motion pictures tended to be classed as "low entertainment". By contrast, Italy's first feature film-makers were the most learned and aristocratic in the world, creating what was dubbed "cerebral cinema". At a time when most other countries still saw film as an amusing novelty, Italy was using it to express the meaning of life.

Early extravaganzas

Early in the 20th century, two directors, Enrico Guazzoni and Piero Fosca, revolutionised Italian films. Both directors' historic and melodramatic tastes perfectly complemented Italy's burgeoning nationalism, and both thrived on glorifying the martial exploits of ancient Rome.

But Guazzoni's significance derives as much from his commercial innovations as from his conceptual ones. *Quo Vadis?* (1913), which established his reputation, ran for two hours and used the world's first gargantuan sets. Guazzoni limited distribution to first-class theatres, and in New York *Quo Vadis?* received

the first personality-spangled premiere. His shrewd marketing enabled future producers to raise unprecedented financial backing. However, *Quo Vadis?* masks any complexity of character with busy sets and costumes, and escapist addiction to costume drama haunts Italian cinema to this day.

Piero Fosca's contribution was more aesthetic and more influential. His grand opus, *Cabiria* (1913), details the adventures of virtuous maidens, strong men, gruesome villains and romantic generals during the wars between ancient Rome and Carthage. Fosca was one of the first to pan cameras across vast scenes, and introduced live orchestras at screenings. More importantly, *Cabiria* showed it was possible to include subtle characterisation within the epic form.

After the successes of *Quo Vadis?* and *Cabiria*, the world woke up to film's great potential. Industrialists saw many opportunities of making money. Also intrigued was the aristocracy, the source of many of Italy's

---

Left: Marcello Mastroianni, Italy's most sophisticated leading man. **Right:** Maciste, an earlier heart-throb.

film-makers and patrons. (Luchino Visconti, first generation neo-realist, was the heir of an aristocratic Sicilian family; a Roman countess provided Roberto Rossellini with the money to begin filming *Roma, Città Aperta*.)

The support of the nobility is one explanation for the high production standards of early Italian cinema. While directors in France and the United States were still pinning up painted backdrops, Italians hired the nation's finest architects to design and construct full-scale sets. Furnishings in histor-

> **BIRTH OF AN EPIC**
>
> Hollywood drew great inspiration from Italy for its own epics. Fosca's *Cabiria* had a direct influence on D.W. Griffith's 1915 *Birth of a Nation*.

credibility were eligible for up to 60 percent state financing. Particularly patriotic endeavours, such as *Scipione l'Africano*, often received total backing from the government.

The final blow to creative competition was dealt by the new National Body for Importation of Foreign Films. It decided which films could be imported, then insisted they be dubbed into Italian. Unable to compete economically, Italy's better directors went into hibernation.

ical dramas were often borrowed from the personal collections of descendants of the depicted heroes, and if a film included aristocrats, authentic aristocrats were invited to make guest appearances.

This so-called Golden Age of Italian cinema hardly had time to blossom before the Fascists came to power. Mussolini instituted several organisations to regulate the film industry, so convinced was he of the power of the medium. The Direzione Generale per la Cinematografia became an official department of the Ministry of Popular Culture. In addition, the Banco del Lavoro helped provide finance for politically acceptable films. Directors who had ideological

Neo-realism

In 1944, while the Germans were still retreating from Rome, Roberto Rossellini, who had launched his career by filming for Mussolini a patriotic panegyric on dashing navy pilots, made *Roma, Città Aperta*, a film whose unflinching confrontation with truth unnerves audiences to this day. The film follows the lives of several Resistance workers. Every scene, except those set in the Gestapo headquarters, was shot on location. *Roma, Città Aperta* has a rough, visceral throb that was revolutionary for the time. Some sequences seem to be documentary footage: the camera jerks and twists, and shots break off suddenly.

Despite the unprecedented, relentless immediacy, *Roma, Città Aperta* has a complex symbolic structure. The film elevates drug addicts, priests, German lesbians and Austrian deserters to levels of wider symbolic import without sacrificing their unique personalities. Pina (Anna Magnani), for example, an agonised mother leading a mob of matriarchs to plunder exploitative bakeries in the neighbourhood, is utterly convincing, yet she also symbolises the desperate plight of Italian housewives during the war.

Federico Fellini, who helped Rossellini write the script for *Roma, Città Aperta*, summarised the atmosphere following World War II that pro-

remarkable homogeneity Italy achieved just after World War II, with the widespread conviction that Fascism was wrong. Neo-realist directors spoke from and for an Italy which could confess, if not to chaos, at least to contradictions.

Resurgence

During the 1960s and early 1970s, economic prosperity triggered a resurgence of Italian film, dominated by Federico Fellini, Michelangelo Antonioni and Francesco Rosi – though this was also the period of Luchino Visconti's *The Damned*, Bernardo Bertolucci's *The Conformist* and Paolo Pasolini's *The Decameron*. Rosi was

duced neo-realism: "We discovered our own country… we could look freely around us now, and the reality appeared so extraordinary that we couldn't resist watching it and photographing it with astonished and virgin eyes."

For the next few years, Rossellini, along with Visconti, Vittorio de Sica and Alberto Lattuada, developed a cinema characterised by rapid, seemingly spontaneous juxtaposition. Neo-realism remains the core of what is considered modern in film. The movement arose from the

born in Naples, and southern Italy is a dominant theme in his films. Antonioni's exploration of existential themes and individual crises reached a climax with *Blow Up* (1967). The tireless Fellini, arguably the greatest Italian director, produced a string of classics. In many ways, Fellini can be viewed as the triumphant culmination of neo-realist philosophy. His characters are torn between the desire to realise their true selves and the urge to conform.

Fellini said that his films were a "marriage of innocence and experience", but they were also about fantasy and loss, tinged with irony, fun and sadness. In *Amarcord* (1975), Fellini's surreal flights of fancy turned Rimini, his home

LEFT: Federico Fellini, the godfather of Italian cinema.
ABOVE: still from *Cinema Paradiso* (1988), Giuseppe Tornatore's nostalgic tribute to cinema.

ITALY IN THE MOVIES

Rome, Tuscany, Sicily and Venice provide the main backdrops to the cinematic illusion of Italy. Such is the power of the movie myth that Sicilian Mafia murders and Tuscan costume dramas are equally convincing. Fellini, who had a virtual monopoly on Roman sensibility, loved to satirise his fellow citizens on film. In *La Dolce Vita* (1960) and *Roma* (1972), he held a distorting mirror to Roman reality. Rome's changing character was confronted more recently by Nanni Moretti in his magical comedy *Caro Diario* (Dear Diary, 1994). Of foreign directors, Peter Greenaway's *Belly of an Architect* (1987) arguably best captures the elusive character of the Eternal City.

Tuscany is a favoured location for foreign films, with the Merchant-Ivory *Room with a View* (1985) both a classic and a cliché, shot in villas in Florence and Fiesole. More quirky are Jane Campion's *Portrait of a Lady* (1996), shot near Lucca, and Tarkovsky's *Nostalgia* (1983), shot in Bagno Vignone, fabulously moody Roman baths south of Siena. Although best-known for *The Last Emperor* (1987), Bertolucci returned to Tuscany to shoot *Stealing Beauty* (1996), set in a rustic villa and idyllic wine estates. Anthony Minghella's *The English Patient* (1996) and *The Talented Mr Ripley* (1999) were lovingly shot in Tuscany, Rome and Ischia, and scenes from Ridley Scott's *Gladiator* (2000) were filmed in Val d'Orcia.

Sicily has long drawn directors of the highest calibre, with Rossellini's *Stromboli* (1950) set on a volcanic island, and Visconti's hymn to faded grandeur and Sicilian decadence, *The Leopard* (1968). Coppola's *Godfather* trilogy was partly shot in Sicily.

Venice provides an ideal location for moody "art house" films. Stanley Kubrick's film *Eyes Wide Shut* (2000) features numerous dramatic Venetian scenes, including a masked ball. Antonioni's masterpiece *Identification of a Woman* (1982) shows Venice as a magical yet murky world. In a similar but more ominous vein, *Don't Look Now* (1973) by Nicolas Roeg brings Donald Sutherland and Julie Christie to an eerily deserted Venice shortly after the death of their child. David Lean's *Summertime* (1955) casts Katharine Hepburn as an American abroad who both falls in love and falls into a canal. Most recently, Venice starred as the lavish backdrop for *Casanova* (2006), directed by Lasse Hallström and starring Sienna Miller and Heath Ledger. in which all the decadence of Venetian life is portrayed. However, the undisputed Venetian masterpiece is Visconti's *Death in Venice* (1970), based on Thomas Mann's classic novella. Visconti wanted "the light of the *sirocco*, the pale, still pearl light" and, with his artistic decision to use dawn and night shoots, forced his stars into sleeplessness.

town, into a virtual-reality world. It was sweet revenge on the "inert, provincial, opaque, dull" Adriatic seaside resort he left for Roman chic. In his 1954 masterpiece *La Strada*, he claimed to have based the central character on the lost innocence of his actress wife, Giulietta Masina, who also starred in the film.

La Dolce Vita (1960) was the first time Fellini worked with his male muse, Marcello Mastroianni, who was chosen for his candour, innocence and "normal face, a face with no personality". The filmic frolicking in Rome's Trevi Fountain turned Anita Ekberg into an international sex symbol.

In 1967, with *A Fistful of Dollars* and *The Good, the Bad and the Ugly*, Sergio Leone presented world cinema with a new genre: the spaghetti Western. These witty and stylised films, which were made on surprisingly low budgets, became the Italian movie industry's most successful exports since Sophia Loren, Gina Lollobrigida and Claudia Cardinale.

In the 1980s the generation of angry young Marxists and Sixties radicals gave way to commercial producers eager to create pale imitations of Hollywood action pictures. Bernardo Bertolucci is an exception in being free to command Hollywood budgets for international blockbusters or to concentrate on more low-key work. Competition from the highly commercial Italian television networks had a detrimental effect on feature films, as did the privatisation of Cinecittà, the once state-owned Roman film studios and former hothouse for Italian directors.

However, after years in the wilderness, Cinecittà is making a comeback. Although the main focus is on television and advertising, rather than on feature films, the state-of-the-art studios, newly equipped with the latest digital technology, are attracting foreign producers. In 2002, Martin Scorsese reconstructed entire blocks of 19th-century New York slums in the studios for *Gangs of New York* – watch out for

The next generation

A new generation of actors and directors are working hard at putting Italian cinema back on the world map. Many regions now have active film commissions generating new movie-making in Campania, Ischia, Capri and Catania. The first Rome Film Festival took place in October 2006 and hopes to become a serious contender to the Venice Film Festival.

Arguably the most popular comedian and actor since the legendary Totò, Roberto Benigni shot to international stardom with his Oscar-winning performance in *La Vita è Bella* (Life is Beautiful, 1997). But Italy's most consistently

the extras, who are all Romans. This heralded a glut of international productions including Mel Gibson's *The Passion of the Christ* (2004), Steven Soderbergh's *Ocean's Twelve* (2004) and a £58 million series made for television, *Rome* (2005), co-produced by HBO and the BBC. The life-size replicas of Roman monuments constructed by Cinecittà's scenery experts have been left in place in the hope of enticing other producers to use the studios for more films set in ancient Rome.

LEFT: Nanni Moretti, scootering around Rome in *Caro Diario* (Dear Diary). **ABOVE:** a break between takes on the set of *Rome*, in the Cinecittà studios.

acclaimed director is witty maverick Nanni Moretti, Rome's left-wing Woody Allen. His film, *The Son's Room*, was awarded the Palme d'Or at Cannes in 2001. Another emerging talent, director and scriptwriter Paolo Sorrentino won several awards for *Le Conseguenze dell' amore* (The Consequences of Love, 2004). This was only his second feature film, but he is already revealing himself as a master of the slow build – in total contrast to the Hollywood appetite for fast, action-packed movies. Most recently, Michele Placido's underworld odyssey, *Romanzo Criminale* (2006), based on a best selling-novel by Giancarlo De Cataldo, has received critical acclaim. ❑

MUSIC AND OPERA

*Italy's contribution to music is unparalleled. And where better
to enjoy the art of opera than where it began and flourished?*

Italy is rightly known as the home of music, and Milan's image is inextricably bound up with La Scala. When opera houses burn down, as they still tend to do in Italy, people cry in public and the country grieves. Fortunately, the country still has an abundance of major opera houses. However, Italy's contribution to Western music goes beyond operatic rococo interiors and impassioned outpourings of Verdi.

A monk, Guido d'Arezzo, devised the musical scale, while a Venetian printer, Ottavino Petrucci, invented a method of printing music with movable type. The language of music remains resolutely Italian, including such terms as *soprano*, *drammatico* and *soprano lirico*. Italy also gave us the piano, the accordion and the fabulous Stradivarius and Guarneri violins and cellos. Cremona has been the capital of violin masters since the 16th century. Indeed, it is not too fanciful to see the curves of violins echoed in the spiral cornices of city palaces.

The food of love

Without the Italian sensibility, the world of music would be without the nobility and intensity of Verdi or the seductive strains of Vivaldi. The lush strings of Albinoni perfectly chime with the public's taste for haunting baroque music, while opera-lovers are rewarded with Rossini's *Il Barbiere di Siviglia*, a comic masterpiece, Bellini's ravishing melodies, and the dramatic flow of Puccini's *Tosca* and *Turandot*. Other musical keynotes are *bel canto*, the traditional Italian art of singing, and Neapolitan love songs, as much part of the passionate city as pizza and Mount Vesuvius.

Opera was Italy's greatest musical achievement, a rousing art form which came into being in 14th-century Florence and was perfected by Monteverdi. In his opera *Orfeo*, the title role was taken by a castrato, a male soprano or contralto with an unbroken voice. Castrati were in great demand during the 17th and 18th centuries, thanks to their strong, flexible yet voluptuous voices. Farinelli (1705–82) was the most

famous, a soprano whose singing and stage presence caused women to faint from excitement. Italian divas have also graced the stages of the great *teatri lirici* (opera houses), including Cecilia Bartoli in the present day, the mezzo-soprano acclaimed for her interpretations of Mozart. Italy, which gave the world Enrico

Caruso and Beniamino Gigli, also boasts a clutch of talented tenors, from Luciano Pavarotti to the romantic Roberto d'Alagna, raised in Paris by Sicilian parents.

The world's their stage

Composers such as the Modernist Luciano Berio also enjoy international renown, experimenting with sound in all its forms, from electronic and rock to folk, jazz and classical. La Scala recently honoured him with a premiere of his opera *Outis*. Gian Carlo Menotti, the founder of the Spoleto Festival, set in a ravishing Roman theatre, is acclaimed for his operas as well as his skills as an impresario. As for conductors, this has been an Italian forte since Toscanini, whose first public performance at the age of 19 was *Aida*, conducted from memory after stepping in at short notice. Riccardo Muti now conducts at Milan's La Scala and runs the Ravenna Music Festival, close to his home. Muti's respected predecessor, Claudio Abbado, directs productions around the world, as well as in Ferrara. Conductors Daniele Gatti, Riccardo Chailly and Giuseppe Sinopoli have also found fame abroad, notably at Amsterdam's Concertgebouw, London's Covent Garden and the Dresden Opera House.

Conductors working abroad are probably or, perish the thought, of mellifluous music, then an Italian audience usually goes home happy, whether the fat lady sings or not.

Opera's golden age

Giacomo Puccini once said of himself, "I have more heart than mind." In these characteristics lies the key to Italian opera. It is essentially sensual and lush, appealing more to the emotions than the intellect.

The bookends of Italian opera's golden age stand clear: on the one side, the 1815 production of Rossini's classic *opera buffa* (comic opera), *Il Barbiere di Siviglia*; on the other, the

relieved to escape their knowledgeable but critical audiences back home. Italian audiences are hard taskmasters, with applause led by the official clapping societies that are present in the major houses. Yet if the opera falls short of perfection, the *loggionisti*, those in the gods, are ready to rain down abuse on fallen divas, with booing and hissing commonplace. Brave visitors who wish to show their appreciation can shout "*bravo*" for tenors, "*brava*" for sopranos and "*bravi*" for all. Ultimately, as long as the opera provides a spectacle, of people-watching

LEFT: Verdi, great opera composer and Italian patriot.
ABOVE: a glittering gala at Milan's La Scala.

THE LEGEND OF "BIG LUCY"

Since his debut in 1961, Luciano Pavarotti has become the world's most recognised tenor. "Big Lucy" began singing for sweets aged five, and his career was launched with the winning of a Welsh choral competition. Throughout his long and prolific career, he has shown himself to be as happy singing Neapolitan love duets and Puccini arias as he is crooning with international rock stars such as Sting and U2. He achieved legendary status in the 1990s singing with Carreras and Domingo as the "Three Tenors". Having been dogged by ill health, his last performance was in 2006 at Turin's winter Olympics opening ceremony. He died at home in Modena in 2007.

ITALY'S OPERA HOUSES

Beyond their gilt-and-stucco interiors, Italy's glittering opera houses *(teatri lirici)* are mostly neoclassical theatres rebuilt after numerous fires. Historically, the rivalry of noble courts gave birth to countless private opera houses, which gradually opened their doors to the public – the first was in Venice in 1637. The fashion for opera spread, and by the 18th century there were 20 in Venice alone. Most historic opera houses are in Lombardy and Emilia-Romagna, linked to great courts such as Cremona, Parma and Mantua.

Milan's La Scala is the premier opera house. All the great Italian composers have written for La Scala, notably Rossini, Donizetti, Bellini, Puccini and Verdi. It underwent a period of glory with performances of Verdi's patriotic works and spent the early 20th century under Toscanini's direction. The historic building, a symphony of red, cream and gold, opened in 1778 with a performance of an opera by Antonio Salieri (who is best known today for being an adversary of Mozart). The theatre, which seats 2,000 and has superb acoustics, celebrated the centenary of Verdi's birth in January 2001. After a long period of restoration the historic venue reopened in 2004 with a performance designed to show off the mechanical marvels of its new acoustics. Since then, the Teatro alla Scala has been dogged by controversy, including an unprecedented walk-out in 2006 by tenor Roberto Alagna, who was booed during a performance of Zeffirelli's *Aida*.

The Teatro San Carlo in Naples enjoys a reputation second only to La Scala. Rebuilt in 1816, it won a name as a "singer's theatre", where vocal gymnastics and artistic rivalry were pre-eminent.

While there are major opera houses in Florence and Rome, La Fenice (the Phoenix) in Venice enjoys greater prestige, despite its tragic history. Venice's "Phoenix" lived to rue its name after fires in 1836 and 1996. Australian diva Joan Sutherland mourned the loss of "the most beautiful opera house in the world; singing in La Fenice felt like being inside a diamond". Now, risen from the ashes once more in December 2003, the red-and-gold rococo confection has been rebuilt exactly as before. Critics complain that it is too bright and brash; supporters praise the state-of-the-art sets and improved acoustics.

On the next rung down in terms of size, but not necessarily in scope, are Parma, Genoa, Bergamo, Modena and Turin. Palermo's Teatro Massimo reopened in 1998 with a glittering production of Verdi's *Aida*, after a scandalous 25-year closure, during which it had opened its doors only once – ironically to allow the filming of *The Godfather: Part III*.

posthumous 1926 opening of Puccini's last and unfinished opus, *Turandot*. Between the two lies more than a century of operatic triumphs.

During the 19th century, when Giocchino Rossini, Gaetano Donizetti and Vincenzo Bellini dominated the scene, Italian opera became infused with vitality, and Europe once again looked towards Italy for operatic innovation. All three composers, born within a decade of one another, shared much in style, and their careers followed similar paths and detours.

Rossini is probably most celebrated for his productions of *Il Barbiere di Siviglia* and *Guillaume Tell*, while Donizetti's masterpieces are

Lucia di Lammermoor and *La Fille du Régiment*. Bellini is celebrated for his *semi seria* works, *La Sonnambula*, *Norma* and *I Puritani*. These operas are part of standard repertoires constantly performed throughout the world.

The three composers shared a small-town background, and all enjoyed great success at an early age, although Bellini was already 22 years old when he made his operatic debut. Each faced the voracious demands of impresarios and the finicky tastes of leading performers, and they all worked with remarkable speed, producing new works in the space of a few weeks. Not surprisingly, there was a fierce and jealous rivalry between them. Upon hearing that Rossini had composed *Il Barbiere di Siviglia* in 13 days, Donizetti shrugged proudly and concluded, "No wonder – he is so lazy."

They acquired gold and glory all over Europe, but, tragically, all three burnt themselves out. Bellini and Donizetti died young, the latter a crazed syphilitic, and Rossini's last triumph was achieved before he reached 40. They were followed by the brightest light in Italian opera.

The brightest star

Giuseppe Verdi was born in 1813 (the same year as Richard Wagner) in Le Roncole, a small village 17 km (12 miles) from Parma. His father

then on, Verdi saw success after success, highlighted by *Rigoletto* (1851), *Il Trovatore* (1853), *La Traviata* (1853), *La Forza del Destino* (1862), *Don Carlo* (1867), *Aida* (1871) and *Otello* (1887). With premieres in London, Paris, St Petersburg and Cairo, along with those in the theatres of Italy, Verdi was a composer of true international stature.

It was a reputation well deserved. Verdi's sharp, almost brutal dynamism freed Italian opera from the lingering vestiges of empty convention. Verdi also refused to tailor his works to the whims of individual singers, something that no composer had dared do in the past. His inde-

was a semi-literate peasant, and the family had no history of talent, musical or otherwise, but young Giuseppe made a mark as the local church organist. In 1832, he was denied admission to the prestigious Milan Conservatory. But the young Verdi was persistent, and, although his first two productions, *Oberto* (1839) and *Un Giorno di Regno* (1840), met with lacklustre receptions at La Scala premieres, rave notices for the epic *Nabucco* (1842) marked the beginning of a long and distinguished career. From

LEFT: poster for a performance of Verdi's *Aida* in La Fenice (1881). **ABOVE:** an animated 19th-century audience in the Teatro San Carlo in Naples.

pendence extended to his personal life. In a very conservative and religious society, he openly lived with his mistress, the soprano Giuseppina Strepponi, for more than a decade before taking her to the altar in 1859.

If Verdi was permitted artistic and personal freedom, he was still constrained by the political realities of his day. Censorship was a constant impediment in an Italy dominated by foreign powers. Verdi was himself an ardent nationalist. His historical works were charged with analogies of the Italians' plight – allusions that were not lost upon native audiences. From 1848, his name became a rallying cry for his countrymen in the fight for freedom from

Austrian domination. The acronym V(ittorio) E(manuele) R(e) D'I(talia) was used as a reference to the first king of Italy, eventually crowned in 1861. A dear friend of Count Cavour, Verdi briefly served in the new chamber of deputies after unification. On his death in 1901, Verdi was mourned not only as a composer but also as a patriot.

The best-loved tunes

Although operas of fine quality continue to be composed today, the golden age of Italian opera drew to a close with the career of Giacomo Puccini, who was inspired by Verdi's *Aida* to become an operatic composer. Others contended for the mantle of Verdi, but Puccini had the advantage of the blessing of the old man himself. "Now there are dynasties, also in art," lamented rival Alfredo Catalani, "and I know that Puccini 'has to be' the successor of Verdi … who, like a good king, often invites the 'crown prince' to dinner!" A dynasty it may have been, but one clearly based on merit. Puccini's success lay as much in his great gift for melody as in his unerring sense of theatre. *La Bohème* (1896), *Tosca* (1900) and *Madama Butterfly* (1904) are today among the best-loved works of opera.   ❑

FESTIVE SPIRITS

Established music festivals have spread their wings. Florence's Maggio Musicale, the oldest music festival in Italy, has gone from strength to strength, celebrating its 70th edition in 2007 with performances involving Daniel Barenboim, Zubin Mehta and Bejart's Ballet. The Stresa Festival, centred on Lake Maggiore, combines world-famous orchestras with smaller concerts in churches around the lake. In Umbria, Spoleto's Festival dei Due Mondi embraces classical, jazz and world music. Newer festivals, such as Cortona's Under the Tuscan Sun, draw an international crowd, presenting performances by major orchestras and literary figures in a picture-postcard medieval town. Most festivals share spellbinding settings, from the Ravello Festival, staged in glorious gardens overlooking the Amalfi Coast, to Sicily, where Taormina's summer showcase presents theatre, ballet, rock and opera in its Greek theatre. In Rome, the Festival of Sacred Music is celebrated in sublime churches. Rome's Notte Bianca (White Nights) mixes music, cinema and the visual arts in surprising settings. On the Adriatic, the Ravenna Festival, linked to Maestro Muti, former conductor at La Scala, focuses on Italian opera. Not far away, Parma, forever associated with Verdi, has an annual festival in his honour. Similarly, Torre del Lago in Tuscany celebrates its illustrious son, Puccini, every summer with opera by the lake.

Sounds of Success

In the last 60 years Italy has developed a home-grown music scene to compete with British and American pop imports – sounds which have some-times found success beyond national boundaries.

This was particularly true in the 1950s when Italian-American singers like Sinatra, Perry Como and Tony Bennett were defining the easy-listening sound. Dean Martin crooned Domenico Modugno's *Volare* to international fame, and his version of *Arriverderci Roma* was a nostalgic hit for people remembering their Italian holidays.

During the 1960s, a group of young pop stars emerged to dominate the domestic market. These included Mina, Rita Pavone, Adriano Celentano, Lucio Battisti and Gianni Morandi. In his 40-year career Celentano sold 70 million records, while Battisti's classics, such as *La Canzone del Sole*, *Mare Nero* and *Aqua Azzurra Acqua Chiara* were the sound-track for a generation of 1970s adolescents.

As the political dissent and liberation movement of the late 1960s took hold, a group of engaged singer-songwriters emerged. Known as *cantautori*, they created some of the most innovative Italian contemporary music, though their lyric-rich compo-sitions were never going to translate abroad.

If we are looking for Italy's Bob Dylan, then Fab-rizio De Andre stakes fair claim, with compositions such as *La Canzone di Marinella* and *La Guerra di Piero*. Singer-songwriter Francesco De Gregori's album *Rimmel* is vintage '70s, while Ivano Fossati peerlessly mined Italy's melancholic soul with com-positions like *I Treni a Vapore*. His *La Canzone Popo-lare* remains an election anthem for the centre-left.

Rome's local *cantautore* Antonello Venditti immor-talised his city in *Roma Capoccia*, and his albums of well-crafted, if sometimes disposable, pop still chart. Neapolitan musical tradition continues with Eduardo Bennato's politically tinged rock. But the city's mu-sical statesman is Pino Daniele; singing in his local dialect, Daniele fuses rock, blues and jazz. His hometown anthem, *Napule E'*, encapsulates the city's melancholic spirit.

Bolognese songwriter Lucio Dalla emerged in the '70s with a lyrical blend of humour, politics and pro-fanity. From the satirical peace anthem *Se Io Fossi Angelo* to the domestic reality of *Anna e Marco*, Dalla

chronicles all aspects of Italian life. Even if you can't follow the lyric, his soaring tribute to opera legend Caruso is essential listening.

Italian rock music has flourished in recent decades. Its health was confirmed in 2004 when Modenese rocker Vasco Rossi performed a free con-cert to 300,000 fans who stood for hours in the rain. And Italian megastar Zucchero scored a rare success in the English market: he reversioned the classic hit *Senza una Donna*, dueting with Paul Young and charting in the UK.

And though the ears of the English-American mar-ket have resisted Italian pop, the rest of the world has embraced two of the nation's singers: Laura

Pausini has racked up global sales of 28 million records, and in 2006 she became the first Italian female to win a Grammy, taking Best Latin Pop Album with *Escucha*; while Roman-born popster Eros Ramazzotti has found fame beyond Italian shores, selling over 36 million records worldwide.

One Italian singer who has become a household name at home and abroad is Andrea Bocelli, who offers a mellifluous blend of classical music, tradi-tional song and pop. He has performed on inter-national opera stages and even sang at the White House. The legacy of popular legends from Caruso to Pavarotti would weigh heavy on any young tenor, but Bocelli, it seems, is more than capable of pick-ing up the baton. ❏

LEFT: performance of Verdi's *Nabucco* with French soprano Sylvie Valayre, at the Verona Opera Festival.
RIGHT: Grammy award-winner Laura Pausini.

PLACES

A detailed guide to the entire country, with principal sights
cross-referenced by number to the maps

Negotiating the tangle of one-way streets in an Italian city takes years of experience. Often a helpful native will point the way, even take you personally to your hotel, restaurant or museum. But if no one materialises, don't panic, simply follow the tourist signs for Centro Storico (historic centre) and Duomo (cathedral), and remember that *senso unico* means "one way". Then find the first *parcheggio* (car park) and abandon your car, for most Italian cities are best explored on foot. If you arrive by train, the station will invariably be in the seedier part of town, so leave it behind for the greener pastures of the Centro Storico.

Modern life has stamped even small villages with a bar and a large population of moped-riding youths. Every town has its Duomo, but how different is the austere Romanesque cathedral of Apulia from the lavish baroque one in Turin. Every town has at least one piazza: in the south they are crowded with men smoking and playing cards; in the north, the men are still there, but so are the women and the tourists.

Our favourite places in Italy include many spots less frequented than the tried and true trio of Rome, Florence and Venice. We suggest that, after visiting Rome, you take an excursion east into Abruzzo or Molise, those hitherto remote regions whose architecture, parks, mountains and beaches rank among the most refreshing vacation spots in the country. Or, if you happen to be exploring the Bay of Naples, rent a car and continue down to Italy's heel and toe – Apulia, Basilicata and Calabria – even taking the ferry across to Sicily.

The north has Florence and Venice, of course, but also Milan and Turin, two very modern cities packed with art and history. You could follow the path of generations of travellers who, with Dante and Ariosto in hand, toured the cities of Lombardy, the Veneto, Emilia-Romagna and Tuscany. If you want to catch your breath and relax, retreat into the green hills of Umbria, home of Italy's beloved St Francis of Assisi. ❑

PRECEDING PAGES: Limone, on Lake Garda; Tricarico, in Basilicata; St Peter's, Rome.
LEFT: the resort of Portovenere near La Spezia.

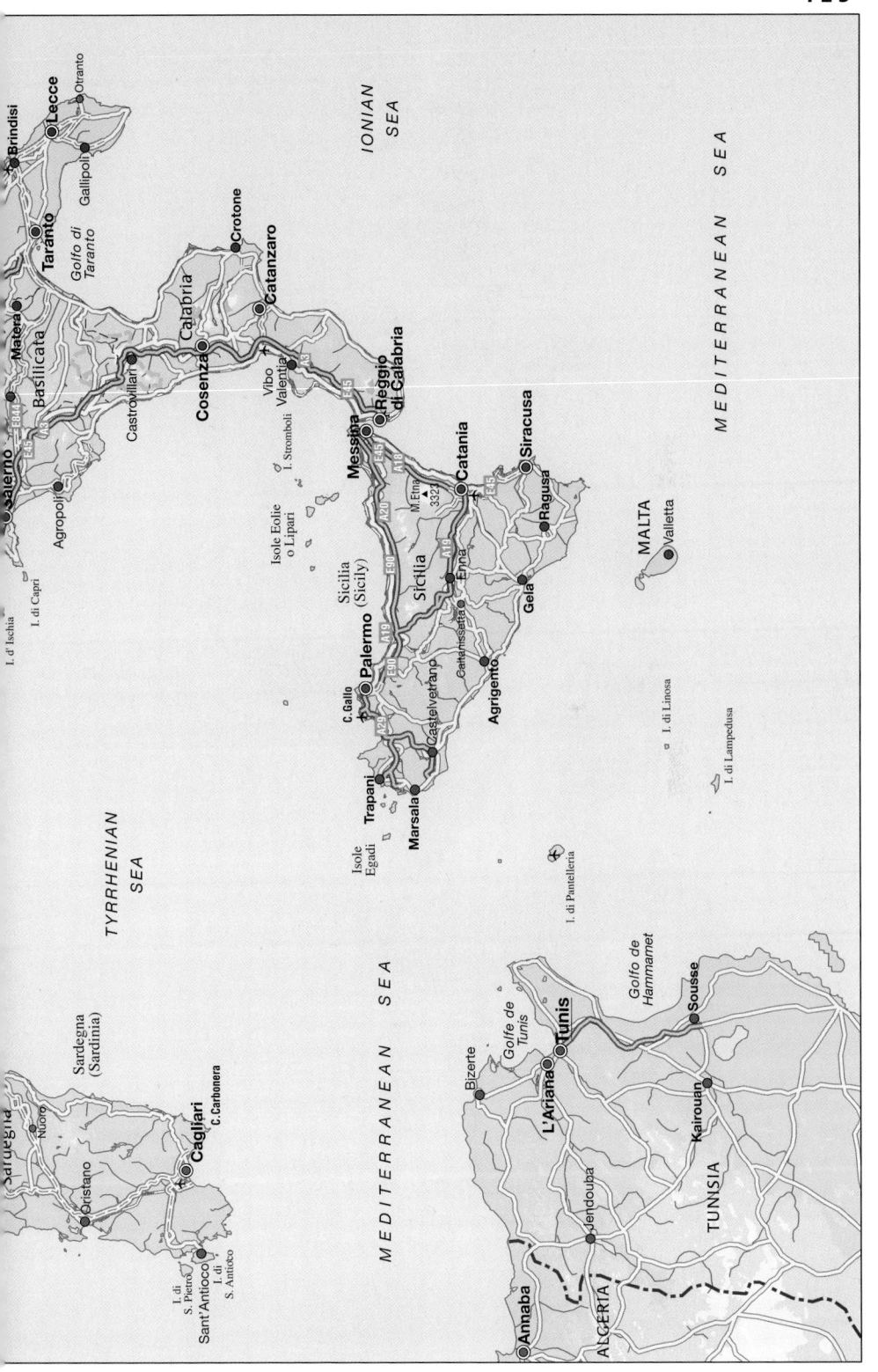

ROME

Follow in the footsteps of emperors and saints,
discovering the monuments and churches that mark Rome
as the capital of Italy and the ancient world

Map on
pages
128–9

ord Byron gave **Rome** (Roma) the epithet "City of the Soul". Poetic
hyperbole perhaps, but the description still strikes a chord among visitors to the city. As a result of Jubilee Year (or Holy Year) Rome is now
resplendent, the 2,000th anniversary of the birth of Christ having been celebrated in unique style with the refurbishment of over 700 temples, churches,
galleries and archaeological sites. Rome can now face the next 2,000 years
with an equanimity bordering on smugness.

The Palatine Hill

The best introduction to Rome is not Piazza Venezia, the terrifying roundabout
at the centre of the modern city, but the more pastoral **Palatino ❶** (Palatine Hill;
daily 8.30am–7.15pm in summer, until 4.30pm in winter, last entry one hour
before closing; entrance fee – ticket also valid for the Colosseum and Forum),
believed by the ancients to be the home of Rome's mythical founder, Romulus.
Its claim to be the site of the original settlement is supported by the remains of
early Iron Age dwellings in the southwestern corner of the hill. Close by are the
remains of the **Tempio di Cibele**, picturesquely planted with an ilex grove. The
cult of the Eastern goddess of fertility, also known as Magna Mater, was introduced to Italy during the Second Punic War (218–201
BC). Though its mystical rites – involving throngs of
frenzied female worshippers, priests committing self-
mutilation, and bull sacrifices – were distasteful to old-
fashioned Romans, the cult spread widely during the
imperial era.

The name Palatine (derived from Pales, goddess of
shepherds) is the root of the word palace. In Roman times
the Palatine Hill was celebrated for the splendour of its
princely dwellings. Earliest, and simplest, of these was
the Domus Augustana. A portion of it, known as the **Casa
di Livia** (Livia was Augustus' second wife), is renowned
for its superb wall paintings and floor mosaics.

To the north, alongside the Palazzo di Tiberio (now
mostly covered by the Farnese Gardens) runs the **Crip-
toporticus**, a cool underground passage with a delicately stuccoed vault, built by Nero to connect the
palaces of Augustus, Tiberius and Caligula to his own
sumptuous Golden House on the Esquiline Hill. To the
southeast of this passage extend the remains of the
Domus Flavia, built at the end of the 1st century AD by
the Emperor Domitian. An infamous sadist who took
pleasure in torturing everything from flies to senators,
Domitian suffered from an obsessive fear of assassination. According to the ancient historian Suetonius,
author of *Lives of the Caesars*, an entertaining if not
entirely trustworthy source, the emperor covered the
walls of the peristyle (the section with an octagonal

LEFT: Piazza della
Repubblica. **BELOW:**
an umbrella pine
shades the ruins of
the Palatine Hill.

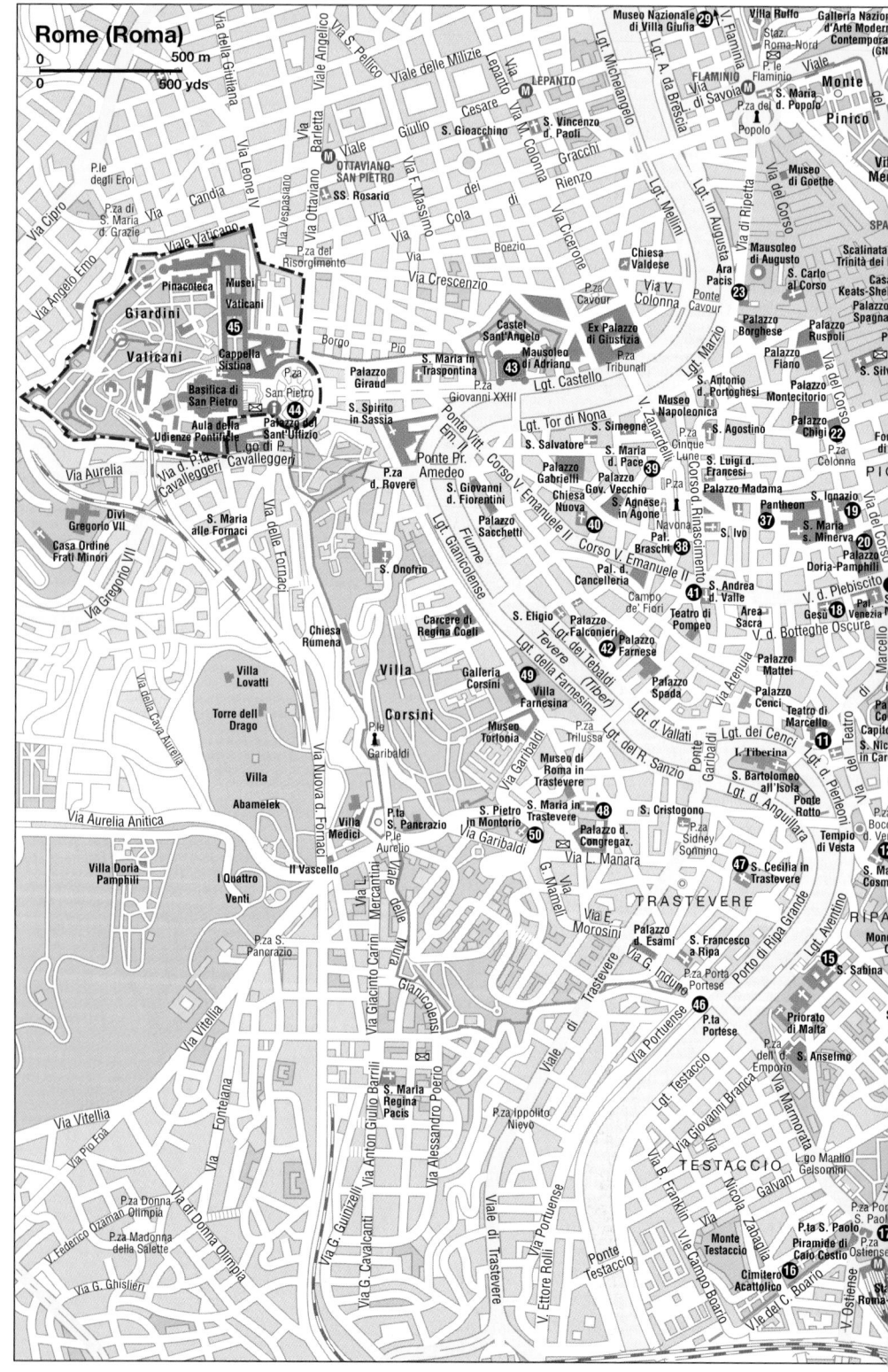

Letters in stone in the Forum.

maze) with reflective moonstone so that no assassin could creep up on him unob‑ served. Next to the peristyle lie the remains of a splendid banqueting hall, hailed by contemporaries as "the dining room of Jove".

Following the fortunes of the city as a whole, the imperial palaces fell into disuse during the Middle Ages. Monks made their home among the ruins, and the power‑ ful Frangipani family built a fortress here. During the Renaissance, when there was a surge of new building throughout the city, Cardinal Alessandro Farnese bought a large part of the Palatine and in 1625 laid out the world's first botanical gardens on the slope overlooking the Forum. The lush **Orti Farnesiani** are delightful, with their formal landscaping, the sounds of fountains and birds, and views over Rome.

For lovers of the picturesque, the ruins of the Palatine are hard to beat. Even archaeological excavations cannot deprive this location of its wild charm. It is the last place in Rome where you can find a landscape as it might have been drawn by Piranesi or Claude Lorraine. Roses, moss and poppies growing amid the crumbling bricks and shattered marble give it a romantic rather than an impe‑ rial splendour. It is the perfect place in which to wander, sketch or picnic.

The Roman Forum

The Clivus Palatinus leads from the domestic extravagances of the emperors down into the **Foro Romano ❷** (Roman Forum; daily 8.30am–one hour before sunset; entrance fee), the civic centre of ancient Rome. This area, once a swamp between the Capitoline and Palatine hills, used as a burial ground by the origi‑ nal inhabitants of the surrounding hills, was drained by an Etruscan king in the 6th century BC. Until excavations began in the 19th century, the Forum – buried under 8 metres (25 ft) of debris – was known as the "Campo Vaccino" (Cow

BELOW: view over the Forum.

Map on pages 128–9

ield) because smallholders tended their herds among the ruins. Today it reveals stupendous array of ruined temples, public buildings, arches and shops.

At the bottom of the Clivus Palatinus, the **Arco di Tito** (Arch of Titus) com-nemorates that emperor's destruction of Jerusalem and its sacred Temple in ᴅ 70. This event marked the beginning of the Diaspora and the shift from the ᴛemple in Jerusalem to local synagogues as the focus of Jewish worship. Until srael was founded in 1948 and the return to Palestine became possible, pious ews refused to walk under this arch.

The Via Sacra leads past the three remaining arches of the **Basilica di Costan-ino**, a source of inspiration for Renaissance architects. Bramante said of his design for St Peter's: "I shall place the Pantheon on top of the Basilica of Con-tantine." The **Tempio di Antonino e Faustina**, also known as San Lorenzo in Miranda, is a superb example of Rome's architectural layering. Originally a ᴛemple erected in ᴀᴅ 141 by the emperor Antoninus Pius, it was converted into ᴀ church in the Middle Ages. During the 17th century a baroque façade was ᴀdded, as was the case with so many Roman churches.

Across the Via Sacra is the lovely, round **Tempio di Vesta** (Vesta was the god-less of the hearth), where the six vestal virgins took turns tending the sacred ᴛire. The punishment for allowing the fire to die down was a whipping by the priest. Service was for 30 years and chastity was the rule. Few patricians were ᴛager to offer their daughters, and the emperor Augustus had to pick girls by lot. ᴌaxity about vows was common, and the emperor Domitian resorted to the ᴛraditional punishment of burying errant virgins alive and stoning their lovers ᴛo death. Living in the lovely **Casa delle Vestali** was some compensation for ᴛhis demanding life. The ruins remain a rose-scented haven.

The Vestals had seats of honour in the circus and theatre, and, in the city, where wheeled vehicles were forbid-den, they alone had the right to travel in a carriage.

BELOW: Arch of Titus.

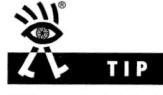

Like modern North Americans, the ancient Romans were keen litigants. Walk past the three elegant columns of the Temple of Castor and Pollux to the **Basilica Julia** (on the left of the Via Sacra), where trials were held, as many as four a a time. The acoustics were terrible, and on one occasion the booming speech o a particularly loud lawyer was applauded by audiences in all four chambers. In cases where an advocate wanted a little extra help, professional applauders called "supper praisers", could be hired. When not employed, these claqueur would loiter on the steps of the basilica and play games. Their roughly carvec boards can still be seen. The Senate met across the way in the Curia, the best preserved building in the Forum. Its sombre, solid appearance fits the seriousness of its purpose.

TIP

Taking a picnic into the Forum or Palatine is not officially allowed, but if you are discreet and tidy, there should be no problem.

At the western end of the Forum rises the famed **Rostra**, where the orator Cicero declaimed to the Roman masses. After his death, during Octavian's anti-Republican proscriptions, Cicero's hands and head were displayed here. Opposite the Rostra is the single **Colonna di Foca** (Column of Phocas). For centuries the symbol of the Forum, it was described by Byron as the "eloquent and nameless column with the buried base". Unburied and named, it is still, as the Italians say, *suggestivo* (atmospheric). To the right is **Arco di Settimio Severo**.

At the end of the Via Sacra, in the shadow of the Capitoline Hill, rise the eight Ionic columns of the **Tempio di Saturno**. The god's festival, called the Saturnalia, marked the merriest occasion in the Roman calendar, when gifts were exchanged and distinctions between master and slave forgotten. Occurring in the middle of winter, this was the feast that Christians later transformed into Christmas. Behind the temple are, from left to right, the Temple of Vespasian and Titus, and the Temple of the Concordia.

BELOW: the Victor Emmanuel Monument.

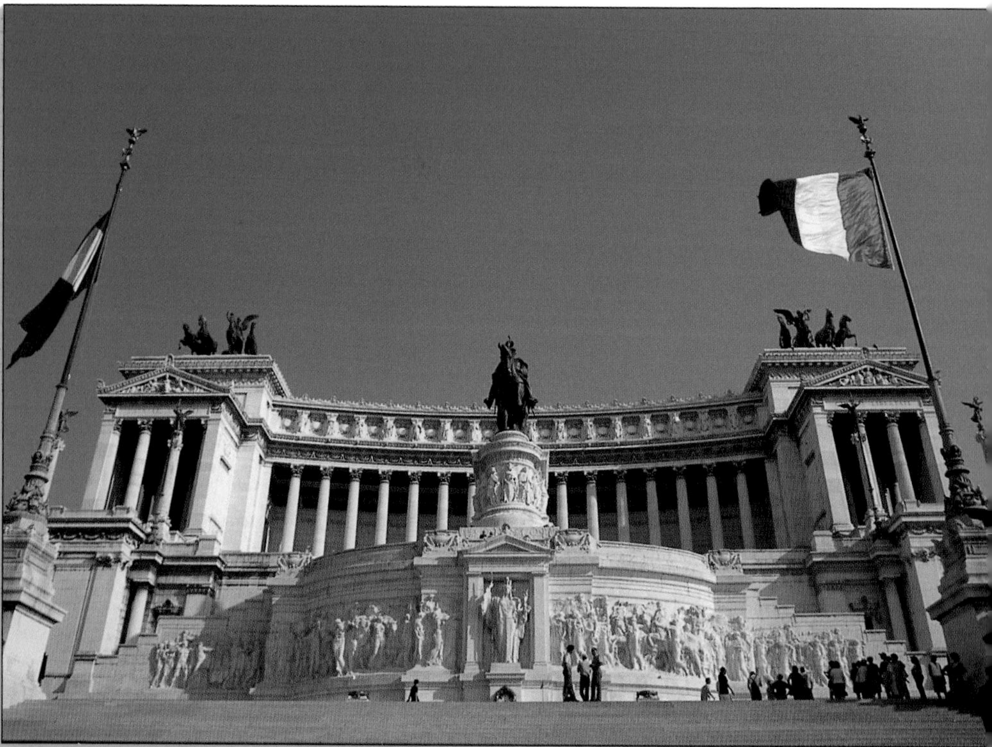

Outside the Forum excavations, across from Pietro da Cortona's Chiesa di Santi Luca e Martina, is the **Carcere Mamertino ❸** (Mamertine Prison; daily 9am–12.30pm, 2.30–6.30pm, until 5pm in winter; donation), home of some of Rome's most famous prisoners. According to legend, this dank, gloomy dungeon was where St Peter converted his pagan guards. Miraculously, a fountain sprang up so that he could baptise the new Christians.

The Capitoline Hill

From the **Capitolino ❹** (Capitoline Hill) the Temple of Jupiter Capitolinus (509 BC) watched over the city. It was here also that modern Italians raised their tribute to Italy's unification. The **Vittoriano** (Victor Emmanuel Monument; daily 9.30am–5.30pm, until 4.30pm in winter; free), completed in 1911 and dedicated to Italy's first king, captures the neoclassical bad taste of the 19th century. The monument is famously despised by locals who call it the "typewriter", "wedding cake" or "false teeth". Beneath the Vittoriano, the **Museo del Risorgimento** (daily 9.30am–6pm; free) contains items relating to the revolution that led to the creation of modern Italy in 1870.

Throughout Rome's history hopes for Italy's future have centred on this hill. In 1300, the poet Petrarch was crowned laureate here; in 1347 Cola di Rienzo roused the Roman populace to support his short-lived attempt to revive the Roman Republic; in the 16th century Michelangelo planned the elegant Campidoglio, thus restoring the Capitoline's status as the architectural focal point of the city.

If you're feeling energetic, climb the 124 steps to the 7th-century **Santa Maria in Aracoeli** (if you happen to be here at Christmas, come for the Midnight Mass). The weak-kneed will probably prefer Michelangelo's regal staircase

Map on pages 128–9

MAMERTINUM
LA PRIGIONE DEI SS APOSTOLI
PIETRO E PAOLO
IL PIÙ ANTICO CARCERE DI ROMA
XXV SECOLI DI STORIA

Vercingetorix, leader of the Gauls, was executed in the Mamertine Prison after Julius Caesar defeated his forces in 52 BC.

BELOW: the *Dying Gaul* in the Museo Capitolino.

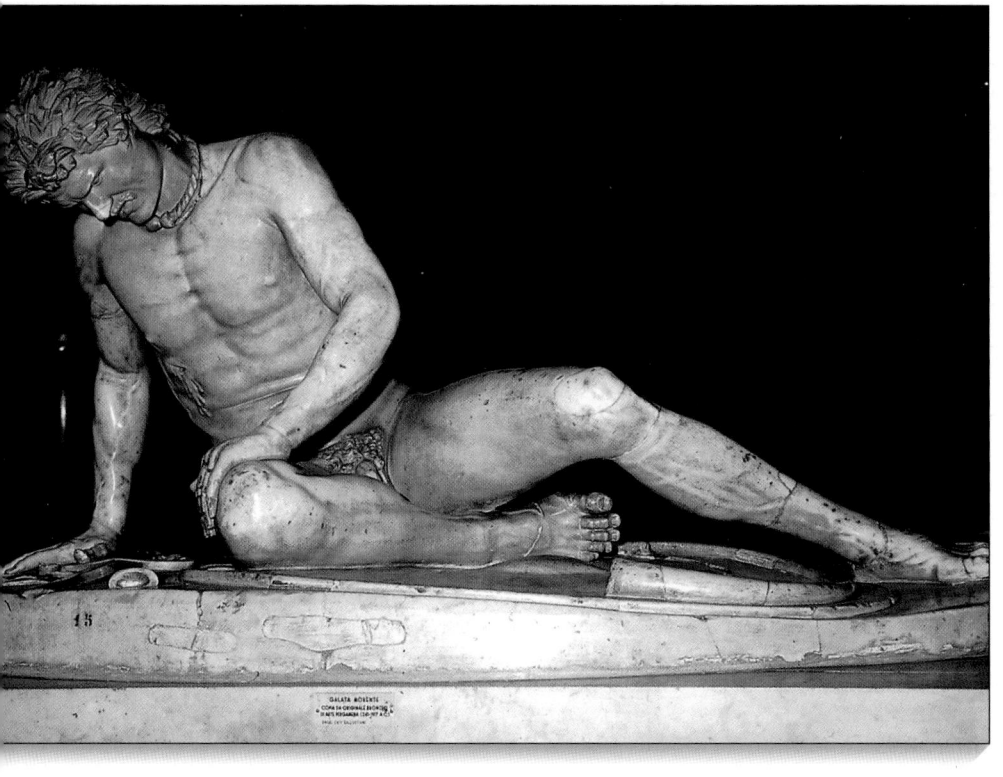

Wine, fish, spices, flowers, shoes, silk – anything could be bought at Trajan's Markets.

BELOW: Trajan's Column, celebrating his victories in Romania early in the 2nd century AD.

(known as the **cordonata**), flanked at the top by monumental statues of Castor and Pollux. In the back of the Campidoglio, Palazzo Senatorio surmounts the ancient Tabularium, dating from Republican times. On the right of Palazzo Senatorio rises **Palazzo dei Conservatori**, and on the left, the **Palazzo Nuovo**. Together they make up the **Capitoline Museums** (Tues–Sun 9am–8pm; entry into the museums is via the Palazzo dei Conservatori; entrance fee), an imposing collection of ancient art and Roman statuary. For an insight into the ancient Roman character, study the busts of emperors in the Sala degli Imperatori in the Palazzo Nuovo.

Mussolini's legacy

Piazza Venezia ❺, at the foot of the Vittoriano, marks the centre of contemporary Rome. You may feel you risk your life by crossing its wide expanse, but usually the torrents of traffic will part to allow a pedestrian passage. The Palazzo di Venezia, Rome's first great Renaissance palace (built in 1455), dominates one side. This was Mussolini's headquarters from 1929. Some of his most famous speeches were delivered from the balcony. The light burning in his bedroom at all hours of the night reassured the Italians that the "sleepless one" was busy solving the nation's problems (though according to Luigi Barzini the light was often left on when Mussolini was not there). Now the palace contains the **Museo di Palazzo Venezia** (Tues–Sun 8.30am–7.30pm, last entry one hour before closing; entrance fee), with a collection of paintings, sculptures and tapestries.

"Ten years from now, comrades, no one will recognise Italy," proclaimed *Il Duce* in 1926. One of the most dramatic changes the Fascists wrought on Rome was the Via dei Fori Imperiali. Mussolini cut down old neighbourhoods (reminders of Rome's decadent period) in order to excavate the fora and build the road. By such brutal means he hoped to create a symbolic connection between Rome's glorious past and his own regime.

West of the Imperial Fora is **Foro Traiano ❻** (Trajan's Forum), dominated by its famous column. Behind are the splendidly preserved and recently restored **Mercati di Traiano** (Trajan's Markets; Tues–Sun 9am–6.30pm, until 4.30pm in winter; entrance fee), a haunt of Rome's ubiquitous *gatti* (cats). In ancient times the five storeys of the market were abundantly stocked with exotic fare. The top floor contained two fishponds while the other held sea water brought from Ostia.

Augustus and Nerva both built their fora to accommodate Rome's growing population and passion for litigation. Statues of them stand opposite their fora.

Finally, at the end of all this ruined splendour rises the **Colosseo ❼** (Colosseum; daily 9am–one hour before sunset; entrance fee – ticket also valid for the Palatine and Forum), stripped of its picturesque wild flowers and weeds, surrounded by buses and snack stands, encircled by a swirling moat of traffic. This symbol of the Eternal City is less splendid than it was in its marble-clad, imperial days; after its restoration in 2001 however, it remains one of the key sights of Rome.

The Colosseum was begun in AD 79 when the emperor Vespasian drained the lake of Nero's **Domus Aurea** ❽ (Golden House; Tues–Fri 10am–4pm; booking required; entrance fee). The message was clear: where Nero had been profligate, emptying the coffers of the empire to construct his own pleasure palace, the Flavian prince built a public monument. Also near by is the **Arco di Costantino** (Arch of Constantine).

Architectural layer cake

From the Colosseum, Via di San Giovanni in Laterano brings you to **San Clemente** ❾ (Mon–Sat 9am–12.30pm and 3–6pm, Sun noon–6pm; entrance fee for excavations), one of Rome's most interesting churches. There are three levels of building. A 12th-century basilica descends to a 4th-century basilica, which in turn leads to a 1st-century Roman apartment building containing, in its courtyard, a Mithraic temple honouring one of the popular cults of imperial Rome.

A little further along, Via di San Giovanni opens up into **Piazza di San Giovanni in Laterano** ❿, containing some of the most important buildings in Christendom. The **Obelisk** is the tallest and oldest in Rome and a suitable marker for the Church of Rome, **San Giovanni in Laterano** (daily 7am–7pm, closes 6pm in winter; free), founded by Constantine the Great. The **Palazzo Laterano** was the home of the popes until the Avignon exile in 1309. The pious may want to ascend the 28 steps of the nearby **Scala Santa** (on their knees of course – daily 6.30am–noon and 3–6.15pm, 3.30–6.45pm Oct–Mar), said to be the steps Christ walked down after being condemned by Pontius Pilate. Constantine's mother, St Helena, retrieved them from Jerusalem.

Map on pages 128–9

TIP

North of the Colosseum lies the traditional *rione* (neighbourhood) of Monti. In parts, particularly in the hilly, leafy streets between Via Panisperna and Via Cavour, it has retained interesting traces of its medieval past, as well as an intimate village atmosphere.

BELOW: the Colosseum.

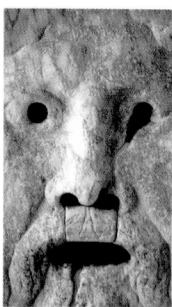

*La Bocca della Verità
– the Mouth of Truth.*

The Ghetto

Rome's old Ghetto lies on the western side of the Capitoline Hill, near the ruins of the **Teatro di Marcello** ⓫. The city has had a substantial Jewish community since the Republican era, but its isolation dates from the Counter-Reformation and the papacy of Paul IV (1555–9). From then on, the gates to the Ghetto were locked from sunset to sunrise, Jewish men had to wear a yellow hat, the women a yellow scarf, and most professions were closed to Jews.

A plaque on Via Portico d'Ottavia is a reminder that just over 60 years ago more than 2,000 Roman Jews were deported to a Nazi concentration camp. Next to the synagogue on Lungotevere Cenci, the **Museo Ebraico** (Jewish Museum; Sun–Thur 10am–7pm, until 5pm in winter, Fri 10am–4pm, until 2pm in winter; entrance fee) sensitively documents the history of Rome's Jewish population.

The Via del Teatro di Marcello leads south to **Piazza Bocca della Verità** ⓬, which yokes together two Roman temples (the Tempio di Portuno and the round Tempio d'Ercole), a baroque fountain and the medieval church of Santa Maria in Cosmedin. In the portico of this church, which uses the Byzantine rites, is the **Bocca della Verità** (daily 9.30am–5.50pm, until 5pm in winter), a marble slab resembling a human face and considered to be one of the world's oldest lie detectors. If a perjurer puts his hand in the mouth, so the legend goes, it will be bitten off. In fact, the slab's origin is sadly prosaic: it once covered a drain.

The oldest and largest of the famed Roman circuses, the **Circo Massimo** ⓭ (Circus Maximus), lies in the valley between the Aventine and the Palatine hills. It once seated 250,000 people. In addition to the main event, vendors, fortune tellers and prostitutes plied their trades beneath the arcades.

BELOW:
Circus Maximus.

If the circus has earned the ancient Romans a bad reputation, their public baths have inspired great praise. In addition to the three pools (hot, warm and cold), the **Terme di Caracalla** ⑭ (Tues–Sun 9am–one hour before sunset, Mon 9am–2pm; entrance fee) offered exercise rooms, libraries and lecture halls, for the improvement of mind and body. But less salubrious activities also went on here, especially when mixed bathing was permitted. Some took their cleanliness to an extreme: Emperor Commodus is said to have taken eight baths a day. But, for the most part, the baths represent a triumph of the Roman public spirit, demonstrating that cleanliness was not limited to those rich enough to have private facilities; they could accommodate up to 1,600 people. These days they are beautifully lit after dark.

Map on pages 128–9

The Aventine and Testaccio

For a contrast to the dusty and barren remnants of the circus and baths, visit the Aventine, one of modern Rome's most desirable residential neighbourhoods. As you climb the Clivo dei Pubblici the smell of roses wafts down from the pretty garden at the top of the hill. Via Santa Sabina leads to **Santa Sabina** ⑮, a perfectly preserved basilican church of the 5th century. Inside, shafts of golden sunlight illuminate the immense antique columns of the nave. Outside, in the portico, are some of the oldest wooden doors in existence (5th century).

Bordered by Via Marmorata to the east is **Testaccio**, a genuine Roman working-class district with a real neighbourhood feel and now the "hip and happening" place for nightlife. There is an excellent produce market on Piazza Testaccio and a few trendy boutiques among the old-fashioned grocery stores.

South of Testaccio, in the shadow of the Piramide Cestio, lies the **Cimitero**

The 2,000-year old Piramide Cestio.

BELOW: Testaccio Market.

TIP

The so-called Protestant Cemetery covers all religions except Catholicism and is divided into two parts: the older section, containing the tomb of Keats, lies to the left of the entrance. Keats fans can also visit the poet's home in Rome (see page 141).

BELOW: San Paolo fuori le Mura.

Acattolico ⓰ (Protestant Cemetery; Mon–Sat 9am–5pm, Sun 9am–1pm; donation), one of the most picturesque spots in Rome. Scores of unfortunate travellers who fell fatally ill on a Grand Tour are buried here. In the old part of the graveyard is Keats's tomb. Its epitaph reads: "Here lies one whose name was writ in water." In accordance with the poet's wishes, the tombstone does not mention Keats by name. The modern part of the cemetery contains Shelley's heart. His body was burnt on the shore near Pisa. As his dear friend Lord Byron put it: "All of Shelley was consumed, except his heart, which could not take the flame and is now preserved in spirits of wine."

Outside the **Porta San Paolo** ⓱ is the basilica of **San Paolo fuori le Mura** (daily 7am–6.30pm), one of the major basilicas of Rome. It is believed to house the tomb of St Paul.

Marble, gilt – and flesh and blood

Exuberant, awe-inspiring and outrageous, baroque architecture offers such an over-profusion of detail, painting, gilt and marble that it often overwhelms. But what pleasure there is in discovering a particularly winning putto winking at you from an architrave, in craning to see a fantastic ceiling by Pietro da Cortona or Andrea dal Pozzo, and in seeing saints and biblical figures made flesh and blood by Caravaggio or Bernini.

The baroque style dominates in Rome, and the best place to start appreciating it is the **Gesù** ⓲. The church was started in 1568 for the recently approved Jesuit Order, champions of the Counter-Reformation. The Council of Trent (1545–63) laid down the rigorous principles for strengthening the Catholic Church against the Protestant heretics. Originally, the Gesù was meant to be

ROME AND THE BAROQUE

The baroque (1600–1750) was born in Rome and nurtured by a papal campaign to make the city one of unparalleled beauty "for the greater glory of God and the Church". One of the first artists to answer the call was Michelangelo Merisi da Caravaggio (1573–1610), whose early secular portraits of sybaritic youths revealed him to be a painfully realistic artist. His later monumental religious painting entitled *The Calling of St Matthew*, in San Luigi dei Francesi, shocked the city by setting a holy act in a contemporary tavern.

The decoration of St Peter's by Gianlorenzo Bernini (1598–1680) was more acceptable to the Romans: a bronze tabernacle with spiralling columns at the main altar; a magnificent throne with angels clustered around a burst of sacred light at the end of the church; and, for the exterior, the classically simple colonnade embracing the piazza (1657).

Bernini's rival was Francesco Borromini (1599–1667), whose eccentric designs were the opposite of Bernini's classics. Many of Borromini's most famous designs hinge on a complex interplay of concave and convex surfaces which can be seen in the undulating façades of San Carlo alle Quattro Fontane, Sant'Ivo and Sant'Agnese in Piazza Navona (1653–63).

Map on pages 128–9

stere; its baroque make-over was performed in the late 17th century. By this me, the Counter-Reformers had discovered art's role as a means of making e intangible more accessible to the faithful. Baroque art also impressed pon the masses the immense power of the Church. Andrea dal Pozzo's altar St Ignatius in the Gesù is particularly sumptuous. But the supreme example of aroque is the Gesù's ceiling, with Il Baciccia's painting *The Triumph of the ame of Jesus*. White statues cling to the gilt vault, some supporting the cenal painting which spills out of its frame.

Another Jesuit church, **Sant'Ignazio ⑲**, this time with a ceiling by Andrea al Pozzo, is also an impressive example of baroque. To appreciate its fantasc perspective, stand in the middle of the nave and look heavenwards: the vault ems to disappear as an ecstatic St Ignatius receives from Jesus the light he ill disperse to the four corners of the earth. Pozzo also painted a fake dome, nce the Jesuit fathers were unable to afford a real one.

Carnival Corso

ia del Corso ("the Corso") stretches from Piazza Venezia to Piazza del Popolo, distance of almost 1.5 km (1 mile). Lined with elegant palaces and crowded ith shoppers, this central artery has always been a good place in which to take e pulse of the city. In ancient times it was the main route north, known as the ia Lata (Wide Way), which gives an idea of how narrow most ancient streets ere. Between the 18th and 19th centuries, it was the scene of the Roman Carival, when aristocrats and riff-raff alike pelted one another with flowers, bonons and confetti. Masked revellers abandoned all discretion, and temporary alconies were attached to palaces to facilitate the ogling of ladies and hurling

The baroque façade of the Gesù.

BELOW: non-stop shopping on Via del Corso.

Egyptian obelisk in the Piazza del Popolo (12th century BC).

BELOW:
Trevi Fountain.

of missiles. This chaotic setting provided a dramatic background for the clima of Hawthorne's *The Marble Faun* (1860). Alas, Rome has sobered up since became the nation's capital, and for Carnival you must now head for Venice.

First stop on a tour of the Corso is **Palazzo Doria Pamphili** ⑳ (Fri–We 10am–5pm; entrance fee), home of the Galleria Doria Pamphili. The collectio is superb (paintings by Titian, Caravaggio and Raphael), but nothing is labelle so unless you're a connoisseur of 16th- and 17th-century art, use the lively audi guide that comes free with the ticket. The star of the collection is Velázquez portrait of Pope Innocent X. Via delle Muratte, to the right off the Corso, lead to the most grandiose and famous of Rome's baroque fountains: the **Fontan di Trevi** ㉑ (Trevi Fountain), where the voluptuous Anita Ekberg frolicked i Fellini's film *La Dolce Vita* (1960).

But the ancient city rears its head even in the most up-to-date places. **Piazz Colonna** ㉒, about halfway down the Corso, is home to the Column of Marcu Aurelius (AD 180–93). Sixtus V (1585–90) crowned this column with a statue o St Paul and Trajan's Column with one of St Peter. (Sixtus was always eager t appropriate Roman triumphal symbols to Christianity: he placed many faller forgotten obelisks in front of churches.)

Two particularly impressive relics of the Augustan era, cleaned up an reassembled during the Fascist era, are the **Mausoleo di Augusto** and the **Ar Pacis Augustae** ㉓ (Tues–Sun 9am–7pm, last entry one hour before closing entrance fee). The emperor's funeral pyre burnt in front of the mausoleum fo five days. In the Middle Ages the ill-fated visionary leader, Cola di Rienzo, wa cremated there. For centuries the Ara Pacis, built from 13–8 BC to celebrat peace throughout the empire, was in pieces. Fragments were to be found as fa away as the Louvre in Paris and the Uffizi in Florence Finally, in 1983, the altar was reconstructed with frag ments and copies of missing parts. The monument ha recently been extensively restored and is now house in a slick travertine-and-glass structure designed by U architect Richard Meier.

The gate of Rome

Everyone – from emperors in triumph to pilgrims o foot – used to enter Rome through the **Porta del Popol** (Porta Flaminia). To the east rises the lush green of th Pincian Hill where, in the Middle Ages, Empero Nero's ghost was believed to wander. The church o **Santa Maria del Popolo** dates from the late 15th cen tury and contains splendidly decorated chapels of dif ferent periods, with works by Pinturicchio, Raphae (the Chigi Chapel) and Caravaggio (*The Conversion o St Paul* and *The Crucifixion of St Peter*).

Take Via del Babuino, on the left of the twin baroqu churches, south to **Piazza di Spagna** ㉔. The piazza i shaped like an hourglass. In the southern section is th Palazzo di Spagna, the seat of the Spanish embassy t the Vatican, which gives the square its name. But it i in the northern part that the famous **Scalinata dell Trinità dei Monti** (Spanish Steps) rises. Neither Nev York's Times Square nor the Champs-Elysées in Pari provides a better location for watching the world go by Caricaturists sketch tourists; old women sell roaste

estnuts or coconuts; tired sightseers rinse their hands in Pietro Bernini's foun-
in; backpackers sunbathe on the steps; hippies play guitars, and shoppers
owd the windows of the elegant shops below. Off this piazza stretch the most
shionable shopping streets in Rome: Via dei Condotti, Via Frattina and Via
orgognona. Underneath the Pincian Hill, the quiet Via Margutta is the place
buy art.

Years ago this area was inhabited by English and American expatriates. John
eats died in the house overlooking the steps, which contains a cluttered col-
ction of memorabilia. The **Keats-Shelley House** (Mon–Fri 9am–1pm and
-6pm, Sat 11am–2pm and 3–6pm – these times do vary, to check tel: 06-678
235; www.keats-shelley-house.org; entrance fee) is essential viewing for all
mantic ghost-seekers. Keep an eye out for plaques marking the past residences
famous foreigners. Henry James stayed in Hotel Inghilterra; Shelley in the
ia Sistina and Via del Corso; George Eliot in the Via del Babuino; Goethe at 18
ia del Corso, where you can visit the **Goethe Museum**, devoted to the writer's
avels in Italy (Tues–Sun 10am–6pm; entrance fee). One of the most grandiose
aques marks James Joyce's residences at 50/52 Via Frattina. Joyce, it says,
nade of his Dublin, our universe".

he bones and the bees

he street between Trinità dei Monti and Santa Maria Maggiore was cut by
ixtus V, a pope bent on improving Rome and glorifying his own name. The
ew down the length of the road is dramatic – culminating in the obelisk which
ixtus raised in front of Santa Maria Maggiore. Once called Strada Felice, the
ad now changes name three times as it cuts through the tangled streets.

Map on pages 128–9

TIP

Via dei Condotti, which
starts at the Spanish
Steps, is Rome's most
opulent shopping
street. Here, and in the
surrounding streets,
you'll find all the Ital-
ian design giants – Ar-
mani, Bulgari, Gucci,
Prada, Valentino et al.

BELOW: Spanish
Steps.

The first leg, Via Sistina, leads down to **Piazza Barberini** 25, in the centre of which is Bernini's sensual **Fontana del Tritone**. The sea creature blows fiercely on a conch shell while a geyser of water shoots above him. In the base is the unmistakable coat of arms of the Barberini family: three bees. The family palace nearby is the work of Carlo Maderno, Bernini and Borromini. Today the Palazzo Barberini houses the **Galleria Nazionale di Arte Antica** (Tues–Sun 8.30am–7.30pm; last entry 30 mins before closing; entrance fee). Don't miss Pietro da Cortona's *The Triumph of Divine Providence*, a baroque celebration of the Barberini Pope Urban VIII – a pope who quarried the ruins of ancient Rome so extensively that he inspired the witticism: "What the barbarians didn't do, the Barberini did."

Via Veneto swoops off the Piazza Barberini. Before strolling along its wide streets or retiring to one of its cafés, stop at the **Chiesa dei Cappuccini**, also known as Santa Maria della Concezione (church open daily 9am–noon and 3–6pm; free; crypt open Fri–Wed 9am–noon and 3–6pm; donation expected) to see its macabre crypt. According to legend, a group of artistically and ghoulishly inclined friars decided to put the dead brothers' bones (4,000 monks in all) to a cautionary use. Four rooms of rococo sculptures contain a playful filigree of hip bones, a garland of spines and an array of skulls stacked as neatly as oranges and apples on a fruit vendor's stall.

The **Via Veneto** became famous after World War II as the centre of Rome's "Dolce Vita", but even after an impressive recent restoration, it's still not the hub of glamorous Roman nightlife that it once was. Buy a magazine, put on your dark glasses and adjourn to one of the streetside cafés for refreshment, then move on to the Villa Borghese, where you can picnic or visit the **Bioparco** 26 (9.30am–6pm, until 7pm at weekends and holidays, 5pm in winter, last entry one hour before closing; tel: 06-360 8211), the city zoo, which has very interesting sections on biodiversity and animal reproduction in the new wing. The Villa Borghese's Orangery is now the location of the **Carlo Bilotti Museum** (Tues–Sun 9am–7pm; entrance fee). There is a permanent collection of works by de Chirico and Warhol. Near the Via Veneto entrance to the park is the **Galleria Borghese** 27 (Tues–Sun 8.30am–7.30pm; visits by reservation only; tel: 06-8413979 or book online at www.ticketeria.it), with works by Bernini, Caravaggio, Raphael, Titian, Rubens and Canova among others. If you are interested in Italy's more recent artistic achievements, visit the **Galleria Nazionale d'Arte Moderna e Contemporanea** 28 (Tues–Sun 8.30am–7.30pm; entrance fee). A wing of the museum opened in 2003 accommodates the collection of paintings, sculptures and prints, largely by Italian artists but including international artists such as Henry Moore, Pollock, Cézanne and Kandinsky, dating from the 1800s to the present.

To the north of the Villa Borghese is another aristocratic palace, built for Julius III. The **Villa Giulia** 29 (for opening times refer to the museum) has a beautiful Renaissance garden and, inside, the fascinating **Museo Nazionale Etrusco di Villa Giulia** (Tues–Sun 8.30am–7.30pm, last entry one hour before closing; entrance fee), full of pre-Roman art. The Etruscan terracotta sculptures are particularly

BELOW: temple in Villa Borghese park.

nteresting. Also well worth seeking out are a touching sarcophagus of a hus-
·and and wife and a magnificent statue of Apollo.

Bernini and Borromini

From the intersection of **Via delle Quattro Fontane** (the extension of Via Sistina)
nd Via XX Settembre you can admire the drama of Roman urban planning: in
three directions obelisks scrape the sky. The Via XX Settembre contains a num-
·er of splendid baroque churches. First is **San Carlo alle Quattro Fontane** ❸,
lso known as San Carlino. This tiny church, whose interior is the same size as
·ne of the piers under the dome of St Peter's, was designed by Francesco Bor-
omini (1599–1667). The undulating façade is characteristic of this eccentric
·rchitect's style. The all-white interior is a fantastic play of ovals. The financially
·ressed monks who commissioned the church were impressed by Borromini's
bility to keep down the costs – by using delicate stucco work rather than marble
·r gilt – without in any way lessening the beauty of the interior.

Up Via del Quirinale, off the other side of Via delle Quattro Fontane, is another
·val gem by Borromini's arch rival, Gianlorenzo Bernini (1598–1680). **Sant'
Andrea al Quirinale** ❸ offers quite a contrast to its neighbour. Every inch of
·his church is covered with gilt and marble. Putti ascend the wall as if in a cloud
·f smoke. Yet the architect's masterful, classical handling of space creates a
·arvellous sense of simplicity.

For another Bernini masterpiece head in the other direction to **Santa Maria
·ella Vittoria** ❸, in Largo Santa Susanna (off Via XX Settembre), where you'll
find his sculpture of the 17th-century Spanish mystic St Teresa of Avila. The artist
·aptures her at the moment when she was being struck by the arrow of divine love.

Map on
pages
128–9

*Gilded door knob in
Santa Maria della
Vittoria.*

BELOW: the Baths of
Diocletian.

Torso of a centurion in the Museo Nazionale Romano.

Across Via XX Settembre, on the north side of Piazza della Repubblica, is **Santa Maria degli Angeli ㉝**, a church Michelangelo created from the tepidarium of the **Terme di Diocleziano** (Baths of Diocletian; Tues–Sun 9am–7.45pm entrance fee), the most extensive baths in Rome, built between AD 298 and 306. The *esedra*, the open space surrounded by porticoes and seats where the Romans would chat, gave its form to Piazza della Repubblica. The **Fontana delle Naiadi** (Fountain of the Naiads) in the centre of the square, dating from around 1900 caused a scandal when it was unveiled, because of the "obscene" postures of the nymphs. The baths were also once the principal venue of the **Museo Nazionale Romano ㉞** *(see box, page 145)*, but this great collection of ancient art was divided up into several sites in a major reorganisation programme carried out in the run-up to the year 2000.

Mary and Moses

Rome has more churches dedicated to the Virgin Mary than to any other saint. The largest and most splendid of these is **Santa Maria Maggiore ㉟** (daily 7am–7pm), one of the four patriarchal churches of Rome. Here the mixture of architectural styles is surprisingly harmonious: early Christianity is represented in the basilican form and in the 5th-century mosaics above the architrave in the nave (binoculars are a must if you want to decipher them). Medieval input includes the campanile (the largest in Rome), the Cosmatesque pavement and the mosaic in the apse. But the overwhelming effect is baroque, and as such it is an appropriate resting place for baroque master, Bernini. The coffered ceiling was supposedly gilded with the gold Columbus brought from America.

BELOW: faded grandeur.

If your head is spinning with the excess of gilt and marble, head down the Via Cavour to **San Pietro in Vincoli ㊱** (daily 7am–12.30pm and 3.30–6pm), where you will find Michelangelo's massive and dignified *Moses*. The statue was to form part of an enormous free-standing tomb for Pope Julius II but politics and constrained finances curtailed Michelangelo's imagination. Of this one statue Giorgio Vasari artist and biographer of artists, said: "No modern work will ever approach it in beauty." Moses sits 3 metres (10 ft) high, every inch the powerful law-giver. The other significant exhibit here is the glass box containing the chains that bound St Peter in his prison cells in Rome and Judaea, hence the name San Pietro in Vincoli (St Peter in Chains).

Near Santa Maria Maggiore, inside the restored Palazzo Brancaccio, is the most important collection of oriental art in Italy, the **Museo Nazionale d'Arte Orientale** (Via Merulana 248, Esquiline Hill; Mon, Wed, Fri and Sat 8.30am–2pm, Tues, Thur and Sun 8.30am–7.30pm, closed first and third Mon of the month; entrance fee).

The living city

During the Middle Ages, most of Rome's population was crowded either into the region between Via del Corso and the Tiber (Campus Martius to the ancients) or into Trastevere *(see page 156)* across the river. The best time to visit these areas is the early morning, when you will be able to admire the façades of buildings alone

nter churches with only the faithful as companions, and watch the Romans start-
ng their day. Windowless shops give directly onto crooked, narrow streets, and
orkers leave their doors open for light and air. Look in and you will see bakers
neading loaves of *casareccio* bread, furniture-restorers rubbing down wood with
rong-smelling waxes, and cobblers hammering heels onto worn boots.

Have a *cornetto* (an Italian croissant) and a cappuccino in Piazza della
otonda and admire the outside of the **Pantheon ㊲** (Mon–Sat 8.30am–7.30pm,
un 9am–6pm, holidays 9am–1pm; free) – the best-preserved of all ancient
oman buildings. For those who question the greatness of Roman architecture
nd dismiss it as inferior to Greek, the Pantheon is an eloquent answer. This per-
ctly proportioned round temple proves how adept the Romans were in shaping
aterior space. Rebuilt by the emperor Hadrian, its architectural antecedents are
ot the Republican round temples – such as the one in the Forum Boarium – but
ne round chambers used in the baths. Western architecture owes the Romans
n enormous debt for their skilful work with vaults and domes. The only light is
rovided by a large hole set in the centre of the dome – the *oculus* – and this
neans that the building has been open to the elements for nearly 2,000 years.

Near the Pantheon, in front of **Santa Maria Sopra Minerva** (daily 8am–7pm),
ernini's much-loved elephant carries the smallest of Rome's obelisks. Inside
ne church (the only one in the Gothic style in Rome) are a chapel decorated by
ra Filippo Lippi and, to the left of the main altar, Michelangelo's statue of *Christ
earing the Cross*. Other ecclesiastical treasures are just a few blocks away. Car-
vaggio frescos adorn both **San Luigi dei Francesi** (*The Calling of St Matthew,
  Matthew and the Angel* and *The Martyrdom of St Matthew*) and **Sant'Agostino**
The Madonna of the Pilgrims). Borromini's **Sant'Ivo** is tucked into the court-

Map on
pages
128–9

*Inside the Pantheon
dome.*

BELOW: a stone
vessel outside the
Baths of Diocletian.

MUSEO NAZIONALE ROMANO

he Museo Nazionale Romano is one of the most important archaeological collections in the world. It is split up
to five main sites. The vast **Terme di Diocleziano** (Baths
f Diocletian; Via Enrico de Nicola 78 – *see page 144*) was
ne original home of the museum. The **Aula Ottagona**
)ctagonal Hall, Via Romita 8), an integral part of the baths,
till contains some important sculptures. But the bulk of the
ollection is at the **Palazzo Massimo alle Terme** (Largo di
lla Peretti 1). Highlights include splendid floor mosaics and
all paintings from the villas of wealthy Romans, seen at
eir best in the delicate frescos from the Villa of Livia. The
alazzo **Altemps** (Piazza Sant'Apollinare 44) is a 15th-
entury palace north of Piazza Navona, with a beautiful
ourtyard which houses a fine collection of antique sculp-
Jres. The **Crypta Balbi** (Via delle Botteghe Oscure 31) –
ne remains of the theatre built by Balbus in 13 BC – docu-
nents the changing face of Rome through history. All sites
pen Tues–Sun 9am–7.45pm. A ticket is valid for all the sites
f the museums for a period of three days. A €20 ticket
rcheologia Card) is also available and includes the four
useum sites, the Colosseum, the Palatine, the Baths of
aracalla, the Tomb of Cecilia Metella and the Villa of the
uintili. Book online at www.pierreci.it or tel: 06-3996 7700.

yard of Palazzo Sapienza. Like San Carlino, this church's interior is dazzling white. Most startling, however, is its spiralling campanile.

Even the crowds of people milling around eating ice cream, the artists sitting on collapsible chairs hoping to sell their paintings, and Roman youths zooming through on their motorbikes cannot mask the elegance of **Piazza Navona** ❸❽. This totally enclosed space was once the Stadium of Domitian, parts of which can still be seen outside the northern end. Hagiographers claim that when the youthful St Agnes was exposed naked in the vaulted areas of the circus beneath the church that bears her name, her hair grew to shield her. Agnes had refused to marry because she had vowed to be a virgin bride of Christ. In another version of her martyrdom, she was banished to a brothel where her chastity was miraculously preserved; a subsequent attempt to burn her was also unsuccessful; finally, she was beheaded.

The church of **Sant'Agnese in Agone** has another curvaceous façade by Borromini. His rival Bernini designed the **Fontana dei Quattro Fiumi** (Fountain of the Four Rivers) in the centre of the piazza. A popular tale claims that the statue of the Nile facing Sant'Agnese is covering its eyes for fear it will collapse. However, the fountain was completed in 1651, before Borromini had even started work on the church.

Stony words

Close by, **Piazza di Pasquino** contains a battered statue that once functioned as the underground newspaper of Rome. The papal censors allowed so little criticism that irrepressible commentators attached their writings to statues in the city. The most famous satirist was Pasquino.

Near the piazza is the elegant church of **Santa Maria della Pace** ❸❾ (Mon–Sa

The Ghetto retains its Jewish heritage, and the medieval streets are dotted with kosher shops and restaurants.

BELOW: fresh fruit at Campo de' Fiori.

CAMPO DE' FIORI

South of the Cancelleria is the lively Campo de' Fiori (Field of Flowers), so named because it used to be a meadow that sloped down towards the Tiber. It has been the site of a produce market for centuries, and was one of the liveliest areas of medieval and Renaissance Rome, when cardinals and pilgrims would rub shoulders with fishmongers, vegetable sellers and prostitutes.

The Campo de' Fiori is the most secular of Roman squares, for although it is as old as Rome itself, it has never been dedicated to any cult, and to this day is free of churches. Its present aspect dates from the end of the 15th century, when the whole area was reshaped. It was surrounded by inns for pilgrims and travellers. In the Renaissance, some of these hotels were the homes of successful courtesans, Vannozza Catanei, mistress of the Borgia Pope Alexander VI, among them. On the corner of the square and Via del Pellegrino you can see her shield, which she had decorated with her own coat of arms and those of her husband and lover.

With its reputation for being a carnal, pagan place, the square must have seemed a natural spot to hold executions. Of all the unfortunate victims, Giordano Bruno was the most important figure to be burnt at the stake here, in 1600. A priest and philosopher, he was accused of heresy and found guilty of freethinking.

Jam–noon and 4–6pm, Sun 10am–noon). Inside there are frescos by Raphael d a beautiful cloister by Bramante which is often filled with exhibitions of the ork of contemporary artists. The front door is often locked, so access is by the ramante cloister. To the north, Via dei Coronari is lit with torches every night.

At the end of Via dei Cornari, take a left turn and you will reach the **Chiesa uova** ⓣ (daily 7.30am–noon and 4.30–7.30pm), dedicated to St Filippo Neri, ne of Rome's patron saints, who lies buried here. The apse contains three fine orks by Rubens, who lived in Rome from 1606 to 1608. The Oratorio dei Fil- pini was built between 1637 and 1662 by Borromini as a place of worship for e fraternity of St Philip Neri, who instituted the musical gatherings that later ecame known as oratorios. The **Museo Barracco** nearby (Corso Vittorio manuele 166/A; Tues–Sun 9am–7pm) showcases a superb collection of Egypt- n, Etruscan and Roman sculpture.

The last baroque church on this tour is perhaps the most ornate. Puccini chose ant'Andrea della Valle ⓣ as a setting for the opening act of *Tosca*. Act II takes lace at the nearby **Palazzo Farnese** ⓣ, the most splendid of Renaissance palaces d suitably intimidating as headquarters for the villainous Scarpia. The palace is ow the French embassy and, alas for the visitor who would like to see Annibale arraci's frescos, it is closed to the public. Other grand palaces in the neighbour- ood include **Palazzo della Cancelleria** (closed to the public) and the **Galleria pada** (Tues–Sun 8.30am–7.30pm; entrance fee), which has a handsome gallery.

Act III of *Tosca* takes place on the west bank of the Tiber, in the notorious astel Sant'Angelo prison (Tues–Sun 9am–7.30pm, last entry one hour before osing; entrance fee). Visiting this fortress takes us from Rome into the Vati- n City, the world's smallest state *(see page 151)*. ❑

Map on pages 128–9

Monti is a district popular with artists and young students drawn by the reasonable rents.

BELOW: spectacular fountains on Piazza Navona.

THE COLOSSEUM: BREAD AND CIRCUSES

"While the Colosseum stands, Rome shall stand; when the Colosseum falls, Rome shall fall; when Rome falls, the world shall fall."

The Venerable Bede's 8th-century prophecy has been taken to heart and the Colosseum shored up ever since. The ancient amphitheatre is the city's most stirring sight, a place of stupendous size and spatial harmony. The Colosseum was begun by Vespasian, inaugurated by his son Titus in AD 80, and completed by Domitian (AD 81–96). Titus used Jewish captives from Jerusalem as masons. The Colosseum had 80 numbered, arched entrances, allowing over 50,000 spectators to be seated within 10 minutes. "Bread and circuses" was how Juvenal, the 2nd-century satirist, mocked the Romans here who sold their souls for free food and entertainment.

FALL AND RUIN

With the fall of the empire, the Colosseum fell into disuse. During the Renaissance, the ruins were plundered to create churches and palaces all over Rome, including the Palazzo Farnese, now the French embassy. Quarrying was only halted by Pope Benedict XIV in the 18th century, and the site consecrated to Christian martyrs. The Colosseum was still neglected on the German writer Goethe's visit in 1787, with a hermit and beggars "at home in the crumbling vaults". In 1817 Lord Byron was enthralled by this "noble wreck in ruinous perfection", while Edgar Allan Poe, another Romantic poet, celebrated its "grandeur, gloom and glory".

During the Fascist era, Mussolini, attracted to the power that the Colosseum represented, demolished a line of buildings to create a clear view of it from his balcony on the Palazzo di Venezia. To celebrate Holy Year (2000) the Colosseum was restored, and it has reopened for festivities and classical drama.

△ **ALL AT SEA**
Renaissance historians believed that in ancient times Roman arenas were sometimes flooded to stage mock naval battles, but there is scant evidence to suggest such a display ever took place in the Colosseum.

▽ **GLADIATORIAL COMBAT**
The price of failure: the Gate of Life was reserved for victorious gladiators, while vanquished gladiators were doomed to the Gate of Death.

△ **BEHIND THE SCENES**
From the higher tiers stretch views down to the arena and a maze of passages. The arena was encircled by netting to prevent beasts escaping. The movable wooden floor was covered in sand, the better to soak up the blood. Below, the subterranean section concealed the animal cages and sophisticated technical apparatus, from winches and mechanical lifts to ramps and trapdoors.

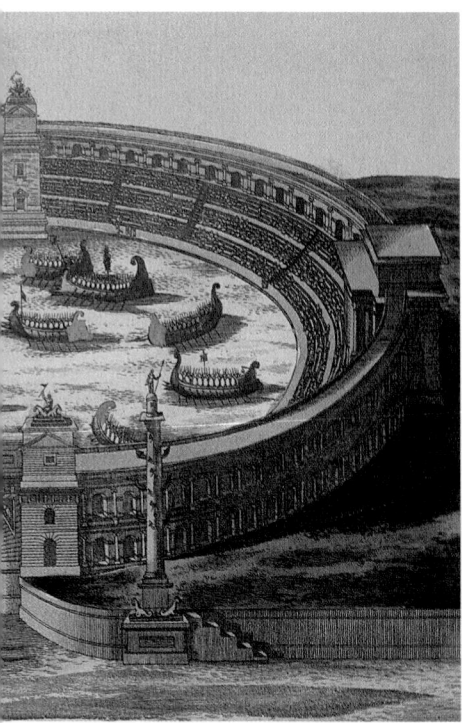

▽ SOCIAL STRATA

Although supremely public, the Colosseum was a stratified affair. The podium, set on the lowest tier, was reserved exclusively for the emperor, senators, magistrates and Vestal Virgins. Above them sat the bourgeoisie, with the lower orders restricted to the top tier, and the populace on wooden seats in the very top rows.

ENTERTAINMENT FOR THE MASSES

The Roman appetite for bloodshed was legendary, with the barbaric *munera*, or blood sports, introduced as a corrupt version of Greek games. The animals, mostly imported from Africa, included lions, elephants, giraffes, hyenas, hippos, wild horses and zebras. The contests were also a way of eliminating slaves and proscribed sects, Christians and common criminals, political agitators and prisoners of war. Variants included battles involving nets, swords and tridents, mock hunts and freak shows with panthers pulling chariots or cripples pitted against clowns. Seneca, Nero's tutor, came expecting "fun, wit and some relaxation", but was dumbfounded by the butchery and cries of "Kill him! Lash him! Why does he meet the sword so timidly?"

In AD 248, the millennium of the founding of Rome was celebrated by contests involving 2,000 gladiators and the slaying of tame giraffes and hippos as well as big cats. Although convicted criminals were routinely fed to the lions, Christian martyrdom in the arena is less well documented. However, St Ignatius of Antioch, who described himself as "the wheat of Christ", was dutifully devoured by lions in AD 107. Gladiatorial combat was banned in AD 404, while animal fights ended in the following century.

◁ IMPERIAL COINAGE

Bearing the head of Emperor Vespasian, this coin depicts no grape-sucking degenerate but a professional soldier who consolidated Roman rule in Britain and Germany. As the founder of the Flavian dynasty and emperor between AD 69 and 79, he began the stadium. The Colosseum is also known as Anfiteatro Flavio (Flavian Amphitheatre).

◁ ROMANTIC ROME

This 18th-century view by Giovanni Volpato reflects the nostalgic sensibility of the Romantic era. Visitors on the Grand Tour were beguiled by the ruins bathed in moonlight or haunted by the sense of a lost civilisation. In Byron's words, "Some cypresses beyond the time-worn breach/ Appeared to skirt the horizon, yet they stood/Within a bowshot – where the Caesars dwelt."

THE VATICAN AND TRASTEVERE

Map on
pages
128–9

*From the spirituality of St Peter's, with its
extensive museums and magnificent art treasures,
to the earthiness of Rome's medieval quarter*

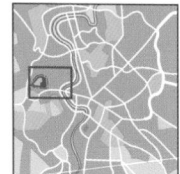

The west bank of the Tiber offers contrasting experiences. Cheek by jowl with the Vatican, with all its papal pomp, is the working-class district of Trastevere, with its tenements, narrow streets and lively street life.
As you cross the Tiber using Ponte Sant'Angelo, it is not the domed heart of the Vatican you see first, however, but the almost windowless walls of the medieval citadel, the **Castel Sant'Angelo** ⓭ (Tues–Sun 9am–7.30pm, last entry one hour before closing; entrance fee). Back in AD 139, this was the site of the mausoleum of the emperor Hadrian. Later it became a fortress and prison, then a residence to which the popes could flee in times of turbulence. Today it is a museum full of 16th-century furnishings and frescos. Puccini's heroine, Tosca, plunged to her death from the parapet where visitors now come to admire the views across Rome. Towering over the battlements is a gigantic statue of St Michael, the warlike archangel after whom the castle is named.

Vatican City

From Castel Sant'Angelo, Via della Conciliazione leads to St Peter's, at the heart of Vatican City. If size were the only measure of a nation's power or importance, the Vatican would warrant hardly any attention at all. Yet it serves as an exception to the rule that tiny nations are famous for little more than their postage stamps.

For centuries the Vatican was the unchallenged centre of the Western world. Its symbolic significance, both past and present, and its enduring international role, as both a religious and a diplomatic force, have put this tiny city-state on a par with nations many million times larger. No matter how secular our world has become, divine authority seems still to count and to make the Vatican much more than a geographic oddity, much more than the academic footnote it might otherwise be.

Covering a total area of slightly more than 40 hectares (100 acres), Vatican City is by far the world's smallest independent sovereign entity. What other nation is as small as New York's Central Park? What other nation can lock its gates at midnight, as the Vatican's doorkeepers do each night, opening them only at the ring of a bell? What other nation can be crossed at a leisurely pace in well under half an hour?

In imperial Roman days, the lower part of what is now Vatican City was an unhealthy bog, an area famous among Caesars and consuls for its vinegary wine, snakes and diseases. But in the 1st century AD, the dowager empress Agrippina had the Vatican Valley drained and planted with imperial gardens. Under Caligula and Nero, the area was turned over to the circus. Chariot racing and executions – including that of St Peter – were regular events on what later became St Peter's Square.

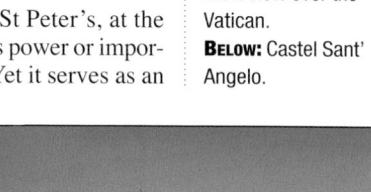

LEFT: view over the Vatican.
BELOW: Castel Sant' Angelo.

The Lateran Treaty of 1929, concluded between Pope Pius XI and Benito Mussolini, established the present territorial limits of the Vatican. The city is roughly trapezoidal in shape, bounded by medieval walls on all sides except on the corner where the opening of St Peter's Square marks the border with Rome and the rest of Italy. Of the six openings to the Vatican, only three are for public use: the Piazza, the Arco delle Campane (south of St Peter's Basilica) and the entrance to the Vatican Museums. Pius XI had a special Vatican railway station built in the early 1930s, a facility which no paying passenger has ever used (even popes use it very infrequently). A heliport has been built on a spot where British diplomats whiled away their days during World War II.

Aside from an impressive array of palaces and office buildings, there is also a Vatican prison, a supermarket and the printing press, which churns out the daily *L'Osservatore Romano* and scripts in a wide range of languages, from Coptic to Ecclesiastical Georgian to Tamil. In short, the Vatican is much more than an oversized museum.

Swiss Guards caught off guard.

Piazza San Pietro

Bernini's spectacular, colonnaded **Piazza San Pietro** ⓸ is, according to one's viewpoint, either the welcoming embrace of the Mother Church or her grasping claws. The Via della Conciliazione, constructed in 1937 to commemorate the reconciliation between Mussolini and Pope Pius XI, changed the original impact of the space. Before this thoroughfare provided a monumental approach to St Peter's, the entrance was by way of smaller streets, winding through the old Borgo and arriving, finally, in the enclosed open space, with the biggest church in the world at one end and an enormous Egyptian obelisk in the centre.

BELOW: St Peter's Square.

Subjects of the Holy See

To be one of the 800 or so citizens with a Vatican passport is to belong to one of the world's most exclusive clubs – the privilege of citizenship hinges on a direct and continuous relationship with the Holy See. The Pope himself carries passport No. 1, and he rules absolutely over Vatican City.

The word "pope" comes from the Greek *pappas*, meaning "father". Despite two millennia having passed since St Peter first assumed the mantle, the Pope's role remains paternal, alternating between concern for humanity and stern warnings against theological or spiritual deviation. John Paul II (1978–2005) asserted his moral authority vigorously. His 1993 encyclical denounced contraception, homosexuality and other infringements of the faith as "intrinsically evil". His successor, Benedict XVI, is cast in the same ethical mould.

The facts and figures

There have been 263 popes. The shortest reign of a pope was that of Stephen II, who died four days after his election in March 752. At the other extreme, the 19th-century's Pius IX, famous for his practical jokes and his love of billiards, headed the Holy See for 32 years. The youngest pope on record, John XI, was just 16 when he took the helm in 931; the oldest, Gregory IX, managed to survive 14 years after his election in 1227 at the age of 86.

While the great majority have been of either Roman or Italian extraction, Spain, Greece, Syria, France and Germany have all been represented, and there has been at least one of African birth (Miltiades, 311–14), and one hailing from England (Hadrian IV, 1154–9). John Paul II was the first Pole to lead the Catholic Church. At least 14 popes abdicated or were deposed from office. Ten popes met violent deaths, including a record three in a row in the 10th century.

The process of electing a new pope is necessarily unique, as the papacy is the world's only elective monarchy. Members of the Sacred College of Cardinals, a largely titular body of 120 bishops and archbishops, are sealed into the Sistine Chapel soon after the death knell tolls in the Vatican Palace. They cannot leave until a new successor has been chosen. Voting can proceed by acclamation, whereby the cardinals all shout the same name at the same time; by scrutiny, in which four ballots are cast daily until one candidate has captured a two-thirds majority plus one; or, as a last resort, by compromise.

All modern popes have been selected by the second method. Paper ballots are burnt after each tally, and onlookers watch the chapel's chimney for dark smoke, which indicates an inconclusive vote, or white plumes, which denote a winner (electors are provided with special chemicals so that there can be no mistake). Finally the cardinal dean announces *"Habemus Papam"* (We have a pope) to the faithful, and the chosen cardinal appears in one of three robes (sized small, medium and large) kept on hand for the occasion. The coronation takes place on the following day. ❏

RIGHT: Pope Benedict XVI at the window of the Apostolic Palace.

Church, museum, mausoleum: the Basilica di San Pietro, **St Peter's** (dail 7am–7pm, until 6pm in winter, dome 8am–6pm, until 5pm in winter; modes dress code; free except for visits to the dome) is all three. No other temple sur passes it in terms of historical significance or architectural splendour. Some ma feel the immensity of the interior is more suited to moving commuters throug a railway station than to inspiring the intimate act of prayer, but the many archi tects and patrons of St Peter's intended the building to symbolise worldly powe as much as spiritual piety. Just about every important Renaissance and baroqu architect from Bramante onwards had a hand in the design of St Peter's. Th idea for rebuilding the original 4th-century basilica had been around since th mid-5th century, but not until Julius II became pope did a complete reconstruc tion get under way. Bramante was succeeded by Raphael, Peruzzi, Michelan gelo (usually credited with the dome), Giacomo della Porta and Bernini.

Pinturicchio's painting of Renaissance pope Alexander VI.

The interior is vast – 186 metres (610 ft) long with a capacity for aroun 60,000 people. On the right, as you walk in, is Michelangelo's *Pietà*, an inspir ation to beholders ever since the sculptor finished it in 1500, at the age of 25 At the end of the nave is the bronze statue of *St Peter*, its toe worn away by th kisses of pilgrims.

Over the high altar, which is directly above the tomb of St Peter, rises Bernini' garish bronze baldachin, resembling the canopy of an imperial bed; Pope Urba VIII stripped the bronze from the Pantheon. But Bernini outdid himself in th design for the Cathedra Petri (the Chair of St Peter) in the apse. Four gilt bronz figures of the Church Fathers hold up the chair. Above, light streams throug the golden glass of a window crowned by a dove (symbol of the Holy Ghost The chair bears a relief of Christ's command to Peter to "feed his sheep". Thu

BELOW: *The Creation of Adam is the most famous scene from Michelangelo's Sistine Chapel ceiling.*

ie position of the Pope is explained and bolstered by Christ's words and the eachings of the Church Fathers, and blessed by the Holy Ghost. Further confirmation of the Pope's sacred trust is found in Christ's words inscribed on the ome: "You are Peter and on this rock I will build my Church and I will give ou the keys to the kingdom of heaven."

Map on pages 128–9

he Vatican Museums

he **Musei Vaticani** ⓰ (Mon–Fri 10am–4.45pm, until 1.45pm in winter, Sat 0am–2pm year round, last Sun of each month 9am–1.45pm, last entry 1hr 5mins before closing; entrance fee) merit a lifetime's study. But for those who ave only a few hours, some sights shouldn't be missed. The **Museo Pio-Clementino** contains the Pope's collection of antiquities. Be sure to visit the 3elvedere Courtyard, home of the celebrated and cerebral *Apollo Belvedere* and he contrasting muscle-bound, sensual *Laocoön*. The Vatican **Pinacoteca** conains superb paintings, including Raphael's *Madonna of Foligno* and *Transfiguation*. **The Raphael Rooms** (the Stanze di Raffaello) comprise four rooms ainted by Raphael, the Sala di Costantino, Stanza di Eliodoro, Stanza della Segatura and Stanza dell'Incendio di Borgo. Downstairs, colourful frescos by Pinuricchio decorate the Borgia Apartments.

But the triumph of fresco painting, not only of the Vatican Palace, but of the ntire world, is the **Cappella Sistina** (Sistine Chapel). The walls are covered in aintings by Botticelli, Pinturicchio and Ghirlandaio, but the breathtaking star of he show is Michelangelo's ceiling, begun in 1508 and completed by 1512. It is shallow barrel vault divided into large and small panels tracing the history of he Creation.

Miracle of the Mass at Bolsena, *one of the Vatican's many works by Raphael.*

BELOW: Giuseppe Momo's helicoidal staircase.

No reproduction can ever do justice to the interplay of painting and architecture, to the drama of the whole chapel, alive with colour (considerably brighter since the controversial cleaning of the frescos finally unveiled to the public in 1994) and human emotion. "All the world hastened to behold this marvel and was overwhelmed, speechless with astonishment," Vasari wrote. The astonishment is no less today than it was in the Renaissance.

Trastevere

One of the gems of the Renaissance is Bramante's Tempietto.

The heart of medieval Trastevere, literally "across the Tiber", is southeast of the Vatican City. Here you can find many reasonably priced restaurants and, at **Porta Portese** ⑯, a popular flea market on Sunday (5am–2pm). Traditionally, Trastevere was a working-class neighbourhood with strong communist leanings. Today it is full of trendy restaurants, shops and wine bars.

South of Viale di Trastevere are two churches worth visiting. **Santa Cecilia** ⑰ (daily 9.30am–12.30pm and 4–6.30pm; entrance fee for crypt) was built on top of the house of a Christian martyr whom the Roman authorities attempted to scald to death in her own caldarium (hot bath). When this failed, she was sentenced to decapitation, but three blows failed to sever her head and she lived for a further three days (enough time to consecrate her house as a church). Carlo Maderno's touching statue of the saint curled in a foetal position was inspired by his observations when her tomb was opened in 1599.

BELOW: shady Piazza Sidney Sonnino.

A contrastingly sublime statue of a woman in her death throes is Bernini's *Blessed Luisa Albertoni* in nearby **San Francesco a Ripa**. This late work of the master captures even more powerfully than his St Teresa the conflict between joy and sorrow felt by a woman who is between this world and the next.

In the piazza of the same name, **Santa Maria in Trastevere** ⑱ (daily 7am–9pm) is one of the oldest churches in Rome. It has some beautiful Byzantine mosaics and it is worth taking a pair of binoculars to enjoy their details. *The Life of the Virgin* series is by Cavallini (1291).

After these sobering places of worship, preoccupied with the horrors of this world and the glories of the next, it is a relief to come to the **Villa Farnesina** ⑲ (Mon–Sat 9am–1pm; entrance fee), a jewel of the Renaissance, worldly and pagan. A ceiling fresco by Raphael details the love of Cupid and Psyche. In the next room, Raphael's *Galatea* captures the moment when the nymph, safe from the clutches of the cyclops Polyphemus, looks round. Upstairs, Baldassare Peruzzi, who designed the entire villa, devised a fantastic *trompe l'œil*. The room seems to open upon a restful village scene. In the bedroom is Sodoma's erotic painting *The Wedding of Alexander and Roxanne*.

To reach another important Renaissance monument, climb the steps up the Gianicolo to the church of **San Pietro in Montorio** ⑳ (daily 8am–noon and 4–6pm; free). In the courtyard is **Bramante's Tempietto** (Tues–Sun 9.30am–12.30pm and 4–6pm, 9.30am–12.30pm and 2–4pm in winter), a circular church that marks what was once mistakenly believed to be the site of St Peter's martyrdom. Climb a little further to the Fontana Paola, an impressive baroque monument that 's now a busy car wash. The shady **Passeggiata del Gianicolo** provides panoramic views over the city. The flat dome of the Pantheon, the twin domes of Santa Maria Maggiore and the Victor Emmanuel Monument are all easy to spot from up here.

Map on pages 128–9

Into the bowels of the earth

Visitors with more time in Rome should try to see remains from the early Christian era. The secretive beginnings of Christianity are recalled in **Sant'Agnese fuori le Mura** ⓮ (daily 8am–noon and 4–8pm; entrance fee) about 2 km (1¼ miles) beyond Michelangelo's Porta Pia on the Via Nomentana. Beneath the church run extensive catacombs (Tues–Sat 9am–noon and 4–6pm; entrance fee), where the martyred Roman maiden St Agnes was buried.

Also in the complex is the incomparable Santa Costanza, the mausoleum of Constantine's daughter. The ambulatory of this elegant round building is encrusted with some of Rome's most beautiful mosaics.

For those not averse to tortuous tunnels winding endlessly past burial niches, there are countless catacombs outside the walls of Rome. The best way to see them is to spend a day on the picturesque **Via Appia Antica**. You can picnic amid the remains of the **Villa of the Quintili** (Tues–Sun 9am–one hour before sunset; entrance fee) or an unnamed crumbling edifice overrun with wild flowers and lizards. Above ground sits what Byron called the "stern round tower" of the Tomba di Cecilia Metella. Below spread the **Catacombs of St Callisto**, the most famous in Rome (Thur–Tues 8.30am–noon and 2.30–5.30pm, until 5pm in winter, closed Feb; entrance fee) and those of saints Sebastian and Domitilla. ❑

San Sebastiano is perhaps the most significant of the catacombs in the Appian Way. The basilica (daily 8am–5.30pm) contains a large fragment of stone which is said to bear Christ's footprints.

BELOW: instrument restorer in Trastevere.

THE ARTISANS' QUARTER

Over the centuries, Trastevere's separation from the rest of the city resulted in the development of its own unique customs, traditions and even dialect, and it became home to a proud people who often came to blows with the city dwellers on the other side of the river. In Roman times Trastevere was primarily inhabited by foreign merchants, whose goods arrived in Rome on the Tiber, and was home to a large Jewish colony which later moved to the other bank. The area's largely medieval character was left intact until the second half of the 19th century when, in order to make way for Viale di Trastevere and the Lungotevere (riverside boulevards), many historic monuments were torn down and an important part of the area's maze-like network of streets erased.

Despite these changes, and the area's increasing penchant for anything touristy and gentrified (the inhabitants are now more bourgeois than working-class), Trastevere retains islands of genuine local atmosphere. Hidden corners remain untouched and provide snap-happy visitors with picturesque photo opportunities of laundry hanging out to dry or old-timers chatting outside their front doors. The winding streets are also the perfect place to seek out an original gift from the area's many artisanal workshops.

ROME'S ENVIRONS

Map on page 160

Explore ancient towns, villas set among beautiful gardens and a reconstructed monastery, then visit the Etruscan tombs to gain a vivid insight into a vanished world

The Fascists boasted that they represented the continuation of ancient Rome; the official art of the regime appropriated forms of Roman grandeur. Mosaics in the style of ancient Roman floors pave the avenue and decorate the walls of the **Foro Italico ❶**, the ambitious sports centre created in 1931 northwest of the capital. Bulky square columns support the Palazzo della Civiltà del Lavoro – commonly called the "Square Colosseum" – at EUR (**Esposizione Universale di Roma**) ❷, an area south of Rome intended by Mussolini to showcase imperial Rome and Fascist achievements. Sixty colossal statues of athletes adorn the Stadio Olimpico in the Foro Italico. Stark lines and impressive bulk characterise the church of SS Pietro e Paolo at EUR. The aesthetic of the regime did succeed in creating some striking effects, but mostly the result was phoney grandeur. In the city itself, urban planners ruthlessly drove roads through areas of historical importance, tearing down medieval quarters, which they considered an inheritance of dark times, and ripping through the very heart of Rome a triumphal way for the new eagles of the regime.

From this point of view, EUR, an area undeveloped before the Fascist era, is the least offensive of *Il Duce*'s efforts in town planning. In 1938 Mussolini undertook to build, with the designs of Marcello Piacentini, a magnificent Third Rome which would be the natural successor to imperial Rome and the Rome of the Renaissance. Plans for an exposition in 1942 to commemorate 20 years of Fascism were overtaken by World War II, and the overall design was only partially completed. In the 1950s new buildings were added, government offices and museums moved here, and EUR evolved into a residential quarter.

The EUR has a number of interesting museums, including the **Museo Preistorico ed Etnografico L. Pigorini** Prehistoric and Ethnographic Museum; Tues–Sun 9am–2pm; entrance fee) and the **Museo della Civiltà Romana** (Tues–Sat 9am–2pm, Sun 9am–1.30pm, last entry one hour before closing; entrance fee), devoted to the history of Rome. The latter contains the famous *plastico di Roma*, a reconstruction of the city in the time of Constantine, as well as the new astronomy museum and the city's recently reopened planetarium.

Ancient apartment dwellers

The town of **Ostia Antica ❸** (Tues–Sun 8.30am–6pm in summer, until 5pm in winter; entrance fee) was founded around the end of the 4th century BC as a fortified city to guard the mouth of the Tiber. Later it developed into the commercial port of Rome as well as its naval base. By the time of Constantine, Ostia had turned into a residential town for middle- and lower-class Romans. Ostia's ruins rival those of Pompeii for showing the layout of an ancient Italian city. Houses

LEFT: the Teatro Marittimo, at Hadrian's Villa, near Tivoli.
BELOW: statuary in EUR's Museo della Civiltà Romana.

Sculpture in the Insula dei Dipinti, Ostia Antica.

unearthed in Ostia offer valuable insights into the type of dwellings the sam classes presumably had in Rome. Each block contained a four-storey house with numerous rooms, built in brick, reaching a maximum height of 15 metres (49 ft) Each room had a window, covered in mica rather than glass. The *domus*, the typ ical Pompeiian residence built for the very rich, usually on one floor only, wa very rare in Ostia. The Roman theatre, enlarged in the 2nd century by Septimiu Severus to hold 2,700 people, houses the summer season of the Teatro di Roma

The **Lido di Ostia** ❹ is an overcrowded but popular seaside resort. Naturist can drive about 8 km (5 miles) south to the laid-back beaches of Tor Vaianica.

Palestrina

Ancient **Praeneste** ❺ (the modern Palestrina) is one of the oldest towns o Latium (Lazio). According to myth, it was founded by Telegonus, son of Ulysse and Circe. The town was flourishing in the 8th century BC, but it wasn't unti the 4th century that it became a part of Rome. During the civil war between Mar ius and Sulla, Marius fled to Praeneste, which was besieged by Sulla's troops and eventually destroyed. Sulla wanted to make amends and so ordered the reconstruction of the sanctuary of Fortuna Primigenia, containing an oracle. The temple, which occupied an area of about 32 hectares (79 acres), was one of the grandest of antiquity. It comprised a series of terraces on the slopes of Moun Ginestro connected by ramps. In the Middle Ages a new town rose on its ruins In 1944 bombs destroyed part of the town bringing the temple to light and prompting excavations. The **Museo Nazionale Archeologico di Palestrina** (daily 9am–8pm; entrance fee) houses many of the local finds, including the incomparable Barberini Mosaic.

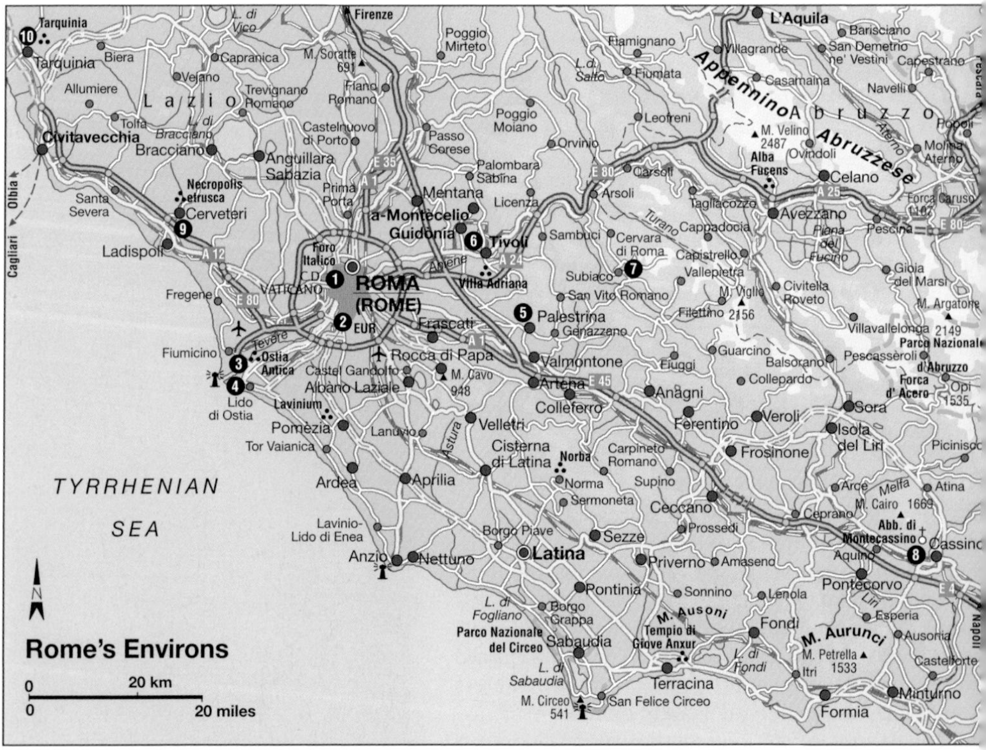

Rome's Environs

0   20 km

0   20 miles

ivoli

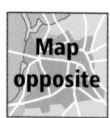

Map opposite

₄ the height of the Roman Empire, the ancient site of **Tibur ❻** (Tivoli), on the
•wer slopes of the Sabine Hills, was a favourite retreat for poets and Rome's
ᴡealthier citizens. The lavish villas scattered around sacred woods and scenic
ᴡaterfalls attracted such famous visitors as Horace, Catullus, Maecenas, Sal-
ᵢst and the emperor Trajan. In AD 117 the emperor Hadrian began building his
ᵢxurious retirement home on the gently sloping plain below the foothills on
ʜhich Tivoli stands. **Villa Adriana** (Hadrian's Villa; daily 9am–one hour before
ᵤnset, last entry one hour 30 mins before closing; entrance fee), which occupies
ȝ hectares (180 acres), was the largest and richest in the Roman Empire.
ᴀdrian wanted to recreate the monuments and places which had impressed him
ᴍost during his extensive travelling in the East (the peaceful Canopus, for exam-
ᵢᴇ, was modelled on a sanctuary of Serapis near Egyptian Alexandria), but
ᴀdrian's overall conception goes beyond mere imitation. The endless succes-
ᴏn of terraces, water basins and baths is a joyful reaction against functionality
ᵢᴅ common sense, but the design doesn't resort to extravagant artifice. Instead,
ᵢs a rigorous, geometrical, classical controlling of nature.

Stone mask in Ostia's theatre.

The spirit which pervades Tivoli's **Villa d'Este** (Tues–Sun 8.30am–one hour
ᵉfore sunset; www.villadestetivoli.info; entrance fee), the sumptuous residence
ᵢat Cardinal Ippolito d'Este, son of Lucrezia Borgia, had the skilful architect
ᵢᵣro Ligorio transform from a Benedictine convent, is very different. The palace
ᵢ light and has a faded grandeur; with its façade overlooking the park and rooms
ᵊcorated with frescos, it is a typical Renaissance mansion.

Water here is the prime element. Long, quiet pools, escorted by rows of elegiac
ᴄypresses extending into the distance, suggest infinity. Water spouts from
ᴏelisks or gurgles from the mouths of mythological
ᴄeatures and monsters, or gaily springs from the nip-
ᵢᴇs of a sphinx or the multiple-breasted Artemis of
ᴏhesus. In this monument, dedicated to the ephemeral,
ᵢ this superb triumph of theatricality, are the begin-
ᵢngs of the baroque.

BELOW: mosaic in
the ancient baths.

Nearby **Villa Gregoriana** (Tues–Sun 10am–6.30pm,
ᵤtil 2.30pm in winter; entrance fee), an oasis of water-
ᴧlls, ravines and grottoes, is well worth a visit. In 1826
ᴇ river Aniene burst its banks, and a catastrophic flood
ᴡept away much of Tivoli. Architect Clemente Folchi
ᴏlved the problem by diverting the river and boring into
ᴇ mountainside to create a spectacular waterfall, with
ᴀthways carved out of the original river bed. After years
ᶠ neglect, the park was recently spruced up and reopened
• the public. Colour-coded walks lead off from the main
ᴀterfall, which plunges 120 metres (394 ft) into the
•cky gorge, and end up at the Temple of Vesta, a round,
ᴇgant structure dating back to the 1st century BC.

ᴍonastic foundations

ᴜbiaco ❼ already existed when the emperor Nero
ᵉgan building his villas overlooking one of the three
ᵣtificial lakes he had created from the waters of the
ᵢver Aniene. The slaves employed in the construction
ᶠ the dam and villa founded the town. Five centuries
ᵢter a rich young man from Norcia, named Benedict,
ᴀme here in search of a place for meditation and prayer.

TIP

The abbey of Monte-
cassino, high on a hill,
is easily spotted from
the Rome–Naples
autostrada.

He stayed for three years, living in a cavern now known as the Sacro Spec
(Holy Grotto). Subiaco, considered the birthplace of Western monasticism, no
comprises a series of convents with their numerous cloisters and churches, be
towers, chapels decorated with frescos and grottoes hewn out of the mountai
side, all connected by picturesque stairways.

Around AD 529 Benedict and his faithful monks left Subiaco and moved t
Montecassino  to continue their mystical experience. Here they established on
of the most important religious and cultural institutions of the Middle Ages. Fi
centuries after Benedict's death in AD 547, the abbey he had founded was one of th
richest in the world (daily 8.30am–12.30pm and 3.30–6pm, until 5pm in winter
The illuminated manuscripts, frescos and mosaics were so skilfully executed th
they became models for others throughout the rest of medieval Europe.

During World War II, Montecassino rose to prominence once more. After U
forces entered Naples, Montecassino became the Germans' front line (the s
called Gustave Line), designed to defend the environs of Rome. When repeate
attacks by the Allies failed to penetrate the powerfully strengthened bulwark,
decision was made to bomb. It resulted in the total destruction of Montecassin
The ancient abbey was swept away. What one sees today is a faithful recor
struction of what existed before the catastrophe.

Cerveteri

Before Rome was the capital of Italy, capital of the popes, or capital of the worl
Italy had a highly refined civilisation: that of the Etruscans. Their zest for li
and emphasis on physical vitality has fascinated many, including D.F
Lawrence, who saw them as a happy contrast to the puritanical Romans.

ABOVE: entrance
mosaic for Villa
d'Este. **BELOW:** the
villa's gardens and
frescos.

The small medieval town of **Cerveteri** ❾, north of Rome on the Via Aurelia, as built on the site of the Etruscan town of Caere. In the 6th and 5th centuries :, Caere was one of the most populated towns of the Mediterranean. It had rong ties with Hellenic lands, the influence of whose merchants and artists ade Caere the centre of a lively and sophisticated cultural life. Its decline began AD 384, when Pyrgi harbour, its main port, was devastated by a Greek incur->n. Eventually the barbaric strength of Rome wiped away what had been a fined and joyous civilisation. Nothing remains today of the ancient town of aere, bar a few walls.

Caere's necropolis occupies a hill outside the city proper, the **Necropoli della anditaccia** (Tues–Sun 8.30am–one hour before sunset; entrance fee). From re it could be seen from the ramparts of the city, gay with painted houses and mples. The oldest tombs (8th century BC) have a small circular well carved to the stone, where the urns containing the ashes of the dead were placed. (Two odes of burial, cremation and inhumation, continued side by side for cen-ries.) The first chamber tombs, also cut into the stone and covered with rocky ocks and mounds *(tumuli)*, appeared as early as the beginning of the 7th cen-ry BC. The noble Etruscans were either enclosed in great sarcophagi with their figies on top, or laid out on stone beds in their chamber tombs.

Decorative water-spout at Villa d'Este.

Excavations of the tombs not already rifled – the Romans were the first collec-rs of Etruscan antiquities – revealed goods of gold, silver, ivory, bronze and ramic. The vases show strong Greek influence as well as the excellent quality the Etruscan craftmanship. Much of this material is now on display in the **useo Nazionale Archeologico di Cerveteri** (Tues–Sun 8.30am–7.30pm; last try one hour before closing; entrance fee), housed in the Ruspoli Castle, in e Museo di Villa Giulia in Rome, and in the Vatican useums *(see page 155).*

BELOW: Roman statue on the canal at Tivoli.

rquinia

he Etruscan town of **Tarquinia** ❿ stood on a hill orthwest of the picturesque medieval town bearing the me name. The town existed as early as the 9th cen-ry BC, and two centuries later was at its height. In 1924 e **Museo Nazionale Tarquiniense** (Tues–Sun 30am–7.30pm; entrance fee) was founded. In it are any Etruscan treasures, including the famous terra->tta winged horses of the 4th century BC.

The **Necropolis of Tarquinia** (Tues–Sun 8.30am–one ur before sunset, until 2pm in winter, last entry 90 mins :fore closing; entrance fee), together with that of Caere, the most important Etruscan necropolis. It stands on a ll south of the original town, occupying an area 5 km (3 iles) long by 1 km (⅔ mile) wide. Some tombs are ainted with frescos that are a precious document of Etr-can lives. Ribbons of bright colours frame the animated enes below: the banqueters and musicians in the Tomba :i Leopardi; the hunters in the Tomba del Cacciatore; the otic scenes in the Tomba dei Tori; the prancing dancers, ving dolphins and soaring birds of the Tomba della eonessa; the beautiful maiden from the Velcha family in e Tomba di Polifemo o dell'Orco. Ironically, visitors ften leave these dusty houses of death feeling shored up y a renewed faith in life and its many mysteries. ❏

Map on page 160

THE NORTH

Above all the sense of going down into Italy – the delight of seeing the North melt slowly into the South – of seeing Italy gradually crop up in bits and vaguely, latently betray itself – until finally at the little frontier village of Isella, where I spent the night, it lay before me warm and living and palpable...

—HENRY JAMES (from his *Letters*, Vol. 1, ed. Leon Edel)

For centuries, most travellers arrived in Italy from the north. They crossed the mountains from Switzerland or France, and often, if physically fit and romantically minded – as was the young Henry James – they made part of the journey on foot. This way Italy came into focus gradually, as they left the cold north behind and made their way south from the lakes to Milan. From there, the cities of the Po Valley beckoned.

If possible, this is still the best way to approach northern Italy. Rather than rush through, with your eyes on the train schedule and your mind checking off each town you have "done", see fewer cities, but see them well. Each one is so rich in history and art that it merits weeks. After all, this is the Italy of Shakespeare – *Romeo and Juliet* (Verona), *The Taming of the Shrew* (Padua) – and of medieval communes and Renaissance princes. The great families – the Viscontis in Milan, the Gonzagas in Mantua, the della Scalas in Verona – are still remembered for the artistic triumphs, as well as the political scandals, of their courts.

In this section of the book we pass from Byzantine Venice to the great cities of the Veneto – Padua, Verona and Vicenza – magnets for university students since the Middle Ages, and then to Milan, the style and shopping capital of Italy, via the magnificent glaciated landscapes of the Alps and the Italian Lake District.

Northern Italians, although generally more aloof and self-contained than the gregarious southerners, are always pleased to answer questions and make suggestions, always willing to spare a moment to give a stranger a little-known fact or their personal opinion on a historical personage. Quite possibly that native will bear more than a slight resemblance to the figures in the 15th-century frescos of the local Duomo – in these regions, the past is always present. ❑

PRECEDING PAGES: brightly painted houses on the Venetian island of Burano.
LEFT: a snow-fed waterfall in the Valle d'Aosta.

VENICE

*...out the wave her structures rise.
As from the stroke of the Enchanter's wand*
—LORD BYRON, *Childe Harold's Pilgrimage* (1812)

Map on
pages
170–1

When Lord Byron arrived in Venice in 1810, the "Queen of the Adriatic" had been in decline for many years. Though nonetheless enchanted by the beauty of the city, the poet describes her palaces as "crumbling to the shore". The seeds of decline were sown at the turn of the 15th century, when the Portuguese stripped Venice of its monopoly of the spice trade. A decade later the League of Cambrai put an end to Venice's hold on crucial cities on the mainland. But even if Venice has been on a downward trend for more than five centuries, it remains one of the most spectacular urban displays in the annals of cultural history. It is not only tourists who are captivated by its charms. For centuries the city has lifted poets, painters and writers to new heights of inspired vision. Proust, James, Waugh and Hemingway are just a handful of the writers who have found her irresistible; few other cities in the world have a more prolific and talented school of painters, from Bellini and Giorgione through Titian and Tintoretto to Tiepolo and Guardi.

Built on over 100 islets, supported by millions of wooden stakes and linked by 400 bridges, Venice is the only city in the world which is built entirely on water. The greatest advantage of this, apart from the obvious aesthetic appeal, is the absence of cars. The biggest disadvantage is the fact that the city is prone to problems of flooding. The sense of precariousness, associated with the city for centuries, inevitably adds to the fascination for the visitor. There is always a feeling that once you turn your back on all this fragile but vibrant glory, the islands, once inhabited by refugees fleeing the hordes of Attila the Hun, will crumble and disappear like a mirage into the sea.

In January 1996 La Fenice, its historic opera house – where Verdi's *La Traviata* and *Rigoletto* were first performed – was razed to the ground. La Fenice finally rose from the ashes once more in December 2003 after a fire which was started by disgruntled electrical contractors. The plush interior, gilt painted ceiling and candelabra lighting have all been recreated. Fittingly, *La Traviata* officially reopened the tiny theatre in 2004, years behind schedule.

LEFT: the ornate Torre dell'Orologio. **BELOW:** St Mark's Square, Basilica and Campanile.

St Mark's Square

The heart of Venice is the vast **Piazza San Marco ❶**. Described by Napoleon as the most elegant drawing room in Europe, this is the great architectural showpiece of Venice. With its café bands and exotic shops under the arcades, it is also the hub of tourist Venice; only in the early evening does it revert to a semblance of solitude. At one end of the piazza, crouching like an enormous, amphibious reptile, the great Basilica di San Marco (St Mark's Basilica) invites visitors to explore its mysterious depths.

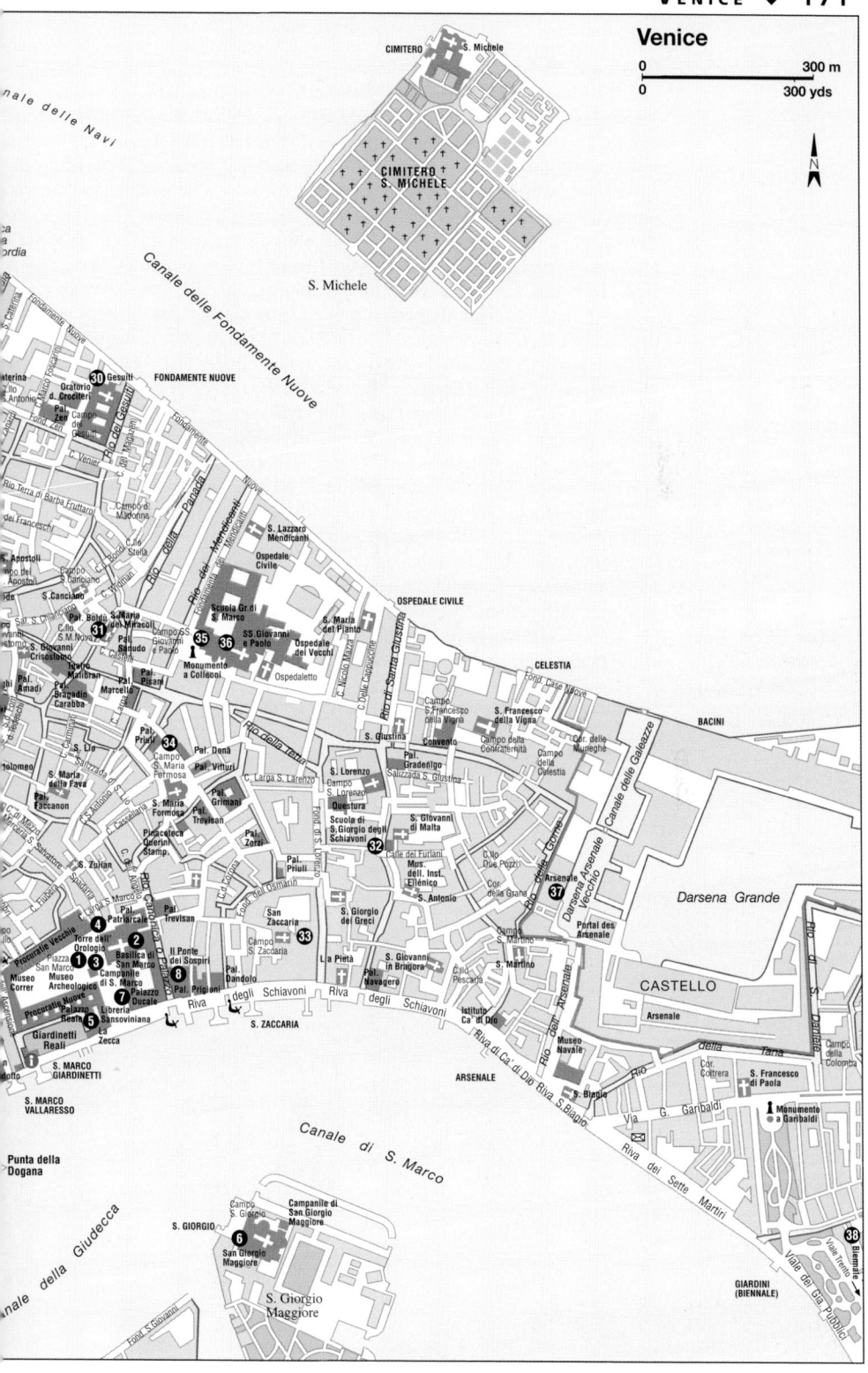

Venice

0 _____ 300 m
0 _____ 300 yds

BELOW:
St Mark's Basilica.

Basilica di San Marco

The **Basilica di San Marco** ❷ (Mon–Sat 9.45am–5pm, Sun 2–5pm, daily fro
7am for worshippers; entrance fee to Sanctuary, Pala d'Oro and Treasury; due
strict security measures all bags now need to be left in the Ateneo San Basso c
Piazzetta dei Leoncini – a free left-luggage service) is named after the evange
ist St Mark, whose remains were recovered (or stolen, depending on your view
point) by the Venetians from Alexandria in the 9th century. The then ruler
Venice, Doge Giustiniano Participazio, built a church on this site to house th
remains. The original church was destroyed by fire a century later, and wa
replaced in the late 11th century by the huge ornate edifice we see today.

Scaffolding has recently been removed from the façades of the Basilica an
the lovely Clock Tower at the landward end of the piazza, revealing the sump
tuous five portals decorated with shimmering mosaics. The only original mosa
– in the doorway to the far left – gives a good idea of the appearance of the bas
ica in the 13th century. Above the main portal are replicas of the famous bronz
horses, thought to be Roman or Hellenistic works of the 3rd or 4th century A
and looted by the Venetians from Constantinople in 1204. They were taken t
Paris by Napoleon in 1797 and returned in 1815, and are now kept inside th
Basilica, protected from pigeons and pollution.

The Basilica's interior, in the shape of a Greek cross, is thought to have bee
inspired by the Church of the Apostles in Constantinople. Above the column
of the minor naves, lining the arms of the cross, are the women's galleries c
matronei, designed in accordance with Greek Orthodox custom, which separate
the sexes. The luxurious atmosphere of the interior is enhanced by the decoratio
of the walls: marble slabs cover the lower part, while golden mosaics adorn th

ults, arches and domes. Following a complex iconographic plan, the mosaics ver 4,000 sq. metres (43,000 sq. ft), which is why St Mark's is sometimes lled the Basilica d'Oro (Church of Gold). For a brief explanation of the osaics, join one of the groups that tour the Basilica.

Among the many gems housed in the church are the **Pala d'Oro**, a jewel-dded gold-and-enamel altarpiece dating from the 10th century. The **Trea-ry** also houses a priceless collection of gold and silver from Byzantium. The **arciano Museum** (daily 9.45am–4.30pm; entrance fee), reached by steep ps from the entrance narthex, affords fine views of the interior as a whole, ile the open-air terrace beyond the museum gives a bird's-eye view of Piazza n Marco. It was here that the doge and other dignitaries gathered to watch lebrations taking place below.

panoramic view

striking feature of the square is the soaring **Campanile ❸** (daily July–Sept m–9pm, Apr–June and Oct 9am–7pm, Nov–Mar 9.30am–3.45pm; entrance fee), aithful replica of the original tower that collapsed in 1902. Inside, a lift – or, for e energetic, a stairway – climbs 100 metres (330 ft) to the top for a sweeping norama of the city and lagoon. The piazza's other tower is Coducci's intricate rre dell'Orologio ❹ (Clock Tower), designed in 1496 (English-language tours on–Wed 10 and 11am, Thurs–Sun 1, 2, 3 and 5pm; book in advance; entrance e). Adjoining the piazza and extending to the waterfront is the **Piazzetta San arco**. On the right as you face the lagoon stands the 16th-century Biblioteca azionale Marciana, also known as **Libreria Sansoviniana ❺** (Apr–Oct daily m–7pm, Nov–Mar daily 9am–5pm; entrance fee, also combined ticket and

Mosaic of Christ in St Mark's.

BELOW:
Doge's Palace.

*Sculptures of Adam
and Eve by Antonio
Rizzo on the façade of
the Palazzo Ducale.*

access via Museo Correr, tel: 041-240 5211), where classical concerts are occasionally staged. Palladio, Italy's greatest 16th-century architect, considered this structure one of the most beautiful buildings ever constructed. Today it houses the **Archaeological Museum** (daily 9am–7pm; entrance fee, combined ticket and access via Museo Correr), the National Library of St Mark and the Venetian Old Library – with a collection of treasures from the city's golden years.

At the lagoon end of the Piazzetta stand two large 12th-century columns, one crowned with a winged lion, the symbol of Venice, the other with a statue of St Theodore, the original patron saint of the city. Originally a marketplace, the area later became known as a gathering place for politicians waiting to attend meetings. Public executions also used to take place between the two columns.

Across the water lies one of Venice's great landmarks – the majestic **Church of San Giorgio Maggiore** ❻ (daily 9.30am–12.30pm, May–Sept 2.30–6pm, Oct–Apr 2.30–4.30pm; entrance fee for Campanile), on the little islet of the same name. This classical masterpiece by Andrea Palladio has a huge white stone interior with works of art by Tintoretto, and the views from the Campanile extend, on a clear day, as far as the Alps.

The Doge's Palace

The **Palazzo Ducale** ❼ (daily Apr–Oct 9am–7pm, Nov–Mar 9am–5pm; entrance fee) flanks the eastern side of the Piazzetta. This "vast and sumptuous pile", as Byron described it, is the grandest and most conspicuous example of Venetian Gothic in the city. The official residence of the doge and the seat of government during the republic, it stands today as eloquent evidence of the power and pomp of Venice in its heyday.

Below: the Rio
Canonica and
Bridge of Sighs.

Inside, the three wings of the palace reveal a seemingly endless series of grandiose rooms and halls. The largest of these is the Sala del Maggior Consiglio (the Great Council Chamber), which could accommodate all 480 (and later 1,700) of the Venetian patricians who sat on the council. The art collection here gives a foretaste of the countless artistic treasures scattered throughout the city, and includes works by the two Venetian giants – Tintoretto and Veronese. Tintoretto's *Paradise* (1588–92) was for many years the largest painting in the world (7 metres by 22 metres/23 ft by 72 ft). In the same room, Veronese's *Apotheosis of Venice* is another compelling masterpiece, though his finest work in the palace is *The Rape of Europa* in the Anticollegio.

Adjoining the palace is the former prison. Once tried and convicted in the palace, prisoners were led across the slender covered bridge to their cell. Since the windowed bridge offered the captive his last glimpse of freedom, it was called **Il Ponte dei Sospiri** ❽ (the Bridge of Sighs). However grim its original purpose, it has a romantic air, and is favoured today by young lovers who believe that if they kiss under the bridge (presumably in a gondola) their love will last.

The *Itinerari Segreti* (Secret Itineraries) are fascinating guided tours of lesser-known parts of the Doge's Palace and prison cells (tours in English run daily Sept–June 9.55am, 10.45am and 11.35am, suspended July–Aug; for information tel: 0415-209 070).

A tour of the Ducal Palace is best rounded off with a coffee break in the piazza. e most famous café here is **Florian**, the once fashionable haunt for high Venan society. Henry James conjures up the atmosphere in *The Aspern Papers* 388): "I sat in front of Florian's café, eating ices, listening to music, talking with quaintances: the traveller will remember how the immense cluster of tables d little chairs stretches like a promontory into the smooth lake of the Piazza."

Map on pages 170–1

e Grand Canal

e **Canal Grande** winds for 3.5 km (2 miles) through the city. This splendid immering thoroughfare is flanked by pastel-coloured palaces in a mixture of zantine, Gothic, Renaissance and baroque styles, built mostly between the th and the 18th centuries.

The best way to see the canal is from a boat. If you are feeling flush, hire a ndola from the San Marco waterfront. Thomas Mann, who commented that e gondolas of Venice were "black as nothing else on earth except a coffin", netheless found their seats "the softest, most luxurious, most relaxing in the orld". Far cheaper, though less romantic and more noisy, is the No. 1 public terbus *(vaporetto)*, which plies the length of the canal at frequent intervals. ternatively, try the faster No. 82 service, which makes fewer stops.

Starting from San Marco, the entrance of the canal is marked on the left bank by e great baroque church of **Santa Maria della Salute ⑨**, designed by the 17th-ntury baroque architect Baldassare Longhena, and erected in thanks for the y's deliverance from the plague of 1630. To the enamoured James, the church as "like a great lady on the threshold of her salon… with her domes and scrolls, r scalloped buttresses and statues forming a pompous crown, and her wide ps disposed on the ground like the train of a robe".

Romantic poet Lord Byron (1788–1824) occupied various palaces on the Grand Canal and often swam its length.

BELOW: Veronese's *Feast in the House of Levi* (Accademia).

On the same side is the **Palazzo Venier dei Leoni ⑩** Ved–Mon 10am–6pm; entrance fee), the famous sidence-museum of the late American patroness of the ts, Peggy Guggenheim (1898–1979). This is Venice's ading contemporary art museum, with a superb eclec- collection of works representing the major artistic d avant-garde movements of the last century. Paint-gs by legendary names including Picasso, Braque, andinsky and Bacon are all on display alongside a rge representation of Surrealist art, which was close to uggenheim's heart – she was briefly married to Max nst, one of the movement's founders. His works, along th those of Dalí, Magritte, Jackson Pollock and de ooning, are all here. The 18th-century *palazzo* was ilt for the noble Venier family and was nicknamed the Nonfinito", because the building remained unfinished, ver progressing beyond the first floor. It is a splen-dly eccentric setting for the collection, with a lovely rden and courtyard where chained lions were once pt, earning it the sobriquet "dei Leoni".

On the right bank opposite is **Ca' Grande ⑪**, a three-orey Renaissance residence by Sansovino, now the ffice of the city magistrate. The first bridge that spans e canal is the wooden **Ponte dell'Accademia ⑫**, built 1932 as a temporary structure but retained through opular demand. It is named after the nearby **Gallerie** ell'Accademia ⑬ (Tues–Sun 8.15am–7.15pm, Mon

8.15am–2pm; entrance fee) housed in the former Scuola della Carità. This co tains the world's finest collection of Venetian paintings, with works by Ma tegna, Bellini, Giorgione *(The Tempest)*, Carpaccio, Titian, Tintoretto, Verone Tiepolo, Guardi and Canaletto, mostly arranged in chronological order.

Further down the canal on the same side stands the imposing baroque pala of the recently restored **Ca' Rezzonico** ⓬ (open Wed–Mon, Nov–Mar 10ar 5pm, Apr–Oct 10am–6pm; entrance fee) housing a museum of 18th-centu Venice, dedicated to the swansong years of Venice's Most Serene Republic La Serenissima. The stately rooms are richly decorated with period painting furniture and frescos. It was here that the poet Robert Browning died in 188

Richard Wagner was staying at the second of the two Gothic **Palazzi Giu tinian** on the left bank when he composed the second act of *Tristan and Isol* during 1858–9. Next door, **Ca' Foscari** ⓯ is a 15th-century palace in the Ven ian Gothic style, named after the family of the great 15th-century doge wl masterminded large Venetian conquests on the Italian mainland.

Beyond the Sant'Angelo landing stage, on the right bank, **Palazzo Corn Spinelli** ⓰ was designed during the early Venetian Renaissance in the Lor bardic style by Coducci. Beyond the next side canal, the **Palazzo Grimani** ⓱ now the Court of Appeal, is a late Renaissance masterpiece by Sanmicheli. front of you, Venice's most famous bridge, **Ponte di Rialto** ⓲, arches over tl canal. The former wooden drawbridges built across the canal at this point a collapsed, necessitating the erection of a more weighty stone structure. Ant nio da Ponte supervised its construction between 1588 and 1592. The singl span, balustraded bridge has two parallel rows of tightly packed shops selli jewellery, leather, masks, silk and souvenirs.

Ca' d'Oro

The most beautiful Gothic palace in Venice, the **Ca' d'Oro** (Tues–Sun 9.15am–7.15pm, Mon 8.15am–2pm; entrance fee) appears on the right at the first landing stage beyond the bridge. When built in 1420 by the wealthy patrician Marino Contarini, it was covered in gold leaf, hence the name "House of Gold". Inside, the Giorgio Franchetti art gallery comprises a varied collection of paintings, frescos and sculpture. Further along, on the left bank, the enormous baroque **Ca' Pesaro** ⓴ is another masterpiece by Longhena; this one houses the Galleria d'Arte Moderna and the Museo Orientale (Tues–Sun, Apr–Oct 10am–6pm, Nov–Mar 10am–5pm; entrance fee). The last building of note before the railway station is **Palazzo Vendramin-Calergi** ㉑, one of the finest Renaissance palaces by Mauro Coducci (1440–1504). Wagner died here in 1883.

The six districts of Venice

The greatest experience the city can offer to the inquisitive visitor is the maze of tiny alleys, the narrow silent canals and the pretty squares and courtyards only minutes away from **San Marco**, the most central of the six districts (sestieri) of Venice. Leading north from the Piazza San Marco, starting at the Clock Tower, is the **Merceria dell'Orologia**. This ancient commercial thoroughfare is still one of Venice's busiest streets, flanked by small shops and boutiques.

Dorsoduro is the most southerly section of historic Venice – an excellent area to stay if you are looking for a quiet *pensione* within easy access of central Venice. To the south, the area is bounded by the **Zattere**, a long, broad and peaceful quayside whose cafés and restaurants afford splendid views across the water to the island of Giudecca. East of the Accademia Galleries, the Dorsoduro is quiet and intimate, characterised by pretty canals, small shops, galleries and chic residences.

Northwest of the Accademia, the area around San Barnaba was traditionally the quarter for impoverished Venetian nobility. Today it is the scene of cafés, artisans and one of the last surviving vegetable barges. Further west, the 16th-century church of **San Sebastiano** ㉒ (Mon–Sat 10am–5pm, entrance fee; Chorus, the association of Venetian churches, issues a special pass allowing access to 16 of the city's most important churches; www.chorusvenezia.org; tel: 041-275 0462) was the parish church of Veronese and provided a classical canvas for many of his opulent masterpieces, painted between 1555 and 1565.

The area becomes increasingly shabby towards San Nicolò dei Mendicoli, erstwhile home of sailors and fishermen. The charming Romanesque church of **San Nicolò dei Mendicoli** ㉓ was expertly restored by the British Venice in Peril Fund in the 1970s.

The island of **Giudecca**, across the Giudecca Canal, is a quiet working-class area of narrow streets. The main landmark on its waterfront is Andrea Palladio's **Redentore** church ㉔ (Mon–Sat 10am–5pm), built in gratitude for the city's deliverance from plague in 1576. On the third Sunday in July, the city commemorates this event by building a bridge of boats from the Zattere to the Redentore, where a special Mass is held. That night, a firework display lights up the sky.

Map on pages 170–1

TIP

The signposted routes between St Mark's, the Rialto and Accademia can get very crowded. For respite from the hordes of tourists, just turn off onto any side canal, where you will find equally attractive buildings and a glimpse of genuine Venetian life.

BELOW: Tiepolo's *Abraham Visited by the Angels* in San Rocco.

San Polo

The *sestiere* of **San Polo** lies within the large bend of the Grand Canal, northwest of San Marco. The quarter around the **Rialto**, the oldest inhabited part of main land Venice, became the gathering place of merchants from the East and thence the commercial hub of the city. It is still a bustling area, with shops and market stalls. Fruit and vegetables are laid out under the arcades of the Fabbriche Vecchie, while the mock-Gothic stone loggia of the Pescheria marks the site of the morning fish market. Arrive early, as the market begins to close by noon.

The major church of San Polo is the majestic brick Gothic **Santa Maria Gloriosa dei Frari ㉕** (Mon–Sat 9am–6pm, Sun 1–6pm; entrance fee, or free with Chorus church pass, *see page 177*), usually referred to as the Frari. The interior houses some of Venice's finest masterpieces, including an exquisite *Madonna and Child* by Bellini, Titian's celebrated *Assumption* (crowning the main altar) and his *Madonna di Ca' Pesaro*. Buried in the Frari are the composer Claudio Monteverdi, the sculptor Canova (who lies in a pyramidal tomb he designed as a monument to Titian) and several doges.

Nearby, the **Scuola Grande di San Rocco ㉖** (Apr–Oct 9am–5.30pm, Nov–Mar 10am–5pm; entrance fee) is celebrated for its series of religious works by Tintoretto, painted on the walls and ceilings in 1564–87. The scenes from *The Life of Christ* culminate in *The Crucifixion,* of which Henry James wrote: "Surely no single picture in the world contains more human life; there is everything in it including the most exquisite beauty. It is one of the greatest things of art."

Santa Croce ㉗, lying north and west of San Polo, is for the most part a relatively unexplored district. Its core is a maze of covered alleyways lined by peeling façades and criss-crossed by canals barely wide enough for the passage of a barge. Its squares are pleasingly shabby, bustling with local life. The only real concession to tourism is the **Piazzale Roma**, the uninspiring arrival point for those coming by road.

The origins of the Ghetto

Cannaregio is the quietest and most remote district in Venice. Its name derives from *canne* (reeds), for this area was once marshland. The *sestiere* forms the northern arc of the city, stretching from the railway station to the Rio dei Mendicanti in the east. At its heart lies the **Ghetto ㉘** its name originated from an iron foundry *(getto)* which once stood here. This was Europe's first ghetto, an area for the exclusive but confined occupation of Jews. Built in the early 16th century, it gave its name to isolated Jewish communities throughout the world. It remained a ghetto until Napoleonic times. Though very few Jews live here, the synagogues, tenements and kosher restaurants lend a distinctive Jewish air, and the area's history is well documented in the **Museo Ebraico** (Sun–Fri 10am–7pm, until 6pm Oct–May, and earlier closing on Fri – before sunset; closed Sat and Jewish holidays; entrance fee), a small museum in the main square.

The northern part of Cannaregio is the most remote and the area around the lovely Gothic church of the **Madonna dell'Orto ㉙** (Mon–Sat 10am–5pm, Sun 1–5pm; entrance fee) the most appealing. Tintoretto was born here and lived at No. 3399, near the Campo dei

Venice's scuole were a cross between professional guilds and charitable societies. Some of them became very wealthy and commissioned fine artists to decorate their headquarters.

BELOW: the arcaded Pescheria, Venice's main fish market.

lori. Forming the northern border of Cannaregio, the Fondamente Nuove is the main departure point for ferries to the northern islands. Across the water you can see the walled cemetery on the island of San Michele. Back from the quayside, the baroque church of the **Gesuiti** ❸ (daily 10am–noon and 5–7pm) has an outrageously extravagant green-and-white marble interior, and contains Titian's dramatic *Martyrdom of St Lawrence*.

It is worth exploring the warren of alleys and canals to the east of Cannaregio. With luck, you will stumble upon the church of **Santa Maria dei Miracoli** ❸ (Mon–Sat 10am–5pm; entrance fee). Designed in the 1480s by Pietro Lombardo and his workshop, it is one of the loveliest Renaissance churches in the city. Decorated inside and out with marble, it is often likened to a jewel-box.

Castello

The city's western section, **Castello**, varies in character from the busy southern waterfront near San Marco to the humble cheek-by-jowl residences of the north. The area behind Riva degli Schiavoni is worth exploring for its pretty canals, quaysides and elegant faded palaces. Essential viewing for those interested in art is the frieze by Carpaccio in the **Scuola di San Giorgio degli Schiavoni** ❸ (Tues–Sat 9am–12pm and 3–6pm, Sun 9.30am–12.30pm; entrance fee) and Coducci's 16th-century church of **San Zaccaria** ❸.

The **Campo Santa Maria Formosa** ❸ (church: Mon–Sat 10am–5pm; entrance fee) is a pleasant market square with a fine Renaissance church, which is home to Palma il Vecchio's splendid *St Barbara and Saints* of 1510. The spiritual heart of Castello is the **Campo Santi Giovanni e Paolo** ❸, better known in Venetian dialect as San Zanipolo. Standing prominently in this spacious square is

Map on pages 170–1

The Ghetto remains at the heart of Jewish life with fine synagogues and workshops selling liturgical objects.

BELOW: 13th-century figure near Campo dei Mori.

Andrea del Verrocchio's masterly bronze equestrian statue of the fierce mercenary Bartolomeo Colleoni. Presiding over the square is the majestic Gothic church of **Santi Giovanni e Paolo ㊱** (daily 7.30am–6.30pm; entrance fee), where 46 doges are buried. Many of their tomb monuments are magnificent, as is Paolo Veronese's *Adoration of the Shepherds* in the Cappella del Rosario.

Part of eastern Castello is occupied by the **Arsenale ㊲**, the great shipyard of the republic where Venice's galleys were built and refurbished. It is now largely abandoned and inaccessible to the public, but you can see a small part from the No. 52 public waterbus, and there is an excellent **Naval Museum** (Mon–Fri 8.45am–1.30pm, Sat until 1pm; entrance fee) alongside the main entrance gate. To the east of the public gardens is the site of the **Biennale ㊳**, an international exhibition of   modern art, film and music (held in odd-numbered years).

Island excursions

There is plenty to see away from the historic centre of Venice. The lagoon was settled from the 5th century, and you can still see the remains of the very first Venetian community on the tiny island of Torcello *(see opposite)*. Frequent ferry services link Venice to the main islands.

The island of **San Michele**, just north of Venice, is occupied by the cemetery (7.30am–4pm) and the early Renaissance church of San Michele in Isola, designed by Coducci. As the first church faced in white Istrian stone, San Michele set a building trend throughout the Veneto. Napoleon, who forbade burials in the historic centre, established the cemetery. Ezra Pound and Igor Stravinsky were two of the eminent visitors to Venice who are buried here. As the island closest to Venice, it is served by ferries from the Fondamente Nuove

Renaissance gateway to the Arsenale, built in 1460 by Antonio Gambello.

BELOW: the Casa Bepi on Burano.

Further north, the island of **Murano** is spread over five islets criss-crossed by canals, which make it seem like a mini-Venice. In the late 13th century Murano became the centre of Venice's ancient glass-blowing industry, as factories were moved from the city centre for fear of fire. The **Museo del Vetro** (Thur–Tues 10am–6pm, until 5pm in winter; entrance fee) is housed in the Fondamenta Giustinian, originally the seat of the bishop of Torcello, which was transferred here after the earlier settlement was abandoned. The museum has exquisite examples of glasswork.

Venice's justly famous lace industry is based in **Burano**, northeast of Venice. This is a colourful island where canals are lined by brightly painted houses and stalls selling lace and linen. Prices in Burano can be cheaper than elsewhere in Venice, but beware of imitation Venetian lace from factories in the Far East.

Torcello, the most remote of these islands (an hour by ferry), is the least populated and, for many, the most interesting. This rural, marshy island was the site of the original settlement in the Venetian lagoon. Still standing is the magnificent Byzantine cathedral. A large striking mosaic of the Virgin, standing above a frieze of Apostles, decorates the chancel apse of the church, while the entire western wall is covered by a huge and elaborate mosaic depicting *The Last Judgement*.

To the south of Venice, on a different route, lies the **Lido**, where Thomas Mann's unhappy Aschenbach loitered too long, feasting his tired eyes on the unattainable boy Tadzio, and died of cholera. The Lido is no longer the fashionable resort depicted in *Death in Venice*, but in the hot summer months, when the city and its sights can be overwhelming, the sands and sea air provide a welcome break. ❑

Map on pages 170–1

Murano glass has been manufactured on the island since 1292.

BELOW: Palladio's San Giorgio Maggiore.

LIFE AS A MASQUERADE

Carnival in Venice is supreme self-indulgence, a giddy round of masked balls and private parties suggesting mystery and promising romance

In Venice, Carnival is a 10-day pre-Lenten extravaganza, culminating in the burning of the effigy of Carnival in Piazza San Marco on Shrove Tuesday. As an expression of a topsy-turvy world, Carnival is a time for rebellion without the risk of ridicule. The essence of the "feast of fools" lies in the unfolding Venetian vistas: masked processions heading towards Piazza San Marco past shimmering palaces, with surreal masqueraders tumbling out of every alley. As the revellers flock to Florian's café in Piazza San Marco, the air is sickly sweet with the scent of fritters and the sound of lush baroque music. Carnival capers include costumed balls, firework displays and historical parades, all staged by the Carnival societies.

SPIRIT OF RESISTANCE

Carnival is often dismissed as commercialised and chaotic, but Venetian traditionalists view it differently. The leader of a venerable Carnival company sees the event as saving his city: "Life in Venice is inconvenient and costly. With the Carnival, we give a positive picture and show the pleasure of living here. Carnival is a form of resistance. By resisting the temptation to leave, we are saving the spirit of the city for future generations."

▽ THE GREAT LEVELLER

A mask makes everyone equal. Masqueraders are addressed as *"sior maschera"* (masked gentleman) regardless of age, rank or even gender. One way of preserving some individuality is face-painting.

△ SELECT CARDS

A select group of Venetians still appears as *tarocchi*, fortune-telling tarot cards. These famous cards supposedly reached Europe from the East through Venice. The star of the pack is the Queen of Swords, her costume rich in silver cabbalistic signs.

▽ WINDOW DRESSING

Masks originally allowed the nobility to mingle incognito with the common people in *casini* (private clubs), but are now an excuse for all-purpose revelry. This shop window displays fantasy masks, which are creative rather than authentic, and appeal to individual tastes.

Mask-makers had their own guild in medieval times, when a *mascheraio* (mask-maker) helped a secretive society run smoothly. Modern masqueraders must choose between masks in leather *(cuoio)*, china *(ceramica)* or papier mâché *(cartapesta)*. Papier mâché and leather masks are the most authentic.

△ THE NOBLE LOOK
Costumes can be historical, traditional or simply surreal. The classic Venetian disguise of the 17th and 18th centuries was known as the *maschera nobile*, the patrician mask. The carnival companies wear noble Renaissance and rococo costumes *(left)* as a matter of course.

▽ VOLTO FACE
The patrician *maschera nobile* and witty *commedia dell'arte* masks are among a number of authentic disguises. While this cumbersome ruff is pure fantasy, the white mask looks to the past for inspiration: it is a modern variant on the slightly sinister *volto*, the traditional Venetian mask.

Antique masks are rare since neither material readily stands the test of time or the Venetian climate. Authentic mask-makers both reinterpret traditional designs and create new ones. In the case of papier-mâché masks, the pattern is made from a fired clay design, which generates a plaster-of-Paris mould. Layers of papier-mâché paste are used to line the mould and thus create the mask. When dry, the paste gives the mask a shiny surface akin to porcelain. Polish and a white base coat are applied before the eye holes are cut and decorative detail is added. This painting process can be simple or highly artistic. Of the alternatives to papier mâché, leather masks are hard to fashion; ceramic designs, ideal as hand-held masks or as wall decorations, are often adorned with fine fabrics. Places to browse include Laboratorio Artigiano Maschere (Barbaria delle Tole, Castello 6657; tel: 041-522 3110) and Ca' del Sol (Fondamenta dell'Osmarin, Castello; tel: 041-528 5549). Nearby is Mondonovo – one of Venice's most creative mask-makers (Rio Terra Canal, off Campo Santa Margherita; tel: 041-528 7344).

Map on pages 186–7

THE VENETO

Two cities with links to Shakespearean heroines
and a chance to surfeit on the buildings of
Italy's greatest Renaissance architect

Shakespeare called Italy's second-oldest university city "Fair Padua, nurser of Arts", and described it as a place where Renaissance Englishmen cam to "suck the sweets of sweet philosophy". Dante and Galileo both lecture at **Padua ❶** (Padova), and in the mid-17th century a learned woman earned doctorate here, the first woman in Europe to do so. (Padua's most famous daugh ter is, without a doubt, Katherina, Shakespeare's tameable shrew.)

But long before the university was established in 1222, Padua was a important Roman town, believed by Virgil to have been founded by the brothe of the Trojan King Priam, after the fall of Troy – though, in fact, it had bee a settlement of pre-Roman tribesmen. (The Roman historian Livy was born i the nearby hills and was always proud to call himself a Paduan.)

Padua is also a magnet for the faithful. Every June, pilgrims come from a over the world to honour St Anthony of Padua, a 13th-century itinerant preache whose spellbinding sermons packed church pews throughout Italy. The **Basilic di Sant'Antonio** (daily 6.20am–7pm, 7.45pm in summer), built over his remain between 1232 and 1307, celebrates his sanctity handsomely, with works b Donatello (who lived in Padua 1443–53), Sansovino and Menabuoi. Venice ❸ *(see pages 169–81)* is, of course, very close to Padua, and Venetian influence i

BELOW: Basilica di Sant'Antonio, Padua.

vident in the church's design. Byzantine domes, an ornate façade and two igh, thin bell towers give the exterior an Oriental appearance. The interior lso has Byzantine decorative details. The chapel of St Anthony, containing he revered tomb, is a 16th-century design by Biosco.

Padua's piazzas

n **Piazza del Santo**, to one side of the basilica stands a famous equestrian statue f Erasmo da Narni, called *Gattamelata*, by Donatello. This sculpture of the reat Venetian *condottiere* (mercenary) is believed to be the first great bronze ast in Italy during the Renaissance. Also in the piazza is the **Oratorio di San Giorgio** (9am–12.30pm and 2.30–7pm, closes at 5pm in winter; entrance fee), riginally a private mausoleum for the prominent Soranzo family. The oratory is lecorated with beautiful frescos by Altichiero and Avanzo. On the corner of the iazza is the entrance to the **Scuola di Sant'Antonio** (daily 9am–12.30pm and .30–7pm in summer, until 5pm in winter; entrance fee) which houses paint-ngs by Bellini, Titian and Giorgione, among others.

The Via Belludi leads to another notable square, the **Prato della Valle**, fronted y the **Basilica di Santa Giustina**. A small park at its centre is reached by cross-ng one of the four stone bridges over a circular moat. In the park, a circle of tatues represents famous past citizens of Padua.

The city centres on the crowded **Piazza delle Erbe**, one of its three market quares. Here stands the **Palazzo della Ragione**, called locally **Il Salone** Tues–Sun 9am–7pm; entrance fee), a massive medieval structure with coats of urms adorning the façade. The interior is decorated with fine frescos, and houses a large wooden horse copied from Donatello's bronze masterpiece.

TIP

The upstairs rooms at the Caffè Pedrocchi are used for concerts and other events. The rooms are worth seeing for their extravagant Egyptian, Moorish, Greek and other decor.

BELOW: the Prato della Valle and Basilica di Santa Giustina.

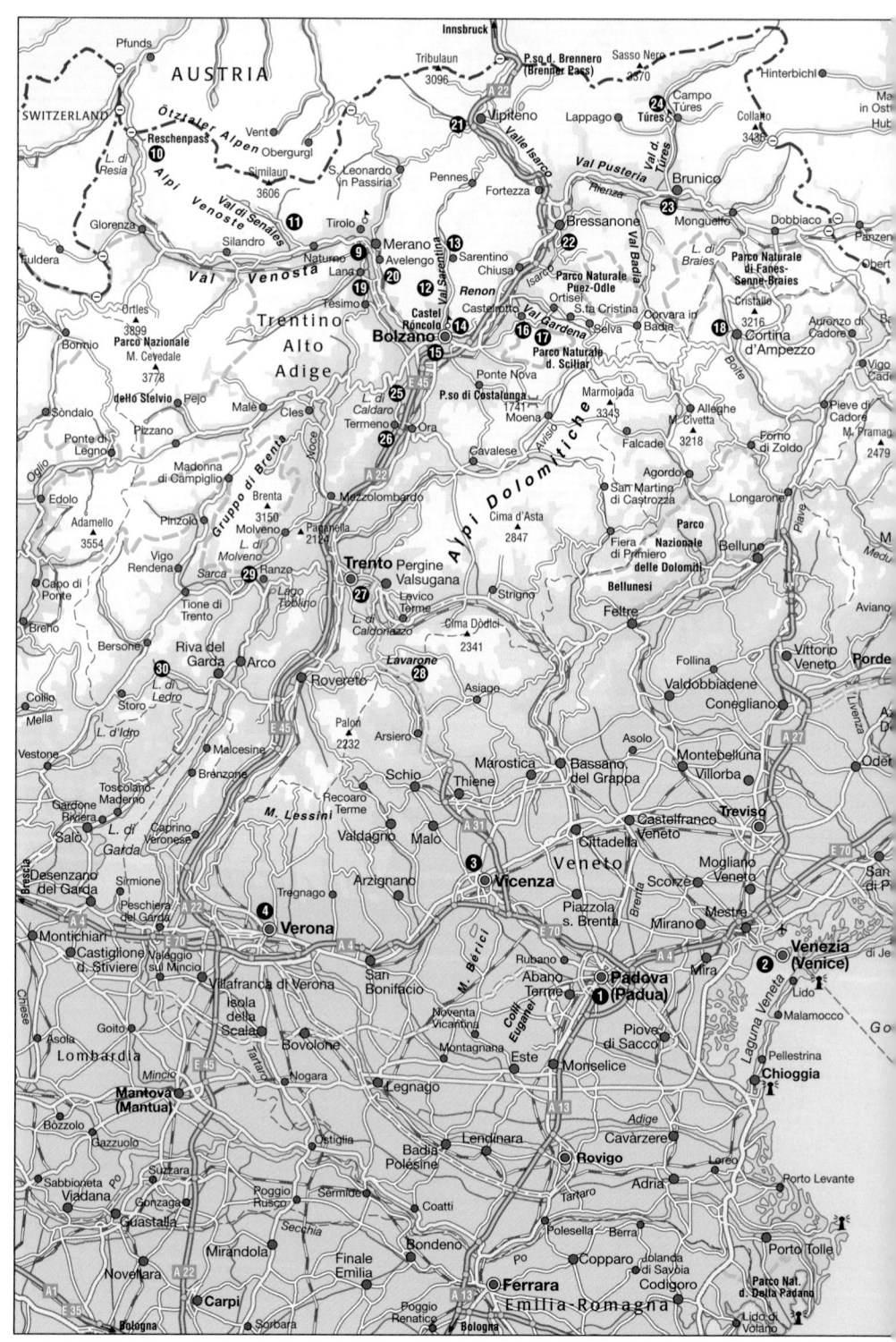

Northeastern Italy

0 ————— 20 km
0 ————— 20 miles

N

AUSTRIA

Heiligenblut

Reißeck
▲ 2965

Obervellach
Gmünd

Hochkreuz
▲ 2708
Möllbrücke

Spittal an
der Drau
Millstätter See
Döbriach
Patergassen

Greifenburg
Techendorf
Latschur
▲ 2236
Radenthein

Kötschach-
Mauthen
Kirchbach
Mösel
Hermagor
Feldkirchen

Gall
S. Stefan
Ossiacher
See

Alpi Carniche
Pontebba
Villach

Paluzza
Podkoren

Chiusaforte
J. di Montasio
▲ 2754
Sava

Tolmezzo
Sella Nevea
▲ 257
Triglav
▲ 2863
Mrzli
studenec

*friuli-
nezia
Giulia*
Gemona
del Friuli
Zaga

Tarcento
Kobarid
Bohinjska
Bistrica

S. Daniele
del Friuli
Tolmin

Spilimbergo
Cividale
del Friuli

Udine

SLOVENIA

Codroipo
Cormons
Gorizia
Idrija

Vito
Tagl
Castions
di Strada
Palmanova
Ajdovscina

Cervignano
d. Friuli
Manfalcone

Latisana
Aquileia
Sezana

Lignano
Sabbiadoro
Castello di
Miramare
Barcola
Trieste

Bibione
Grado
Kozina

Caorle
*Golfo di
Trieste*
Koper

Rt Savudrija

Umag
Buje
Buzet

Venezia

CROATIA

Porec
Baderna
Pazin

Vrsar
Zminj

Rovinj
Labin

*ADRIATIC
SEA*

Pula

Behind Il Salone is **Caffè Pedrocchi** famous throughout Italy as a gathering place for intellectuals. During the Risorgimento *(see page 55)*, liberals from the nearby university met here to discuss the founding of the new nation.

From here it is only a short walk through **Piazza dei Signori** to Padua's **Duomo**. Although the cathedral was designed by Michelangelo, many alterations were made to his plans, and the result is rather disappointing. The most interesting corner of the church is the frescoed baptistery (Mon–Sat 7.30am–noon and 3.30–7.30pm, Sun 8am–1pm and 3.30–8.45pm; baptistery open daily 10am–6pm; entrance fee).

Miser's Madonna

To the north of the university lies the **Cappella degli Scrovegni** (daily 9am–7pm; by appointment only, tel: 049-201 0020, lines open Mon–Fri 9am–7pm, Sat 9am–6pm; entrance fee includes Eremitani Museum). Enrico Scrovegni commissioned this richly decorated chapel in 1303 to atone for his father's miserliness and usury. It contains a recently restored cycle of frescos by Giotto, dedicated to the Virgin, the Life of Christ and The Last Judgement. The panels rank among Giotto's masterpieces. The solidity and emotional depth of the figures marked a turning point in Western painting. "In my opinion," wrote Giorgio Vasari in the 17th century, "painters owe to Giotto, the Florentine painter, exactly the same debt they owe to nature, which constantly serves them as a model and whose finest and most beautiful aspects they are always striving to imitate and reproduce."

Thankfully, the chapel escaped the fate of the nearby **Eremitani** church whose apse, covered with precious Mantegna frescos, was bombed during World War II – Italy's greatest art loss of the war.

This bare-walled church stands in poignant contrast to the rich collection of paintings, frescos, bronzes and mosaics in the **Eremitani Museum** (daily 9am–7pm; entrance fee includes Scrovegi Chapel) alongside, which contains outstanding art works, such as Bellini's *Portrait of a Young Suitor* and Tintoretto's *The Crucifixion*.

Vicenza

Andrea di Pietro, nicknamed Palladio, and the most prominent architect of the Italian High Renaissance, worked for most of his life (1508–80) in **Vicenza ❸** Rich and eager to decorate their city with new buildings, the local gentry gave Palladio many opportunities to use his talents. As a result, there is hardly a stree in central Vicenza not graced by a Palladian mansion, despite the destruction o 14 of Palladio's buildings during World War II.

In **Piazza dei Signori**, at the city's heart, stand two of Palladio's master pieces. The **Basilica**, his first major work, is not a church but a remodelling of Gothic courthouse (called *basilica* in the Roman sense – a place where justice is administered). Palladio's elegant design features two open galleries, the lowe one with Tuscan Doric columns and the upper one with Ionic columns. Facing the Basilica is the **Loggia del Capitaniato**, a later Palladian work commissione in 1571 to honour the victory over the Turks at Lepanto.

The city's Gothic-style **Duomo** stands just behind the Basilica. It was badly bombed during World War II but has since been completely rebuilt. The interio is unremarkable. A Palladian cupola tops the roof.

North of the Duomo is **Corso Palladio**, the city's main street, lined with many fine villas. Number 163 is the so-called **Casa del Palladio**. With its classic lines and precise geometric proportions, it is a typical example of Palladio's work Another excellent example of the Palladian style is the **Palazzo Chiericati**, in the Piazza Matteotti, at the end of Corso Palladio. This beautiful building houses the **Museo Civico** (Tues–Sun 9am–5pm; entrance fee) and the city's art collec tion. Tintoretto's *Miracle of St Augustine* and works by Flemish artists are on permanent display. In addition to the fine works in the city museum, the new

Palladio's addition of open galleries to Vicenza's Basilica was not just a way of embellishing the market square – the galleries were designed to strengthen the older building, which was suffering from subsidence.

BELOW: Palladio's Villa Rotonda, outside Vicenza.

Galleria di Palazzo Leoni Montanari (Contrà di Santa Corona 25; Tues–Sun 10am–6pm, but variable; tel: 800-57 88 75; entrance fee) has a superb collection of Venetian paintings, including works by Canaletto and Pietro Longhi. On the top floor there is also a notable collection of Russian icons.

Palladio wasn't the only great architect to work here. The younger Scamozzi, who learned much from Palladio, designed the **Palazzo del Comune** on the Corso Palladio; it reflects his strict interpretation of classical architecture.

The finest example of Scamozzi and Palladio's joint work is the **Teatro Olimpico** (Tues–Sun 9am–5pm; entrance fee), said to have been the first covered theatre in Europe when it was built between 1580 and 1582. Palladio died before its completion, and Scamozzi took over. The theatre is a wood-and-stucco structure with a permanent stage set of a piazza and streets in perfect perspective. The theatre is still in regular use today.

Map on pages 186–7

Elegant Verona.

Excursions from Vicenza

Monte Berico, a forested hill visible from all parts of Vicenza, is well worth a visit. Take a bus from the Piazza Duomo, or walk for approximately one hour to reach the **Madonna del Monte**, a 17th-century rebuilding of a chapel that commemorated the site of two apparitions of the Virgin. The final section of the approach is covered by a portico with 150 arches and 17 chapels. Inside, the basilica is spacious and airy, and works of art include a *Pietà* by Montagna. During World War I, the mountains beyond Vicenza were the scene of many great battles. The **Piazzale della Vittoria**, close to the church, is a memorial to all the Italians who died close to here.

To the southeast of the town centre is **Villa Capra**, better known as La Rotonda (grounds: mid Mar–mid Oct Tues–Thurs 10am–noon, 3–6pm; interior:

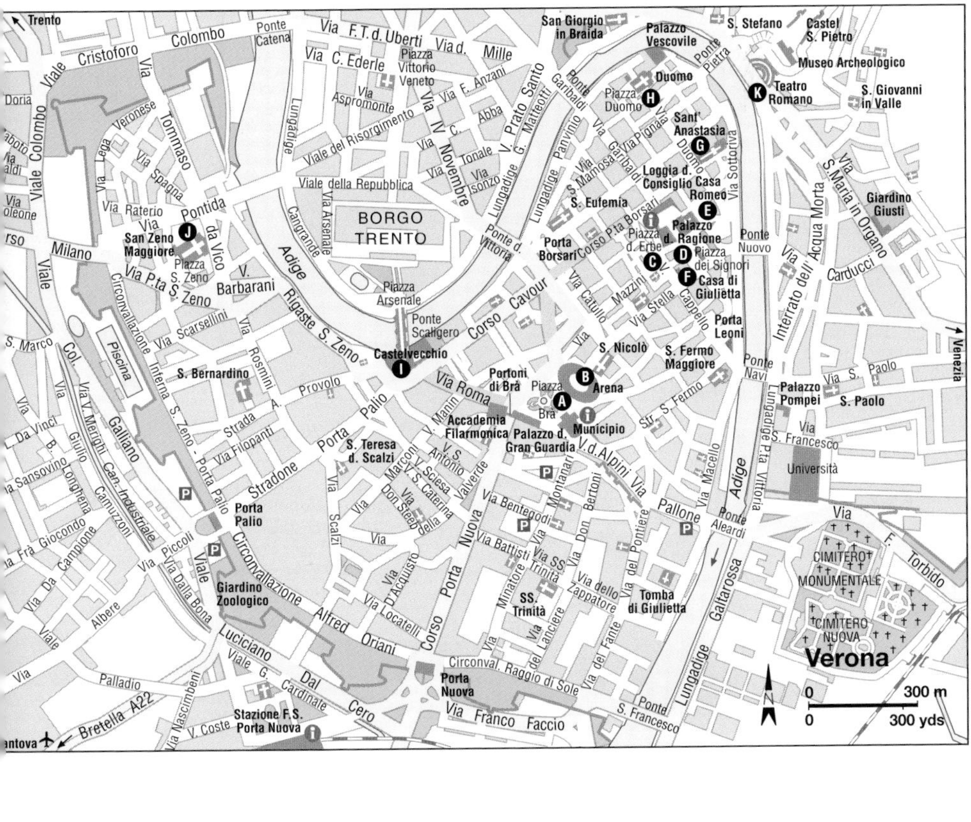

Verona

Verona's Giardino Giusti, a superb example of a Renaissance garden, is dotted with statuary.

BELOW: Piazza Brà.

Wed only, same hours; tel: 044-321 793; entrance fee), a famous belvedere buil by Palladio in 1551 with a distinctive circle within a cube design. Another fine villa nearby was built in 1688 by Antonio Muttoni. Known as the Villa ai Nani (Villa of the Dwarfs) on account of the statues of comical figures topping the garden wall, it is decorated with the delightful illusionistic frescoes of father and son, Giambattista and Giandomenico Tiepolo.

Verona

Built in the distinctive local pink marble, **Verona ❹** has a rosy hue, as if the sun were constantly setting. What was once a thriving Roman settlement is today one of the most prosperous and elegant cities in Italy.

The **Piazza Brà ❹** is where the Veronese gather day and night to talk, shop and drink together. They sit or stroll in the shadow of the glorious 1st-century AD Roman **Arena ❸** (Aug–May Tues–Sun 8.30am–7.30pm, June–July same times plus Mon 8.30am–5pm, but Thurs closing 2pm; last entry one hour before closure; tel: 045-800 3204; entrance fee), the third-largest structure of its kind in existence. The highest fragment, called the Ala, reveals the Arena's original height. It is often used for city fairs and, in summer, up to 25,000 people at a time fill it to attend performances of popular Italian opera – notably Verdi's *Aida* (if you are fortunate enough to get tickets, take a cushion and do not drink for several hours beforehand – the loos are virtually impossible to reach). *See page 406–7 for details of booking.*

The Roman Forum was located in what is now **Piazza delle Erbe ❹**, off the **Via Mazzini**. This large open space has a quirky beauty, due to the variety of *palazzi* and towers that line its sides. Among the most impressive is the baroque **Palazzo Maffei**, next to the **Torre del Gardello**, the tallest Gothic structure in the square. The palace with the attractive double-arched windows on the corner of **Via Palladio** is the medieval guild house – the **Casa dei Mercanti**.

The adjoining **Piazza dei Signori**  is more formal than its neighbour. The **Palazzo della Ragione**, a massive structure with heavy exterior decoration, stands on the border of the two squares. The interior courtyard has a delicate Gothic stairway. Opposite rises the **Loggia del Consiglio**, considered the finest Renaissance building in the city. Nearby are the tombs of the della Scala family (the Scaligeri), one-time rulers of Verona. The elaborately sculpted monuments stand outside the tiny church of Santa Maria Antica, surrounded by a wrought-iron fence featuring the family's staircase motif (della Scala means "of the stairs").

Verona is, of course, the city of *Romeo and Juliet*. Though the Capulet and Montague families immortalised by Shakespeare did exist, the story of the star-crossed lovers was entirely fictional. However, what is now a rather seedy bar on the Via delle Arche Scaligeri was allegedly the **Casa Romeo** ❺. Rather better maintained is **Juliet's House** ❻ (Tues–Sun 8.30am–7.30pm, Mon 1.30–7.30pm; entrance fee) at No. 23 Via Cappello, near Piazza delle Erbe, a medieval town house complete with balcony and museum. It is also possible to visit Juliet's purported final resting place. The "tomb" (Tues–Sun 8.30am–7.30pm, Mon 1.45–7.30pm; entrance fee) is several miles out of the centre on the Lungoadige Capuleti.

If your taste runs to the Gothic, head for **Sant'Anastasia** ❼, which houses a magnificent painting by Pisanello of St George, and frescos by Altichiero and Turone. Verona's **Duomo** ❽ (Mar–Oct Mon–Sat 10am–5.30pm, Sun 1.30–5.30pm, Nov–Feb Tues–Sat 10am–1pm and 1.30–4pm, Sun 1–5pm; contribution) is nearby. Inside is Titian's *Assumption of the Virgin*.

The **Castelvecchio** ❾ (Tues–Sun 8.30am–7.30pm, Mon 1.30–7.30pm; entrance fee) on the River Adige is a reminder of one of the grimmer chapters in the history of "fair Verona". The castle was first built in 1354 by the hated tyrant Cangrande II Scaliger for protection if a rebellion occurred. But he met his end not at the hands of the mob but through the treachery and ambition of his own brother, who stabbed him. As elsewhere in Italy, this fortress is now an excellent museum with works by Veronese and Tiepolo.

A saint and a prophet

Every Italian city must have a patron saint, and Verona is no exception. Little is known about St Zeno, a 4th-century holy man, though it seems he was a fisherman. His most famous miracle is depicted by Nicola Pisano on the porch of the **Basilica di San Zeno** ❿ (Mar–Oct Mon–Sat 8.30am–6pm, Sun 1–6pm, Nov–Feb Tues–Sat 10am–1pm and 1.30–4pm, Sun 1–5pm; entrance fee). According to the story, the saint was out fishing when he saw a man being dragged into the Adige by crazed oxen. St Zeno made the sign of the cross, exorcised the devils and the man continued safely on his journey. The bronze doors of the church are of splendid workmanship, though the artists are unknown. Most people are drawn to Verona because of *Romeo and Juliet* and other Shakespeare plays which are frequently performed in the **Teatro Romano** ⓚ, an ancient construction of perfect proportion and superb acoustics. ❏

Relief in the Castelvecchio.

BELOW: Romeo's beloved Juliet immortalised in bronze.

FRIULI-VENEZIA GIULIA

The influence of successive invaders has given Italy's northeastern corner a cosmopolitan feel, combining flavours of Italy, Austria and Slovenia

Map on pages 186–7

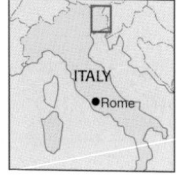

Since the 2nd century BC – when the Romans took over the northeastern corner of the Italian peninsula – Friuli-Venezia Giulia has been a victim of foreign invasions. The Visigoths poured into the area in AD 403; Attila the Hun earned his nickname "the Scourge of God" here in 452, and in 489 came Theodoric and the Ostrogoths. Many of the most gracious modern towns, including **Cividale del Friuli**, began as barbarian outposts. As a result, Cividale has an outstanding collection of sculpture, jewellery and weapons from this period, displayed in the **Museo Archeologico** (Mon 9am–1.30pm, Tues–Sun 8.30am–7pm; entrance fee) and the **Museo Cristiano** in the cathedral (Mon–Sat 9.30am–noon, 3–6pm, Sun 3–6pm, until 7pm in summer). A short walk away from the cathedral is the **Tempietto Longobardo** (Apr–Sept Mon–Sat 9.30am–12.30pm, 3–6.30pm, Sun 9.30am–1pm, 3–7.30pm; Oct–Mar Mon–Sat 9.30am–12.30pm, 3–5pm, Sun 9.30am–12.30pm, 2.30–6pm; entrance fee). This prestigious monument is an 8th-century Lombardic relic with fine 14th-century frescos. Subsequent invaders – the Venetians and the Austrians – left their mark, adding to the cosmopolitan flavour of this region, which shares a convoluted border with Slovenia. The border runs through the heart of the bilingual city of **Gorizia**, which has a fascinating castle (Tues–Sun 9.30am–1pm, 3–7.30pm, until 6pm in winter; entrance fee) and a small war museum. On the coast, the spa town of **Grado** was founded by the Hapsburgs; nowadays it is lined with parasols and sun-loungers, and is a very popular seaside resort.

Trieste

Of all Friuli's foreign "invaders", perhaps the best-known is James Joyce, who arrived in **Trieste ❺** in March 1905. He may not be Trieste's favourite son – he was constantly in debt, often drunk, and given to shouting in the theatre – but the city was to become his home for the following 10 years.

Today the city has an air of faded elegance. Once Venice's rival for trade on the Adriatic, later the maritime gateway for the Austro-Hungarian Empire, Trieste is now a port without a hinterland, a city that history left behind. In the Città Nuova, long, straight avenues flank a Grand Canal where tall ships once anchored. Southwest of the canal is the café-filled **Piazza dell'Unità d'Italia** – the largest sea-facing piazza in Italy, and a favourite promenade area. On the east side of the piazza stands the ornate **Municipio** (town hall), of 19th-century Austrian inspiration. At its foot, across the railroad tracks, stretches the long quay with its **Acquario Marino** (Apr–Oct Tues–Sun 9am–7pm, Nov–Mar 9am–1pm; entrance fee) exhibiting fish from the Adriatic Sea.

LEFT: boats line the Grand Canal, Trieste.
BELOW: Sunday parade in Cividale del Friuli.

The old city

Behind the Municipio are the narrow, winding streets of the **Città Vecchia**. Stairs by the **Teatro Romano** (closed to visitors) ascend steeply to the 6th-century **Duomo di San Giusto**. Two 5th-century basilicas were here combined into a single four-aisled structure in the 14th century. Up on the hill behind the Roman Theatre are the remains of a 1st-century BC dwelling, the **Antiquarium** (Thur 10am–noon; for visits after closing hours tel: 040-43631 (Cultural Heritage Office of the Friuli-Venezia Giulia region)). The site was constructed from the middle of the 2nd century to the end of the 7th century for funeral purposes. At the top of the hill here rises the 15th-century Venetian **Castello di San Giusto** (Piazza Cattedrale 3; Apr–Sept daily 9am–7pm, Oct–Mar 9am–5pm), with a sweeping view of the city and harbour. The **Museo del Castello di San Giusto** (Tues–Sun 9am–1pm; entrance fee) inside the castle has exhibits of weapons from the 13th–19th century, plus a small art collection. On your way back down, you may want to stop at the **Civico Museo di Storia ed Arte** (Tues, Thur–Sun 9am–1pm, Wed until 7pm; entrance fee), which features relics from the various invaders and inhabitants of Friuli-Venezia Giulia. Also worth a visit is the 12th-century **Basilica of San Silvestro** on the hillside. Overlooking Piazza Venezia is the **Museo Revoltella** (Via Diaz 27; Mon and Wed–Sat 9am–6pm, Sun 10am–6pm). This was once the grand residence of Trieste's most important merchant, but now showcases modern art.

Seven km (4 miles) west of Trieste, set in lush green gardens, is the fairytale **Castello di Miramare**, near the seaside town of **Barcola** ❻. Built between 1856 and 1860, this mock medieval fortress was the summer home of Archduke Maximilian. This was his dream palace, built with his wife Charlotte, daughter of Leopold I of Belgium, between 1856 and 1860. As the name suggests, it is set

While living in Trieste, James Joyce finished Dubliners, *wrote the final draft of* Portrait of the Artist as a Young Man, *and conceived* Ulysses.

BELOW: magnificent mosaics in San Giusto Cathedral.

on a promontory overlooking the sea, and the rooms are designed like the interiors of ships. It is Italy's best relic of the Austro-Hungarian Empire. The old conservatories house a butterfly garden. A museum (daily 9am–6pm, Mar and Oct until 5pm; park open daily 8am–7pm, until 5pm in winter; entrance fee) honours the ill-fated archduke, who later became Emperor of Mexico and died in front of a revolutionary firing squad.

Only 15 km (9 miles) from Trieste is the **Grotta Gigante e Museo Speleologico** (Giant Cave and Speleological Museum; guided tours Tues–Sun in summer every half-hour 9am–noon and 2–6.30pm, in winter every hour 10am–noon and 2.30–4.30pm; tel: 040-823859/327312; museum Tues–Sun 9am–5pm, until 5.30pm in summer; entrance fee). This vast cavern is part of the system of the underground river Timavo, which enters the karst in Slovenia.

The Romans based their Northern Adriatic fleet at **Aquileia** ❼, which now lies several miles inland. Here you can see the ruin of a once-vast harbour, dating from the 1st century AD. Best of all is the **Basilica** (daily, summer 9am–7pm, winter 9am–1pm and 2–5pm), begun in AD 313. This jewel of Friuli-Venezia Giulia has a stunning Roman mosaic floor depicting Biblical tales and mythological scenes. Stretching the entire length of the nave, it was laid down in 314, but the current building was consecrated in 1031 under Patriarch Poppo, who had the mosaics covered. They did not see daylight again until 1909, and in 2000 a major restoration took place when the mosaics were polished stone by stone.

Udine ❽ has an appealing style all its own. Echoes of Venetian rule are everywhere: the 16th-century **Castello** that towers over the city was built as the residence for Udine's Venetian governors and now houses the city's art and archaeology museums (Tues–Sat 9.30am–12.30pm and 3–6pm, Sun 9.30am–12.30pm). At the foot of the castle hill, lining the monumental Piazza della Libertà, are elegant buildings, Venetian in style, including the graceful **Porticato di San Giovanni**, built in 1523, and the **Loggia del Lionello**, the city hall constructed in the 15th century. This building shows a distinct Venetian influence, with its layered pink-and-white masonry and windows and arches with pointed tops. The **Galleria d'Arte Moderna di Udine** (GAMUD; Tues–Sat 9.30am–12.30pm and 3–6pm, Sun 9.30am–12.30pm; tel: 0432-295891) showcases both Italian and foreign 20th-century art.

Tiepolo, the greatest Venetian baroque painter, did some of his best work here. The city's **Duomo** has three chapels decorated by him in golds and pinks.

Northwest of Udine, the hillside town of **San Daniele del Friuli** is one of the world's capitals of raw *prosciutto*, which, thanks to the ideal climate here, has been produced since the time of the Celts. Today, every year some 2 million sweet-cured *prosciutto* hams are produced in over 26 establishments. Some people say San Daniele ham is superior even to Parma ham. San Daniele pigs are kept outside so their flesh is leaner, and their diet of acorns gives it a distinctive flavour. It is produced in much smaller quantities than Parma ham, which makes it even more expensive. ❏

TIP

The Caffè degli Specchi (the Mirror Café) is one of the most lavish symbols of the *belle époque* and one of the oldest cafés in Trieste.

BELOW: Piazza della Libertà in Udine, with the 15th-century Palazzo del Comune.

TRENTINO-ALTO ADIGE

The limestone peaks of the Dolomites frame an area of castles, lakes and ancient spas, with its own distinctive mix of Italian and German culture

Map on pages 186–7

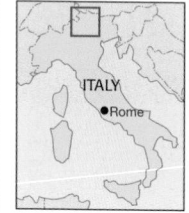

This mountainous region, which stretches north to the Italian-Austrian border, first came to the attention of tourists in the English-speaking world in 1837 when John Murray, the London publisher, brought out a handbook for travellers. The book's description of the Dolomites sparked interest particularly among mountaineers who had conquered the Swiss Alps and were looking for new challenges: "They are unlike any other mountains, and are to be seen nowhere else among the Alps. They arrest the attention by the singularity and picturesqueness of their forms, by their sharp peaks or horns, sometimes rising up in pinnacles and obelisks, at others extending in serrated ridges, teethed like the jaw of an alligator."

Today, Trentino-Alto Adige (also known as the South Tyrol, or Südtirol in German) is a popular holiday retreat for hikers, skiers and watersports enthusiasts. It is marked by contrasts, in the landscape as well as in the culture. Here it is possible to hike around a secluded Alpine lake in the morning, sample wine in an Italian vineyard at noon, stroll along the palm-lined promenade of a Continental spa in the afternoon and then slip into bed in a medieval castle at the end of the day.

Trentino-Alto Adige actually consists of two different provinces. Trentino, historically a part of Italy except for a period during the 19th and early 20th centuries when it was ruled by Austria, has a definite Italian flair. Alto Adige, on the other hand, was a part of the Austrian Tyrol for six centuries, first becoming an Italian domain in 1919 when the Austro-Hungarian Empire was carved up and the European borders were redrawn.

LEFT: the majestic landscape of the Dolomites.
BELOW: Germanic traditions are still flourishing.

Forced assimilation

The Germanic traditions, culture and language have remained, despite post-World War I efforts by Mussolini to stamp them out. The dictator Italianised not only the names of the towns, mountains and rivers, but even went so far as to force the South Tyrolean people to adopt Italian family names. Schools were forbidden to teach in German, and huge numbers of Italians were sent into the region to run both the government and industries, as well as to tip the ethnic balance within the population.

The South Tyroleans, however, insisted on clinging steadfastly to their cultural heritage, turning, in the 1960s, to acts of terrorism in an attempt to gain more autonomy for the province. Today, the atmosphere is once again peaceful as Italians and Germans live side by side, accepting and even appreciating each other's differences. The province is officially bilingual.

The mix of cultures is just one of the factors which makes Trentino-Alto Adige so diverse. The landscape in the east and north is marked by the awe-inspiring peaks of the rocky Dolomites, while the rolling green hills of the south central region are blanketed with

vineyards and orchards. The castles, of which there are more than 350, vary from crumbling overgrown ruins reminiscent of the one described in *Sleeping Beauty* to those that have been comprehensively restored and now house restaurants, hotels or well-appointed museums documenting the region's history.

Merano

The sleepy spa town of **Merano ❾** (Meran), with its palm-lined promenades, exclusive shops, fine restaurants and grand old hotels, offers the visitor a taste of old Europe. Merano has played host to the great and the gracious for well over a century. Those who can afford it come to relax and take the cure in a Mediterranean-like climate. The city owes its famously mild climate to its position in a deep basin, protected to the north by the massive Alpine peaks and opening to the Etsch Valley in the south. Merano flourished between the late 13th and early 15th centuries, when it was the capital of the Tyrol. Thereafter, it passed into relative insignificance until its value as a spa town was discovered. Merano hosts one of the biggest wine festivals in Italy in the first weekend of November. It also offers "grape cures" which involve a copious diet of grapes for the duration of the regime.

Just a short distance north of Merano is **Castel Tirolo**, one of the only castles in the world to have lent its name to an entire region. During the summer, concerts are performed in the castle. Just down the hill is **Castel Brunnenburg**, where Ezra Pound (1885–1972) spent the last years of his life.

To the west of Merano, the **Venosta** (Vinschgau) Valley extends all the way to the Swiss-Austrian-Italian border. The route leading over the **Reschen Pass ❿** was first constructed during Roman times as an important link between Augs-

A medieval belfry in Graun.

BELOW: view from the Stelvio Pass, near Venosta Valley.

urg and the Po Valley. Vinschgauer bread, a speciality of the region which is baked in small flat loaves and flavoured with aniseed, is worth sampling.

The **Val di Senales** ⑪ (Schnals Valley), which branches to the north, just past Naturno, passes through the region of the Similaun glacier. It was here that the 5,000-year-old "Similaun Man" was found by hikers in 1991. This frozen corpse is now on view in Bolzano (*see page 200*).

In the heart of Alto Adige lies the **Val Sarentina** ⑫ (Sarn Valley), a place where time seems to have stood still. Old farms perch precariously on the mountainsides, rushing brooks carve deep gorges through the mountain walls, and the people themselves, celebrating traditional festivals dressed in colourful costumes, add to the feeling of yesteryear. The ancient craft of *federkielstickerei*, or embroidering with peacock quills, is still practised here. The quill is split lengthways with a razor-sharp knife into thin threads used to embroider leather goods such as shoes, braces, handbags and book covers. In **Sarentino** ⑬ (Sarnthein) you can watch the craftsmen at work.

The road leading out of the valley towards the provincial capital of Bolzano winds through numerous tunnels before emerging at **Castel Roncolo** ⑭ (Schloss Runkelstein) (Tues–Sun 10am–6pm, last entry 5.30pm; entrance fee), built on a towering cliff in 1250 and today housing a museum with Gothic frescos.

Bolzano

Bolzano ⑮ (Bozen) itself provides one of the most vivid examples of the coexistence of Italian and Germanic cultures. The old part of the city, gathered around Piazza Walther and the arcades of the Via dei Portici, is marked by patrician

Map on pages 186–7

Bilingual road sign.

BELOW: fresco in Castel Roncolo.

houses and German Gothic architecture. Adjacent to Piazza Walther is the impressive Gothic **Duomo**, built in the 13th and 14th centuries and reputedly the oldest hall church in Alto Adige. The **Museo Archeologico dell'Alto Adige** (Tues–Sun 10am–6pm, daily July–Aug; entrance fee) has a fascinating collection including, famously, the mummified body of "Ötzi", the Iceman. Found by chance in the Ötzaler Alps in 1991, the extraordinarily well-preserved remains, including his clothing and copper axe, are estimated to be over 5,000 years old. He is on display in a refrigerated capsule, maintaining the mummy's temperature at –6 °C (21°F), and protected behind bulletproof glass.

On the other side of the River Talfer, in "New Bolzano", the Italian influence is seen in the austere Mussolini-era buildings. As a part of the Italianisation effort after World War I, the city was industrialised, and today Bolzano, outside the old town, is an unattractive mass of factories and smoking chimneys.

From Bolzano a cable car takes visitors on a scenic journey up to the **Renón** (Ritten) **Plateau**, a popular resort area. On a clear day, the views of the Dolomite formations are spectacular.

Just east of Bolzano is the **Sciliar** (Schlern) massif, towering like a great stone fortress above the surrounding area. At its base is the **Alpe di Siusi** (Seiser Alm), Europe's largest expanse of mountain pastureland, comprising almost 50 sq. km (20 sq. miles) and offering an abundance of hiking and ski trails.

Following the road from Sciliar to **Castelrotto** ⑯, one emerges in the **Val Gardena** (Grödner Valley) ⑰, with the popular ski resorts of **Ortisei** (St-Ulrich), **Santa Cristina** and **Selva** (Wolkenstein). This valley is also famous for its woodcarvers. From **Wolkenstein**, the Sella Joch Pass winds its way between the jagged peaks of Mount Langkofel and the majestic Sella massif. Travellers

TIP

The Alto Adige produces some good wines. Try the white wines, such as Pinot Grigio or aromatic Gewürztraminer, or the light red wines, which are very good chilled.

BELOW: Cortina d'Ampezzo.

rough this pass enjoy a panoramic view of Mount Marmolada, the region's ighest mountain, standing at 3,343 metres (10,965 ft). This route connects with ae Great Dolomite Road which leads east to **Cortina d'Ampezzo** ⑱, in the 'eneto, the site of the 1956 Winter Olympics and a very chic winter resort, and est over the **Costalunga** (Karer Pass) to Bolzano. The road from Bolzano asses the **Catinaccio** (Rosengarten) massif. During twilight hours, the rose-oloured rays of the setting sun bathe the cliffs of the Rosengarten (literally rose garden") in red, which is known as the *enrosadira*.

Lana ⑲, located between Bolzano and Merano, is the centre of the apple-rowing region. The parish church in **Niederlana** contains Alto Adige's largest ate-Gothic altarpiece, over 14 metres (46 ft) in height. Across the valley is **velengo** ⑳ (Hafling), home of the famous Hafling breed of horses.

In central Alto Adige, the **Isarco** (Eisach) **Valley** has, for the past 2,000 years, erved as the major route connecting the German north to the Latin south via ae Brenner Pass. The former commercial importance of **Vipiteno** ㉑ (Sterzing), he northernmost town on this route, is still evident today in its patrician houses.

Map on pages 186–7

The Gothic Duomo in Bolzano.

3ressanone

3ressanone ㉒ (Brixen), the region's oldest settlement, was a bishopric from 990 ntil 1964, when the bishop moved to Bolzano. Interesting sights include the rince-bishop's palace and the baroque Duomo, which features impressive marble vork and fine ceiling frescos. A stroll through the Gothic cloisters adjacent to the)uomo is worthwhile. The frescos here, dating from 1390 to 1509, are among he best examples of Gothic painting in the Alto Adige. The Romanesque chapel f St John at the southern end of the cloisters was built as a baptismal church.

BELOW: grazing under Mount Marmolada.

Just north of Bressanone, stretching to the east, is the **Pusteria Valley**. Th
valley's main town is **Brunico** ㉓ (Bruneck), with its lovely main street lined wit
houses from the 15th century. West of Brunico, the **Badia Valley** (Gadertal), wher
the Ladin language is still spoken, branches to the south. From Brunico, the **Túre
Valley** leads north to **Campo Túres** (Sand in Taufers), site of **Castle Túres** ㉔
The castle has been restored with many of its original furnishings and is open to th
public (for information on guided tours check with the regional tourist office; te
0474-678076). The Pusteria Valley is the gateway to the Sexten Dolomites, wher
the majestic Three Pinnacles and the Sexten Sundial formations are located. Th
latter was used by early astronomers as a point of orientation.

*The Adige is one of
Italy's longest rivers.
It rises on the border
with Switzerland and
Austria, and flows
down through
Trentino and the city
of Verona, before
emptying into the
Adriatic at Chioggia.*

Trentino and the Adige Valley

In direct contrast to the rugged mountainous north, the **Adige** (Etsch) **Valley** i
south central Alto Adige is marked by a more tranquil landscape. The fertil
hills are blanketed with vineyards, while orchards stretch across the plains. I
addition to the wealth of castles, this region is also the site of numerous aristo
cratic residences dating from the late 16th and early 17th centuries, when i
was the fashion among the Tyrolean nobility to build country houses in the Ital
ian Renaissance style. Many of these now serve as luxurious hotels and restaur
ants. **Lago di Caldaro** ㉕ (Lake Kalterer), nestled between vineyards and
waterfowl preserve, is one of the warmest lakes in the Alps. Further south i
Termeno ㉖ (Tramin), home of the Gewürztraminer grape.

The capital of the province of Trentino is **Trento** ㉗, site of the Council o
Trent which was held intermittently between 1545 and 1563. It was during thes
sessions, called by the Catholic Church to discuss the rising threat o

BELOW: snow in
Brunico.

utheranism, that the seeds of the Counter-Reformation were sown. Note-
orthy sights include the **Duomo**, built between the 13th and 14th centuries in
austere Romanesque-Gothic style, and the **Castello del Buonconsiglio**, one
f Italy's grandest castles and the residence of the prince-bishops who ruled the
ty for centuries. Today it houses a museum of local art (Tues–Sun 10am–6pm
summer, 9.30am–5pm in winter; entrance fee).

The region of **Lavarone** ⓟ is located to the southeast of Trento. Here one
nds dark green forests, mountain pastures, lakes and caves full of stalactite
nd stalagmite formations. It was on the shores of the small **Lago di Lavarone**
at Sigmund Freud liked to stroll on the lakeside path, later named after him.

The **Paganella Mountains**, considered by many to be the most beautiful in
aly, range to the north of Trento. At the foot of this massif are the lakes of
erlago, **Santo** and **Lamar**. Further south is **Lago Toblino**, with a short hiking
ath leading to **Ranzo** ⓠ, a small village with a breathtaking panorama over
e valley of the lakes. More ambitious trekkers can follow the *translagorai*
ute through the wild **Catena dei Lagorai** in the eastern part of the province,
assing by numerous serene Alpine lakes.

Just west of Lake Garda is **Lago di Ledro** ⓡ. Items from here dating from
e 4,000 BC stilt village can be seen at the Rocca di Riva museum in Riva del
arda (Tues–Sun mid-Mar–end June and Sept–early Nov 10am–12.30pm and
.30–6pm; July and Aug daily; entrance fee). The northern tip of Lake Garda is
cated within Trentino. Although many towns on the lake have, in the past,
een obliged to close their beaches due to pollution, the northern waters remain
ncontaminated and off limits to motorboats, so they are well worth exploring
see page 225).   ❏

Map on
pages
186–7

TIP

Castel Toblino, the
lakeside fortress, is
one of the most
romantic castles in
Trentino. Now
sensitively converted
into a restaurant it is
open in summer (late
March–Oct) Wed–Mon;
tel: 0461 864036.

BELOW: vineyard in
Termeno.

MILAN

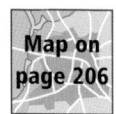

Map on page 206

or Henry James, Milan's reserved Northern European flavour made it more "the last of the prose capitals than the first of the poetic". But there is poetry in Milan in spite of its modernity

Milan (Milano) is one of the world's fashion capitals, and home to both Leonardo's *Last Supper* and the world's premier opera house, La Scala. Above all, Milan is the centre of business in Italy, and it is here and in rovincial Lombardy that the demand for federalism – embodied by the right-ing Northern League – is strongest. The prosperous Milanese are courteous ut reserved towards visitors.

There is no better place to begin a tour of Milan than at its spiritual hub, the **uomo** Ⓐ (daily 8.30am–6.45pm; crypt daily 9am–noon and 2.30–6pm), escribed by Mark Twain as "a poem in marble". This gargantuan Gothic cathe-ral (the third-largest church in Europe after St Peter's in Rome and Seville's athedral) was begun in 1386 but not finished until 1813. Decorating the exte-or are 135 pinnacles and over 3,400 marble statues from all periods. The Madonnina", a beautiful 4-metre (13-ft) gilded statue, graces the top of the uomo's highest pinnacle, soaring 109 metres (358 ft) above ground. The build-g requires continuous restoration.

nside the Duomo

he English novelist D.H. Lawrence called the Duomo an imitation hedgehog of a cathedral", because of its ointy intricate exterior. But inside the church is sim-le, majestic and vast. Five great aisles stretch from the ntrance to the altar. Enormous stone pillars dominate e nave, which is big enough to accommodate some 0,000 worshippers. In the apse, three large and intri-ate stained-glass windows attributed to Nicolas de onaventura shed a soft half-light over the area behind e altar. The central window features the shield of the isconti, Milan's ruling family during the 13th and 4th centuries. It was Duke Gian Galeazzo Visconti, e most powerful member of the family, who com-issioned the Duomo.

A gruesome statue of the flayed St Bartholomew, car-ying his skin, stands in the left transept. In the right ransept is an imposing 16th-century marble tomb made or Giacomo di Medici by Leone Leoni after the style f Michelangelo. The crypt contains the tomb of the Counter-Reformation saint Charles Borromeo. This 6th-century Archbishop of Milan epitomised the Lom-ard virtues of energy, efficiency and discipline. His nbending character led to frequent battles with the lay uthorities, especially when he tried to ban dancing, rama and sport.

Outside, a lift goes up to the roof of the Duomo Apr–mid-Sept 5.45–9pm, closing times vary, tel: 02-202 2656, last entry 45 mins before closing), among the

LEFT: Galleria Vittorio Emanuele.
BELOW: the roof of the Duomo.

Milan

0 _____ 400 m
0 _____ 400 yds

nnacles and carved rosettes. The view from the top is spectacular: on a clear day
stretches as far as the Alps.

Come down into the recently restored **Piazza del Duomo ⑧**, where
ilan's many worlds converge. The large equestrian statue standing at one
d of the square honours Italy's first king, Victor Emmanuel (after whom
ajor boulevards in cities throughout Italy are named). The piazza is lined
n two sides with porticoes, where Milanese of all ages and styles love to
ther. To the north is the entrance to the **Galleria Vittorio Emanuele ◉**,
aly's oldest and most elegant shopping mall. Its four-storey arcade is full
f boutiques, bookshops, bars and restaurants. But, before you sit down to
atch the world go by, be forewarned: the cafés here are pricey. Among the
alleria's best cafés and restaurants are the Art Nouveau Camparino at No.
8, a classic spot for an *aperitivo*, especially a campari – Davide Campari, the
ventor of the drink, was born here on the first floor. Other perfect people-
atching spots include Biffi and the new Gucci café next door. While not
leap, its tasty and sophisticated snacks are far more affordable than the con-
nts of the adjoining Gucci shop.

See map opposite

At the other side of the Galleria is **Piazza della Scala ◍**, site of the famed
a Scala opera house, which has now been opulently restored. It was built
etween 1776 and 1778 by Giuseppe Piermarini, and it was here that Verdi's
tello and Puccini's *Madama Butterfly* were first performed. The **Museo
eatrale alla Scala ◎** (Opera House Museum; daily 9am–12.30pm and
30–5.30pm; entrance fee) is now housed again at La Scala after its temporary
ome on Corso Magento. There is a rich collection of memorabilia, includ-
g original scores by Verdi, Liszt's piano and other objects connected to great
usicians and composers. The visit includes a look
to the theatre itself from one of the boxes – as long as
ere are no rehearsals under way.

A bust of Verdi in the Opera House Museum.

BELOW: Pinacoteca di Brera.

Follow the Via Verdi from La Scala to the **Pina-
oteca di Brera ◑** (Tues–Sun 8.30am–7.15pm; tel:
2-722631; entrance fee; www.brera.beniculturali.it),
ome of one of Italy's finest art collections. Paintings
f the 15th to the 18th century are especially well rep-
esented. Famous works included in the collection are
Mantegna's *The Dead Christ* (viewed from the pierced
oles of his feet), Caravaggio's *Supper at Emmaus*, and
ne restored 15th-century *Madonna and Saints* by Piero
ella Francesca. Raphael's beautiful *Betrothal of the
'irgin (Lo Sposalizio)*, a masterpiece of his Umbrian
eriod, was his first painting to show powers of com-
osition and draughtsmanship far in advance of his
iggest stylistic influence, Perugino.

A despot's dwelling

Off the Piazza del Duomo is Via Mercanto. From
here, Via Dante leads to the **Castello Sforzesco ◎**
daily 7am–6pm, until 7pm in summer; entrance fee
or the museum), stronghold and residence of the
Sforza family, the despotic rulers of Milan in the 15th
entury (*forza* means strength in Italian). The great-
st of the Sforzas was Francesco, a mercenary gen-
ral who became the fourth duke of Milan. To design
is stronghold, Francesco employed a local architect,

Fresco of St Ambrose in the Basilica di Sant' Ambrogio.

Giovanni da Milano, but the decoration of the principal tower was unde. taken by Filarete, a Florentine.

The residential part of the castle, the Corte Ducale, contains a magnifice collection of sculpture, including Michelangelo's last work, the unfinishe *Pietà Rondanini*, an almost abstract work charged with emotion. Michelange worked on this *pietà* until within a few days of his death in 1564, and now has been cleaned it is especially evocative.

Three blocks west of the castle stands the church of **Santa Maria del Grazie ⓗ** (daily 7.30am–noon and 3–7pm), begun in 1466 but expanded in 149 by Bramante, who also built the exquisite cloister. Next door, the **Cenacolo Vi ciano ⓘ** (Tues–Sun 8.15am–7.30pm; booking necessary, tel: 02-8942 114 entrance fee), once a refectory for Dominican friars, is home to Leonardo's icon *Last Supper* (1495–7). Leonardo painted on dry plaster which would allow hi more time to retouch the work, using an experimental mix of tempera and or However, excessive humidity combined with the faulty mixture used for bindir the paint caused the fresco to deteriorate even during Leonardo's lifetime. Restora tion of the work began in 1977 and took 22 years to complete.

Whatever your view of its controversial restoration, the *Last Supper* remains powerful and moving work. It is far larger than expected – some 9 metres (30 f wide and 4.5 metres (15 ft) high. Not all the expressions on the disciples' face can be discerned, but the careful composition of the work remains completel clear. On either side of Jesus sit two groups of three Apostles, linked to each othe through their individual gestures and glances. It vividly captures the moment whe Jesus announces that one of them is about to betray him. This painting was sem inal to the perception of the artist as a creative thinker rather than just an artisan

BELOW: Leonardo da Vinci's masterpiece, *The Last Supper.*

Since the newly restored work was unveiled in 1999, visitor numbers have been
stricted, with visits limited to 15 minutes. More recently, of course, the painting's
pularity has been even further enhanced by the huge success of Dan Brown's
riller *The Da Vinci Code*, made into a big budget film in 2006. If you don't
anage to secure an advance booking, there is a very small chance of getting
urns on the day at the booking office (opposite Santa Maria delle Grazie).
From Santa Maria delle Grazie, proceed to the **Basilica di Sant'Ambrogio** ❶
aily 8am–noon and 2.30–7pm; Via Carducci). This is the finest medieval build-
g in Milan and dedicated to the city's patron saint, St Ambrose. To enter, step
wn from street level and cross an austere atrium. The church is dark and low,
t compelling in its antiquity. Founded between 379 and 386 by St Ambrose,
en bishop of Milan – it was he who converted St Augustine – the basilica was
larged first in the 9th century and again in the 11th. The brick-ribbed square
ults that support the galleries are typical of Lombardic architecture. The **Museo**
lla Basilica (daily 10am–noon and 3–5pm; entrance fee) has many treasures
cluding St Ambrose's robe and illuminated manuscripts.
Down Via San Vittore from the basilica is the **Museo della Scienza e della**
cnologia Leonardo da Vinci ❼ (Tues–Fri 9.30am–5pm, Sat–Sun 9.30am–
30pm; entrance fee). Although the large section devoted to applied physics
ll probably be of interest only to specialists, everyone will enjoy the huge
llery filled with wooden models of Leonardo da Vinci's most ingenious inven-
ns. It remains one of the most important science and technology museums in
e world. Don't miss the reconstruction of his famous flying machine.
Return in the direction of the Duomo to the **Pinacoteca Ambrosiana** ❶,
art gallery founded by Cardinal Federico Borromeo in 1618, along with a

Map on
page 206

TIP

For a gruesome
glimpse of the past,
venture down into the
crypt of Sant'Ambrogio
to see the skeletal
remains of St
Ambrose, Milan's
patron saint, along
with those of two early
Christian martyrs.

BELOW:
Buon appetito!

ASHION FOR FOODIES

isitors come to Milan as much to shop and dine as to take
in Leonardo's *Last Supper*. As with the fresco, you will
ed to book in advance if you plan to eat at a top establish-
ent. One is the very grand Savini (Galleria Vittorio Emanuele
tel: 02-7200 3433), where you can try the definitive *risotto*
a Milanese. Just as exclusive is the two Michelin-starred
acco-Peck, at Via Victor Hugo 4, where you can enjoy a six-
urse gastronomic menu (tel: 02-876774). The two Miche-
-starred Sadler restaurant in the Navigli district (Via Troilo
; tel: 02-5810 4451) is another expensive temple to gas-
nomy, but for more reasonable prices try the stylish off-
oot, Sadler Wine and Food restaurant and wine bar, located
tween the city centre and the exhibition zone (Fiera) at Via
nte Bianco 2/A (tel: 02-481 4677). If your budget doesn't
ow for the full gastronomic blow-out, you can always shop
picnic ingredients at Gastronomia Peck, Via Spadari 9 (tel:
-8023161), choosing from the huge and enticing selection
top-quality gourmet cheeses, meats and pastries on dis-
ay. When in the Quadrilatero, at the intersection of Monte
poleone and Sant'Andrea, seek refuge from the haughty
les staff in the Antico Caffè Cova. *For more restaurant rec-*
mmendations in Milan, see page 392.

major library. The newly restored gallery houses a collection of paintings dati‐
from the 15th to the 17th century (Tues–Sun 10am–5.30pm; entrance fee
Most notable among the works are Leonardo's *Portrait of a Musician*, Titian
Adoration of the Magi and Caravaggio's *Basket of Fruit*.

Fashion avenue

For a break from sightseeing and a glimpse of a key aspect of Milanese life, str‐
down **Via Monte Napoleone** Ⓜ, which extends off Corso Vittorio Emanue‐
between the Duomo and Piazza Santa Babila. The "Vie" Monte Napoleone, Sa
t'Andrea, della Spiga and Manzoni are home to all the great designer shops. V
Monte Napoleone takes in Emilio Pucci – one of the longest-established fashi‐
houses – a Prada flagship store, Versace glitz, Gucci glamour, sumptuous cas
mere from Loro Piana, Alberta Ferretti and their younger brand "Philosophy"
the adjoining shop – and much more. Other designers include Salvatore Ferra‐
amo, Fratelli Rossetti, Valentino, Tanino Crisci, Cartier, Etro and Louis Vuitto‐

Ultra chic Via della Spiga is home to Dolce & Gabbana, Moschino, Rober‐
Cavalli, Agnona – the womenswear arm of Ermenegildo Zegna, Krizia, Serg‐
Rossi, Gianfranco Ferre, Bottega Veneta, Tod's, Prada, Bulgari, Chopard a‐
Genny. Be prepared to stretch your credit card to the limit, or else stick to wi‐
dow shopping. This elegant street is overlooked by the Carlton Hotel Baglioni
terrace champagne bar and tea lounge. *(For more on the Milan fashion scen‐
see page 212.)*

Also within Milan's designer area is the excellent, if eccentric **Museo Baga‐
Valsecchi** (Via Gesù; Tues–Sun 1–5.45pm; closed Aug; entrance fee).The Baga‐
Valsecchi brothers were avid collectors of late 19th century items. They spent mu‐

TIP

The canal quarter
has some excellent
markets. Every
Saturday the Darsena
and Naviglio Grande
are taken over by the
Fiera di Senigallia,
with stallholders
displaying bric-a-brac
along the canal banks.

BELOW: window
cleaning in style.

their lives collecting antiques from all over the country, and commissioned ·riod-style furnishings from skilled Lombard craftsmen in order to recreate an ·thentic Renaissance atmosphere in their own home. The resulting museum, ·used in a delightful neo-Renaissance *palazzo*, is a collector's paradise, where it ·fun to try to distinguish authentic 16th-century pieces from the reproductions.

In this cutting-edge city, cutting-edge art is showcased at the **Padiglione ·Arte Contemporanea (PAC)** (Via Palestro 14; Tues–Sun 9.30am–7pm, Thur ·til 9pm; www.comune.milano.it/pac). Large, experimental works of con-·mporary art feature in all their forms in this museum.

The **Museo Poldi-Pezzoli** (Via Alessandro Manzoni 12; Tues–Sun 10am–·m; www.museopoldipezzoli.it; entrance fee) is a treasure trove amassed by ·e extremely wealthy Giacomo Poldi-Pezzoli in 1881, who bequeathed his ·me to the city on his death. The interior is a testament to 19th-century patrician ·stes. It is filled with paintings (by Botticelli, Bellini, Piero della Francesca and ·antegna), jewellery, porcelain, timepieces and sundials, tapestries, ancient ·maments and period furniture.

If you have time on your visit to Milan, there are two more churches which ·e worth seeking out. In the Via Torino, near the Piazza del Duomo, stands **San ·tiro** ❶, built by Bramante in 1478–80. Inside, the architect cleverly used ·cco to create an illusionistic effect, giving the impression that the church is far ·rger than it actually is. **San Lorenzo Maggiore** ❷, nearby on Corso di Porta ·cinese, attests to Milan's antiquity. The basilica was founded in the 4th century ·d rebuilt in 1103. Martino Bassi restored it in 1574–88, but its octagonal shape ·d many beautiful 5th-century mosaics are original. The vast dome creates an ·ve-inspiring interior.   ❑

Map on page 206

Milan's Central station is under-going a facelift. The historic entrance will be left intact, but the whole area will be transformed with new ticket offices, lifts and conveyor belts for passengers. A new shopping area will be created to host at least 100 shops.

BELOW: façade of the Duomo.

Planet Fashion

Milan has become a brand, Planet Fashion, a glitzy galaxy where you can live by fashion alone. After waking up in Frette sheets in the Bulgari design hotel (Via Privata Fratelli Gabba), breakfast in the glass-domed Gucci café, trim your designer stubble in the Dolce & Gabbana barber's and take a dip in Gianfranco Ferre's spa retreat. That's before sipping cocktails at a fashion show in Just Cavalli, and dancing the night away (on a beige carpet, naturally) in Privé, Giorgio Armani's exclusive nightclub (private members only).

Piazza Duomo, Milan's main square, is as good a spot as any to plan a shopping campaign. Overlooking the cathedral is **Rinascente**, the city's slick department store where Giorgio Armani started his career as a window-dresser. This is the perfect place for exploring your taste before succumbing to hot chocolate in the rooftop café. From here, fashionistas will be drawn to the designer honey-pots of the Golden Triangle. Known as the **Quadrilatero d'Oro**, this chic (but physically square) fashion district is bounded by Via della Spiga, Via Manzoni, Via Montenapoleone, Via Sant'Andrea and Corso Venezia. In this partly pedestrianised district, discreet courtyards and classical palaces conceal the most ostentatious of international brands.

A way of life

All the designers are getting in on the lifestyle act, adding spas or bars with gay abandon. **Gianfranco Ferré** (Via Sant'Andrea 15) has a tranquil E'Spa spa attached to his boutique, while **Dolce & Gabbana** menswear emporium (Corso Venezia 15) has a grooming salon and Martini bar. **Roberto Cavalli** (Via della Spiga), where more is always more, responds with a goldfish bowl, a fashionable bar framed by an aquarium with models parading around in the latest tactile collection. Less theatrically, **Armani Superstore** (Via Manzoni 31) pays homage to the master of minimalism and showcases his main collections, from Armani Casa to prêt-à-porter, Emporio Armani and Armani Jeans. Diehard fans will salivate over Armani books, cutlery and designer chocolate in the store's Armani Café and swanky Nobu bar and restaurant (partly owned by actor Robert de Niro).

Fashionistas are easily satisfied, but the city also caters to a more conservative set. For dapper Italian politicians, the king of ties is **Angelo Fusco Cravatte Sette Pieghe** (Via Montenapoleone 25; tel: 02-7631 8933). Created as an amusing sideline by Angelo, a practising cosmetic surgeon, the firm produces intricate designer ties made of seven-times-folded jacquard silk, hand-stitched and presented in a wax-sealed box.

For couples with a wedding list, Italy between the sheets is best represented by **Frette** (Via Montenapoleone 21; tel: 02-783950). The firm is the leading creator of desirable bed linen, embracing linen sheets, baby blankets, cashmere throws and silk cushions, tempting lovers of luxury.

For those on a non-designer budget, salvation lies in the form of **Il Salvagente** (Via

LEFT: A Prada shop window with the inevitable tempting display.

Fratelli Bronzetti 16; tel: 02-7611 0328; www.salvagentemilano.it). This is one of Milan's most reliable discount outlets for designer clothes, particularly at sale time, when prices are reduced by a further 60 percent. During sale times, the store can turn into a scrum, with squabbles over cut-price Armani, Prada and Alberta Ferretti.

At the other end of the spectrum, the most beguiling shopping experience in Milan remains the very stylish **10 Corso Como** (Corso Como 10; tel: 02-2900 2674; www.10corsocomo.com), Milan's sexiest concept store. Designed by Carla Sozzani, former editor of *Elle*, this sprawling, bazaar-like emporium is the haunt of style gurus and supermodels.

After celebrity-spotting over handbags or home furnishings, slip away from the designer clothes to the store's stylish design gallery or the café in the conservatory (where low-carb menus attract the waif-like models).

Design capital

Milan is as much a design capital as it is a fashion capital. For cutting-edge furniture and lighting, make tracks for **Via Durini.** Dominating "Design Street" are the rival showrooms of B&B Italia, Armani Casa, Cassina and Meritalia. **High Tech** (Piazza XXV Aprile 12; tel: 02-624 1101) is an eclectic homeware store housed in the former ink factory for *Corriere della Sera.* Mid-range contemporary furniture and home furnishings are offset by knick-knacks such as hand-crafted candles. For seductive design icons, **Alessi** is a contemporary style guru who specialises in corkscrews and coffee pots, cutlery and kitchenware. Choose between the convenient Milan store or the factory shop on Lake Orta, which offers superb deals on signature household objects (Alessi, Corso Matteotti 9, Milan; tel: 02-795726; or Alessi Factory Outlet, Via Privata Alessi 6, Crusinallo, Omegna, Lake Orta; tel: 0323-868648; wwww.alessi.it).

Not far from fashion central is the elegant **Brera district**, centred on Via Solferino, and home to upmarket yet bohemian boutiques. The funky **Navigli canal district** is the coolest quarter, boasting the city's hippest shops and

liveliest nightlife. Antonioli (Via Pasquale Paoli 1) sells cutting-edge fashion labels in a former cinema, while Kitchen (Via E. De Amicis 45) is packed with cooking utensils, cookbooks and foodstuffs.

A short train ride from Milan, Como is to silk what Milan is to fashion and Venice is to glassware. The city remains the country's leading centre for luxurious silk creations, and is a lovely place to shop. **La Tessitura**, a sleek outlet run by Mantero, Como's famed silk factory, claims to be the world's sole concept store "dedicated to the art of silk". The store is housed in an old textile mill, built in 1870. The building has been totally revamped, keeping its original glass ceiling, cast iron columns and exposed beams. Combine brunch in the store's Loom Café with live music and shopping for silk (Viale Roosevelt 2A; tel: 031-321666). Alternatively, **Frey** is a small but well-established silk shop selling ties and scarves (Via Risorgimento 49; tel: 031-927538). Como is a delightful interlude, but Milan's masters of merchandising will soon tempt you back to Planet Fashion. ❑

RIGHT: Stainless-steel seasoning shakers from Alessi – every home should have one.

LOMBARDY

Beneath is spread like a green sea / The waveless plain of Lombardy, / Bounded by the vaporous air, / Islanded by cities fair
— PERCY BYSSHE SHELLEY

Map on pages 216–7

From the heights of the central Alps to the low-lying plains of the Po Valley, the province of Lombardy is remarkably diverse. Contrasts abound in this land named after the Lombards, one of the barbarian tribes that invaded Italy in the 6th century. Its cities, renowned for their elegance since Renaissance times, are complemented by dramatic scenery. The Italian Lakes jut into the heart of a steep mountain range, offset by fertile farmlands and fields of gently swaying poplars.

An easy day trip from **Milan ❶**, or a stopover on a longer journey south, is the **Certosa di Pavia ❷** (Charterhouse of Pavia; May–Sept Tues–Sun 9–11.30am, 2.30–6pm, Oct–Mar until 4.30pm, Apr until 5.30pm). This world-famous church, mausoleum and monastery complex, founded in 1396, is a masterpiece of Lombardic Renaissance architecture, complete with relief sculpture and inlaid marble. The interior of the church is Gothic in plan, but highly embellished with Renaissance and baroque details. Inside stand the tombs of Ludovico Visconti and his child-bride, Beatrice d'Este. Their bodies are not actually buried here, but life-sized effigies on top of the tombs portray them in all their lifetime splendour.

Behind the Certosa is the magnificent Great Cloister where Carthusian monks, who had taken vows of silence, once lived in individual dwellings. Each cottage is two storeys high, with two rooms on the ground floor and a bedroom and loggia above. Each monk, living in seclusion, took delivery of his food through the small swing portal at the right of his doorway.

Nowadays, Pavia is a country backwater, but between the 6th and 8th centuries it was the capital city of the Lombards. Pavia's fame was augmented in 1361 when the university was founded, and to this day it remains a prestigious centre of learning.

On the Via Diacono, in the old centre of town, is the church of **San Michele**, consecrated in 1155. Here the great medieval Lombard leader, Frederick Barbarossa, was crowned king of Italy. Look for the carefully sculpted scenes of the battle between good and evil above the three doorways. Inside, San Michele is plain and sombre; only the columns are highly decorated.

Eclectic and electric

To reach the **Duomo**, follow the Strada Nuova from San Michele. This cathedral is an eclectic mixture of four centuries of architectural styles. The basic design is Renaissance (Bramante and Leonardo worked on it), but the immense dome, the third-largest in Italy, is a late 19th-century touch, and the façade was added in 1933. The rest of the exterior is unfinished.

If you continue on the Strada Nuova you will arrive at the **Università**, where 17,000 students currently attend classes. One of Pavia's most famous past graduates was Alessandro Volta, the physicist who discovered and

LEFT: the cloister of the Certosa di Pavia.
BELOW: a sculpture on its façade.

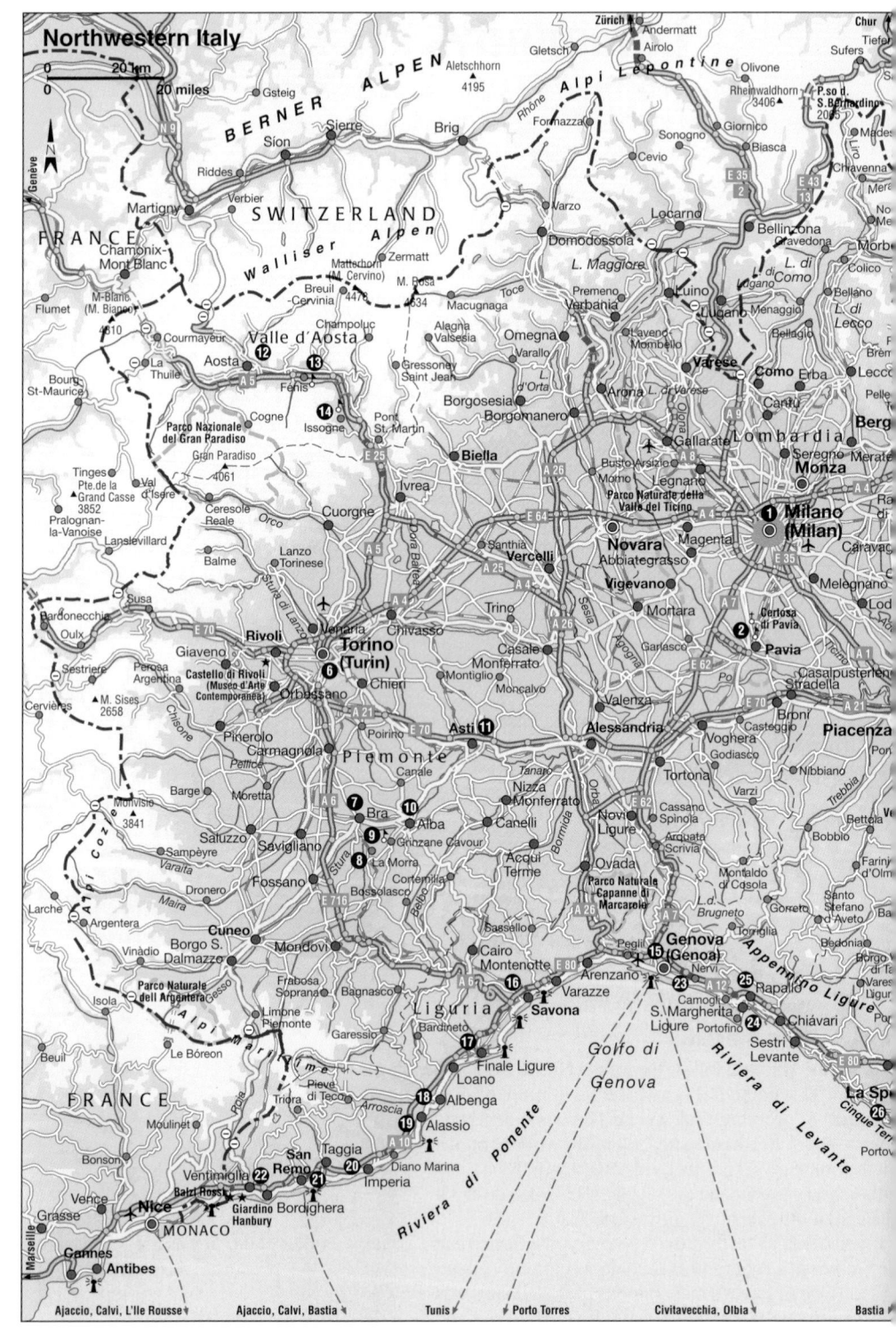

Northwestern Italy

0   20 km
0   20 miles

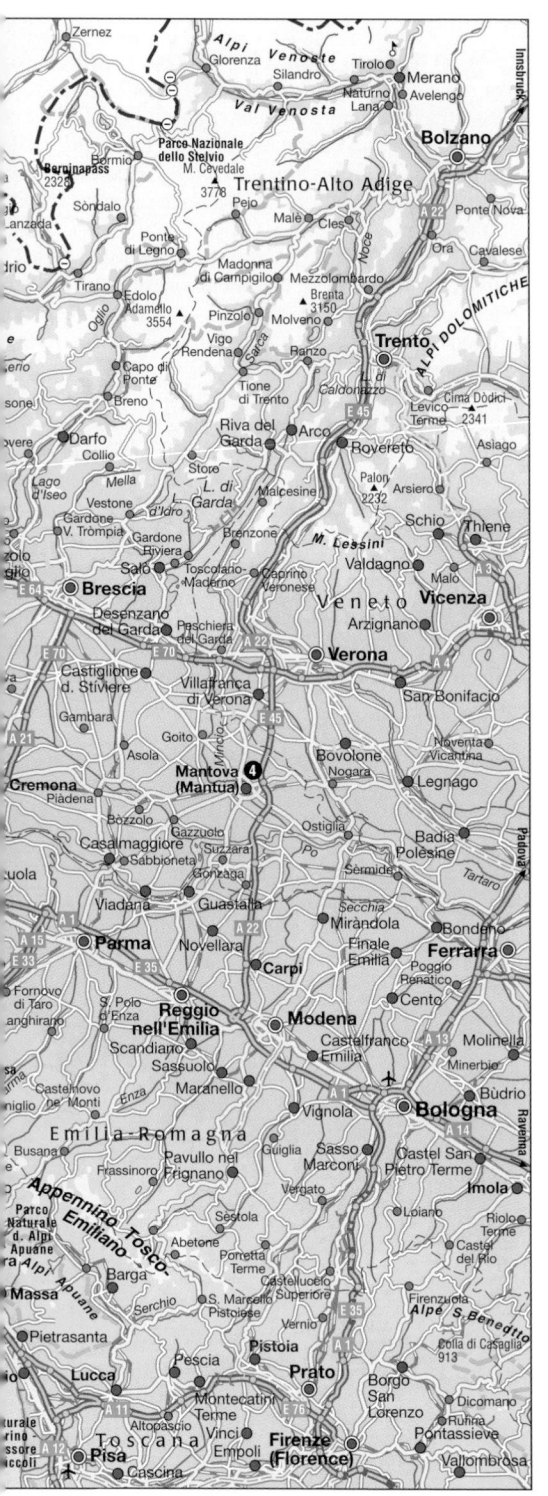

gave his name to electrical volts. His statue stands in the left-hand court of the university complex.

At the end of the Strada Nuova stands the **Castello Visconteo**, an imposing square fortress built in 1360–5. Today, the castle is the home of the **Museo Civico** (Tues–Sun 10am–6pm, July–Aug and Dec–Jan 9am–1.30pm; entrance fee). Included in the museum's collection are many fine Lombardic Romanesque sculptures and remnants of Roman Pavia, including inscriptions, glass and pottery.

Go west from the castle to reach **San Pietro in Ciel d'Oro**, a fine Lombardic Romanesque church, smaller than San Michele, but quite similar. A richly decorated Gothic arch at the high altar is said to contain the relics of St Augustine.

Before leaving Pavia, have a bowl of the town's speciality, the hearty *zuppa alla pavese*, a recipe said to have been concocted by a peasant woman for Francis I of France. The king was about to lose the battle of Pavia (1525) to the Spanish when he stopped for a bite to eat at a nearby cottage. His hostess wanted her humble minestrone to be fit for a king, so she added toasted bread, cheese and eggs.

Cremona

About two hours' drive from Pavia lies the city of **Cremona ❸**, a pleasant market town on the banks of the Po River and world-famous centre of violin-making. The greatest of Cremonese violin-makers was Antonio Stradivari (1644–1737), whose secret formula for varnish may account for the beautiful sound of a Stradivarius violin. Some of these glorious instruments are on display in the grandiose 13th-century **Palazzo de Comune** (Tues–Sat 9am–6pm, Sun 10am–6pm) in the Civic Collection (open same times but Apr–June and Sept–Oct only; entrance fee) on Corso Vittorio Emanuele and the modern **International School of Violin-Making** nearby.

The pink marble **Duomo** was built in the Lombardic Romanesque style. Although consecrated in 1190, it was not completed until much later. Inside the church, 17th-century tapestries on the *Life of Samson* surround some of the heavy columns.

TIP

Try to visit Mantua on a Thursday, when Piazza delle Erbe, Piazza Mantegna and nearby streets become an enormous market.

Mantua

Because **Mantua** ❹ (Mantova) lies on a peninsula in the River Mincio, surrounded by a lagoon on three sides, it is known as Piccola Venezia (Little Venice). But history has given the city a more resonant name: "Ducal Mantua" because from 1328–1707 the enlightened but despotic Gonzaga family ruled the town from its sombre fortress. Mantua has a slightly musty, medieval atmosphere: the quiet cobbled streets at night could easily be a stage set from a Shakespearean comedy or a Verdi opera.

During the Renaissance, the Gonzaga court was one of the bright lights of Italian culture, especially under the influence of the Marchioness Isabella d'Este (1474–1539), who modelled her life on *Il Cortegione*, a textbook for courtiers and ladies written by Castiglione. She even gave Castiglione a palace in Mantua. She also hired Raphael, Mantegna and Giulio Romano to decorate the Reggia dei Gonzaga (**Palazzo Ducale**), once the largest palace in Europe. The public can visit a selection of the palace's 450 or so rooms by joining a tour (May–Sep Tues–Sun 8.45am–7.15pm, last entrance 6.30pm; entrance fee). Particularly worth seeing are the nine tapestries in the Appartamento degli Arazzi that were made in Flanders from drawings by Raphael. The Camera degli Sposi (the matrimonial suite) is decorated with frescos by Mantegna depicting scenes from the lives of the Marquess Ludovico Gonzaga and his wife, Barbara of Brandenburg.

Across town is the **Palazzo Te** (Tues–Sun 9am–6pm, Mon 1–6pm, times vary when exhibitions are on; entrance fee), the supremely elegant Gonzaga summer residence. Designed by Giulio Romano in 1525, this palace is delicate and pleasing. Many rooms are decorated with frescos of summer scenes, and there is a lovely garden.

BELOW: a violin workshop in Cremona.

Mantua's **Duomo**, located near the Reggia, has a baroque façade added in 1756. Inside, the cathedral has a Renaissance design and stucco decoration by Giulio Romano. Also worth a visit is the **Basilica di Sant'Andrea** in Piazza Mantegna. The Florentine L.B. Alberti designed most of Sant'Andrea, starting in 1472, but the dome was added in the 18th century. Inside, Sant'Andrea is both simple and grand. The frescos that adorn the walls were designed by the great painter Andrea Mantegna, who died in 1506, and executed by his pupils, among them Correggio.

Map on pages 216–7

Bergamo

If you want to escape from the hot stillness of "the waveless plain of Lombardy", there is no more restful or picturesque town than **Bergamo ❺**, too often bypassed by tourists racing along the autostrada between Milan and Venice. Bergamo is, in fact, two cities: Bergamo Bassa and Bergamo Alta.

Though pleasant and spacious, the modern **Bergamo Bassa**, where the railway station is situated, is less dramatic than its parent town which rises upon a rough-hewn crag. Beneath its shadow runs Via Pignola, lined with elegant palaces built between the 16th and 18th centuries. But the real treasure of Bergamo Bassa is the **Accademia Carrara** (Tues–Sun 10am–1pm and 2.30–5.30pm; entrance fee). Where else but in Italy can you find, in a small city, a collection of paintings that the grandest metropolis would be proud to have? In this case, it is thanks to the good taste of the 18th-century Count Giacomo Carrara. There is no need to queue to look at paintings by Pisanello, Lotto, Carpaccio, Bellini and Mantegna, since the museum is often virtually deserted except for the cordial guards. Opposite the Carrara, the **Galleria d'Arte Moderna e Contemporanea** (Tues–Sun 10am–1pm and 3–7pm) hosts excellent exhibitions by contemporary artists and sculptors.

If you enjoy mountain-climbing, take the creaking funicular to **Bergamo Alta**, a medieval town built in warm brown stone. The best spot in which to sit and admire it is the central **Piazza Vecchia** – a good place to find the local speciality *polenta con gli uccelli* (polenta with quail). The piazza is flanked by the 17th-century Palazzo Nuovo and the 12th-century Palazzo della Ragione. Beyond the medieval building's arcade is the small Piazza del Duomo, packed with ecclesiastical treasures: the Romanesque **Santa Maria Maggiore** and the Renaissance **Colleoni Chapel** (daily 9am–12.30pm and 2–6.30pm, Nov–Feb Tues–Sun until 4.30pm), designed by Amadeo who contributed to the Certosa di Pavia, and with an 18th-century ceiling by Tiepolo. The chapel is dedicated to the Bergamesque *condottiere* Bartolomeo Colleoni. The mercenary fought so well for the Venetians that he was rewarded with an estate in his native province, which, at that time, was under Venetian rule. Operatic composer Gaetano Donizetti is buried here. He was born in Bergamo in 1797 to a seamstress mother and pawnbroker father. He died here in 1848, quite insane, having composed 75 operas, of which the best-known today is *Lucia di Lammermoor*. Just behind the Citadella is the **Museo Donizettiano** (Donizetti Birthplace Museum; June–Sept Tues–Sun 9.30am–1pm and 2–5.30pm, Oct–May mornings only). Within are several of the composer's artefacts, such as his piano and portraits. ❑

The Palazzo Ducale in Mantua.

BELOW: the richly sculpted stonework of Cappella Colleoni in Bergamo Alta.

THE LAKES

Map on pages 222–3

ITALY
●Rome

lthough close to the Alps, the Italian Lakes enjoy cool summers and mild winters which make the region ideal for hikers, windsurfers, or anyone who enjoys magnificent landscapes

The Italian Lakes have long been a retreat for romantics. Writers drawn to their shores include Pliny the Younger, Shelley, Stendhal and D.H. Lawrence. "What can one say of Lake Maggiore, of the Borromean Islands, of Lake Como, except to pity people who do not go mad over them?" rote Stendhal. Today, they are also a playground for the rich, as well as a popular destination for tourists and honeymooners from all over the world, drawn to their ravishing scenery. But despite the number of visitors, and the lakes' proximity to Milan's international airport (Lake Como, for instance, is a 90-minute drive away), the region has lost none of its allure.

There are five major lakes in the Italian Lake District (from west to east: Lakes Maggiore, Lugano, Como, Iseo and Garda), and each has its own character. The lakes were formed during the last Ice Age, which ended around 11,000 years ago, and are the result of glaciers thrusting down from the Alps and gouging out deep valleys wherever softer rock created an easy pathway for the ice. Later, as the ice melted, the lakes were formed in the valley bottoms. All run roughly north to south and all enjoy sheltered microclimates that make them warm and mild in winter especially on the southern shores which benefit from winter sunshine – the northern shores tend to be overshadowed by Alpine peaks).

LEFT:
Lake Maggiore.
BELOW: the shoreline at Lake Garda.

Another phenomenon, which makes the lakes – particularly Lake Garda – popular with sailors and windsurfers, is the dependable offshore wind, caused by temperature and air-pressure differences between the warmer water and the cooler surrounding mountains. unbathers on the shores of the lake can bask in warm till air, while a stiff wind blows on the lake itself.

Lake Maggiore

The westernmost lake, **Lago Maggiore ❶**, has a special attraction: the **Borromean Islands ❷**, named after their owners, a prominent Milanese family whose members included a cardinal, a bishop and a saint. **Isola Bella**, the most romantic of the three islands, was a desolate ock with just a few cottages until the 16th century, when Count Charles Borromeo III decided to civilise the island in honour of his wife, Isabella. With the help of the architect Angelo Crivelli, Charles designed the splendid palace and gardens (mid-Mar–Oct daily 9am– oon and 1.30–5.30pm; entrance fee).

Isola dei Pescatori is, as the name suggests, a fishing village. Another Borromean palace and elaborate botanical gardens decorate **Isola Madre** (same opening times as Isola Bella). All three islands are served by ferries from the main lakeside towns.

The most famous and liveliest settlement on the shores of Lake Maggiore is **Stresa ❸** (put on the literary map

Ceiling decoration in Como's cathedral. The building was started in 1396 and only completed in the 18th century.

by Hemingway's *A Farewell to Arms*), with its many beautiful *belle époque* vi las. Two famous villas adjoining the landing stage are the **Villa Ducale**, res dence of the philosopher Antonio Rosmini (1797–1855), and the **Vill Pallavicino** (daily Mar–Oct 9am–6pm; entrance fee) just outside town on th road to Arona, remarkable for its fine gardens. From Stresa, it's a short drive c cable-car ride from Stresa Lido to the summit of **Monte Mottarone**, from wher there is a stunning view of the Alps, the lake and the town below.

Baveno **4**, northwest of Stresa, is a small, quiet town near the islands and th site of many villas, among them the **Castello Branca** where the British Quee Victoria spent the spring of 1879. The drive south from Stresa to **Arona 5** alon the Lungolago is especially pretty: the road is tree-lined, the views of the lake and islands spectacular. Arona itself is a rather unremarkable resort town, but does contain a number of attractive 15th-century buildings.

Lake Lugano

Much of **Lago di Lugano 6** lies within Swiss territory; only the very eastern ti is Italian, plus the enclave of Campione d'Italia, a little lakeside town tha remains proudly and typically Italian, whilst being entirely surrounded by Swis territory (and using Swiss currency and postage stamps). Visitors come to Cam pione for the casino and its nightlife.

Lake Como

Lago di Como 7, known locally as "the Lario", is the most dramatic of th lakes. It is almost 50 km (30 miles) long and up to 5 km (3 miles) across; at 41 metres (1,345 ft), it is the deepest inland lake in Europe. At many points th

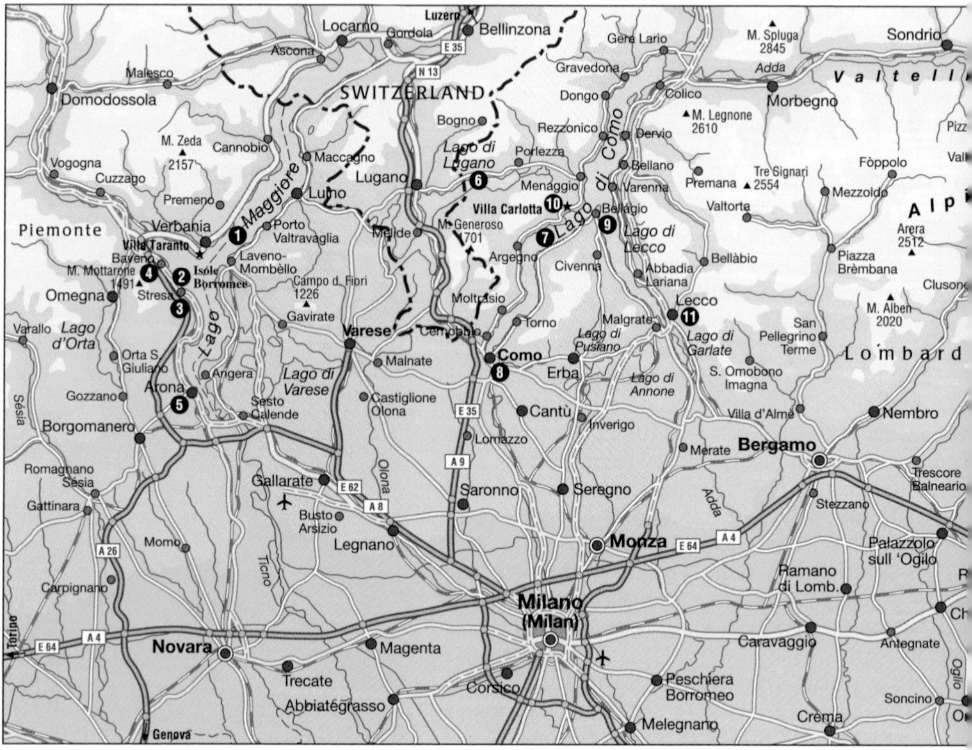

Map below

hore is a sheer cliff, and the Alps (providing year-round skiing on the glaciers, though they are receding) loom like a wall at the northern end of the lake. **Como** itself is a historic yet thriving town. Silk-weaving, which for many years was onfined to homes and small workshops in Como, is now concentrated in several factories.

Como's **Giardini Pubblici** are a pleasant place to relax and look over the lake. n the midst of these gardens stands the Tempio Voltiano (Tues–Sun 10am–noon nd 3–6pm in summer, 10am–noon and 2–4pm in winter; entrance fee), a classic rotunda dedicated to Alessandro Volta, who gave his name to the volt. Many f the instruments he used in his electrical experiments are on display.

It's an easy walk across the town to **Santa Maria Maggiore** (daily 7am–noon nd 3–7pm), Como's 14th-century marble cathedral. The intricately carved portal is flanked by statues of the two Plinys, who were among the earliest admirers of Lake Como. "Are you given to studying, or do you prefer fishing or unting, or do you go in for all three?" the younger Pliny asked a friend, and oasted that all three activities were possible at Lake Como.

The 11th-century church of **Sant'Abbondio** (daily 9am–noon and 3–6pm) n the outskirts of Como will transport you back to Como's pre-resort days, vhen it was a pious and prosperous medieval village. Chances are that you will ave this solemn Lombardic church to yourself. The 14th-century frescos of the *ife of Jesus*, in the apse, make it worth the trip.

Although the distance between the two cities is not great as the crow flies, it an take an hour of driving on narrow, twisting roads to reach **Bellagio ❾**, "the ewel of the lake", from Como. Going by public boat from Como's pier is a more pleasant way of getting there. Bellagio sits on the point of land that divides Lake

After the murder of celebrity designer Gianni Versace in 1998, it was here, in the grounds of his beloved Montrasio villa, that his family chose to scatter his ashes.

BELOW: sculpture by Canova in Villa Carlotta, across the lake from Bellagio.

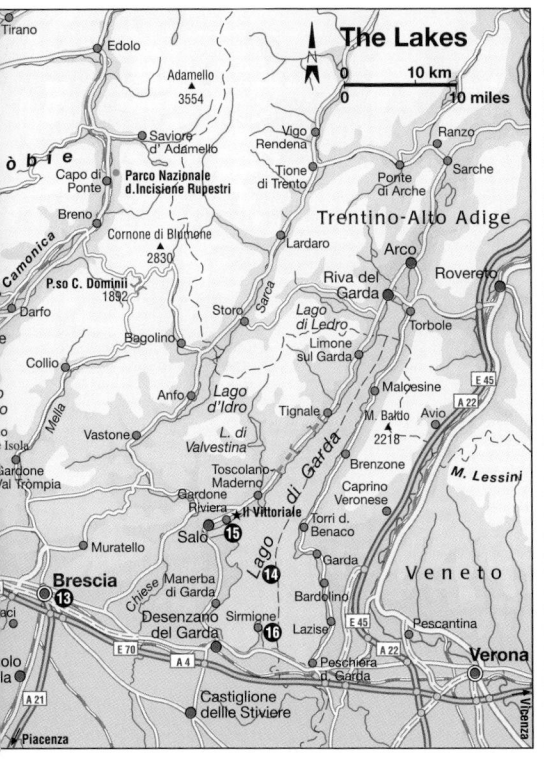

TIP

The lifestyle store La Tessitura is a temple to silk awash with garments, textiles and furnishing accessories by Mantero, Como's historic silk manufacturer. Viale Roosevelt 2/a, Como; Tues–Sat 11am–7pm; tel: 031-321666; www.latessitura.com.

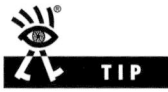

Como into three parts. From here you can see the entire expanse of the lake an enjoy a spectacular view of the Alps. "Sublimity and grace here combine to a degre which is equalled but not surpassed by the most famous site in the world, the Ba of Naples," wrote Stendhal in *The Charterhouse of Parma*. The Frenchman set th opening scenes of his novel in the **Villa Carlotta** ⑩ (across the lake from Bellagio after staying here as a guest. Today the villa (Apr–Sept daily 9am–noon and 2–6pm Mar and Oct until 4.30pm; entrance fee), originally built by a Prussian princess fo her daughter, and its idyllic gardens provide the perfect setting for a picnic lunch

Lecco ⑪, a pleasant city at the southeastern end of Lake Como, is famous a the setting of Alessandro Manzoni's *The Betrothed*, a 19th-century novel whic is a classic of Italian literature, and a revealing piece of social history. The autho Italy's greatest 19th-century novelist, was a native of Lecco and a politica activist instrumental in bringing about Italy's unification. Visitors can explore hi childhood home, the **Villa Manzoni** (Tues–Sun 9.30am–5.30pm; entrance fee)

Among the more antique attractions of the city is the **Basilica**, with its fin frescos from the 14th century depicting *The Annunciation*, *The Deposition* an *The Life of St Anthony*. The oldest monument in the city is the bridge spannin the River Adda, the **Ponte Azzone Visconti**, built between 1336 and 1338.

Lake Iseo

Lago d'Iseo ⑫ is the fifth-largest of the lakes, measuring 24 km (15 miles) lon by 5 km (3 miles) wide. Views of the lake all focus on the large island that sits i the middle: graphically named **Monte Isola** (Mountain Island), at a height o 600 metres (1,970 ft), this is the largest island of any European lake, and it typ ifies the rugged, mountainous appeal of this lake and its surroundings. Northeas

Below: Santa Giulia Museo della Città, Brescia.

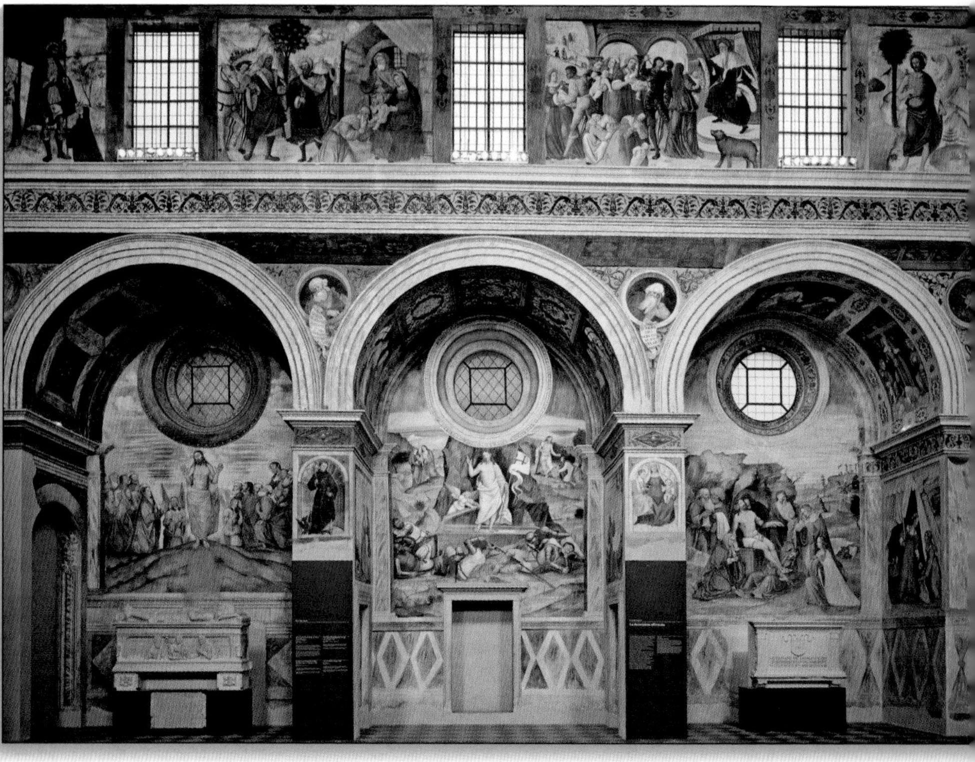

f the lake, the town of **Capo di Ponte** makes a good base for exploring the **Val
amonica**, renowned for its prehistoric rock carvings and designated a Unesco
/orld Heritage Site. Some 158,000 rock carvings have been found, 75 percent
f them in the Capo di Ponte area; dating from as far back as 8,000 years ago,
ey are a record of the hunting and farming activities of the local Camoni tribe.
he local tourist office sells guides to the **Parco Nazionale delle Incisioni
upestri** (National Rock Engravings Park; Tues–Sun 8.30am–7pm, until 4pm
 winter; entrance fee) with five colour-coded trails, or call 0364-42212 for a
uide (Società Archeocamuni).

Southeast of the lake is Lombardy's second city, **Brescia** , which has an
xceptional museum – indeed, **Santa Giulia Museo della Città** (Tues–Sun
.30am–5.30pm; entrance fee) is one of the best historical and archaeological
useum complexes in Italy. Santa Giulia showcases Brescia's past in monu-
ents from the Bronze Age to the present day. It incorporates an 8th-century
unnery, the Renaissance church and cloisters of Santa Giulia, the Romanesque
ratory of Santa Maria, and the Lombard basilica of San Salvatore. The church
one is a major monument, with Byzantine, Lombard and Roman remains. Also
 Brescia, the **Museo delle Armi** in the medieval castle houses Italy's finest
ollection of antique weapons (June–Sept Tues–Sun 10am–5pm, Oct–May
ues–Sun 9.30am–1pm and 2–5pm; entrance fee).

*Lily from Gardone
Riviera.*

ake Garda

ago di Garda  is the cleanest and largest of the Italian lakes. It is especially
opular with Northern European tourists, who come to sail, windsurf and water-
ki. Its equable climate is responsible for Soave and Valpolicella wines.

BELOW: the water-
front at Lake Iseo.

On the shores of this lake is a garish remnant of the
ascist era – **Il Vittoriale** – the home of the flamboyant
alian poet and patriot Gabriele d'Annunzio which was
iven to him by his greatest admirer, Benito Mussolini
ark and gardens daily Apr–Sept 8.30am–8pm,
ct–Mar 9am–5pm; guided tours of house Tues–Sun
pr–Sept 9.30am–7pm, Oct–Mar 9am–1pm and
–5pm; entrance fee). Located in **Gardone Riviera** ⑮,
 one time Lake Garda's most fashionable resort, Il Vit-
riale is more than a house, it is a shrine to d'Annun-
io's dreams of Italian imperialism. Included in the
state is the prow of the warship *Puglia,* built into the
illside. In the auditorium, the plane d'Annunzio flew
uring World War I is suspended from the ceiling.

From Salò and Gardone Riviera it takes no more than
n hour to reach **Sirmione** ⑯, a medieval town built
n a spit of land extending into the lake. The **Rocca
caligera** (Mar–mid-Oct 8.30am–7pm, mid-Oct–Feb
ntil 5pm; entrance fee), a fairytale castle, dominates
e town's entrance. It was originally the fortress of the
caligeri family, rulers of Garda in the 13th century,
nd it is said that they entertained the poet Dante here.
n enjoyable hour or two can be spent exploring the
ocal shops, dipping into churches and following the
ootpath that leads to the tip of the peninsula, with its
xtensive ruins of a Roman spa, the **Grotte di Catullo**
Tues–Sun 9am–7pm, 8.30am–4.30pm in winter;
ntrance fee). ❑

Map on
pages
222–3

Maps:
Area 216
City 228

PIEDMONT, VALLE D'AOSTA AND LIGURIA

*If it is not so Italian as Italy it is at least more
Italian than anything but Italy*

— HENRY JAMES

ITALY
●Rome

BELOW: the city's
symbol, the Mole
Antonelliana.

Piedmont (Piemonte) may strike today's visitor, as it did Henry James, a
not very Italian. The bordering nations of France and Switzerland hav
contributed much to the cultural life of this northwestern region. Mor
over, the Alpine landscapes of Piedmont, especially in the dramatic Val
d'Aosta, are very different from scenery elsewhere in Italy. But the particula
Piedmontese twist on Italian life is not unappealing. It's as if the cool mountai
breezes have bestowed a calming effect on the people. No wonder that it was
Piedmontese king, Victor Emmanuel, and his Piedmontese adviser, Cour
Camillo Cavour, who guided Italy to independence.

Turin ❻ (Torino), the capital of Piedmont, is a genuinely Italian city, but i
proximity and centuries-old ties to France give it a strong Gallic flavour. Durin
the Middle Ages, it was part of a Lombardic duchy, but in the 16th century
became the capital of the French province of Savoy. Following the Risorgiment
(see page 55), it was the capital of united Italy from 1861 to 1865.

Today, Turin is headquarters for some of Italy's most successful industrie
including the Fiat automobile company. But the factories of Turin are a long wa

om the city's gracious centre, with its wide streets and beautiful squares, gar-
ens and parks where visitors can soak up the sun and sample the spirit of this
ost modern of Italian cities. Turin hosted a successful 2006 Winter Olympics,
ndorsing its prestige. Many of the Alpine events were held at the ski resort Ses-
iere, part of the extensive Franco-Italian Milky Way area.

istoric town centre

he hub of civic life in Turin is the fashionable **Via Roma**, an arcaded shop-
ing street that connects the **Stazione Porta Nuova Ⓐ** with **Piazza Castello
Ⓑ**, a huge rectangular Renaissance square planned in 1584. In the centre stands
alazzo Madama**, a 15th-century castle that houses the **Museo Civico di Arte
ntica** (Museum of Ancient Art). Included in this museum's collections is a
opy of part of the famous *Book of Hours* of the Duc de Berry, illustrated by Jan
an Eyck.

Palazzo Madama.

Another fine building on the Piazza Castello is the baroque church of **San
orenzo**, once the royal chapel. The royal residence was the 17th-century
alazzo Reale Ⓒ** (Tues–Sun 8.30am–7.30pm; guided tours; entrance fee; gar-
en open daily). From its balcony, Prince Carlo Alberto declared war on Austria
1 March 1848. Nearby is the **Armeria Reale** (Royal Armoury; Tues–Fri
am–2pm, Sat–Sun 10am–7pm; entrance fee; tel: 011-543889).

Behind the Palazzo Reale, in **Piazza San Giovanni**, are the **Duomo Ⓓ** (Catte-
rale di San Giovanni Battista; Mon–Sat 7am–12.30pm and 3–7pm, Sun
am–12.30pm and 3–7pm) and **Campanile**. The former is a Renaissance con-
truction designed by the Tuscan Meo del Caprino; the Campanile is the work of
baroque architect. The Duomo was damaged by fire in 1997, but fortunately
1e flames did not consume the **Cappella della Sacra
indone** (Chapel of the Holy Shroud; daily 8am–noon
nd 3–7pm; entrance fee) – a work of Guarino Guarini.
t contains the Turin Shroud, for centuries believed to
e the shroud in which Christ was wrapped after the
rucifixion. The cloth is imprinted with the image of a
earded man crowned with thorns. Although carbon
ating suggests that the shroud is the work of clever
1edieval forgers, recent tests imply death by crucifix-
on. For four centuries the royal House of Savoy owned
he shroud, but on his death in 1983, the exiled king
Jmberto left the relic to the Vatican. It will, however,
emain in Turin, but only a copy is on view. The real
hing is shown every 25 years – every jubilee – the next
eing 2025.

The Piedmontese capital may seem an unlikely centre
or the study of Egyptian art, but it is home to the
vorld's second-largest museum devoted to ancient
gypt after Cairo: the **Egyptian Museum** (June–Aug
ues–Sun 9.30am–8.30pm, 8.30am–7.30pm in winter;
ntrance fee) is housed in the **Palazzo dell'Accademia
elle Scienze Ⓔ**, off Via Roma. The collection was
ssembled by Charles Emmanuel III, and includes the
ascinating tomb of the architect Kha. The same *palazzo*
lso contains a good picture collection on the second
loor in the **Galleria Sabauda** (Tues, Fri, Sat and Sun
.30am–2pm, Wed–Thurs 2–7.30pm; entrance fee).
Made up of the main art collection of the House of

BELOW: the authen-
tic Al Bicerin café in
Turin, for coffee and
chocolates.

Turin

N

0   500 m
0   500 yds

Savoy, this is one of the country's richest repositories of paintings from the 14th to 18th centuries. Highlights in the Italian Masters section include works by Veronese, Bellini and Mantegna, as well as a selection by Piedmontese artists such as Gaudenzio Ferrari and Defendente Ferrari. Famous Dutch and Flemish artists such as Van Dyck and Jan Van Eyck are well represented, as are French works, including landscape paintings by Claude Lorrain and Poussin.

Cine scene

Turin's enduring city symbol, the Mole Antonelliana, now houses the great **Museo Nazionale del Cinema ⓕ** (Tues–Sun 9am–8pm, until 11pm on Sat; entrance fee). From 1906 to 1916 Turin was the world film production capital, until it was overtaken by Hollywood (and, in Italy, by Rome). Spread over five levels, the museum outlines the story of cinema. Costumes range from Marilyn Monroe's bodice to Fellini's scarf, coat and hat. At the heart of the museum is the Aula del Tempio, where clips of films of yesterday and today are screened. In the Macchina del Cinema section, the craft of film-making is explored – such as editing, sound effects and casting. The ride to the top of the Mole is by panoramic, glass-walled lift (Tues–Fri 10am–8pm, Sat 10am–11pm, Sun 10am–8pm; entrance fee) which in less than a minute soars up to 85 metres (279ft), from where there are spectacular views over the city and the amphitheatre of the Alps.

Vintage car in the Museo Nazionale dell'Automobile.

The **GAM ⓖ** (Galleria Civica d'Arte Moderna e Contemporanea; Tues–Sun 10am–6pm; entrance fee) has excellent visiting exhibitions and an illustrious permanent collection featuring works by such luminaries as Picasso, Modigliani, Chagall, Renoir and Klee.

BELOW: inside the Museo Nazionale del Cinema.

Car capital

It is no surprise that the automobile capital of Italy has a fine museum of cars. It can take hours to explore the **Museo Nazionale dell'Automobile ⓗ** (Tues–Sun 10am–6.30pm; entrance fee). Exhibits include the earliest Fiat, the Itala that won the world's longest automobile race (between Peking [Beijing] and Paris in 1907) and an elegant Rolls-Royce Silver Ghost. This area south of the city centre was the heart of Turin's car industry. The Fiat company (Fabbrica Italiana Automobile Torino), founded in 1899, made Turin *the* city of cars. The areas of Lingotto, Italia 61, Mirafiori and Millefonti, once the powerhouse of the industry, have now been spruced up and transformed into a multi-million-euro "suburbs project", with many new sporting facilities constructed for the 2006 Winter Olympics. Lingotto, the cultural and trade centre risen on the site of the historical Fiat factory, was the epicentre of the 2006 Games. Under the skilful eye of architect Renzo Piano, the area was transformed into a multi-purpose exhibition centre. Today, it is the setting for big events and exhibitions, such as the biannual Salone del Gusto, the international Slow Food Movement fair. Lingotto also encompasses an auditorium, a vast shopping mall and two hotels, the Meridien and Art+Tech. Hotel guests can use the former Fiat test track on the roof for jogging.

Also on the Lingotto rooftop is the Pinacoteca Giovanni e Marella Agnelli (Tues–Sun 10am–7pm; entrance fee; tel: 011-006 2713). Designed by Renzo Piano and known as "Lo Scrigno" (the jewel case), it showcases treasures from the art collection of the Agnelli family, the owners of Fiat, including works by Picasso and Renoir.

BELOW: Gran Paradiso National Park, south of Aosta.

To the west of the city at the entrance to the Valle di Susa lies the Castello di Rivoli, which houses the **Museo d'Arte Contemporanea** (Tues–Thur 10am–5pm, Fri–Sun 10am–9pm; entrance fee) Here the imposing old baroque building, designed by Juvarra, contrasts with the very, very new. Works by avant-garde artists such as Jeff Koons and Maurizio Cattelan contrast dramatically with the stuccoed interior. There are around 400 pieces in the permanent collection, and major temporary exhibitions are also staged. There is a good museum café and excellent restaurant, the Combal.Zero.

Cross the Po to visit the **Monte dei Cappuccini ❶**, a small hill crowned by a Capuchin convent. From here, take a bus or the rack railway to the **Basilica di Superga** (Apr–Oct Mon–Fri 9am–noon and 3–6pm, Sat–Sun 9am–12.45pm and 3–6.45pm, Nov–Mar closes one hour earlier), a "great votive temple" (Henry James) by Juvarra which houses the tombs of the kings of Sardinia and the princes of Savoy. This basilica sits on a hill commanding a splendid view of the natural amphitheatre of the Alps. The circular church is dominated by the 75-metre (246-ft) dome, flanked by twin 60-metre (196-ft) high bell towers.

Hills and valleys

Southeast of Turin, Piedmont turns into a region of rolling hills and long valleys. In some ways it is reminiscent of Tuscany, and like Tuscany it is an excellent wine-growing area. From Turin head towards Alba along the autostrada. If you have time, make a stop at **Bra ❼**, birthplace of the Slow Food Movement *(see page 97)*, to see a fine baroque church, **Sant'Andrea**, and an attractive Gothic building called the **Casa Traversa**. The hills surrounding the small town of **La Morra ❽**, 10 km (6 miles) from Bra, are the source of one of Italy's greatest

wines, Barolo. In **Grinzane Cavour** ❾, between La Morra and Alba, is the Castello Cavour, an imposing 13th-century castle, the feudal home of Count Cavour, which also houses a wine museum (Wed–Mon 9.30am–7pm, last entry 6.30pm; closed Jan; entrance fee).

Alba ❿ has long been a favourite with gourmets. It sits at the centre of an area famous for white truffles. These treats are the principal attraction at the city's October fair. Alba also has a fine late 15th-century Gothic cathedral, with a 16th-century inlaid wooden choir.

For more taste treats, proceed to **Asti** ⓫, a city at the centre of a valley that produces Asti Spumante and other famous wines. The Gothic cathedral is a splendid edifice, with three ornate portals and circular openings above. The nearby baptistery of San Pietro, dating from the 12th century, is the most interesting of the city's medieval monuments.

Maps:
Area 216
City 228

Valle d'Aosta

The beautiful Alpine valleys around Piedmont have much to offer. The region is noted for its glaciers, hilltop castles, clear mountain lakes and streams, pine forests and green meadows. The most striking area is the Valle d'Aosta. Here rise Europe's highest mountains: Mont Blanc, Monte Rosa and the Cervino (Matterhorn). The capital, **Aosta** ⓬, was an important city in Roman times and has many interesting Roman ruins. Roman walls surround the city, and the ruins of the **Roman Theatre** (daily 9am–8pm Apr–Aug, until 7pm Mar and Sept, until 6.30pm Feb and Oct, until 5pm Nov–Jan), in the northwest corner of Aosta, include the well-preserved backdrop of the stage. Emperor Augustus nicknamed Aosta the "Rome of the Alps", and it is the Arch of Augustus that guards the main entrance to the city.

Some of Italy's finest wines come from Le Langhe, the hilly region south of Turin.

Dating from Aosta's medieval period are the cathedral and several smaller churches. Among the latter group, the **Church of Sant'Orso** (outside the walls on Via Sant'Orso) is the most interesting. The architecture is a strange mix of Gothic and Romanesque. St Orso – who converted the first Christians in the Valle d'Aosta – is buried beneath the altar. Be sure to visit the cloister, which dates back to the 12th century and is known for its unusual carved pillars.

The valley southeast of Aosta contains many fine castles, in particular those at **Fénis** ⓭, now magnificently restored (Mar–Sept daily 9am–6.30pm, July and Aug until 7.30pm, Oct–Feb Wed–Mon 10am–noon and 1.30–4.30pm; entrance fee), and **Issogne** ⓮ (daily 9.30am–6.30pm in summer, 10am–4.30pm in winter; entrance fee), which were used as both residences and fortresses. The Lord of Verrès, Giorgio de Challant, commissioned construction of the castle at Issogne in 1497.

BELOW: medieval castle in the Valle d'Aosta.

The region of Liguria

A narrow strip of coastline sandwiched between sea and mountains, Liguria curves and twists in an east–west arch from the French border to Tuscany. Known as the Italian Riviera, the region is favoured by a year-round mild climate, excellent beaches and the dramatic Maritime and Ligurian Apennines, which plunge in sheer cliffs or slope gradually to the sea. It is an area of sudden

In celebration of 2004, Via Garibaldi, "the street of palaces", now links the three most prestigious palazzi – home to the city's most celebrated art museums – to become a museum-street. Palazzo Rosso and Bianco are joined by the Palazzo Grimaldi-Doria Tursi, formerly the town hall, and the most important building on the street.

BELOW: Genoa's historic streets.

contrasts, not merely between rocky shores and deep green-blue water, but between cosmopolitan resorts and isolated villages, bustling ports and quiet inlets.

Genoa ⓯ (Genova) rises above the sea like a great theatre. Its tiers are elegant *palazzi* and its pit is a noisy, strong-smelling port, the most important in Italy. La Superba, as the city was known in its heyday, rose to prominence between the 11th and 15th centuries, growing rich on trade with the East, and economic and cultural control of Liguria and the island of Corsica. In 2004 it was designated a European City of Culture.

Immediately behind the docks, the lower city begins. Here streets are ancient and narrow with twisting alleys – called *carrugi* – nowadays lined with exotic shops. The afternoon *passeggiata* in Genoa takes place on the elegant **Via Luccoli Ⓐ**, a *carrugio* of slightly wider proportions than most. Strolling along with the prosperous Genoese, you can decide for yourself whether Mark Twain was right to consider the Genoese women the most beautiful in Italy.

Not far from the dock that serves large luxury liners is the **Stazione Principe Ⓑ**, an airy building facing a small square with a striking statue of Christopher Columbus, the most famous Genoese of all time. From the railway station follow the Via Balbi, an avenue lined on both sides with sombre Renaissance palaces. Stop at No. 10, the 17th-century **Palazzo Reale Ⓒ**, famous for the Galleria degli Specchi (Hall of Mirrors) and its art collection (Tues–Wed 9am–1.30pm, Thur–Sun 9am–7pm; entrance fee).

Continue towards the centre on Via Balbi until it becomes the patrician **Via Garibaldi Ⓓ**. This street splits Genoa in two; to your right are the twisting alleys of the old town, and to the left are the newer sections on the hillside. No. 11 Via Garibaldi is one of the most magnificent of Genoese palaces, **Palazzo Bianco Ⓔ**

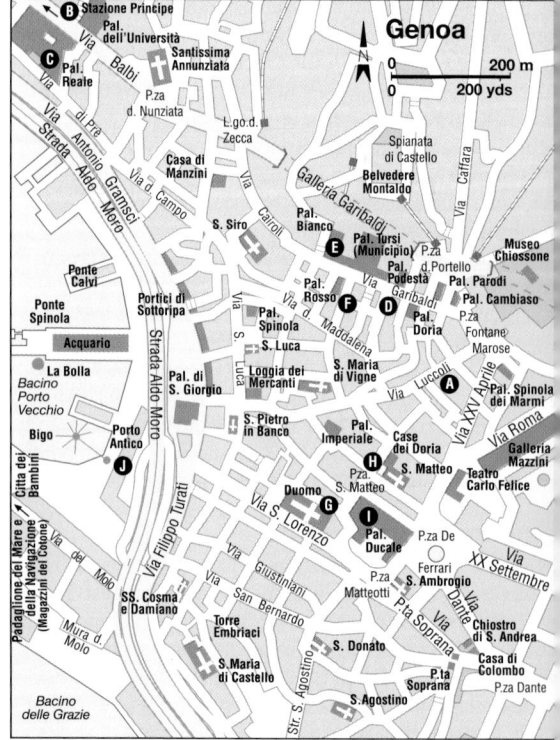

Genoa

0   200 m
0   200 yds

Tues–Fri 9am–7pm, Sat and Sun 10am–7pm). This 16th-century structure was originally white, but the stone has darkened with time. The façade is baroque, due to major remodelling in the early 18th century. Inside, an art collection features many extraordinary works by Flemish masters.

Across the street is the **Palazzo Rosso** ❼ (gallery open Tues–Fri 9am–7pm, Sat–Sun 10am–7pm; entrance fee), featuring a beautiful courtyard. Most of the other Renaissance residences on Via Garibaldi are privately owned and can only be admired from the outside. According to legend, the Romanesque-Gothic **Duomo** ❼ (12th–14th-century) was founded by St Lawrence in the 3rd century. However, history dates the building to 1118. One of its Gothic portals bears a relief sculpture of the Roman saint's gruesome martyrdom. While being burnt alive, St Lawrence said to his tormentors: "One side has been roasted, turn me over and eat it."

The Doria family, who ruled Genoa in the Middle Ages, built their houses and private church around the **Piazza San Matteo** ❼, lying just behind the cathedral. Each of the buildings on this small, elegant piazza has a black-and-white façade. Between San Matteo and the port lies the most beguiling part of old Genoa, best explored by day. Also near the cathedral is the 16th-century **Palazzo Ducale** ❼, once the seat of government and now a cultural centre.

Door knocker in the Palazzo Ducale.

Towards the medieval city's eastern limits is the **Porta Soprana**, the twin-towered gateway and the **Casa Colombo de Cristoforo** (Sat–Sun 10am–6pm; entrance fee). This is the reconstructed boyhood home of Genoa's most famous son, Christopher Columbus (1451–1506).

Port area

From here it is a short stroll through labyrinthine alleys to the **Porto Antico** ❼. This recently renovated port area maintains its raffish charm, with rough and ready dockside cafés, although the old warehouses and customs buildings have been converted to other uses.

Today's famous Genoese son is the architect, Renzo Piano, who did so much for the Columbus celebrations in 1992, marking the 500th anniversary of the discovery of the Americas. Building upon his transformation of the harbour, the Porto Antico was given a facelift for the city's celebrations as European City of Culture in 2004.

Those with children in tow should visit Renzo Piano and Peter Chermayeff's visionary **Acquario** (daily Mar–June and Sept–Oct 9am–7.30pm, Sat–Sun until 8.30pm, July–Aug 8.30am–10pm, Nov–Feb 9.30am–7.30pm, Sat–Sun until 8.30pm; last entrance usually two hours before closing; entrance fee), Europe's largest aquarium. Among more than 600 different species are sharks, dolphins and the highly popular penguins.

Next to the Aquarium, Renzo Piano's **La Bolla** (daily Mar–Oct 10am–7pm, Nov–Feb until 5pm; entrance fee) is a futuristic glass-and-steel bubble containing tropical plants and a collection of rare ferns among which butterflies flit around freely. **Il Grande Bigo** (Tues–Sun 10am–11pm, Mon 4–11pm; times reduced in winter; admission charge) is an enormous crane, visible for miles, which whisks passengers 40 metres (130 ft) high in a cylindrical lift for panoramic views over the city and waterfront.

BELOW: in the Acquario.

The dockyards (Darsena) have been restored and renovated, creating a hug
area of entertainment and culture dedicated to the sea. A vast museum com
plex with over 20 exhibition areas presents a voyage through time, coverin
every aspect of maritime culture. **The Galata Museo del Mare** (Museum c
the Sea; daily Nov–end Feb Tues–Fri 10am–6pm, until 7.30pm Sat and Su
Mar–Oct Tues–Sun 10am–7.30pm, last entry one hour 30 mins before clos
ing; entrance fee) is housed in the old cotton warehouses. It features a perma
nent exhibition of ships, artefacts, and a new room dedicated to the voyages c
Christopher Columbus.

Also within the cotton warehouses (Magazzini del Cotone) is the Città de
Bambini (July–Sept Tues–Sun 11.30am–7.30pm, Oct–June 10am–6pm
entrance fee) a hands-on, high-tech interactive space for three- to 14-year-old

The Italian Rivieras

Flanking Genoa on either side are two famous and beautiful coasts; each offer
ample doses of sand, sun and sea, but they are quite different. The western **Rivier
di Ponente**, stretching from Genoa to the French border, is the longer of the tw
and the one with more popular resorts. The eastern **Riviera di Levante** is cha
acterised by rocky cliffs and promontories, and has a large naval port at La Spezi

Heading towards France from Genoa, you'll pass **Savona ⑯**, a port and indus
trial centre. With the exception of a small art gallery on Via Quarda Superior
Savona offers little of interest to the tourist. The town of **Finale Ligure ⑰**,
30-minute drive further on, is a more inviting place. Visit the **Church of Sa
Biagio**, which has an octagonal Gothic bell tower adjoining.

The most important town on the Riviera di Ponente from an artistic and his
toric point of view is **Albenga ⑱**. The Romans founde
a port on this site in 181 BC, but over the centuries th
topography has changed, and today the old centre i
about a mile from the beach. Surrounding the town is
well-preserved medieval wall and three large 17th
century gates. The cathedral of **San Michele** dates bac
to the 5th century. Even older are the Roman aqueduc
and the ruins of a Roman amphitheatre. In addition t
the historic monuments are fine facilities for swimmin
and boating. The nearby resort of **Alassio ⑲** has lon
been popular with celebrities. It lies in a pretty bay wi
a 3-km (2-mile) sandy beach.

Imperia ⑳ was once two separate seaside town
Oneglia and Porto Maurizio. It was Mussolini's idea t
unite the two and name the city after a nearby river. **Cors
Matteotti**, a wide boulevard with magnificent views c
the coast, links the two town centres. **Oneglia**, in the eas
known for its olive oil and pasta production, is the mor
industrial and modern sector. A large cathedral, **San Mau
rizio**, towers over the narrow streets of **Porto Maurizi**

The large resort of **San Remo ㉑** was once a gath
ering spot for European aristocracy. The partially ren
ovated resort offers two enjoyable diversions
walking along the famous palm-lined promenade an
gambling at the casino. Near the tourist office at th
city's centre is an authentic Russian Orthodox churc
(1913), the **Chiesa Russa** (daily 9.30am–12.30p
and 3–6.30pm, 6pm in winter; small entrance fee

TIP

If you're visiting the
resort of Alassio don't
miss the Caffè Roma in
the centre of town. It
has a wall – the
Muretto – decorated
with tiles bearing the
signatures of, among
others, Ernest Heming-
way, Sophia Loren and
Sir Winston Churchill.

BELOW: Camogli.

Another landmark is the Art Nouveau **Villa Nobel**, where inventor and philanthropist Alfred Nobel (1833–96) lived.

The gateway to France is nearby at **Ventimiglia ㉒**, a centre of flower cultivation and a pleasant city with an excellent Friday market and a delapidated medieval quarter. The major architectural attraction is the 11th-century **Duomo**. Set on the Cape about 6 km (4 miles) from Ventimiglia in the village of Mortola is the **Giadino Hanbury** (Mar–mid-June daily 9.30am–5pm, mid-June–mid-Sept daily 9.30am–6pm, mid-Sept–mid-Oct daily 9.30am–5pm, mid-Oct–Feb 9.30am–4pm; entrance fee), where you will find the colourful flora of five continents.

West of Ventimiglia, virtually on the French frontier are the prehistoric caves, **Balzi Rossi** (Tues–Sun 9am–12.30pm and 2–6pm in summer, 9am–1pm and 2.30–6pm winter; free; museum same opening; entrance fee). In addition to skeletons dating from over 100,000 years ago, there are fossils, wall drawings, tools, weapons and fertility figures.

San Remo's Russian Orthodox church.

Riviera di Levante

Among the eastern suburbs of Genoa is **Quarto dei Mille**, famous as the starting point of Garibaldi's valiant 1,000-man expedition that liberated Sicily and led to the unification of Italy. Nearby **Nervi ㉓** is the oldest winter resort on the eastern coast. Here you can take warm sea baths, or follow a 3-km (2-mile) cliff walk.

After the quaint but chic former fishing village of **Camogli**, take the branch off the main road that leads to **Portofino ㉔**, the most exclusive resort on the Riviera. A tiny waterfront village of extraordinary concentrated beauty, it was discovered by wealthy visitors after World War II. Once, only fishing boats docked in the narrow, deep-green inlet, edged on three sides by high cliffs, but it is now a berth for luxury yachts. Part of Portofino's attraction is its size. There are no beaches, and few large shops and restaurants. The pleasures of the port are visual – the reflection of brightly painted houses in the clear water, the ragged edges of stone heights set against the brilliant blue sky. **Rapallo ㉕** is a welcoming family resort, with a large beach and many moderately priced hotels. Other attractions include the 17th-century **Collegiata**, and the 16th-century church of **San Francesco**.

"Paradise on earth" is how Lord Byron described the cluster of five little fishing villages that make up **Le Cinque Terre ㉖**. Monterosso al Mare, Vernazza, Corniglia, Manarola and Riomaggiore cling perilously to the steep rocky coast just north of La Spezia. From Dante to Shelley, the Gulf of La Spezia has been praised so often by poets that it is also known as the Golfo dei Poeti. On its western point the elongated orange and yellow houses of **Portovenere ㉗** stretch up the precipitous mountain.

Anglophiles and romantics should make a pilgrimage to the grotto from where the virile Lord Byron began his famous swim across the Gulf to visit Shelley in **Casa Magni**. If you take the 20-minute boat ride to **Lerici ㉘** you will appreciate what a powerful swimmer the poet must have been. Shelley had less luck against the waves when his ship sank off the coast. A plaque on Casa Magni commemorates the tragedy: "Sailing on a fragile bark he was landed, by an unforeseen chance, in the silence of the Elysian Fields." ❑

BELOW: picturesque Portovenere.

CENTRAL ITALY

Subtle differences in art, cooking, fashion sense and attitude to life – even between neighbouring towns – help to form a destination that appeals to both the heart and the head

To many travellers, Central Italy is the true Italy – that is, the Italy they know from Merchant-Ivory films of E.M. Forster novels, or from the pictures that adorn all the tour brochures. Ironically, the people of this region are reluctant to admit to being Italian at all. They are Tuscan, Florentine, Sienese, Bolognese or Perugian – not a semantic distinction, but a deeply held conviction based on history, culture, and even tribal and genetic differences from the pre-Roman era. And this is an area where history is not the dry stuff of academic books, but a living part of the culture – for anthropologists, Central Italy has long been fertile ground for testing the belief that competition for resources leads people to emphasise their differences. If you want to see this process in action, visit any Umbrian or Tuscan town during its annual festivities – not to mention Siena during Palio, or Florence during Calcio in Costume (Football in Costume) – and feel the intense and elemental atmosphere of inter-parish rivalry.

Such rivalries are reflected in myriad ways that make exploring the region a delight for the sensitive and enquiring traveller. Food is an obvious indicator, whether it be the subtle differences between sheep's-milk cheeses, the more emphatic distinctions between a crisp Orvieto wine and a soft, fruity Chianti, or whether it be the view firmly held by every seafront restaurant along the Tuscan Riviera that theirs is the only authentic fish soup *(cacciucco)*, and that it is far superior to anything the French produce.

Art and architecture is another indicator: labels, such as Florentine, Umbrian School, Lombardic or Pisan Romanesque, at first seem designed to confuse the uninitiated, until continued exposure to some of the world's finest artistic creations leads you to the point where you can distinguish between the light-filled limpidity of the School of Perugino and the crisply delineated and boldly coloured frescos of Benozzo Gozzoli – unmistakably Florentine even when encountered in the tiny Umbrian hill town of Montefalco. ❏

PRECEDING PAGES: Siena's Piazza del Campo.
LEFT: a medieval street in Perugia, decorated for a festival.

EMILIA-ROMAGNA

The gastronomic heart of Italy is also noted for its medieval cities and the late-Roman mosaics of Ravenna – all of which are rewarding reasons for visiting this prosperous region

Maps:
City 242
Area 246

milia-Romagna's winters are cold, wet and foggy, and its summers long and hot. Together with the rich soil of the Po Valley, this climate makes it one of Italy's most prosperous farming regions, famous for its succulent ams and flavoursome Parmesan cheeses.

Emilia-Romagna also has a rich cultural past. The Via Aemilia, a road first uilt by the Romans, cuts through the centre of the region, linking Rimini, ologna, Modena, Parma and Piacenza – all founded by the Romans as way ations along the road from the Adriatic to the interior. The other major cities of milia-Romagna, Ferrara and Ravenna, are off this main thoroughfare. In the enaissance, Ferrara was home for the d'Este family, whose court was a cen- e of culture and learning. Ravenna was a great international centre from the th to the 8th century, originally as the last capital of the Western Empire, then s the seat of the Byzantine emperors.

Bologna ❶, the capital of Emilia-Romagna, is a city of less than half a million eople and famous for its university, its cuisine, its traditional left-wing stance nd its beautifully preserved historic centre. The old buildings are of a soft range-red brick, and have handsome marble or brick porticoes which shelter hoppers and pedestrians from inclement weather.

The old city evolved around two adjoining squares, **'iazza Maggiore ❹** and **Piazza del Nettuno ❸**. On e south side of the former stands **San Petronio ❹**, the rgest church in Bologna. Originally, the Bolognese ad hoped to outdo St Peter's in Rome, but Church uthorities decreed that some funds be set aside for the onstruction of **Palazzo Archiginnasio ❹** nearby. San 'etronio's design is by Antonio di Vincenzo, and lthough construction began in 1390, the facade is still nfinished. The completed sections are of red-and-vhite marble and decorated with reliefs of biblical cenes. The interior is simple but elegant. Most of the are brick walls remain unadorned. In the fifth chapel n the left is a spectacular 15th-century altarpiece of the *Martyrdom of St Sebastian* by Lorenzo Costa.

Centre of learning

3ehind San Petronio is the **Archiginnasio**, former seat f Europe's most ancient university, in whose 17th-entury **Sala Anatomica** (Mon–Fri 9am–6.45pm, Sat 'am–1.45pm; summer hours vary, tel: 051-276811) ome of the first dissections in Europe were performed.

The Piazza del Nettuno has many attractions. At its entre is the **Fontana di Nettuno ❺**, a 16th-century ountain with bronze sculptures by Giambologna of a nuscle-bound Neptune surrounded by cherubs and nermaids. On its west side is the majestic **Palazzo Comunale ❻**, the medieval town hall remodelled in

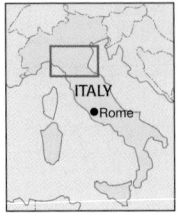

LEFT: the last of Bologna's high towers.
BELOW: delicacies on display in a Bologna deli.

Santo Stefano was originally a complex of seven churches; only four remain today. In the court-yard is a fountain in which Pontius Pilate is said to have washed his hands of the fate of Christ.

the Renaissance by Fieravante Fieravanti. Part of the palace is now a touri office. The bronze statue above the gateway is of Pope Gregory XIII, a native c Bologna. To the left is a beautiful terracotta Madonna by Niccolò dell'Arc Inside are grand public rooms and a fine collection of works by Bolognese arti Giorgio Morandi (1890–1964) (Museo Morandi; Tues–Fri 9am–3pm, Sat–Su 10am–6.30pm), one of the greatest still-life painters of modern times.

Bologna's leaning towers

From Piazza del Nettuno follow the **Via Rizzoli**, a picturesque street lined wit cafés, down to **Piazza di Porta Ravegnana ⑦** at the foot of the **Due Torri**, th "leaning towers" of Bologna. In medieval days, 180 of these towers were built b the city's leading families; now only a dozen remain. Legend has it that the tw richest families in Bologna – the Asinelli and the Garisenda – competed to buil the tallest and most beautiful tower in the city. However, the Torre Garisenda wa built on weak foundations and was never finished. For safety's sake it was shor ened between 1351 and 1360, and is now only 48 metres (157 ft) high and lean more than 3 metres (10 ft) to one side. The **Torre degli Asinelli** (daily 9am–6pm until 5pm in winter; entrance fee) is still standing at its original height of 97 metre (318 ft), but it too leans more than 1 metre (3 ft) out of the perpendicular. It's stiff climb to the top up 498 steps, but worth the effort for the wonderful views.

The **Strada Maggiore** leads east from the two towers along the original lin of the Via Aemilia to the **Basilica di San Bartolomeo ⑧**. Inside, look for th *Annunciation* by Albani in the fourth chapel of the south aisle, and a beautifu Madonna by Guido Reni in the north transept. Further down the Strada Mag giore is **Santa Maria dei Servi ⑨**, a well-preserved Gothic church.

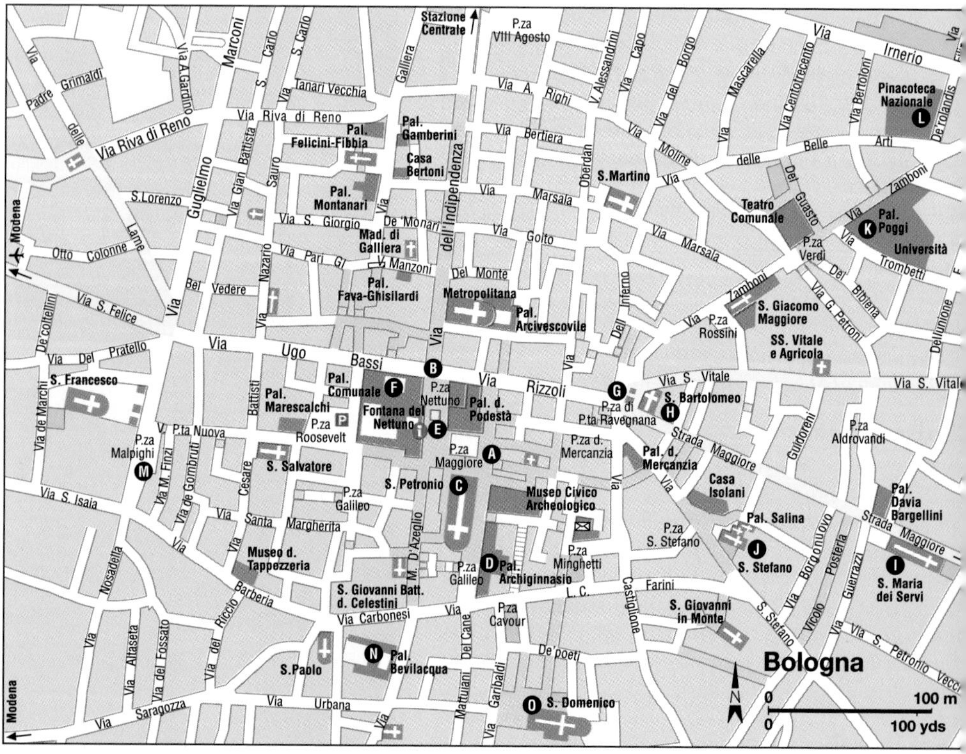

Bologna

The **Abbazia di Santo Stefano** 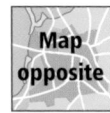 (daily 9am–noon and 3.30–6.30pm) – a complex of churches all dedicated to St Stephen – is located off Via Santo Stefano, just south of the Casa Isolani, a well-restored 13th-century house. Of the several churches, the most interesting is **San Sepolcro**, where San Petronio, patron saint of Bologna, is buried near the striking Romanesque pulpit. To the left is **Santi Vitale e Agricola**, the oldest church of the group, a 5th-century structure containing several Roman capitals and columns. In San Sepolcro is the entrance to the 12th-century **Cortile di Pilato**, "Pilate's courtyard", and beyond this open courtyard is the church of **Santa Trinità**, a dark 13th-century building.

Bologna's **University**, the oldest in Italy, an institution founded in the 11th century and famous in its early days for reviving the study of Roman law, is located on **Via Zamboni**. Petrarch attended classes here, as did Copernicus. Today, although faculties are spread throughout the city, the official seat is the 16th-century **Palazzo Poggi** Ⓚ.

Past the university, on the left, is the **Pinacoteca Nazionale** Ⓛ, where the National Art Gallery (Tues–Sun 9am–7pm; entrance fee) is home to an interesting and varied collection of Italian paintings. The emphasis is on the development of Bolognese and Emilian art from the Middle Ages to the 1700s, including works by Vitale da Bologna (especially the painting of *St George and the Dragon*) and Guido Reni. The stars of the collection are Raphael's great *Ecstasy of St Cecilia* (1515) and Perugino's *Madonna in Glory* (1491).

South and west of the Piazza Maggiore, Bologna has more architectural treasures. Follow the Via Ugo Bassi west to **Piazza Malpighi** Ⓜ. On the west side of this piazza rises **San Francesco**, a church constructed between 1236 and 1263, with a design of French-Gothic inspiration. The larger of San Francesco's two towers and the surrounding decorative terracotta are the work of Antonio di Vincenzo. Though badly damaged in the war, the tower has been skilfully restored.

From San Francesco walk southeast until you reach **Palazzo Bevilacqua** Ⓝ, a 15th-century building in the Tuscan style. Here, the Council of Trent met for two sessions after fleeing an epidemic in Trent. It is the boldest of Bologna's senatorial palaces and has a sandstone facade, wrought-iron balconies and a courtyard surrounded by a loggia. Nearby, **San Domenico** Ⓞ dominates Piazza San Domenico. Dating from 1228, it was remodelled in Baroque style but incorporates Romanesque walls. The interior displays the tomb of St Dominic, founder of the Dominican Order, decorated with sculptures by Nicola Pisano and Arnolfo di Cambio of the Pisan School, as well as two by the young Michelangelo.

Bologna has earned a number of epithets: "La Dotta" (The Learned One), "La Turritta" (The Turreted One), "La Rossa" (The Red One, as much for the rich red of its buildings as for its politics) and finally "La Grassa" (The Fat One), for here the rich cooking of Emilia-Romagna is at its best. Specialities are mortadella sausage, tortellini and tagliatelle, said to have been invented for the marriage feast of Lucrezia Borgia and the duke of Ferrara. The Bolognese dress their tagliatelle, never spaghetti, with *ragù*, which in its home town is a rich blend of beef, ham, vegetables, cream and butter.

San Domenico contains several statues by Michelangelo.

BELOW: typical arcaded street in Bologna.

Modena

Since the Romans conquered **Modena ❷** in the 2nd century BC, the city has thrived. In the past, the sources of Modena's wealth were the rich farmland of the Po plateau that surrounds it, and its position on the Via Aemilia. This famou Roman road still runs through the centre of Modena, but the city has new riche the car factories where Maserati and Ferrari sports cars are manufactured.

Modena's massive and magnificent Romanesque **Duomo** sits right off the V Aemilia. It dates from the end of the 11th century, when Countess Matilda of Tu cany, ruler of Modena, commissioned a cathedral which would be worthy to recei the remains of St Geminiano, patron saint of the city. Matilda engaged Lanfranco, t greatest architect of the time, to mastermind the project. The pink Verona marb structure is a mirror of the medieval mind, with friezes of saints and monsters, p grims and knights, griffins and doves, dragons and deer. The **Museo del Duom** (Tues–Sun 9.30am–12.30pm and 3.30–6.30pm) contains impressive 12th-centu metopes, low reliefs which once surmounted the flying buttresses.

The partly Gothic, partly Romanesque bell tower that stands to one side is th famous **Torre Ghirlandina**. It contains a bucket whose theft from Bologna 1325 sparked off a war between the two cities. The poet Tassoni immortalise the incident in his celebrated poem *La Secchia Rapita* (The Stolen Bucket).

Frequently seen strolling around Modena are the smartly dressed students c the **Accademia Militare**, Italy's military academy, housed in a 17th-centur palace in the centre of Modena. Another Modenese palace, **Palazzo dei Muse** contains several galleries, including the Galleria Estense (Tues–Sun 8.30am 7.30pm; entrance fee), and the **Biblioteca Estense** (Mon–Sat 9am–1pm entrance fee), the library of the d'Este family, dukes of Modena as well as Fer

TIP

Motoring enthusiasts will enjoy a visit to the Galleria Ferrari at Via Dino Ferrari 43 in Maranello, 20 km (12 miles) south of Modena (tel: 0536-943204). Exhibits tell the history of the Ferrari company.

BELOW: stone lion outside Modena's Romanesque Duomo.
BELOW RIGHT: Piazza Grande in Modena.

...ra. On permanent display in the library is a collection of illuminated manu-
...ripts, a 1481 copy of Dante's *Divine Comedy*, and the stunning Borso d'Este
...ible, which contains 1,200 miniatures.

...arma

...here is no better place to become a connoisseur of *parmigiano* (Parmesan), the
...ard, sharp-flavoured cheese, than in **Parma ❸**, where the cheese is made. It
... a medium-sized city that enjoys a cooler, fresher climate than other towns in
...e muggy Po Valley. The history of Parma is full of interesting personalities.
...apoleon's widow, Marie Louise, was ceded this city after her husband's death.
...espite her reputation for immodest behaviour, she did good things for Parma,
...uilding roads and bridges and founding orphanages and public institutions.
...he also founded the Galleria Nazionale (Tues–Sun 8.30am–1.45pm; entrance
...e) in the 16th-century **Palazzo della Pilotta**, a palace which also contains the
...eatro Farnese, a Palladian theatre with Italy's first revolving stage.

However, the main aesthetic attraction of Parma is the **Duomo** (daily
...am–12.30pm and 3–7pm) and adjoining Baptistery. Its nave and cupola are dec-
...rated with splendid frescos by Correggio. Contemporaries gushed over them:
...itian said that if the dome of the cathedral were turned upside down and filled
...ith gold it would not be as valuable as Correggio's frescos. Vasari wrote of the
...*ssumption*: "It seems impossible that a man could have conceived such a work as
...his is, and more impossible still, that he should have done it with human hands."

The brilliantly restored **Baptistery** (daily 9am–12.30pm and 3–6.30pm;
...ntrance fee) is the work of Benedetto Antelami, who built this octagonal building
... rich rose-pink Verona marble and then sculpted the reliefs that adorn both the

Map on pages 246–7

The king of Italian cheeses.

BELOW: Parma hams.

...ARMA HAM AND PARMESAN

Parma ham and Parmesan cheese *(parmigiano)* are
intricately linked, because it is the whey – the waste-
...roduct from Parmesan production – that is used to feed
...he pigs that produce Parma ham. True Parma ham is
...randed with the five-pointed crown of the medieval dukes
...f Parma, and is produced in the Langhirino hills, south of
...arma. Here the raw hind thighs are hung in drying sheds
...or up to 10 months. The air that blows through the sheds is
...aid to impart a sweet flavour to the meat – unlike cheap,
...nass-produced *prosciutto crudo*, which is injected with
...rine and artificially dried to speed up the curing process.

Try it as a starter (antipasto) in any Parma restaurant,
...sliced into wafer-thin slivers for eating with bread, melon
...or figs; end your meal, perhaps, with slivers of superior
...*parmigiano-reggiano*, the king of Parmesans, which is
...especially delicious partnered with apples, pears or a good
...red wine. A lower-quality Parmesan is known as *grana*.

Another speciality of the region is *aceto balsamico* (bal-
...samic vinegar), made from sweet grape juice, boiled
...slowly and reduced to a syrup, mixed with vinegar and
...then aged in wooden casks for many years. It can be used
...in salads or as a marinade, or even drizzled over fresh
...berries or ice cream.

interior and the exterior. Inside is a superb cycle of frescos. Antelami's earliest known work, the *Depositione* (1178), can be seen in the Duomo. This deeply moving sculpture was hewn from a single piece of marble.

In the dome of **San Giovanni Evangelista**, another splendidly sensuous Correggio fresco (*c*.1520) can be seen. It depicts St John gazing up at heaven where the Apostles are gathered, and is matched by frescos by Parmigiano. Nearby are Renaissance cloisters, a refectory and a library used by the resident Benedictine community. Of particular interest here is the **Benedictine Dispensary** (pharmacy Tues–Sun 8.30am–1.45pm, June and Sept Mon–Fri 8.30am–6pm, Sat–Sun until 7pm; entrance fee), complete with 16th-century apothecary's jars.

If you are driving northwest on the Via Aemilia towards Piacenza, consider making a quick stop in **Fidenza** ❹ to see another glorious Romanesque cathedral. Just beyond Fidenza is the turn-off for the little town of **Roncole Verdi** ❺, where you can visit the humble cottage in which Giuseppe Verdi (1813–1901) was born (Tues–Sun 9.30am–12.30pm and 3–7pm Apr–Sept, until 5pm in winter; entrance fee).

In the revolutionary year of 1848, when Prince Charles Albert of Savoy called for Italians to assemble under his leadership and form an independent nation, the citizens of **Piacenza** ❻ were the first to respond in a plebiscite. This vote of rebellion was a remarkable event in Piacenza's otherwise peaceful history. Situated at the point where the Via Aemilia meets the Po, Piacenza has been a lively trading post since 218 BC. Nothing remains of the Roman period, though there are many fine medieval and Renaissance buildings. At the centre of the city is the massive **Palazzo del Comune** (not open to the public), called "Il Gotico". This town hall was built during Piacenza's "Communal Period" (approximately

Giorgio de Chirico, who immortalised Ferrara castle in his surreal city-scapes, called this former dukedom the most magical and metaphysical of places.

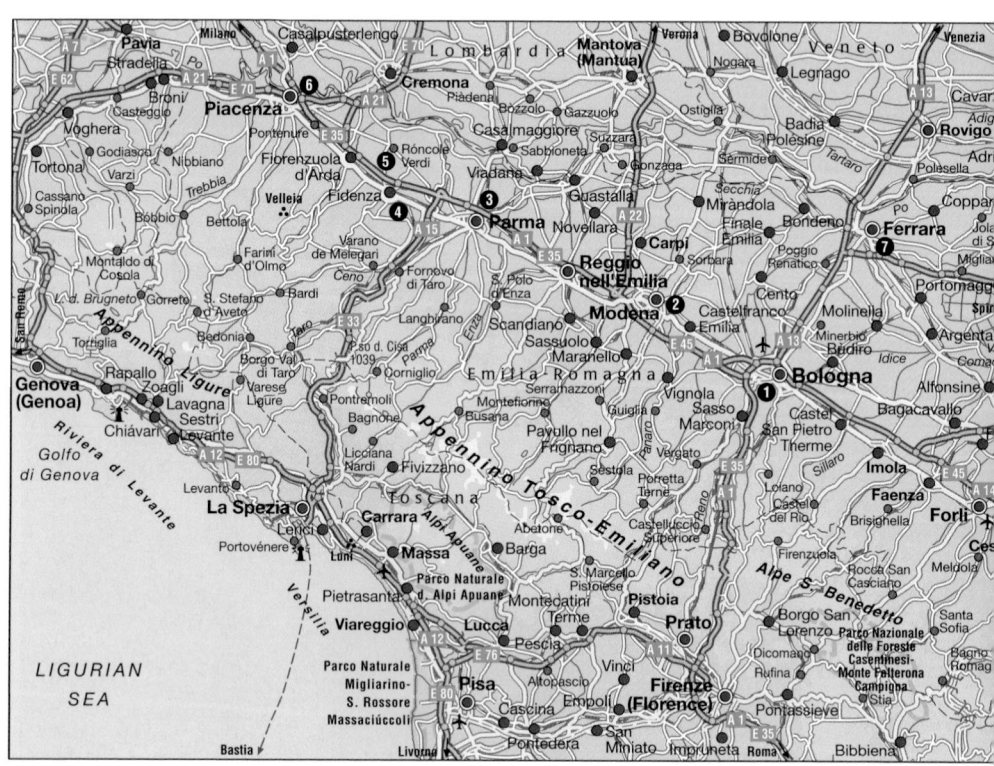

200–1400) when the city was an independent and important member of the Lombard League that defeated Emperor Frederick II of Hohenstaufen in his bid to conquer Italy. Il Gotico, begun in 1280, is a remarkably well-preserved building of brick, marble and terracotta. In front of it stand two massive baroque equestrian statues of Piacenza's 16th-century rulers, the Farnese dukes. At the end of the Via Venti Settembre stands Piacenza's Romanesque **Duomo** (daily 7.30am–noon and 4–7pm). Although gloomy on the inside, the cathedral is worth a visit for the frescos on the columns near the entrance.

Ferrara

A prosperous market town on the banks of the misty River Po, **Ferrara ❼** seems at first glance peaceful and provincial. But the city has a colourful history and splendid treasures. At the southern end is a well-preserved medieval town, and to the north are long broad avenues lined with Renaissance palaces and carefully groomed gardens. The d'Este family ruled Ferrara from the late 13th century until 1598, a time of prosperity when their court attracted poets, scholars and artists. The Renaissance, the city's golden age, is reflected in all the major monuments.

Dominating Ferrara's skyline is the restored medieval **Castello Estense**, complete with moats, drawbridges and towers (Tues–Sun 9.30am–5.30pm; entrance fee). Just behind the castle is Ferrara's 12th-century **Duomo**. Among the noteworthy paintings here and in the adjoining museum (Museo della Cattedrale; Tues–Sun 9am–1pm and 3–6pm; entrance fee) are Cosimo Tura's *St George* and his *Annunciation,* and Jacopo della Quercia's *Madonna della Melagrana* (1408). Across from the Duomo is the **Palazzo del Comune** (not open to the public), a medieval building with a beautiful Renaissance staircase. The piazza in front of

Ariosto, Petrarch, Tasso, Mantegna and Bellini were just some of the great Italian poets and painters patronised by the d'Este family of Ferrara.

BELOW: the richly sculpted facade of Ferrara's cathedral.

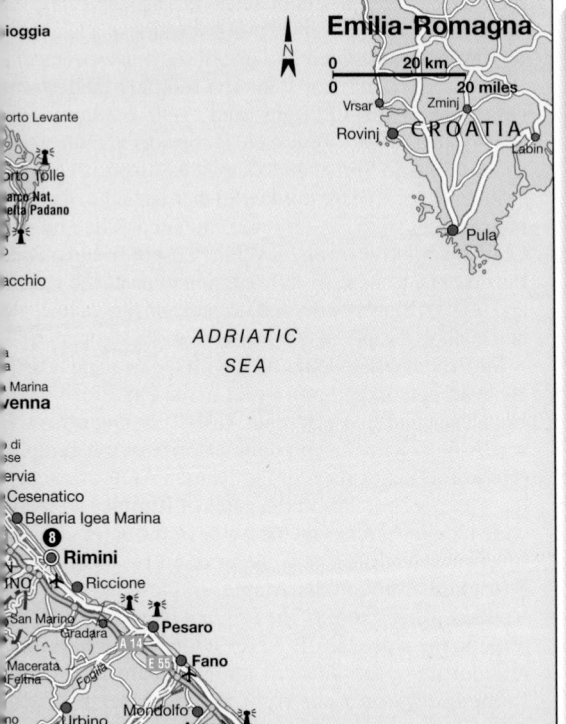

this town hall is the hub of life in modern Ferrara, and teeming with bicycles, the number one method of transport in this very flat region of the Po Valley.

Many of the medieval streets south of the cathedral are lined with fortified houses, and, stretching across the **Via delle Volte**, a narrow street near the Po there are a number of elegant arches. At the beautiful **Palazzo Schifanoia** (Tues–Sun 9am–6pm; entrance fee), one of the d'Este family's summer residences, you can climb the steep stairs to the Salone dei Mesi, a large, high room decorated with colourful frescos of the months. However, most have deteriorated and their colours dulled. These were executed for the duke of Borgo d'Este by masters of the Ferrarese School, including Ercole de' Roberti.

Just around the corner is another d'Este palace, the **Palazzo di Ludovico il Moro**, designed by the famous Ferrarese Renaissance architect Biagio Rossetti. This houses the Museo Archeologico Nazionale (Via XX Settembre; Tues–Sun 9am–2pm; entrance fee), which has a fine collection of Etruscan artefacts.

North of the Duomo, Ferrara is a city of broad avenues. Along one of the prettiest streets, Corso Ercole d'Este, is Rossetti's **Palazzo dei Diamanti** (Tues–Sat 9am–2pm, Thurs until 7pm, Sun until 1pm; entrance fee), with an art gallery, the Pinacoteca Nazionale, concealed behind a large Renaissance structure with a unique facade. The diamond, emblem of the d'Este family, is repeated 12,600 times.

Rimini

Today **Rimini ❽** is two cities: the old medieval and Renaissance town, and the ultra-modern beach resort a mile distant. In the skyscraper hotels that line Rimini's coast you are more likely to hear German or English spoken than Italian, but the old centre retains its charm despite the influx of tourists.

The infamous ruler Sigismondo Malatesta has left his mark everywhere in Rimini. It was this anticlerical patron of art who presided over the transformation of a 13th-century Franciscan church into one of the most spectacular Renaissance buildings in Italy. The **Tempio Malatestiano** (Mon–Sat 8am–12.30pm and 3.30–6.30pm, Sun 9am–1pm and 3.30–7pm; free) is considered more a personal tribute to Sigismondo's mistress, Isotta degli Atti (who later became his third wife) than a church. But perhaps that is what Sigismondo intended, since he and Church authorities were never the best of friends. Pope Pius II even went so far as to excommunicate the violent and sensual Sigismondo, and to condemn him publicly to hell, calling the site "a temple of devil-worshippers".

Sigismondo had better luck with women and artists. He was patron of such great artists as Piero della Francesca and Leon Battista Alberti, among others. It was Alberti who designed the exterior of the Tempio. (He found inspiration in the Roman Arch of Augustus which still stands at the gates of Rimini.) Note the wide classical arches on each side of the entrance. The interior rebuilding was supervised by Matteo de' Pasti, and although the simple, single-nave plan and wooden-trussed roof of the original Franciscan church remain, the side chapels (some added and others only redecorated) are opulent and intricate in design. Immediately on your right as you enter is Sigismondo's tomb. It is decorated with his initials inter-

Film director Federico Fellini (1902–93) was born in Rimini. His Oscar-winning film Amarcord *immortalised the area in the 1970s, and the Felliniesque atmosphere is still evident in the narrow streets and small houses around the Borgo San Giuliano. The famous "old lady" of Adriatic hotels, the Grand, stands in the park named after him.*

BELOW: the beach and Grand Hotel, Rimini.

wined with Isotta's. Note also the fresco of Sigismondo praying at the feet of St Sigismond, by Piero della Francesca.

To the left of the Tempio is **Piazza Tre Martiri**, which was named in honour of three Italian partisans hanged by the Nazis in this square in 1944. The piazza is also the site of the ancient Roman forum, whose columns now support the porticoes of the two eastern buildings.

Walk out of the piazza along **Corso di Augusto** for four blocks. At the end stands the **Arco di Augusto**, dating from 27 BC. With this archway the Romans marked the junction of the Via Aemilia and the Via Flaminia, the primary road north from Rome to the Adriatic Sea.

Ravenna

When the unstoppable barbarians overran Rome in the 5th century AD, **Ravenna ❾** benefited, gaining the honourable rank of capital of the Western Empire. This Adriatic port town continued as capital under the Ostrogoths, and the barbarian leaders Odoacer and Theodoric also ruled their vast dominions from here. Later, when the Byzantine emperor Justinian reconquered part of Italy, he too made Ravenna his seat of power, liking it for its imperial tradition under the barbarians and – perhaps more importantly – for its direct sea links to Byzantium.

Under Justinian's rule the Ravenna we know today began to take shape. New buildings arose all over the city, including a handful of churches that are among the wonders of Italian art and architecture. There is no preparation in their simple brick exteriors for the brilliant mosaics within. It is these mosaics that make modern Ravenna, if no longer capital of the Western world, at least a capital of the Western art world.

Map on pages 246–7

TIP

Ravenna's medieval Piazza del Popolo is a good place to relax with a cup of coffee after seeing the mosaics.

BELOW: mosaics at the Mausoleo di Galla Placidia.

Amazing mosaics

Start with **San Vitale** (daily 9am–7pm; entrance fee), the city's great 6th-century octagonal basilica, famous for the mosaics in its choir and apse. These "monuments of unaging intellect", as the Irish poet W.B. Yeats called them, immediately draw the eye with their marvellous colours and intricate detail. Bright ducks, bulls, lions, dolphins and a phoenix intertwine with flowers and oddly angled corners of buildings to frame Old Testament scenes and portraits of Byzantine rulers with humour and exactitude.

In the dome of the apse a purple-clad and beardless Christ sits on a blue globe flanked by archangels and, at the far sides, St Vitalis and Bishop Ecclesius. Christ hands the saint (Ravenna's patron) a triumphal crown, while the bishop (who founded the church in 521) carries a model of the building as it finally appeared many years after his death. Below stretch imperial scenes of Justinian with his courtiers and Theodora, his beloved wife, with hers.

San Vitale is not the only place to see mosaics in Ravenna. Nearly every church contains a pristine example of the art. Just north, another set may be seen at the **Mausoleo di Galla Placidia** (daily 9am–7pm; entrance fee). This interesting lady was born a Roman princess, sister to Emperor Honorius, but after she was captured by the Goths, she married their leader, Athaulf, and ruled with him. He, however, soon died, and she next married a Roman general to whom she bore a son. This son became Emperor Valentinian III. As Valentinian's regent, and a woman with connections in the highest barbarian circles, Galla Placidia played a powerful role in the world of "the decline". The building that houses her tomb has a simple exterior, but inside the walls, floors, and ceiling are covered with glorious mosaics, the oldest in Ravenna. Built between 425 and 450, it is bathed in green light which becomes aquamarine higher up the walls. The mystical atmosphere is intensified by the strikingly simple style of the mosaics, including the cobalt-blue sky sprinkled with gold stars. Despite the simple Christian iconography, the realism of the figures reflects the naturalistic Roman style as much as a nascent Christian one.

Through the gate that lies between San Vitale and Galla Placidia are two Renaissance cloisters that now house the **Museo Nazionale** (Tues–Sun 8.30am–7pm; entrance fee). The museum includes, as one might expect, many mosaics, as well as other relics from Ravenna's past. There is glass from San Vitale and also fabrics from the tomb of St Julian at Rimini.

The baroque Duomo

A pleasant walk along Via Fanni, Via Barbiani and left onto Via d'Azeglio leads to Ravenna's **Duomo** – originally constructed in the 5th century but redone in baroque style in the 1730s. Far more attractive than the cathedral itself is the adjoining **Battistero Neoniano** (daily 9.30am–7pm; entrance fee), a 5th-century octagonal baptistery that was once a Roman bathhouse. The interior combines spectacular Byzantine mosaics with marble inlay from the original.

Across Piazza Caduti from the cathedral complex is **San Francesco**, another 5th-century church almost completely redone in the baroque style. To the left stands the

The glorious mosaics depicting an ethereal blue sky sprinkled with gold stars which fill the vaulted ceiling of the Mausoleo di Galla Placidia are said to have inspired Cole Porter to write his timeless song Night and Day.

BELOW: the apse of San Vitale, with a mosaic of Christ handing a crown to the martyr, Vitale.

Tomba di Dante (daily 9.30am–6.30pm in summer, 10am–4pm in winter), not a remarkable building architecturally, but of great historic interest. Dante, the author of *The Divine Comedy*, was exiled from his home in Florence for his political outspokenness and found refuge in Ravenna in 1317. He spent the remaining four years of his life here, putting the finishing touches to his great work.

After Dante's death, the repentant Florentines would dearly have loved to honour their famous son with a splendid tomb, but proud Ravenna refused to give up the poet's remains. The battle over the bones continued for hundreds of years. At one point in 1519, it looked as if Ravenna would lose. The powerful Medici of Florence sent their representatives to Ravenna with a papal injunction demanding the relics. The sarcophagus was duly opened, but the bones were not inside. Someone had been warned of the Florentine scheme and had removed the bones to a secret hiding place. They were not found again until 1865, and now rest within the sarcophagus that is on display. To this day, the city of Florence provides the oil for the lamp which burns on his tomb.

Down the Via di Roma is another church full of mosaics, **Sant'Apollinare Nuovo** (daily 9am–7pm; entrance fee). Flanked by a cylindrical bell tower, it was built between 493 and 496. The scenes are of processions, one of virgins and the other of martyrs who appear to be moving towards the altar between rows of palms. Above, the decorations depict episodes from the *Life of Christ*. Opposite stands the basilica of **San Giovanni Evangelista** (daily 7.30am–noon and 3.30–6.30pm), with a sculpted marble portal. Dating from the 5th century but much altered, it was built by Galla Placidia. Legend has it that she had vowed to build the church in return for surviving a shipwreck on a voyage from Constantinople. ❏

Map on pages 246–7

Take Via Barbiani to visit the excavated mosaic floors known as Domus di Tappeti di Pietra *(Carpet of Stones). This underground mosaic pavement was unearthed within a 14th-century church and reveals the dining room of a classical Roman villa.*

BELOW: mosaic of the three Magi in Sant'Apollinare Nuovo in Ravenna

FLORENCE

One of the world's great artistic centres, packed with aesthetic masterpieces, Florence is the essential destination for students of Renaissance art and architecture

Map on pages 254–5

ITALY
Florence
●Rome

Florence (Firenze) is the city that gave birth to the Renaissance, and many visitors come here to trace the development of this extraordinary outpouring of artistic talent in the 15th century. A huge number of Renaissance works have remained in the city where they were created; many paintings, statues and whole buildings, such as the Palazzo Pitti, were bequeathed to the people of Florence by Anna Maria Lodovica of the Medici family, whose death in 1743 brought an end to the dynasty that had ruled Florence since 1434.

Her far-sighted bequest ensured that the Medici collections remained intact and were not dispersed all over the globe. Napoleon stole a few choice pieces during his adventures in Italy (including the *Medici Venus*, now in the Louvre), and English collectors bought some splendid paintings very cheaply in the 19th century when the so-called "primitives" were out of fashion. Despite this, you can still see in Florence many of the paintings and frescos that Vasari, the first art historian, mentions in his entertaining and anecdotal *Lives of the Artists*, first published in 1550. Nearly all works have been superbly restored since the great flood of November 1966, and the bulletproof glass installed to protect the most important paintings in the Uffizi proved effective when a terrorist bomb exploded in May 1993, reducing some minor masterpieces to shreds.

LEFT: Piazza della Signoria.
BELOW: texting on the steps of the Duomo.

Where the Renaissance started

To see where the Renaissance began, it is traditional to begin with Piazza del Duomo. Approaching this massive square, you file through sober streets lined with buildings presenting a stern defensive face. Suddenly the 19th-century face of the **Duomo ❶** (cathedral; Mon, Tues, Wed, Fri 10am–5pm, Thur 10am–3.30pm, Sat 10am–4.45pm, Sun 1.30–4.45pm; free) is revealed, all festive in its polychrome marble – green from Prato, white from Carrara and red from the Maremma. The design echoes that of the tall **Campanile** (daily 8.30am–7.30pm; entrance fee) alongside, designed by Giotto in 1331. You can climb the 414 steps of the bell tower for intimate views of the cathedral dome and roofline, or simply enjoy the flamboyant exterior of the cathedral from one of the open-air cafés on the south side of the square.

The little octagonal **Battistero** (Baptistery; Mon–Sat noon–7pm, Sun 8.30am–2pm; entrance fee), to the west of the cathedral, dates to the 6th century, though the interior was redesigned and given its ceiling mosaics of the *Creation* and *Last Judgement* in 1300. The Baptistery has three sets of bronze doors, and those to the north have an important place in art history. If it is possible to pin down the start of the Renaissance to a particular event, then it was the competition held in the winter of 1401 to choose an artist to design these doors. Of the six artists who entered the competition, Ghiberti and Brunelleschi were

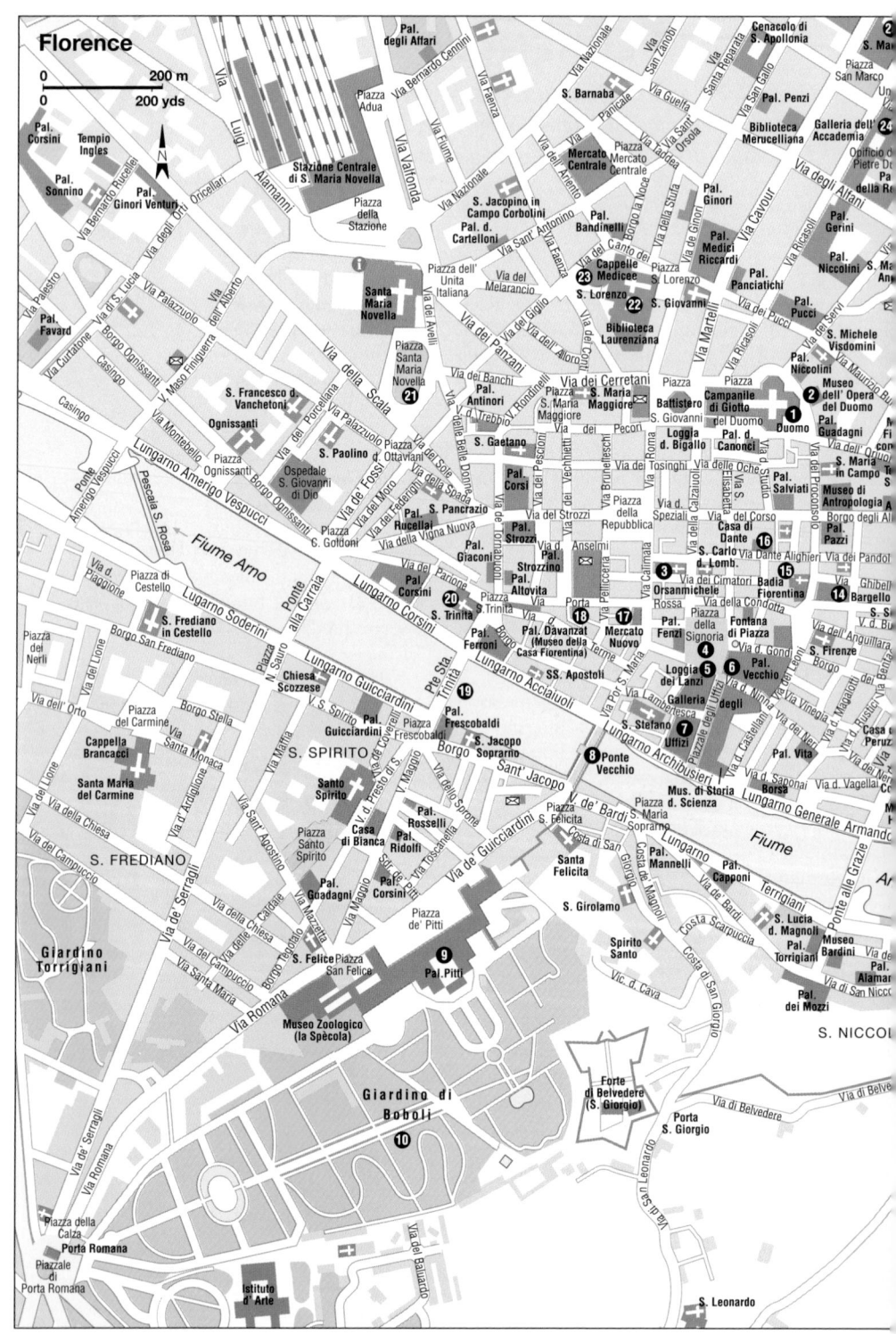

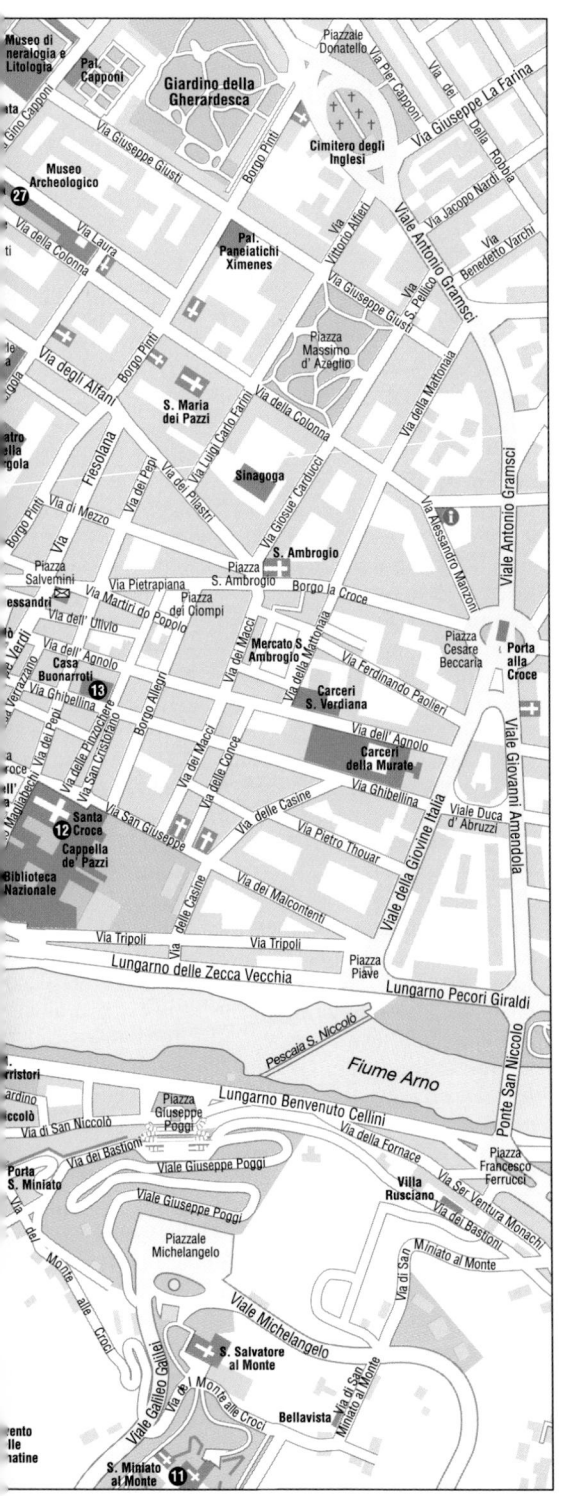

adjudged joint winners, but Brunelleschi, a fiery-tempered genius, refused to work with Ghiberti and went off in a huff to Rome.

Ghiberti, left with sole responsibility for the doors, did not complete them until 1424, but the resulting work shows many of the key features that define Renaissance art: the realistic depiction of people, fully worked-out perspective, and narrative clarity combined with dramatic tension. Ghiberti was immediately commissioned to design another set of doors, this time for the east portal, and these were unveiled in 1452 when Michelangelo hailed them as fit to serve as the "gates of Paradise"; they are known to this day as the Paradise Doors. The third set of doors, to the south, are the work of Andrea Pisano (1330) and tell the story of John the Baptist, patron saint of the city.

Biggest dome in the world

Brunelleschi, meanwhile, spent his time in Rome studying ancient Roman architecture, and he returned to Florence full of confidence that he could accomplish a task that had defeated other architects, namely to complete the cathedral by erecting the vast **dome**. In typically Florentine fashion, the city had decided to build the biggest dome in the world without actually knowing how to achieve it. If you enter the cathedral and climb the 436 steps to the top (Mon–Fri 8.30am–7pm, Sat 8.30am–5.40pm; entrance fee) you can study how the problem was solved – by building a light inner shell of interlocking brick which serves as the support for the outer roof of the dome.

Brunelleschi was hailed as a new Icarus (the mythical hero who similarly defied gravity by taking to the skies), and the city passed an ordinance forbidding the construction of any building taller than the dome out of respect for his achievement; to this day, the massive dome rises supreme above the red roofs of the city, rising almost higher than the surrounding hills. Brunelleschi was also buried in the cathedral – an honour granted to him alone – and his tomb can be seen in the **crypt** (Mon–Wed and Fri 10am–5pm, Sat until 4.45pm; entrance fee), among the

Lorenzo Ghiberti took themes from the Old Testament for the East Doors (the "gates of Paradise") of the Battistero. This is a detail from the Battle with the Philistines.

BELOW: figure of a saint in an external niche of Orsanmichele.

excavated ruins of Santa Reparata, the city's first (4th-century) cathedral.

Much of the rest of the cathedral is bare. There is an interesting fresco on the north aisle wall, painted by Paolo Uccello in 1436, depicting Sir John Hawk wood, the English mercenary who served as captain of the Florentine army from 1377 to 1394. Otherwise, to see the cathedral treasures you must visit the **Musee dell'Opera del Duomo ❷** (Mon–Sat 9am–7.30pm, Sun 9am–1.45pm; entrance fee) on the east side of Piazza del Duomo. This restored and expanded museum is full of outstanding sculptures, from Donatello's haggard *Mary Magdalene* carved in wood in the 1460s, to the same artist's superb *cantoria* (choir gallery) decorated with angels and cherubs engaged in frenzied music and song. The star exhibit here is Michelangelo's *Pietà*, begun around 1550. Michelangelo intended this for his own tomb, but left it unfinished (a pupil rather clumsily attempted to finish the work). Its magnetic hold over visitors derives from the fact that the tall hooded figure of Nicodemus is Michelangelo's self-portrait.

Showpiece of the guilds

From the cathedral square, **Via dei Calzaiuoli** leads south. This was the principal street of Roman and medieval Florence, and, having been restored after World War II bombing, it is lined with good shops. Part-way down, on the right, is the church of **Orsanmichele ❸** (Tues–Sun 10am–5pm), a contraction of Orti di San Michele – the Gardens of San Michele Church, which once stood here. The niches around the exterior walls are filled with Renaissance statues sponsored by the guilds and depicting their respective patron saints. Of these, Donatello's *St George*, made for the Guild of Armourers, is the most important, and for that reason it has been removed to a place of honour in the Bargello museum *(see page 261)* and replaced by a copy.

The same fate befell Michelangelo's *David*, which once stood in the **Piazza della Signoria ❹**, just to the south. The original was moved to the Galleria dell'Accademia *(see page 262)* in 1873, but the copy that now stands in front of the Palazzo Vecchio is faithful to the original. David's companions are *Hercules* (1534 by Bandinelli), the mythical founder of Florence, and Ammannati's licentious *Neptune Fountain* (1575). Nearby, the **Loggia dei Lanzi ❺** (1382) shelters Cellini's *Perseus* (1554) and Giambologna's *Rape of the Sabine Women* (1583), alongside ancient Roman statues.

Most of the statues gathered here are symbolic, not least David himself, carved by Michelangelo to represent the aspirations of the Florentine people not long after the citizens had declared themselves independent of all rulers except for God. The fledgling Florentine republic was threatened by a number of tyrannical Goliaths, including the Pope, the Holy Roman Emperor and the Medici. The combined forces of all three held the city to siege in 1530, and shortly afterwards Cosimo I was crowned duke of Florence.

This Cosimo was a very different character from his earlier namesake, the humanist, classics scholar and patron of the arts, Cosimo il Vecchio, who ruled the city from 1434 to 1464 without ever holding office. Cosimo I was a no-nonsense military man who set about conquering all those cities in the region not already ruled

y Florence. Cosimo I created the Tuscany of today by these means, and he set
p an efficient administration to rule his dukedom, which remained in place
ntil Tuscany joined the united kingdom of Italy in 1861.

That administration was based in the **Palazzo Vecchio ❻** (daily 9am–7pm,
ntil 2pm on Thur; entrance fee), which remains the town hall of Florence, and
vhich was comprehensively redesigned during the reign of Cosimo I. Visiting
he ancient town hall, you can see the delicately decorated entrance courtyard
vith its little fountain – Vasari's copy of the original *Putto and Dolphin* fountain
nade by Verrocchio in 1470. By contrast, the vast Salone dei Cinquecento (Hall
f the Five Hundred) was originally intended as the council chamber of the 500
itizens who governed during the republic. Cosimo I set his stamp on the cham-
er by commissioning a series of vast frescos, painted by Vasari, which glori-
ied his military triumphs. Other rooms of the palace contain mementos of
arious prominent Florentines, such as portraits of the Medici popes Leo X and
lement VII. A small bust of Machiavelli is located in the little room that he
sed during his term of office as chancellor of Florence.

A copy of Michelan-gelo's David *in Piazza della Signoria.*

The Uffizi

Jnder Cosimo I, Tuscan bureaucracy grew to the point where new offices
vere required to house the burgeoning army of lawyers and notaries, the guilds
nd the judiciary. Thus it was that the **Uffizi ❼** (Tues–Sun 8.15am–6.50pm,
ntil 10pm Tues and Wed July–Sept, last entry 45 mins before closing;
ntrance fee) came to be built alongside the Palazzo Vecchio – now a world-
amous art gallery but originally intended to serve a far more utilitarian pur-
ose (the word *uffizi* simply means offices).

BELOW: the Duomo.

TIP

Queues for the Uffizi can be achingly long, but tickets can be reserved in advance. Call Firenze Musei, tel: 055-294883, where, for a small fee, you're given a booking number, or log on to www. uffizi.com at least one day in advance (subject to a booking fee). Pre-booked tickets are picked up at a separate entrance.

BELOW: the Ponte Vecchio, built in 1345.

Vasari was the architect, and he built a well-lit upper storey, using iron reinforcement to create an almost continuous wall of glass running round the long inner courtyard of the Uffizi. It was this glass wall that caused so much damage when a terrorist bomb exploded near the west wing of the Uffizi in May 1993, sending splinters of glass everywhere and destroying a number of paintings in the process. In the 16th century, such lavish use of glass was novel, and Cosimo's heirs decided that the airy upper corridor of the Uffizi would make a perfect exhibition space for the family statues, carpets and paintings.

Thus began what has grown to be the greatest collection of Italian art in the world. It is arranged chronologically so that you can trace, almost in textbook fashion, the development of Florentine art from the formal style of the Gothic era (13th and 14th centuries), to the greater realism of the early Renaissance (15th century), and finally to the painterly use of exaggerated colours and the contorted poses designed to show off the artist's skill that are so characteristic of the High Renaissance and Mannerist periods (16th century).

The famous names and familiar works come thick and fast as you explore the collection; essential viewing includes Botticelli's *Primavera* (1480) and the *Birth of Venus* (1485). You should also seek out the portraits of the Medici family that are gathered in the octagonal Tribune, including Bronzino's *Portrait of Bia*, illegitimate daughter of Cosimo I (1542). The corridors of the gallery are lined with ancient Roman and Greek statues, and look out too for Michelangelo's influential *Holy Family (Doni Tondo*; 1506–8), Raphael's tender *Madonna of the Goldfinch* (1506) and Titian's erotic *Venus of Urbino* (1538).

When Vasari planned the Uffizi, he incorporated an aerial corridor (the Corridoio Vasariano) into the design. This consists of a continuous covered walkway linking

ʰe Palazzo Vecchio to the Pitti Palace, passing through the Uffizi and along the top f the Ponte Vecchio. The Medici dukes used this corridor to walk between their ʲarious palaces without having to mix with their subjects in the streets below. The ʲorridoio Vasariano opening is subject to change. It is usually by appointment ɔnly (tel: 055-265 4321), but tours are conducted by Uffizi staff on some mornings ɔften Wednesday and Friday): there are no fixed rules.

En route to the Pitti Palace, the corridor passes over the **Ponte Vecchio** ❽. The ʲridge was built in 1345, and its workshops were used by butchers and tanners until ʰese noxious trades were banned by ducal ordinance in 1593. Today it has been ɑken over by jewellers, buskers and streams of tourists shopping for trinkets. It ʲas the only Florentine bridge to be spared by the Germans in World War II.

Good shops line the route south of the bridge into the Oltrarno district, where ʲou will find the churches of **Santo Spirito**, an architectural masterpiece by ʲrunelleschi, and **Santa Maria del Carmine** (Wed–Sat and Mon 10am–5pm, ʲun 1–5pm; entrance fee), where the Brancacci Chapel contains Masaccio's ʲresco cycle on the *Life of St Peter*. This is one of the great works of the early ʲenaissance, and the Brancacci Chapel is tiny, with room for only 30 people at ɑ time, so there are likely to be queues at the entrance. Visits are limited to 15 ɱinutes (tel: 055-238 2195 to book).

ʲesidence of the Medici Grand Dukes

ʲpace is not a problem at the vast and fortress-like **Palazzo Pitti** ❾. This became ʰe residence of the Medici Grand Dukes in 1550 and, like the Uffizi, it is stuffed ʲith artistic treasures, housed in museums including the Palatine Gallery, the ʲlodern Art Collection, the Argenti (Silver) Museum and the Costume Museum.

The most rewarding of these is the **Palatine Gallery** ʲTues–Sun 8.15am–6.50pm, ticket office closes 45 ɱins earlier; entrance fee), especially the richly deco-ʳated rooms with ceiling frescos by Pietro da Cortona. ʲhese illustrate the education of a prince under the tutor-ʲhip of the gods. In Room 1, the prince is torn from the ɑrms of Venus (love) by Minerva (knowledge), and in ʲubsequent rooms learns about science from Apollo, war ʲrom Mars and leadership from Jupiter. Finally the ʲrince takes his place alongside Saturn, who, in ancient ɱythology, presided over the Golden Age.

Among the paintings displayed in these rooms are ʲome wonderful portraits by Titian, who even manages ʲo turn the reformed prostitute, Mary Magdalene, into ɑ delectable study of the delights of the female form. ʲlore disturbing is Rubens' celebrated masterpiece, *The Consequences of War* (1638), an allegory of the Thirty Years War. The artist explained in a letter that the fig-ʲure in black represents "unfortunate Europe who, for so ɱany years now, has suffered plunder, outrage and mis-ʲery". Next to her, Venus is trying to restrain the war god, Mars, who is trampling over books, symbolising his dis-regard for civilisation.

The **Giardino di Boboli** ❿ (daily Jan–Feb and Nov–Dec 8.15am–4.30pm, Mar and Oct until 5.30pm, Apr–May and Sept until 6.30pm, June–Aug until 7.30pm; closed first and last Mon of month; entrance fee), behind the Palazzo Pitti, was laid out in the 16th

Map on pages 254–5

So rich is the Uffizi's collection that many of its masterpieces are kept in storage for lack of room to display them. Proposals for expansion have been under discussion for many years, but the powers that be seem incap-able of agreeing, and, for now at least, plans remain on the table.

BELOW: the opulent interior of the Palazzo Pitti.

The Bargello was built in 1255 and became a national museum in 1865.

century. Here you will find box hedges clipped into formal geometric patterns se against wild groves of ilex and cypress to create a contrast between artifice an nature.

Jewel on the hill

On one of the hills above Florence sits **San Miniato al Monte** ⓫ (daily 8am–7pn in summer, 8am–12pm and 3–6pm in winter), a jewel-like Romanesque church Catch the No. 12 or 13 bus up, and come back down on foot via **Piazzale Michelangelo**, a terrace set high above the city dotted with reproductions o Michelangelo's famous works and with fantastic views across the Arno of th city below.

Prominent in the view, to the east of the city, is the massive Gothic church o **Santa Croce** ⓬, which features in E.M. Forster's novel (and the Merchant Ivory film) *A Room with a View* (church: Mon–Sat 9.30am–5.30pm, Sun 1 –5.30pm, 7.30am–7pm for services; entrance fee; Cloister, Capella de' Pazz and museum: Mon–Sat 9.30am–5.30pm, Sun 1–5.30pm; entrance fee). Here you will find frescos by Giotto and his pupils, and the tombs and monument of famous Florentines, including Michelangelo, Machiavelli and Galileo (born in Pisa but protected by the Medici after his excommunication for holding the heretical view that the earth goes round the sun, rather than the reverse).

Weaving your way back from the church through the alleys of the Santa Croce district you pass the **Casa Buonarroti** ⓭ (Wed–Mon 9.30am–2pm; entrance fee) a house owned by Michelangelo and now containing one of his earliest works the *Madonna della Scala*, created when he was only 16 years old. Call in at the **Bar Vivoli Gelateria** (Via Isole delle Stinche 7), which serves the best ice cream

BELOW: Santa Croce's facade.

n Florence. From here it is a short step to the **Bargello** ⑭ (daily 8.15am–1.50pm, except closed 2nd and 4th Mon and 1st, 3rd and 5th Sun of the month; entrance fee), once a prison and place of execution but now a museum devoted to sculpture and applied art where you can see works by Donatello, Michelangelo, Cellini and Giambologna. Dante was born in this district, and opposite the Bargello you can see the abbey church, the **Badia Fiorentina** ⑮, where the poet watched his beloved Beatrice attending Mass. Round the corner, in Via Dante Alighieri, is the **Casa di Dante** ⑯ (Tues 10am–4pm, Wed and Fri until 3pm, Sat–Sun until 5pm; entrance fee), the house in which the poet is supposed to have been born in 1265.

Continuing west, you will reach another important shopping street, Via Roma, which leads south into Via Calimala and the **Mercato Nuovo** ⑰ (Mon–Sat). Despite its name, the "New Market" has been here since 1551, and was known as the Straw Market in the 19th century, on account of its specialism in raffia goods. The little bronze boar, **Il Porcellino**, on the south side of the market, has a shiny nose because of the number of visitors who have rubbed it for good luck.

From the north side of the market, Via Porta Rossa will take you to the **Palazzo Davanzati** ⑱, a delightful 14th-century town house; known as the **Museo della Casa Fiorentina**, sections of it are open to the public (Tues–Sat 8.15am–1.50pm, and 1st, 3rd and 5th Sun of month and 2nd and 4th Mon). Complete with frescoed walls, it presents a vivid picture of domestic life in late medieval Florence.

You are now close to the **River Arno** and the bridge called **Ponte Santa Trinità** ⑲, after the adjacent church. The bridge, which features statues of the *Four Seasons*, was blown up by the retreating Nazis in 1944 and dredged up from the river bed to be restored to its original design.

The church of **Santa Trinità** ⑳ (Mon–Sat 8am–noon and 4pm–6pm, Sun

Map on
pages
254–5

Relief on a door at Santa Trinità.

BELOW: fresco by Gozzoli in the Palazzo Medici-Riccardi.

Map on pages 254–5

Sculpture in the Accademia.

BELOW: atrium of the Annunziata.
RIGHT: sketch of Dante by Bronzino.

4–6pm) contains frescos by Ghirlandaio showing the *Life of St Francis* set against a background of Florentine buildings. North from here, **Via de' Tornabuoni** is lined with the chic boutiques of high-class couturiers, such as Salvatore Ferragamo and Gucci. At the top of the street, the Palazzo Antinori contains an excellent wine bar and restaurant, but if the prices are too steep you can sample the cheap Chinese restaurants in **Piazza Santa Maria Novella ㉑**, with a view of the Basilica di Santa Maria Novella. The latter features in Boccaccio's *Decameron*, and contains colourful frescos by Ghirlandaio on the *Life of the Virgin*. In the adjoining **museum** (Mon–Thur and Sat 9am–5pm, Sun 9am–2pm; entrance fee) you can see what remains of Paolo Uccello's masterpiece, the *Universal Deluge* fresco, depicting the flood that drowned all but Noah and his entourage, a fresco that was, ironically, badly damaged by the Florentine floods of 1966.

Popular market

Heading back to the heart of Florence, it is easy to get lost in the streets around **San Lorenzo ㉒**, the venue of a street market most days of the week. At the back of San Lorenzo is the entrance to the **Cappelle Medicee ㉓** (daily 8.15am–6pm, also 1st, 3rd, 5th Sun and 2nd, 4th Mon of the month; entrance fee), the mausoleum of the Medici family, for which Michelangelo carved two splendid tombs featuring the allegorical figures of *Night* and *Day, Dusk* and *Dawn*. The church itself is an example of Renaissance rationalism in architecture, all cool whites and greys and restrained classical decoration. By contrast, the two huge pulpits carved by Donatello with scenes from the *Life of Christ* are full of impassioned emotion, and Michelangelo's staircase leading to the **Biblioteca Medicea Laurenziana** (Laurentian Library; Sun–Fri 9.30am–1.30pm; entrance fee during special exhibitions), off the cloister, is considerably more exuberant.

Just off Piazza di San Lorenzo is the **Palazzo Medici-Riccardi** (Thur–Tues 9am–7pm; entrance fee), the first Medici seat, containing a frescoed chapel, state rooms and a library.

Michelangelo's most famous work, *David*, is in the **Galleria dell'Accademia ㉔** (Tues–Sun 8.15am–7.15pm, Mon until 2pm; entrance fee), two blocks away in Via Ricasoli. Other highlights include Michelangelo's unfinished *Four Slaves*, the plaster cast of Giambologna's *Rape of the Sabines* (on display in the Loggia dei Lanzi) and Fillipino Lippi's striking *Deposition from the Cross*, which was finished by Perugino on the former's death. The collection has been recently expanded to incorporate a display of musical instruments.

The nearby convent of **San Marco ㉕** (church: Tues–Sun 8.15am–6pm; museum: Mon–Thurs 8.15am–1.50pm, Fri until 6pm, Sat–Sun until 7pm; closed 1st, 3rd, 5th Sun and 2nd and 4th Mon every month; entrance fee) contains nearly every painting and fresco ever produced by the saintly artist Fra Angelico.

Return to the city centre via the **Piazza della Santissima Annunziata ㉖**, with its delicate Renaissance colonnade fronting the **Innocenti** orphanage, the work of Brunelleschi, and the **Museo Archeologico Nazionale ㉗** (Mon 2–7pm, Tues and Thur 8.30am–7pm, Wed and Fri–Sun 8.30am–2pm; entrance fee), with its ancient Etruscan and Egyptian treasures. ❑

Florentine Firsts

From something as down-to-earth as street paving and eyeglasses to grand concepts such as capitalism and the theory of the universe, it is sometimes difficult to grasp the breadth of Florence's contributions to the modern world.

Old records show that street paving began in Florence in the year 1235, and by 1339 the city had paved all its streets – the first in Europe to do so. And while Florentines had little to do with the discovery of the New World, Amerigo Vespucci provided the word "America", and Leonardo da Vinci created the first world maps showing America. A tablet in Santa Maria Maggiore Church documents another first: "Here Lies Salvino d'Amato degli Armata of Florence, the Inventor of Eyeglasses, May God Forgive His Sins, Year 1317."

Two developments in music are among the most solidly documented Florentine firsts. The pianoforte was invented in Florence in 1711 by Cristofori, and the origins of opera are traced to the performance, in 1600, of *Euridice*, a new form of musical drama written by Iacopo Peri in honour of the marriage in Florence of Maria de' Medici to Henry IV of France. An earlier marriage was the impetus for modern table manners. When Catherine de' Medici wed the future Henry II and moved to France, she was apparently appalled at the French court's table manners; in contrast to Florence, no one used a fork. Before long, all of Paris society was imitating her. It is also possible that Catherine, equally appalled at French food, sent for her own chefs, and was responsible for the birth of French haute cuisine.

The arts

Many other firsts, of course, are related to the arts. Donatello's *David* (1430) is regarded as the first free-standing nude statue of the Renaissance. Donatello is also credited with the first free-standing equestrian statue of the Renaissance.

The grandiose claim that Brunelleschi is the father of modern architecture is one of the least contested. He was the first Renaissance architect to evolve the rules of linear perspective, and he developed a new approach, detailing specifications in advance and separating design from construction.

Machiavelli, through *The Prince* and other works, is credited with inventing both modern political science and modern journalism. Another literary great was Dante. Though much of his work was written in exile, Dante's highbrow Florentine language was so admired that it became the basis for modern Italian. Also in literature, Guicciardini is credited with laying the groundwork for modern historical prose, Petrarch for modern poetry and Boccaccio for the modern prose narrative.

In the financial world, it is arguable that 13th-century Florentine banks were responsible for modern capitalism, and that the city's medieval merchants were the first of a new, and eventually dominant, social class. But there is less doubt that those early Florentine financiers originated credit banking and double-entry bookkeeping, both of which contributed to the success of capitalism. Finally, it is well documented that in 1252 Florence became the first city to mint its own gold coin, the florin, which was widely used throughout Europe. ❏

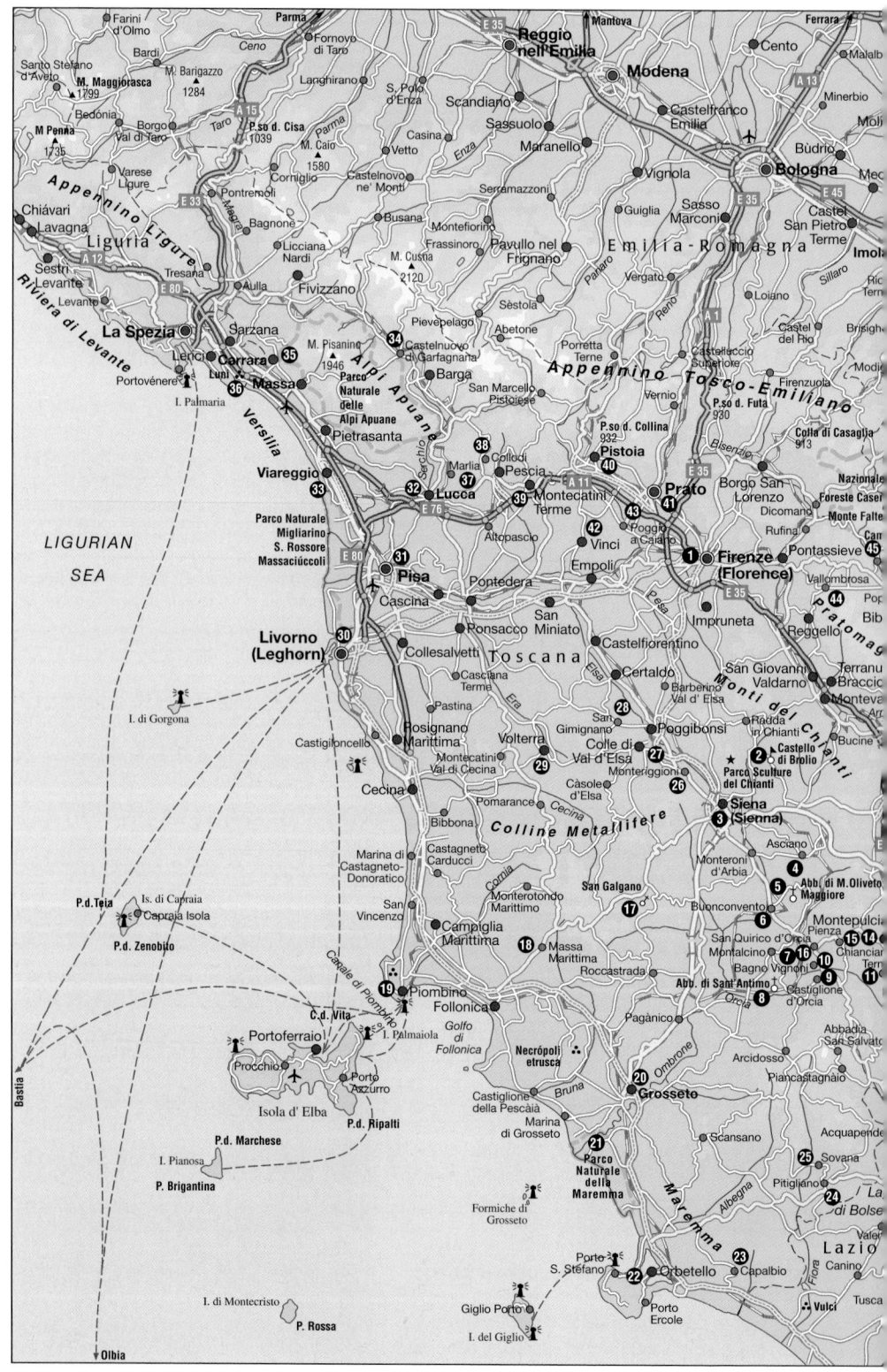

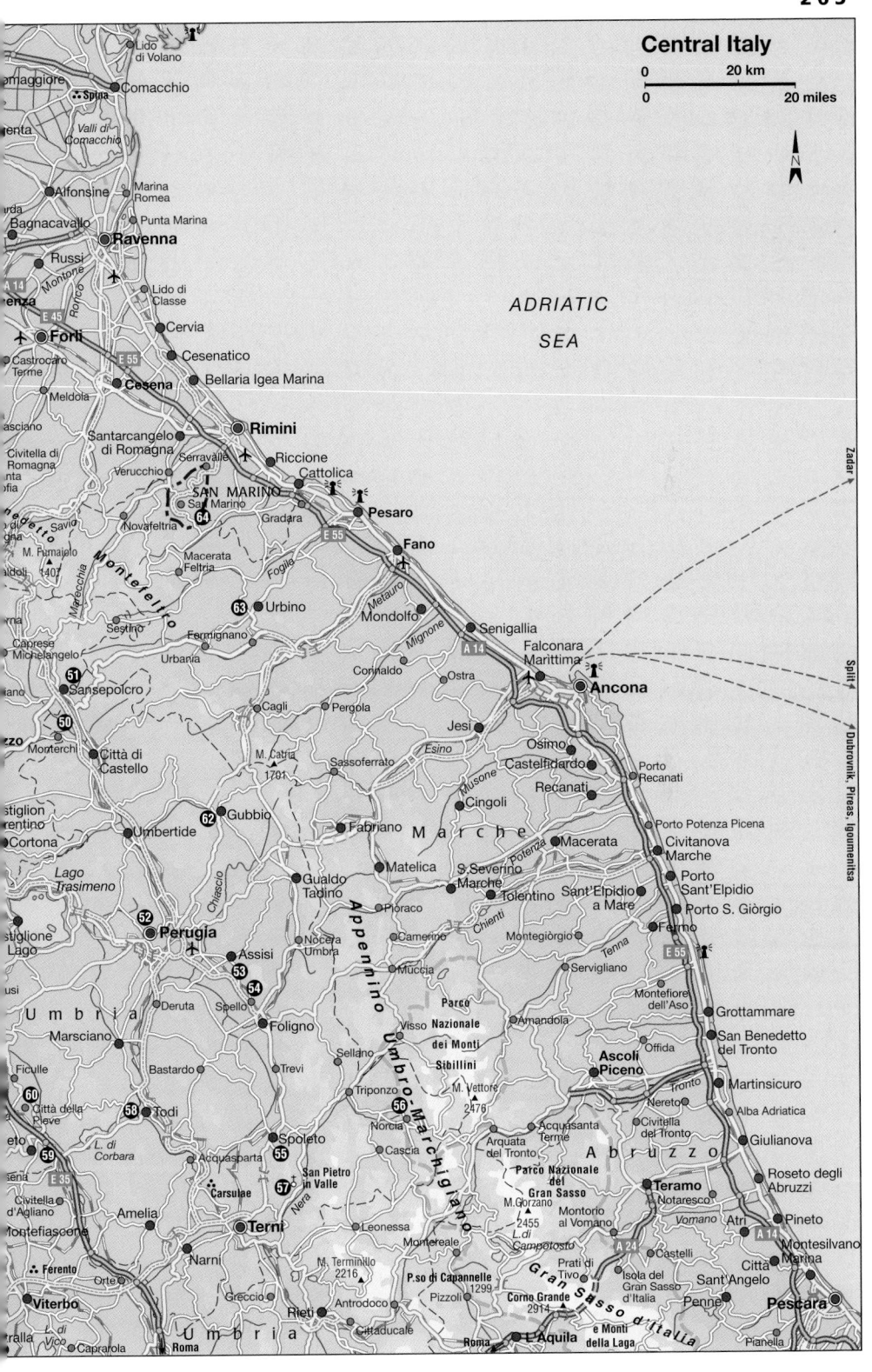

Central Italy

ADRIATIC

SEA

TUSCANY

Strong architecture, evocative landscapes and soft red wines form an essential part of this region's appeal, and the cities of Siena and Pisa have much to recommend them

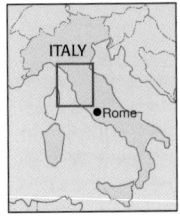

For those not fascinated by frescos, the delights of **Florence ❶** can quickly fade, and the desire to escape the cauldron-like atmosphere of this hot, dry city can prove overwhelming, as it did in the case of the English writer Laurie Lee: "I'd had my fill of Florence, lovely but indigestible city. My eyes were choked with pictures and frescos… I began to long for the cool uplands, the country air, the dateless wild olive and the uncatalogued cuckoo."

Lee escaped by walking south along the Chiantigiana, the Chianti Way, shown on maps as the N222 road, which takes you to Siena via several pretty towns in the Chianti Classico wine-growing region. If you are driving, the journey will take little more than an hour, unless you are tempted to stop along the route at the scores of *fattorie* (wine estates) offering free tastings and wine sales direct to the public *(vendita diretta)*. This is one way to learn about the region's famous red wines; another is to leave the N222 at Castellina in Chianti and drive east, stopping for a walk round the pretty town of Radda in Chianti before rejoining the N429 to the **Badia a Coltibuono** (gardens and cellars May–Oct daily 2–5pm), a 12th-century abbey set among pines, oaks, chestnuts and vines. Below the abbey are cellars filled with Chianti Classico, the abbey's traditional living. Wine, together with locally produced olive oil and chestnut honey, can be bought on the premises or savoured in the excellent abbey restaurant (tel: 0577-749031; www.coltibuono.com).

South of Gaiole in Chianti is **Castello di Brolio ❷** (Apr–Oct Mon–Fri 9am–7.30pm, Sat–Sun 11am–6.30pm, Nov–Mar Mon–Fri 9am–1pm and 2–5.30pm; entrance fee) the birthplace of the modern Chianti industry. It was here, in 1870, that Barone Bettino Ricasoli established the formula for making Chianti wines that has been used ever since, requiring a precise blend of white and red grape juice and the addition of dried grapes to the vat to give the wine its softness and fruit-filled flavour.

City of narrow medieval lanes

Knowledgeable about the region's wines, you can tackle the traffic headaches that await in **Siena ❸**. Finding space to park may prove difficult, but the medieval core of the city is largely traffic-free, because the alleys that thread between high palaces of rose-pink brick are too narrow for vehicles. All roads in Siena eventually lead to the **Campo Ⓐ**, the huge main central square, which is shaped like an amphitheatre – the Sienese say that it is shaped like the protecting cloak of the Virgin, who, with St Catherine of Siena, is the city's patron saint.

From the comfort of a pavement café on the curved side of the Campo you can note the division of the paved surface into nine segments, commemorating the beneficent rule of the Council of Nine Good Men which governed

LEFT: classic Tuscan landscape.
BELOW: a door knocker, typical of the Tuscan nobility's taste for elaborate decoration.

A statue by the Duomo shows Remus and the she-wolf. Remus' son is said to have founded Siena.

Siena from the mid-13th century to the early 14th, a period of stability and pros perity when most of the city's main public monuments were built. Twice a year on 2 July and 16 August, the Sienese recreate their medieval heritage in the Palio a sumptuous pageant-cum-horserace around the Campo. This is no mere tourist event; the residents of the city's 17 *contrade*, or districts, pack the square as their representative horses and riders career around the Campo, and the rider who wins the race and the Palio, a heraldic banner, becomes an instant local hero. At the square's base is the **Palazzo Pubblico**, with its crenellated facade and waving ban ners. Erected in the 14th century, it housed the offices of the city government. At its left corner is the slender bell tower, the **Torre del Mangia** (Mar–Oct daily 10am–7pm, Nov–Feb 10am–4pm; entrance fee). Climb more than 500 steps for a panorama of the city.

Although bureaucrats still toil in parts of the *palazzo*, as they have for some seven centuries, much of the complex is now devoted to the **Museo Civico** Ⓑ (daily 10am–7pm in summer, until 6pm in winter; entrance fee), which houses some of the city's greatest treasures. Siena's city council once met in the vast **Sala**

Siena

0   200 m
0   200 yds

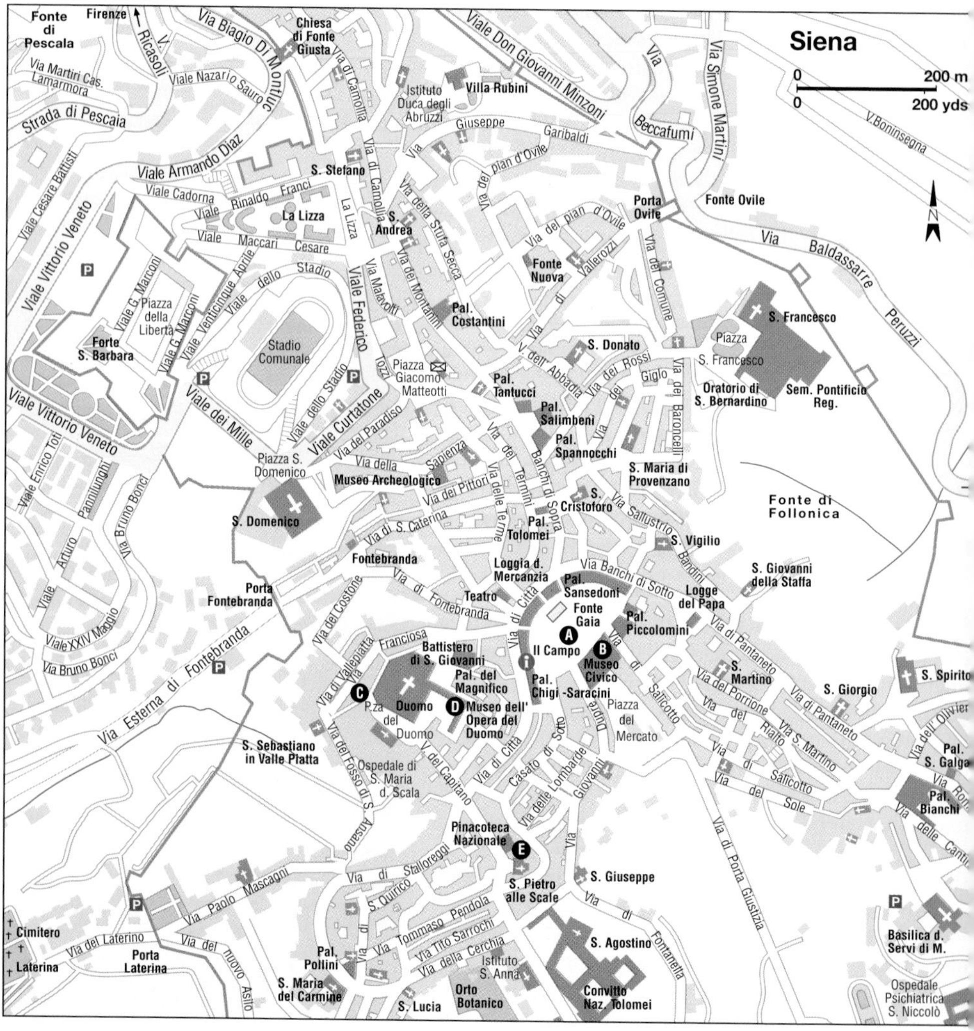

el **Mappamondo**, although the huge globe that then graced the walls has disappeared. What remains are two frescos attributed to the medieval master Simone Martini: the majestic mounted figure of Guidoriccio da Fogliano and, opposite, e *Maestà*. The *Maestà* is signed in Simone Martini's own hand, but in recent ears doubts have been cast on the authenticity of the Guidoriccio. A smaller fresco cently uncovered below the huge panel may be Simone Martini's original, and e Guidoriccio may have been executed long after the artist's death.

In the Sala della Pace is Ambrogio Lorenzetti's *Allegory of Good and Bad overnment*. Intended as a constant reminder to the city fathers of their responbilities, it depicts the entire sweep of medieval society, from the king and his urt down to the peasants working the terraced hillsides outside the city walls.

Exiting again to the Campo, turn left and head up the hill via one of the winding reets to **Piazza del Duomo** ❸. The facade of the vast striped cathedral (June–Aug Ion–Sat 10.30am–8pm, Sun 1.30–6pm, Mar–May and Sept–Oct Mon–Sat).30am–7.30pm, Sun 1.30–5.30pm, Nov–Feb Mon–Sat 10.30am– 6.30pm, Sun 30–5.30pm; entrance fee) is a festival of green, pink and white marble, which ill help prepare you for the stunning black-and-white geometric patterns of the iterior. Take special care to study the 15th- and 16th-century marble inlaid paving f the Duomo, which depicts allegories and scenes from the New Testament (unfornately, many are covered most of the year to protect them from wear and tear). ff the north aisle is the decorative Libreria Piccolomini, built in 1495 to house ie personal papers and books of Pope Pius II. The frescos by Pinturicchio show :enes from the life of the pope, and in the centre of the room is the famous *Three races*, a Roman copy of a sculpture by the Greek artist Praxiteles.

Siena has two other important museums: the **Museo dell'Opera del Duomo** ❶ (Cathedral Museum; daily 9.30am–7pm in sumier, June–Aug until 8pm, Nov–Feb 10am–5pm; ntrance fee), to the right (south) of the cathedral, and ie **Pinacoteca Nazionale** ❺ (Picture Gallery; ues–Sat 8.15am–7.15pm, Sun until 1.15pm, Mon .30am–1.30pm; entrance fee), in the Palazzo Buongnori on the Via San Pietro, just south of the Campo. 'he Cathedral Museum's main attraction is the room evoted to the works of Duccio di Buoninsegna, ɪcluding his moving *Madonna dei Francescani*, the 'irgin enthroned.

₹ounded hills of the Crete

iena sits at the geographical centre of Tuscany, and /hichever way you drive you will be spoilt for choice in ?rms of attractive historic towns and beautiful counyside. Drive southwest along the N438 to unpromising ₅sciano ❹ and you will pass through the dramatic 'rete region, the Tuscany that appears on countless ostcards and posters. Here the bare, rounded clay hills ave no trees except for the occasional stately avenue f cypresses, winding across the landscape and markɪg the way to an isolated farm, a simple Romanesque hurch or a *borgo*, a small defended village.

Asciano's main street, Corso Giacomo Matteotti, is ɪned with smart shops and classical *palazzi*. At the top nd is the simple Romanesque **Collegiata** and the Ɩuseo **Archeologico e d'Arte Sacra** (Tues–Sun

Maps:
Area 264
City 268

Fresco in Monte Oliveto Maggiore.

BELOW: rooftops of Siena.

Church in the well-preserved town of Buonconvento.

BELOW: 5th-century Tomb of the Monkey, Chiusi.

10am–1pm and 3–7pm), a revamped museum of Sienese sculpture and archaeo logical finds from the area. The **Museo Etrusco** (daily 10am–12.30pm an 3–6pm, closed Tues pm), on Corso Matteotti, is a typical small Tuscan museur that celebrates Etruscan inheritance.

A short drive on is the **Abbazia di Monte Oliveto Maggiore** ❺ (dail 9.15am–noon and 3.15–6pm, until 5pm in winter), a 14th-century Benedictin monastery with an air of aloof dignity, set among groves of cypress trees. The Grea Cloister is covered in frescos on the *Life of St Benedict*, begun by Luca Signorel in 1495 and completed by Sodoma from 1505. The excellent monastery guideboo gives a detailed description. In one scene Sodoma portrays himself with his pe badgers (one wearing a scarlet collar) looking like a pair of well-trained dogs.

Buonconvento ❻ is worth a brief stop, if only to admire the massive mediev: city gates of iron-bound wood, before driving through fertile countryside, sca tered with vineyards, to the hilltop town of **Montalcino** ❼, a wine-producin town where every other shop seems to sell the famed Brunello wines. It is also town of timeless character, with several old-fashioned wood-panelled bars wher vineyard workers shelter from the midday sun. The streets are narrow and steer and from the airy heights of the walls there are entrancing views. The highest poin is the **Fortezza** (Fortress), housing a wine centre or *enoteca* (daily 9am–8pm ii summer, 9am–6pm in winter; entrance fee to enter the castle towers), wher regional vintages can be sampled and purchased and the ramparts explored.

Romanesque abbey church

Further south again is another sight that features on postcards, but which is fa more beautiful in the flesh. The ancient abbey church of **Sant'Antimo** ❽, bui f creamy travertine and set against tree-clad hills, has inspired numerous poets nd painters. The main part of the church was built in 1118 in a style that owes uch to the influence of French Romanesque. The simple interior has capitals arved with biblical scenes, and recorded plainsong echoes around the walls as ou explore. The small community of Augustinian monks who tend the church ng the Gregorian chant at Mass every Sunday afternoon throughout the year.

A tortuous mountain route will take you through **Castiglione d'Orcia** ❾ and **Rocca d'Orcia**, both with medieval castles built to watch over the valley of the River Orcia, and down to the tiny, fashionable spa town of **Bagno Vignoni** ❿. At its heart, where the main square ought to be, this has a large stone-lined pool where sulphurous vapours rise above the hot, bubbling waters which well up rom volcanic rocks deep under the earth. Some famous bodies have bathed in his pool in times past, including St Catherine of Siena. Bathing is now forbid-en, but there are several spas and swimming pools nearby.

Just north of Bagno Vignoni, a minor road takes you east along the wide vale f the River Orcia and then up to **Castellúccio** and **La Foce** ⓫, from where here are spectacular views of a cypress-lined, ancient Etruscan road zigzag-ing up the hill. The next town is **Chianciano Terme** ⓬, a popular spa resort vith chic shops and a historic town centre. More interesting is **Chiusi** ⓭, one f the most powerful cities in the ancient Etruscan League. Chiusi's pride is he **Museo Archeologico Nazionale** (daily 9am–8pm; entrance fee), which has ne of the finest collections of its kind in Italy – a thoughtfully arranged display f Etruscan funerary urns, canopic jars, sculptures and Greek-style vases exca-ated from local tombs. Arrangements can be made at the museum to visit one f the tombs in the vicinity (using the same ticket).

Map on pages 264–5

People have been taking the therapeutic waters of Tuscany since Roman times. Lorenzo the magnificent, ruler of Florence, who suffered from arthritis, was one notable spa enthusiast.

BELOW: the timeless Tuscan landscape.

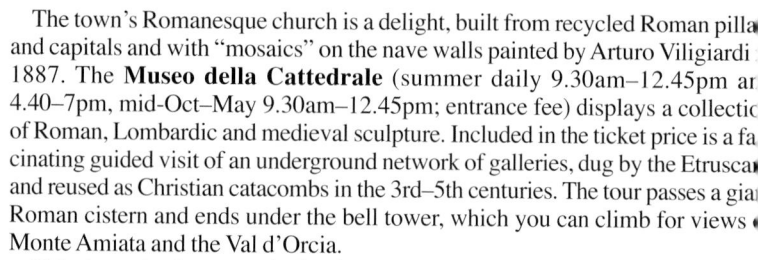

The town's Romanesque church is a delight, built from recycled Roman pilla and capitals and with "mosaics" on the nave walls painted by Arturo Viligiardi 1887. The **Museo della Cattedrale** (summer daily 9.30am–12.45pm ar 4.40–7pm, mid-Oct–May 9.30am–12.45pm; entrance fee) displays a collectic of Roman, Lombardic and medieval sculpture. Included in the ticket price is a fa cinating guided visit of an underground network of galleries, dug by the Etrusca and reused as Christian catacombs in the 3rd–5th centuries. The tour passes a gia Roman cistern and ends under the bell tower, which you can climb for views o Monte Amiata and the Val d'Orcia.

Chiusi stands almost on the border with Umbria, but our Tuscany tour conti ues north, up the fertile Val di Chiana, where cattle are bred to supply the restauran of Florence with the raw ingredients of *bistecca alla fiorentina* (steak Florentine then west to **Montepulciano** ⑭. This splendid hilltop town deserves long an leisurely exploration, with stops to sample the local Vino Nobile wines, either in th city's rock-cut cellars, or in the elegant Caffè Poliziano (Via del Corso Voltaia 27

The spacious main square, the **Piazza Grande**, sits at the town's highest poin On one side is the 15th-century **Palazzo Comunale** (Town Hall), a miniatur version of the Palazzo Vecchio in Florence. On the other side, Sangallo's intr guing 16th-century **Palazzo Contucci** now houses a hotel and wine cella (closed 12.30–2.30pm). Between the two is the gloomy **Duomo** (dail 9am–12.30pm and 3–6pm), which contains a masterpiece of the Siena Schoo the huge *Assumption* triptych (1401) by Taddeo di Bartolo over the high altar.

As the road to Pienza leaves Montepulciano, it is worth diverting right for th church of the **Madonna di San Biagio**, perched on a platform below the wall of the city. This domed church of honey- and cream-coloured stone, a Renais sance gem begun in 1518, is the masterpiece of Anto nio da Sangallo.

Model Renaissance city, built for a pop

Pienza ⑮ is an exquisite Renaissance tiny town. It is als famous for sweet sheep's-milk cheeses, and the fact tha the future Pope Pius II was born here in 1405. He decide to rebuild the village of his birth as a model Renaissanc city, but was swindled by his architect, Bernard Rossellino, who embezzled most of the funds. Only th papal palace and the cathedral were completed and bot are now suffering from serious subsidence.

Despite the great cracks and buckled pillars, the cathe dral is uplifting, and flooded with light from the grea windows that the Pope requested – he wanted a *domu vitrea*, a house of glass, to symbolise the enlightenment o the Humanist Age. The **Palazzo Piccolomini** (mid Mar–mid-Oct Tues–Sun 10am–6.30pm, in winte Tues–Sun until 4.30pm, closed Jan–mid-Feb; guide tours only; entrance fee) alongside is filled with th Pope's personal possessions, and the loggia at the rea was designed to frame views of Monte Amiata, the dis tant, cone-shaped peak of an extinct volcano.

The last stop after Pienza is **San Quirico d'Orcia** ⑯ with its splendid Collegiata, whose Romanesque wes portal is carved with dragons and mermaids.

Back in Siena, the N73 will take you southwestward on a winding and often empty road through the gree

Some of the best producers of Vino Nobile di Montepulciano are Avignonesi, Le Casalte and Poliziano.

BELOW: view along Pienza's town walls.

Map on
pages
264–5

nd sparsely populated foothills of the Colline Metalliferre, the Metal-Bearing
ills, so called because they have been a rich source of iron, copper, silver and
ad ores since ancient Etruscan times.

Some 20 km (12 miles) out of Siena, be sure to stop off at the ruined Cistercian
bey of **San Galgano** ⑰, with its huge and roofless abbey church, where
wallows skim in and out of the glassless Gothic windows and sunlight plays on
e richly carved capitals of the nave. On a hill above the church is the beehive-
aped oratory built in 1182 on the site of San Galgano's hermitage. Look out for
e sword in the stone, thrust there by the saint when he renounced his military
reer to become a hermit. An excellent shop alongside sells local herbs, wines, toi-
tries and books on the history and sights of the region.

Massa Marittima is the ancient mining capital of the region, but there are
 ugly industrial scars, just two museums devoted to the history of mining in the
gion (which flourished in the 13th century) and one of Tuscany's finest
omanesque churches, decorated with humorous sculptures illustrating the
dventures of St Cerbone, the town's patron saint. Massa Marittima is the gate-
ay to Tuscany's south, a holiday land with many fine and unspoilt beaches and
 Mediterranean climate, notably different from that only a short way north.

From **Piombino** ⑲ ferries take visitors to the island of **Elba**, either on day trips
 see the villa where Napoleon spent a short period in exile, or for a relaxing week
 one of the island's many family-friendly hotels. Further south along the busy
oastal road, the Via Aurelia, the city of **Grosseto** ⑳ is worth a stop only if you
ant to visit the excellent **archaeology museum** (Nov–Apr Tues–Sun 9am–1pm
d 4–6pm, May–Oct Tues–Sun 10am–1.30pm, 5–8pm; times may vary, tel:
564-488752; free). This has displays and finds that will help you understand the

The symbol of Massa Marittima's "New Town".

BELOW: the harbour of Porto Ercole, on Monte Argentario.

Giglio is the second-largest island after Elba in the Tuscan archipelago, a chain of seven islands between the Ligurian and Tyrrhenian seas. It is very popular with weekending Romans, daytrippers and divers, and makes for a lovely excursion. It can be reached by ferry from Porto Santo Stefano on the rugged Argentario peninsula (accessed via Orbetello).

BELOW: one of the medieval towers of San Gimignano.

ruins of nearby Etruscan cities such as **Vetulonia** (22 km/13 miles northwest of Grosseto) and **Roselle** (7 km/4 miles north).

Just south of Grosseto is the **Parco Naturale della Maremma** ㉑ (daily; entrance fee), a protected traffic-free nature reserve, rich in wildlife, with a long stretch of beautiful unspoilt beaches. The park office in **Alberese** (Mar–Sep 8am–5pm, Oct–Mar 8.30am–1.30pm) issues tickets and supplies information on walking trails.

Another wildlife haven is the lagoon north of Orbetello, an important wintering spot for birds. In the 16th century **Orbetello** ㉒ was a Spanish garrison town, and the baroque architecture reflects this fact. The sea laps right up to the stout city walls, and visitors come from afar for the excellent restaurants specialising in fish.

Inland, tiny villages like **Capalbio** ㉓ specialise in more robust Tuscan dishes such as wild boar and even baked porcupine (both are hunted locally). For a totally sybaritic experience, you can swim beneath the stars in the hot falls just south of **Saturnia** before heading into the town for a leisurely meal.

The other villages of this beautiful region, known as the forgotten corner of Tuscany, are situated above dramatic cliffs of soft tufa. These are especially spectacular at **Pitigliano** ㉔, where local people have excavated caves in the rock for storing wine and olive oil, and at **Sovana** ㉕, where the ancient Etruscans excavated tombs in the soft rock below the town. The tiny one-street village has two outstanding proto-Romanesque churches.

West of Siena

More spectacular sights await to the west of Siena. Taking the N2, you will first pass **Monteriggioni** ㉖, a hilltop town built in 1213 to guard the northern border of Sienese territory, encircled by walls and 14 towers.

Next, drive through the lower, modern town of **Colle di Val d'Elsa** ㉗ and, taking the Volterra road, head for the more ancient upper town. Here the main street is lined with 16th-century *palazzi* of unusual refinement and, at one point, the stately procession of buildings is interrupted by a viaduct from which there are splendid views of the surrounding landscape. The shops here are filled with fine glass and crystalware made in the glass factories down in the valley.

Perhaps the most spectacular sight anywhere in Tuscany is the town of **San Gimignano** ㉘, bristling with medieval towers, scarcely changed in appearance since the Middle Ages and richly rewarding – despite the huge number of visitors. (It is best to stay overnight here, in one of the characteristic hotels, to savour the peaceful beauty of the town in the evening and early morning after the day-trippers have gone.) The main street is lined with shops, many of them selling quality crafts as well as locally produced Vernaccia wines and wild-boar ham.

The tall defensive towers lining the two squares at the highest point of the town were built as status symbols rather than for genuinely defensive purposes. These alone make a visit here worthwhile, but the town also possesses such an embarrassment of artistic riches that few visitors get to see everything. The highlights are the *Wedding Scene* frescos in the **Museo Civico** (daily; Mar–Oct 9.30am–7pm, Nov–Feb 10am–5.30pm)

ntrance fee), showing the newly married couple taking a bath together and
limbing into bed, plus the frescos that cover every inch of wall space in the
Collegio, the collegiate church, depicting the *Last Judgement* and stories from
he Old and New Testaments.

Volterra ㉙ is another rewarding place, sited high on a plateau with distant
iews to the sea. The entrance to the city is dominated by a Medicean castle,
ow used as a prison, and if you wander through the park that lies beneath its
alls you will come to the **Museo Etrusco Guarnacci** (daily mid-Mar–Oct
am–6.45pm, Nov–mid-Mar 9am–1.45pm; entrance fee) in Via Don Minzoni.
This is packed with ancient Etruscan urns excavated from cemeteries uncov-
red by landslides in the 19th century. The *Married Couple* urn is a masterpiece
f realistic portraiture, and even more stunning is the bronze statuette known as
'Ombra della Sera (The Shadow of the Night), resembling a Giacometti sculp-
ure but cast in the 5th century BC.

The attractive main square of Volterra has some of the oldest civic buildings
n Tuscany, dating from the 13th century, and provides a showroom for the local
labaster-carving industry; galleries selling alabaster are located all over the
own. The cathedral has a wealth of carvings from an earlier age, including a
alletic *Deposition*, sculpted in wood in the 13th century.

As one drives west or north from Volterra, the landscape changes rapidly from
illy terrain to flat marshy coastline. You could be forgiven for missing out
Livorno ㉚, for, although it has an interesting harbour area and a famous Renais-
ance statue (the *Four Moors* monument), World War II bombing and modern
ndustry have stripped the city of its character.

Pisa ㉛, by contrast, is a must. All the main attractions lie in the northwestern

Map on
pages
264–5

*Getting the picture by
Pisa's baptistry.*

BELOW: Pisa's
Campo dei Miracoli.

angle of the city walls, around the well-named **Campo dei Miracoli** (the Field of Miracles). The appearance of the cathedral and baptistery owes much to the influence of Islamic architecture, which Pisan merchants and scholars experienced through their extensive trade contacts with Moorish Spain and North Africa. The gleaming marble surfaces of these buildings are covered in arabesques and other ornamentation, as densely patterned as an oriental carpet. The **Duomo** (Apr–Sep 10am–8pm, Mar and Oct 10am–7pm, Nov–Feb 10am–1pm and 2–5pm; entrance fee), built between 1068 and 1118, is one of Italy's major monuments and contains one of its greatest sculptures, the magnificent pulpit by Giovanni Pisano. The **Battistero** (Apr–Sept 8am–8pm, Mar and Oct 9am–6.30pm, Nov–Feb 10am–5pm) built in the same Pisan Romanesque style as the cathedral, has another fine pulpit sculpted in 1260 by Giovanni's father, Nicola.

In 2001, after more than a decade under wraps to halt the dramatic tilt, the iconic **Leaning Tower** (Torre Pendente; daily Apr–Sept 8.30am–8.30pm, mid-June–mid-Sept until 11pm, Mar and Oct 9am–7pm, Nov–Feb 10am–5pm; no entry to children under eight years; www.opapisa.it; entrance fee) reopened to the public. Visitors are now limited to 40 people at a time and queues develop quickly, so get there at opening time if you can, or book in advance through the website. It may be possible to buy tickets on the day from the Campo dei Miracoli information office to the right of the Tower, open daily 9.30am–6.30pm.

Lucca ㉜, a short way north, is a city of many seductive charms, not least the ramparts encircling the city, which were transformed into a tree-lined promenade in the 19th century. The city has more than its fair share of splendid Pisan-Romanesque churches, with ornate facades of green, grey and white marble. The best include **San Michele** (daily 9am–noon and 3–6pm), with

ts tiers of arcading and hunting scenes, **San Frediano** (daily 9am–noon and –5pm), with its massive Romanesque font, and the splendid **Duomo di San Martino** (Mon–Fri 9.30am–5.45pm, Sat until 6.45pm, Sun 9–9.50, 1.20–11.50am and 12.50–4.45pm). The Duomo contains one of the most famous relics of medieval Europe, the *Volto Santo* (Holy Face), said to have been carved by Nicodemus, who witnessed the Crucifixion – hence it was believed to be a true portrait of Christ (in fact, the highly stylised figure is probably a 13th-century copy of an 11th-century copy of an 8th-century original). Each year on 13 September, this greatly revered relic is paraded through the candlelit streets in a huge procession that takes over the whole town.

Lucca is the gateway to several regions of Tuscany which all have their own special character. To the west is the Tuscan Riviera, a string of coastal towns known as the **Versilia**. The beaches here are regimented (you pay for access but get facilities such as sun-loungers, showers, beach cabins and a bar or restaurant). **Viareggio 33** is most interesting for its Liberty-style (Art Nouveau) architecture, its plentiful fish restaurants specialising in *cacciucco* (a hearty fish soup) and its atmospheric harbour area. It is the oldest of the coastal towns in the Versilia and is famous for its February Carnival. Floats are built to a specified theme and are usually spiced up with political satire and irony.

To the north is the **Garfagnana**, a wild area of high mountains, seemingly covered in snow all year round because the peaks are made of marble. Designated as a huge nature reserve, this is a paradise for walkers. Information on waymarked trails is available from the region's main town, **Castelnuovo di Garfagnana 34**. On the fringe of the region is the marble town of **Carrara 35**, with several quarries offering guided tours and workshops. Just outside Carrara is **Luni 36**, once a Roman town and now a place of well-preserved ruins.

Nearer to Lucca, there are several ornate villas and gardens open to the public, notably the **Villa Pecci-Blunt** (formerly known as the Villa Reale; guided tours of the garden Mar–Nov Tues–Sun on the hour from 10am–noon and 3–6pm; entrance fee), at **Marlia 37**, whose Teatro Verde (Green Theatre), surrounded by clipped yew hedges, is the setting for concerts during Lucca's summer music festival. Another splendid villa, with theatrical gardens spilling down the steep hillside, is the **Villa Garzoni** (garden open daily 8.30am–sunset in summer, Mon–Fri 9am–noon and 2–5pm and Sat–Sun 8.30am–sunset in winter; entrance fee; villa currently closed for renovation) at **Collodi 38**. Collodi was also the pen name of Carlo Lenzini, the author of *The Adventures of Pinocchio* (1881), who spent his childhood here. The Pinocchio theme park in the village (open daily 8.30am–sunset) is a welcome distraction for children and is dotted with sculptures based on episodes from the book.

Montecatini Terme 39 is the most elegant spa town in Tuscany, with ornate buildings surrounded by flower beds and manicured lawns. You can buy day tickets that allow you to sample the waters and admire the marble-lined pools, splashing fountains and Art Nouveau tile pictures of water nymphs at the **Terme Tettuccio** (www.termemontecatiniweb.it).

Map on pages 264–5

Terracotta by della Robbia in Pistoia's Ospedale del Ceppo.

Below: statue at Collodi.

*The chapterhouse of
Prato's Church of
San Francesco
contains splendid
frescos by Niccolò
Gerini.*

Medieval and modern sculpture

Pistoia **40** and its neighbour, Prato, are both industrial towns specialising in tex
tiles and metalworking, but with attractive historic centres. Pistoia's Piazza de
Duomo is graced with the Romanesque **Cattedrale di San Zeno** and Baptistery
The town's churches contain a remarkable number of carved fonts and pulpit
from the pre-Renaissance period; they include Giovanni Pisano's pulpit of 1301 ii
Sant'Andrea church, which art historians consider to be his masterpiece, mor
accomplished even than the pulpit he made for Pisa's cathedral in 1302. In th
Palazzo del Tau, you can also see the work of one of Italy's best-known moder
sculptors, Marino Marini (1901–80), now the **Museo Marino Marini** (Mon–Sa
10am–6pm, until 5pm Oct–Mar; entrance fee), on Corso Silvano Fedi.

Prato **41** was the birthplace of Francesco di Marco Datini (1330–1410), wh
died one of the richest men in Europe and left his money to city charities. Anothe
local merchant married a Palestinian woman in 1180 and discovered that he
dowry included the Virgin's girdle. The relic is exhibited four times a year from
Donatello's external pulpit on the Duomo facade. Inside are superb frescos by Fra
Filippo Lippi and Agnolo Gaddi. Prato's textile heritage can be seen in the excel
lent **Museo del Tessuto** (Mon–Fri 10am–6pm, Sat until 2pm, Sun 4–7pm
entrance fee). Also worth visiting is the 13th-century **Castello dell' Imperator**
(9am–5.30pm, 4.30pm in winter; entrance fee), the only one of its kind in Italy
built for the Holy Roman Emperor Frederick II of Swabia.

City of Leonardo

South of Pistoia is the tiny hilltop village of **Vinci** **42**, birthplace of Leonardo da
Vinci, where the castle has been turned into an entertaining **museum** (daily
9.30am–6pm; entrance fee) dedicated to the great ma
and his inventions. The displays consist of wooden mod
els of a bicycle, a submarine, a tank, a helicopter, etc.
beautifully crafted and based on Leonardo's notebooks

From Vinci, you can take a winding rural road into Flor
ence, stopping at **Poggio a Caiano** **43** (daily June–Aug
8.15am–7.30pm, Apr–May and Sept until 6.30pm, Ma
and Oct until 5.30pm, Nov–Feb until 4.30pm, closed 2n
and 3rd Mon each month, guided tour only), the vill
built for Lorenzo de' Medici which became the arche
type for many others. Skirting Florence, you can spee
south to Arezzo on the A1 autostrada, or break the jour
ney by leaving at the Incisa intersection and following
signs for **Vallombrosa** **44**. The reward is the splendi
beech wood that surrounds it; the poet John Milton, vis
iting in 1638, was so impressed that he wrote a descrip
tion of Vallombrosa's autumnal leaves in *Paradise Lost*

More delights await if you go north and take the N70
to **Stia** **45**. From here, you can visit two sacred sites se
high in spectacular woodland, cut by mountain stream
and waterfalls. One is the hermitage at **Camaldoli** **46**
(open only to male visitors), 17 km (10 miles) east o
Stia; the other is the monastery at **La Verna** **47** furthe
south, best reached by driving east from Bibbiena. I
was here that the hands and feet of St Francis were
miraculously marked with the stigmata in 1224. The
monastery commands panoramic views.

On the way south from here to Arezzo, it is also worth

seeking out little **Caprese Michelangelo** ❽, which has a sculpture park in the grounds of the castle where Michelangelo was born. The views over Alpine countryside explain why Michelangelo attributed his good brains to the mountain air he breathed as a child.

Arezzo ❾ has an **archaeological museum** (daily 8.30am–7.30pm, closes earlier in winter; entrance fee) full of Arretine tableware, fashionable during the Roman period. For most visitors, though, the highlight will be Piero della Francesca's painstakingly restored fresco cycle in the church of **San Francesco** (Mon–Fri 9am–7pm, Sat 9am–6pm, Sun 1–6pm; essential to pre-book; tel: 0575-352727). The frescos illustrate the *Legend of the True Cross*, a complex story whereby the wood of the Tree of Knowledge, which bore the fruit that Adam and Eve ate, becomes the Cross on which Christ died and then is instrumental in converting Constantine the Great, who made Christianity the religion of the Roman world.

The artist's style, compelling and mysterious, attracts superlatives from art historians, and you can easily become hooked on his work, following the Piero della Francesca trail, like the heroine of *A Summer's Lease*, a novel by the English writer John Mortimer. If so, the trail leads from here to **Monterchi** ❺, 25 km (15 miles) west along the N73, where a former schoolhouse displays his striking *Madonna del Parto*, the Pregnant Madonna. From there, you should continue 12 km (7 miles) north to **Sansepolcro** ❺, the town where Buitoni pasta is produced. Here the **Museo Civico** (mid-June–mid-Sept daily 9.30am–1.30pm and 2.30–7pm, other months closes 6pm; entrance fee) has della Francesca's 1463 masterpiece, *The Resurrection*, hailed by Aldous Huxley as "the best picture in the world". To complete the trail, you should visit **Urbino**, in the Marches, to see *The Flagellation of Christ* and other works in the Ducal Palace (*see page 291*). ❏

Map on pages 264–5

The Casentino region, north of Arezzo, is much loved by walkers. It is also well known for its plentiful wild mushrooms. The Oscar-winning film La Vita è Bella (Life is Beautiful) was filmed here, and a trail of the film locations covers the main sights.

BELOW: the terracotta roofscape of Arezzo.

ROLLING HILLS, CYPRESS TREES AND TOWERS

The distinctive Tuscan countryside has for centuries been a favourite haunt of travellers looking to escape the madding crowds of the cities

As glorious as its historic cities and artistic treasures may be, Tuscany's timeless landscape has long been a draw to visitors. After a hectic, sticky visit to Florence, Siena, Pisa or any of the other major towns, the relative coolness and freshness of a rural ride out is a welcome treat. Small medieval towns, perched on hills to benefit from cooling breezes, overlook a rolling landscape which embraces both controlled agriculture and nature at its wildest. Terraces of vines and silvery groves of olives vie for attention with Tuscany's own peculiar landmark – tall, slender cypresses, often planted in rows as windbreaks. These elegant trees have studded the skyline here for centuries, prompting the writer D.H. Lawrence to accuse them of hiding the secrets of the Etruscans, the early settlers of these parts. He described them as "… the sinuous, flame-tall cypresses/That swayed their length of darkness all around/ Etruscan-dusky, wavering men of old Etruria." These and other images of the Tuscan countryside feature strongly in the background of some of the greatest works of Renaissance art.

▷ **HIDDEN GEMS**
The domed 16th-century church of Santa Maria Nuova lies just beyond the ancient Etruscan walls of Cortona. Churches like this would stand out in any other environment, but in Tuscany their simple, elegant forms and the colour of the local stone blend in with the other visual delights of the countryside.

▷ **FLORA AND FAUNA**
The backdrop to the 12th-century church of Sant'Antimo provides a fine example of Tuscan nature at work. Wild flowers (best seen in late spring) fight for room with ancient olive trees and coarse shrubs and grasses. These provide a habitat for moths, lizards and cicadas, whose song is heard in summer.

TOWERS OF POWER AND WEALTH

△ **OLIVE GREEN**
The silvery leaves of olive groves bring a distinctive colour to a Tuscan hillside. Some wine estates now produce very high-quality (and highly priced) olive oils. Badia a Coltibuono also offers cookery courses in which you can learn how best to appreciate its wines and oils.

▽ **CULTIVATION CULTURE**
Tuscan farmers use their land for a variety of purposes. Olives, fruit and tobacco are just some of the crops produced alongside cereals like barley and maize. Chianina cattle, native to the region, provide the meat for *bistecca alla fiorentina*, the classic Florentine steak dish.

In the Middle Ages, towers protected the wealthiest families in times of internal and external strife; today, they mark out some of Tuscany's oldest towns, catching the traveller's eye from afar. No better example exists of this distinctive skyscape than San Gimignano *(above)*, which has 13 towers – although at one time it had more than 70.

San Gimignano's many towers date from the 12th and 13th centuries, and are mostly windowless, possibly to afford further protection; families could retreat into the many rooms inside for months at a time. Defence was not the only purpose of these lofty extensions, however: they were also status symbols. Building a tall, imperious tower was a way of flaunting your wealth and social standing.

Another theory about the towers concerns the textile trade for which San Gimignano was noted. Towers may have been built to house and protect valuable dyed fabrics, as there was little room to spread them out at ground level.

As many of Tuscany's medieval towns were built on hilltops, a climb to the top of a tower is usually rewarded with magnificent views over the town and the beautiful surrounding countryside.

CHIANTI COUNTRY
uth of Florence, the hills are minated by rows of vines owing predominantly ngiovese grapes, which are essed to make Chianti wines. me vineyards are centred ound medieval castles; any of these offer tastings d sell wine to visitors.

BURNT SIENNA
e hills around the city of ena are known for their ddish-brown clay, which is ed for brick-making and the nstruction of most of the y's buildings. The stinctive pigment in the clay s become internationally own as burnt sienna.

UMBRIA AND THE MARCHES

*Castles cling to ravines, and woodland cloaks the
wild mountains in the green heart of Italy,
home to one of Christianity's best-loved saints*

Map on
pages
264–5

Perugia ⑫ is the sun around which the other towns of Umbria orbit. Like
so many of its neighbours, the city suffered considerable damage during the
series of violent earthquakes that hit Umbria during the autumn of 1997.
Following the earthquakes, many historic churches and buildings were closed as
a precautionary measure. Many have since reopened, while some remain resolutely closed. Even so, most towns in Umbria are attractive in their own right,
and worth visiting even if you cannot get into every church, museum or gallery.

Perugia's **Piazza IV Novembre** is freshened by the 13th-century **Fontana
Maggiore**. This splendid fountain is one of the great works of the Pisan sculptors
Nicola Pisano and his son, Giovanni. Carved in 1277, it is covered in elegant figures representing sundry subjects: the *Labours of the Months*, Adam and Eve,
scenes from Aesop's *Fables*. Such accomplished art, used to decorate a fountain, reveals just how important a reliable water supply was to the survival of any
medieval city. Just to the north of the fountain, the steps of the Gothic cathedral
are where people and pigeons gather to preen and flirt. Inside, the mystic *Deposition*, painted by Barocci while under the influence of poison fed to him by a
rival, inspired the famous painting by Rubens known as *The Antwerp Descent*.

Sweeping down from the piazza is the **Corso Vannucci**. On the right is the
13th- to 15th-century **Palazzo dei Priori** (Town Hall).
Up its steps is the **Sala dei Notari**, painted at the end
of the 13th century and since restored.

LEFT: Urbino.
BELOW: St Francis,
Umbria's best-loved
son.

Work of local artists

In the same building is the **Galleria Nazionale dell'
Umbria** (Tues–Sun 8.30am–7.30pm; entrance fee) containing works by the most important of the many artists
who lived in Umbria, including Francesco da Rimini, Fra
Angelico, Piero della Francesca and Pinturicchio. Next
door to the gallery is the 15th-century **Collegio del Cambio** (daily 9am–12.30pm and 2.30–5.30pm in summer,
Tues–Sun 9am–2pm in winter, Sat 9am–12.30pm all
year; entrance fee), distinguished by frescos of Perugino
and his school, and by 17th-century inlaid woodwork.

The rest of the Corso Vannucci is best appreciated at
night. Relax in one of the cafés on the street and watch
the students watching you. Stop at the end of the Corso
in the **Giardini Carducci** to enjoy the second-best view
in Perugia: the hills twinkling under the stars.

South of the town is **San Pietro**, with its 16th-cen-
tury choir stalls, carved with a whole medieval bestiary
– ducks, crocodiles and elephants included. Closer is the
barn-like **San Domenico**, with a little-visited tomb that
ranks as one of the finest of its age in Italy – that of Pope
Benedict XI, who died in Perugia in 1304 having eaten
poisoned figs. The adjacent cloister contains Umbria's
Museo Archeologico (daily 9am–1pm and 2.30–5.30pm;

entrance fee), with vast quantities of ancient Etruscan pottery and metalwork. West of the city centre is the church of **San Bernardino**, its façade decorated with angels and musicians in diaphanous robes, like the figures in Mucha's Art Nouveau posters, except that these date to 1451, not the 1890s.

Assisi and the Vale of Spoleto

There is no place quite like **Assisi ㊵**. Despite the crowds, despite the damage caused by the 1997 earthquakes, it remains an inspiring and spiritual city. The sight, as you approach Assisi, of the mighty arches supporting the Basilica di San Francesco, rising above the perpetual Umbrian haze, and of Monte Subasio, the great peak towering behind, is sufficient to make the rest of the world seem blissfully far away. The streets are almost too postcard perfect: cascades of flowers fall from wall sconces, alleyway gardens hoard every scrap of sunlight, and the smell of roses and wood smoke permeates the air.

The **Basilica di San Francesco** (daily – Lower Church: 6am– 6.45pm in summer, until 5.45pm in winter; Upper Church: from 8.30am; closed Sun am for services; audio guides available from tourist office opposite; entrance free) is perfectly situated for sunsets. The façade, designed by a military architect, is like the saint it commemorates, beautiful in its poverty. The main doors lead into the Upper Basilica, decorated with Giotto's famous fresco cycle on the *Life of St Francis*. The frescos have been restored following the 1997 earthquake: several saints have been reinstated, though the cycle will never look like it used to; the restoration is fragmentary yet faithful. With this cycle, Giotto revived the art of fresco painting in Italy and this is his most accomplished work (though it is now believed that at least three other artists contributed to the cycle, including Pietro

BELOW: San Bernardino in Perugia.
BELOW RIGHT: Assisi's Basilica di San Francesco, Upper Church.

Cavallini), admired by all the great artists of the Renaissance for the degree to which it introduced realism into Western art.

The walls of the Basilica Inferiore (Lower Basilica) are a jigsaw puzzle of frescos by many hands, all of them inspired by the example and life of St Francis. They vary between the sweetly cheerful frescos of Simone Martini, where even the horses seem to smile, to the sternly didactic vault frescoes depicting the monastic virtues of Chastity, Poverty and Obedience. Equally stern is the crypt where St Francis is buried, but the face of the little monk, painted in the transept by Cimabue and said to be a faithful portrait, tells a different story.

Chronologically, a tour of the rest of Assisi begins with the **Roman Forum** beneath the **Piazza del Comune**. The forum's above-ground vestige is the **Tempio di Minerva** (Minerva's Temple), whose interior has been revamped in an unfortunately gaudy manner. In the northeast sector of town, the **Anfiteatro Romano** (Roman Amphitheatre), where live naval battles were staged, has been topped by homes that follow its original oval structure.

The **Rocca Maggiore**, grim and immobile above the town, destroyed and rebuilt, was part of a string of towers guarding Assisi. The **Duomo** (12th-century, dedicated to San Rufino) is best appreciated for the carving of its Romanesque exterior details; its interior was revamped in 1571.

The newly restored **Chiesa Santa Chiara**'s pink-and-white exterior is supported by buttresses that are decidedly feminine in their generous curves. The chapel houses a 12th-century crucifix said to have spoken to St Francis.

To experience something of the solitude and spirituality that matched the lives of St Francis and St Clare, it is worth visiting a couple of churches on the outskirts of Assisi. **San Damiano**, just 2 km (1 mile) south of the town, is the con-

Map on pages 264–5

BELOW: *Francis Casts off His Clothes,* from Giotto's fresco cycle in San Francesco.

Assisi's weeping lion.

BELOW: Ponte delle Torri, Spoleto.

vent where St Clare spent most of her reclusive life, and it retains the air of a simple religious retreat. More rural still is the favourite hermitage of St Francis the **Eremo delle Carceri** (daily 6.45am–sunset), a tranquil spot nestling into the tree-covered slope of Monte Subasio, 3 km (2 miles) east of the town.

Unrivalled views of the region can be had from the summit of **Monte Subasio** (1,290m/4,230ft). For centuries the mountain was quarried for its pink stone from which so many of the buildings in the area are made. The road through the Parco Regionale del Monte Subasio begins at the hermitage car park (the barrier is raised at 6am and lowered at 6pm).

Assisi sits on the rim of a dried-up lake bed called the Vale of Spoleto, which was drained of water in the 16th century. Several other towns of great character line the eastern shore, including **Spello ㊴**, which has renowned frescos by Pinturicchio, one of the main artists of the Umbrian school. **Spoleto ㊶** sits at the southernmost point of the former lake, a city of great cosmopolitan sophistication renowned for its summer arts jamboree, the Festival dei Due Mondi (of the Two Worlds, meaning Europe and the Americas). The emphasis in this festival is on the avant-garde, and the legacy is a number of modern sculptures dotted about the town, plus numerous art galleries selling work of dubious merit.

The town's dominant building, the **Rocca Albornoziana** (guided tours only usually on the hour; Tues, Wed and Sun 9am–6pm, Thurs–Sat until 7.30pm, Mon 10am–6pm; entrance fee) was built as a papal stronghold, became the home of Lucrezia Borgia, served as a prison where members of the Red Brigades were held and is now a national museum and art gallery. Alongside is the striking **Ponte delle Torri**, spanning the gorge that yawns between the castle and the opposite hill. The Bridge of the Towers, as the name translates, was built as an aqueduct in the

13th century, and you can walk across the top of the (now dry) water channel.

Spoleto's outstanding treasure is the 12th-century **Duomo** (daily 8am–12.30pm and 3–7pm in summer, until 5.30pm in winter). Its medieval porch is surmounted by a rose window. The cathedral floor has an intricate herring-bone and spiral Romanesque design. The chapel to the right was decorated by Pinturicchio. The apse is ablaze with Filippo Lippi's final work, the coronation of an exquisite Madonna surrounded by a rainbow and an arc of angels.

On the north side of the stairs leading to the Piazza del Duomo is the 12th-century **Chiesa Sant'Eufemia**; its chaste perfection contrasts with the cathedral's grandeur. Note Sant'Eufemia's massive and ancient stone throne behind the altar.

Visitors to Spoleto with time and a taste for the wild can use the town as a base for exploring the mountainous area to the east of Umbria, where winding narrow roads carry you up to the snowy peaks of the **Monti Sibillini** range, part of the Apennines. You can drive, via Triponzo, to **Norcia 56**, the birthplace of St Benedict and a major centre of the truffle and salami industries. From here, roads climb ever higher to the spectacular **Piano Grande**, a vast open plain that is covered in rare Alpine plants in summer. On the return journey you can take in the pleasing 8th-century monastery at **San Pietro in Valle 57** (10.30am–12.30pm and 2.30–4.30pm, tel: 0744-780129 to check; the monastic complex is now a hotel, but the church is open to the public), with its Lombardic sculpture and 12th-century frescos.

Hilltop Todi

West of Spoleto is the hilltop town of **Todi 58**. Here the lovely view from the **Piazza Garibaldi** is enhanced by the fragrance of a garden beneath. Nearby is

The Edicola, or Tempietto, in Norcia is a curious structure. The 14th-century tower is covered with inscriptions and reliefs of Christian and Masonic symbols.

BELOW: the view from Monte Subasio.

Map on pages 264–5

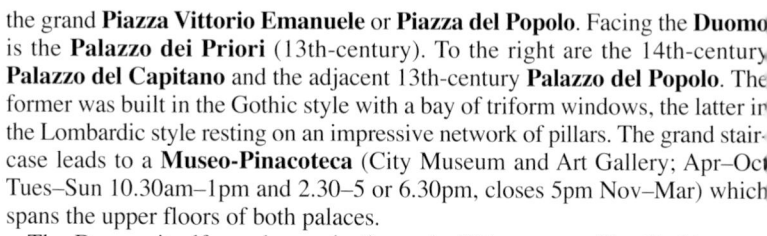

The interior of Santa Maria della Consolazione.

the grand **Piazza Vittorio Emanuele** or **Piazza del Popolo**. Facing the **Duomo** is the **Palazzo dei Priori** (13th-century). To the right are the 14th-century **Palazzo del Capitano** and the adjacent 13th-century **Palazzo del Popolo**. The former was built in the Gothic style with a bay of triform windows, the latter in the Lombardic style resting on an impressive network of pillars. The grand staircase leads to a **Museo-Pinacoteca** (City Museum and Art Gallery; Apr–Oct Tues–Sun 10.30am–1pm and 2.30–5 or 6.30pm, closes 5pm Nov–Mar) which spans the upper floors of both palaces.

The Duomo itself was begun in the early 12th century. The Gothic campanile, built 100 years later, strays from the fine Romanesque style. The Duomo's rear wall is decorated by a Ferraù da Faenza fresco. To the right is a 16th-century Giannicola di Paolo painting of the Madonna. The interior is softly lit by some of the finest stained glass in the region.

A brisk walk around the hill will bring you to the church of **San Fortunato**. The structure was begun in 1292 and built in stages over a period of 200 years during the architectural revolution. The central portal's sculptures deserve close examination for their tiny, whimsical depictions of humans and beasts. The interior is light and airy; the eggshell whiteness of the stone is enhanced by the deep sable colour of the carved choir and the formidable pillar-mounted lectern.

Through the **Parco della Rocca**, replete with good views, and on down the mountain, the **Tempio di Santa Maria della Consolazione** is perched on a little shelf of green. The 16th-century structure was long thought to be the work of Bramante because of the similarities with St Peter's in Rome, but it is now attributed to one Cola di Capsorala. The altar may seem to some a bit too much, but the space is light and airy, the intricate sunburst of stones on the floor a marvel of geometrics.

Vine-growing Orvieto

The hill which supports **Orvieto ⑤** is volcanic in origin, and therefore porous and in danger of bringing the city down as it crumbles. The volcanic slopes are covered in the vineyards that produce Orvieto's famously crisp white wines.

After climbing up serpentine curves and through scaffolding-clad streets, you will burst into the unexpected expanse of the **Piazza del Duomo**. With any luck, the late-afternoon sun will be glittering off the mosaics of the 14th-century cathedral's astonishing façade. The cathedral's steps are generally crowded with a mixture of visitors, Orvietans and soldiers garrisoned just down the street. Also on Piazza del Duomo, opposite the cathedral, is the recently renovated **Museo Claudio Faina e Civico** (Tues–Sun 9.30am–6pm in summer, Tues–Sun 10am–5pm in winter; entrance fee). This is home to one of Italy's most important collections of archaeological finds, including Etruscan artefacts and many Greek ceramic works, dating back to the 6th century BC.

The cathedral was begun on 15 November 1290 to house relics of the miracles of Bolsena (1263): principally a chalice cloth onto which blood flowed from the host during a celebration of the Mass. Although the identity of the original architect is a matter of some

BELOW: Santa Maria della Consolazione in Todi.

debate, by its completion the Duomo's construction required the input of legions of architects, sculptors, painters and mosaicists. The façade, designed by Lorenzo Maitani, is bolstered by striped horizontals of basalt and travertine.

Inside the cathedral, the black-and-white stripes point up the curvilinear arches. The wall of the apse is decorated with scenes from the *Life of the Virgin*. These were begun by Ugolino di Prete Ilario and completed by Pinturicchio and Antonio Viterbo during the late 14th century. On the left-hand side of the altar is the **Cappella del Corporale**, painted by Ugolino and his assistants and depicting *The Miracle of Bolsena*. To the right side of the altar is the **Cappella Nuova**, whose decoration was begun by Fra Angelico in 1447 and completed by Luca Signorelli at the turn of the next century.

Via Duomo and **Corso Cavour** are lined with shops selling Orvietan ceramics of medieval and Etruscan design. Nearby are elegant restaurants, chic clothiers and more shops selling wood sculptures. To the right, off Corso Cavour, is the striking 12th-century **Palazzo del Popolo**.

Straight ahead are the **Palazzo Comunale** and the church of **Sant'Andrea** in the **Piazza della Repubblica**. To the left is the **Old** or **Medieval Quarter**, which is easily the most delightful part of the town, with its ancient walls hung with pots of tumbling geraniums, and tiny cave-like workrooms of Orvietan artisans.

Lakeside pursuits

The road north from Orvieto will take you to **Città della Pieve** ❻₀, birthplace of Perugino, father of the Umbrian School of painting. The town has several of his works, including *The Adoration of the Magi*, which features Lake Trasimeno in the background.

Map on pages 264–5

TIP

Orvieto has lent its name to a white wine of variable quality. Orvieto Classico, though, refers to a special classification and can be very good. Look for wines by Antinori and Bigi. *Secco* wines are dry, while *amabile* are semi-sweet.

BELOW: Orvieto cathedral.

Today that lake is Umbria's summer holiday playground, ringed by campsites offering tennis, swimming and trekking on horseback. **Castiglione del Lago ❻** is the lake's capital, and there are splendid views from the ramparts of the 14th-century castle.

North of the lake, the road through Umbertide takes you to **Gubbio ❷**, once known as the "city of silence" because of its desolate position in the Umbrian backwoods. Now, thanks to modern roads it is a town within easy reach of those who love good food and architecture. Gubbio clings to the side of Monte Ingino, and its major buildings just fit on the narrow terraces that step up the mountainside. At the top of Monte Ingino (take the funicular railway from the station in Via San Geraloma to the top, then walk back down) rises the **Basilica di Sant'Ubaldo**. The remains of the saint are kept here in a crystal urn above the altar. The basilica also displays the three immense candles with which the sturdy men of Gubbio race up the hill in a celebration of the saint's day every 15 May.

Returning to the town, your path should take you to the fine **cathedral** to see the great Gothic ribs of the vault and the 13th-century stained glass. Across a small passage from the cathedral is the **Palazzo Ducale** (Tues–Sun 8.30am–7.30pm; entrance fee), begun in 1476 by Federico da Montefeltro, duke of Urbino.

The outstanding element of Gubbio's skyline, the bell tower of the 14th-century **Palazzo dei Consoli**, is under restoration, but the **Museo Civico** is open (daily 10am–1pm and 3–6pm in summer, 10am–1pm and 2–5pm in winter; entrance fee). Its Great Hall houses a quixotic collection of medieval paraphernalia, including examples of medieval plumbing. A room on the left of the main hall contains the **Tavole Eugubine**: seven bronze plates upon which a precise hand has translated the ancient Umbrian language into Latin.

BELOW: the Corso dei Ceri festival in Gubbio, which takes place in May.

The Marches

After the stunning hill towns of Umbria, the neighbouring region of the Marches holds very few sights that can compete, with the singular exception of **Urbino ❸**, with its stronghold of the wise old warrior Duke Federico da Montefeltro. Here he constructed one of the great treasures of 16th-century architecture. Urbino is an eyrie of a town whose golden buildings are set high amid spectacular mountains. Urbino remains one of the few hill towns left in Italy not ringed by the unsavoury intrusions of modernity. The original old city remains almost completely "unimproved", perched at the top of its two peaks.

The **Piazza del Popolo** is a tourist centre by day. By night, groups of university students recline here on the steps or in the cafés, or stand in the street and discuss politics, the latest foreign film, or last night's poetry reading. The façades are old; the faces are generally young. The contrast exemplifies the relaxed symbiosis that exists between Urbino's walls and the lives they enclose.

The duke and his Humanist contemporaries felt man was the centre of the universe – a significant break with Christian philosophy. The courtyard of his **Palazzo Ducale** is paved with a hub, with radiating spokes of marble to symbolise man's central position. The building itself is part palace and part fortress: a graceful, secure nest in the rarefied mountain air for the duke to feather with marvellous works of art. The **Galleria Nazionale delle Marche** (Tues–Sun 8.30am–7.15pm, Mon 8.30am–2pm, last entry 75 mins before closing; entrance fee), now housed in the palace, has several fine works by Piero della Francesca, including his enigmatic and disturbing *Flagellation of Christ*, and by the town's most famous artist, Raphael. Also remarkable is the *trompe l'œil* inlay work in the duke's study.

Down the street from the ducal palace is **Casa di Raffaello** (Mon–Sat 9am–1pm and 3–7pm, Sun 10am–1pm in summer, Mon–Sat 9am–2pm, Sun 10am–1pm in winter; entrance fee) where Raphael spent his first 14 years. In the courtyard is the stone upon which Raphael and his father, Giovanni, also an artist, ground their pigments.

Pocket-sized republic

Urbino stands a little inland from the Adriatic, a sunny coastline marked by hectare after hectare of orchards growing peaches and nectarines for export, and regimented beaches and seaside hotels. You will see something of this if you visit the **Republic of San Marino ❹**, a self-governing state within Italy that has remained independent for 1,700 years. Stamp collectors will know it as a republic that issues big pictorial postage stamps in a variety of shapes other than square – the philatelic output is on show in its specialist museums.

The republic stands on the peak of Monte Titano, with sweeping views to Rimini and the Adriatic beyond. You can do a complete circuit of the town's historic walls, visiting the several museums that are housed in the bastions, and the diminutive building that serves as the parliament of this pocket-sized republic.

Just west of San Marino is Federico's hilltop fortress of **San Leo**, one of the most impressive sights in Italy, which inspired Dante to use it in the landscapes of his *Divine Comedy*. In the 18th century, the alchemist Cagliostro was imprisoned here. ❑

Map on pages 264–5

Urbino was not on any major trade routes and had few natural assets, so Federico brought wealth to the town by offering himself and his army as mercenaries.

BELOW: the citadel of San Marino.

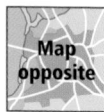

Map opposite

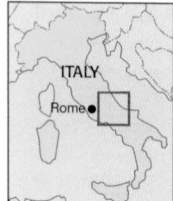

ITALY

Rome ●

ABRUZZO AND MOLISE

*Two huge national parks, Abruzzo and Gran Sasso,
make this a region where the wonders of
nature rule supreme*

From the Alpine peaks of the Gran Sasso to the wild wolves in the national park; from craggy medieval hill towns to 193 km (120 miles) of Adriatic coastline – Abruzzo offers everything an Italophile could wish for.

For years the region's wild beauty was hidden from the world by the Apennines. But now, with regular flights to Pescara, this once hidden corner is emerging from the shadows and many have hailed it as the "new Tuscany". The region boasts a unique landscape and a history which may be the oldest in Italy. Molise, which split off from Abruzzo to form an autonomous region in 1963, retains its wild spirit more completely than its more populous neighbour.

Pescara

The energetic town of **Pescara ❶** is a meeting point for travellers. A stepping stone to the Adriatic for the ancient Romans, its modern-day motor and railway links have turned the city into an industrial and business capital with a bustle and punch more typical of northern Italian towns. Pescara would win few beauty contests – much of the local building is more commercial than artistic – but, with an eye on becoming an Adriatic Riviera hotspot, Pescara is changing. In the last five years, the *centro storico* has smartened itself up, with much of the action

BELOW: the peaks
of Gran Sasso.

gravitating around Corso Manthone and Via Delle Caserme. Come here in the day to stroll the pedestrianised streets with their Liberty-style façades, including the birthplace of Italy's great poet, D'Annunzio (Course Manthonè 116; daily 9am–2pm; entrance fee). Come here in the evening and join Pescara's designer-clad beau monde as they bar-hop before heading into the nightclubs.

Chieti

Half an hour inland from Pescara is the ancient hilltop town of **Chieti ❷**. Known since antiquity for its views across mainland Abruzzo and the sea, it is home to the remains of three Roman temples located along the Corso Marrucino – just behind the post office. The recently modernised **Museo Archeologico** (daily 9am–7pm; entrance fee) has a fine collection of coins, but most significantly is home to the symbol of Abruzzo – the 6th-century BC Capestrano Warrior.

As you travel south down the coast from Pescara on the coast road towards Vasto the natural beauty of Abruzzo reveals itself. Beach umbrellas disappear

The local delicacy in Chieti is torrone di fichi secci, or nougat with figs.

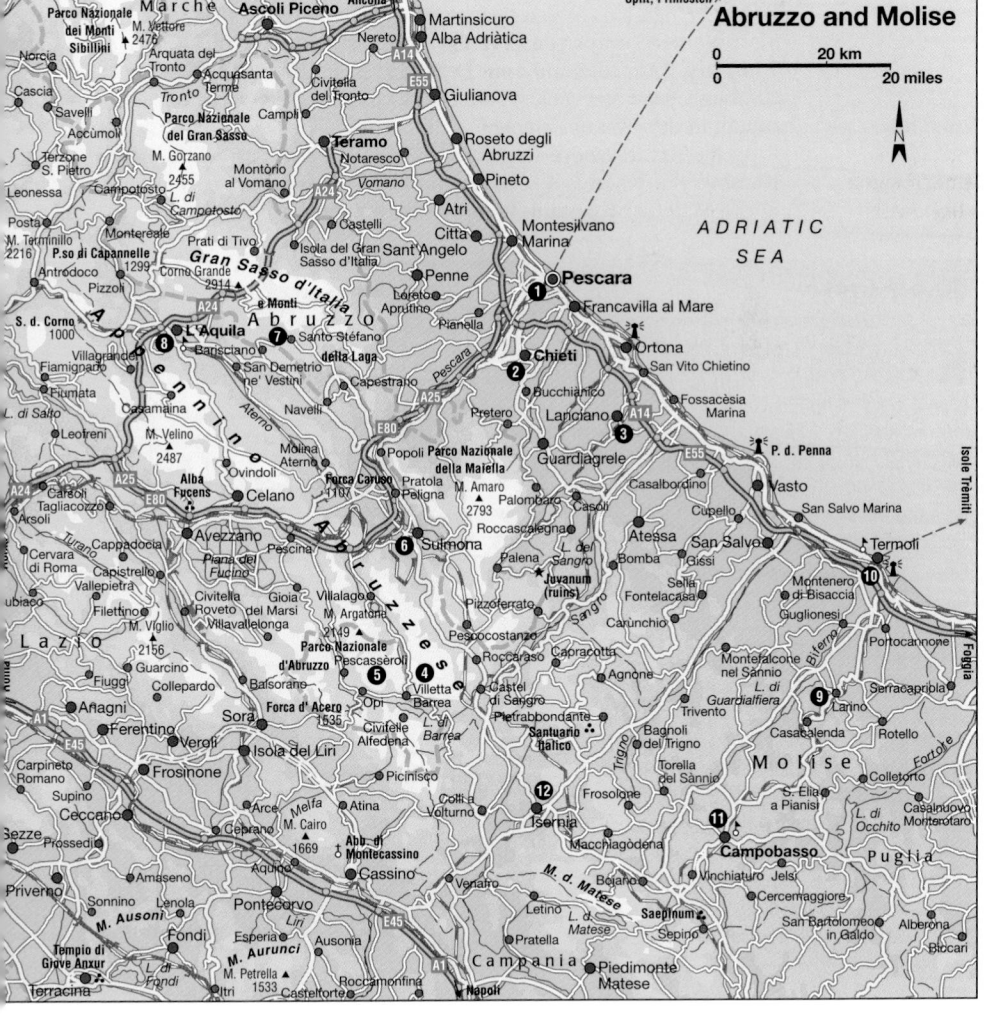

Quadri in the Sangro Valley is known as the town of truffles. Stop by at Luigi's shop, Il Tartufo di Quadri (Via G. Marconi 23), and choose from a fabulous selection of truffle products. June–Aug black truffles are on sale; Oct–Dec the coveted white truffle is in season.

as you reach the coast of the *trabocchi*. Fishermen weave tales of these fantastical wooden fishing platforms, which have been there for over 600 years. Legend says they were created by local farmers too timid to take a fishing boat out to sea – today many are owned by enthusiasts who fish from them at the weekend.

Sangro Valley

Inland from the coast runs the Sangro Valley, which takes you to **Lanciano ❸**. Every year 600,000 pilgrims come here to visit the Church of San Francesco (just off the central Piazza Plebiscito). The church marks the site of the 8th-century miracle of San Legonziano – a doubting monk was given a divine response when the Host (bread) turned to flesh and the wine to blood. The relics are held in the church to this day. Lanciano also boasts a fine cathedral and an imposing clock tower built on brick bridges which may date back to Roman times.

After the war many Sangro Valley farmers left their hill towns to look for work. Building regulations were negligible, and many towns were surrounded by low-cost rings of concrete apartment blocks. An exception is Roccascalegna, where the fabulous St Peter's Church and Castle balance on top of a limestone bluff – a beacon for conservation. The castle (10am–1pm and 3–6pm, until 7pm July, 8pm Aug and 5pm Dec–Jan; entrance fee) is home to the blood-curdling legend of a wicked baron who was murdered when he made a local girl submit to the *droit de seigneur*.

As the River Sangro forges down the valley, it pauses to form the lake at **Bomba**. The water is a good location for family holidays. With its backdrop of the Maiella Mountains National Park, there is plenty to do here. You can

BELOW: wolves are a rare sight in Abruzzo National Park.

PARK LIFE

Known as the "Region of Parks", one-third of Abruzzo's territory is given over to environmental protection – including the Abruzzo, Maiella and Gran Sasso-Laga National Parks. The oldest and most diverse is the **Abruzzo National Park**, home to the last 40 or so Marsican bears left on earth. Rangers escort the public on bear-watching trips, where visitors have a reasonable chance of viewing the 500lb (227 kg) Marsicans.

The park also contains some 50 Apennine wolves. Though no longer endangered, these shy animals are rarely seen – even the rangers only catch sight of them five or so times a year. But if you can't see them, Ecotour (Via Piave 7; tel: 0863-912760) leads groups on wolf-howling sessions. A recorded soundtrack of howling wolves is played and the wild wolves respond. Visitors to the park may also catch sight of roe deer, red deer and wild boar.

cruise the lake on the Valsangro Boat (tel: 0872-940484) and spot fish jumping from the water, and diving herons; you can water-ski, canoe, or simply sit by the shore and watch the sun go down to the sound of a frog chorus. If you enjoy trekking, head up into Monte Palano, with its oak and chestnut-tree woods underscored by a seasonal explosion of cyclamen, wild roses, broom and rare orchids.

The nearby ruins of **Juvanum** are a reminder of ancient times. Walk in the footsteps of legionaries at this Roman settlement sitting among farmers' fields against the backdrop of the Maiella Mountains (park open until dusk, museum 10am–1pm and 4–7pm).

At the top of the Sangro Valley is the entrance to Abruzzo's treasured **Parco Nazionale**. Founded in 1923, the park covers 777 sq. km (300 sq. miles) and is home to some of Europe's rarest animals. A good starting point for a visit is the medieval *borgo* of **Barrea ❹**. With characteristic terracotta tile roofs and beautifully kept local stone buildings, the old town sits above a deep blue lake.

Across the valley from Barrea is the hillside town **Civitella Alfedena**, known as the "village of the wolves". Sightings of wolves and lynxes living in semi-captivity are frequent. From Alfedena it's a short drive down to **Pescasseroli ❺**, an unusual mixture of Alpine buildings and a traditional *centro storico*. It is base camp for trekkers and nature-lovers, who can arrange for local guides to take them up into the mountains *(see box opposite)*.

Heading away from the national park towards L'Aquila, you pass the town of **Sulmona ❻**. *"Sulmo mihi patria est"* (Sulmona is my homeland) proclaimed its most famous son, the classical poet Ovid, whose statue takes pride of place in Piazza Settembre. Since the 1400s, Sulmona has been a candy town, a fac-

TIP

Inspired by the landscape of Abruzzo, Point 101 are offering art and photography holidays in the region. Visiting the most evocative hotels and locations it is guaranteed to bring out the hidden artist in you. Contact tel: 020-7241 1113; www.point101.com.

BELOW: *trabocchi*, traditional wooden fishing platorms.

tory for *confetti* – sugar-coated almonds which are given at weddings.

Sulmona's pride is the **Palazzo della Santissima Annunziata**, once a combination of hospital, church and storehouse. It wears its four centuries of architecture in style: with a Gothic portal on the left, a Renaissance central doorway, and the entrance on the right built in 1522. On the first floor is a museum of local archaeology (Tues–Sun 10am–1pm and 4–7pm; entrance fee).

The road between Sulmona and L'Aquila (Route 261) offers one of the most spectacular drives in Abruzzo – following the Aterno River Valley past a number of medieval villages, each with its ruined castle and its church. Along this road the Gran Sasso mountain starts to dominate. This is the high point of the Apennines – 2,914 metres (9,560 ft) of majestic rock, amidst a range resembling the limestone Alps of the Tyrol.

Santo Stefano

Just inside the Gran Sasso Park is the celebrated village of **Santo Stefano ⑦**, a once unknown *borgo* now renowned throughout Italy *(see box below)*. Peering down on Santo Stefano is **Rocca Calascio**, a picturesque stony hamlet of limestone houses. Beyond here stretch the plains of Campo Imperatore. This Alpine highland resonates to a soundtrack of cowbells and bleating sheep. Known as "the little Tibet", in summer its dried ravines and river beds contrast with vivid green pasture – an ideal place to trek, walk and cycle.

Fountain of 99 spouts

BELOW: entrance to Santa Maria di Collemaggio.

On a plateau below the Gran Sasso mountain range is **L'Aquila ⑧**. The capital of Abruzzo is peppered with remnants from its rich past. It is best known for

VILLAGE PEOPLE

A decade ago the medieval hamlet of Santo Stefano (www.sextantio.it) was crumbling into the hills of Abruzzo, and was well on the way to being a ghost town. Then the motorcycling philosopher and entrepeneur Daniele Kihlgren rode by. Smitten by a vista unchanged for 500 years, he bought up the empty buildings and hatched an idea, a "diffuse hotel". The hotel, which opened in 2006, has some 40 period rooms located in different houses throughout the village. Each bedroom is faithful to its medieval origins; ancient 15-cm (6-inch) long iron keys open timeless doors; traditional bed covers are hand woven and dyed in Santo Stefano's own craft workshop.

Santo Stefano is the flagship for Kihlgren and his team's mission to awaken the *Mezzogiorno* to its popular heritage. In the last 50 years southern Italy has paid scant attention to the aesthetic and economic importance of conserving and respecting its buildings. The rejuvenated Santo Stefano itself has been dubbed the most beautiful village in southern Italy, with Romano Prodi and Umberto Eco among its visitors. Kihlgren, who is working on further ruined villages in Abruzzo, continues to campaign for enforceable planning regulations which will preserve the region's character. *For more information see page 386.*

Map
on page
293

the curious legend of 99. The story goes that the city was created with 99 palaces, 99 churches and 99 squares – and in 1272, in commemoration of this numerical coincidence, the city commissioned a fountain of 99 spouts. The **Fontana delle Novantanove Cannelle** is one of the highlights of the city, its courtyard of red-and-white stone echoing to the sound of water from the fountains. L'Aquila's best-known monument is the 13th-century church of **Santa Maria di Collemaggio** (Mon–Sat 8.30am–1pm and 3–8pm, Sun 8am–8pm). Located outside the city wall on the southeast corner of town, its striking red-and-white façade features three rose windows. The church was begun in 1277 under the guidance of Pietro da Morrone, whose Renaissance tomb can be seen to the right of the apse inside.

The church of **San Bernardino** (Mon–Sat 7–10am and 5.30–6.30pm, Sun 7.30am–noon and 5.30–6.30pm) is arguably the finest Renaissance monument in the Abruzzo. The interior, completely rebuilt after after the earthquake of 1703, is dominated by its baroque ceiling and organ.

On weekday mornings in the **Piazza del Duomo** there is a vibrant open-air market where local cane, wool, lace and copper are sold. The Duomo itself – also destroyed by the earthquake – was rebuilt in the 1900s.

Defensive "ears"

L'Aquila's **Museo Nazionale d'Abruzzo** (Tues–Sun 8.30am–7.30pm; entrance fee) is located in the castle at the north end of town. The *castello* itself, built in 1532, is known for its four protruding "ears", which enabled soldiers to cover every possible angle of approach. The archaeological collection has an amusing Medusa's-head frieze and the remains of a prehistoric mammoth found locally.

Pietro da Morrone, a local hermit, was crowned Pope Celestine V at the age of 85. He served only five months in office, claiming that his inexperience with the ways of the world made him unfit to sit on the throne of St Peter.

BELOW: the village of Santo Stefano.

Map
on page
293

Molise

If you take the train from Termoli to Campobasso between 25 and 27 May, stop at the medieval village of **Larino** . The Sagra di San Pardo, Larino's annual festival, will be taking place, when ox-carts are paraded through the streets. While there, visit the old cathedral, with its beautiful façade, and climb up the monumental staircase of the Palazzo Reale. Larino is one of the least-known places in Italy, yet one of the most rewarding to visit.

Termoli , on the Adriatic, is a popular beach resort whose old town on the promontory offers fine views in all directions. Well garrisoned behind a small castle built by Frederick II are labyrinthine streets and a fine cathedral.

The town that best illustrates the difference between the old and the new in Molise is **Campobasso** , the region's capital. Presided over by the 15th-century Castello Monforte, from which tumble the steeply stepped streets of the old town, Campobasso's modern quarters spread out to the station below. It is in the new town that two of Campobasso's best-known features can be found: a top-security prison and a training school for the *carabinieri*, the Italian police. Ask here for directions to the old town, in particular to San Giorgio, the 12th-century Romanesque church.

Ninety minutes away by train is **Isernia** , rich in regional legend and a good starting point for exploring the remote hill towns. In 1979, an ancient settlement was discovered on the outskirts. No human remains were found, but there is evidence that man lived here a million years before the birth of Christ. Bones of elephants, rhinoceroses, hippos, bison and bear were also discovered, some now displayed in the excellent archaeological museum, the **Museo Santa Maria delle Monache** (daily 9am–7.30pm; entrance fee). ❑

Boats leave from Termoli for the Isole Tremiti, a group of off shore islands celebrated for their mysterious grottoes.

BELOW: L'Aquila's Fountain of 99 Spouts.
BELOW RIGHT: harvesting Trebbiano grapes.

Wines of Abruzzo

Abruzzese wines have a profound regional identity. In the last decade they have stepped out of the (unjustified) shade of more famous neighbours, to take their place among the top wines of Italy. Abruzzo is Italy's 5th-largest producer, with around half the production registered as DOC (Denominazione di Origine Controllata).

Their signature wine is Montepulciano d'Abruzzo. In Abruzzo this is the name of the vine (the Tuscan Montepulciano is made with the Sangiovese grape), and they have been planting the grape here for over 200 years. Top of the range Montepulciano has a brilliant ruby-red colour, a dry, mellow, pungent and slightly tannic taste.

Nicola Santoleri produces a DOC Montepulciano d'Abruzzo and Trebbiano d'Abruzzo from his vineyard near Guardiagrele. His father planted the vines in 1962, and under Nicola's care the Santoleri wines have gained a reputation for discreet quality. In recent years Nicola

has moved towards more "natural" production to give colour and intensity to the Montepulciano. The Santoleri cantina in the centro storico of Guardiagrele is a charming, beautifully lit vault. If you are in the area, it's worth calling to arrange a visit (tel: 39-0871-893301; www.nicolasantoleri.it).

The Zaccagnini winery was founded in 1978. With 14 wines, including 6 DOCs, the brand now produces 500,000 bottles a year. The Zaccagnini cantina sits on the hills above the vineyards at Contrada Pozzo, and the elegant and high-tech vinery building reflects Marcello Zaccagnini's pursuit of quality. It also marks Marcello's interest in modern art, with several sculptures by Joseph Beuys gracing the new cantina. Marcello and his oenologist cousin Concerzio have turned out a top-class reserve Montepulciano and a fabulous Clematis dessert wine. The production is limited to an annual 4,800 bottles, but it is worth going out of your way for. To get to the vineyards, take Autostrada 25 exit Torre de' Passeri and follow road signs for Bolognano (tel: 39-085-8880195; www.cantinazaccagnini.it). ❑

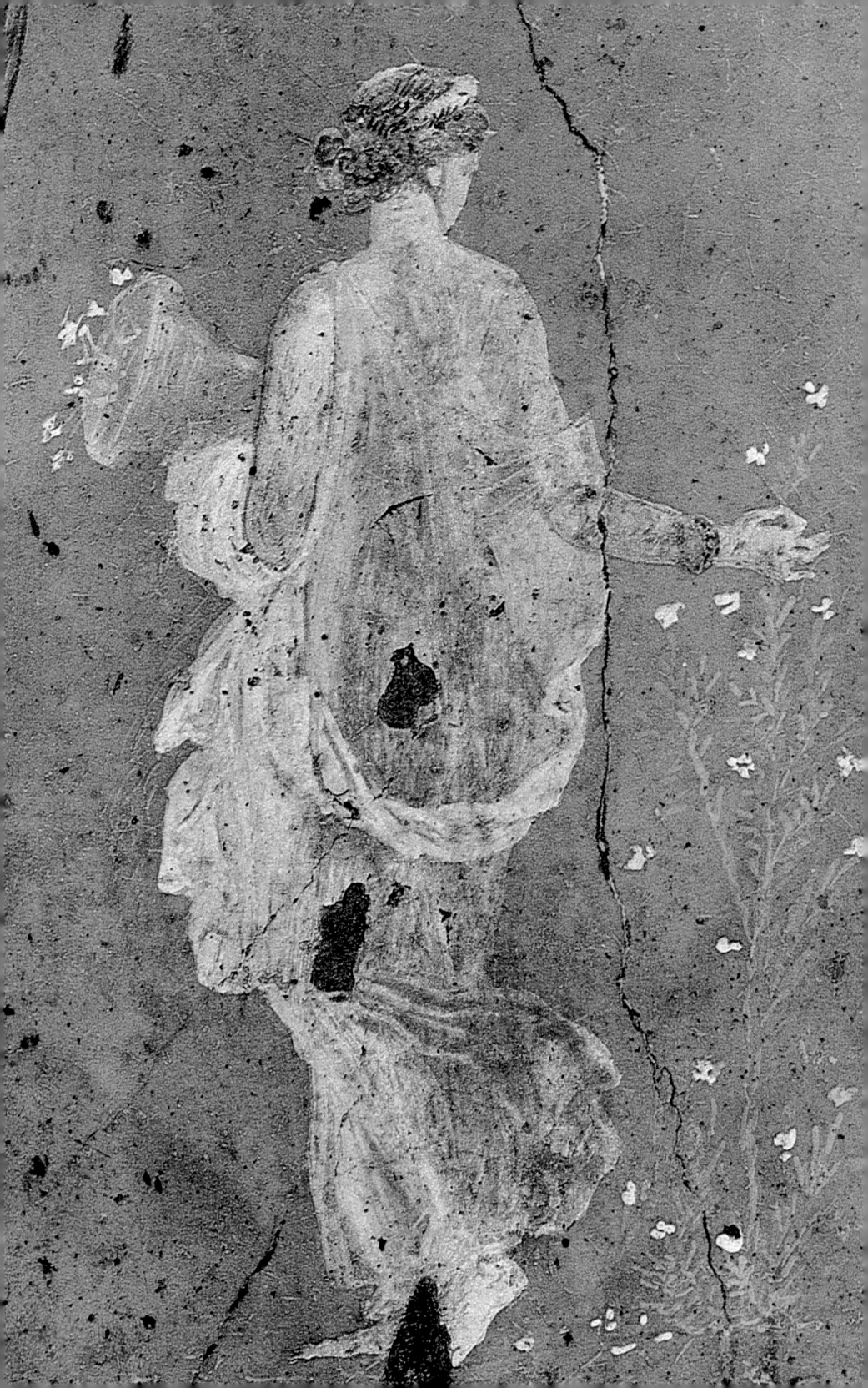

THE SOUTH

To discover one of Europe's most interesting regions, venture beyond Naples and Sicily into the Mezzogiorno

When foreign travellers visit the remote parts of Puglia, Basilicata and Calabria, they are sometimes greeted by stares. The stares are not hostile, nor are they necessarily suspicious. They're just surprised. So few foreigners – few northern Italians, even – visit these sun-baked regions that anybody who does is looked upon as a bit of a maverick.

This was the case when the English writer Norman Douglas visited in 1911; it was the case when the anti-Fascist Carlo Levi was banished here in 1935. So few people came to this area for pleasure or insight that nobody knows of the pleasures and insights to be found. The growing number of travellers who do come, follow the footsteps of the Greeks and Romans to Naples, Pompeii, Cumae and Capri. They flock to Sicily and its temples. But Puglia? Basilicata? Calabria? Italy's heel? Her instep? Her toe?

Then there is northern prejudice. Northerners are industrial, pragmatic, fair-skinned. The southerners are agricultural, superstitious, dark. The northerners are rich. Although there is a wealthy southern upper class, many southerners are poor, and emigrate if they get the chance. Nobody moves south to take their place.

The truth is that southern Italy is one of the most interesting places to visit in Europe. It is a romantic land of castles and churches, vast, wheat-covered plains, and misty mountains where shepherds roam. Puglia is a place for novel architectural forms: the Puglian Romanesque, Leccian baroque, castles by Frederick II and odd, conical, peasant dwellings known as *trulli*. In Basilicata are the *sassi* cave-dwellings carved into the side of a ravine, many adorned with frescos, and La Trinità, an unfinished 11th-century Benedictine monastery covered with Roman inscriptions. In Calabria visitors rediscover the Greeks – in particular, two Greek statues made of bronze, recently dredged up by fishermen off Riace. There are Norman castles, Byzantine churches, rich red wines and landscapes which were first described by Homer.

Naples, the Bay of Naples and Sicily are the richest regions historically, and this is reflected in this guide. Apart from the chapter on Naples, which is best explored on foot, the descriptions are geared towards travelling by car. A car is especially important in the *Mezzogiorno*, where sights are too scattered to justify spending long hours waiting for infrequent trains. ❑

PRECEDING PAGES: the typical Basilicata landscape, unchanged for centuries.
LEFT: an ancient fresco of *Spring* in Naples' Archaeological Museum.

NAPLES

*Noisy and crowded, but thrilling, Naples has it all –
fine buildings, world-class museums
and cosmopolitan verve*

Map on
pages
306–7

Naples (Napoli) has always been the black sheep of Italian cities, the misfit, the outcast, the messy brother that nobody knew quite what to do with. It is burdened by poverty, unemployment, bureaucratic inefficiency and organised crime, but, prompted by a popular mayor, the city has undergone a transformation over the past decade in the renovation of its centre and a less anarchic approach to urban life. However, the irrepressible Neapolitan spirit remains. That Naples is, in fact, one of the most beautiful Italian cities, with a friendly population and a long cultural heritage, evidenced in art, churches, castles and pizza, does not deny its less appealing side. In the end, like all black sheep, troubled Naples is the most interesting member of its family.

Orientation

The city has its own special shape, defined partly by landscape, partly by chance and partly by government edict. The only way to get a feel for the place is to walk its different quarters. To orientate yourself, find **Piazza Garibaldi** ❶. From here, the long **Corso Umberto I** juts down to the southwest to **Piazza Bovio** ❷, where, changing its name to Via Agostino Depretis, it continues on to **Piazza Municipio** ❸. The thoroughfare was forced through the narrow, crowded streets that surround it in 1888, in an effort to improve air circulation following a cholera epidemic. The rather drab **Università** ❹ looms halfway down, on the right-hand side.

From Piazza Municipio and the nearby **Piazza Plebiscito** ❺ the city fans out to the east, the north and the west. Directly north, up Via Toledo, also known as Via Roma, is the red *palazzo* housing the **Museo Archeologico Nazionale**. East of the museum, in the triangle it forms with the Piazza Plebiscito and the Piazza Garibaldi, lies most of Old Naples, with its medieval streets and churches. North, on a hilltop, stands the art gallery of **Capodimonte**. Further south, on a spur of land out in the bay, rises the egg-shaped Castel dell'Ovo and, along the waterfront, Via Partenope, where the city's most expensive hotels overlook the water. The shoreline then curves away west, passing the delightfully restored **Villa Comunale**, with its famous aquarium, to the marina at **Mergellina**, near Virgil's tomb. From Mergellina views stretch back over the entire city, with Mount Vesuvius looming in the background haze.

The city's roots

The name Naples derives from Neapolis, the New City founded by settlers from Cumae in the 6th century BC. Nearby stood Paleopolis, the Old City, founded in the 9th century BC, also by Greeks from Cumae. The two cities grew side by side like brother and sister until their violent overthrow by Samnites in 400 BC. Rome wrested

LEFT: Via Tribunali, in the historic quarter.
BELOW: Neapolitan personality.

them away after a three-year siege in 326 BC, at which point they began to grow into a single entity called Neapolis. From the beginning, Romans flocked here, drawn by the mild climate, the sparkling bay and the political freedom which retention of the Greek constitution allowed. Virgil wrote the *Aeneid* here; emperors built gardens and bathed.

Eight dynasties

The Dark Ages were indeed dark in Naples – nobody knows quite what happened – and until shortly after the first millennium the city was ruled by dukes loosely allied to Byzantium. Then, in 1139, Roger the Norman took Naples under the wing of his kingdom of Sicily. The seven dynasties that followed produced most of the architectural landmarks that can be seen today. Their statues, together with one of Roger, peer out from niches in the façade of the Palazzo Reale at the centre of town: Frederick II of Hohenstaufen, who founded the university; Charles I of Anjou, who lived here and left his mark; Alfonso I of Aragon, Charles I of Austria, Charles I of Bourbon, Joachim Murat and Victor Emmanuel II. They line up like wrinkles in the building's broad face, testimonies to the city's past.

Castles and music

When Charles I of Anjou built the **Castel Nuovo** ❻ (Museo Civico: Mon–Sat 9am– 7pm; entrance fee) in 1282, he could not have known that seven centuries later it would still serve as the political hub of the city. The Municipal Council of Naples meets in the huge **Sala dei Baroni**, where Charles is said to have performed some of his bloodiest executions. The finest architectural element in this imposing fortress is the Triumphal Arch, built from 1454–67 to commemorate Alfonso I's defeat of the French. It is the only Renaissance arch ever to have been built at the entrance to a castle.

A short walk up Via San Carlo brings you swiftly to the **Teatro San Carlo** ❼ (www.teatrosancarlo.it), the largest opera house in Italy and one of the finest in the world. It is all red velvet and gold trim, with six tiers of boxes rising from the

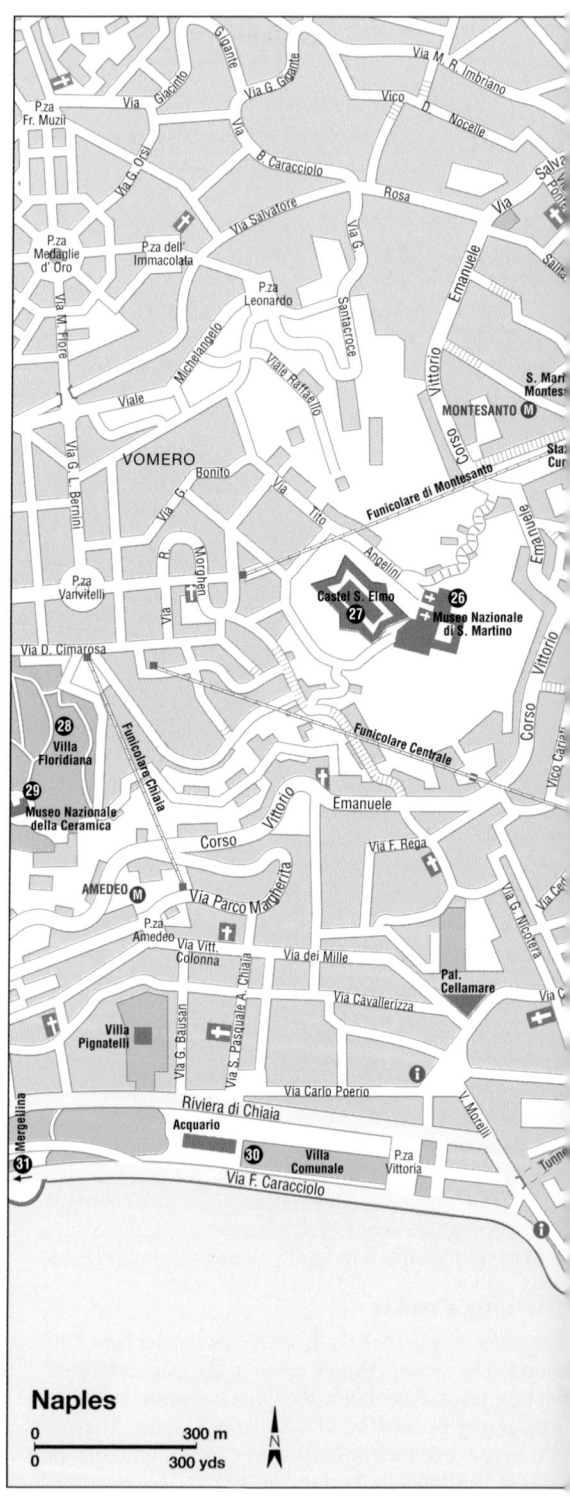

Naples

0   300 m

0   300 yds

N

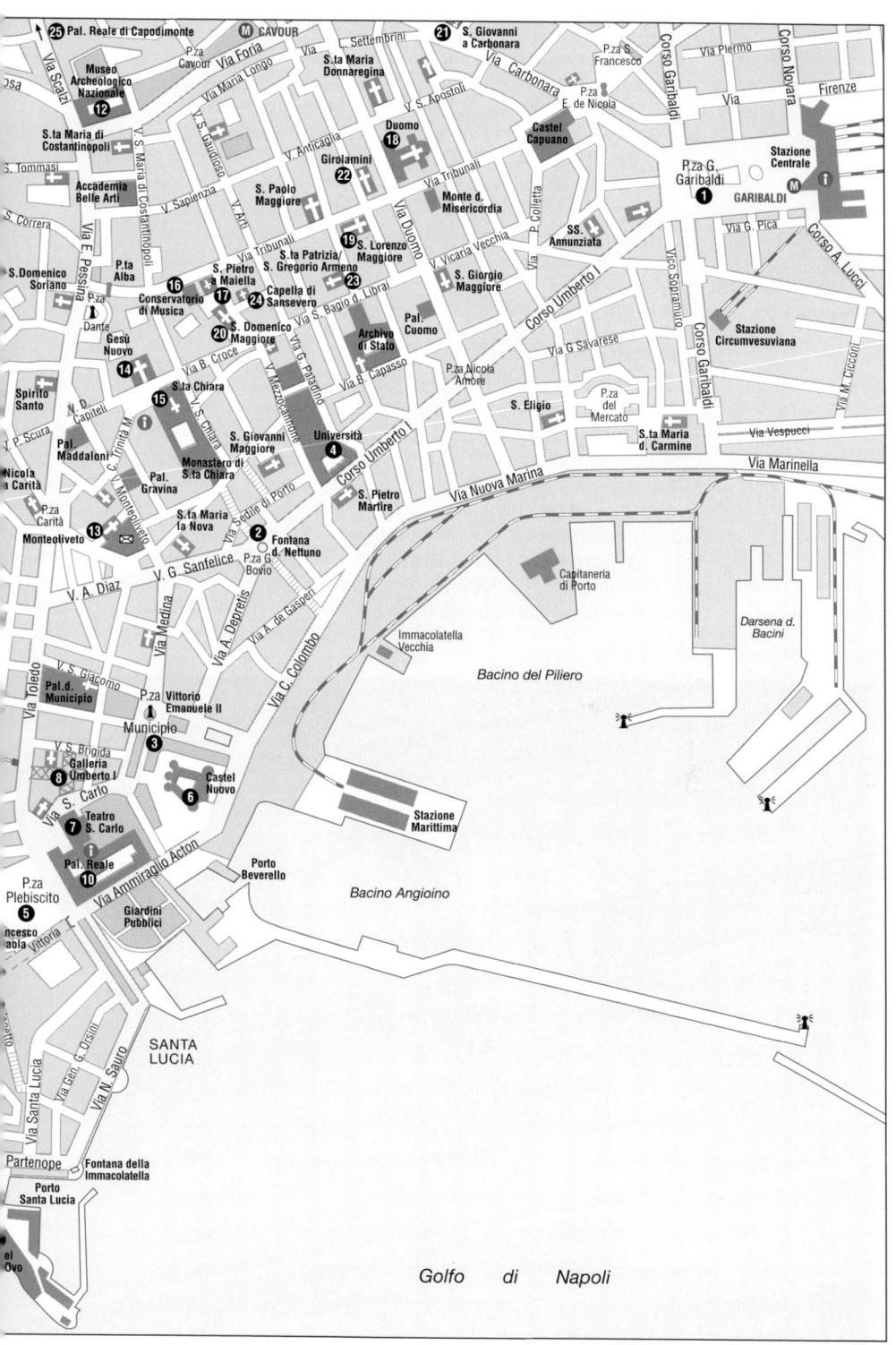

25 Pal. Reale di Capodimonte
M CAVOUR
21 S. Giovanni a Carbonara
P.za Cavour
Via Foria
L. Settembrini
Via Carbonara
P.za S. Francesco
Via Piermo
Corso Garibaldi
Corso Novara
Firenze
Via
Museo Archeologico Nazionale 12
Via Maria Longo
S.ta Maria Donnaregina
V. S. Apostoli
P.za E. de Nicola
Via
Via S. Gaudioso
V. S. Maria di Costantinopoli
S.ta Maria di Constantinopoli
Duomo 18
Girolamini
18
Castel Capuano
Stazione Centrale
Accademia Belle Arti
V. Anticaglia
22
Via Tribunali
S. Paolo Maggiore
S.ta Maria di Costantinopoli
V. Sapienzia
V. Arti
Monte d. Misericordia
P. Colletta
SS. Annunziata
P.za G. Garibaldi 1
GARIBALDI M
S. Domenico Spriano
P.ta Alba
16 S. Pietro a Maiella
19 S. Lorenzo Maggiore
Via Vicaria Vecchia
Corso A. Lucci
Via G. Pica
Via Tribunali
S.ta Patrizia/ S. Gregorio Armeno
S. Giorgio Maggiore
Corso Umberto I
Gesù Nuovo
Dante
17 Conservatorio di Musica
24 Capella di Sansevero
23
Via S. Bagio d. Librai
Stazione Circumvesuviana
20 S. Domenico Maggiore
Pal. Cuomo
Archivio di Stato
Via G Savarese
Corso Garibaldi
14 Gesù Nuovo
V. Mezzocannone
P.za Nicola Amore
Via M. Ciccioni
Spirito Santo
N. D. Capitoli
15 S.ta Chiara
S. Eligio
P.za del Mercato
S.ta Maria d. Carmine
Via Vespucci
V. P. Scura
15 i
S. Giovanni Maggiore
Università 4
Via B. Capasso
Via Marinella
Nicola a Carità
Pal. Maddaloni
V. Trinità M.
Monastero di S.ta Chiara
Corso Umberto I
Pal. Gravina
S. Pietro Martire
Via Nuova Marina
P.za Carità
S.ta Maria la Nova
2 Fontana d. Nettuno
Capitaneria di Porto
13 Monteoliveto
V. G. Sanfelice
P.za G. Bovio
Immacolatella Vecchia
Darsena d. Bacini
V. A. Diaz
V. A. Depretis
Via A. de Gasperi
Via C. Colombo
Bacino del Piliero
V. S. Giacomo
Via Medina
Pal. d. Municipio
P.za Vittorio Emanuele II
Municipio 1
Via Toledo
3
V. S. Brigida
8 Galleria Umberto I
S. Carlo
6 Castel Nuovo
Stazione Marittima
7 Teatro S. Carlo
Pal. Reale 10
Via Ammiraglio Acton
Porto Beverello
Bacino Angioino
P.za Plebiscito
5
Giardini Pubblici
ncesco aola
Vittoria
SANTA LUCIA
Via Santa Lucia
Via Gen. G. Orsini
Via N. Sauro
Partenope
Fontana della Immacolatella
Porto Santa Lucia
el Ovo
Golfo   di   Napoli

Street vendor.

stage. Constructed in 1737, under the direction of Charles III of Bourbon, the theatre retains its perfect acoustics, helped by the insertion, after a fire in 1816 of hundreds of clay pitchers between the walls. Even on the sixth tier, you can sit on a red velvet seat in your own private box.

Across the street is the **Galleria Umberto I** ❽, erected in 1887 on a neo-classical design similar to that of its older brother in Milan. Its glass ceiling, 56 metres (184 ft) high, and its mosaic-covered floor were reconstructed after bomb damage in World War II. Pleasant cafés permit a moment's rest.

The wide Piazza Plebiscito around the corner is embraced by the twin arcade of the **Chiesa di San Francesco di Paola** ❾ (1817–32), modelled after the Pantheon in Rome. The square is closed to traffic and is popular with local artists who often exhibit their work under the arches of the church.

Reminder of turbulent times

The sprawling red façade of the **Palazzo Reale** ❿ (Royal Apartments; Thurs–Tues 9am–8pm; entrance fee) looms across the street with its eight statues illustrating the eight Neapolitan dynasties. At the foot of its monumental marble staircase stand the original bronze doors from the Castel Nuovo. The cannonball lodged in the left door is a reminder of an early siege. Upstairs are a throne room and a small but lavish theatre. Further rooms stretch off in a seemingly endless series of period furniture and Dresden china.

Another famous castle, the **Castel dell'Ovo** ⓫ (Mon–Sat 9am–6pm, Sun 9am–1pm; free) on the waterfront, is used for hosting exhibitions and cultural events. Its oval shape (hence the name) was commissioned by the Spanish viceroy Don Pedro de Toledo in 1532, but the original castle was built by

BELOW: the Castel Nuovo, built in 1282.

William I in 1154, finished by Frederick II and enlarged by the not-to-be-outdone Charles I of Anjou. Pleasant restaurants line the shore, children bellyflop from the causeway, and the speedboats of the Guardia di Finanza (Fraud Squad) lurk just along the quay.

House of history

The **Museo Archeologico Nazionale di Napoli** ⑫ (Wed–Mon 9am–8pm, last entry 7pm; entrance fee) is one of the great museums of the world, housing the most spectacular finds from Pompeii and Herculaneum and fine examples of Greek sculpture. A trip to the museum will take an entire morning. The highlights include the so-called "Secret Cabinet" (Gabinetto Segreto), which reopened in 2000 after 26 years of unusual Neapolitan prudery (it had been semi-open until 1967). It contains erotic images which lift the lid on the racy ancient world. Graphic sex scenes are depicted on Greek vases, Roman terracottas and Etruscan mirrors.

The ground floor is devoted to classical sculpture and Egyptian art. In the main entrance hall, a monolithic sarcophagus depicts a famous and important scene: Prometheus creating man out of clay. Another awesome sarcophagus presents a raucous Bacchanalian celebration. Through a doorway to the right, a pair of statues of Harmodius and Aristogeiton, who killed the tyrant Hipparchus, fairly leap out at you as you enter the room. These are actually Roman copies of originals once installed in the Agora in Athens.

In a further room stands a Roman copy of the famous statue of Doryphorus by Polycleitus (440 BC), considered the "canon of perfection" of manly proportions. This statue, found at Pompeii, and others of its period are evidence of the refined tastes of early Greek settlers. The Farnese Collection includes a Hercules and the *Farnese Bull* (the largest piece of antique sculpture ever found) from Rome's Baths of Caracalla.

The rich collection of mosaics on the mezzanine floor at the back of the building come from the floors, walls and courtyards of houses unearthed at Pompeii. The freshness and colour of these works after centuries buried in ash are an amazing tribute to the craftsmanship of their ancient makers.

The Nile scenes in Room LX, from a later period, feature ducks, crocodiles, hippopotami and snakes. These mosaics originally framed the *Battle of Issus*, in Room LXI. In this scene, Alexander the Great is presented in his victorious battle against the Persian emperor Darius III in 333 BC. The thicket of spears creates the illusion of an army far larger than that actually shown.

Rooms on the first floor show paintings of Pompeii and a reconstruction of the Villa of the Papyri in Herculaneum, including an extraordinary collection of marble and bronze sculptures.

Through the large Salone dell'Atlante at the top of the stairs is a series of rooms containing wall paintings from various Campanian cities. Especially startling is the 6th-century BC *Sacrifice of Iphigenia*, the Greek equivalent of the biblical sacrifice of Isaac. The deer borne by Artemis in the top of the picture replaced Iphigenia at the last minute, just as Isaac was replaced by a ram. Far happier is *The Rustic Concert*, in which Pan and nymphs tune up for a Roman celebration.

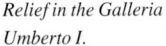

Map on pages 306–7

Relief in the Galleria Umberto I.

BELOW: a flying leap off the Castel dell'Ovo.

Neapolitan churches

The churches of Naples, like the churches of any Italian city, offer glimpses into Italian life. In Italy, a visit to a church, a quick confession, a genuflection in front of an altar are still a daily ritual for many people. Because of this, churches open every day (but close 1–4.30pm), so no opening times are given.

The church of **Monteoliveto** ⓭, about halfway up Via Roma, contains a wealth of Renaissance monuments hidden away in surprising corners. Far in the back of this aisleless basilica, begun in 1411, stands a bizarre group of terracotta figures by the artist Guido Mazzoni. The eight statues, looking almost alive in the dim light that filters into the chapel, represent the *Pietà*, and are said to be portraits of Mazzoni's 15th-century friends. Further back, down a side passage, is the Old Sacristy, containing frescos by Vasari and wooden stalls inlaid with biblical scenes. In the very front of the church, to the left of the entrance, another passage leads to the Piccolomini Chapel, where a relief of a Nativity scene by the Florentine Antonio Rossellino (1475) is a delight to behold.

Unlike in Rome, which is heavily baroque, no single architectural style dominates Naples. The Gothic, the Renaissance and the baroque are all represented. The late 16th-century church of **Gesù Nuovo** ⓮ at the top of the street called **Trinità Maggiore** presents perhaps the most harmonious example of the Neapolitan baroque. The embossed stone façade originally formed the wall of a Renaissance palace. At noon on Saturdays, when weddings take place here, the massive front doors are thrown open to give a splendid view of fully lit baroque at its best. The interior has a unique design, being almost as wide as it is deep. The coloured marble and bright frescos seem to spiral up into the dome. Directly above the main portal, just inside the church, stretches a wide fresco by Francesco Soli-

Wall painting taken from a house in Pompeii depicting Perseus, son of Zeus, and Andromeda, whom he rescued from a sea monster.

BELOW: the Battle of Issus mosaic from the House of the Faun, Pompeii.

nena (1725) depicting Heliodorus driven from the temple. The ubiquitous Soli-
nena dominated Neapolitan painting in the first half of the 18th century.

Robert the Wise

Map on pages 306–7

A more austere, and older, architectural approach is demonstrated by the Gothic
church of **Santa Chiara** ⓯, just across the street. Founded between 1310 and
1328 by Robert the Wise for his queen, Sancia, the huge church – the biggest in
Naples – became the favourite place of worship of the Neapolitan nobility. Unfortunately, extensive bomb damage during World War II destroyed many important works of art and 18th-century decorations, but worth seeking out in its vast
interior is the tomb of Robert the Wise (1343) behind the main altar. Through a
courtyard to the left of the church is the entrance to its immense and peaceful
cloister (built in the 15th century but much altered in the 18th), where majolica-
tiled pathways meander through a wild and beautiful garden of roses and fruit
trees. The cloister was recently carefully restored and medieval frescos under the
arcades were recovered and the garden replanted with the same species grown
here in Bourbon times. Many brightly coloured mosaics discovered in the excavations can also be seen. A museum of sculpture and archaeology is also on site.

The steep **Via Santa Maria di Costantinopoli** leads up to the **Conservatorio
di Musica** ⓰, founded in 1537, the oldest musical conservatory in Europe. It
has an important library and museum (tel: 081-564 4411), but it is also enjoyable to wander through its courtyard listening to the music of violins, organs,
harps and pianos spilling down from upper storeys. Just down the block, the
church of **San Pietro a Maiella** ⓱, built between 1313 and 1316, has one of the
most famous ceilings in Italy. The Calabrian Mattia Preti began painting it in

ABOVE and **BELOW:**
majolica tiles in
Santa Chiara.

1656, at the age of 43, a few months after leaving his
native Taverna for the more rigorous artistic challenges
of Naples. Five years later he completed his work, establishing himself as one of the most talented painters of
his generation. The panels in the nave tell the story of St
Celestine V, while the panels in the transept present the
life of St Catherine of Alexandria, the virgin martyr who
was beheaded for out-arguing pagan scholars.

Reliable miracles

The Naples **Duomo** ⓲ is a magnificent Gothic ware-
house of relics from every period of the city's history. In a
chapel off the right aisle are the head of San Gennaro, the
patron saint of the city, and two phials of his blood (chapel
Mon–Sat 8am–12.30pm and 4.30–7pm, Sun
8am–1.30pm and 5–7.30pm). The mysterious powers of
the congealed blood are the subject of what Mark Twain
called "one of the wretchedest of all the religious impos-
tures in Italy – the miraculous liquefaction of the blood".
The miracle has been taking place every year on the first
Saturday in May, 19 September and 16 December since
the saint's body was brought to Naples from Pozzuoli, the
place of his martyrdom, by Bishop Severus in the time of
Constantine. It is said that if the blood fails to liquefy a
disaster is in store for the city. The last great eruption of
Vesuvius in1944 and the earthquake northeast of Naples
in 1980 occurred in years that the blood did not liquefy.

Other notable churches, all in the historical centre of

Display of the sweet lemon liqueur known as Limoncello.

BELOW: view from Castel Sant'Elmo.

the city, include **San Lorenzo Maggiore** ⓙ, where archaeological excavation have revealed the old Decumano (main street) running through its cloister; the Gothic **San Domenico Maggiore** ⓴; the 14th-century **San Giovanni a Carbonara** ㉑; **Girolamini** ㉒; and **Santa Patrizia** ㉓, with its **monastery of San Gregorio Armeno**. Via San Gregoria Armeno is famous for its workshops producing *presepi* (Christmas cribs), an important Neapolitan tradition.

The **Cappella di Sansevero** ㉔ (Mon and Wed–Sat 10am–5.40pm, Sun 10am–1.10pm; entrance fee), a small unconsecrated church near the church of San Domenico Maggiore, should not be missed. It contains a moving and remarkably realistic sculpture known as the *Cristo Velato* (Veiled Christ) carved out of a single piece of marble by Giuseppe Sammartino. The chapel was once the workshop of Prince Raimondo, a well-known 18th-century alchemist who was excommunicated by the Pope for dabbling in the occult. In the crypt are the gruesome results of some of his experiments.

Museums with a view

Two of the greatest museums in Naples stand high on bluffs overlooking the city. The National Gallery of Naples, formerly in the **Museo Nazionale**, has been relocated to the **Palazzo Reale di Capodimonte** ㉕ (Wed–Mon 9am–8pm; entrance fee), the 18th-century palace of King Charles III, set in a shady park directly north of the museum. The gallery contains some of the best paintings in southern Italy. At its heart is the important Farnese collection, which by the late 18th century numbered over 1,700 paintings. Among the high points are Masolino da Panicale's *Foundation of Santa Maria Maggiore in Rome*, in which Christ and Mary ride a cloud as if it were a magic carpet; Bellini's *Transfigu-*

ration; various works of Titian; two startling allegorical paintings by Pieter Brueghel the Elder *(The Blind Leading the Blind* and *The Misanthrope)*; and, perhaps the most famous of all, Caravaggio's *Flagellation.* The Salottina di Porcellano is lined throughout with magnificent Capodimonte porcelain tiles which were made in King Charles III's factory in 1757. These originally adorned the queen's parlour in the royal palace at Portici.

A trip up the Montesanto funicular brings the visitor to the top of the Vomero hill, home of the **Certosa e Museo di San Martino**  (Thur–Tues 8.30am– 7.30pm; entrance fee), located in the Carthusian monastery of the same name. Like so many buildings in Naples, the Certosa di San Martino was built in the 14th century, but had a complete baroque make-over a few hundred years later, and has recently been beautifully restored. Some of the top painters of the Neapolitan baroque are represented here, including Salvator Rosa, Francesco Solimena and the prolific Luca Giordano. Belvederes give access to the best views in town – the wide sweep of the Bay of Naples.

Good views can also be had from the **Castel Sant'Elmo** (Thur–Tues 8.30am–7.30pm; entrance fee) next door, a 14th-century fortress long used as a prison for political troublemakers. The stately gardens of the **Villa Floridiana** (daily 9am to 1 hour before sunset; free), also on the Vomero, are favoured among young mothers as a place to teach infants to walk. The gardens house the **Museo Nazionale della Ceramica** (Wed–Mon 8am–2pm; entrance fee), which contains one of the most extensive collections of porcelain in Italy.

A secret known to sailors in navies around the world is that the Bay of Naples is one of the most beautiful ports in Europe. To appreciate the splendour of the bay, walk through the pleasant and popular **Villa Comunale gardens** to the far western district of **Mergellina**, from where boats depart to the islands in the bay. The Villa Comunale itself is a mile-long public garden containing a small **aquarium** (Tues–Sat 9am–6pm, Sun 9.30am–7.30pm in summer; Tues–Sat 9am–5pm, Sun 9am–2pm in winter; entrance fee), where 200 species of fish cavort in murky tanks.

Birthplace of the pizza

The **Piazza Sannazzaro**, at the heart of the Mergellina district, repays walkers with some of the best pizza in Naples. Pizza was originally born in Naples, and genuine Neapolitan pizza is unbeatable. Its secret, aside from the fact that it is made with fresh mozzarella – another speciality of the Naples region – lies in the baking. It is cooked quickly, at a high temperature, in a dome-shaped brick oven, over a wood fire. Other local specialities invariably available include octopus *(polpo)*, mussel soup *(zuppa di cozze)*, numerous varieties of fish, various spaghettis made with a fish sauce, such as the Neapolitan catch-all *spaghetti alla pescatora* (fishwife's spaghetti), various kinds of cheese and ham, swordfish, fried mozzarella and spaghetti alla mozzarella.

Naples is a big, brawling city that exists for nobody, ultimately, but itself. It neither actively discourages visitors nor makes any real attempt to draw them in. It just continues on its crowded, noisy, irremediable way, a gypsy caravan of all that is best and worst in Italy. ❏

Map on pages 306–7

TIP

The Campania Artecard costs €13 and is valid for 3 or 7 days. During this period it allows you free entry into two museums and half price for another four. Available at participating museums, the main station and tourist information centres (freephone: 800-600601; www. campaniartecard.it).

BELOW: preparing pizza.

THE CAMPANIA COAST

*An endless succession of jewel-like coves
ripples down the Naples coast,
with Pompeii and Herculaneum just inland*

Map on
page 316

In Greek times, Naples was a mere stripling overshadowed by its powerful parent **Cumae ❶** (Cuma), 30 km (19 miles) to the west. Founded by Aeolians from Asia Minor around 750 BC, Cumae had become by the 6th century BC the political, religious and cultural beacon of the coast, controlling the Bay of Naples and its islands.

Here Aeneas came to consult the Sybil before his descent into the underworld. The famous **Antro della Sibilla Cumana** (Cave of the Cumaean Sybil; daily 9am–1 hour before sunset*; entrance fee), recently uncovered by archaeologists, consists of a trapezoidal *dromos* (corridor), 44 metres (144 ft) long, punctuated by six airshafts. At the far end is a rectangular chamber cut with niches where the Sybil apparently sat and uttered her prophecies. The eerie echo of footsteps in the corridor recalls Virgil's description of "a cavern perforated a hundred times, having a hundred mouths with rushing voices carrying the responses of the Sybil". From the cave's mouth it is possible to climb up to the acropolis, whose ruined, lizard-haunted temples offer fine views of the coastline and the sea.

The region between Cumae and Naples, known traditionally as the **Campi Flegrei** (Burning Fields), has been a centre of volcanic activity for the whole of recorded history. Unexpected rumblings and gaseous exhalations from below have linked the area to the mythical Greek underworld. The **Lago di Averno**, a once gloomy lake in the crater of an extinct volcano, is the legendary "dark pool" from which Aeneas began his descent into Hades. No bird was said to be able to fly across this lake and live, due to the poisonous gases. For many years this theory was cruelly tested at the **Grotta del Cane** on the nearby Lago d'Agnano. Dogs were subjected to the carbon dioxide that issued from the floor of the cave until knocked out or killed. "The dog dies in a minute and a half – a chicken instantly," reported Mark Twain. The experiment was repeated nine or 10 times a day for the benefit of tourists.

LEFT: the Amalfi Coast.
BELOW: the trapezoidal corridor of the Sybil Cave at Cumae.

Volcanic crater

Pozzuoli ❷, a wealthy trading centre in Greek and Roman times but later devastated by wars and malaria, is now famous for its **Solfatara** (daily 8.30am–1 hour before sunset; entrance fee), a volcanic crater releasing jets of sulphurous gases. The Solfatara is thought to have inspired Milton's description of Hell in *Paradise Lost*. Pozzuoli also boasts a magnificent amphitheatre, now newly restored (daily 9am–1 hour before sunset; entrance fee) and used for summer concerts. Pozzuoli was also the birthplace of actress Sophia Loren. On the waterfront, enclosed in a small park, lies a rectangular structure formerly known as the **Serapeo** (Temple of Serapis), but now thought to have been a *macellum* (marketplace). Shellfish encrustation around the bases

TIP

From Naples, the best
way to reach Pompeii
and Vesuvius is to
take the Circum-
vesuviana railway to
either destination.
For a convenient route
to the top of Vesuvius,
take the same train
to Ercolano Scavi,
then take a bus and
walk the final stretch
(20 minutes).

of its four Corinthian columns has led to speculation that the ground once sank 5 metres (16 ft) below sea level before rising again to its present height.

Baia ❸ derives its name from Baios, Odysseus's navigator. Here Roman society came to swim. The modern town, with its view across the Gulf of Pozzuoli, contains extensive ruins of Roman palaces enclosed in a picturesque **Parco Archeologico** (daily 9am–1 hour before sunset; bookings required, tel: 081-868 8868; entrance fee) on the hillside. At the lowest level of the park is a rectangular *piscina* (bathing pool) from which an arched pathway, hidden in foliage, leads to a domed building believed to have been a bathhouse. Archaeologists have pinpointed this perfect circular structure as the model for the Pantheon in Rome.

Pompeii and Herculaneum

The two Roman cities of **Pompeii ❹** (Apr–Oct daily 8.30am–7.30pm, Nov–Mar daily 8.30am–5pm, last entry 90 mins before closure; special night openings in summer; tel: 081-8575348; entrance fee; for general information on Pompeii and Herculaneum, tel: 081-8575347; www2.pompeiisites.org) and Herculaneum, buried by the eruption of Mount Vesuvius in AD 79, have solved what the archaeologist Amedeo Maiuri has called "the essential problem in the history of civilisation: the origin and development of the house". Pompeii, originally settled by indigenous Oscans some time before the 8th century BC and later ruled by Etruscans, Greeks and the warlike Samnites, was a commercial centre at the time of its sudden immersion in pumice stone and ash. It was a city of shops, markets and comfortable town houses, with paved streets, a stadium, two theatres, temples, baths and brothels. Its rediscovery during land reclamation oper-

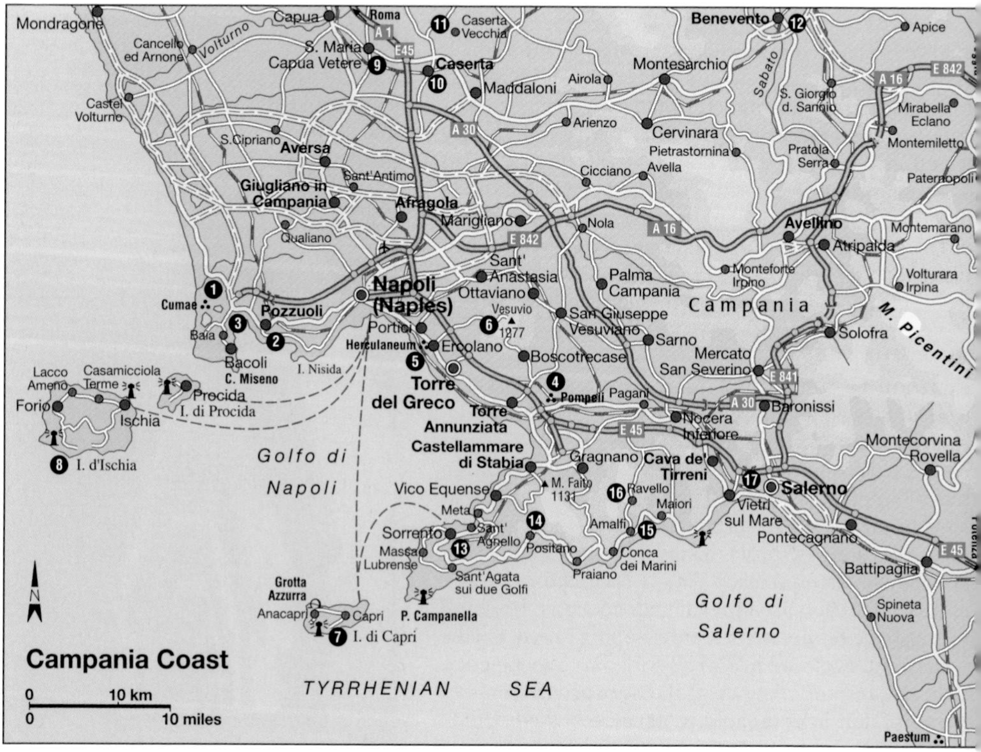

Campania Coast

TYRRHENIAN SEA

0 _____ 10 km
0 _____ 10 miles

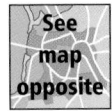

tions in the 16th century, and subsequent years of excavation (sometimes pirat-cal but increasingly respectful) have revealed an intimate picture of life in a st-century Roman city.

The Pompeian house is thought to have evolved from the relatively simple design of the Etruscan farmhouse. The structure was built around a central court-yard *(atrium)* whose roof sloped inwards on all four sides to a rectangular open-ng in the centre known as the *compluvium*. Through the *compluvium*, rainwater ell into a corresponding rectangular tank called the *impluvium*. Around the *atrium* itself were the various family quarters, including the bedrooms *(cubic-*la), the dining rooms *(triclinia)* and, directly opposite the narrow entranceway *vestibule)*, the living room *(tablinum)*, the most important room in the house.

As the plan developed, a further peristyle courtyard was added, often con-aining a fountain. Shops were built into the front of the house; sections of the nouse were blocked off and rented out, with separate entranceways, to strangers for example, the **Villa di Julia Felix**); another storey was added up top, until the Etruscan prototype had metamorphosed into the comfortable and palatial town nouses typified by the **Casa dei Vettii** and the **Casa del Fauno**.

Wedding whips

A striking feature of the Pompeian house was the colourful and often highly refined artwork covering its walls. Many of the most beautiful frescos have been taken to the Museo Archeologico Nazionale in Naples *(see page 305)*, but at the **Villa dei Misteri**, just outside the Porto Ercolano, a series of 10 scenes, apparently depicting the initiation of brides into the Dionysiac mysteries, has been left *in situ*. The meaning of these paintings, which depict, among other things, the whipping of a young bride, is still far from clear, although it is gener-ally agreed that the woman in the final scene is probably a portrait of the mistress of the house, who may have been a Dionysiac priestess.

ABOVE: faun in the Casa del Fauno.
BELOW: fresco at Villa dei Misteri.

The most remarkable thing about Pompeii is the mass of detail. Carved into the polygonal paving stones of the streets, for instance, are small phalluses pointing to the centre of the city. These are thought by some to have warded off evil spirits, by others to have pointed to the brothel district. And walls and monuments throughout the city are covered with inscriptions of every kind, from lists of upcoming plays to the scribbled accounts of shopkeepers, from election notices to billets-doux. "It is a wonder, O Wall," wrote one cynic on the wall of the basilica, "that thou hast not yet crumbled under the weight of so much written nonsense."

Herculaneum ❺ (Ercolano) (Apr–Oct daily 8.30am–7.30pm, Nov–Mar daily 8.30am–5pm, last admission 90 minutes before closure; tel: 081-7777008; entrance fee) was built for the enjoyment of sea breezes and views across the Bay of Naples. Instead of the compact town houses of Pompeian businessmen, there are sprawling villas of wealthy patricians. There is a free, spontaneous form of architecture, and the houses, freed of the mud in which they were encased for so long, are generally in a better state of preservation than those of Pompeii.

One of the pleasures of Herculaneum (aside from the fact that it is less crowded with tour groups than

Transport on Ischia.

Pompeii) is the carbonised pieces of wooden furniture, door mouldings and screens still inside the houses. Fine frescos, such as *The Rape of Europa* in the **Casa Sannitica**, adorn the walls, and carpet-like mosaics cover the floors. Particularly striking are the black-and-white mosaics on the floor of the **Casa dell 'Atrio a Mosaico**. But the finest building here is the **Casa dei Cervi** (The House of the Stags), which features superb frescos and statues. After lengthy excavations the **Villa dei Papiri** opened in 2003. Built by Julius Caesar's father-in-law, it is believed to contain the "lost library" of Latin and Greek literary masterpieces. Prior booking is essential for visits. Reservations and tours for Herculaneum (and Pompeii) can be made through Pompeii's tourism office by calling 081-8507255.

Herculaneum is the best starting point for an afternoon ascent of **Mount Vesuvius ❻**, which looms directly over the modern city of **Ercolano**. Buses leave regularly from the Ercolano Scavi train station and drop passengers at the roadhead, from where there is a 20-minute climb up a well-beaten track.

Just before the infamous eruption of AD 79, trees and olive groves covered Vesuvius up to its very peak. In the 20th century, a constant plume of smoke billowed from a cone inside the crater until 1944, when, during the volcano's last major eruption to date, the cone was destroyed. Aware that 1 million people are sitting on a time bomb and that a major eruption is a matter of when and not if, the Italian authorities are offering each family €25,000 to move, but the take-up from Neopolitans has been minimal.

BELOW: heading for the Blue Grotto, Capri.

Islands of pleasure

Of the three islands just outside the Gulf of Naples, **Capri ❼**, on the Sorrento side, has traditionally been the most popular. Its mild climate, luxuriant vegetation and seemingly inaccessible coast have drawn visitors for centuries. Emperor Tiberius retired here in AD 27, either to pursue his lifelong love of privacy or to indulge in the secret orgies which the historians Tacitus and Suetonius claim characterised the closing years of his reign. While on Capri, writes Suetonius, the emperor "devised little nooks of lechery in the woods and glades… and had boys and girls dressed up as Pans and nymphs posted in front of caverns or grottoes; so that the island was now openly and generally called 'Caprineum' because of his goatish antics." The writer Norman Douglas, who also lived on Capri, attributed such legends to the idle exaggerations of resentful peasants.

The modern traveller, arriving by ferry or hydrofoil from Naples or Sorrento, can reach the remains of **Tiberius' Villa** (Villa Jovis; daily 9am–1 hour before sunset; entrance fee) by bus from the town of Capri. The most famous sight on the island, however, is the **Grotta Azzurra** (Blue Grotto), a cave on the water's edge.

From **Anacapri**, on the far side of the island, you can take a chair-lift up **Monte Solaro** (from Piazza Vittoria; entrance fee). Its 360-degree view encompasses the southern Apeninnes, Naples, Vesuvius, Sorrento and Ischia. In Anacapri itself, the church of **San Michele** (daily 9am–7pm, 9.30am–3pm in winter) is worth a visit for its majolica-tiled pavement depicting *The Story of Eden*.

Ischia ❽, the largest island off Naples, is famous for

ts hot mineral springs. The island is of volcanic origin. Some say the giant Typhoeus, struck by Zeus' thunderbolt, was buried under Ischia, the cause of the occasional groanings and shakings that have marked its long history. Compared with Capri, Ischia is larger, wilder and decidedly less manicured than its chic but more touristy neighbour.

The town of **Lacco Ameno**, on the coastal road, is known for its mud baths, which contain the most radioactive waters in Italy. **Sant'Angelo** has some of the best beaches on the island. At **Ischia Ponte**, a causeway crosses to the **Castello Aragonese**, built by Alfonso I of Naples in 1450. The crypt of the ruined cathedral is adorned with frescos in the style of Giotto. The nearby convent has an interesting cemetery where departed sisters were placed upright in chairs.

Procida, the smallest of the islands in the Bay of Naples, has good beaches and a thriving fishing industry. It is quiet and has not succumbed to mass tourism.

Old Campania

Inland from Naples, at **Santa Maria Capua Vetere** ❾, are the remains of the second-largest amphitheatre in Italy after the Colosseum (Tues–Sun 9am–5.30pm). Few tourists are aware of this magnificent crumbling structure, where visitors can actually climb down into the subterranean passages where wild beasts roamed.

Caserta ❿ is often called the Versailles of Naples for its lavish **Reggia** (Royal Palace; Wed–Mon 8.30am–7pm; gardens 8.30am–7pm, until 3.30pm in winter; entrance fee), designed by Luigi Vanvitelli in 1752 for the Bourbon king Charles III. The brick-and-stone colossus doesn't quite achieve the elegant beauty of Versailles, but it is impressive nonetheless, and the vast gardens alone make an excursion worthwhile. **Caserta Vecchia** ⓫, on a hilltop 10 km (6 miles) northeast, is

Map on page 316

The royal palace of Caserta took 22 years to complete. The façade is 249 metres (815 ft) long, it has 2,000 windows, and its 1,200 rooms are spread across five floors connected by 34 stairways. Most impressive of all are the 120 hectares (300 acres) of magnificent parkland.

BELOW: the village of Corricella, on the island of Procida.

The freshness and quality of local produce in Campania are superb.

one of the most beautiful towns in Campania. Founded in the 8th century, it still looks much as it did then. Its Romanesque cathedral has a wonderful façade with a cow over the central portal. Inside is a monolithic 4th-century font in which baptism by full immersion was practised.

One of the most important cities in Campanian history is **Benevento ⑫**, where the noble king Manfred voluntarily died in battle after the defection of his allies in 1266. The city was named Beneventum upon becoming a Roman colony in 268 BC. In the centre of town, on the route of the ancient **Via Appia** from Rome to Brindisi, stands the **Arch of Trajan**. Of the splendid reliefs depicting scenes from Trajan's life, those on the side facing Rome celebrate the emperor's domestic policies while those on the side facing Brindisi record his foreign policies. The **Museo del Sannio** (Tues–Sun 9am–7pm; entrance fee) is worth visiting not only for its collection of local antiquities but also for the hunting scenes on the column capitals that surround its 12th-century cloister.

Paradise regained

The visitor to **Sorrento ⑬**, whether arriving from the noisy streets of Naples or from the scorched ruins of Pompeii, will find a cool and peaceful town of lemon groves, with a small beach and plentiful cafés. There's not much more to Sorrento, save for a 15th-century **loggia** with fine column capitals on the Via San Cesareo, and the fact that the poet Tasso was born here in 1544, but that is exactly why the town is such a popular resort among Italians and foreigners alike. It's an excellent starting point for excursions to Capri and the **Amalfi Coast**. This dramatic coast stretches from **Positano** to **Salerno** and has some of the most spectacular scenery in Italy. The **Amalfi Drive** faithfully follows its length, keeping a respectful distance above the waves but doggedly following each frightening twist of the shoreline. Pastel-painted houses cling to the slopes, and gardens descend in steps to the sea.

Positano ⑭ consists of a semicircle of houses set back in a cove, with numerous hotels, good swimming and wonderful views. The road then passes through several tunnels before reaching the **Grotta di Smeraldo**, famous for its emerald-green light. Through yet more tunnels (watch out for cyclists) lies **Amalfi ⑮**, a major trading centre in Byzantine times and now a major tourist centre. From the main piazza, with its fountain, a flight of steps ascends to the 11th-century bronze door of Amalfi's **Duomo**. In the crypt lies the body of St Andrew the Apostle, delivered from Constantinople in 1208. On either side of the main altar are ambones with fine mosaics.

The loveliest town on the Amalfi Coast is **Ravello ⑯**, famous for its architecture, its gardens and admirers. Ravello's **Duomo** is celebrated for its bronze doors by the Puglian Barisano da Trani. Cast in Trani in 1179, the doors were transported to Ravello by ship. Inside, the floor slopes upwards towards God and a fine marble pulpit supported by pillars rests on the backs of six hungry lions. The pulpit was presented to the church in 1272 by Nicola Rufolo and his wife, Sigilgaida, who built the splendid **Villa Rufolo** (daily 9am–8pm, until 6pm in winter; entrance fee) opposite. The villa's lush gardens and Moorish cloister overlook the sea several miles away. The best view, however, is from the more extensive gardens

BELOW: Ravello.

at the **Villa Cimbrone** (daily 9am–8pm, until 6pm in winter; entrance fee), built at the end of the 19th century by a wealthy Englishman, Ernest William Beckett.

Salerno and Paestum

It was just south of **Salerno ⑰** that the Allies began their assault on Italy on 9 September 1943. Recently, there has been a belated restoration of the historic centre and a successful revival of the medieval Fiera Vecchia, a large food and handicrafts fair held in May. The city, strung out along the shore, has a good beach and one of the loveliest cathedrals in southern Italy, which is reached through an atrium incorporating 28 columns from Paestum. Inside, as the removal of 18th-century plaster continues, more medieval frescos are coming to light.

The English writer George Eliot regarded the **Temple of Neptune** at **Paestum** (daily 9am–1 hour before sunset, last entry 1 hour earlier; entrance fee) as "the finest thing, I verily believe, we have seen in Italy". Her words echo the sentiments of many 19th-century travellers for whom this Greek city was the final stop on the Grand Tour. There are few sights so arresting as Paestum's three well-preserved Doric temples standing empty on the grassy plain that surrounds them. The Temple of Neptune, the most majestic of these, was built in the 5th century BC of a reddish travertine whose warmth, as Eliot wrote, "seems to glow and deepen under one's eyes".

The so-called **basilica** beside the Temple of Neptune dates from the 6th century BC. The third temple, the **Temple of Ceres**, is separated from the other two by the **Roman forum** and **baths**, and a **Greek theatre**. Across the street, in the **museum** (daily 8.45am–7pm; closed 1st and 3rd Mon of the month; entrance fee) are famous mural paintings from the **Tomb of the Diver** (480 BC). ❑

Map on page 316

Temple of Neptune at Paestum.

BELOW: the pastel-hued houses of Positano.

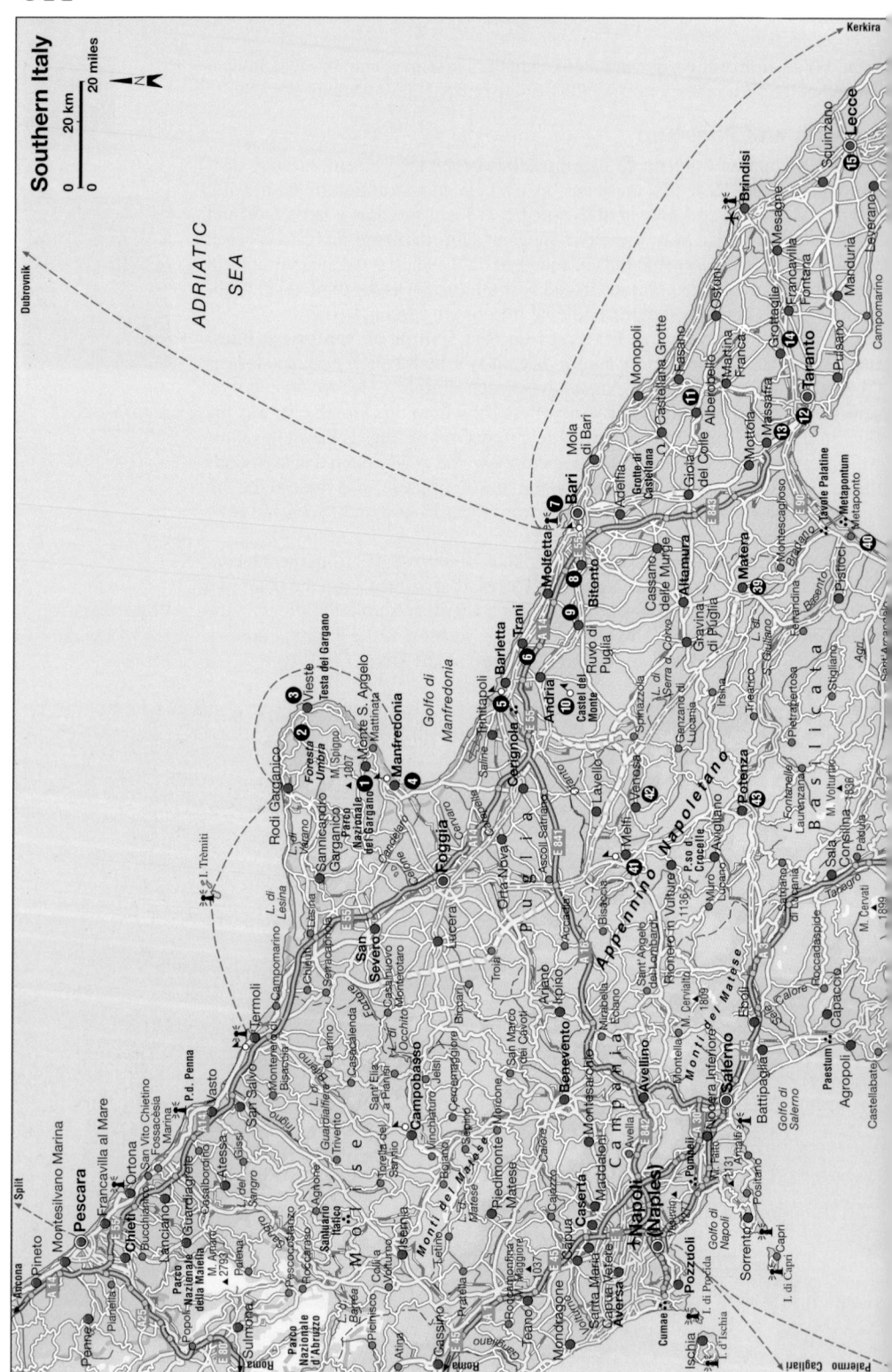

Southern Italy

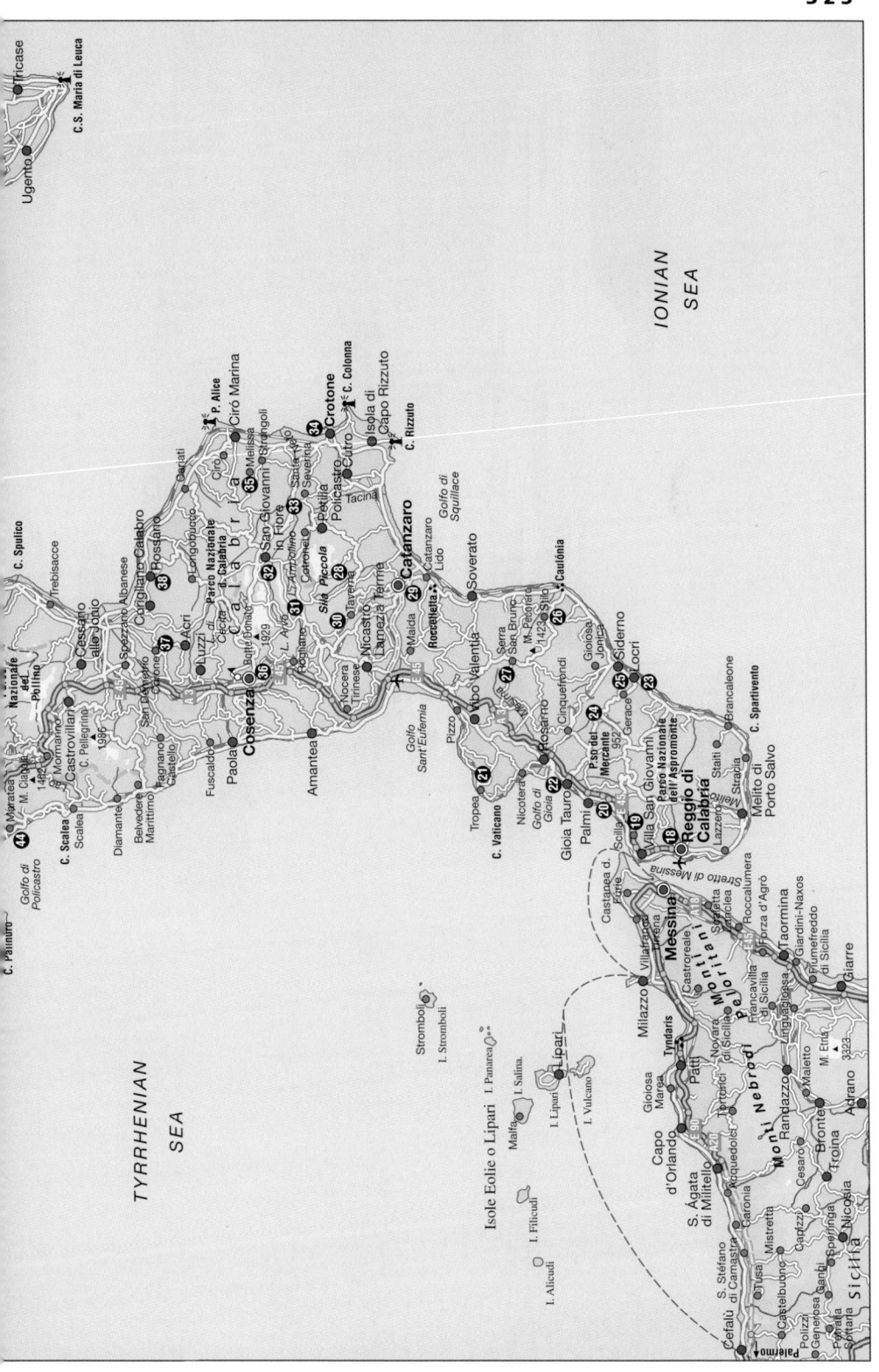

PUGLIA

*Forming the heel and spur of Italy's boot,
Puglia is a region of glorious churches, castles
and sun-bleached beaches*

Map on
pages
322–3

ITALY
Rome●

Some people visit Puglia for its architecture, some for its landscape, some for its archaeology and some for its food, but all go away haunted by memories of a single man: Frederick II of Hohenstaufen, Holy Roman Emperor, king of Germany and king of Sicily. Known to Dante as "the father of Italian poetry" and to his 13th-century contemporaries as *stupor mundi et immutator mirabilis* – wonder of the world and extraordinary innovator – Frederick built most of the castles that are still the dominant architectural feature of the region.

He also founded many of Puglia's most splendid churches, carrying on the tradition of the Puglian Romanesque begun by his Norman predecessors a century before. An enlightened ruler who waged a bitter and ultimately unsuccessful feud with the popes in Rome, he was also an avid sportsman whose brilliant treatise on falconry still ranks among the most accurate descriptions of the subject. His just laws and tolerance of the Islamic beliefs of the Saracens are legendary. Frederick's death in 1250 and the tragic defeat of his illegitimate son, Manfred, at the battle of Benevento in 1266 ushered in a period of economic and spiritual decline that is only now being reversed, the former often by illegal means (Puglia has become the preferred gateway for contraband – cigarettes and arms – now flooding into the border-free Europe from former Yugoslavia).

LEFT: Ostuni, a white hill town.
BELOW: the white sands of the Gargano.

If Frederick II is the dominant figure in Puglia's long and varied history, the Puglian Romanesque is its most important architectural legacy. The style, fusing Byzantine, Saracenic and Italian decorative techniques with the French architectural forms introduced by the Normans, first appeared in the church of San Nicola at Bari in 1087. The plans of most other Puglian churches of the period derived from this elegant cathedral with its short transepts, three semicircular apses corresponding to three naves and three portals, a tall, plain façade, and richly decorated doorways carved with animals, flowers and biblical scenes.

The visiting Archangel

The landscape of northern Puglia is dominated by vast inland plains planted with wheat. The only real mountains are clustered on the Gargano promontory, a thickly forested peninsula that juts out into the Adriatic to form the "spur" of the boot of Italy. Here, in the medieval town of **Monte Sant'Angelo ❶**, is the **Santuario di San Michele** (July–Sept daily 7.30am–7.30pm, Oct–June daily 7.30am–12.30pm and 2.30–5pm; entrance fee), a cave where the Archangel Michael is said to have revealed himself to local bishops in AD 490, 492 and 493. The cave is entered through a pair of bronze doors made in Constantinople in 1076 and decorated with the numerous deeds of the Archangel; brass rings in the doors were

TIP

From Vieste you can catch a ferry to the Tremiti Islands, 40 km (25 miles) offshore, which are sparsely populated but offer good beaches and clear water.

supposed to be knocked loudly to wake the Archangel within. This pleasant town also has a fine **municipal museum** (Monte Santangelo, Piazza San Francesco; Tues–Sun 9am–1pm, 3.30–7pm; entrance fee) devoted to the popular arts of the Gargano. Particularly interesting are the presses once used to make wine and olive oil, and a stone flour mill originally turned by mules.

Monte Sant'Angelo is a good place to buy components for a picnic lunch in the **Foresta Umbra ②**, a parkland in the centre of the peninsula where 100-year-old beech, oak and chestnut trees shade winding trails and pleasant picnic spots. From here, you can drive along the coastline to **Vieste ③**, a bright town on the tip of the promontory containing a castle built by Frederick II. The road continues west along a serpentine coastline studded with beaches and grottoes, passing en route an impressive 20-metre (66-ft) high rock formation known as *Pizzomuno*, referred to by locals as "the top of the world".

Manfredonia ④, back on the mainland, is a port and beach resort with a pretty historic centre including a castle, begun by Manfred (son of Frederick II) in 1256 and later enlarged by Manfred's enemy, Charles I of Anjou. Near Manfredonia are the beautiful medieval churches of **Santa Maria di Siponto**, with a 5th-century crypt and an altar made from an early Christian sarcophagus, and **San Leonardo**, with a façade guarded by two stone lions. Siponto, once a thriving medieval port, also has good, if crowded, sandy beaches.

Coastal route

The coastal route to Bari is lined with seaport towns, all doing a brisk trade in vegetables, fruit and wine. The oldest, most important and, today, least attractive of these is **Barletta ⑤**, where Manfred established his court in 1259. Here, at the

BELOW: Trani's Duomo.
BELOW RIGHT: frying polenta.

intersection of the corsos Garibaldi and Vittorio Emanuele, stands the intriguing **Colosso**, a 4th-century Byzantine statue thought to represent the emperor Valentinian I (364–75). Only the head and torso are original; the rest was recast in the 15th century. Behind rises the **Basilica di San Sepolcro**, with a nice Gothic portal and an octagonal cupola reminiscent of Byzantine designs. Barletta's **Duomo** is a confusing edifice built on a Romanesque plan, with five radiating apses in French Gothic style and a Renaissance main portal. By the sea lies Manfred's 13th-century castle, much expanded in later centuries.

A far more picturesque town, 13 km (8 miles) south of Barletta, is **Trani ❻**, the prosperous centre of the local wine trade. Its Romanesque cathedral (daily 9am–noon and 3.30–6pm in summer, reduced hours in winter), founded in 1097 but not completed until the middle of the 13th century, is perhaps the most beautiful church in Puglia. Beneath its richly carved rose window is a smaller window flanked by pillars resting on the backs of elephants. The wonderful bronze doors are the work of the local artist Barisano da Trani, who is also responsible for the celebrated doors on the cathedral at Ravello. The interior of the church, bright and austere, has the usual three apses and three naves, with triforium arcades above the side-aisles supported, here, by six pairs of columns on either side. Steps descend to the underground church of **Santa Maria della Scala** and the crypt. Even further down is the underground **Ipogeo di San Leucio**, 1.5 metres (5 ft) below sea level, containing two primitive but delightful frescos.

Windy Bari

Ancient **Bari ❼**, founded by the Greeks and developed by the Romans as an important trading centre, was destroyed by William the Bad in 1156 and restored by William the Good in 1169. Today it is the largest and most important commercial centre in Puglia. The city is divided into two distinct parts: the intriguing Città Vecchia, situated at the end of Corso Cavour, with its tight tangle of medieval streets and dazzling white houses, and the Città Nuova, the modern city, with wide, grid-like boulevards. The tortuous alleyways of the Moorish-style old city protected the inhabitants from the wind and from invaders. Nowadays, travellers are often warned by the locals to take care when visiting the maze of alleys in case of getting lost.

The church of **San Nicola** was founded in 1087 to house the relics of St Nicholas, patron saint of Russia – stolen from Myra in Asia Minor by 47 sailors from Bari. Its façade bears many resemblances to that of the cathedral at Trani, though it is even plainer. A small round window (oculus) crowns three bifora windows, a monofora window, and a richly carved portal flanked by columns borne by a pair of time-worn bulls.

The interior of the church is best visited in the evening, when sun shines through the windows of the façade, creating unusual lighting effects on the three great transverse arches (structural additions of 1451). Among the many noteworthy objects in this church are the beautiful column capitals of the choir screen separating the nave from the apse, and the *ciborium* (free-standing canopy) over the high altar, dating from the early 12th century. Behind the *ciborium* is the church's best-known work of art, an

Map on pages 322–3

BELOW: in the old city of Bari.

Window of the Castel del Monte.

11th-century episcopal throne supported by three grotesque telamones. To the left is a Renaissance altarpiece, *Madonna and Four Saints*, by the Venetian Bartolomeo Vivarini. The crypt contains the precious relics of St Nicholas, said to exude a wonder-working oil and visited by pilgrims for centuries. The Byzantine icon of St Nicholas in the central apse of the crypt was presented to the church by the King of Serbia in 1319.

Bari's **Duomo**, a short walk west of San Nicola, was erected between 1170 and 1178 over the remains of a Byzantine church destroyed by William the Bad during his rampage through the city in 1156. Basilican in plan, the church follows San Nicola in most details of its design, with deep arcades along both flanks and a false wall at the rear that masks the protrusions of the three semicircular apses. A particularly fine window adorns the rear façade.

Nearby, off the Piazza Federico II di Svevia, is the **Castello** (Tues–Sun 9am–1pm and 3–7pm; entrance fee), built in Norman times, refurbished by Frederick II, and considerably enlarged by Isabella of Aragon in the 16th century.

Bari's **Pinacoteca Provinciale** (Tues–Sat 9am–1pm and 4–7pm, Sun 9am–1pm; entrance fee), containing paintings from the 11th century to the present, is in the Città Nuova, along the Lungomare Nazario Sauro. The best painting is undoubtedly Bartolomeo Vivarini's *Annunciation* in Room II. Further rooms contain Giambellino's startling *San Pietro Martire* and a number of works by Neapolitan baroque painters, including Antonio Vaccaro and the prolific Luca Giordano. Francesco Netti, the Italian Impressionist, a native son of Bari, is also represented, and there is a new collection of contemporary art.

BELOW: the Duomo in Bitonto.

Around Bari

An interesting one-day excursion into Puglia's architectural past begins 18 km (11 miles) west of Bari in the olive-oil centre of **Bitonto 8**, whose famous cathedral, built between 1175 and 1200, represents perhaps the most complete expression of the Puglian Romanesque. The beautiful façade has a rose window and an elegantly carved portal, flanked by the usual lions. The pelican above the doorway is a symbol of Christ – in medieval times, the pelican was thought to peck at its own flesh to feed its young. Bitonto has an attractive historic quarter, and is worth an excursion from Bari.

The town of **Ruvo di Puglia 9**, 18 km (11 miles) further west, was known as Rubi in Roman times, when it was famous for its ceramics. The 13th-century **Duomo** was widened in the 17th century to provide room for baroque side-chapels, and, though restorations have shrunk the interior's width back to its original Romanesque proportions, the wide façade retains its baroque girth, giving the church a somewhat squat appearance. Fortunately, the medieval sculpture on the façade largely remains; the seated figure at the top is thought to represent the ubiquitous Frederick II. Beneath the nearby **Chiesa del Purgatorio** lie some Roman remains. Ruvo's excellent **Museo Archeologico Jatta** (Mon–Thurs and Sun 8.30am–1.30pm, Fri–Sat until 7.30pm; free) is devoted to Rubian ceramics excavated from nearby necropolises and dating from the 5th to the 3rd century BC.

On a hilltop 30 km (19 miles) west of Ruvo stands the **Castel del Monte**  (daily 10.15am–7.45pm in summer, 9.15am–6.45pm in winter; entrance fee), often cited, as is the Colosseum in Rome, as a supreme example of the architectural aims of an age. The eight-sided building has two storeys and eight Gothic towers; curiously enough, the main entrance is adorned with a Roman triumphal arch. Historians differ as to whether Frederick II erected the small fortress as a hunting lodge or as a military outpost, but all agree that he married his daughter, Violanta, to Riccardo, Count of Caserta, here in 1249. In 1266 the implacable Charles I of Anjou imprisoned the hapless sons of Manfred after their father's tragic defeat – and subsequent suicide – at Benevento. The castle served as a refuge for the noble families of Andria, a nearby town, during the plague of 1665, and was later abandoned, becoming a hideout for brigands and political exiles. Restoration began in 1876. The eerie emptiness of the building is reinforced by its isolated position on a hilltop perch that's visible for miles around.

The town of **Alberobello** ⓫, 50 km (32 miles) southeast of Bari, is known for its distinctive peasant dwellings known as *trulli*. Nobody knows the exact origins of these conical whitewashed houses (the oldest date back to the 12th century), but they did allow for easy home-extension through the addition of another unit, and modern building in the area is often based on the *trulli* shape. Now many of them have been turned into gift shops or are let to foreigners. South of Alberobello, the pleasant hilltop village of **Locorotondo** is another place to find *trulli*. It is also a good centre for local wines.

The **Grotte di Castellana** (daily 8.30am–7pm; guided tours on the hour or half hour depending on tour length; entrance fee; www.grottedicastellana.it) is another of the region's great tourist attractions. The 20-km (12-mile) network of caves con-

TIP

To stay in a *trullo* in Alberobello, contact Trullidea, a company based in the town (tel: 39-0804-323860; email: info@trullidea.it).

BELOW: *trulli* houses in Alberobello.

TRULLI EXTRAORDINARY

With their triangle-top roofs, whitewashed walls and mystical graffiti, Puglia's *trulli* are Italy's most curious houses. Originally built as overnight lodgings for farmers, a 15th-century tax dodge led to a whole town of *trulli* springing up at Alberobello. The count of Conversano enjoyed feudal rights over Alberobello, but did not enjoy paying his masters for the privilege. The emperor taxed every home in the count's domain – but not farmer's lodgings. So the crafty count ordered that the only buildings in Alberobello would be *trulli*.

The Albererobelesi became people of the *trulli*. Everything they built was a whitewashed brick "O" with a tepee-shaped slate hat. There are 1,500 of them, and even a double-topped *trullo*, once home to two brothers who fell in love with the same woman. The girl was promised to the elder, but fell for the younger, and the brothers fought until the only solution was to divide the house.

The *trulli* roofs are painted with primitive symbols: hearts and crosses blending Christian and erotic love; icons to Saturn, Jove and Mercury; to the pagan powers of the earth, sun and sky. You look on and wonder if the architect of the first *trullo* was a madman or a poet – truth is, he was both.

Flamboyant decoration on the façade of Sant'Irene, which also houses one of Lecce's most spectacular baroque altars.

BELOW: Piazza Sant' Oronzo in Lecce.

tains pools, grottoes and ceilings that drip with stalactites. You can opt for a one- or two-hour trip; the latter takes in the spectacular Grotta Bianca (White Cave).

To the east is the whitewashed hilltown of **Ostuni**, with its beautiful 15th-century cathedral and narrow streets that are a delight to wander around.

Spartan Taranto

Taranto ⑫, the ancient Taras founded by Spartan navigators in 706 BC, was in the 4th century BC the largest city in Magna Graecia, boasting a population of 300,000 and a city wall 15 km (9 miles) in circumference. It was, like many towns on this coast, a centre of Pythagorean philosophy and visited by such luminaries as Plato and Aristoxenus (author of the first treatise on music). Today the city, much damaged in World War II, is the home of one of Europe's most important ironworks. The old town is effectively an island separated from the modern and industrial quarters by canals.

Taranto's **Museo Nazionale** (currently closed for restoration), in the modern quarter, is the second-most important museum in southern Italy, rivalled only by the Museo Archeologico in Naples for the splendour of its antiquities, and recalls Taranto's importance as a centre of Magna Graecia. The collection includes Greek and Roman sculpture, a series of wonderful Roman floor mosaics and one of the most complete collections of ancient ceramics in Italy. While the museum is being restored, a significant proportion of the collection is temporarily on view at the nearby Palazzo Palanteo (Lungomare Vittorio Emanuele; daily 8.30am–7.30pm; entrance fee).

In Taranto's old city is the church of **San Domenico Maggiore**, founded by Frederick II in 1223, rebuilt in 1302 by Giovanni Taurisano, and much altered in baroque times. Nearby, on the Via Cariati, is a lively fish market. Taranto's **Duomo** contains fine mosaic floors and antique columns from pagan temples.

For those with the time, a fascinating side trip (21 km/13 miles) can be made from Taranto to the nearby town of **Massafra** ⑬, known for its early Christian cave churches hewn into the sides of a deep ravine that snakes through the centre of the town. The Santuario della Madonna della Scala contains a 12th-century *Madonna and Child* fresco. It can be reached via a baroque staircase from the town centre. At the bottom of the ravine is the Farmacia del Mago Gregorio – a maze of caves and tunnels once used by monks as a herb store. Ask in the town about access to these and other cave churches, but avoid visiting in the middle of the day when there will be very few people around.

From Massafra by back roads (37 km/23 miles), or from Taranto by *superstrada* (22 km/14 miles), you can reach **Grottaglie** ⑭, a hilltop town where you can watch Puglian potters make the ceramic pitchers, plates, bowls and cups available in gift shops across the region. The decorative spaghetti plates produced in the town are known throughout Italy.

Baroque Lecce

Lecce ⑮ is known for its profusion of baroque houses and churches. The city owes its appearance to the malleable characteristics of the local sandstone, which is easy to carve when it comes out of the ground but hardens with time. The growth of religious orders, particularly the Franciscans, Jesuits and Theatines, in the 17th and 18th centuries led to intensive building which created an architectural uniformity unique in southern Italy. Churches drip with ornate altars and swirling columns. Outside, shadeless streets meander past curving yellow palaces bright with bursts of bougainvillea.

The heart of Lecce is the cobblestoned **Piazza Sant'Oronzo**. At its centre stands a single Roman column once part of a pair in Brindisi that marked the southern terminus of the Via Appia from Rome. A bronze statue of St Orontius, patron saint of the city, stands on top of the column. The southern half of the square is dominated by excavations of part of a well-preserved **Roman amphitheatre** (Mon–Fri 10am–1pm, weekends 6–9pm; entrance fee) dating from the 2nd century AD. Discovered in the 1930s, it was reopened in 2000 as a concert venue, after a six-year restoration. A small museum on the site displays some fine frescos and mosaics. The unusual Renaissance pavilion used to be the town hall but now houses the tourist information office.

Lecce's harmonious **Piazza del Duomo**, just off the **Corso Vittorio Emanuele**, is framed by the façades of the **Duomo**, the **Palazzo Vescovile** and the **Seminario**, all built or reworked in the 17th century. The Duomo actually has two façades: the lavish one facing the Corso, with its statue of St Orontius, and the more austere (and older) one facing the Palazzo Vescovile. The altars inside the Duomo, carved with flowers, fruit and human figures, are typical of the ornate local style.

Bright basilica

The most complete expression of Leccian baroque is the **Basilica di Santa Croce** (daily 8am–1pm and 4–7.30pm), built in 1549–1679. Its exuberant façade sports a balcony supported by eight grotesque caryatids. The bright interior has an overall restraint that unifies the different designs of its chapels. A chapel in the left transept contains a series of 12 bas-reliefs showing the life of St Francis of Paola.

Lecce's modern and informative **Museo Provinciale** (Viale Gallipoli 28, Mon–Sat 9am–1.30pm and 2.30–7.30pm; free), just outside the old city, is built around a spiral ramp reminiscent of the Guggenheim Museum in New York.

The rewards of travelling in Puglia, as in its neighbours Basilicata and Calabria, include the pleasure of ending the day on a beach. Puglia has the longest coastline in Italy, a fact which has made it peculiarly attractive to foreign invaders, from the ancient worshippers of Zeus to the sun-worshipping visitors of today. Lecce is within easy reach of beaches at **Gallipoli** ⑯ on the Ionian Sea and **Otranto** ⑰ on the Adriatic. Otranto has the added attraction of a Romanesque cathedral (daily 8am–noon and 3–7pm in summer, 8am–noon and 3–5pm in winter) with an impressive mosaic floor.

In the peace and the wave-song of the pristine Puglian sands, you could lie dreaming for many months, lost in reveries on the passage of so many heroes through these parts, from wily Odysseus to the broad-minded, gallant, brooding Frederick II. ❑

While so much baroque architecture is overblown, "Lecce baroque" is both dazzlingly ornate and exuberant, and at the same time refined. This lovely city is known to many as the "Florence of the South".

BELOW: elaborate figures on the façade of the Basilica di Santa Croce.

CALABRIA

*When Rome was still a village of shepherds, Pythagoras was
teaching philosophy here. But today, behind miles of
shoreline, Calabria conceals some of the remotest spots in Italy*

Map on
pages
322–3

Calabria is closer in spirit than any other region in Italy to the Italy of Byron
and Shelley – the land of crumbling ruins that inspired the romantic
thoughts of 19th-century travellers. But the region is fast changing. The
completion of the autostrada from Salerno to Reggio Calabria, government support for housing and industry, and vast improvements in the quality of hotels
have begun to lure both northern entrepreneurs and foreign tourists to this long-
isolated part of Italy. But the tourist industry is still in its infancy here and much
of Calabria's heritage lies buried among the roots of the many olive trees.

The landscape of the region is dominated by a backbone of mountains that
descend in a series of fantastic foothills to the sea and only 9 percent of the
territory consists of flat land. Not surprisingly, it was from the sea that Calabria's first invaders, the Greeks, came in the 8th century BC, crossing the Straits
of Messina from Sicily.

Spectacular treasure trove

Also from the sea are the **Bronze Warriors** – Calabria's most celebrated
reminder of those early settlers. Discovered by fishermen off Riace in 1972,
these two colossal Greek statues – thought to have been lost overboard from a
ship sailing between Calabria and Greece 2,000 years
ago – are the star attractions in the **Museo Nazionale
della Magna Graecia** in **Reggio di Calabria** ⓲
(Tues–Sun 9am–7pm; entrance fee).

The coastline just north of Reggio was first
described by Homer in Book XII of the *Odyssey*, the
earliest navigational guide to the Tyrrhenian Sea. Here
lurked the infamous monster Scylla, whose "six heads
like nightmares of ferocity, with triple serried rows of
fangs and deep gullets of black death" did away with
six of Odysseus' best men. Today the Rock of Scilla
forms the foundations of a youth hostel. **Scilla** ⓳ itself
is a charming fishing town whose spirit, dialect and
traditions feel more Sicilian than Calabrian. The view
over the Straits of Messina at sunset is stunning, and is
set to remain so now that controversial plans for a suspension bridge have been shelved. Take a stroll down
to Chianalea and explore the picturesque fishermen's
neighbourhood. The houses are built on the water, so
each one has two entrance ways – one facing the sea
and the other facing the street. Further north, **Palmi**
⓴ is worth visiting for its **ethnographic museum**
(Mon–Fri 8am–2pm and 3–6pm; entrance fee), which
has an extensive collection of ceramic masks designed
to ward off the evil eye, and collections of agricultural
and maritime life. The museum is housed in a modern
complex just outside the town.

Tropea ㉑, suspended from a cliff over one of the

LEFT: Tropea.
BELOW: sunset at
Scilla.

many fine beaches that line the shore, is perhaps the most picturesque town on the coast. The old town has a beautiful Norman **cathedral**. Behind the high altar is the *Madonna di Romania* – a portrait that is said to have been painted by St Luke.

Highway SS111 is the loneliest road in Calabria. It twists across the central mountain chain following what is believed to be an ancient trade route connecting **Gioia Tauro** ㉒ on the Tyrrhenian with **Locri** ㉓ on the Ionian Sea. Fierce brigands once ruled the woods through which it passes. From the **Passo del Mercante** ㉔, the road's highest and loneliest point, both seas are visible. From here the road descends to the beautiful town of **Gerace** ㉕, situated on the hump of a nearly inaccessible crag. It is best to visit Gerace in the evening on foot, to appreciate the romantic sunset views from the grassy ruins of its castle. Before the 10th century, a miracle-working saint – San Antonio del Castello – conjured up a spring of pure water in a cave in the cliff that surrounds the castle. The imprint of the saint's knees, they say, can be seen in the floor of the cave.

Gerace is a city of many layers, justifying the phrase, "If you know Gerace, you know Calabria." Its cathedral is the largest in Calabria. It was begun in 1045 on top of an older church – now in the crypt. Both cathedral and crypt contain columns from the Greek settlement at Locri. Some parts of this 7th-century BC town, including walls and temples, can still be seen.

The famous **Cattolica** at **Stilo** ㉖, one of the best-preserved Byzantine churches in existence, is a reminder that in medieval times Calabria's rugged interior was a vibrant religious centre. The tiny 9th-century church, built on a square floor plan with five cylindrical cupolas, clings to the flank of Monte Consolino, just above Stilo, like a miniature castle overlooking its town. Its

It is said that in the 10th century the inhabitants of Gerace survived an Arab siege by subsisting on ricotta cheese made from mother's milk.

BELOW: a Bronze Warrior in the Reggio di Calabria Museum.

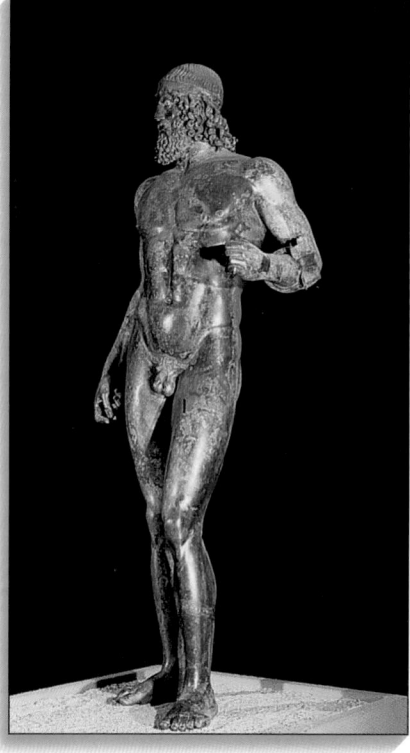

THE RIACE BRONZES

In 1972, a young man on holiday from Rome saw a bronze arm emerge from the Riace Marina. Fate decreed that it appear at exactly the same spot where the locals immersed the reliquary of the Saints Cosma and Damiano to summon rain. For the faithful, there was no doubt that this was the divine intervention of the two miraculous martyrs. The two "Bronzes of Riace" have brought great fame to the Ionian coastal town. They were sent to Reggio for eight years of meticulous restoration, and it was not until 1980 that they were put on display in Florence. The exhibition was a phenomenal success, and the following year the president had the bronzes publicly exhibited at the Quirinale Palace in Rome. They then returned "home" to the Museo Nazionale di Reggio di Calabria.

During the first months of exhibition in Reggio, many visitors tried to "feel" the statues and lifted babies to touch them. The atmosphere was similar to that of a southern Italian religious festival, in which young children participate in divinity through touch. These glorious, virile 2-metre (7½-ft) warriors are a patriotic reminder for the Calabrese that their remote toe of the Italian boot was once home to some of the Western world's most important cities in a land of philosophers and artists.

bright interior is adorned with fragments of frescos. The four columns supporting the vault are from a pre-Christian temple, but were placed upside-down to symbolise the Church's victory over paganism.

Another important religious centre further inland is the Carthusian monastery at **Serra San Bruno** ㉗, where you can visit the Museo della Certosa (Tues–Sun 9am–1pm and 3–8pm in summer, 9.30am–1pm and 3.30–6pm in winter; entrance fee).

Where shepherds wander

Of Calabria's four great mountain clusters – the Aspromonte, the Sila Piccola, the Sila Grande and the Sila Greca – the **Sila Piccola** ㉘, in the middle, has most to offer. Among its dense pine groves and cool meadows shepherd boys still wander with their flocks. The climate up here is refreshing after the dry heat of the coast. The twisting road up to **Catanzaro** ㉙ climbs first to **Taverna** ㉚, a serene town whose name suggests that it was once a way-station. In 1613, the baroque painter Mattia Preti was born here. He left Calabria at the age of 43 to become one of the most influential painters in Naples. The church of **San Domenico**, just off the main square, contains the best of Preti's local work; paintings of his may also be seen in the churches of **Santa Barbara** and **San Martino**.

A few "tourist villages" have been developed in the vast pine-covered area of the inner Sila as skiing or fishing centres, but they have not altered its sense of isolation. The roads are empty and winding, and barred when the snow gets too deep in winter. Even the **Lago Ampollino** ㉛, a man-made lake created in the early 20th century to encourage tourism and produce electricity, lacks the crowds found at even the most remote Italian holiday spots. Here, nature still rules.

Map on pages 322–3

In the Serra San Bruno monastery, 16 bearded, white-robed monks live according to the vows of silence prescribed by Bruno of Cologne in the 11th century. The monks eat no meat but make excellent cheese which is sold in the town.

BELOW LEFT: medieval rooftops of Gerace.
BELOW: the Cattolica at Stilo.

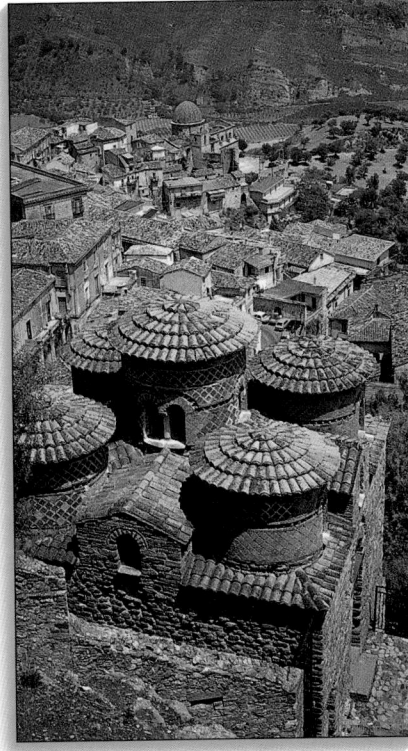

San Giovanni in Fiore ㉜, the biggest town in the Sila, is noted for the black-and-purple costumes of its women. More compelling is the lovely hilltop town of **Santa Severina** ㉝, famed for its medieval scholastic tradition. Attached to the cathedral is an 8th–9th-century Byzantine baptistery built originally as a *martyrium* (a shrine for the sacred relics of honoured members of the local Christian community) when it stood alone. At the entrance to the town, the Byzantine church of **San Filomena** has a cylindrical dome of Armenian inspiration, and three tiny apses that seem to anticipate Romanesque design. The long central Piazza Vittorio Emanuele leads to the 10th-century castle which is now a school.

The coastal town of **Crotone** ㉞ was founded by Greeks in 710 BC. Here the mystical mathematician Pythagoras came up with his theorem on right-angled triangles and taught the doctrine of metempsychosis, in which the soul is conceived as a free agent which, as John Donne later imagined, can as easily attach itself to an elephant as to a mouse before briefly inhabiting the head of a man. Other than these scholarly associations, the modern town on its crowded promontory has little to offer the tourist apart from an interesting **archaeological museum** (daily 9am–7.30pm, closed first and third Mon in the month; entrance fee) and an excellent wine from the nearby village of **Melissa** ㉟.

Northern Calabria

The old town of **Cosenza** ㊱ stands on a hilltop surrounded by the flat and sprawling modern city that has grown around it. In the heart of the *centro storico* stands a beautiful Gothic cathedral, consecrated in the presence of Frederick II in 1222. In the **Tesoro dell' Archivescovado** behind the cathedral is a Byzantine reliquary cross that Frederick II donated to the church at the time of its

More porcini mushrooms are harvested in Calabria than in any other region in Italy. They grow in the forests of the Sila and the Serre, along with more than 3,000 other varieties of mushroom.

BELOW: poppies in the Sila Grande.

consecration. The partially ruined **Castello** (daily 8am–8pm; free) at the top of the old town has excellent views.

When the travel writer Norman Douglas visited the Albanian village of **San Demetrio Corone** ➌ in 1911, he was told by the amazed inhabitants that he was the first Englishman ever to have set foot in the town. Although tourists are no longer a rarity in these parts, be prepared for the curious stares of barbers, policemen, shopkeepers and women in bright Albanian dresses. The Albanians first fled to Calabria in 1448 to escape persecution by the Arabs. Today they form the largest ethnic minority in the region. They have their own language, literature and dress, and their own Greek Orthodox bishop. As isolated as San Demetrio is in the backhills of the Sila Greca, this was once one of the most important centres of learning in Calabria, the site of the famous Albanian College where the revolutionary poet Girolamo de Rada taught for many years. Inside the college, the little church of Sant' Adriano contains a Norman font and a wonderful mosaic pavement.

On the Ionian Coast, overlooking the sea, stands lonely **Rossano** ➌, the most important city of the south between the 8th and 11th centuries. It is home of the famous **Codex Purpureus**, a rare 6th-century Greek manuscript adorned with 16 colourful miniatures drawn from the Gospels and the Old Testament. This extraordinary book can be seen in the **Museo Diocesano** (June–mid-Sept daily 9am–1pm and 4.30–8pm, mid-Sept–May Tues–Sat 9.30am–12.30pm and 4–7pm, Sun 10am–noon and 4.30–6.30pm; entrance fee) beside the cathedral. At the top of the greystone town, the five-domed Byzantine church of **San Marco** offers breathtaking views across the valley. Below the old town lies the bustling resort of Rossano Scalo. ❑

Map on pages 322–3

A true Calabrese breakfast, typical of Reggio and the Ionian Coast up to Crotone, features several round brioches soaked in a glass of iced almond milk.

BELOW: San Marco church, Rossano.

BASILICATA

*Between forests, sandy coves, castles, excavations and
rock-hewn churches, there's plenty to explore
in this region entirely off the beaten track*

Map on
pages
322–3

Even for Italians, Basilicata is relatively unknown. But the region's forests, sandy coves and castles have much to offer the tourist. The area's most beguiling city is **Matera** ㊴, a fabulous troglodyte town of prehistoric grottoes, cave tabernacles, abandoned hovels and Renaissance houses – all excavated into the luminous limestone tufa.

The rock-cut dwellings – known as the Sassi – date back to Byzantine times. Up until the 1950s the caves were home to peasants who lived alongside their donkeys in dark hovels. Then the Italian government, embarrassed by the poverty, rehoused the entire population.

By the 1980s a number of intrepid Materani started to return. Two decades later the Sassi are the region's main tourist attraction – recognised by Unesco as the finest example of "cave architecture" in the Mediterranean.

A hill splits the Sassi into two areas: Sasso Caveoso and Sasso Barisano. The best way to explore them is on foot, stopping at the bars and shops to see the inventive use of the cave interiors. You can pick up maps and itineraries from the tourist office (Via de Viti de Marco 9; tel: 0835-331983).

Across the canyon from the Caveoso and Barisano are the original cave habitations. These date back to 6 BC, and stake a claim to be the second-oldest habitation in the world. This Stone Age history is documented in the excellent **Museo Ridola** (Via Ridola 24; Tues–Sun 9am–8pm, Mon 2–8pm; tel: 0835-310058).

The great legacy of Byzantine civilisation in Basilicata are the so-called *chiese rupestri*: 9th–15th-century rock-hewn churches carved out of the tufa with built-in altars, pilasters, domes and frescos. There are around 150 of these churches, with some 48 in the Sassi themselves. Among the most important and best preserved are Santa Barbara, Santa Maria de Idris, Santa Lucia alle Malve, San Nicola dei Greci, the Madonna delle Virtù, the Convicinio di Sant'Antonio and Santa Maria della Valle. They are not easy to find or access, so the best way to visit them is with a guide, who will often have keys to unguarded churches.

Other interesting visits include the 17th-century **Palazzo Lanfranchi** (Piazza Giovanni Pascoli; Tues–Sun 9am–1pm and 4–7pm; tel: 0835-256262), which houses Italian paintings from the 13th–18th century and a modern art collection.

The baroque Chiesa del Purgatorio, dedicated to the medieval cult of the Holy Souls of Purgatory, features a curvaceous façade and gruesome Halloween-style decorations carved in the tufa of the main doorway.

At the junction of Via Ridola and Via del Corso is the 17th-century Chiesa di San Francesco, home to painting by the early Renaissance master Bartolomeo

LEFT: Matera.
BELOW: the perfect vehicle for the narrow Sassi streets.

The doorway of San Giovanni in Matera.

Vivarini. The nearby Piazza del Sedile, dominated by the 16th-century home to the local *conservatoire*, leads into Via Duomo, with its 13th-century Romanesque cathedral. The façade features a great rose window and statues of the Archangel Michael. The church is dedicated to Matera's patron saint, the Madonna della Bruna, visible in the Byzantine-style fresco above the first altar to the left. Of the rock churches, **Santa Lucia** contains the two most famous frescos in Matera, the *Madonna del Latte* and *San Michele Arcangelo e San Gregorio*, both dating from the second half of the 13th century.

Historic sites

It's a short, easy day trip from Matera to Basilicata's Ionian coastline, which is dotted with ancient ruins. Just north of **Lido di Metaponto** ⓵ are the remains of the Greek colony of Metapontum. This is the only ancient Mediterranean colony where archaeologists have completely mapped the urban layout. The first group of ruins includes a theatre and traces of four temples. Even more evocative are the **Tavole Palatine** (daily 9am until one hour before sunset; tel: 0835-745327), the remains of 15 standing columns from the 6th-century BC Doric Temple of Hera.

Like Metaponto, **Policoro** is a new town with little to detain a visitor except a dip in the sea. Excavations are still in progress at the **Parco Archeologico di Policoro** (daily 9am until one hour before sunset), where the remains of the 5th-century BC Acropolis of Heraclea are on view. The **Museo della Siritide** (Wed–Mon 9am–8pm, Tues 2–8pm; entrance fee) contains local finds such as bronzes and statuettes, as well as exhibitions on traditional games and sports.

The area around **Melfi** ⓵, between Foggia and Potenza, combines natural

BELOW: the Sassi at sunset.

landscape and historic sites. Melfi itself is a small, unprepossessing town. The Norman conqueror Robert Guiscard was crowned duke of Puglia and Calabria in the castle, and Pope Urban II launched the First Crusade from here in 1089. The castle (Tues–Sun 9am–8pm, Mon 2–8pm; entrance fee) is an imposing fortress with a double perimeter wall and eight polygonal towers. Once the stronghold for the Holy Roman Emperor Frederick Barbarossa's Swabian dynasty, it is now home to the Museo Nazionale del Melfese.

The region around Melfi is dominated by the Vulture mountain range. Its extinct volcanic craters are filled by two lakes, the Laghi di Monticchio. A cableway between Lago Grande (Big Lake) and Lago Piccolo (Small Lake) takes you up to Monte Vulture (1,326 metres/4,350 ft). Another splendid view is from the heavily restored Norman Abbazia di San Michele, located on the wooded slopes of the Lago Piccolo crater.

Roman Venusia

Less than an hour away from Melfi is **Venosa** ㊷. Originally the successful Roman city of Venusia, it has survived thanks to its dominant position above the surrounding territory. For centuries it was a centre of learning, and it was fought over by the powerful families of the region. The Latin poet Horace (65–8 BC) was born here and, according to legend, lived in Vico Orazio, where remains of a Roman structure known as the Casa di Orazio are located (not open to the public, but visible from behind the gate). In 1443, Venosa came under the control of Pirro del Balzo, who enriched it with several monuments, including the Castello, now home to the **Museo Archeologico** (Wed–Mon 9am–8pm, Tues 2–8pm; entrance fee). Pirro demolished the cathedral, which was rebuilt in Piazza del Municipio.

Map on pages 322–3

Sassi art ceramicist Maria Bruna Festa (Ceramiche D'Arte Via Buozzi 99, Sasso Caveoso; tel: 338-1555660; 10am–1pm and 5–8pm) collects antique roof tiles fallen from abandoned Sassi, handpaints and re-fires them to make

BELOW: the Norman castle at Melfi.

The Via Frusci leads out of the town centre to one of the most interesting areas in Basilicata, the **Parco Archeologico di Venosa**. The park centres on the unfinished Abbazia della Trinità, and includes Roman and palaeo-Christian remains, Jewish and Christian catacombs, a thermal complex and a 10,000-seat amphitheatre.

The name Basilicata comes from basilikòs, the Byzantine administrator who governed here before the Normans arrived in the 11th century. The region is also known as Lucania, from the Lucani, who lived here in the 5th century BC.

The abbey (May–Sept Wed–Sun 9am–7pm, Tues 2–5pm, Oct–Apr variable; tel: 0972-34211) is one of the most intriguing buildings in southern Italy. It is made up of the *chiesa vecchia* (the old Norman church), and the roofless *chiesa nuova*, a huge basilica (70 metres by 48 metres/230 ft by 157 ft) planned by Benedictines in 1135 but never completed. Built of stones from an earlier pagan temple on the site, the abbey is a treasure trove of inscriptions, sarcophagi and frescos emerging from the small grove of olive trees.

Potenza and the Apennine Dolomites

Built on a spur of rock between two valleys, the historic centre of **Potenza** ❹❸ looks down on modern suburbs scattered at its feet. The capital of Basilicata's history has been dominated by earthquakes. The last big tremor hit in 1980, and reconstruction has not exactly been miraculous.

With the exception of the Museo Archeologico Provinciale (Via Ciccotti; Tues–Sun 9am–1.30pm and 4pm–9pm, Mon 9am–1.30pm), which is a 25-minute walk downhill from the centre, and some attractive churches clustered along Via Pretoria, there is little worth seeing. South from Potenza stretch the **Lucano Apennines**. Along the River Basento these peaks adopt a surprisingly "dolomitic" look, their bare, pointed rocks sculpted into bizarre forms by the elements. The most famous tourist attraction is **Pietrapertosa** (southeast of

BELOW: the town of drilled stone, Pietrapertosa.

Potenza, off the SS407), named after the *pietra forata*, or drilled stone. The town sits at 1,088 metres (3,570 ft) above sea level. It is surrounded by spires which take on the shape of objects and animals, and dominated by an unusual fortress carved out of the mountain.

Map on pages 322–3

The Portofino of the South

Maratea ❹ looks down on the coastal villages of Porto di Maratea, Fiumicello, Castrocucco and Acquafredda, which spread along a spectacular, jagged coastline. The so-called "city of 44 churches" looks out onto the blue Gulf of Policastro, and these days more Italians come here to swim and be seen than to pray.

Maratea's unmistakable landmark is a statue of Christ the Redeemer – a gift from local patron Count Rivetti, who placed it there to fend off bad times. The Redeemer's charms worked during the 1960s when Maratea earned the nickname the Portofino of the South. Its credentials were underlined by a visitor list which included Frank Sinatra and Richard Burton. But in the 1970s the resort fell into decline, a stagnation which lasted until the last few years during which, thanks to a large pot of private money, Maratea has recaptured its glory. Much of this renaissance centres on the Santa Venere resort, where a Turinese construction group has invested some £40 million in the area and its famous hotel (www.mondomaratea.it).

Up on the hill, Maratea's old town looks down on Santa Venere's renewed swank with insouciance. Lolling along the side of Monte Saint Biagio, its medieval houses and churches still bear the cracks of the earthquake which struck in the 1980s. The old town retains its downbeat, friendly feel and the renewed influx of tourists is welcome. ❏

Built into a hillside across the valley from Matera is the Church of the Madonna delle Tre Porte, with an exquisite fresco of the Vigin.

BELOW: Piano Ruggio in Pollino National Park.

A WALK ON THE WILD SIDE

Maratea is sandwiched between two national parks. On the Calabrian side is the **Parco Nazionale del Pollino** (www.parcopollino.it) – a great place for walking and wildlife. Founded in 1991, the enormous park stretches across 200,000 hectares (500,000 acres) of wilderness which host many protected species, including a colony of wolves, black squirrels, golden eagles, vultures, falcons, buzzards and otters. The park's symbol is the rare loricate pine. It has declined since the last Ice Age as the climate has warmed, and is only found here and in the Balkans. There are underground caves with bat colonies and craft workshops demonstrating the art of bagpipe-making. The park is also home to ethnic Albanians who tenaciously preserve their Arbëreshe (Italian-Albanian).

To the north, the **Parco del Cilento** is the second-largest park in Italy. It stretches from the Tyrrhenian Coast to the foot of the Apennines in Basilicata, and it includes the peaks of the Alburni Mountains, a wild calcareous mountain chain with caves, large beech forests and stark rocks. An endangered population of wolves and wildcats survive in a few remote corners of the park, alongside over 1,800 species of plants. For more information on all parks in all regions visit www.park.it.

SICILY

The island of Sicily, set in the middle of the Mediterranean and once the centre of the known world, has the finest array of classical and Moorish sites in Italy

Map on page 346

Nature and history have made Sicily a land of considerable and striking contrasts. The greatest island in the Mediterranean Sea, Sicily was for centuries the centre of the known world. Its peculiar geographic position – smack in the middle of the Mediterranean – made the island vulnerable to attacks by foreigners, but at the same time a meeting place of Mediterranean civilisations, a bridge between East and West. Witness the Greek colonisation (8th–3rd century BC), the Arab invasions (9th–10th century) and the Norman domination (11th–12th century). These were Sicily's great epochs, when commercial towns were founded and developed along the coast.

Invaders generally confined themselves to the coast because of the difficult, mountainous terrain inland. Sicily's volcanic features, represented by Mount Etna and the Aeolian Islands, testify to relatively recent geological origins. The island still suffers occasional violent earthquakes, and intermittent lava flows have made the plain below immensely fertile *(see page 354)*.

The reasons for the island's relative state of underdevelopment are rooted in its feudal past. Land in the interior is still organised along semi-feudal lines, while industry suffers from mismanagement and Mafia involvement.

LEFT: Arab-Norman cloisters at Monreale.
BELOW: under the almond trees, near Etna.

The Ionian coastline

A ferry crosses between Villa San Giovanni in Calabria and **Messina ❶** in half an hour. Travellers arriving at Messina are invariably surprised to find themselves in a modern grid-like city with low-rise buildings and wide avenues; the surprise turns to astonishment when they see the wonderful scenery which is offered by the **Peloritani Mountains** that cradle the city.

Although founded in the Classical Age by Greek settlers and developed mostly between the 15th and 17th centuries, Messina has little to show for its ancient origins. On a fateful morning in 1908, terrifying earthquake jolts, followed by a violent seaquake, shook the city and razed it to the ground. Despite this disaster, several fine churches survived, including the **Duomo** and the nearby Orion fountain, by a pupil of Michelangelo, Giovanni Montorsoli. At midday, the astronomical clock of the Duomo's campanile puts on a spectacular show with mythological and religious figures and sound effects such as a cock crowing and a lion's roar.

In the shadow of Etna

After 45 km (28 miles), the road from Messina winds up to a town that is the essence of Sicily. "It is the greatest work of art and nature!" exclaimed Goethe in *Italian Journey*. **Taormina ❷** knows no greys. Its beauty is made up of light, colour and sea. Lying on a short terrace of the coast against a mountain, it slopes down a

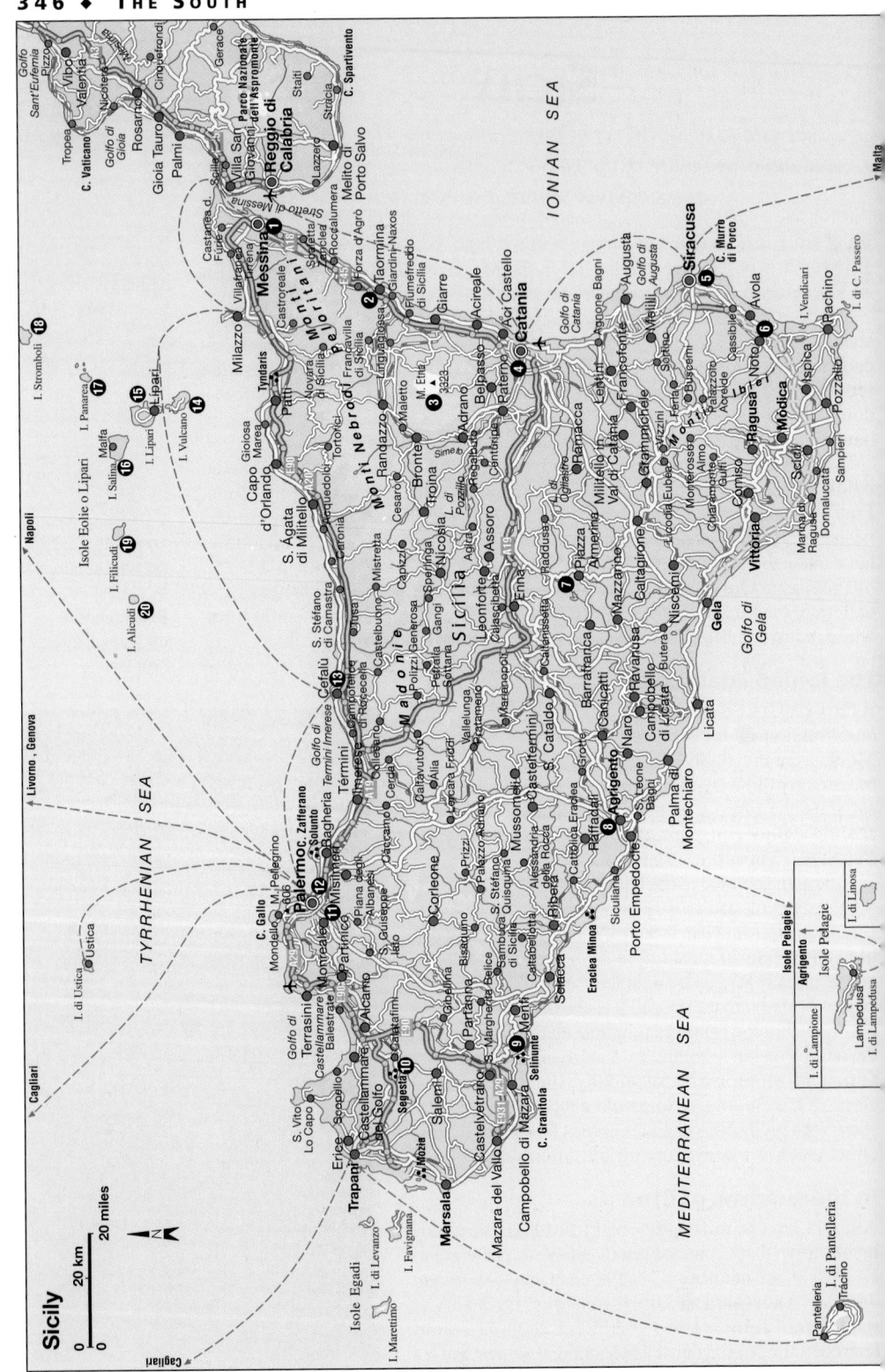

Sicily

cliff "as if", wrote Guy de Maupassant, "it had rolled down there from the peak". Its shoulders are embraced by the looming Mount Etna.

Climb the hill to the **Greek Theatre** (daily 9am–7pm in summer, until 4pm in winter; entrance fee; also open for summer concerts, opera and drama July–Sept, tickets and information from the tourist office, tel: 0942-23301), Taormina's most famous monument, celebrated by many writers for its magnificent position. Built in the 3rd century BC, but completely remodelled by the Romans in the 2nd century AD, it illustrates the Greeks' knack of choosing settings where nature enhances art. The jagged coastline of Taormina is dramatic: outcrops of rocks are intercut by narrow creeks, ravines and inlets.

In town, **Corso Umberto**, which cuts through the old centre, is the place for shopping and people-watching. The bars here are usually packed with an international crowd, but the atmosphere somehow remains that of a village. You can see this village in its churches or in the grand *palazzi* with their mullioned windows, marble tracery, scrolls and billowing balconies. The village atmosphere, however, does not disguise the fact that Taormina is a resort for the well-heeled.

Sicily's smokestack

The landscape south of Taormina is dominated by **Mount Etna ❸**, the majestic volcano (3,323 metres/10,959 ft) with its snow-capped peak. It is one of only a few volcanoes in the world which are active. Its surface is punctuated by about 200 cones, smaller craters, accumulated layers of lava, gashes and valleys. Etna's history is a series of more or less ruinous eruptions, from the one in 396 BC which halted the Carthaginians, to one in 1981, which destroyed part of the cableway. Even a smaller eruption in 1992 required help from the US marines to staunch the lava flow. The volcano has been in eruptive mode again since 1999 – the last major eruption was in October 2002. What happens next, of course, is as unpredictable as ever. To discuss options of getting close to Mount Etna, usually by the northern route via Linguaglossa, contact Etna Natural Touring (tel: 095 643613; www.naturaltouring.it). For general advice on current conditions and hiking routes visit the Etna Regional Park in Nicolosi (tel: 095-821111), or visit the information centres in Catania or Taormina.

In the fertile plain stretching from the southern foot of Mount Etna rises the city of **Catania ❹**. It was an important Greek and Roman colony, and suffered from the various powers that succeeded in dominating the island. Destroyed twice by violent earthquakes (in 1169 and 1693), the city was covered in 1669 by lava which even advanced into the sea for about 700 metres (2,300 ft).

Catania is the economic centre of the richest area of Sicily: its continuing development is based mainly on citrus fruits, vineyards and market gardening, but commercial and high-tech enterprises also flourish.

Catania has a modern feel, with an urban plan characterised by wide streets designed in the 18th-century baroque style. Its main axis is the elegant, austere **Via Etnea**, where people gather for the *passeggiata* and window-shopping. But Catania's baroque soul is better tasted in the smaller **Via Crociferi**, in which churches and monastic buildings open like wings of a

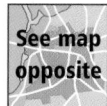

See map opposite

Traditional puppets of Crusader knights.

BELOW: the rich interior of Catania's Duomo.

Sicilian bread comes in a variety of shapes.

BELOW: Greek Theatre at Syracuse.

theatre. The street is covered by a baroque arch leading to **San Benedetto**, a vast yet unfinished Benedictine monastery.

Another landmark in the history of the baroque style is the church of **San Nicolò**, which is reached by following Via Gesuiti. And any visit would be incomplete without seeing **Castello Ursino** (Mon–Sat 9am–1pm), erected by Emperor Frederick II (1239–50) and since sympathetically restored. The Swabian castle contains an art museum. You can then rest in the landscaped gardens of **Villa Bellini**.

Town of tyrants

From the wide plain of Catania head for **Syracuse ❺** (Siracusa) through landscapes of classical beauty, counterpointed by archaeological remains. Built in 734 BC by a group of Corinthian farmers who settled on the small isle of **Ortigia**, Syracuse developed so rapidly that in a short time it was establishing new colonies along the Sicilian coast. In 485 BC, when it had developed into a prosperous town, it was conquered by the tyrant Gelon. Syracuse then enjoyed its greatest political, economic and artistic magnificence, becoming one of the most important centres of the Mediterranean. It defeated the Carthaginians, Etruscans and even Athenians and eventually it ruled over almost the whole of Sicily. After a short dalliance with democracy, Syracuse flourished under despotism. Dionysius, the city's most enlightened tyrant, presided over Syracuse's golden age.

Great monuments and public works testify to the epoch's glory and wealth. After many years of decay, Syracuse is benefiting from restoration work – much-needed work, which has brought a new confidence to the city. In the ancient but still lively heart of town, you can admire the monumental and grandiose **Tempio di Atena** (5th century BC), which later became the **Duomo**.

Leave Ortigia across the **Ponte Nuovo** and head north to **Neapolis** (daily 9am to two hours before sunset; entrance fee), the sprawling archaeological park with the **Teatro Greco**, one of the greatest theatres in the Greek world (spanning 138 metres/ 452 ft in diameter and with a capacity of 15,000 seats). Here, in summer, a series of high-quality classical performances are held; if you buy a ticket, you may end up in the very spot where Plato or Archimedes sat for their night on the town. Call the tourist office for details (tel: 0931-464255).

Nearby lie the **Latomie**, which are ancient honeycombed quarries. Later, these were used as prisons for Athenians sentenced to hard labour. In the **Latomia del Paradiso** there is a man-made cave known as Dionysius' Ear, which has an amazing echo. A whisper is amplified by the walls, a phenomenon that permitted the tyrant Dionysius to eavesdrop on prisoners. If you relish ancient legends, stop at the lively bars by the **Arethusa Fountain** back in Ortigia. According to local lore, the beautiful nymph jumped into the sea in order to escape from the river god Alfeus and was transformed into this spring.

An interesting destination close to Syracuse is the small town of **Noto ⑥**. It stands on a ridge of the **Iblei Mountains**, furrowed by a long and straight road which widens out into wonderful inclined squares. Here Spanish baroque architecture triumphs in churches, palaces, monasteries and squares, all in a golden-coloured stone. Noto's most interesting vantage point is Piazza Municipio, a baroque square that encompasses a riot of pilasters, adorned windows, loggias, terraces and bell towers. Another highlight is **Palazzo Villa-Dorata**: a façade incorporating Ionic columns and baroque balconies awash with lions, cherubs, gorgons and monsters.

Map on page 346

The original town of Noto was destroyed by an earthquake in 1693. A Spanish-Sicilian noble, Giuseppe Lanza, was put in charge of the rebuilding, and he decided to start the town afresh, 16 km (10 miles) further south.

BELOW: mosaics from the Villa Romana del Casale in Piazza Armerina.

At the cloisters in Monreale, 109 groups of capitals were ornately decorated by 12th-century craftsmen.

Sicily's harsh and imposing heart

From the coast, an excursion leads through the bare interior, with its reddish sulphur mines, vivid vegetation and little villages clustered on hills. One hilltop town is **Piazza Armerina** ❼, famous for the **Villa Romana del Casale** (daily 8.30am–6pm; entrance fee), an imperial mansion or grand hunting lodge outside the town. This is a complex construction, built between the 3rd and 4th centuries when the great noble families of the Roman Empire relaxed in the countryside. Designated a Unesco World Heritage Site, the villa possesses a series of extraordinary mosaics, the work of African and Sicilian artists, representing hunting scenes, imaginary creatures and natural landscapes; an entire ancient world comes to life before your eyes. This is Sicily's greatest Roman wonder.

Also of interest is the baroque **Duomo**, crowning a terraced hill back in the heart of the town. Theatrical staircases also accentuate the spacious belvedere and the Duomo's baroque façade. A Catalan-Gothic campanile with arcading remains from the original church sets the tone for the lavish interior.

Land of the gods

The neglected landscapes of the mining area lead to the solar beauty of **Agrigento** ❽, described by the Greek poet Pindar as "the most beautiful city of mortals". The symbol of the city is a group of magnificent temples occupying a valley. The origins of Agrigento (Akragas to the Greeks) date from 581 BC. The 5th century marked the apogee of the town, and it was then that the main temples were erected. The town was later conquered by the Carthaginians and the Romans. Its importance diminished under the successive Byzantine and Arab dominations, but grew again with the arrival of the Normans. The classical city, **Valle dei Templi** (Valley of the Temples; main zone daily 8.30am–7pm; entrance fee) comprises magnificent temples and tombs. The finest are: Tempio di Giove (Olympian Zeus), the largest Doric temple ever known; Tempio di Giunone (Juno/Hera), which commands a view of the valley; and Tempio della Concordia, one of the best-preserved temples in the world, despite the present need for some scaffolding. Opposite the Temple of Olympian Zeus is the Kolymbetra Mediterranean garden.

The splendid temples of **Selinunte** ❾ (daily 9am–7pm, until 4pm in winter; entrance fee) can be seen from afar, on a promontory between a river and a plain in the middle of a gulf with no name. Selinunte looks like a puzzle made of stone pieces: divided columns, chipped capitals, and white and grey cubes are all heaped together, as if a giant hand had mixed the pieces to make the reassembling of the original image more difficult. However, the stones speak volumes, revealing libraries, warehouses, courthouses, temples – all testifying to a prosperous ancient town in the middle of fertile lands. Amid the stones grows *selinon*, the wild parsley which gave its name to the powerful Greek colony.

Selinunte was destroyed in its attempt to expand at the expense of Segesta: in 409 BC, 16,000 citizens of Selinunte were slain by their Carthaginian rivals. To

BELOW: the Tempio della Concordia at Agrigento.

complete the plunge into the past, go to the rival **Segesta** ⑩ (daily 9am–7pm in summer, until 4pm in winter; entrance fee). In spite of the frequent devastations of wars between the Greeks and the Carthaginians, an imposing Doric **temple** has survived. It stands on the side of an arid, wind-beaten hill, and is propped up by 36 columns. Further up is the **Theatre** (Teatro), constructed in the 3rd century AD over the top of Mount Barbaro and from which stretches a splendid view over the **Gulf of Castellammare**; during July and August there are open-air performances.

The Conca d'Oro

Enclosed by a chain of mountains, the Conca d'Oro, an evergreen valley that widens as it approaches the sea, is still irrigated and cultivated according to old custom. The valley is dominated by **Monreale** ⑪, which was founded in the 11th century around the famous Benedictine abbey bearing the same name.

Next to the monastery is the **cathedral** (daily 8am–6pm, chapel and terraces closed noon–3.30pm), a masterpiece of 12th-century Norman architecture. The

Maps:
Area 346
City 351

Fortified Marsala wine was first created by an English trader, John Woodhouse, in 1773. You can still buy Marsala created by his company, sold under the name Florio.

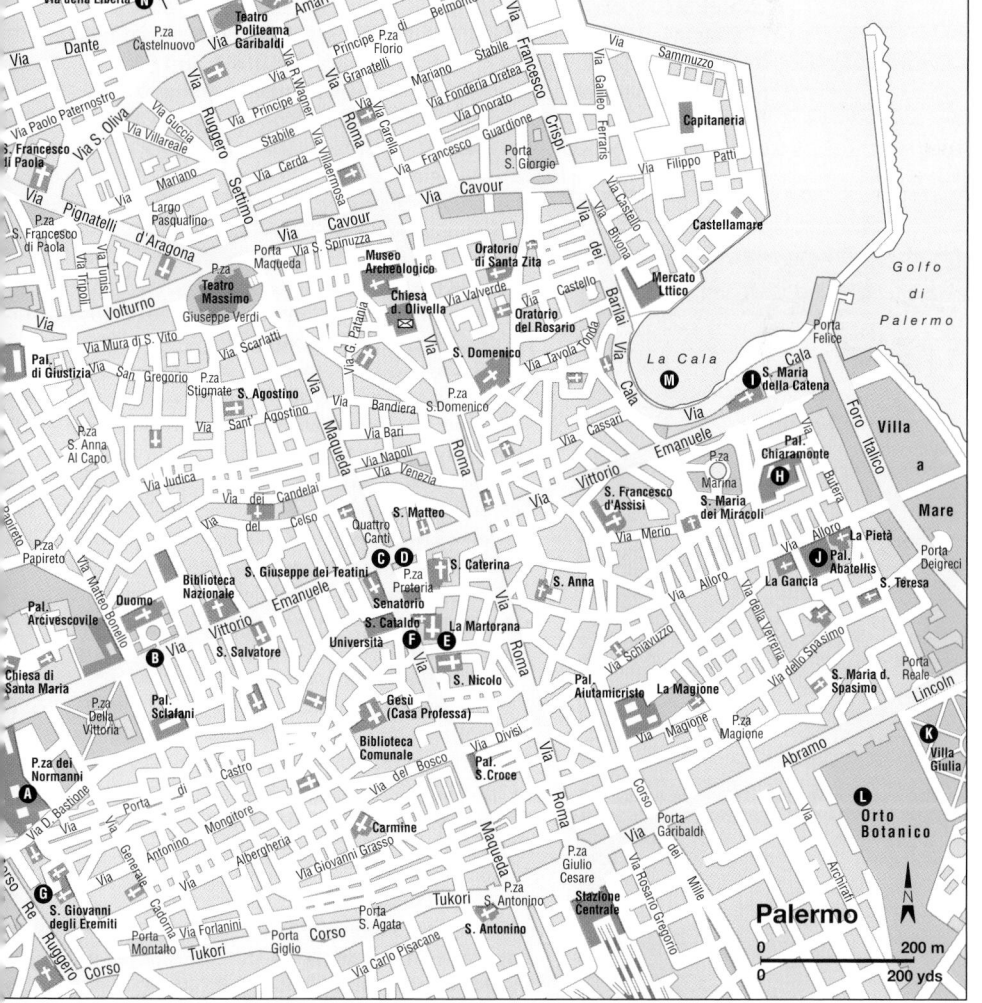

Palermo

The puppet theatre in Sicily goes back centuries, retelling the story of the battles between Charlemagne's knights (the Paladins) and the Saracen invaders.

BELOW: in the gardens of Villa Giulia.

church owes its fame to the mosaics, made by Byzantine and Venetian artists and craftsmen. The mosaics illustrate biblical scenes, from the Creation to the Apostles, in a golden splendour which fades away into grey, giving a tone of "sad brightness" summed up by the gesture and glance of the huge Pantocrator (Almighty). To pass from the cathedral to the cloister is to move from the East to the West. Here, the beauty lies in the 109 groups of capitals whose sculptures show an unusual freedom in execution, typical of the Romanesque style.

After admiring the view of the Conca d'Oro from the church's terraces (180 steps), proceed to **Palermo ⑫**, chief town and port of Sicily, at the bottom of a wide bay enclosed to the south by Capo Zafferano and to the north by Mount Pellegrino, which Goethe described as "the most beautiful promontory in the world".

Discovering Palermo

The best place to start an itinerary is from the **Palazzo dei Normanni Ⓐ**, the splendid Norman palace and seat of the Sicilian parliament (also known as the Palazzo Reale). Inside are the **Cappella Palatina** (Mon–Sat 9–noon and 2–5pm, Sun 8.30am–2pm; entrance fee) and the **Sala di Re Ruggero** (guided tours available; enquire at Cappella Palatina), featuring glittering chambers enlivened with mosaics of Eastern influence. From there, follow the city's oldest thoroughfare, the **Via Vittorio Emanuele Ⓑ**. This street leads down to the **Quattro Canti Ⓒ**, a busy crossroads in the centre of the old town, cut by **Via Maqueda**, the other axis of Palermo. Here the baroque dominates in four monuments decorated with fountains and statues. Another beautiful 16th-century fountain stands in nearby **Piazza Pretoria Ⓓ**. Once nicknamed the Piazza Vergogna (Square of Shame), due to its saucy nudes cavorting in its fountain, the Piazza Pretoria celebrated the 500th anniversary of

this sculptural masterpiece by unveiling the restored fountain in 2004. In Piazza Magione, the Cistercian church, **La Magione**, has been restored. Near to the Vucciria market is the **Oratorio di Santa Zita** and the nearby **Oratorio del Rosario di San Domenico**.

A few more steps lead to the Norman Age, when Palermo was defined by the geographer Idrisi as the "town which turns the head of those who look at it". Here are two churches: the **Martorana Ⓔ**, decorated with Byzantine mosaics, and **San Cataldo Ⓕ**, which preserves three red Moorish domes. The nuns of the church of Martorana are famous for inventing *pasta reale,* the popular marzipan fruit-shaped sweets.

Between Via Maqueda and the Palazzo dei Normanni extends the **Albergheria Quarter**. In spite of the desolation, it is still possible to discover old Palermo near the lively **Ballarò market** in the quarter's centre. Isolated by an oasis of green is the small church of **San Giovanni degli Eremiti Ⓖ** (Mon–Sat 9am–7pm, Sun 9am–1.30pm), a masterpiece of medieval architecture. Its five Moorish domes recall the 500 mosques that once dotted the town, as described by the traveller Ibn Hawqal in the 10th century. The dilapidated southeastern quarter of the old town, called the **Kalsa**, is at the heart of an urban regeneration programme. A witness to its turbulent history is the splendid 14th-century **Palazzo Chiaramonte Ⓗ** (not open to the public), a Catalan-Gothic fortress which became the headquarters of the Inquisition in the 17th century. Nearby in the ancient harbour, the church of **Santa Maria della Catena** ❶ is a synthesis of Gothic and Renaissance art. Via Alloro, the hub of the quarter, contains Sicily's most important art gallery in the imposing **Palazzo Abatellis** ❿. The **Galleria Regionale della Sicilia** (Mon and Fri–Sun 9am–1pm, Tues–Thurs 9am–1.30pm and 2.30–7.30pm; entrance fee) has a collection of medieval paintings.

Stroll in the park of **Villa Giulia** ⓚ, a typical Italian garden, planted in 1777 with rigorous symmetry. Close by is the **Orto Botanico** ⓛ (Mon–Fri 9am–6pm, Sat–Sun 8.30am–1.30pm; entrance fee), among whose exotic plants and rare trees Goethe loved to rest. You can then continue along the **Foro Italico**, an esplanade leading to the **Cala** ⓜ, the old port. Although it no longer functions as a port, the Cala remains a picturesque shelter for gaily coloured fishing boats. Today's city centre is in **Via Ruggero Settimo** and the first part of the bland **Viale della Libertà** ⓝ. Here are the most elegant shops, several bookstores and cinemas. Palermo's picturesque side is still visible in the food market of the **Vucciria** and in the **Castello di Zisa** in the suburbs (Mon–Sat 9am–6.30pm, Sun 9am–1pm; entrance fee), built in 1160 by William I, which recalls the time when Palermo was virtually the centre of the known world.

Along the Tyrrhenian Coast

Along the intense blue Tyrrhenian Sea the road is bordered by flowers and luxuriant citrus and olive groves. The winding road offers glimpses of **Cefalù** ⓭. A panoramic view of the town, possible only from the sea, is extraordinary: a little town clinging to a promontory at the foot of an enormous rock and, to the west, a beautiful sandy beach crowded with bathers and flanked by hotels. Cefalù's fame lies in its medieval charm and great Norman cathedral.

Aeolian Islands (Isole Eolie)

The Sicilian experience should end with a taste of adventure. The best place for this is an archipelago of seven little isles emerging in the **Golfo di Patti** off the north coast of Sicily: the **Aeolian Islands**, a name alluding to Aeolus who, in Greek mythology, is the god of the winds. **Vulcano** ⓮, the first stop for the ferry, offers yellow sulphurous baths and volcanic craters. **Lípari** ⓯, the largest and most populated island, is the most complex geologically and the richest historically. Its pumice beach has the only white sand in the whole archipelago. **Salina** ⓰, the highest and the greenest, is topped by two symmetrical volcanos.

The smallest and most exclusive island is **Panarea** ⓱. With its little white houses framed by luxuriant vegetation, it is a refuge for rich tourists and luxury yachts. **Stromboli** ⓲, the "black giant", has just two villages, separated by burning lava flows. Like Etna, it is constantly active, and rumblings can be heard at between 5- and 25-minute intervals.

The visitor to **Filicudi** ⓳ and **Alicudi** ⓴ has to forget modern comforts, for there is no running water on these islands. Despite such inconvenience, they are a paradise not only for divers and marine-life enthusiasts but also for people who love peace and solitude. ❏

Maps:
Area 346
City 351

Palermo's superb archaeological musum has a large collection of classical finds. In the inner courtyard amidst lush vegetation, you can see fine examples of Egyptian and Greek statuary .

BELOW: a freshly caught swordfish in Lípari.

THE LIVING EARTH: ITALY'S VOLCANOES

Bubbling, seething and angry, or silent, solemn and threatening, Italy's volcanoes dictate the way of life of those in their shadow

The area from the island of Sicily north to Campania on the Italian mainland is notoriously unstable geologically. Here, the earth's crust continues to suffer earthquakes, changes in land levels and volcanic activity. From Vesuvius brooding over the Bay of Naples to imperious, seething Etna on Sicily, Italian volcanoes have shaped the way of life of local people for centuries. The destruction and devastation that has followed major eruptions has on the one hand caused trepidation and exodus but, on the other, has offered long-term compensation in the legacy of fertile soil enriched with volcanic extract.

SPREADING THE WORD

The fame of Italy's volcanoes owes much to its classical writers. Virgil and Pliny the Younger both described the might of volcanic activity in the region. Pliny, in particular, left us a detailed account of the eruption of Vesuvius in AD 79 which saw the death of his uncle, Pliny the Elder, and destroyed the towns of Herculaneum and Pompeii. In turn, Vesuvian mud and ash has preserved for us a unique picture of life in Roman times *(see page 316)*.

▽ VOLCANIC ISLES

Stromboli, one of the volcanic Aeolian Islands northeast of Sicily, was believed by the ancient Greeks to be the home of Aeolus, the god of the winds. The waters around these islands are enriched with minerals and are known for their curative properties, making them popular with bathers.

△ THE TOURIST TRAIL

Volcano tourism really began in the 19th century when Vesuvius, then Etna *(above)* became part of the traveller's itinerary. Sedan chairs or donkey power was used to convey lazy visitors to the top, and wily, business-minded local guides led the way.

▷ FIRE PREVENTION

Vesuvius, although officially "active", has not shown any major activity since 1944. Etna, however, remains a constant threat. In 2001 lava flows reached the nearby town of Nicolosi and in 2002 the volcano was awakened again by earthquakes.

▷ MUD, GLORIOUS MUD

The seas around the Aeolian Islands can be radioactive and in places are warmed by underwater jets of steam. Sulphurous mud pools are sought out for the treatment of rheumatism. The island of Lípari also has the notable hot springs of San Calogero, where the water temperature rises to over 60°C (140°F).

THE MIGHT AND POWER OF GODS

The power of Italy's active volcanoes is a phenomenon which defied explanation in ancient times. The Romans attributed the fiery convulsions to Vulcan, the god of fire and metal-working, whom they believed lived deep beneath the Aeolian island of Vulcano. In addition, the poet Virgil told of the giant Enceladus who, he declared, was interred below Mount Etna, his groanings and rumblings accounting for the earth-shaking, violent eruptions.

Early Christians, too, saw divine activity in volcanic outbursts. In the year 253, the mere production of the veil covering the tomb of the recently martyred St Agatha was said to have staunched the lava flow from Etna that threatened to envelop Catania and its people. Even in relatively modern times, the citizens of Naples have been quick to turn to their patron saint, Januarius, for help whenever Vesuvius has begun to belch smoke.

However, some observers over the centuries have been more pragmatic about the causes of volcanic activity. One anonymous Roman poet suggested that the phenomenon was wind-induced: "It is the winds which arouse all these forces of havoc: the rocks which they have massed thickly together they whirl in eddying storm…"

◁ **KEEP YOUR DISTANCE**
Etna is Europe's largest active volcano and Italy's highest mountain outside the Alps. Though it is prone to eruption, and the area around the main crater is now out of bounds, it is possible to climb – providing common sense and local advice are heeded. Wear warm clothing and strong shoes.

△ **ROCKY RAVINE**
Etna's Valle del Bovo (Valley of the Ox) is a bleak, rocky chasm, 5 km (3 miles) wide, on the mountain's eastern face. It was created by a volcanic explosion and pot holes still puff out plumes of smoke. Geologists marvel at the clear stratification of rock forms in the valley walls.

▷ **RIVERS OF FIRE**
Awesome rivers of fire like this lava flow on Etna reveal the raw power of volcanoes and the wonder they have induced over the centuries. In Le Speronare, Alexandre Dumas described Etna's immense crater, roaring, full of flames and smoke; Heaven above one's head, Hell beneath one's feet."

Map on page 358

SARDINIA

Seven thousand prehistoric stone towers, countless beaches and more sheep than people make Sardinia the perfect place to get away from it all

S ardinia has little in common with the rest of Italy. The Mediterranean's second-largest island offers a restricted diet of art and architecture; rather, its appeal lies in its beaches and rugged landscape. Much of its 1,600-km (1,000-mile) coastline is given over to duney sands and romantic coves nestling in pine and juniper woods. Much of its interior, where sheep outnumber humans, is wild and mountainous, and covered in a knotty carpet of herby, shrubby *macchia*. Even the island's cuisine is different from the mainland's. Here, robust, country fare comes in the form of pecorino cheese made from ewe's milk, roast lamb and suckling pig, *seadas* or cheese pastries served with honey, and *carta da musica* – crisp, wafer-thin bread said to resemble sheets of music.

Most holidaymakers come for stay-put beach holidays. Many base themselves in the purpose-built, ritzy resorts that have put the island on the tourist map, but there are more down-to-earth alternatives. The large distances involved and the paucity of sights make Sardinia less than ideal for a touring holiday. There are, however, some unique attractions, notably the intriguing remnants of the prehistoric nuraghic civilisation: an astonishing 7,000 stone towers, or *nuraghi*, which from a distance look like giant dung heaps, litter the countryside.

BELOW: Capriccioli beach, Costa Smeralda.

Lying within Gallura, the sparsely inhabited northeastern region of Sardinia where pinky, granite rocks tower like castles over swathes of *macchia* and juniper, cork and oak woods, is the **Costa Smeralda** ❶, or Emerald Coast. In the early 1960s, the Aga Khan and associates bought up this impossibly picturesque little piece of coastline – a mere 10 km (6 miles) end to end by road – and turned it into a hedonistic bolt-hole, now the flagship of the island's tourism. Development is rigorously controlled. Virtually every hotel and apartment complex comes in regulation "Mediterranean" style, with pantiled roofs, and pink-and-russet walls, distressed to give the appearance of age.

Even if you can't afford to partake in the jet-set lifestyle, it makes a great spectator sport. Head for **Porto Cervo**, the only resort where Armani and Versace boutiques compete for attention with extravagant yachts, and **Cala di Volpe**, half Moorish castle, half rustic homestead and the most stylish of the hotels. Many of the gorgeous coves are inaccessible, but you can wander through groves to those on the Cappriccioli peninsula. Impressive **Cala Liscia Ruja**, just south, is the area's biggest beach. The resort of **Baia Sardinia**, just north of the Costa Smeralda proper, is equally contrived, but far less pretentious and more affordable.

Much of the rest of the Galluran coastline is being spoilt by the onset of ranks of apartments and self-catering villages. This is true of scruffy **Palau**, the departure point for ferries to **La Maddalena** ❷, part of the Maddalena archipelago. The island is a NATO military zone, but there is public access to good beaches, and it is connected to **Caprera** ❸, where you can visit the house in which Garibaldi spent his last years. Back on the mainland, **Santa Teresa di Gallura** ❹ is a study in pink, and there are a couple of great sandy beaches at nearby **Capo Testa**, fringed by bizarre rocks the size of houses.

Alghero

Northwestern Sardinia is a more benign, softer region than the northeast, with sandy strands cupped in pine woods. But its big draw is **Alghero** ❺, the only resort on the island which has genuine character and history: in the 14th century, the port was occupied by Catalans, and street names are still written in that language.

Its old centre, half surrounded by medieval walls, could hardly be more entrancing: cobbled lanes are lined with high-sided, shuttered buildings dripping in peeling stucco and washing. The best beach in the vicinity is **Spiaggia di Maria Pia**, and there is a popular boat trip across the bay to the **Grotta di Nettuno** ❻, a cave system at the foot of a towering, tilted cliff with memorable rock formations. Untouristy **Sassari** ❼, a 45-minute drive inland, is Sardinia's second city, and has enjoyably earthy backstreets between the overblown, neo-Gothic **Piazza d'Italia** and the baroque-fronted cathedral, and a large **archaeology museum** (Tues–Sun 9am–7.30pm; entrance fee), which, after Cagliari's, is the best place to immerse yourself in the nuraghic culture.

Sardinia's dramatic interior – with imposing tablelands, pine woods, massive walls and granite amphitheatres – is the historic, cultural and geographic heart of the island. Here, safely sheltered from foreign invaders, a population of shepherds developed a fierce and isolated society.

There are no urban centres of interest – **Nuoro** ❽, the

TIP

Alghero is arguably the best place on the island for fresh seafood. Stop at the market in Via Sassari for lobster, sea urchins and squid, or try the local restaurants.

BELOW: Capo Testa, the promontory of huge granite boulders.

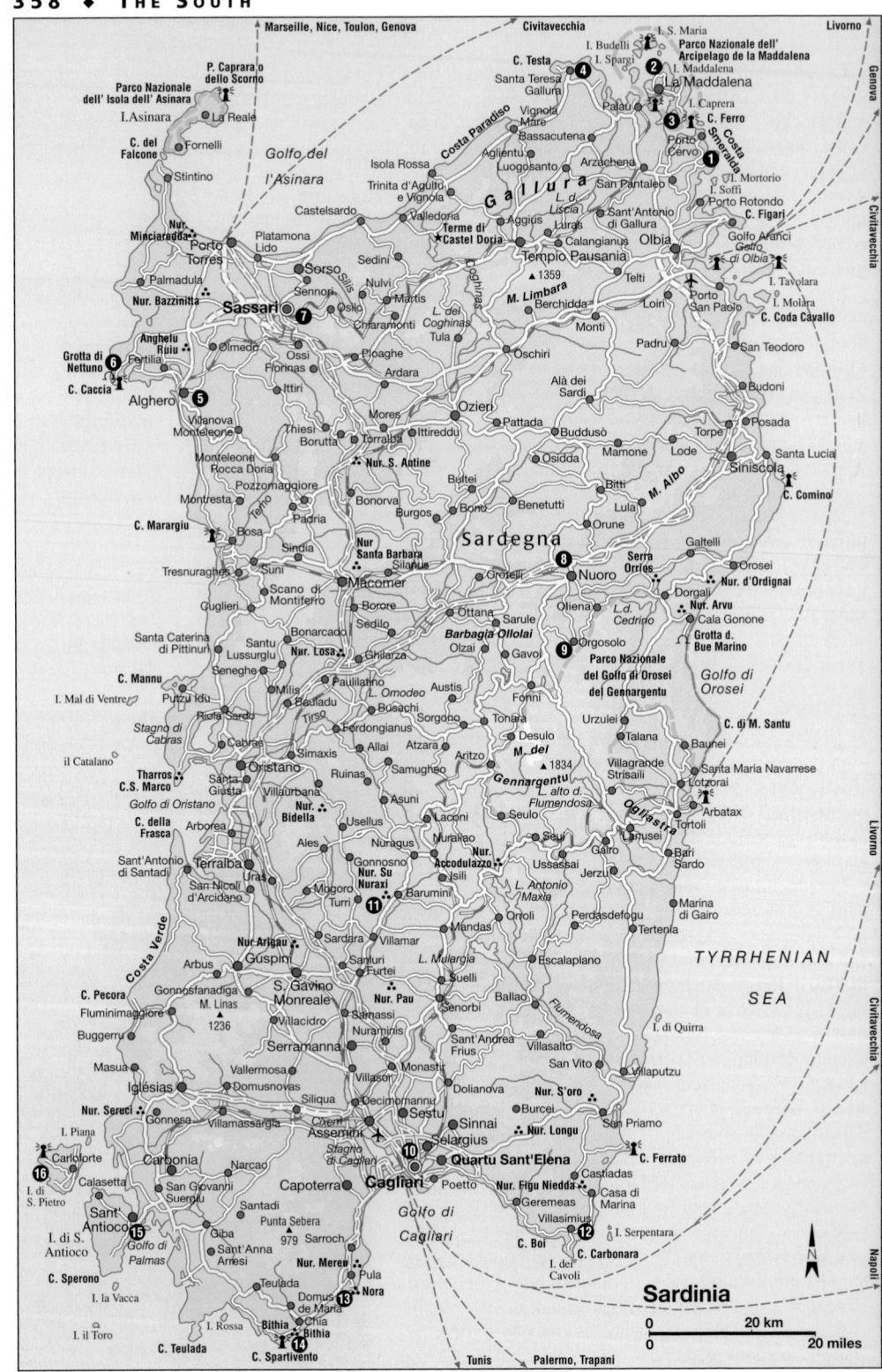

Sardinia

Marseille, Nice, Toulon, Genova
Civitavecchia
Livorno
Genova
Civitavecchia
Livorno
Napoli
Tunis
Palermo, Trapani

TYRRHENIAN SEA

Golfo di Cagliari

Sardegna

0   20 km
0   20 miles

N

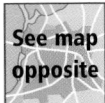

See map opposite

area's capital, is only worth visiting for its folk museum, the **Museo della Vita e delle Tradizioni Sarde** (mid-June–Sept daily 9am–8pm, Oct–mid-June 9am–1pm and 3–7pm; entrance fee). Immediately south is the most accessible part of the region, where vineyards and olive groves are intensively cultivated on the hillsides. Many visitors end up at the **Hotel Su Gologone** near Oliena, which lays on superb Sardinian cooking and guided expeditions into the mountains. Just down the road lies unwelcoming but fascinating **Orgosolo ⑨**, once the Barbagia's "bandit capital", where anti-capitalist murals cover much of the wall space along its high street. The long, lonely drive south on the SS125, which clings unnervingly to mountainsides from Dorgali to Arbatax and beyond, is the island's most exhilarating.

The south

Cagliari ⑩, the island's hectic capital, is rewarding if you ignore the traffic-ridden port and climb up into **Castello**, the medieval centre where steep, gloomily atmospheric streets lie within 13th-century walls and towers. The cathedral, a hotchpotch of styles, and a Roman amphitheatre are outshone by the **Museo Archeologico Nazionale** (Tues–Sun 9am–8pm; entrance fee), famous for exquisite bronze statuettes and votive boats from the nuraghic culture.

An hour's drive north, skirting the fertile **Campidano** plain, brings you to the island's most impressive *nuraghe*, **Su Nuraxi ⑪** (open daily May–Sept 9am–7pm, winter closes between 4 and 6pm; entrance fee) at Barumini. Dating from the 13th–16th century BC, the colossal fortification is made up of beautifully formed, beehive-shaped rooms; the maze of low stone walls at its base was once a dependent village.

The coastal road east from Cagliari leads to enormous tranches of the finest sand in the island's isolated southeastern corner. However, **Villasimius ⑫** and the **Costa Rei**, the unfancy resorts that have grown up around them, are rather characterless, comprising mainly campsites and self-catering complexes.

The gentle, pine-clad coastline southwest from Cagliari, scattered with holiday homes and a few smart hotels, is more interesting. Punic and Roman **Nora ⑬** (open daily 9am–8pm, winter 5.30pm; entrance fee) is Sardinia's most extensive classical site, with clearly defined houses and mosaics and a temple and small theatre. Equally rewarding is the waterside location, on a little peninsula next to a long curve of sand. Many of the finds from Nora are housed in the **Museo Archeologico** (Tues–Sun 9am–8pm, winter 5.30pm; entrance fee) in nearby **Pula**. A few miles south lies the **Forte Village**, a luxurious, beautifully landscaped and family-orientated complex where the service runs to flower petals being placed in bedroom lavatory bowls. It sits next to a good beach, but the area's best is at **Chia ⑭**, backed by hillock-high dunes. The drive beyond along the **Costa del Sud** passes craggy headlands and azure waters in deep inlets on its way to **Sant'Antíoco ⑮**. Linked to the mainland by an ancient causeway, the island's eponymous town has Christian catacombs under its main church.

Ferries run to **San Pietro ⑯**, known for the bloody *mattanza* in early summer, when schools of tuna are slaughtered en masse. ❑

Traditional folk costume.

BELOW: Cattedrale di Santa Maria, Cagliari.
OVERLEAF: door of San Zeno, Verona.

INSIGHT GUIDES

TRAVEL TIPS

ITALY

TRAVEL TIPS

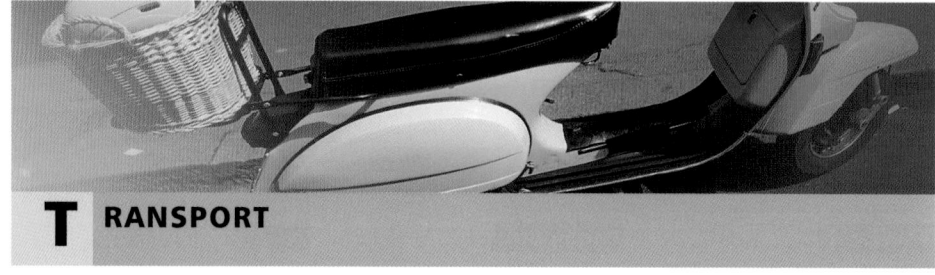

T RANSPORT

GETTING THERE
AND GETTING AROUND

GETTING THERE

By Air

Low-cost airlines now operate from many of Italy's smaller provincial airports, thus opening up Italian routes to greater competition. In addition to the national airline, Alitalia, many major scheduled airlines fly direct to Italy, as well as charter flights, which tend to offer lower fares, and often fly to more convenient provincial airports. (Alitalia, for instance, only flies directly to Rome or Milan; to reach other Italian destinations, you have to catch a connecting flight.) However, transfers into the nearest town may be less easily available than at the smaller airports, so it might be worth considering hiring a car, especially if arriving late in the evening.

The country has two airports designed for intercontinental flights: Roma Leonardo da Vinci (Fiumicino) and Milano Malpensa 2000.

Rome
Leonardo da Vinci/Fiumicino
Rome's main airport is 35.5 km (22½ miles) southwest of central Rome, and is Europe's fourth-busiest airport. Rome is a good gateway to other destinations, including Naples, the south and even parts of Tuscany. (Fast, reliable trains connect the city with Chiusi-Chianciano, for instance.) The airport is served by most major carriers, from Alitalia to British Airways and British Midland.

There is a direct **train service** that runs every 30 minutes (daily 6am–11.30pm) between Fiumicino airport and Termini station. Tickets (around €11) are sold at the airport and all

counters at the station, as well as from vending machines, and many newsagents. The train journey takes 35 minutes. Another slower local train (around €5) runs roughly every 15 minutes to the stations of Trastevere, Tiburtina and Ostiense, from which taxis, metro and bus services are available; the journey to Trastevere takes about 40 minutes.

Catching a white **taxi** with a meter (unofficial taxis can charge extortionate fares and may even be dangerous) from the airport can be a good alternative to public transport, but do negotiate a fare beforehand. Surcharges are made for luggage and for travel at night and on Sunday, and there is also a special airport supplement. Typical fares are in the region of €45, even more at night.

Roma Ciampino
The low-cost airlines EasyJet and Ryanair are just two of many carriers which fly to Ciampino. At the arrivals hall you can buy a one-way or return ticket for an efficient and private **bus shuttle service** to Via Marsala, near Termini station (for more information see www.terravision.it; tickets can also be bought in advance online). Alternatively, an **airport bus** (COTRAL) goes roughly every 30 minutes from the airport to Anagnina metro station at the end of Linea A. From there, it's 30 minutes to Termini and the centre of town (trains leave every 5 minutes until 9pm, when the metro is replaced by an efficient bus service, see page 367). Bear in mind that airport buses stop running at 11pm, so late arrivals will need a taxi. **Taxis** are far more convenient and typically cost around €36–40. If you're travelling by **car**, take the GRA ring road, coming off at exit 23 for Rome.

Northern Italy
Bergamo
Bergamo airport is small, but convenient for exploring the Lakes, including Lake Iseo and Lake Como, as well as Milan, Mantua and the rest of Lombardy. Among other airlines, Gandals flies here from London City airport.

Brescia
Brescia airport is very convenient for Lake Garda, Lake Iseo, Verona, the Dolomites and Trentino-Alto Adige, and is used by budget airlines such as Ryanair (from London Stansted).

Genoa
Genoa airport (Genova) is convenient for exploring Genoa and the Ligurian Coast. This small airport is served by Ryanair, which runs from London Stansted and by BA from Gatwick.

Milan
Milano Malpensa 2000, Milan's intercontinental airport, is served by major carriers, from Alitalia to Lufthansa, British Airways, British Midland, EasyJet, BMI Baby and Flybe. The airport is 46 km (28½ miles) from the centre of Milan, which is rather inconvenient.

The **Malpensa Express** runs from the airport's Terminal One to the centre of Milan (Cadorna station, which is on the metro; note that this is different from Stazione Centrale, Milan's main railway station). The service takes about 50 minutes and operates from 5.30am to 1.30am.

Alternatively, an **Air Pullman** shuttle bus ferries passengers between the airport and the Air Pullman office outside Stazione Centrale. You can buy a ticket (around €8) up to a few minutes before departure from the Air

Pullman office. The journey takes approximately 50 minutes and shuttles run every 30 minutes.

For **drivers**, a new link road to central Milan is under construction, but in the meantime follow signs to the A8 autostrada (motorway) that runs to Milan. A **taxi** to the centre will take about 45 minutes and cost around €80; it's sensible to try and negotiate a price beforehand.

Milano Linate, Milan's other airport, is around 8 km (5 miles) from the centre. International flights are being phased out from Linate, but some carriers continue to use this airport rather than Malpensa, including EasyJet from the UK. The **ATM bus 73** runs regularly (5.30am–midnight) from in front of the airport (Piazzale del Aeroporto) to its terminus on Piazza San Babila at the corner of Corso Europa. There's also the **STAM shuttle** to Milan's Stazione Centrale, running about every 30 minutes.

Turin
Turin airport is small but very handy for exploring the Piedmontese hinterland and the vineyards of Barolo and Bardolino, as well as the Gran Paradiso National Park and even the Valle d'Aosta. The airport is served by British Airways, Alitalia and Ryanair.

Scheduled Airlines

Aer Lingus: tel: 353-0818-365000; www.aerlingus.com
Air Malta: tel: 0845-607 3710; www.airmalta.com
Alitalia: reservations, tel: 0870-544 8259; 020-8814 7700; www.alitalia.com
American Airlines: tel: 1-800-433-7300; www.aa.com
BMI Baby: tel: 0871-224 0224; www.bmibaby.com
British Airways: tel: 0870-850 9850; www.ba.com
British Midland: reservations, tel: 0870-6070 555; from outside the UK: 44-1332-648181; www.fly-bmi.com
EasyJet: tel: 0871-244 2366; www.easyjet.com
Flybe: tel: 0871-700 0535; www.flybe.com
Meridiana: tel: 0845-3555 588; www.meridiana.it
MyTravel: tel: 0870-241 5333; www.mytravel.com
Ryanair: reservations, tel: 0871-246 0000; www.ryanair.com
Thomsonfly: tel: 0870-190 0737; www.thomsonfly.com
Volareweb: tel: 39-070-460 3397; www.volareweb.com

Venice
Venice's **Marco Polo airport** is at Tessera on the mainland 9 km (5.5 miles) north of Venice. The airport is served by major carriers, from Alitalia to British Airways and EasyJet to Volare and Thomsonfly. To reach Venice there is a **public bus** to Piazzale Roma (30 minutes), a private **land taxi** (20–25 minutes) or the hourly **Alilaguna waterbus**, which crosses the lagoon to Piazza San Marco via the Lido and takes about 75 minutes, depending on your stop. The waterbus *(vaporetto)* is quicker between 11.30am and 3.30pm and it costs €10; for further details, tel: 041-541 6555. The luxury option is to take one of the private **water-taxis**, identifiable by their black-on-yellow numbers; these cost about €85 and carry up to four people with luggage.

Venice/Treviso
Treviso airport is an alternative for travellers to Venice or the Lakes. Charter flights are available from London Stansted, and a reliable coach service runs to Venice. When some low-cost airlines (eg Ryanair) refer to "Venice airport", they actually mean Treviso airport.

Verona
Verona airport is probably the most convenient for the Lakes or the Veneto region. Charter flights arrive from cities including London, Paris and Frankfurt, and British Airways also flies here. Again, there is often confusion about which airport is correct for Verona. Ryanair's "Verona airport" is actually Brescia airport.

Central Italy
Ancona
Ancona airport is small but convenient for exploring the Marche region, as well as parts of Tuscany, Emilia and Umbria. Ryanair flies here from London Stansted.

Bologna
Bologna Marconi airport is handily placed for exploring Emilia Romagna, or even travelling on to Florence and Tuscany. The airport is served by Alitalia and British Airways. A **shuttle bus service** called Aerobus goes to the city centre and takes 20 minutes; a **taxi** takes 15 minutes, but it will cost around three times as much as the bus.

Bologna's second airport at **Forlì**, 60 km (38 miles) south of the city, is served by Ryanair. Forlì is convenient for exploring the southern "Romagna" part of the region and the Adriatic beaches.

Florence
Peretola-Florence is 4 km (2 miles) northwest of the city centre. Some international flights land here, but these tend to be more expensive than flights to Pisa *(see below)*. From the UK, Meridiana flies regularly to Florence.

Parma
Parma airport is small but a handy alternative to Bologna for exploring Emilia Romagna. Ryanair has introduced a new service.

Pescara
Pescara airport is served by Ryanair and is a good option for exploring the lesser-known central regions of Abruzzo and Molise.

Pisa
Galileo Galilei airport is the more usual airport for international visitors to Florence, although Bologna provides an acceptable alternative *(see above)*. Pisa airport is served by charter and scheduled airlines, including Ryanair, Mytravelite, BMI Baby, British Airways and Thomsonfly. **Trains** to Florence (hourly; journey time about one hour) leave from just outside the airport.

Rimini
Rimini airport is small but handy for exploring the Adriatic Coast and the rest of Emilia Romagna. Mytravelite flies from Birmingham and Volare from Luton.

Southern Italy
Bari and Brindisi
Both city airports are handy for exploring Italy's heel – the regions of Puglia and Basilicata. Alitalia, British Airways and Ryanair all operate services to Bari, and Brindisi is served by Ryanair.

Calabria
Calabria's **Lamezia Airport** may be in the middle of nowhere, but it's convenient for the north coast of Sicily, since you can catch the ferry at the port of Villa San Giovanni (every half-hour until 10pm, then hourly throughout the night) to Messina. Cheap carriers, such as Ryanair, offer incredible savings on standard fares.

Naples
Naples airport is served by major carriers from Alitalia to British Airways and EasyJet. The airport **bus** stops outside the terminal every hour and takes just 20 minutes to reach Piazza Municipio in Naples. A **taxi** takes the same time and costs about €20 –

make sure that the meter has been turned on before the journey begins. For **drivers**, the autostrada A2 exits into the Naples bypass *(tangenziale)*, which is also a toll road.

Sardinia

Cagliari-Elmas is the main airport on Sardinia, but there are also airports at **Olbia** (the airport for the famous Costa Smeralda) and **Alghero**. Ryanair flies to Alghero from London Stansted. Meridiana flies to Sardinia (Olbia) via Florence, while Alitalia also runs regular flights.

Sicily

Palermo's **Punta Raisi airport** is 32 km (20 miles) west of Palermo. The airport is served by major carriers and charters. Scheduled flights involve a change at Milan or Rome, but many charter flights are direct and save time. The airport is small but convenient for Palermo and Sicily's north and west coasts.

Fontanarossa airport, Sicily's other main base, is 7 km (4 miles) southwest of Catania and is served by such carriers as Alitalia, Air Malta and British Airways, as well as a large number of charters. This airport, too, is small, but it's handy for Sicily's east and south coasts, from Taormina to Siracusa.

By Car

When calculating the cost of travelling to Italy by car, allow for the price of motorway tolls as well as accommodation en route and petrol. A number of new motorways have been built in recent years, including one on the north coast of Sicily and others around Milan. The most heavily tolled motorway is the one along the Ligurian Coast.

The usual route from France is via

Car Trains

The following rail services will transport cars to Italy:
• Paris–Milan
• Boulogne–Lille–Milan
• Schaerbeek (Brussels)–Milan
• Hertogenbosch (Holland)– Domodossola–Genoa–Milan
• Hertogenbosch–Chiasso–Milan
• Düsseldorf–Cologne–Milan–Genoa
• Hamburg–Hanover–Verona
• Munich–Rimini
• Düsseldorf–Cologne–Bolzano
• Vienna–Venice
• Boulogne–Bologna
• Boulogne–Rome
• Boulogne–Alessandria
• Boulogne–Livorno

the Mont Blanc Tunnel (between Chamonix and Courmayeur) or from Switzerland through the Gran San Bernardo Tunnel (between Bourg St Pierre and Aosta). Some of the many Alpine passes are seasonal, so it is best to check with the tourist board or a motoring organisation before setting off.

To take your car into Italy, you will need a valid driving licence (with an Italian translation if it's not the standard EU licence), the vehicle registration document (which must be in the driver's name or be supported by the owner's written permission for the driver to use the vehicle) and the insurance documents. You must carry a warning triangle in case of breakdown. Most petrol stations accept credit cards, as do toll booths, but cash is always welcome, especially in the south.

By Coach

The cost of travelling to Italy from the UK by coach is not much cheaper than by air. National Express Eurolines runs coaches from London Victoria, via Paris and Mont Blanc, to Aosta, Turin, Genoa, Milan, Venice, Bologna, Florence and Rome. To book from London, contact: National Express Eurolines, tel: 0870-514 3219; www.eurolines.com.

By Rail

Compared with flying, travelling to Italy by rail is slow (although the service through France is constantly improving) and not particularly cheap (except Inter Rail, which provides a month's unlimited rail travel in Europe for anyone under 26 at a very reasonable price). However, it can be a very attractive way to travel, especially if you are planning to stop off en route. From the UK the usual route when travelling to Rome, for example, is on Eurostar as far as Paris, where you change trains (from Gare du Nord to Gare de Lyon). Arriving in Rome's impressive Termini station is a pleasure, and the station has both left-luggage lockers and a left-luggage office.

ES (Eurostar), IC (Inter City) and EN (Euronight) trains are top-of-the-range trains running between the main Italian and European cities. A special supplement is charged and seat reservation is obligatory.

For train information, call the same number from anywhere in Italy: 89 20 21. The Italian rail system is operated by Trenitalia (www.trenitalia.it).

The Rail Pass, Family Card and Kilometric Card (which allows one or

more people to travel a specified number of kilometres at a special rate) can be purchased at any major train station in Italy. The fastest trains operate on the networks between the major cities, while the regional trains are fairly slow.

Be aware that with paper tickets, you must stamp your ticket in the yellow machines found at the head of the platform before boarding. Failure to do so will result in a fine.

Ticketless, a new venture by Trenitalia, allows you to book tickets online or by phone up to 10 minutes before the train's departure time. You will then be given a booking code, which will be checked by the ticket inspectors on board. The service is available on all Eurostar trains and on most Inter City trains. Book through www.trenitalia.it.

GETTING AROUND

Travelling within Italy

Local newspapers offer reasonably trustworthy information on bus, train and ferry timetables, including up-to-date telephone numbers of bus and ferry companies. If you are planning to travel much by train, it's worth buying an *Orario Generale* (General Timetable), an infallible yet inexpensive source of information. Booking (including train tickets) through a travel agency often proves easier than doing it yourself.

The latest transport novelty in a few Italian city centres is the "Motobeep", an egg-shaped capsule on wheels that is a cross between a covered scooter and a tiny car. (The passenger sits in an covered seat behind the driver, who acts like a tour guide.) Motobeeps are proving popular in Palermo and Rome, and are due to be introduced in Naples.

By Air

The major cities – Rome, Milan, Florence, Venice, Naples – and other tourist centres are connected by flights, most provided by Alitalia. Smaller Italian airlines include AirOne (www.flyairone.it), Alisarda (www.alisarde.it) for Sardinia, and the budget airline blu-express (www.blu-express.com), which flies from Rome to Milan and Bari. Flying in Italy is expensive compared to the train, but it can be useful for long distances. Discounts are often available if you are prepared to travel on certain days, but these must be booked in Italy. For information, contact your nearest

Train Information

Train information is available from staff at *Uffici Informazioni* at most major stations.

For train information anywhere in Italy, tel: **892 021** or **199 166 177** (in Italian). From the UK call Rail Europe on **08708-371 371**; **www.raileurope.co.uk**

You can also check routes on the official railway website: **www.trenitalia.it**

travel agent or Alitalia office. Children under two (accompanied by an adult) get a 90 percent discount, and those between two and 12 get a third off.

By Rail

In general, the cheapest, fastest and most convenient way to travel in Italy is by train. For long distances or major lines, the fast Inter City (IC), Euro City (EC) and Eurostar (ES) services (reservations obligatory) are well worth the extra cost for comfort and time. The Pendolino is the fastest and most comfortable train, and requires a "supplement" *(supplemento)* and a reservation. It is also worth reserving a seat for long journeys as trains tend to be crowded, especially in peak season. You can book at most travel agencies and at train stations.

Local trains are called Regionale, Diretto, Interregionale and, rather inappropriately, Espresso – much slower than you might expect.

In the south, especially in Sicily, buses are the better option because many southern train services are poorly maintained. Exceptions to this rule are the fascinating Circumetnea service around Etna and the Naples Circumvesuvio, which is the best way of seeing Pompeii, Herculaneum and other classical sites.

Significant reductions and special offers are available for groups and young travellers; make enquiries on arrival in Italy.

Train Tickets

Tickets are valid for two months. You must stamp tickets in the station before boarding and if for any reason that is not possible, you must find the conductor before he finds you.

By Bus

Each province in Italy has its own inter-city bus company and each company has its own lines. This can lead to some confusion since, particularly in Sicily, the rival firms do

not provide information about one another and connections are not always co-ordinated. However, in some areas, such as the south, and if you are going into the mountains, buses are the best method of travel. The journey from Siena to Florence is also faster by bus than by train. Some of the main bus companies operating long-distance travel from the principal cities are listed below.

Rome

COTRAL (www.cotralspa.it) covers the region of Lazio efficiently. Buses leave from different metro stations around town.

Milan

Autostradale, Piazzale Castello 1, tel: 02-801161. Services across Lombardy and the Lakes, and to Venice and Turin. The firm uses the fastest motorway routes and also organises guided tours, which can be booked through tourist offices.

Trentino

Atesina, tel: 0461-821000, is a bus company based in Trento; it runs services throughout Trentino and further afield, including abroad.

Alto Adige

SAD, Via Conciapelli 60, Bolzano, tel: 0471-450111, www.sad.it. This company operates services in the province of Bolzano and further afield, including the entire Alto Adige (South Tyrol) Dolomites area.

Florence

Lazzi, Via Mercadante 2, tel: 055-215154, www.lazzi.it. This firm runs services to Tuscany and all over Italy. **Sita**, Viale dei Cadorna 105, tel: 055-278611. Sita operates services to most of Italy.

Ferries and Hydrofoils

There are daily car-ferry connections between Reggio di Calabria and Sicily, Villa San Giovanni and Sicily, Naples and Sicily; between Civitavecchia and Sardinia, Livorno and Sardinia; and between Naples and the islands of Capri and Ischia. Regular boat services link Genoa, Sardinia, Naples and Sicily and connect the mainland with Italy's many smaller islands. Ferries and hydrofoils also operate between towns and sites on the northern lakes of Como, Garda and Maggiore. A number of towns on the lakes are also linked by car ferry: Lake Maggiore–Verbania-Laveno; Lake Como–Menaggio-Bellagio-Varenna; Lake Garda–Maderno-Torri del

Benaco. Timetables tend to change at least twice a year, but the routes remain quite constant. For information and timetables, contact the local tourist office or ask at the ticket offices on the jetties *(imbarcaderi)*. The following websites have useful information on the lakes:
www.navigazionelaghi.it
www.distrettolaghi.it
www.lagodigarda.it
www.maggiore.ch
www.lakelugano.ch
www.lakecome.org

Ferry information can be found online at the following websites:
www.traghetti.com
www.fun.informare.it
www.viamare.com

By Car

Italian motorways *(autostrade)* are generally fast and uncrowded, except in summer and on key holidays, such as Easter. Nearly all *autostrade* charge tolls, which can be paid for by cash or by major credit cards. A convenient method of payment is by ViaCard, a prepaid card that will take off the amount for each toll that you go through. It can be bought from various outlets, including the main motorway service stations and some tobacconists. Entering the automatic toll-meter lanes if you haven't already pre-registered may incur a fine.

Note that it is compulsory to wear seatbelts at all times. Infants up to nine months must travel in a baby seat, and children up to four years must sit in the back seat of the car.

It is obligatory to use headlights

Taxis

In Italy, cabs are found at taxi ranks or may be booked by phone. Hailing them in the street is less common. When you telephone, you will be given the call letters of the taxi and approximately how long it will take to arrive. Fares are clocked up on meters but do check that the driver has switched the meter on when you set off. There is a fixed starting charge, then a charge per kilometre (and a standing charge for traffic jams). If asked, taxi drivers are obliged to show the current list of additional charges, which should also be posted on the back of the seat. Extra charges are added for journeys at night (10pm–7am), on Sundays and holidays, for luggage and trips outside town.

The general rule for tipping is to round off the fare to the nearest few euros or so.

on motor vehicles during the day as well as at night.

Hitchhiking is forbidden on motorways and is not advised for solo women, especially in the south.

When travelling into the mountains in winter, check road conditions with the nearest tourist information centre, or ring the Italian Automobile Association (ACI) on 803-116. When there is ice and snow on the roads, you will need to put chains on your wheels.

Parking

Pay attention to street signs advising "no parking" because Italian police are strict and will remove vehicles found in these areas. You'll need plenty of cash to reclaim your car. Try to park in a garage for the night: it will be fairly expensive but much safer. Ideally, leave your car in your hotel car park, a designated car park (of which there are few) or an official car park. Never leave valuables inside, and do not leave any objects visible to passers-by.

In the south, especially in Naples, Palermo and Catania, where it is hard to find parking, it is best to leave your car with official car-parking attendants – although there are also few of these. Many locals leave their car (often with the keys) with unofficial attendants, but this is not recommended.

Car Rentals

Hiring a car is expensive in Italy, as is petrol. Car rental firms, such as Avis, Hertz and Europcar, are represented in most cities and all airports, though local firms often offer better rates – look in the Yellow Pages (Pagine Gialle) under Autonoleggio. Collision damage waiver and breakdown recovery are usually included in the price, but check this; additional insurance cover is usually available at fixed rates. Ensure that the fee includes the 19 percent VAT (IVA).

The renter must be over 21 and must be in possession of a valid driver's licence (an EU licence, an international driving licence or a national driving licence with Italian translation). A deposit equal to the cost of hiring the vehicle is usually required, or a credit-card imprint.

Speed limits

Urban areas:
50 km/h (30 mph)
Roads outside urban areas:
90 km/h (55 mph)
Dual carriageways outside urban areas:
110 km/h (70 mph)

Motorways (autostrade):
130 km/h (80 mph);
for cars less than 1,100cc:
110 km/h (70 mph)

Inner-City Travel

Rome

Most visitors have to rely on public transport, taxis and their feet to access the centre of Rome, as only residents' cars are allowed there. There is a large underground car park at the foot of the Gianicolo, with space for 800 cars and 200 coaches, so you can park there and take public transport or a taxi into the centre. There are plenty of taxi ranks, or you can call for one on 06-3570, 06-4994 or 06-5551.

The Roman metro covers a limited area but it is efficient. There are also night buses and tourist bus routes. Other options include hiring a Vespa or rollerblades (the latter from Villa Borghese).

Buses

Tiburtina station is the main terminus for buses coming from or going to places outside Rome and the surrounding Lazio region. To reach the centre from Tiburtina, take metro line B towards Termini, the main train station.

ATAC/COTRAL bus information is available from the kiosk in Piazza dei Cinquecento in front of Termini or from tourist offices. Free route maps are available at main metro stations, such as Ottaviano. Buses run 5.30am–midnight, after which time there is a night service. Tickets, once validated, are good for 75 minutes on all ATAC (orange, red or green) buses and for one journey on the metro or on some urban railways, excluding Roma–Lido di Ostia, the beach route.

Ticket machines are located in every metro station, but tickets can

Roma Pass

If you're in Rome for a few days, the Roma Pass, a three-day tourist card, is a worthwhile investment. The €18 pass includes travel on the entire transport network, free entrance to the first two museums or archaeological sites you visit, plus further discounts on entrance to galleries, museums, concerts and events. A map and events guide are also included. The Roma Pass can be bought from the sites themselves, or from the green tourist information kiosks around town. Tel: 06-0606; www.romapass.it.

Roman Travel

Public transport information:
freephone: 800-431784;
www.atac.roma.it
Train enquiries: tel: 892 021.

also be bought from most tobacconists (marked with a large T outside) or newsagents. A standard single-use ticket (biglietto a tempo) is valid for a journey of up to 75 minutes. A one-day ticket (the Metrebus, also known as a biglietto integrato giornaliero) allows you to use all modes of transport excluding the airport bus and the so-called "tourist bus" (line 110); it expires at midnight on the day purchased. Three-day (biglietto turistico integrato), weekly and monthly passes are also available.

Bus and metro tickets must be validated with a time stamp from the machines at the entrance to the metro and at the rear of buses. If a ticket inspector catches you without a ticket you will be given a hefty on-the-spot fine.

Of the public buses, number 64 is especially useful since it connects Termini with Piazza Venezia and the Vatican. As for tourism, the 110 open (an open-top double-decker bus; www.trambusopen.com) covers all the main sites, including the Colosseum, Piazza Navona and St Peter's, in a two-hour tour that leaves every 15 minutes from Piazza dei Cinquecento in front of Termini daily between 8.40am and 8.25pm. Tickets allow you to get on and off all day and can be bought from the kiosk on Piazza dei Cinquecento, or on board if you get on at another stop.

To minimise pollution, the city has several "electric buses" which can cope with the narrow alleys of the historic centre. Line 119, for instance, connects Piazza Venezia with Piazza del Popolo via the Trevi Fountain and Piazza di Spagna, while the 116 passes through or close to Piazza Navona, Campo de Fiori and St Peter's.

Metro

The metro system (Metropolitana) has two lines, A and B, which meet at Termini, the city's main train station, and runs between 5.30am and 11.30pm (until 12.30am on Saturdays). (Until 2008 Line A will close down early at 9pm for major engineering and renovation work. Between 9–11.30pm (12.30pm on Saturdays) the service is replaced by two above-ground buses, MA1 and

MA2, that follow more or less the same route as the metro.

Milan

Milan's **bus** and **tram** service (ATM) is fast and efficient. Standard tickets must be purchased in advance at tobacconists (tabacchi) or news kiosks, and are valid for 75 minutes of travel.

The **Metropolitana Milanese** (MM) is the best subway in Italy. MM has four lines, including the blue Passante Ferroviario (in addition to red MM1, green MM2 and yellow MM3), which serve almost all the city and the hinterland. Tickets are sold at machines in stations and in most tobacconists (tabacchi) and news kiosks; they must be validated at the start of travel. Once metro tickets are stamped, they can be used for other forms of transport within the specified time period. Although basic tickets allow 75 minutes of travel, they cannot be used twice on the metro. However, there is also a flat-fare day ticket, valid on all forms of transport and for multiple journeys. You can also buy 24-hour tourist tickets, 2-day tickets, carnets (books of 10 tickets) and weekly passes.

For **taxis**, which are all white, go to one of the many ranks (eg at San Babila or Stazione Centrale) or call 02-8383, 02-6767 or 02-8585.

Florence

The main **bus** company is ATAF, and its office at Piazza Stazione should have a free bus map of the city. Tickets are sold at bars, tobacconists (tabacchi) and news kiosks with the ATAF sticker and at machines near bus stops.

Milanese Travel

Milan Linate airport: tel: 02-74851
Milan Malpensa airport: tel: 02-74851
Public transport (ATM): freephone: 800-016857
Train information: 892 021
Malpensa Express rail service: tel: 02-27763.
The Malpensa Express Train connects Malpensa airport to Milan (Cadorna station). The service is operated by the Ferrovie Nord. The 40-minute train ride round trip leaves Cadorna every half-hour from 5.50am to 8.20pm and Malpensa every half-hour from 6.45am to 9.45pm. Malpensa Shuttle Buses go to and from Milan's central train station (Stazione Centrale).

Florentine Travel

Train information: 892 021
Florentine public transport: freephone: 800-424500
To learn more about Florentine transport, call the Florence tourist office (see page 418) or check the traffic situation on: www.comune.firenze.it

They are valid for 60 or 120 minutes of travel, and you can change buses during that time. You can also buy 24-hour and multiple tickets.

Cars are discouraged from the city centre, with strict traffic and parking regulations, but large car parks are provided on the edge of town (eg Piazza Independenza), linked by public transport. The city has a complex traffic system known as ZTL (Zona a Traffico Limitato). In certain zones, only pedestrians are allowed, while in others, residents may drive, deliver or even park at some times of day. Really, the simplest and most reliable way of getting around is on foot.

Venice

The city is small enough to be covered on foot, but a good map is essential for exploring the maze of small streets and squares. Pick one up from one of the tourist offices. Note that Venice's tourist offices do not supply public transport maps.

The main form of public transport in Venice is the **vaporetto** (water-bus). Routes and times are subject to change, and information is available at the ACTV water-transport offices on Piazzale Roma, tel: 041-528 7886, or consult their website, www.actv.it. The cost of maintaining Venice and the difficulties of protecting this unique environment prompted increases in the cost of water transport, particularly a high fare for tourists travelling the Grand Canal. A single fare is €3.50 (plus €3.50 for each piece of luggage). 24-hour tickets are €10.50, and a 3-day travelcard costs €22.

The most scenic, but slowest, line remains the No. 1 Accelerato, which takes you down the Grand Canal. Line 82 provides a faster service on the same route, taking 25 minutes and making only six stops; it goes west as far as Tronchetto (the car-park island) and east to San Zaccaria (and the Lido in summer). The 52 provides an enjoyable circular ride around the periphery of Venice and takes in Murano.

Buy a ticket before boarding, or you will be surcharged. Day

(24-hour) and three-day passes are available. Children under 1-metre (just over 3-ft) tall travel free, but there are surcharges for excess luggage – a suitcase costs as much as an adult.

Water-taxis take up to four people and, like regular taxis, display meters. You can find water-taxi "ranks" at main points in the city. The system of charges for water transport is complex; pick up a free copy of A Guest in Venice from any major hotel, or look out for Meeting in Venice, a similar publication.

The flat rate for hiring a **gondola** during the day is around €60 for 50 minutes and about €30 for each 25 minutes thereafter, and after 8pm it's €80, though it is advisable to haggle. A singing gondolier costs extra. A maximum of six people are accepted, and gondolas booked as a group convoy may be cheaper. A recommended route is Bridge of Sighs–Santa Maria Formosa–Rialto Bridge–Grand Canal.

Very much cheaper are traghetto gondolas, which cross the Grand Canal where there are no bridges.

Naples

In general, Neapolitan transport has improved dramatically in terms of efficiency, reliability and safety. Napoli Centrale, the main railway station, is now tightly controlled by the police and therefore safer than stations in many cities.

Buses run to most places in the city and they are the only public transport along the waterfront. However, they are generally very crowded during rush hours. Owing to congested traffic, **taxis** are not much faster than buses, although they are much more expensive.

Naples's main **metro** line, the Metropolitana FS, covers most of the city and suburbs. It connects Piazza Garibaldi with Piazza Cavour, Monte Santo, Mergellina, Campi Flegrei and Bagnoli.

Two good **local railways** for tourists include Circumvesuviana, which goes from Piazza Garibaldi to Pompeii, Herculaneum and Sorrento, and the Circumflegri, which leaves from Piazza Montesanto for Cuma.

Neapolitan Travel

Train enquiries: tel: 892 021.
Taxis: take one from an official rank or call: 081-556 0202/ 081-556 4444 (Napoli taxis).
A flat-fare **ticket** is available covering city buses and metro.

ACCOMMODATION

EATING OUT

ACTIVITIES

A – Z

LANGUAGE

A CCOMMODATION

WHERE TO STAY

Italy has a wonderful variety of accommodation in all categories, from luxury villa hotels and palatial apartments to small family-run hotels, rustic retreats and an increasing number of B&Bs.

Hotels

The once stuffy hotel scene has smartened up its act in recent years with the creation of new concepts from grand guesthouses, chic chalets and fortified farmhouses, to hip boutique hotels, Zen-like spa-hotels, industrial conversions, and urban design dens.

Boutique hotels

Given the Italians' sense of style and aptitude for family-run businesses, it is no surprise that the country is studded with boutique hotels. The best of the current crop aspire to being the embodiment of chic, understated luxury rather than glitzy palaces awash with gold and marble.

Creative conversions

The choices are many and varied. In Sicily, Antica Stazione Ficuzza, a former station that once served the Bourbon Kings' hunting estates, has been transformed into a tiny hotel and jazz venue. In Venice, a former flour mill and local landmark, has been reborn as palatial loft-style apartments. In deepest Basilicata, Matera's cave dwellings carved out of tufa-stone, have been transformed into hip hotels with views over a lunar landscape. In Puglia, the *masseria fortificata*, the authentic rural residence, doubled as a fortress and family-run working farm. But many, such as gorgeous Masseria Torre Coccaro, have been converted into luxurious country retreats.

Designer hotels

The country's celebrated designers have happily leapt into the hotel business, from Ferragamo and Ferretti to Bulgari and Benetton. The Ferragamo dominate the Florentine hotel scene while the Alberta Ferretti fashion dynasty has several designer hotels on the Riviera Romagnola, from an art deco villa in Cattolica to a castle resort, Montegridolfo, complete with drawbridge, gatehouse and church. In Milan, the design capital, the Bulgari is the epitome of cool, with its seductive spa and a peaceful botanical garden. In Venice, Benetton's stately Hotel Monaco & Grand Canal is at odds with the company's casual clothing aesthetic.

Eco hotels

Eco hotels are the new buzzword, and presented as the answer to rural depopulation. Both enlightened eco-warriors and green-minded locals are looking for alternatives to the classic "agriturismo" (farm-stay) concept *(see page 371)*. In Abruzzo, the ancient hamlet of Santo Stefano di Sassanio has been restored, but not prettified, leaving the smoke-blackened walls and unwieldy iron keys as a tribute to those who once eked out a living here. It is a model for rural tourism and sustainable development, attracting summer ramblers and winter skiers.

Set in gentle hills around Urbino, Locanda della Valle Nuova flaunts its impeccable green credentials. On the farm, guests appreciate the rural rooms as much as the organic wine, vegetables, and the home-made bread, pasta and jams. Underpinning it all is a green conscience: water is purified while heating is solar or from wood stoves, supplied by pruned branches from the woods.

Gastro-hotels

Gastro-hotels, run by celebrity chefs, have flourished, by creating cookery schools, wine estates and even spas. Two of the best-known are L'Albereta, near Lake Iseo, run by chef Gualtiero Marchese, and L'Andana in Tuscany, linked to Alain Ducasse and E'SPA.

Villa hotels

In the lake district, popular with the stars, Lake Como and Lake Garda are home to some of the country's finest villa hotels. Villa Feltrinelli, overlooking Lake Garda, was Mussolini's last bolthole but is now the ultimate hideaway, from fabulous frescos to a private boat and personal chef. In the Dolomites, chic chalets offer skiing in style: Virgilius Resort is a zen-like lodge tuned into its alpine ambience, with a soothing spa and panoramic views over the Italian Tyrol. On the Amalfi Coast, the revamped Caruso is considered the most romantic of historic grand hotels.

Spa hotels

Italian spa hotels used to be synonymous with scary doctors in white coats, but there is now a sharp divide between clinical spa hotels and those dedicated to pampering. Many of the sybaritic hideaways are in Tuscany (Fonteverde, Grotta Giusti and Saturnia) or in Ischia, where they make use of radioactive springs and thermal mud.

Spiritual retreats

The country abounds in religious retreats that have been transformed into leading luxury hotels. Outstanding examples include San Domenico in Taormina, San Michele in Florence, or San Clemente, set on its own island in the Venetian lagoon. But there are also perfect pads in sanctuaries that retain their spiritual vocation. In Piedmont, for instance, you can stay up in the mountains, in the Santuario d'Oropa, a prestigious Marian Sanctuary.

Hotel Groups

The following is a selection of the most noteworthy hotel groups.

Abitare La Storia: Operating under the banner of "Living History", this is an association of independently run hotels, each of which occupies an historic palazzo or villa, often with lovely grounds. General enquiries, tel: 0322 772156; www.abitarelastoria.it

Boscolo Hotels: This Italian-owned hotel group has luxury hotels in Bologna, Florence, Rome, Treviso, Venice and Verona. Boscolo Luxury Hotels are five-star hotels; Boscolo First Class are four-star hotels. From the UK tel: 0800-2672 6565; from the US tel: 1888-626 7265; www.boscolohotels.com

Charming Hotels: This group of luxurious, independent hotels is characterised by its impeccable taste in atmospheric locations, antiques and excellent traditional cuisine. There are Charming Hotels in Como, Siena and Venice, among other places. You can book through head office in Rome: Via G. Caccini 1, tel: 06-9777 4591. Call, toll-free, outside Italy from Australia, Belgium, France, UK, Spain, Switzerland and US 800-24276464; in Italy call 840-707575; www.thecharminglife.com

Intercontinental Hotels Group: The world's largest hotel company owns hotels throughout Italy. In Italy, tel: 800-877399; from the UK, tel: 0870-400 9093; from the US, tel: 800-424 6835; www.ichotelsgroup.com

Jolly Hotels: Formed in 1949, this is now the largest Italian hotel group; tel: 00800-0005 6559 (toll-free); www.jollyhotels.it

Leading Hotels of the World/ Leading Small Hotels of the World: Consortium of upmarket properties. From the UK, tel: 00800-1010 1111; 020-7290 1000; www.lhw.com

Logis d'Italia: Similar to the French group, Logis de France, this group has hotels all over Italy and these are listed in the Logis d'Italia guide. The group's principles are founded on value for money, size and hospitality (many are small and family run). Book through a central reservations system in Milan, tel: 02-4851 9285, or directly with hotels, www.logis.it

Rocco Forte Hotels Group: This luxury hotel group has hotels in Florence and Rome. In the UK,

tel: 020-7493 6020; in Italy book through the Rome office, tel: 06-3288 8841; www.roccofortehotels.com

Sina Hotels: This small hotel group, founded by an Italian aristocrat, runs stylish and luxurious hotels in Milan, Parma, Viareggio, Florence, Venice, Turin, Perugia and Rome. They have a certain elegance and formality in common. You can book directly or through Sina Hotels in Rome: Piazza Barberini 23, tel: 06-487 0222. For central reservations, tel: 800-273226; www.sinahotels.com

Starhotels: This Italian group specialises in hotels in the heart of cities, such as the four-star Savoia Excelsior in Trieste. For reservations from the UK, tel: 00800-313132; from the USA, tel: 800-816 6001; in Italy, tel: 800-860200; www.starhotels.it

Starwood Hotels and Resorts: Upmarket properties located throughout Italy and the world. For reservations from the UK, tel: 0800-353 535; www.starwood.com

Turin Hotels: This group began in Turin and manages traditional, classic hotels in the regions of Piedmont and Liguria. The hotels are characterised by high Piedmontese standards of service, classical or Neo-classical buildings and excellent cuisine. They are all 4-star and can be booked through Turin Hotels International, Turin, tel: 011-515 1911, www.thi.it.

Travelling Around Italy Hotels: This chain has just 14 elegant hotels, which are closely linked to their surrounding areas and cater for lovers of good food and wine. The group is based at Via della Purificazione 4, Rome, tel: 06-487 2001; fax: 06-485994; www.travellingarounditaly.com.

Una Hotels: This Italian hotel group has reliable 4-star hotels in Milan, Bergamo, Bologna, Brescia, Catania, Florence and Naples. Book through the head office at Via Cusani 13, Milan; tel: 02-8560 2910 or through www.unahotels.it

B&Bs and Guesthouses

Italy was slow to get onto the B&B bandwagon but a raft of recent laws has led to a boom in Bed & Breakfast, but the concept is now established and the B&B sector thriving. However, particular cities and regions appear to be better-provided for than others. Venice, Bologna and Siracusa offer a huge range of options, but Rome is the city where the Bed & Breakfast system has taken off, particularly for budget travellers. Although the quality of accommodation is extremely variable,

places are generally clean, simple and welcoming.

In many sought-after cities, chic guesthouses have replaced the peeling pensione, a category that no longer exists, officially at least. The model is, curiously enough, the English guesthouse, but the Italian version is keener on eclecticism than cosiness. Whether B&B or guest-house, expect much more than a room with a view.

For full, up-to-date B&B listings visit: www.caffelletto.it (upmarket), www.bbitalia.it (general) or www.b-b.rm.it (Rome).

Agriturismo

For longer holidays, rural farm stays (agriturismo) have long been an option, embracing everything from a real farm to a converted granary or country estate. Tuscany and Umbria are probably the two areas where agriturismo is most developed. In Tuscany, most of the best places are around Florence, Siena and San Gimignano. In the Chianti area properties are prized for their proximity to wine estates, while many of those in Lucca are in exquisite patrician villas. Lesser-known areas such as the Mugello (north of Florence), wild Lunigiana, Massa Marittima and the Lucca hinterland can also be promising places to stay.

Most regional tourist offices (and a number of those in cities and provinces) should be able to supply lists of agriturismo properties. The term can mean different things in different areas, so check carefully what is on offer when you book. For information on farmhouse stays throughout Italy log on to www.agriturismoinitalia.com or www.agriturist.it. For Tuscany consult www.agriturismoregionetoscana.it

Villa Holidays

Private villas with their own pool usually cost a premium in Italy, and such properties tend to be booked up very quickly. Some so-called "villas" are actually apartment complexes, so always ask exactly what you're getting.

Tuscany tends to be the most expensive region but Umbria is catching up in terms of price and quality; there are also a number of magnificent Palladian villas in the Veneto, but the weather can be disappointing compared with areas further south. In the south, except for some chic sites in Sardinia, Capri and the Amalfi coast, prices tend to be lower than elsewhere.

Selected operators in Italy, the UK and USA who offer villa holidays:
www.anotheritaly.co.uk
www.bridgewatertravel.co.uk
www.citalia.co.uk
www.cuendet.com
www.cottagestocastles.com
www.indiv-travellers.com
www.interhome.co.uk
www.italiantownandcountry.com
www.italtourism.com
www.landmarktrust.org.uk
www.luxuryretreat.com
www.tuscandream.com
www.villaescapes.com
www.villasitalia.com

Apartment Holidays

Venetian Apartments, tel: 020-8878 1130, www.venice-rentals.com, are market leaders for Venice but they also have apartments in Rome, Verona and Florence.

Italtourism, tel/fax: 020-8879 0345, www.italtourism.com, offers over 1,000 self-catering apartments; most of their rural properties have pools.

Carefree Italy, tel: 01293-552277, www.carefreeitaly.com offers apartment and other self-catering holidays in locations throughout Italy.

Caffelletto, tel: 02-331 1814/ 331 1820, www.caffelletto.it, has a selection of villas, castles, stylish country manors and city apartments, some on a bed and breakfast basis, others self-catering.

UK Tour Operators

Abercrombie & Kent, tel: 0845-0700610; www.abercrombiekent. co.uk.
Andante Travels, tel: 01722-713800; www.andantetravels.co.uk.
Citalia, tel: 0870-909 07555; www.citalia.co.uk.
Simply Sardinia, tel: 020-7433 2675; www.simplytravel.co.uk.
Exclusive Italy, tel: 020-8256 0231; www.exclusiveworldwide.com.

Italian Connection, tel: 01424-728900; www.italian-connection.co.uk.
Italian Expressions, tel: 020 7433 2675; www.expressionsholidays.co.uk.
Italian Journeys, tel: 0870-733 3000; www.italianjourneys.com.
Long Travel Southern Italy, tel: 01694-722193; www.long-travel.co.uk

US Tour Operators

Adagio Travel, tel: (314) 761-9336; www.adagiotravel.com
AMTA, tel: 1-800-228-0877; www.amta.com
Bella Italia Tours, tel: (303) 283-0944; www.bellaitaliatours.com
Bella Vista Tours, tel: 877-723 0802; www.bellavistatours.com
Crystal Tour Unlimited, tel: (305) 534-5507; www.crystal-tours.com
Hidden Treasures of Italy, tel: 888-419-6700; www.htitaly.com
Visit Italy Tours, tel: 800-255 3537; www.visititalytours.com

ACCOMMODATION LISTINGS

ROME

Rome has an impressive range of accommodation, particularly at the top end of the scale. However, the large demand means that, like in Venice, prices are relatively high, and it is worth booking in advance if you wish to stay in a good hotel. The alternative is to book with a reputable tour operator, who ought to have a fixed allocation in some of the best hotels. The following websites offer a wide choice of places to stay: www.venere.com; www.expedia.it; www.hotelreservation.it; www.gotoroma.com

Grand Hotels

Aldrovandi Palace Hotel
Via Ulisse Aldrovandi 15
Tel: 06-322 3993
www.aldrovandi.com
This imposing 18th-century palace overlooking the Villa Borghese gardens is in the prestigious Parioli district and its suites are among the most expensive in the city. Decor is sumptuous rather than stylish – a

mood that is reflected in both the facilities and service. The hotel's many amenities include an outdoor swimming pool – exceptional for Rome. €€€€

Baglioni Regina
Via Veneto 72
Tel: 06-421111
www.baglionihotels.com
Without resorting to the formal or the frumpy, the 62-room Regina in Rome is elegantly decorated in period style bringing a touch of class back to the Via Veneto, which had lost some of its sparkle. €€€€

Capo d'Africa
Via Capo d'Africa 54
Tel: 06-772801
www.hotelcapodafrica.com
One of a recent slew of boutique hotels in Rome. The dramatic, palm-tree lined entrance bodes well and the 64 rooms are cosy yet refreshingly contemporary – one suite has its own private terrace. Views are delightful and the Colosseum only a five-minute walk away. Any worries that you won't be in

the thick of things will vanish once you realise how well connected you are. €€€–€€€€

Cavalieri Hilton
Via Cadlolo 101
Tel: 06-3509 2031
www.cavalieri-hilton.it
This resort-style hotel with superb views has great sports facilities, including two swimming pools, a fitness centre, jogging track and tennis courts. It has two renowned restaurants – La Pergola and Giardino dell'Uliveto – an executive floor and several shops. €€€€

Celio
Via Santissimi Quattro 35/C
Tel: 06-7049 5333
www.hotelcelio.com
This boutique hotel is just a stone's throw from both the Colosseum and the Forum. It occupies a charming *palazzo* that has been completely and sensitively restored, including its fine mosaics. The atmosphere is elegant and the bedrooms achieve a particularly high standard of comfort. €€€

Hotel De Russie
Via del Babuino 9
Tel: 06-328881
www.hotelderussie.it
A favoured 19th-century haunt of the Russian imperial family, dignitaries and luminaries, this hotel was later frequented by Picasso and Jean Cocteau. Set among terraced, shady gardens, and beautifully restored, it's a verdant, tranquil oasis in the heart of town. Designed in an elegant minimalist style, it offers the ultimate in luxury blended with up-to-the-minute technology. A fully equipped health spa and a superb restaurant – Le Jardin du Russie – make it very popular with celebrities. €€€€

D'Inghilterra
Via Bocca di Leone 14
Tel: 06-699811
www.royaldemeure.com
Old-fashioned it may be, but this hotel, in the main shopping area close to Trinita dei Monti, is arguably the most atmospheric of the grand hotels. Bedrooms are mostly spacious and

elegant, with marble bathrooms. In the public areas, frescos, antiques and chandeliers add to the elegant atmosphere. Lizst, Ernest Hemingway, Anatole France and Alec Guinness all stayed here. The roof garden is one of the loveliest in the city. €€€€

Forum
Via Tor dei Conti 25
Tel: 06-679 2446
www.hotelforumrome.com
This is a lovely hotel close to the Colosseum with a view of the ancient city, including the Forum, from its roof garden. 80 rooms. €€€–€€€€

Grand Hotel Parco dei Principi
Via G. Frescobaldi 5
Tel: 06-854421
www.parcodeiprincipi.com
Beautifully located in a park on the edge of the gardens of the Villa Borghese, this luxurious, modern hotel prides itself on exquisite attention to detail. Excellent facilities include a swimming pool, well-appointed rooms, 20 panoramic suites and three restaurants. €€€€

Hassler-Villa Medici
Piazza Trinità dei Monti 6
Tel: 06-699340
www.hotelhasslerroma.com
Located at the top of the Spanish Steps, this hotel is one of the best in Rome. It provides excellent food and service and even has free bicycles available for exploring the city. The bedrooms are luxurious, and some have four-poster beds. The roof-garden restaurant has fine views over the city. €€€€

Lord Byron
Via Giuseppe de Notaris 5
Tel: 06-322 0404
www.lordbyronhotel.com
Situated close to the Villa Borghese in the exclusive Parioli district, this distinguished hotel has the elegant, ambience of a private club, sustained by old-fashioned decor and individually designed rooms with Irish linen sheets, French beds and good Roman service. There's a piano bar and the renowned Sapori del Lord Byron restaurant. €€€€

St Regis Grand
Via VE Orlando 3
Tel: 06-47091
www.starwoodhotels.com
Between the railway station and the Via Veneto area, this exclusive and dignified hotel occupies a patrician palace, graced with Oriental rugs, chandeliers and antiques. It has recently been beautifully restored, but retains its original style. Facilities include tea-rooms, a bar and gourmet restaurant. Personal butler service available. €€€€

Westin Excelsior
Via Vittorio Veneto 125
Tel: 06-47081
www.starwoodhotels.com
This grand hotel has been a meeting place for celebrities and society figures since the 1950s. The hotel claims that this was the location of the Ingrid Bergman–Roberto Rossellini affair, and where the last Shah of Iran courted his future wife. To many, this hotel is synonymous with Roman *dolce vita*, even if some of this indefinable quality has otherwise moved on from the Via Vittorio Veneto. €€€€

Small Hotels

Casa Howard
Via Capo La Case (off the Spanish Steps)
Tel: 06-6992 4555
www.casahoward.com
Tucked away on a secluded second-floor *palazzo* is a delightful "home-from-home" created by style gurus Massimiliano Leonardi and Jennifer Howard Forneris. Modelled on an English guesthouse, its design aesthetic is far more eclectic. Instead of a concierge, "house-genie" Cristy oversees the guesthouse, from the Turkish *hammam* (steam bath) to the "honesty fridge" and five themed bedrooms. The mood is stylish yet intimate, and dotted with curious furniture and ethnic objets d'art. As guests you have the keys to the house. €€€

Columbia
Via del Viminale 15
Tel: 06-488 3509
www.hotelcolumbia.com
This charming hotel is centrally located near to the Via Nazionale. Rooms are large and elegantly furnished. There is also a roof terrace where you can enjoy breakfast. €€–€€€

Dei Consoli
Via Varrone 2/d
Tel: 06-6889 2972
www.hoteldeiconsoli.com
Occupying a 19th-century building that has been well restored in the Empire style, this new hotel overlooks St Peter's. The cupola is visible from the spectacular rooftop terrace and from many of the 28 bedrooms. There is direct internet connection in each room. €€–€€€

Gregoriana
Via Gregoriana 18
Tel: 06-679 4269
www.hotelgregoriana.it
Close to the Spanish Steps, this former 17th-century mansion is now a three-star hotel with a quiet, cosy atmosphere. Especially admirable is the art deco interior. There is no restaurant, but the hotel does have a pleasant terrace where breakfast is served. €€

La Residenza "A"
Via Vittorio Veneto 183
Tel: 06-486700
www.hotelviaveneto.com
On the first floor of a *palazzo* in the swanky but dull Via Veneto, this features modern rooms with art on the walls. Computers with free internet in every room. €€€

Mozart Hotel
Via dei Greci 23
Tel: 0845-227 0141 (UK)
www.hotelmozart.com
Warm, elegant atmosphere in the heart of Rome with its ancient history and modern shopping, just a few steps from Piazza di Spagna and Via dei Condotti. €€€

Margutta
Via Laurina 34
Tel: 06-322 3674
Near Piazza del Popolo, this little hotel occupies an 18th-century *palazzo*. Rooms are simple and there is no restaurant, but atmosphere and value are compensation enough. €€

Santa Maria
Vicolo del Piede 2
Tel: 06-589 4626
www.htlsantamaria.com
This small jewel of a hotel takes its name from the nearby church of Santa Maria in Trastevere. A former 17th-century cloister, it has been sympathetically renovated and offers high standards of comfort. There is an attractive courtyard garden which is an oasis of calm, yet close to all the main sights of Trastevere. €€

Teatro di Pompeo
Largo del Pallaro 8
Tel: 06-6830 0170
www.hotelteatrodipompeo.it
Just off picturesque Campo de' Fiori, this popular family-run hotel stands on the site of Pompey's Theatre, dating from 55BC. The walls of the cosy breakfast room have been hewn from the theatre's tufa stone. The bedrooms are a cosy blend of cream decor and terracotta-flagged floors. €€

Other Options

aRoma
Via Palestro 49
Tel: 34-0284 7643
www.aromabb.it
Set in the centre of Rome, not far from the main station, this is a popular B&B in a quiet *palazzo* with vaulted ceilings. €–€€

The Beehive
Via Marghera 8
Tel: 06-4470 4553
www.the-beehive.com
A chic but incredibly cheap option near Termini station run by an American couple with a dorm room, apartments and private rooms decorated in a colourful and contemporary style. It has a welcoming garden, its own café for guests and knowledgeable staff. €

PRICE CATEGORIES

Price categories are for a double room without breakfast:
€ = under €80
€€ = €80–160
€€€ = €160–280
€€€€ = more than €280

MILAN

Always book a Milan hotel well in advance because, except in July and August, rooms tend to be scarce. During the main trade fairs it can be almost impossible to find a room, leaving no alternative but to stay outside the city. If no rooms are available, consider saying on Lake Como, which is only 30–40 minutes from the centre of Milan and can be easily reached by train.

Distinctive Milanese Hotels

Hotel Ariston
Largo Carrobbio 2
Tel: 02-7200 0556
Set in a rather noisy, traffic-filled area, this ecologically minded hotel is an experiment in healthy living and an asthma-sufferer's dream: rooms come equipped with atomisers and ionisers. Recycled paper and biodegradable products are used and the restaurant uses organic products. Decor is minimalist. €€€
Carlton Hotel Baglioni
Via Senato 5
Tel: 02-77077
www.baglionihotels.com
In the heart of Milan, overlooking the ultra chic Via della Spiga, this luxurious hotel offers the ultimate in elegance and refinement. Rooms are furnished with exquisite silk brocades, antiques and marbled bathrooms. There are 92 sound-proofed rooms, some of which have sunroofs, and nine opulent suites. Outside terrace with very fashionable tented "shisha bar" – hubblybubbly pipes and Middle Eastern nibbles.There is also a large indoor car park. €€€€

Hotel Bulgari
Tel: 02-805 8051
www.bulgarihotels.com
Set a short stroll away from the style capital's most famous fashion street, Via Montenapoleone, this luxury hotel can compete with the best designer boutiques. The Bulgari has an inviting spa and a peaceful botanical garden. Honey-mooners may opt for the Bulgari suite, with views from the dark teak terrace. Shopaholics should bear in mind that sales are held the first two weeks of January and July. €€€
The Gray
Via San Raffaele 6
Tel: 02-720 8951
www.thegray@sinahotels.it
In the heart of Milan, very close to the Duomo, the Scala and Galleria Vittorio Emanuele, this designer boutique hotel has become one of the city's most fashionable. The 21 rooms are all individually styled and there is a very pleasant restaurant. €€€
Park Hyatt
Via Tommaso Grossi 1
Tel: 02-8821 1234
www.milan.park.hyatt.com
Cool understatement has been combined with opulence here. Beautiful bedrooms with travertine-clad walls, Venetian stucco and lovely touches such as hand-blown Venetian-glass light sconces. Just a stone's throw from La Scala, the Duomo and a Prada shop. €€€€
UNA Hotel Century
Via Fabio Filzi 25b
Tel: 02-67504
www.unahotels.it
Despite occupying a tower, this hotel located close to Stazione Centrale has a friendly atmosphere and offers both the luxury of space and a sense of privacy. The 150 bedroom-suites are probably the largest in their price range in Milan. Other amenities include a small fitness centre and a good restaurant which serves Milanese and classic Italian cuisine. €€€€

Grand Hotels

Excelsior Gallia
Piazza Duca d'Aosta 9
Tel: 02-67851
www.excelsiorgallia.it
Located beside Stazione Centrale, this luxurious historic hotel is now part of the Le Meridien group, but still feels like a real Milanese institution. Public rooms are gracious and appealing, and the bedrooms vary greatly in style and size; most feature wonderful original art deco marble bathrooms. €€€€
Four Seasons
Via Gesù 8
Tel: 02-77088
www.fourseasons.com
This is one of Milan's most exclusive hotels assuring attentive, but unobtrusive service. The setting is delightful, with the former monastic cells converted into supremely luxurious bedrooms. Many choose the hotel for its proximity to the prestigious Quadrilatero shopping district. Book well in advance. €€€€
Hermitage
Via Messina 10
Tel: 02-318170
www.monrifhotels.it
Elegant and characterful hotel with 119 rooms (and eight suites). A lovely garden and veranda, plus stylish decor and attentive service have made this hotel very popular with celebrities. €€€–€€€€
Principe di Savoia
Piazza della Repubblica 17
Tel: 02-62301
www.luxurycollection.com
This hotel revels in old-fashioned luxury, with a self-consciously grand interior. More than 400 rooms include the most splendid presidential suite in the city, favoured by celebrities, super-models and heads of state. The suite's private pool is an over-the-top fantasy inspired by Pompeiian baths. Apart from such glitzy touches, this is essentially a classic luxury hotel, offering superb service and excellent facilities. The rooftop fitness centre includes a sauna and pool, with glorious views over the city. €€€€
The Westin Palace
Piazza della Repubblica 20
Tel: 02-63361
www.westin.com
The third main hotel on the Piazza della Repubblica, the Palace offers wonderful fitness facilities, notably its indoor golf range. Guests have access to the Principe di Savoia's rooftop pool and fitness club. The renovated bedrooms, some with steam rooms, are comfortable, and the restaurant has a sound reputation. €€€€

Small, Old-fashioned Inns

Antica Locanda dei Mercanti
Via San Tomaso 6
Tel: 02-805 4080
www.locanda.it
This intimate hotel has only 14 rooms and is cosy as an inn, despite its setting in the heart of the financial district. It has no sign (and no TV), and guests are woken in the morning by an old-fashioned bell before being served breakfast in bed. There are well-stocked bookshelves and the rooms have fine views. €€€
Antica Locanda Solferino
Via Castelfidardo 2
Tel: 02-657 0129
Old-fashioned furniture and a gracious atmosphere create a pleasant ambience in this 11-bedroom hotel in the elegant Brera quarter. In tune with the low-key mood, breakfast is served in your room. Book well in advance. €€€

Small, Friendly Hotels

Antica Locanda Leonardo
Corso Magenta 78
Tel: 02-463317
www.leoloc.com
Small, family-run hotel with 20 rooms offering a warm welcome. Close to the church of Santa Maria delle Grazie and Leonardo's Cenacolo. €€€

Aspromonte
Piazza Aspromonte 12–14
Tel: 02-361119
www.venere.it/milano/aspromonte
Small and gracious with very attentive service from the young proprietors. In summer breakfast is served in the garden. €€

Hotel Gran Duca di York
Via Moneta 1
Tel: 02-874863
www.ducadiyork.com
Close to the Duomo, this is a very popular boutique hotel with just 33 rooms. It is housed in a former 18th-century *palazzo*, recently very stylishly renovated.

Service is attentive and professional and this good-value hotel attracts a faithful following. €€–€€€

Hotel Spadari al Duomo
Via Spadari 11
Tel: 02-7200 2371
www.spadarihotel.com
Exclusive little jewel of a hotel just around the corner from the Duomo and La Scala. The first "art hotel" in Italy, it was developed around a private collection of contemporary art and designer furniture. The result is a collection of 40 lovely, individually styled rooms. Professional, friendly

service. Rooms 72 & 74 also have jacuzzis. €€€€

Hotel Vittoria
Via Pietro Calvi 32
Tel: 02-545 6520
This pleasant, family-run three-star hotel, with friendly, helpful staff, is about ten minutes' walk from the cathedral. All 18 bedrooms have air-conditioning and noise insulation, although some are a little small (typical for Milan). The cosy breakfast room overlooks a nice garden where breakfast is served in fine weather. The hotel does not have a restaurant but there's a

24-hour bar. Car park (supervised) nearby. €€€

Standard Business Hotels

Jolly Hotel President
Largo Augusto 10 (corner of Piazza Luigi di Savoia). Tel: 02-77461
A good, large chain hotel. There are three other Jolly hotels in Milan. €€€–€€€€

Michelangelo
Via Scarlatti 33
Tel: 02-67551
Close to the Central Station, this is one of Milan's best-run business hotels. €€€–€€€€

LOMBARDY AND THE LAKES

Many of the best hotels in Lombardy, Piedmont and the Veneto occupy lakeside sites, with glorious views. The resort of Como has a handful of good hotels on the lakeside and, of the other resorts around the lake, Bellagio, although tiny and touristy, is the nicest. Although less exclusive and intimate than Lake Como, Garda has its own appeal and is excellent for water-sports. Sirmione is one of the loveliest resorts, followed by Gardone Riviera and Riva del Garda.

Bergamo

Excelsior San Marco
Piazza della Repubblica 6
Tel: 035-366111
This modern hotel offers slick service, good facilities and a roof garden. €€€

Brescia

Il Santellone Resort
Via del Santellone 116
Tel: 030-241 1112
www.santelloneresort.it
The resort occupies an 11th-century abbey close to Franciacorta wine country on the outskirts of Brescia. It is connected with Vita E Spa (www.vitaespa.it), the most seductive spa in the area, which occupies part of a Romanesque Benedictine monastery. Both the resort and spa

manage to be ultra cool while remaining understated. The design of the bedrooms and public spaces, in off-whites and earth tones, complements the spare grandeur of the abbey walls. €€€

Lake Como

Grand Hotel Tremezzo
Via Regina 8, Bellagio
Tel: 0344-42491
www.grandhoteltremezzo.com
Set on the western bank of Lake Como, this art nouveau-style villa-hotel has fine views over the lake on one side and an Alpine panorama on the other. The Grand, popular as a congress centre, has three restaurants, one of which produces gourmet feasts. Enjoy the floating swimming pool in the lake waters. €€€–€€€€

Grand Hotel Villa Serbelloni
Via Roma 1, Bellagio
Tel: 031-950216
www.villaserbelloni.it
This fabulous patrician villa has been converted into one of the finest hotels in northern Italy. The views, grounds, facilities (including two swimming pools, tennis courts and health spa) and service are all impeccable. The terrace restaurant overlooks the palm-filled grounds and the lake. €€€€

Hotel du Lac
Piazza Mazzini 32, Bellagio
Tel: 031-950320
www.bellagiohoteldulac.com
Very centrally located, overlooking the embarkation point for boats. Pleasant roof garden and dining room with excellent, panoramic views. Good value. €€–€€€

Lake Garda

Hotel Gardesana
Torri del Benaco
Piazza Calderini 20
Tel: 045-722 5411
www.hotel-gardesana.com
This delightful medieval harbour-master's house, which overlooks Lake Garda, has been converted into a welcoming, well-furnished three-star hotel. Bedrooms on the third floor are the quietest and they have lovely views over the lake. €€€

Grand Hotel Terme
Viale Marconi 7
Tel: 030-916261
www.termedisimione.com
Elegant hotel overlooking the lake. Excellent sports facilities include a swimming pool, sauna and fitness centre. €€€€

Hotel du Lac et du Parc
Viale Rovereto 44
Tel: 0464-566600
www.hoteldulac-riva.it
This part-old, part-modern hotel in Riva del Garda enjoys a lakeside location where motor boats are

banned. As well as the hotel, there are holiday chalets in the spacious grounds and facilities include restaurants, a piano bar, tennis courts, a sailing and wind-surfing school and a fitness centre. €€€–€€€€

Villa Feltrinelli
Via Rimembranza 38–40, Gargnano
Tel: 0365-798000
www.villafeltrinelli.com
Villa Feltrinelli, overlooking Lake Garda, was Mussolini's last bolthole in his doomed Republic of Salo. Now a seductive villa-hotel, it is the ultimate hideaway and the height of decadence, from fabulous frescoes to Frette sheets. You can sail *La Contessa* on a cocktail cruise before being served dinner cooked by your personal chef. €€€–€€€€

Lake Iseo

L'Albereta
Via Vittorio Emanuele 11, Erbusco, Provincia di Brescia
Tel: 030-776 0550
www.albereta.it
This hotel is a destination for gastronomes, as its restaurant is run by one of Italy's best-known chefs, Gualtiero Marchesi. The "hotel" is actually a compact rural estate, consisting of a couple of farmhouses and a tower-house. €€€

TURIN

Though most of its hotels still cater largely to a business clientele, Turin is trying to broaden its appeal. The fact that low-cost airlines now fly here has made the city an increasingly popular city break destination.

Art Boston
Via Massena 70
Tel: 011-500359
www.hotelbostontorino.it
Tasteful hotel, designed with a sense of exclusivity and originality. All the common areas are hung with works of contemporary art and there is an oriental theme in some of the bedrooms. €€–€€€

Jolly Hotel Ambasciatori
Corso Vittorio Emanuele II 104
Tel: 011-5752
Freephone tel: 167017703
www.jollyhotels.it
This typical Jolly hotel is

favoured by a business clientele. It is large, modern and efficient and offers a good location and service. €€€

Le Meridien Art+Tech
Via Nizza 230, Lingotto
Tel: 011-664 2000
www.lemeridien-lingotto.it
Renzo Piano's renovation of Fiat's former Lingotto plant. The high-tech vision is clear in the vertiginous lifts and glass-roofed, cavernous central hall. Expect ultra-designed bedrooms, with signature pieces by Philippe Starck and Gio Ponti. The rooftop racing track is now a jogging track with fabulous views. €€€€

Turin Palace Hotel
Via Sacchi 8
Tel: 011-562 5511
www.thi.it
This, the flagship of the Turin Hotel Group, is a

classic, elegant hotel, designed in grand Piedmontese style, and handy for Porta Nuova station. The public rooms house large paintings and period furniture. The staff are highly professional and the cuisine is good. €€€

Hotel Victoria
Via Nino Costa 4
Tel: 011-561 1909
www.hotelvictoria-torino.com
This hotel has few rivals for atmosphere and service at three-star prices. It is rather like stepping into an English country house full of antiques and objets d'art collected by the owners on their travels far and wide. Each of the 106 spacious bedrooms is individually and pleasingly decorated, while downstairs there is an open fire and bar and

pleasant conservatory-style breakfast room. In summer, breakfast is served in the garden under the gazebo. It is also centrally situated, close to Piazza San Carlo and Via Roma. €€–€€€

Villa Sassi
Strada Traforo del Pino 47
Tel: 011-898 0556
www.villasassi.com
Housed in a splendid 18th-century villa, in the Torinese foothills and surrounded by lovely parkland. There are only 16 bedrooms, some of which have private terraces overlooking the park. Expect excellent service and every comfort. Rooms on the first floor are more romantic than those on the modern floor above. Dinner is served in the elegant, frescoed dining room. €€€

PIEDMONT AND VALLE D'AOSTA

Piedmont (Piemonte) has considerable appeal, especially for wine-lovers, who are attracted to the many specialist wine tours on offer in the region, and nature-lovers, wanting to visit its national park. Albi is popular as a chic desti-nation, and in winter the ski resorts of Sestriere, Sansicario, Sauze-d'Oulx and the rest of the "Milky Way" ski circuit featured in the 2006 Winter Olympics, are pulling in a growing number of visitors.

Alba

I Castelli
Corso Torino 14
Tel: 0173-361978
www.hotel-icastelli.com
Modern hotel built of cement and glass in the heart of town. Bedrooms are spacious and elegantly furnished. Covered parking.
€–€€

Aosta

Europe
Piazza Narbonne 8

Tel: 0165-236363
Set in the historic centre, this is a traditional hotel, noted for its tranquillity and elegance. €€–€€€

Milleluci
Località Porossan Roppoz 15
Tel: 0165-235278
www.hotelmilleluci.com
Pleasant, traditional inn with 31 rooms in a panoramic and peaceful position with views over the city. Swimming pool. €€

Asti

Hotel Reale
Piazza Alfieri 6
Tel: 0141-530240
www.hotel-reale.com
This lovely palazzo in the heart of the old town has been a hotel since 1793. The reception area and 24 rooms are tastefully decorated and some are quite spacious. €–€€

Biella

Santuario di Oropa
Biella Oropa
Tel: 015-2555 1200
www.santuariodioropa.it

This sanctuary hotel provides comfortable period suites in a prestigious Marian Sanctuary up in the mountains, just north of Biella. A wonderful setting for meditation, walks, or even wine-tasting and gourmet trails. At the same time, consider visiting Chiostro San Sebastiano (tel: 015-252 3112, Via Quintina Sella, Biella), which serves simple regional fare in the romantic cloisters of a former abbey. €€

Bra

Albergo dell'Agenzia
Via Fossano 21, Pollenzo
(7 km/4 miles southeast of Bra)
Tel: 0172-458600
www.albergoagenzia.it
Four-star hotel housed in part of what was once King Carlo Alberto's neo-Gothic residence, now part of the premises of the University of Gastronomic Sciences. The 47 rooms are spacious and elegantly furnished and each bears the name of a famous "cru" of Barolo,

Barbaresco and Roero, underlining the strong link between the area and its culture, faithful to the philosophy of Slow Food.
€€€

Cogne

Hotel Miramonti
Viale Cavagnet 31
Tel: 0165-74030
This friendly family-run hotel is an ideal base for exploring Gran Paradiso National Park. It's furnished with antiques and antiquarian books, with a blazing fire in winter. The hotel's Coeur de Bois restaurant has a cosy, panelled interior and is noted for its local specialities and mouth-watering desserts. Pool and fitness centre. €€–€€€

Canelli

Agriturismo La Casa in Collina
Località Sant'Antonio 30
(2 km/1 mile west of Canelli)
Tel: 0141-822827
www.lacasaincollina.com

This lovely house sits on a hill overlooking vineyards and enjoys stunning views of the snowy Alpine peaks in the distance. There are six spacious and

comfortable rooms furnished with period pieces and antiques. Views from the breakfast room are breathtaking. Very good value. €

Sestriere

Miramonti
Via Cesana 3
Tel: 0122-755333
www.miramontisestriere.com

Panoramic hotel with an enviable position on the ski slopes and golf course. The spacious wooden-clad bedrooms are cosy and welcoming. €€–€€€

LIGURIA AND THE ITALIAN RIVIERA

Genoa has a shortage of individual and historic hotels in the city centre. However, this is more than compensated for by the huge range of stylish accommodation on the Ligurian coast. Note that a number of the hotels, especially standard beach hotels, close in winter.

Genoa

Bristol Palace
Via XX Settembre 35
Tel: 010-592541
www.hotelbristolpalace.com
Traditionally Genoa's grandest hotel, the Bristol Palace is on the city's most elegant shopping street, close to Old Genoa. The modest entrance belies its history and though rooms vary greatly in quality, some have appealing features, such as old marble bath-rooms. €€€–€€€€
Jolly Hotel Marina
Molo Porto Calvi
Tel: 010-25391
www.jollyhotels.it
This purpose-built hotel set on a pontoon was modelled on an ocean liner so is decked out with brass and mahogany nautical fittings. As the only hotel in Porto Antico marina, it enjoys sweeping views of the Old Port and the new architec-tural installations. €€€
Locanda di Palazzo Cicala
Piazza San Lorenzo 16
Tel: 010-2518824
www.palazzocicala.it
Facing the cathedral, this perfectly located 16th-century palace is a subtle showcase of contemporary design, with sleek bed-rooms equipped with computers and internet access. The hotel has equally charming period apartments nearby, and at mid-range rates. €€€

Alassio

Beau Rivage
Via Roma 82
Tel: 0182-640585
www.hotelbeaurivage.it
This late 19th-century villa has an old-fashioned charm. Some rooms feature frescoed ceilings; others have terraces. Guests have use of a private beach nearby. €€

Bordighera

Grand Hotel del Mare
Via Portico della Punta 34
Tel: 0184-262201
www.grandhoteldelmare.it
This exclusive hotel overlooks the sea and is popular for its peace, comfort and beautiful rooms. €€€–€€€€
Parigi
Lungomare Argentina 16–18
Tel: 0184-261405
www.hotelparigi.com
Centrally located with panoramic views over the beach and sea, this elegant hotel is very comfortable. The rooms are spacious and there is also a fitness centre. €€€

Camogli

Cenobio dei Dogi
Via Cuneo 34
Tel: 0185-7241
www.cenobio.com
Overlooking the sea and surrounded by a lovely park, this hotel offers beautiful rooms, a good restaurant, salt-water pool, solarium and private beach. €€€–€€€€

Portofino

Eden
Vico Dritto 20
Tel: 0185-269091
www.hoteledenportofino.com
This three-star hotel, set in a 1920s' Ligurian villa, is a

lovely family-run alternative to the Splendido *(below)*. Only 12 rooms but the ambience is delightful, as are the gardens. €€–€€€
Splendido
Viale Barratta 16
Tel: 0185-267801
www.hotelsplendido.com
One of the finest hotels on the Ligurian Riviera is set in an exclusive little port. It's a peaceful oasis with a splendid view of the Portofino promontory. Every comfort is provided, plus fine dining, health and beauty centre, and a private speedboat. €€€€

Rapallo

Excelsior Palace Hotel
Via San Michele di Pagana 8
Tel: 0185-230666
www.thi.it
This elegant hotel is beautifully appointed, overlooking the Gulf of Tigullio and Portofino. It combines a rich history with every modern, stylish amenity, including pools and a health spa. €€€€
Hotel Europa
Via Milite Ignoto 2
Tel: 0185-669521
Part of the Turin Hotels group, this art-nouveau hotel was restored to its former glory a few years ago. It now houses a fine restaurant, as well as a fitness centre. €€

Santa Margherita Ligure

Imperiale Palace
Via Pagana 19
Tel: 0185-288991
www.hotelimperiale.it
This grand hotel is located in the neighbouring, but less chic, resort to Portofino. The appeal lies in the old-fashioned decor, antique furnishings, spacious rooms

and excellent service. Private beach. €€€–€€€€

San Remo

Royal
Corso Imperatrice 80
Tel: 0184-5391
www.royalhotelsanremo.com
This luxurious hotel is the choice of high-rollers at the casino and Italian stars during the annual San Remo Song Contest in February. Large rooms overlook sea or hills and facilities include a fitness centre, pool, tennis courts and Fiori di Murano restaurant. €€€€

Sestri Levante

Grand Hotel dei Castelli
Via alla Penisola 26
Tel: 0185-487220/485780
www.hoteldeicastelli.com
The Grand, in a pleasant setting opposite a church, is surrounded by a large park. It features a converted tower and retains some original features, including stone fireplaces. There's a lift down to the private beach. Good service. €€€

Ventimiglia

La Riserva di Castel d'Appio
Castel d'Appio 71
Tel: 0184-229533
www.lariserva.it
Set 5 km (3 miles) outside Ventimiglia, this is a small place with a wonderful view of the Riviera dei Fiori and the Costa Azzurra. €€–€€€

PRICE CATEGORIES

Price categories are for a double room without breakfast:
€ = under €80
€€ = €80–160
€€€ = €160–280
€€€€ = more than €280

VENICE

Since there is almost no off-season in Venice, only a small blip in late January, many hotels are full all year round. Unfortunately, this means that many hoteliers try less hard than they might to keep guests happy. Hotel prices here can be up to 30 percent higher than on the mainland. The basic rules are: book early, check what view your room has and ask what the price differential is between "good" rooms and "bad" rooms (the same hotel can offer expensive large rooms overlooking the canal and pokey back rooms with little natural light.)

Top Hotels

Cipriani
Isola della Giudecca 10
Tel: 041-520 7744
www.hotelcipriani.it
A small oasis on the tip of the Giudecca, the Cipriani is the most glamorous of Venetian hotels. Lavish bedrooms are furnished with Fortuny fabrics, and amenities include one of the only private swimming pools in Venice. There are gardens, tennis courts, a yacht harbour, piano bar and a water-launch service, which whisks guests to San Marco. On the down side, service can be indifferent and quality of individual rooms is variable. €€€€

Danieli
Riva degli Schiavoni 4196, Castello
Tel: 041-522 6480
www.hoteldanielivenice.com
In a dominant position on the bustling waterfront, just a stone's throw from St Mark's Square, this prestigious hotel is rich in memories of eminent guests: George Sand, Alfred de Musset, Dickens, Balzac and Wagner. The splendid covered Gothic foyer, built around a courtyard, is an attraction in itself, and the rooms in the old part of the hotel are very plush, with parquet floors and gilded bedsteads. Avoid the modern extension, which is devoid of charm. Unless you are a celebrity, a regular or a big tipper, service can be supercilious to the point of arrogance. €€€€

Gritti Palace
Campo Santa Maria del Giglio 2467, San Marco
Tel: 041-794 611
www.hotelgrittivenice.com
The 15th-century Gritti, decorated with Murano-glass chandeliers and 16th-century damask furnishings, is the most legendary Venetian hotel and has a price tag to match. Renowned for its formal luxury, fabulous setting on the Grand Canal and discreet, attentive service, it has hosted Ernest Hemingway, Winston Churchill and Greta Garbo. Distinguished cuisine can be enjoyed on the canalside terrace. €€€€

Londra Palace
Riva degli Schiavoni 4171, Castello
Tel: 041-520 0533
www.hotelondra.it
This elegant hotel on the scenic Riva degli Schiavoni, overlooking the lagoon, has been restored to its neoclassical splendour. Tchaikovsky composed his *Fourth Symphony* here in 1877. The hotel has a romantic bar and an excellent restaurant. The staff are welcoming and far less supercilious than in many other Venetian top hotels. Rooms differ greatly, so it is worth paying extra for one overlooking the waterside. €€€€

Westin Europa & Regina Hotel
Corte Barozzi 2159, San Marco
Tel: 041-240 0001
www.europaregina@westin.com
Five minutes from San Marco, facing the baroque church of Santa Maria della Salute, this luxury hotel occupies a newly renovated 18th-century palace; the stucco-work and tapestries are now shown to great effect. The spacious bedrooms and suites are all decorated in traditional Venetian style. The restaurant spills onto a romantic terrace, and the service is first-class. The pastel rooms overlooking the Grand Canal are in great demand. €€€€

Superior Hotels

In terms of comfort and degree of luxury, but alas also in price, there is sometimes little to choose between these hotels and the "top hotels", but there can be big price differentials between "star", "superior" and "standard" rooms.

Hotel Giorgione
SS Apostoli 4587
Tel: 041-522 5810
www.hotelgiorgione.com
Situated near the Ca d'Oro, quite close to San Marco and the Rialto Bridge. The hotel interior is a tribute to Venetian style, with lots of chandeliers and Murano glass. Superior rooms are considerably bigger than standard ones, and are worth the slightly higher price. The restaurant, Osteria Giorgione, is very good. €€€–€€€€

Luna Baglioni
Calle Larga dell'Ascensione 1243, San Marco
Tel: 041-528 9840
www.baglionihotels.com
The Luna is the oldest hotel in Venice, dating back to 1118, when it was founded as a lodge for pilgrims travelling to Jerusalem. Countless restorations and refurbishments mean that it does not really look its age. The decor is currently in traditional Venetian style: a riot of Murano glass, inlaid marble and swagged curtains. The breakfast room is the grandest in Venice. €€€€

Metropole
Riva degli Schiavoni 4149, Castello
Tel: 041-520 5044
metropole.hotelinvenice.com
This popular patrician residence is decorated in fine 19th-century style and dotted with well-chosen antiques. There are excellent views over courtyards and the lagoon. The hotel is a little tricky to find, so request directions or, better still, take a private gondola to the jetty. €€€€

Molino Stucky
Giudecca 753
Tel: 041-522 1267
www.molinostuckyhilton.com
This former flour mill, transformed into a luxurious Hilton for 2007, occupies 13 industrial buildings and is situated just 5 minutes from Piazza San Marco. The hotel complex includes over 500 rooms (with 50 suites) as well as 14 meeting rooms and Venice's largest conference centre, not to mention five restaurants and bars, a rooftop outdoor swimming pool and a luxurious spa. €€€€

Monaco & Grand Canal
Calle Vallaresso 1332, San Marco
Tel: 041-520 0211
www.hotelmonaco.it
Benetton's stately hotel occupies a prime spot opposite Santa Maria della Salute Church, where the Grand Canal flows into the lagoon. It has been revamped with a contemporary twist: a glass-roofed lobby now forms part of the Ridotto, a private casino that was once the haunt of Casanova. €€€€

Saturnia & International
Calle Larga XXII Marzo 2398, San Marco
Tel: 041-520 8377
www.hotelsaturnia.it
A distinctive hotel housed in a historic 13th-century palace close to a busy shopping street by Piazza San Marco. The hotel has a medieval air, which, depending on taste, comes across either as romantic or austere. Rooms are intimate and comfortable. €€€

Small Hotels

Accademia Villa Marevege
Fondamenta Bollani 1058, Dorsoduro
Tel: 041-523 7846
www.pensioneaccademia.it
Set in the Dorsoduro district at the Grand Canal end of Rio San Trovaso within easy walking distance of the Accademia gallery, this remodelled Gothic palace maintains its charm, with delightful gardens front and

back. Reserve months in advance. €€€

Bucintoro
Riva San Biagio 2135, Castello
Tel: 041-522 3240
www.hotelbucintoro.com
This is a simply furnished, family-run two-star hotel on the waterfront, with splendid views over the Basin of San Marco and the island of San Giorgio Maggiore, especially from those on the top floor. The side rooms have a sweeping vista over the Riva degli Schiavoni. €€–€€€

DD.724
Dorsoduro 724
Tel: 041-277 0262
www.dd724.it
This intimate, arty design hotel, named after its postcode, is a softly lit urban retreat. Expect geometric lines and muted earth colours. The Guggenheim collection is next door. €€€–€€€€

Flora
Calle dei Bergamaschi 2283/a (off Larga XXII Marzo), San Marco
Tel: 041-520 5844
www.hotelflora.it
This friendly three-star hotel is set in a quiet alley off a prestigious shopping street, just five minutes'

walk from Piazza San Marco. The art nouveau-style touches, such as the staircase, are particularly appealing. Bedrooms vary enormously. Among the best are numbers 45, 46 and 47. There's a secluded garden and the courtyard provides a lovely breakfast setting. €€–€€€

La Fenice et des Artistes
Campiello della Fenice 1936, San Marco
Tel: 041-523 2333
www.fenicehotels.it
This highly individual hotel is set within a stone's throw of La Fenice, and has traditionally been popular with actors, musicians and artists. €€–€€€

San Cassiano Ca' Favretto
Calle della Rosa, Santa Croce 2232
Tel: 041-524 1768
www.sancassiano.it
One of the few hotels actually on the Grand Canal, the three-star San Cassiano is a converted 14th-century *palazzo*. About half the rooms have canalside views looking across to the Ca' d'Oro, but they vary dramatically in size and quality. The stairs are steep and there is no lift, so less agile

visitors are advised to stick to rooms on the ground floor. The hotel has its own jetty, so you can arrive in style in a gondola. €€–€€€

Hotels on the Lido

Des Bains
Lungomare Marconi 17
Tel: 041-526 5921
desbains.hotelinvenice.com
This prestigious four-star hotel is remembered for its role in Thomas Mann's *Death in Venice* and still finds favour with stars who flock to the September Venice Film Festival. It has a private beach across the road. A more atmospheric and characterful choice than the Westin Excelsior *(below)*. €€€–€€€€

Westin Excelsior Hotel
Lungomare Marconi 41
Tel: 041-526 0201
www.westin.com
Situated on the Lido, a short ferry-ride from San Marco, this huge five-star beach hotel is the grandest on the Lido, its impressive facade reminiscent of a Moorish castle. Attractions include numerous sports facilities and a free launch service into Venice. The

beach location makes it a popular choice for visitors with young families. €€€€

Venetian Apartments

Given the high cost of Venetian hotels (and the poor quality offered by many of them), apartments, particularly for a family or small group, can represent not just a more attractive option, but also excellent value for money.

Venetian Apartments
403 Parkway House, Sheen Lane, London SW14 8LS
Tel: 020-8878 1130
www.venice-rentals.com
Based in London, Venetian Apartments has a wide selection of individualistic apartments on offer. €€–€€€

Palazzetto Pisani
Canale Grande
Tel: 041-523 2550
www.palazzettopisani.com
Set close to the Accademia Bridge on the Grand Canal, this patrician palace offers a choice of two apartments, the larger of which has delightful views over the Grand Canal, and a vast drawing room. €€–€€€€

THE VENETO

At the top end of the market, the Veneto has a good selection of Palladian villas, which make a good alternative to hotels. The Veneto is home to Italy's most prestigious winter ski resort, Cortina d'Ampezzo, and accommodation here should be booked well in advance for the winter season. Verona and Vicenza have long been sought-after destinations.

Asolo

Asolo, with its picturesque historic centre, is a popular destination for foreign visitors and it makes a handy base for exploring Verona, Vicenza, Treviso and even Venice.

Hotel Villa Cipriani
Via Canova 298

Tel: 0423-523411
This luxurious ochre-washed Palladian villa was once the home of Robert Browning. Set in the low Veneto hills, the romantic Cipriani has a welcoming, lived-in feel. The pastel-coloured bedrooms overlook manicured grounds. Local facilities include golf, tennis courts and horse-riding. €€€€

Bassano del Grappa

This old-fashioned town is popular with foreigners in search of peace, quiet and *grappa*.

Bonotto Hotel Belvedere
Piazzale Giardino 14
Tel: 0424-529845
Some rooms in the centrally based Belvedere are nicely old-fashioned,

while others are more modern, and consequently have less character. The hotel also has a noted restaurant, Il Ristorante di Buon Ricordo. €€–€€€

Padua (Padova)

If Venice is fully booked or too pricey, consider making Padua your base. This historic city, famed for its ancient university and Giotto's frescoes, has much to offer and, while it lacks the obvious romance of Venice, it has culture aplenty. And Padua is infinitely preferable to the garish resorts nearby (such as Lido di Jesolo), or so-called "mainland Venice", the grim commercial and industrial area around Mestre.

Majestic Toscanelli
Via dell'Arco 2
Tel: 049-663244
www.toscanelli.com
This small, cosy four-star hotel lies in the heart of the old quarter, close to Piazza delle Erbe. Some of the bedrooms are lovely, if rather small. There is no restaurant, but the hotel is handy for exploring haunts in historic Padua, including the good local *osterie* and boutiques. €€€€

PRICE CATEGORIES

Price categories are for a double room without breakfast:
€ = under €80
€€ = €80–160
€€€ = €160–280
€€€€ = more than €280

Verona

One of Italy's most romantic destinations, Verona is ideal for a city break, particularly since several low-cost airlines now run flights here. Beds can be hard to find during the annual wine trade fair (Vinitaly, held in early April) or when operatic performances are being staged at the Roman Arena.

Due Torri Baglioni
Piazza Sant' Anastasia 4
Tel: 045-595044
www.baglionihotels.com
This grand classical *palazzo*, a Veronese institution, has been refurbished and converted into a luxury hotel. It has an excellent, if rather formal, restaurant with a fine wine list. There are eight suites as well as luxurious bedrooms. €€€€

Giulietta e Romeo
Vicolo Tre Marchetti 3
Tel: 045-800 3554
www.giuliettaeromeo.com
Set in the historic centre, close to the celebrated Roman Arena, this is a popular, good-value hotel. The comfortable rooms are decorated in good taste and have spacious bathrooms, but there is no restaurant. €€

Victoria

Via Adua 8
Tel: 045-590566
In the heart of the old quarter of Verona, this historic 12th-century *palazzo* has been creatively yet sensitively converted. The bedrooms are inviting and the reception rooms feature original Roman and medieval decoration. The staff are generally helpful. €€–€€€

Vicenza

Giardini
Via Giuriolo 10
Tel: 0444-326458
www.hotelgiardini.com
This recently renovated *albergo* is modern, comfortable and offers good value for money. €€–€€€

Villa Michelangelo
Via Sacco 35
Arcugnano, near Vicenza
Tel: 0444-550300
Set in Arcugnano, 7 km (4½ miles) south of Vicenza, this handsome 18th-century villa surveys the vine-clad slopes from its eyrie on a hill. Now converted into a stylish four-star hotel, it has a well-regarded restaurant. €€–€€€

TRENTINO–ALTO ADIGE (SOUTH TYROL)

Trentino is best known for its ski stations in the Dolomites. The jewel in the crown is Madonna di Campiglio, Italy's most prestigious ski resort after Cortina d'Ampezzo. Prices are relatively high but you can also choose to stay in furnished apartments, which are less expensive than hotels. Lake Garda is the other area in Trentino that is in great demand throughout the year (a hotel at Riva del Garda is listed on page 375). The overriding atmosphere of Alto Adige is Germanic rather than Italian, as befits this bilingual province. The accommodation ranges from quaint flower-bedecked Tyrolean chalets to family-run inns and grand castles.

Cavalese

Hotel La Stua
Via Baldieroni 2
Tel: 0462-340 235
This rustic-style hotel is set in the heart of the Alpine resort of Cavalese, which is popular both for winter skiing and summer rambling. La Stua is named after the traditional large mountain stove that is on display here. Pleasant wood-panelled rooms are cosy, individualistic and well equipped. The hotel has a steam room, sauna and hay baths, a popular therapeutic treatment here that involves lying under a huge pile of clean hay and sweating your cares away. The restaurant serves filling local specialities. €–€€

Cognola

Villa Madruzzo
Via Ponte Alto 26
Tel: 0461-986220
This grand hill-top villa is set in lovely grounds and is generally more appealing than most of the hotels in Trento, the provincial capital, 3 km (1½ miles) away. The villa's elegant interior is matched by pleasing service and good traditional cuisine, with dishes featuring mushrooms a local speciality. It's a good base for exploring Trento and the Dolomites, and non-residents can eat at the restaurant. €–€€

Lana

Virgilius Mountain Resort
Vigiloch Mountain
Tel: 0473-556600
www.virgilius.it
Designed as a chic chalet, Virgilius is a Zen-like lodge tuned into its alpine ambience, as soothing as it is functional and eco-friendly. The resort suits keen hikers, skiers and spa-worshippers, as well as those there for the hearty Tyrolean cuisine and panoramic views over a remote part of German-speaking Italy.

Levico Terme

Imperial Grand Hotel Terme
Via Silva Domini 1
Tel: 0461-706104
www.imperialhotel.it
This grand, sensitively restored Habsburg villa is a lasting reminder of what this area must have been like under Austrian domination. The atmosphere here is formal rather than welcoming but the impressive facilities include a health and fitness centre, indoor and outdoor pools, tennis courts. There is also a convention centre. €€–€€€

Madonna di Campiglio

Biohotel Hermitage
Via Castellatto Inferiore
Tel: 0465-441558
www.chalethermitage.com
This serene and welcoming hotel is one of the most fashionable places in this stylish ski resort. A good place to stay summer or winter. €€–€€€

Diana
Via Cima Tosa 32
Tel: 0465-441011
www.hoteldiana.net
This Alpine chalet is extremely popular during the skiing season. Bedrooms are in quiet good taste. Facilities include a sauna, steam room and solarium. Here, as in many other ski resorts, you will be encouraged to take half-board at peak periods. €€–€€€

Merano

Castel Rundegg
Via Scena 2
Merano
Tel: 0473-234100
www.rundegg.com
This fairytale Tyrolean castle (in fact a 12th-century fortified manor), set in landscaped grounds close to Merano, is promoted as a health and beauty farm. Some rooms have Gothic vaulting, beams and panelling. It's atmospheric, though the style may seem a little too contrived for some tastes. The upmarket restaurant can cope with special diets as well as Mediterranean cuisine. Facilities include an indoor pool, gym, fitness centre and a sauna. There is also a golf course nearby. €€€–€€€€

Villa Tivoli
Via Verdi 72
Tel: 0473-446282
www.villativoli.it

Peacefully located within its own gardens, this small Liberty-style hotel is an oasis of tranquillity, and deservedly attracts high acclaim. In summer, meals are served on a panoramic terrace. €€–€€€

Trento

Hotel Accademia
Vicolo Colico 4–6
Tel: 0461-233600
Set in a medieval building in the historic heart of Trento, this family-run hotel has great character. The charm

lies in such details as wooden shutters, geranium-filled window boxes, vaulted ceilings and gentrified rustic bedrooms, which have been fully modernised. The restaurant serves good local dishes and there is also an *enoteca*, for snacks

and sampling the local wines. Good service. €€€
Hotel del Buonconsiglio
Via Romagnosi 16–18
Tel: 0461-272888
This pleasant modern hotel is comfortable well equipped and close to the historic centre. €€€

FRIULI-VENEZIA GIULIA

Trieste

Grand Hotel Duchi d'Aosta
Piazza Unità d'Italia 2
Tel: 040-760 0011
This luxurious hotel, set in a handy position in the old part of town, is old-fashioned and dignified. Big, well-furnished rooms

are matched by efficient service. €€€–€€€€
Jolly
Corso Cavour 7
Tel: 040-760 0055
www.jollyhotels.it
This modern hotel is typical of the Jolly style, so good service and comfort abound. The downside is

the anonymous decor, in keeping with the chain's desire to also attract a business clientele. €€

Udine

Astoria Hotel Italia
Piazza XX Settembre 24
Tel: 0432-505091

www.hotelastoria.udine.it
Set in the historic centre of this lovely old town, this is a delightful and peaceful spot, with traditionally decorated rooms. Staff provide attentive and professional service; there is parking and a business suite. €€–€€€

EMILIA-ROMAGNA

Emilia Romagna has a great range of accommodation, with fine hotels in Bologna, Ferrara and Modena. There's a particularly good choice of bed and breakfast accommodation in Bologna, which compares favourably with 2/3-star hotels in terms of price, atmosphere and location but early booking is essential.

Bologna

Beatrice
Via dell Indipendenza 56
Tel: 051-246016
www.bb-beatrice.com
Set on the main city boulevard, linking the historic centre with the station, this lofty apartment has two guest bedrooms (shared bathroom) and views over the rooftops from the terrace. Convenient location for restaurants and sightseeing. €–€€
Break 28
Via Marconi 28
Tel: 051-649 4950
www.break28.it
An apartment on the top floor of a Rationalist tower with a minimalist designer interior to match. The location is central, between the historic centre and the station. €–€€

Ca' Fosca Due Torri
Via Caprarie 7
Tel: 051-261221
www.cafoscaduetorri.com
Set in the shadow of Bologna's medieval "twin towers", this central B&B boasts a gracious art nouveau-inspired interior, with breakfast served in the art deco winter garden. €€
Casa Zambeccari
Via Barberia 22
Tel: 051-332363
An upmarket B&B spot in a central, 17th-century *palazzo* with trompe l'œil frescoes and sophisticated yet quirky touches, such as Murano chandeliers and art deco beds matched by a breakfast banquet. €€–€€€
Dei Commercianti
Via dei Pignattari 11
Tel: 051-233052
www.bolognarthotels.it
Set in a side street close to San Petronio, this frescoed medieval palace is home to a stylish and seductive city-centre hotel. Well-restored public rooms lead to romantic bedrooms under the eaves, many of which have lovely views over the rooftops; free use of bicycles. €€€–€€€€
Grand Hotel Baglioni
Via dell' Independenza 8
Tel: 051-225445

www.baglionihotels.com
As the dowager of Bologna hotels, this 300-year-old *palazzo* is awash with Murano chandeliers, gilded mirrors, period furnishings and even its own section of Roman pavement. The elegant, frescoed Caracci restaurant is popular with visiting celebrities, such as Woody Allen and John Grisham. Weekend rates are good value. €€€€
Orologio
Via IV Novembre 10
Tel: 051-231253
www.orologio.hotel-bologna.net
In the heart of the historic centre, this former *palazzo* offers every comfort and excellent service. There are 29 very stylish rooms and five suites. €€€
Porta Saragozza
Viale Carlo Pepoli 26
Tel: 051-644 7437
Set in a quiet residential zone just outside the city walls, this is a charming bed and breakfast retreat; the reception rooms are studded with antiques; the two bedrooms have a shared (but spacious and modern) bathroom. €€
Royal Carlton
Via Montebello 8
Tel: 051-249361
This large hotel is very

comfortable and close to the centre of Bologna. The professional ambience and convenient location makes this a popular choice for executives and tourists alike. €€€€

Ferrara

Duchessa Isabella
Via Palestro 70
Tel: 0532-202121
This small, frescoed 15th-century *palazzo* is the finest hotel in Ferrara. Authentic features include inlaid ceilings and the reception rooms are studded with antiques. Facilities on offer include bicycles, a very popular form of transport in flat Ferrara. In summer, breakfast is served in a lovely garden. €€€–€€€€
Hotel Ripagrande
Via Ripagrande 21
Tel: 0532-765250
www.ripagrandehotel.it
This refined Renaissance

PRICE CATEGORIES

Price categories are for a double room without breakfast:
€ = under €80
€€ = €80–160
€€€ = €160–280
€€€€ = more than €280

palace, with good cuisine (served in the courtyard in summer), is set in the heart of historic Ferrara, close to the former Jewish ghetto. The only jarring note is the huge difference in size and quality between the bedrooms. €€€

Parma

Jolly Stendhal
Via Bodoni 3
Tel: 051-4216296
www.jollyhotels.it
Unlike standard Jolly hotels, the Stendhal rejects blandness in favour of character. Set in a period palace in the heart of town, it combines stylishness with sophistication and sheer comfort. La Pilotta serves classic cuisine in an elegant setting. €€
Villa Ducale
Via del Popolo 35/a
Tel: 0521-272727
A charming, welcoming villa set in award-winning grounds. Staff provide attentive service. €€€

Ravenna

Bisanzio
Via Salara 30
Tel: 0544-217111
This modern, comfortable hotel lies close to the city's Byzantine monument of San Vitale. It offers marble-clad interiors, spacious rooms, good breakfasts and a pleasant garden. €€–€€€
Palazzo Manzoni
Azienda Agrituristica, Via Ponte della Vecchia 23
Ravenna-San Zaccaria
Tel: 0544-554634
Set just off the Adriatic coast, but a world apart, this rustic 15th-century working estate doubles as a small country inn and cookery school. Expect rural charm, period furnishings – and bicycles. €€

Rimini

Duomo Hotel
Via Giordano Bruno 28
Tel: 0541-24215/6
www.duomohotel.com
The concept of this much-

hyped Ron Arad hotel comes complete with a Roman fish market, red lacquer doors, a bronze bar, resident DJs, and one-off design features, all devised by the world's most innovative hotel designer. €€€
Castello di Montegridolfo
Montegridolfo, Rimini
Tel: 0541-855350
www.montegridolfo.com
A medieval hill village, complete with drawbridge, gatehouse and church, is the centrepiece of this charming resort owned by celebrated local fashion designer, Alberta Ferretti. Apart from the boutique hotel itself, Palazzo Viviani, there are apartments elsewhere in the village, as well as five restaurants, golf, tennis, fishing and cycling. €€€–€€€€

Riviera Romagnola

Carducci 76
Viale Carducci 76
Tel: 0541-954677

www.carducci76.it
This curvy coastal art deco villa is also owned by the Ferretti fashion family and is the best-known of the Riviera Romagnola's trio of design hotels. Not far away, the Riviera golf resort offers accommodation in a series of eco-style villas. €€€
Agriturismo Paradiso
Via Palmegiana 285
Bertinoro, near Faenza
Tel: 0543-445044
This traditional farm estate lies among the vineyards, olive groves and woods between Bologna and Forli, only 15 km (9 miles) from the Adriatic. Two swimming pools, bicycles and fresh produce aplenty. €€
Il Villino
Via Ruggeri 48 Santarcangelo di Romagna
Tel: 0540-685959
Stylish inn set in a 17th-century residence in a village just inland from Rimini. The tone is set by the deft mix of antiques and design objects. €€

FLORENCE

Florence has lots of good accommodation but prices are quite high and you need to book well in advance if you want to have any chance of staying in a good hotel, or book with a reputable tour operator. Instead of staying in the city centre, which can be very hot in summer, you could head for the cool hills above the city, in such engaging villages as Fiesole.

Grand Hotels

Brunelleschi
Piazza Santa Elisabetta 3
Tel: 055-27370
www.hotelbrunelleschi.it

Close to the Duomo, this luxurious place was once a medieval prison. It is one of the most atmospheric city-centre hotels in Florence, with a beautifully restored church, Byzantine tower, some Roman remains and a private museum incorporated into the building. The bedrooms and suites overlook the Duomo. The Santa Elisabetta restaurant specialises in Tuscan dishes. €€€–€€€€
Grand Hotel Baglioni
Piazza dell'Unità Italiana 6
Tel: 055-23580
www.hotelbaglioni.it
This classic hotel retains its air of discreet elegance while providing luxurious and extremely comfortable rooms. €€€€
Grand Hotel Villa Medici
Via Il Prato 42
Tel: 055-277171
www.villamedicihotel.com
With its huge bedrooms, roof-garden restaurant and swimming pool, this

18th-century villa-hotel offers everything you could desire, including a good location near the station. €€€€
Helvetia & Bristol
Via dei Pescioni 2
Tel: 055-26651
helvetiabristol.warwickhotels.com
This is among the best luxury small hotels in the city, with many famous names on its guest list. Elegant and extremely comfortable rooms and suites (45 rooms, 13 suites). There is a good restaurant and a delightful winter garden. €€€€
Hotel de la Ville
Piazza Antinori 1
Tel: 055-2381805
www.hoteldelaville.it
This is a quiet and elegant hotel located in the centre next to Via de' Tornabuoni. The atmosphere is elegant but understated, and the service is discreet but correct. Bar, sitting room and terrace. €€€–€€€€

JK Place
Piazza Santa Maria Novella
Tel: 055-2645181
www.jkplace.com
This coolly elegant boutique hotel is the embodiment of chic, luxurious in a style that blends contemporary with tradition. Despite its understated luxury, it aims for a "home from home" style, assuming one's home has the requisite glamour, of course. €€€€
Lungarno Hotels
www.lungarnohotels.com
Lungarno hotels are a delectable group of boutique hotels and apartments clustered along the Arno, owned by the Ferragamo fashion dynasty. Each of the hotels has its own character.
Hotel Gallery Art is a contemporary space and has a noted sushi restaurant. In contrast, **Hotel Lungarno**, which overlooks the river, is a stylish take on a classic hotel, including a suite with a canopied bed

set in a medieval tower.
Hotel Continentale is intentionally hipper, and has a great rooftop restaurant. Central booking system for all hotels in the group. €€€€
Savoy
Piazza della Repubblica 7
Tel: 055-27351
www.hotelsavoy.it
Set on one of the city's grandest squares, the Savoy is a Florentine institution. It is still undoubtedly an Italian classic in style and service, with many rooms decorated in the Venetian style. €€€€

Small Hotels

Annalena
Via Romana 34
Tel: 055-222402
www.hotelannalena.it
Located across the Ponte Vecchio, opposite the rear entrance to the Boboli Gardens, this little hotel offers a lovely Florentine experience at a reasonable price. The frescoed entrance

leads to tasteful antique-furnished bedrooms. €€€
Beacci Tornabuoni
Via de' Tornabuoni 3
Tel: 055-212645
www.tornabuonihotels.com
This small and atmospheric hotel occupies the top floors of a Renaissance *palazzo* on the most elegant shopping street in Florence. Roof-garden restaurant; half-board compulsory. €€€
Regency
Piazza Massimo d'Azeglio 3
Tel: 055-245247
www.regency-hotel.com
This small 19th-century villa is perfect for those in search of tranquillity and 5-star luxury. The hotel has a lovely garden, beautiful furniture, a gourmet restaurant, impressive service, a central position and a price to match. €€€€

Florentine Hills

The hills around the city are always an attractive proposition, especially in

the hot summer months. Fiesole, 8 km (5 miles) outside the city, makes a good summer base.
Pensione Bencistà
Via Benedetto da Maiano 4
Fiesole
Tel: 055-59163
www.bencista.com
Situated between Fiesole and San Domenico, this small 15th-century villa is decorated with low-key rustic good taste and attracts a loyal clientele for its peaceful grounds, pleasant summer terrace and typically Tuscan cuisine. Half-board only. Closed December and January. €€
Villa Le Rondini
Via Bolognese Vecchia 224
Trespiano
Tel: 055-400081
www.villalerondini.it
Set in the hills 4 km (2½ miles) from Florence, this period villa has been modernised out of all recognition yet remains a characteristic villa in lovely

grounds. Reception rooms are airy, bedrooms are comfortable, and the restaurant is excellent, serving produce from the owners' family farm. What really sets this hotel apart from most of the city-centre hotels is the sense of space and the great views over the city. Facilities include a heliport, tennis court and a delightful pool set in olive groves. Regular shuttle service to the centre of Florence. €€€–€€€€
Villa La Massa
Via della Massa 24, Candeli
Tel: 055-6261
Fax: 055-633102
www.villalamassa.com
Situated 7 km (4 miles) north of Florence, this cluster of beautifully converted 17th-century villas radiates elegance. In addition to a piano bar and riverside restaurant, there are facilities for swimming and tennis and a free shuttle bus into the city centre. €€€€

TUSCANY

As a region with centuries of tourism behind it, Tuscany has the best range of accommodation in Italy. However, the popularity of Chianti and the delightful medieval hill-top towns makes bargains scarce. A popular option is to book a villa holiday or stay in an *agriturismo* property *(see page 371)*.

Arezzo

Arezzo is a prosperous city thanks to the gold jewellery trade and other local enter-prises. The surrounding countryside is worth exploring, particularly the rugged Casentino.
Castello di Gargonza
Monte San Savino
Tel: 0575-847021
www.gargonza.it
This meticulously restored medieval hamlet lies in the Tuscan hills between Arezzo and Siena. Accommodation is in modernised 13th-century apartments and

cottages. The excellent restaurant serves Tuscan dishes and there is a pool in the grounds. The hotel is part of the excellent Abitare La Storia hotel group of independent historic hotels (www.abitarelastoria.it). €€–€€€
Hotel Patio
Via Cavour 23
Tel: 0575-401962
www.hotelpatio.it
Innovative hotel in an old *palazzo* in the historic heart of Arezzo, not far from San Francesco. The colourful decor of each of the seven rooms was inspired by the writings of widely travelled novelist, Bruce Chatwin. €€–€€€
Val di Colle
Località Bagnoro, Scopeto
Tel: 0575-365167
www.valdicolle.it
Set in a tranquil position, this beautifully restored 14th-century house is 4 km (2½ miles) from the centre of Arezzo. There are eight elegant bedrooms with a rustic theme. €€

Lucca

Hotel Villa Rinascimento
Santa Maria del Giudice
Tel: 0583-378292
www.villarinascimento.it
This beautifully restored Renaissance villa lies on the road to Pisa, 9 km (5 miles) from Lucca, with panoramic views. The interior is simple yet lovely and the grounds include a pool and olive groves. Open March to October. €€–€€€
San Martino
Via della Dogana 7
Tel: 0583-469181
www.albergosanmartino.it
A warm, welcoming hotel in a quiet location, within the city walls, a stone's throw from the Duomo. Nearby private car-parking organised by the hotel. €€
Vallicorte
Compignano, 55050 Massarosa
Tel: +44 (0) 20 7680 1377
www.vallicorte.com
Good-value B&B in a beautifully restored Tuscan villa between Pisa and

Lucca. In spring and autumn the owners also run cookery classes, led by Gianluca Pardini, which you can join on an ad-hoc basis. €€
Villa La Principessa
Via Nuova per Pisa 1616, Massa Pisana
Tel: 0583-370037
www.hotelprincipessa.com
This rambling villa is deco-rated in stately 18th-century Parisian style. Bedrooms are dotted with antiques, while public rooms are hung with works of art. In a peaceful spot, 4.5 km (3 miles) from Lucca. €€€–€€€€

Pisa

Ariston
Via Cardinale Maffi 42
Tel: 050-561834
Literally in the shadow of the Leaning Tower, this hotel has been recently renovated to a high standard. €€
Hotel Locanda La Lanterna
Via S. Maria 113
Tel: 050-830305
www.locandalalanterna.com

Pleasant, no-frills bed and breakfast hotel, close to the Leaning Tower. Very good value for money. €–€€
Hotel Relais dell'Orologio
Via della Faggiola 12–14
Tel: 050-830361
www.hotelrelaisorologio.com
Conveniently located between the Campo dei Miracoli and Piazza dei Cavalieri, this gracious 14th-century manor house has been transformed into a stylish and elegant boutique hotel. Romantic courtyard garden. A luxurious treat. €€€€
Royal Victoria
Lungarno Pacinotti 12
Tel: 050-940111
www.royalvictoriahotel.it
The most characterful hotel in the city opened in 1842 and played host to Dickens and other Grand Tourists. Old-fashioned atmosphere. Rooms overlooking the Arno are in great demand, though they can be noisy. Private garage. €€€

San Gimignano and Chianti Country

Belvedere di San Leonino
Località San Leonino
Tel: 0577-740887
www.hotelsanleonino.com
Imposing 15th-century country house surrounded by grounds with olive trees and vineyards. Swimming pool. €€€
Hotel La Cisterna
Piazza della Cisterna 23
Tel: 0577-940328
www.hotelcisterna.it
Medieval *palazzo* with a recommended restaurant. One of the most atmospheric and popular hotels in town. €€–€€€
Hotel Pescille
Localita Pescille
Tel: 0577-940186
www.hotelpescille.it
Converted manor house 3 km (2 miles) southwest of San Gimignano. Outdoor spa, swimming pool and tennis facilities. €€
Tenuta di Ricavo
Località Ricavo 4
Tel: 0577-740221
www.ricavo.com
A highly rated hotel

occupying a series of rustic houses in a medieval hamlet, 5 km (3 miles) from Castellina. Pool; good quality restaurant. Open March–October. €€€
L'Ultimo Mulino
Loc. La Ripresa di Vistarenni
Tel: 0577-738520
www.ultimomulino.it
Atmospheric hotel in a converted mill. An ideal setting for exploring Chianti; pool. €€–€€€
Villa Miranda
Radda in Chianti
Tel: 055-787 4647
www.villamiranda.it
An appealing Chiantishire villa, run by the same family since the 1840s, which is ideally placed for trips into the vineyards. €€
Villa San Paolo
Strada per Certaldo, (Casini)
Tel: 0577-955100
www.villasanpaolo.com
This delightful classical villa is set on a hillside 4 km (2½ miles) from San Gimignano, and its terraced grounds include a pool and tennis courts. The bedrooms are very cosy and the service is friendly. €€€

Siena

Visitors choosing Siena as a base need to decide between a historic city hotel or a rural retreat in Siena province. City accommodation can be scarce in summer, particularly during the Palio race in July and August.
Certosa di Maggiano
Strada di Certosa 82
Tel: 0577-288180
www.certosadimaggiano.com
This unique 14th-century Carthusian monastery is the oldest such building in Tuscany. Now converted into a five-star hotel, it is adorned with antiques and offers a prestigious restaurant, library and lovely cloisters. €€€€
Garden
Via Custoza 2
Tel: 0577-47056
www.garden-hotels.it
This 18th-century patrician villa is now a comfortable hotel with formal Italian gardens and an indoor swimming pool. The hosts

are welcoming and the restaurant has panoramic views. €€€
Palazzo Ravizza
Piano dei Mantellini 34
Tel: 0577-280462
www.palazzoravizza.it
This atmospheric family-run villa is five minutes' walk from the historic centre of Siena. Although it is far from being one of the most expensive city hotels, it remains one of the most appealing and arguably the most typically Sienese. The breakfast room over-looks the garden and there is a good restaurant. Half-board encouraged in summer. €€€
Santa Caterina
Via Enea Silvio Piccolomini 7
Tel: 0577-221105
www.hscsiena.it
Friendly hotel set in a garden just outside the city walls, near Porta Romana. €€
Villa Scacciapensieri
Via Scacciapensieri 10
Tel: 0577-41441
www.villascacciapensieri.it
This delightful villa is set on a hill 3.5 km (2 miles) from Siena, with sweeping views of the city centre. It is surrounded by landscaped classical gardens. Simple rooms; swimming pool. €€€

South of Siena

Le Case
Castiglione d'Orcia
Tel: 0577-888983
www.agriturismolecase.com
A delightful hilltop farmhouse overlooking the Val d'Orcia. This is ideal hiking country, close to Castiglione d'Orcia and the spa centres of Bagni San Filippo and Bagno Vignoni. This rural B&B is run by an English-speaking Italian couple and comprises 5 double rooms each with private bathroom. Break-fast is included. €
I Savelli
Località Gallina, Castiglione d'Orcia
Tel: 0577-880266
www.isavelli.it
An oasis of peace in the middle of the unspoilt Val d'Orcia landscape, south of Siena. Set close to the spa centres of Bagni San Filippo

and Bagno Vignoni, these are sensitively renovated rural apartments with an outdoor pool. €€
Il Borghetto
Via Borgo Buio 7, Montepulciano
Tel: 0578-757535
www.ilborghetto.it
Three 16th-century *palazzi* in the heart of town, converted into a hotel. Rooms are small, but comfortable. Be sure to request one with views over the valley. The owner is also a tour guide. €€
Il Chiostro di Pienza
Corso Il Rosellino 26, Pienza
Tel: 0578-748400
www.relaisilchiostrodipienza.com
Beautifully converted medieval convent, with a quiet cloister, in the heart of Pienza. Very welcoming atmosphere. €€€–€€€€
Il Giglio
Via Saloni 5, Montalcino
Tel: 0577-848167
www.albergoilmarzocco.it
Small family-run hotel suspended above the city walls. Its 12 rooms all offer fine views over the lush Val d'Orcia. €€–€€€
Locanda dell'Amorosa
Località L'Amorosa
Tel: 0577-677211
www.amorosa.it
Sinalunga is certainly not the most attractive of Tuscan towns but it matters little to guests at the Locanda. This lovely medieval complex is famed for its gastronomic excellence, but the romance of the building means that the 14 bedrooms and six suites are as sought after as the restaurant tables. Swimming pool. €€€
Palazzo Contucci
Via del Teatro 1, Montepulciano
Tel: 0578-757006
www.residenzecontucci.it
This palatial 16th-century building designed by Sangallo still belongs to the aristocratic Contucci family. The Contessa rents out an apartment above the wine cellars. €€€

Grosseto and the Maremma

L'Andana
Tenuta La Badiola, Castiglione della

Pescaia
Tel: 0564-944800
www.andana.it
The former estate of grand
duke Leopold II has been
transformed into a refined
hotel by one of France's
most celebrated chefs, Alain
Ducasse, who has also set
up his own winery here. The
height of luxury. €€€€
La Parrina
Km 146 Via Aurelia, Albinia

Tel: 0564-862626
www.parrina.it
Genuine *agriturismo* set
among vineyards, olive
groves and orchards on
the Maremman plains. It
has retained the tradi-
tional decor of a country
estate. Excellent buffet
breakfast on garden
terrace. Swimming pool,
chapel, farm shop and
bicycles. €€

Hotel Il Pellicano
Località o Sbarcatello, Porto Ercole
Tel: 0564-858111
www.pellicanohotel.com
Chic hotel enjoying a
superb, isolated clifftop
position. Bedrooms are
housed in various buildings;
terraces lead down to the
private beach. Tennis courts
and swimming pool. Weekly
barbecues in summer. An
expensive treat. €€€€

Torre Di Cala Piccola
Stefano on the Strada Panoramica,
Argentario (8 km/5 miles) from
Porto Santo
Tel: 0564-825111
www.torredicalapiccola.com
Charming cliff-top hotel,
built around a 17th-century
Spanish lookout tower.
Rooms and apartments with
private beach and superb
views. Open March–
October. €€

UMBRIA AND THE MARCHES

Accommodation in Umbria,
Tuscany's rival, is plentiful
and varied, ranging from
period villas and aristocratic
town palazzi to small B&Bs,
country inns, converted
abbeys and farm lodgings in
beautiful rural settings. The
Marche, with the notable
exception of Urbino, is less
developed, although this is
changing with the increasing
number of low-cost flights to
the region.

Assisi

Subasio
Via Frate Elia 2
Tel: 075-812206
www.hotelsubasio.com
Assisi's most famous
hotel, next door to the
Basilica, a privilege you pay
for and one enjoyed by the
likes of Charlie Chaplin and
Elizabeth Taylor. Many
rooms have views and
terraces. €€€
Umbra
Vicolo degli Archi 6
Piazza del Comune
Tel: 075-812240
www.hotelumbra.it
A charming 13th-century
palazzo, set in an
atmospheric spot in the
heart of Assisi. The 25
rooms are comfortable,
though small and low-key.
The restaurant is very good,
with alfresco service on the
terrace in summer. €€

Gubbio

Hotel Bosone Palace
Via XX Settembre 22
Tel: 075-922 0688
Dante was once a guest in
the aristocratic palace, now

an upmarket hotel. The
rooms are comfortable, but
not all of the same
standard. The rooms and
suites overlooking the
valley are best. €€–€€€
Park Hotel ai Cappuccini
Via Tifernate
Tel: 075-9234
www.parkhotelaicappuccini.it
Set at the foot of the Gubbio
hills, this austere 17th-
century convent is now a
striking upmarket hotel.
Modern comforts include a
good restaurant, heated
pool, gym, tennis courts,
solarium and Jacuzzi, as well
as a very good collection of
modern art. €€€

Perugia

Brufani Palace
Piazza Italia 12
Tel: 075-573 2541
www.brufanipalace.com
This luxurious, recently
remodelled 19th-century
hotel is furnished with
antiques. The terrace of the
restaurant, where truffles
are a speciality, offers
lovely views across the
valley. €€€–€€€€
Hotel Fortuna
Via Bonazzi 19, Perugia
Tel: 075-572 2845
www.umbriahotels.com
A comfortable mid-range
hotel, just off Corso
Vannucci. Some rooms have
a small terrace. The garage
is a big plus point for
drivers. €–€€
Hotel Priori
Via dei Priori
Tel: 075-572 3378
www.perugia.com/hotelpriori
This elegant but affordable
hotel is conveniently located

in the centre of the city.
Some of the comfortably
furnished rooms overlook
the historic church of San
Filippo Neri, and others look
out to the valley below.
There is a huge terrace with
panoramic views; weather
permitting, this is where
breakfast is served. €–€€
Le Tre Vaselle
Via Garibaldi 48, Torgiano, Perugia
Tel: 075-988 0447
www.3vaselle.it
Umbria's only five-star hotel
outside Perugia, is a
historic manor house
belonging to the Lungarotti
wine estate. Modern
additions include two pools
and a health spa. The hotel
restaurant is one of the
region's best. €€€

Spello

Hotel Palazzo Bocci
Via Cavour 17
Tel: 0742-301021
www.palazzobocci.com
A stately hotel with a
frescoed interior and lovely
hanging garden and
breakfast terrace. Rooms,
though, are disappointingly
dull. €€–€€€

Spoleto

Hotel Gattapone
Via del Ponte 6
Tel: 0743-223447
www.hotelgattapone.it
A romantic hotel, oozing
charm and atmosphere,
with chic 1960s styling, a
curvaceous bar and picture
windows overlooking the
Ponte delle Torri. A popular
choice so book early.
€€–€€€

Il Castello di Poreta
Loc. Poreta (just off the SS3
Flaminia)
Tel: 0743-275810
www.ilcastellodiporeta.it
An enchanting castle
rescued from ruin by an
American ex-pat and a co-
operative of local volunteers,
now run as an excellent
country hotel and a top-
notch restaurant. A short
drive from Spoleto. €–€€

Todi

Agriturismo La Ghirlanda
Loc. Saragano, Gualdo Cattaneo
Tel: 0742-98731
www.laghirlanda.it
Former hunting lodge of a
rich Todi land-owner, lying
among vineyards and olive
groves, transformed into the
homeliest of *agriturismo*
establishments, with a
couple of cosy sitting
rooms, a bar and small
horizon pool overlooking the
Martani Hills. A 15-minute
drive from Todi. €€–€€€

Urbino

Bonconte
Via delle Mura 28
Tel: 0722-2463
Freephone: 176867148
Fax: 0722-4782
www.viphotels.it
This delightful villa-hotel is

PRICE CATEGORIES

Price categories are for a
double room without
breakfast:
€ = under €80
€€ = €80–160
€€€ = €160–280
€€€€ = more than €280

set within the famous walled town, near the Ducal palace. The interior is comfortable and elegant and the restaurant is well reputed. €€–€€€

Locanda della Valle Nuova
La Capella 14, 61033 Sagrata di Fermignano
Tel/fax: 0722-330303
www.vallenuova.it
In gentle hills surrounded by ancient oaks and within sight of Urbino, this large farm produces fine organic meat, vegetables and wine,

and schools horses. An unexpectedly modern conversion has given La Locanda the feel of a discreet modern hotel, where perfectly turned sheets lie on perfectly crisp and clean beds. Breads, pastas and jams are home made; water is purified; heating is solar or from wood stoves, supplied by the prunings from the farm woods where truffles are gathered in autumn. There is a lovely pool. €€

Valle Umbra

Il Chiostro di Bevagna
Corso Matteotti 107
Bevagna
Tel: 0742-361987
www.ilchiostrodibevagna.com
A warm welcome and a good night's sleep are guaranteed at this serene hotel in a converted Dominican convent near Bevagna's main square. Breakfast is served in the upper cloister gallery. €

Hotel Villa Pambuffetti
Viale della Vittoria 20
Montefalco
Tel: 0742-379417
www.villapambuffetti.com
Set in shady grounds of oak, cedar and cypress trees, this villa-hotel just outside Montefalco is a peaceful refuge. Breakfast is served in the courtyard in summer and the restaurant extends on to the terrace on warm evenings. Swimming pool. €€€

ABRUZZO AND MOLISE

Although gradually improving, these regions are still woefully behind most others in Italy in their range and quality of accommodation. However, the same does not apply to Abruzzese cuisine, which is popular across Italy.

L'Aquila

Hotel Duomo
Via Dragonetti 6
Tel: 0862-410893
A stone's throw from the Piazza del Duomo, this hotel is charming and offers a warm welcome. Very reasonably priced. €–€€

Sextantio Albergo Diffuso
Santo Stefano di Sassanio
Tel: 085-497 2324
www.sextantio.it
An abandoned hilltown, painstakingly restored and converted into guest

accommodation with some 40 period rooms in different houses throughout the village. €

Villa Dragonetti
Via Oberdan 4, Paganica
(7 km/4 miles from L'Aquila)
Tel: 0862-680222
www.villadragonetti.it
This hotel on the borders of the Gran Sasso National Park occupies a 16th-century residence with elegant bedrooms, a large park and a 16th-century Italian garden. €

Bomba

Isola Verde
Via G. Carboni 1, Lago di Bomba
Tel: 0872-860475
There is a campsite here at Isola Verde Tourist Centre, as well as cottages with 4–5 beds. The hostel with 28 beds is a cheaper option.

There is a swimming pool, and facilities for fishing, mountain bike rides and boat trips, making it a great place for family holidays. €–€€

Chieti

Masciarelli
Via Gamberale 1
San Martino sulla Marrucina
Tel: 0871-85241
www.masciarelli.it
This 17th-century baronial palace has been saved by local wine maker, Gianni Masciarelli. He and his wife have tirelessly preserved the building's authenticity, with giant wine presses, oak barrels and the chapel all restored to recreate the *palazzo*'s original character. There are 14 rooms and an apartment available. €€

Pescara

Esplanade
Piazza 1 Maggio 46
Tel: 085-292141
Elegant hotel with a modernised interior with spacious rooms. The Esplanade overlooks the beach. €€–€€€

Santo Stefano di Sassanio

Renaissance Palazzo delle Logge
Tel: 085-497 2324
www.sextantio.it
The revitalisation of this semi-abandoned hamlet is a model for rural tourism and sustainable development. There are currently six rooms in the Renaissance Palazzo delle Logge but the complex is being expanded (see page 296).

NAPLES

Caravaggio
Piazza S.Riario Sforza 157
Tel: 081-211 0066
www.caravaggiohotel.it
This 17th-century buildling behind the Duomo has 11 comfortable guest rooms. It is within walking distance of the city's most famous sights, churches and monuments. €€–€€€

Chiaja
Via Chiaia, 216 (1st floor)
Tel: 081-415555
www.hotelchiaia.it
Charming hotel close to

Piazza Plebiscito, popular with visiting musicians and artists performing at the nearby Teatro San Carlo. Good breakfast and very helpful staff. €€

Grand Hotel Parker's
Corso Vittorio Emanuele 135
Tel: 081-761 2474
www.grandhotelparkers.com
Established in 1870, this chic hotel is considered to be one of Naples' finest. The rooms are light and airy with wonderful views of the bay. €€€€

Grand Hotel Santa Lucia
Via Partneope 46
Tel: 081-764 0666
www.santalucia.it
One in a row of grand seafront hotel that manages to be refined without being stuffy. In a prime position opposite the Castel dell'Ovo. The rooms are spacious and some have hot tubs. €€€€

Paradiso
Via Catullo 11
Tel: 0861-2475111
www.bestwestern.it

Elegant hotel in Posillipo, away from the noise and pollution of the city. Its best asset is the panoramic view of the bay and Vesuvius. A bit of a trek to the centre. €€€

Parteno
Lungomare Partenope 1
Tel: 081-245 2095
www.parteno.it
Homely and perfectly positioned B&B on the first floor of a *palazzo* right next to the Villa Comunale. The corner room is best. €€

CAMPANIA COAST AND ISLANDS

Capri, Ischia and the Amalfi Coast are the main poles of attraction in Campania, with tiny Positano and the chic island of Capri taking most of the laurels (and the euros). Ischia is increasingly sought after, particularly for the spas. Sorrento has long been popular with package tourists and it still has great appeal. It is also a good base for exploring the Amalfi coast, Pompeii and Capri.

Amalfi

Hotel Luna Convento
Via Pantaleone Comite 33
Tel: 089-871002
Ibsen penned much of *The Doll's House* in this converted 13th-century monastery. In summer, breakfast is served in the Byzantine cloister. The hotel restaurant and pool are housed in the Saracen tower opposite. €€€–€€€€
Hotel Cappuccini Convento
Via Annunziatella 46
Tel: 089-871877
The monastic cells of this former monastery have been converted into comfortable rooms featuring period furniture. There is a pleasant garden, an Arab-Norman cloister and panoramic views. €€–€€€

Capri

Capri Palace Hotel
Via Capodimonte 2, Anacapri
Tel: 081-978 0111

www.capri-palace.com
Impeccable service and 85 tasteful rooms, four of which have their own swimming pool. One suite has its own star-gazing Jacuzzi. Capri's choice for the rich and famous. A serious splurge. €€€€
Villa Brunella
Via Tragara 24
Tel: 081-837 0122
www.villabrunella.it
Small, quiet hotel with a lovely flower-filled terrace, comfortable family atmosphere and classically elegant rooms. The restaurant has panoramas over the sea and the surrounding landscape. Swimming pool. €€
Villa Sarah
Via Tiberio 3/A
Tel: 081-837 7817
www.villasarah.it
Good value three-star hotel by Capri standards. In a tranquil setting, a 10-minute walk from the Piazzetta. Rooms with balconies facing onto well tended grounds. Breakfast on the garden terrace. €

Ischia

Il Monastero
Castello Aragonese, Ischia Ponte
Tel: 081-992435
www.castelloaragonese.it
Fairytale hotel in the former convent of the Castello Aragonese. Tastefully decorated with incredible views. A couple of rooms

have their own terraces, but those without can make use of the lovely communal terrace. €–€€
L'Albergo della Regina Isabella
Piazza Restituta 1, Lacco Ameno
Tel: 081-994322
www.reginaisabella.it
Rooms range from tasteful, country-house chic to contemporary opulence, with plunge pools or Jacuzzis on the balconies of the best suites. Friendly staff and a superb restaurant complement a somewhat clinical spa that is still one of the best on the island, brimming with thermal cures. €€€€

Positano

Le Sireneuse
Via Colombo 30
Tel: 089-875066
www.sireneuse.it
Luxury hotel in a patrician villa. Highlights include wonderful views from the terrace and most bedrooms and delicious Campanian cuisine in the atmospheric restaurant. There's a fitness centre, private boats, a cooking school and a lovely swimming pool. €€€€
Palazzo Murat
Via dei Mulini 23
Tel: 089-875177
www.palazzomurat.it
This hotel occupies a charming 18th-century *palazzo*. Recitals, concerts and exhibitions are

sometimes held here. Good value compared with Le Sireneuse. €€€–€€€€
Villa Franca
Via Pasitea 318
Tel: 089-875655
www.villafrancahotel.it
First-rate family-run hotel with 28 well-decorated and comfortable rooms, most with tiled floors and arched windows that look out onto the sea. Pool with magnificent views. €€€

Sorrento

Grand Hotel Ambasciatori
Via Califano 18
Tel: 081-878 2025
www.manniellohotels.it
A quiet Sorrento retreat, with a swimming pool and a large garden. €€€
Grand Hotel Excelsior Vittoria
Piazza Tasso 34
Tel: 081-807 1044
www.exvitt.it
The most refined of the grand cliff-top hotels, set among citrus trees. Most rooms have marble ensuite bathrooms and a balcony overlooking the sea or the grounds. Pool and private lift to the sea. €€€
Hotel Rivage
Via Capo 11
Tel: 081-878 1873
www.hotelrivage.com
A great budget alternative on the western edge of town, most rooms with small terraces facing the water. €–€€

PUGLIA

Although Puglia has largely been overlooked by package holidays, green tourism looks set to be the future for the region. Regional accommodation includes the delightful *trulli (see below)* in Alberobello, and *agriturismo*. Villa holidays and specialist holidays are also beginning to open up here. The experience of staying in a *masseria pugliese*, a fortified manor house, is something quite unique to Puglia.

Alberobello

This village is famed for its *trulli*, quaint conical stone houses *(see page 329)*.
Dei Trulli
Via Cadore 32
Tel: 080-432 3555
www.hoteldeitrulli.it
Furnishings here are simple to the point of austerity but that is all part of the fun. However, if the novelty of living in a cone does start to wear off, the pleasant grounds with swimming pool

may compensate. Half-board is available in summer. €€–€€€
Trullidea
Via Monte Nero 15-70011
Tel: 080-432 3860
www.trullidea.it
Trullidea is made up of 25 *trulli*, dating from the 15th century, all situated in the historic centre. Bookings can be self-catering, but there is a restaurant and a breakfast and dinner option. Bike hire is available. €€

Savelletri

Masseria San Domenico
Località Petolcchia (65 km/40 miles from Bari; 54 km/33 miles from Brindisi)

PRICE CATEGORIES

Price categories are for a double room without breakfast:
€ = under €80
€€ = €80–160
€€€ = €160–280
€€€€ = more than €280

Tel: 080-482 7990/482 7769
www.imasseria.com
Luxurious *masseria fortificata* with ancient origins, designed as both a fortress and a family-run working farm. Set in secluded gardens in a peaceful location, with swimming pool, gracious bedrooms, attentive service and a very pleasant outdoor terrace. €€€

Masseria Torre Coccaro
Savelletri di Fasano
Tel: 080-482 9310
www.torrecoccaro.com
This *masseria* is now a luxurious yet curiously authentic Puglian country residence. The setting embraces formal gardens, orchards, olive groves and a lake-style pool. Inside the hotel, a subterranean Aveda spa competes with a

hotel chapel, a bar set in a tower, atmospheric grotto-like bathrooms, and rooms occupying vaulted towers or old hay-lofts. Organic Puglian restaurant and a more international beach club restaurant. €€€–€€€€

Cisternino/Ostuni

Il Frantoio
(5 km/3 miles from Ostuni)

Tel: 0831-330276
www.masseriailfrantoio.it
This gentle old *masseria* B&B nestles in the Itria Valley, not far from the medieval town of Ostuni, and close to the sea. It is attached to a bio-farm which produces organic olive oil among other things. Superb Puglian country cooking is also on offer. €€–€€€

CALABRIA AND BASILICATA

These two sparsely populated areas in Italy's toe offer a wild, unspoilt beauty. Accommodation in Basilicata is centred around Maratea on the beautiful Cilento coast, Matera and its cave dwellings, Melfi and Potenza. Calabria's main hubs are Cosenza and Reggio di Calabria, the jumping-off point for Sicily.

Cosenza

Grand Hotel San Michele
Località Bosco 8–9 (55 km/ 34 miles from Cosenza, 16 km/ 10 miles northwest of Cetrano)
Tel: 0982-91012
This hotel is in a magnificent setting, with a sheer drop down to the sea. It offers all comforts, including tennis courts, a swimming pool and a lift to the beach. €€€
Excelsior
Piazza Matteotti 14, Cosenza, Calabria
Tel: 0984-74383
Simple but serviceable

hotel on a main piazza, near the train station. 44 rooms. €–€€

Maratea

Hotel degli Argonauti
Lido di Macchia, Marina di Pisticci
Tel: 0835-470242
www.argonauti.com
This large modern hotel complex on the Ionian coast features an enormous swimming pool and lots of summer leisure facilities. €€–€€€
La Locanda delle Donne Monache
Via Carlo Mazzei, 4
Tel: 0973-877487
La Locanda is a four-star hotel converted from a 300-year old convent. No vows of poverty here though: its rooms face onto a pool terrace and garden; the decor blends ancient and modern – bedrooms feature wrought-iron beds draped in designer covers. Room 9 has a multilevel bathroom in a grotto carved into the rocky hillside. €€

Santavenere Hotel
Via Santavenere 28/A, Fiumicello
Tel: 0973-876910
www.hotelsantavenere.it
In the '60s, Santavenere was the signature hotel for the *dolce vita*. A bound-leather guest book at reception tells stories of the legendary years, with names such as Burton and Taylor, and Frank Sinatra. With a cliff-top bar and restaurant, spas and a docking place for your yacht, this is discreet luxury at a price. €€€€

Matera

Locanda di San Martino
Via di San Fiorentini
Tel: 0835-256600
www.locandadisanmartino.it
To sample caveman chic, try this unique place incorporating a deconsecrated church and cosy rooms in cave dwellings, connected by *cunicoli*, secret passages in the rocks. Located in the

heart of Matera's *sassi* Historical District, and well placed for the city centre. €–€€
Sassi Hotel
Tel: 0835-331 0009
www.hotelsassi.it
This hip cave hotel is enjoying great success as a result of the makeover in Matera inspired by Mel Gibson's controversial movie, *The Passion of Christ*. It is one of several cave hotels that are undergoing a dramatic reinvention. Expect a labyrinth of Stone Age walls, carved facades, niches and curious-shaped courtyards. €

Reggio di Calabria

Grand Hotel Excelsior
Via Vittorio Veneto 66
Tel: 0965-812211
www.excelsior@reggiocalabriahotels.it
This first-rate hotel which faces the Museo Nazionale offers comfortable rooms and some of the best facilities in the region. €€€

SICILY

Accommodation in Sicily has improved greatly in recent years. Taormina

remains the prime resort on the island, but other centres, from Cefalù to Agrigento and Erice, are gaining in popularity.

Agrigento

Villa Athena
Via Passeggiata Archeologica 33
Tel: 0922-596288
A stylish 18th-century villa hotel very close to the

Temples (building permission would never be granted today), with a very fine view of the Temple of Concord. The rooms are modern and comfortable and the restaurant and service are both good. €€€

Cefalù

Cefalù is the rival resort to Taormina but, despite a

wonderful Norman cathedral, it does not have the prestige, nor the facilities or luxury hotels, of that established east-coast holiday spot. Nevertheless, it can make quite a good base for exploring Palermo and the north coast of Sicily. Note that, unlike in Taormina, hotels here close between October and March.

Baia del Capitano

Località Mazzaforno (5 km/3 miles east of Cefalù)
Tel: 0921-420003
This is a comfortable recently renovated Mediterranean-style modern hotel in an olive grove 5 km (3 miles) west of the town. There's a swimming pool and tennis courts at the hotel and a beach nearby. €€–€€€

Kalura

Via Cavallaro 13, Località Caldura
Tel: 0921-421354
www.kalura.it
Lying 2 km (just over a mile) out of town, this hotel has spacious rooms, all with a terrace. The grounds are attractive and there is a pool, as well as access to a private beach. Good for families, with an emphasis on sports facilities. €€–€€€

Erice

This lovely old village makes a far better base than Trapani for exploring the west of the island. The sea is some distance away but Erice is restful and atmospheric.

Baglio Santa Croce

Tel: 0923-891111
www.bagliosantacroce.it
Set just outside the village of Erice on the flanks of Mt Erice, this 17th-century former farmhouse with beamed ceilings and brick floors is the loveliest place to stay in this area. It has a swimming pool and great views towards Trapani. €€

Elimo

Via V. Emanuele 73
Tel: 0923-869377
www.charmerelax.com
This is a welcoming, cosy boutique hotel, tastefully converted from a 17th-century palazzo set in the middle of Erice. Panoramic views. €€–€€€

Moderno

Via V. Emanuele 63
Tel: 0923-869300
This is a pleasant if unremarkable hotel in the heart of the village. It's fairly old fashioned and decorated in simple yet good taste. Acclaimed restaurant. €€

Ficuzza

Antica Stazione Ferroviaria Ficuzza

Via Vecchia Stazione, Ficuzza
Tel: 091-846 0000
www.anticastazione.it
This is a former railway station that once served the Bourbon Kings' hunting estates. Now a small rural hotel, restaurant and jazz and blues venue run by an enthusiastic Sicilian jazz fan. Bedrooms, tucked under the station roof, are quiet, but with skylights rather than windows. €€

Palermo

Excelsior Palace

Via Marchese Ugo 3
Tel: 091-625 6176
Set off the chic and central Viale della Libertà, the Excelsior offers old-world charm, comfort and excellent cuisine, although it is now looking rather faded. It overlooks a pleasant park and is well located for a visit to the beach at Mondello. Note that there is a considerable difference between the size and quality of individual rooms. €€€€

Grand Hotel et des Palmes

Via Roma 398
Tel: 091-602 8111
This old-fashioned, slightly dilapidated but centrally located historic hotel has art nouveau-style public rooms and a chequered history that includes a Mafia convention on the premises. It is also where Wagner composed his Parsifal. Rooms variable in quality and size. €€€

Grand Hotel Villa Igiea

Via Salita Belmonte 43
Tel: 091-631 2111
Near the Lido di Mondello, under Monte Pellegrino 3 km (2 miles) north of the city, this is Sicily's most prestigious hotel. The palace was built for the Florio dynasty and has lush gardens, sea views and a grand dining room. The villa was designed to look like a Norman palace from the outside, although the interior is richly decorated with stucco-work and art nouveau furnishings. €€€€

Principe de Villafranca

Via G. Turrisi Colonna 4
Tel: 091-611 8523
www.principedivillafranca.com
This charming boutique hotel is very popular. Spacious rooms have vaulted ceilings and there is a pleasing blend of contemporary and antique furnishings. Very good bar and restaurant. €€€

Siracusa

Grand Hotel Villa Politi

Via Maria Politi Laudien 2
Tel: 0931-412121
This elegant, restored hotel is set in landscaped grounds overlooking the archaeological zone. It is slightly inconvenient for those without a car, but the delightful secluded atmosphere makes up for it. Good service. €€€

Hotel Roma

Via Roma 66
Tel: 0931-465626
www.hotelroma.sr.it
This very attractive small hotel is set in the heart of the lovely island of Ortigia. Recently totally renovated, it still retains its palazzo elegance and style and has plenty of period features. The restaurant, Vittorini, is very good. €€€

Taormina

This is Sicily's most prestigious resort, so accommodation can be difficult to find here. Bear in mind that a number of Taormina hotels try to insist on guests taking half-board, especially in high season.

Grand Hotels

Grande Albergo Capo Taormina

Via Nazionale 105
Tel: 0942-572111
Set just below the village, with stunning views of the bay, this large modern hotel is carefully landscaped into the rocks. Rooms are spacious and calming, with lovely views. Other big attractions include the grounds and the pool overlooking the rocky private beach. Of the hotel's two main restaurants, the best

one, the fish restaurant Il Pirata, is romantically set on the beach. Ask for a room with a view overlooking Etna or Isola Bella. €€€€

Grand Hotel Timeo & Villa Flora

Via Teatro Greco 59
Tel: 0942-23801
This exclusive place is one of Taormina's top hotels, with spectacular views over the Greek Theatre, the coast and Mt Etna. It has an elegant, old-world atmosphere, impressive public rooms and sleek service. €€€€

San Domenico Palace

Piazza San Domenico 5
Tel: 0942-613111
This is one of the best hotels in Sicily. The 15th-century monastery has been converted into a glorious luxury hotel and has an elegant swimming pool. San Domenico is famous for its location, its floral park and the vast, high-ceilinged rooms with extraordinary views over Mt Etna and the sea. €€€€

Villa Hotels

Villa Ducale

Via Leonardo da Vinci 60
Tel: 0942-28153
This small villa with only 13 rooms has a delightful atmosphere. The cosy mood is enhanced by a small library and period furniture. There is also a romantic breakfast terrace for breakfast and views of Etna from some rooms. €€€

Villa Fiorita

Via Pirandello 39
Tel: 0942-24122
This atmospheric villa has lovely gardens and grand reception rooms. The bedrooms are decorated in good taste; some have balconies or even terraces. Breakfast can be taken on the terrace. Pool. €€€

Villa Sant'Andrea

Via Nazionale 137 (in Mazzaro, 5 km/3 miles east of Taormina)
Tel: 0942-23125
This elegant, old-fashioned villa, dotted with antiques, is surrounded by exotic gardens, and the gorgeous setting includes a break-fast terrace overlooking the sea. €€€€

E ATING OUT

RECOMMENDED RESTAURANTS, CAFES & BARS

What to Eat

Italian **breakfast** *(colazione)* is usually a light affair, consisting of a *cappuccino* and *brioche* (pastry), biscuits or crispbreads, or simply a *caffè* (black, strong *espresso*).

Lunch *(pranzo)* is traditionally the main meal of the day but this is gradually changing as Italy comes more into line with Northern Europe, particularly in the north of Italy and in the industrialised cities. A traditional lunch is increasingly the preserve of the south or the leisured classes. However, when Italians have the time to indulge in such lunches, then an ideal one might run as follows: after an *antipasto* (hors d'oeuvre), there follows a *primo* (pasta, rice or soup) and a *secondo* (meat or fish with a vegetable (known as a *contorno*) or just a salad. To follow, comes cheese or fruit. Italians usually drink an *espresso* after lunch and sometimes a liqueur, such as *grappa*, *amaro* or *sambuca*. Traditionally, **dinner** *(cena)* is similar to lunch, but lighter. However, where it has become more normal to eat less at lunchtime,

dinner is the main meal of the day.

Every region in Italy has its own typical dishes: Piedmont specialises in pheasant, hare, truffles and *zabaglione* (a hot dessert made with whipped egg yolks, sugar and Marsala wine). Lombardy is known for *risotto alla Milanese* (saffron and onions), minestrone, veal and *panettone* (a sweet, Christmas bread made with sultanas and candied fruits). Trentino-Alto Adige is the place for dumplings and thick, hearty soups to keep out the cold; Umbria is best for roast pork and black truffles, and Tuscany is good for wild boar, chestnuts, steak and game. Naples is the home of Mozzarella cheese and pizza and is good for seafood, and Sicily is the place to enjoy delectable sweets.

Italy still claims the best ice-cream in the world, as well as the Sicilian speciality *granita* (crushed ice with fruit juice or coffee).

Where to Eat

With such a variety of restaurants on offer, how should you choose where

to eat? Even the names are confusing – what is the difference, for example, between a *ristorante* and an *osteria*? Although *osteria* means an inn, it can refer to a chic restaurant decorated in a gentrified rustic style. The number of courses may seem confusing too: if you don't want a multi-course meal, you could have a snack at a bar, *tavola calda* or *rosticceria* (grill), or forego the *antipasto* and take a *primo* and a *secondo* instead.

Address Tip

If there is an "r" in a restaurant's address after the street number, this identifies the property as commercial premises.

Restaurant Listings

It is hard to generalise about prices since much depends on the choice of dishes and menu selection – even noted chefs may offer a cheaper set menu alongside the main menu. The price ranges should therefore only be used as guides to value.

RESTAURANT LISTINGS

ROME

Agata e Romeo
Via Carlo Alberto 45
Tel: 06-446 6115
www.agataeromeo.it
This little temple to gastronomy has been the proud bearer of a Michelin star for over eight years. Traditional and modern Roman and southern Italian cuisine are seamlessly

blended and the wine list is among the best in Rome. Vegetarians are well catered for. Reservations essential. Closed Sat, Sun and Aug. €€€€

Agustarello
Via Giovanni Branca 98
Tel: 06-574 6585
Traditional, long-established *trattoria* specialising in real

cucina romana or offal. The owners use every part of the animal and create delicious offerings such as *coda alla vaccinara* (oxtail with tomatoes, pinenuts, raisins and bitter chocolate). Popular with the locals, so reservations are recommended. Closed Sun and mid-Aug–early Sept €€

Alberto Ciarla
Piazza San Cosimato 40
Tel: 06-581 8668
Set on Trastevere's friendliest square, this elegant fish restaurant is one of Rome's best and in contrast with the chaos of the market outside. Reserve. Dinner only. Closed Sun. €€€€

Bio Restaurant
Via Otranto 53
Tel: 06-4543 4943
As its name suggests this place is organic. You will eat well in this calming, earth-toned surroundings. Closed Sun. €€

Cantina Cantarini
Piazza Sallustio 12
Tel: 06-485528
Informal, bustling taverna serving simple but very good dishes. From Thursday to Saturday evening only fish features on the menu. At other times the menu is meat-based Roman and marchigiana (from the Marche region). Closed Sun and two weeks in Aug. €€

Checchino dal 1887
Via Monte Testaccio 30
Tel: 06-574 3816
The place for an authentic old-time family atmosphere, plus Roman cuisine of the offal variety – hardly surprising since this area, Testaccio, was the home of the slaughterhouse and Roman meat-processing industry. Not one for vegetarians. Reserve. Closed Sun, Mon, Aug and Christmas. €€€–€€€€

Cul de Sac
Piazza Pasquino 73
Tel: 06-6880 1094
One of the best-stocked wine bars in Rome. Middle Eastern influenced snacks, hearty soups and salads are on the menu. It gets packed so be prepared to queue as bookings are not taken. €–€€

Da Benito e Gilberto
Via del Falco 19
Tel: 06-686 7769
Tucked away in the Borgo area between St Peter's and the Castel Sant'Angelo, this intimate, family-run restaurant is a great favourite with locals. Its speciality is superb fresh seafood and there is no menu, but you are guaranteed a gourmet feast. Reservations essential. Dinner only. Closed Sun and Mon. €€€

Da Giggetto
Via Portico d'Ottavia 21a
Tel: 06-686 1105
Long a feature of the Ghetto area, this restaurant serves up tasty Jewish-Roman cuisine, specialising in carciofi (artichokes). The atmosphere is friendly and bustling, and the location – right next to the 1st-century Portico d'Ottavia is spectacular. €€

Dar Poeta
Vicolo del Bologna 45
Tel: 06-588 0516
Hailed by many as Rome's best pizzeria, A great selection of pizzas is matched by rich desserts. Be prepared to queue as bookings are not taken. €

Ditirambo
Piazza della Cancelleria 74
Tel: 06-687 1626
Numerous vegetarian options such as ricotta flan with raw artichokes and pomegranate vinaigrette. Extensive wine list. €€

Il Convivio Troiani
Vicolo dei Soldati 31
Tel: 06-686 9432
Run by three brothers, Il Convivio is one of the city's foremost temples to food and innovation. Equal emphasis is placed on vegetable, fish and meat, always combined with the unexpected. Closed Mon lunch and Sun. €€€€

Il Gonfalone
Via del Gonfalone 7
Tel: 06-6880 1269
This smallish space is a quiet gourmet experience. Lovely outdoor seating on a quiet street. The bread is home-made and the cuisine is a nouvelle take on Mediterranean. Closed Mon. €€

Il Pagliaccio
Via dei Banchi Vecchi 129
Tel: 06-6880 9595
This smart restaurant has a limited but creative menu with an emphasis on beautiful presentation and quality ingredients. Closed Mon lunch and Sun. €€

Il Simposio
Piazza Cavour 16
Tel: 06-320 3575
This Liberty-style restaurant adjoins the Bacchanalian paradise of the Costantini enoteca (wine bar). The cellars hold over 4,000 bottles of wine to match the delicious, creative food. Reserve. Closed Sun and Aug. €€€–€€€€

La Pergola
Via Cadlolo 101
Tel: 06-3509 2165
This sophisticated, rooftop restaurant with three Michelin stars belongs to the Cavalieri Hilton Hotel. The views are spectacular, the interior sumptuous and the menu a gastronome's dream. Reservations essential. Dinner only. Closed Sun, Mon and part of Jan and Aug. €€€€

Matricianella
Via del Leone 3–4
Tel: 06-683 2100
For the traditional, family-run trattoria experience, look no further than this popular restaurant near Via del Corso. The kitchen serves up classic, no-frills Roman fare, and service is friendly. Book. €€

Myosotis
Vicolo della Vaccarella 3/5
Tel: 06-686 5554
Fresh seafood, fresh pasta and excellent meats reflect the owners' commitment to using only the best raw materials. Closed Sun, Mon lunch and Aug holidays. €€

Obikà
Via dei Prefetti 26 (corner of Piazza Firenze)
Tel: 06-683 2630
Rome's only Mozzarella bar, but they serve plenty of main courses too. Minimal but welcoming setting. Cheap lunch menus available. €€

Piperno
Via Monte de' Cenci 9
Tel: 06-6880 6629
Traditional yet discreetly upmarket trattoria on a little piazza in the heart of the Ghetto district. The menu features classic Roman dishes such as veal and offal. Closed Sun dinner, Mon, part of Aug and Christmas. €€€–€€€€

Roscioli
Via dei Giubbonari 21
Tel: 06-687 5287
This deli-cum-restaurant has had rave reviews for its authentic produce and inventive food combinations. Try their signature dish, tonnarelli with grouper, pistachios and fennel seeds. €€

Il Sanpietrino
Piazza Costaguti 15

Tel: 06-688 06471
Located in the former stables of a fabulous 18th-century palazzo, Oscar di Mauro's acclaimed restaurant offers a mixture of ghetto food and Roman dishes Food is served with award-winning wines from his family vineyard. Reserve. Dinner only. Closed Sun. €€€

Sora Lella
Via di Ponte Quattro Capi 16
Tel: 06-686 1601
This authentic Roman trattoria is in a palazzo situated on the magical Isola Tiberina, next to Trastevere. Here you will find traditional food and home-made pasta. Reserve. Closed Sun and Aug. €€€

Taverna Angelica
Piazza Amerigo Capponi 6
Tel: 06-687 4514
This is a warm and welcoming establishment, ideal for a romantic, candlelit dinner. It is set in the labyrinth of lanes in front of St Peter's, known as the Borgo area. A constantly changing menu reflects the seasons, with an emphasis on seafood. Must book. Closed Mon–Sat lunch. €€€–€€€€

Trimani Wine Bar
Via Cernaia 37b
Tel: 06-446 9630
This very popular enoteca is the place to enjoy a glass or two chosen from an extensive selection of wines. Tasty snacks include torte salate (savoury tarts). There's also a fine daily specials menu. Closed Sun and Aug holidays. €€

Zi Fenizia
Via Santa Maria Del Pianto 65
Tel: 06-689 6976
Seasonal ingredients on fresh tasting pizza dough make Michele and Cinzia's kosher pizza among the best in Rome. Closed Fri pm and Sat. €

PRICE CATEGORIES

The price of a three-course meal for one (not including wine):
€ = under €25
€€ = €25–45
€€€ = €45–70
€€€€ = more than €70

ROME'S ENVIRONS

When the Roman heat gets too much to bear, escape to the sea at Ostia, or consider a trip to the Castelli Romani, the Alban Hills to the southeast of the city. Tivoli, with its lovely water gardens, makes for a good excursion in summer – you can dine out on the way back to Rome. Frascati, of wine fame, is one of the best-known towns just outside Rome, but there are many others that are equally good. Frascati is the place to eat *porchetta* (suckling pig). Nemi has a strawberry festival, where the red fruit is served in white wine. Castel Gandolfo is the place to try *guanciale* (similar to bacon), smoked with olive, oak and laurel wood and flavoured with red pepper. Quite a few places in this area offer special tasting menus (*degustazione*) at reasonable prices.

Civitavecchia

L'Angoletto
Via P. Guglielmotti 2
Tel: 0766-32825
Good, traditional seafood, soups and home-made pasta. Warm welcome and attractive setting near the promenade. Closed Mon and Christmas. €€

Frascati

Cacciani
Via A. Diaz 13
Tel: 06-942 0378
In the centre of Frascati with views over the hills from the terrace. Local dishes and fish are the specialities and, of course, Frascati wine. Closed Mon, 2 weeks in Jan and 2 weeks in Aug. €€€

Nemi

La Taverna
Via Nemorense 13
Tel: 06-936 8135
This inn is rustic and charming and serves traditional food. Reserve. Closed Wed and Jan. €€

Ostia

Allo Sbarco di Enea
Vicolo dei Romagnoli 675
Tel: 06-565 0253
Set in a Roman seaside port, this restaurant is perennially popular. Closed Mon and Feb. €€€

Palestrina

Stella
Piazza della Liberazione 3
Tel: 06-953 8172
Modern ambience combined with regional cuisine in this long-established hotel. €€

Tarquinia

Arcadia
Via Mazzini 6
Tel: 0766-855501
The young owners offer a warm welcome in this very pleasant, central restaurant. Fish is the speciality. Closed Mon (except July–Aug) and Jan. €€–€€€

Tivoli

Adriano
Via di Villa Adriana 222
Tel: 0774-535028
Close to the entrance of the Villa Adriana (Hadrian's Villa), this elegant restaurant features good, local specialities. Reserve. Closed Sun dinner in winter. €€€

Vesta
Piazza della Mole 19
Tel: 0774-333786
A fairly new restaurant which offers a contemporary take on Italian cuisine. Lots of fish and various home-made interpretations of the beloved *tiramisù* dessert. Dinner only except Sun; closed Wed. €€–€€€

MILAN

Milan is home to some of the best restaurants in Italy, many of which are institutions, such as Boeucc or Savini (*see below*), as famed for their formality and stuffiness as for their cuisine. Milanese food is fine, if you like risotto and escalopes, but most gastronomic menus also offer classic Italian dishes. There is also a huge range of foreign cuisine on offer here, plus culinary examples from every Italian region.

Restaurants in the centre of the city vary greatly, ranging from gourmet temples to *pizzerie* and fast-food joints. If you want a lively, more bohemian atmosphere, try Milan's canal quarter, the Navigli. The Brera is the place for fashionable dining. Since Milan is essentially a business city, some top restaurants close during high summer.

Alla Cucina delle Langhe
Corso Como 6
Tel: 02-655 4279
This is an exclusive Piedmontese restaurant offering such typical dishes as *tartuffo bianco* (white truffle) and *carpaccio*. Closed Sun and Aug. €€€

Al Mercante
Piazza di Mercanti 17
Tel: 02-805 2198
This friendly restaurant is in a great central location on the lovely Piazza di Mercanti. Specialises in local cuisine and a rich selection of antipasti. In summer, the ancient *loggia* is a very pleasant place to eat. Best to reserve. Closed Sun, Aug and 1–7 Jan. €€€

Armani/Nobu
Via Pisoni 1
Tel: 02-6231 2645
Innovative cuisine in the Emporio Armani. There is a sushi bar and a restaurant which offers fusion food combining the flavours of Japan with South America and the West. Reserve. Closed Sun and Mon lunch, Aug and Christmas. €€€–€€€€

Bice
Via Borgospesso 12
Tel: 02-7600 2572
This is a Milanese institution of the best kind: a reliable top-class restaurant serving exquisite food with friendly, attentive service. Classic Italian dishes, with some Tuscan specialities. During the seasonal fashion shows or when there is a big event in town, Bice tends to be full. Book in any case, since it is among the trustiest of celebrity restaurants in Milan. Closed Mon, Tues lunch and Aug. €€€–€€€€

Bistrot Duomo
Via San Raffaele 2, 7th floor, La Rinascente, Piazza del Duomo
Tel: 02-877120
This modern restaurant is on the top floor of La Rinascente, Milan's swanky department store. Recommended as much for its view of the Duomo as for the cooking. Milanese specialities predominate but classic Italian cuisine is also on offer. Closed Sun, Mon lunch and 3 weeks in Aug. €€€

Boeucc
Piazza Belgioioso 2
Tel: 02-7602 0224
This temple of old-school gastronomy is a Milanese institution. The atmosphere is formal but more characterful than that of its rival, Savini. Classic Italian cuisine is leavened with Milanese dishes and there is a cool portico for summer dining. Smart dress; book in advance. Closed Sat and Sun lunch, Aug and Christmas/New Year. €€€€

Cracco-Peck
Via Victor Hugo 4
Tel: 02-876774
This Michelin two-starred bastion of gourmet cuisine

is now under the guidance of top chef, Carlo Cracco, a disciple of the fabled Alain Ducasse. Expensive and outstanding. Reservations essential. Closed Sat and Sun lunch, mid-June–Aug lunch, and Christmas/New Year. €€€€

Il Luogo di Aimo e Nadia
Via Montecuccoli 6
Tel: 02-416886
Acclaimed as one of the top places to eat in Italy, with one Michelin star. Some Tuscan influence characterises the deceptively simple but superbly executed dishes. Reservations are essential. Closed Sat lunch, Sun, Aug and Christmas. €€€€

Il Teatro
Hotel Four Seasons, Via Gesù
Tel: 02-7708 1435
Superlatives abound in descriptions of Milan's Four Seasons Hotel and its two restaurants – especially Il

Teatro, where the cuisine is hard to fault. Reservations essential. Dinner only. Closed Sun, 1st week of Jan, and August. €€€€

Joia
Via Panfilo Castaldi 18
Tel: 02-2952 2124
Very popular restaurant specialising in creative vegetarian and fish dishes. The Swiss owner/chef, Pietro Leemann, holds a Michelin star. Reflecting his time in the Far East, many of his dishes have exotic touches. Reservations essential. Closed Sat lunch, Sun and Aug holidays. €€€€

Sadler
Via Conchetta corner of Via Ettore Troilo 14
Tel: 02-5810 4451
Creative cuisine in a modern, prestigious setting, with two Michelin stars. Professional service. Specialities include fish and white truffles (in

season). Must book. Dinner only. Closed Sun and part of Jan and Aug. €€€€

Sadler Wine and Food
Via Monte Bianco 2/a
Tel: 02-481 4677
Elegant, but informal, this is a smaller version of Sadler on Via Conchetta, with Innovative cuisine based on classical favourites. Open non-stop noon–11pm. Closed Sun and part of Jan and Aug. €€–€€€

Savini
Galleria Vittorio Emanuele 11
Tel: 02-7200 3433
Formal décor, an ultra-professional approach and classic Italian cuisine can be expected from a restaurant that has been perfecting its formula since 1867. However, the effect is somewhat marred by supercilious service and a cool atmosphere. Reservations and smart dress required. Closed

Sun, Aug and first week of Jan. €€€–€€€€

Torre di Pisa
Via Fiori Chiari 21
Tel: 02-874877
Set in the liveliest street in the elegant Brera district, this is an intimate and appealing Tuscan *trattoria* with gourmet cuisine inspired by seasonal produce. Arrive early to allow time for a drink in one of the Brera's numerous bars – try the Orient Express (Via Fiori Chiari 8), which recreates the atmosphere of the legendary train. Closed Sat lunch and Sun. €€€

Trattoria Aurora
Via Savona 23
Tel: 02-8323 3144
In the Navigli district, this atmospheric, very popular restaurant specialises in Piedmontese cuisine. Service in the delightful garden in summer. Closed Mon. €€–€€€

LOMBARDY AND THE LAKES

Also see the entries under *Where to Stay, page 375*, as a number of the best hotels in the Lakes have equally good restaurants. Villa-hotels, in particular, often provide lovely lakeside settings, and the cuisine makes use of fish from the lakes, as well as some more traditional Lombard specialities.

Bergamo

Da Vittorio
Viale Papa Giovanni XXIII 221
Tel: 035-213266
One of Italy's top restaurants, the young chefs are very creative, using the finest, seasonal ingredients. This is matched by attentive service. Two Michelin stars. Reservations essential. Closed Wed and Aug. €€€€

Lio Pellegrini
Via San Tomaso 47
Tel: 035-247813
Set in an atmospheric former sacristy, this restaurant serves Tuscan specialities in the garden in

summer. Must book. Closed Mon and Tues lunch. €€€–€€€€

Taverna Colleoni dell'Angelo
Piazza Vecchia 7, Città Alta
Tel: 035-232596
Lombard specialities are served in a 14th-century palace. This elegant restaurant has been open since 1740. Excellent service. Closed Mon. €€€

Trattoria del Teatro
Piazza Mascheroni 3, Città Alta
Tel: 035-238862
This old-fashioned restaurant serves simple but delicious, traditional food where specialities include polenta. Closed Mon. €–€€

Cremona

Martinelli
Via degli Oscasali 3
Tel: 0372-30350
This is an elegant restaurant located in an 8th-century *palazzo* specialising in local, traditional cuisine and fish dishes. Closed Sun, Wed and Aug. €€€

Gardone Riviera

Villa Fiordaliso
Corso Zanardelli 150
Tel: 0365-20158
Set in a luxurious villa, this excellent restaurant (one Michelin star) is one of the best in the region, perhaps even in the country. Mussolini entertained his mistress, Claretta Petacci here. Expect creative cuisine, with lots of fish, seafood and pasta. Closed Mon and Tues lunch, and Nov–mid-Feb. €€€€

Mantua (Mantova)

Il Cigno Trattoria dei Martini
Piazza Carlo d'Arco 1
Tel: 0376-327101
Set on a lovely piazza, Cigno offers delicious regional food and excellent service. Reserve. Closed Mon, Tues and Aug. €€€

Pavia

Il Cigno
Via Massacra 2
Tel: 0382-301093

Well-presented creative and modern cuisine is served in this small, atmospheric and intimate restaurant. The historic town of Pavia is 35 km (22 miles) from Milan. Reserve. Closed Mon, Aug and early Jan. €€€

Sirmione

Vecchia Lugana
Piazzale Vecchia Lugana 1
Tel: 030-919 6023/919 012
Set in an ancient palace close to the Sirmione peninsula, this *trattoria* on the lake was a favourite of Maria Callas and numerous Italian literary figures. Fish features heavily. One Michelin star. Closed Mon and Tues, 7 Jan–15 Feb; Nov open only Fri dinner, Sat and Sun. €€€–€€€€

PRICE CATEGORIES

The price of a three-course meal for one (not including wine):
€ = under €25
€€ = €25–45
€€€ = €45–70
€€€€ = more than €70

PIEDMONT

Piedmontese cuisine is considered one of the best in Italy and worthy of a gastronomic pilgrimage in itself. The keynotes are elegant French flourishes and filling country food. Dishes include truffle-scented risotto, creamy, buttery risotto, game, and Alpine cheeses. Typical dishes can be tasted in Turin's grandest hotels and restaurants. The region has a monopoly on many of Italy's best wines, including Barolo and Barbaresco, which are produced in vineyards on the western shore of Lake Maggiore. The success of the wine business has brought quiet prosperity to the villages of Asti and Alba, places traditionally connected with truffles and other gastronomic delights.

Alba

Locanda del Pilone
Frazione Madonna di Como 34
(5 km/3 miles southeast of Alba)
Tel: 0173-366616
Overlooking the hills and vineyards, this elegant Michelin-starred restaurant specialises in local cuisine. In autumn the *crema al parmigiano e tartufo bianco d'Alba* (parmesan and white truffle soup) is sublime. Desserts are excellent too. The Locanda also has six rooms if the gourmet experience becomes all too overwhelming. Reservations essential. Closed Tues and Wed lunch, Christmas/New Year and 20 July–20 Aug. €€€€

Asti

L'Angolo del Beato
Via Guttuari 12
Tel: 0141-531668
Entering the discreet doorway of this small, family-run restaurant is like going into someone's home. The décor has a distinct French touch and the cuisine relies heavily on

the regional and seasonal. Rabbit is often on the menu, often paired with tuna sauce; peppers with bagna cauda and delicious zabaglione with Moscato d'Asti also feature on the menu. Closed Sun, Christmas/New Year and 3 weeks in Aug. €€

Barolo

Locanda nel Borgo Antico
Piazza Municipio 2
Tel: 0173-56355
Highly acclaimed restaurant, Michelin-starred, set in Barolo's old centre in a country nobleman's house. The speciality is creative Piedmontese cuisine where the menu varies according to the season. There are two wine lists, one just for Barolo, the "king of wines", the other for a wide selection of international wines. €€€€

Rivoli

Combal.Zero
Piazza Mafalda di Savoia
Tel: 011-956 5225
This highly acclaimed restaurant in the Castello di Rivoli (home of the Museo d'Arte Contemporaneo) continues its tradition of innovative gourmet cuisine. Specialities include fish with black truffles, foie gras, beef – especially *gelatina di manzo al Porto*. Excellent service, and the restaurant is the proud holder of one Michelin star. €€€–€€€€

Turin

Al Garamond
Via Pomba 14
Tel: 011-812 2781
This elegant restaurant in the heart of the city specialises in creative modern cuisine. Antipasti are a speciality, and set menus featuring either fish or meat, or both together such as fish carpaccio with foie gras, are excellent value.

Home-made bread and delicious puddings are also very tempting. This is one of Turin's best-loved restaurants, so advance reservations are recommended. Closed Sat lunch and Sun. €€–€€€

Del Cambio
Piazza Carignano 2
Tel: 011-546690
This formal establishment, which opened in 1757, is one of the most impressive-looking restaurants in Italy, decorated with grand 19th-century furniture. The equally formal staff serve classic Italian cuisine with an excellent selection of Piedmontese wines. It is strange to think that Casanova, the great libertine, appreciated this symbol of restraint. Reservation recommended. Closed Sun and Aug. €€€€

La Pista
Via Nizza 262 (pedestrian entrance)
Via Nizza 294 (entrance by car which takes you up the amazing spiral ramp)
Lingotto
Tel: 011-631 3523
Named after the rooftop car test track on top of the Lingotto centre, this elegant restaurant has spectacular views over the city framed by the amphitheatre of the snow-peaked Alps in the distance. The food is excellent with traditional Piedmontese dishes alongside creative, original delicacies and a long, well-chosen wine list. Must book. Closed 1 week in Jan and 3 weeks in Aug. €€€

Sotto La Mole
Via Montebello 9
Tel: 011-817 9398
Opposite the Museo Nazionale del Cinema, overlooked by the Mole Antonelliana, this brick-vaulted little restaurant is very popular. Lovers of offal will be in their element, but if that is not to your taste there are plenty of Piedmontese

classical and innovative dishes to tantalise the taste buds. Booking advised. Dinner only except Sun. Closed Wed, 3 weekends in June, and Christmas. €€

Spada Reale
Via Principe Amedeo 53
Tel: 011-817 1363
This modern *trattoria* and restaurant is especially popular with young professionals, not only for its eclectic mix of Tuscan and Piedmontese cuisine but for its lack of stuffiness. Wine and beer are both available. Booking recommended. Closed Sat lunch, Sun and Aug. €€–€€€

Tre Galline
Via Bellezia 37
Tel: 011-436 6553
Tre Galline is a typical old-fashioned *piola*, and has recently been refurbished. As well as the Piedmontese specialities, there are lighter salads, pastas, soups and cheeses. Reservation recommended. Closed Sun, Mon lunch and Aug. €€

Villa Sassi-Toula
Strada Traforo del Pino 47
Tel: 011-898 0556
This 18th-century former cardinal's villa converted into a chic small hotel has an equally exclusive restaurant. Superb, subtle cuisine, including *carpaccio* and asparagus *frittata*, with sea bass to follow. Reservations necessary. Closed Sun and Aug. €€€€

Le Vitel Etonné
Via San Francesco da Paola 4
Tel: 011-812 4621
Very close to Piazza Castello, this is a very buzzing *vineria*-cum-restaurant. Perfect for a glass of wine and nibbles, for a light lunch or full dinner, the menu changes daily but, faithful to its name, always features *vitello tonnato* (veal in tuna sauce). A spiral staircase leads down to the very atmospheric wine cellar. Closed Wed and Sun dinner. €€€€

VALLE D'AOSTA

Fontina, arguably the best cow's milk available, comes from the Valle d'Aosta, a region that is also noted for its fondues, salami, terrines and cured meats. *Larda*, a rasher of pure fat, is traditionally served here with a plate of cold cuts. In the chilly Alpine region of Valle d'Aosta, the locals might recommend a warming *caffe valdostano nella grolla*, coffee laced with wine and *grappa*, which is set alight.

Aosta

Le Foyer
Corso Ivrea 146
Tel: 0165-32136/41845

Located just outside Aosta, this renowned hotel belongs to Classhotel Aosta. The restaurant offers "tastes of Aosta" – especially good cheeses. Closed Mon dinner and Tues. €€–€€€
Vecchio Ristoro
Via Tourneuve 4
Tel: 0165-33238
This former watermill is now home to one of the best restaurants in the area. It has one Michelin star for its excellent seasonal cuisine which features fish and specialities such as *bollito misto* (beef broth). Good, attentive service and very pleasant atmosphere. Must book.

Closed Sun and Mon lunch, June and 1–7 Nov. €€€€

Breuil-Cervinia

Les Neiges d'Antan
Località Cret Perrères 10
Tel: 0166-948775
Situated on a mountain around 4.5 km (2 miles) southwest of Breuil-Cervinia, this quiet inn comes into its own during the skiing season, when it is much in demand. Typical Valdostana cuisine predominates, from soufflés to trout. The *fonduta* (fondue) is particularly tasty, and there is an excellent wine list. Reservation essential.

Seasonal opening: 6 Dec–1 May and July–15 Sept. €€€

Gignod

Locanda La Clusaz
Località La Clusaz, Statale Gran San Bernardo (St Bernard motorway)
Tel: 0165-56075
Located 9 km (6 miles) north of Aosta, this delightful inn (with 14 rooms) offers specialities including grain soups, polenta and warming dishes made with chestnuts or bacon. Dinner only except Sat, holidays and Aug. Closed mid-May–mid-June and 3 Nov–3 Dec €€€

LIGURIAN RIVIERA

Ligurians have the longest lifespan in Italy, thus prompting hordes of researchers to investigate the merits of the local diet. Certainly, the cuisine is one of the healthiest in Italy and it has the greatest appeal to vegetarians of all Italian regional diets. Oddly, the Ligurians do not eat nearly as much fish as one would expect of a coastal region. Typical dishes include basil-scented *pesto* sauce, the region's signature dish, often served with *trennette*, ribbon-shaped pasta. Other specialities include olive oil, second in prestige only to Tuscan oil, salt-cod stew, excellent artichokes, salad leaves, and a range of vegetables.

Genoa

In the past, Genoa has had a reputation as an unsafe city, and the locals may try to dissuade you from exploring the restaurants of the historic centre at night. To avoid the centre, however, would mean missing out on much of what is best about the city: the rough-and-ready atmosphere of the tiny

trattorie hidden in the back streets. If you feel remotely nervous, you could take the precaution of checking out a few places for lunch and then returning to one nearby in the evening. If you dress down a little, walk confidently, and know roughly where you are going, then you should be as safe as you would be anywhere else. At heart, Genoa is a city for culinary surprises: don't be afraid to peer into a few places before deciding, on impulse, on a place that suits your mood. Most such tucked-away eating places are fairly cheap and yet they often have far more atmosphere than the grander restaurants in the rather soulless modern quarter.
Antica Osteria del Bai
Via Quarto 12, Quarto dei Mille
Tel: 010-387478
This illustrious restaurant set inside a fortress overlooking the sea is where Garibaldi dined in 1860 – not, however, its only claim to fame. On offer are Genoese dishes, although much richer than is generally typical of the local cuisine, and seafood

also plays a greater role, whether in pasta sauces or as elaborate Adriatic fish dishes. Must book. Closed Mon. €€€€
Gran Gotto
Viale Brigata Bisagno 69r
Tel: 010-564344
Set near Stazione Brignole, this is a classic and elegant spot dedicated to regional cooking and seafood. Try the seafood pasta, the hot seafood *antipasto* or the *trenette al pesto*, Genoa's signature dish. Reserve. Closed Sat lunch and Sun. €€€
La Bitta nella Pergola
Via Casaregis 52r
Tel: 010-588543
This acclaimed, elegant restaurant specialises in fresh seafood and offers regional cooking in a comfortable maritime atmosphere. One of Genoa's best restaurants, it has one Michelin star. Must book. Closed Sun dinner, Mon, and Aug; also Sun lunch in July. €€€€
Le Cantine Squarciafico
Piazza Invrea 3 Rosso
Tel: 010-247 0823
Lying between the old town and the port, the restored wine cellars of a lovely 16th-century *palazzo* make

this an atmospheric wine bar and restaurant. Wines from every region of Italy are on offer, accompanied by, predominantly, Ligurian dishes. Closed Sun, and lunch in summer. €€
Pansön dal 1790
Piazza delle Erbe 5
Tel: 010-246 8903
This lovely restaurant is situated in a safe but slightly dilapidated square close to Via XX Settembre. The restaurant is very popular with the locals, especially with families. Many Genoese dishes are on offer, including *pansoti al sugo di noci* (pasta with walnuts) and *pesto alla genovese* (pasta with basil sauce). Closed Sun dinner and 2 weeks in Aug. €€€
Zeffirino
Via XX Settembre 20
Tel: 010-591990
Set in the centre of the city, off the smart shopping

PRICE CATEGORIES

The price of a three-course meal for one (not including wine):
€ = under €25
€€ = €25–45
€€€ = €45–70
€€€€ = more than €70

TRANSPORT
ACCOMMODATION
EATING OUT
ACTIVITIES
A – Z
LANGUAGE

district, Zeffirino is a prestigious restaurant and was once frequented by Frank Sinatra. It is famous for the *pesto alla genovese*. However, veal, lobster and fresh fish are cooked fairly inventively. The chef is renowned for giving away his cooking secrets, so ask, if you're interested in the recipe. Reserve. €€€–€€€€

Lerici

La Calata
Via Mazzini 7
Tel: 0187-967143
This restaurant in the port is known for its seafood prepared with top-quality fresh ingredients. In summer you can dine on the terrace with fabulous

views over the Gulf. Closed Tues and Dec. €€€

Portofino

This is a chic destination, so expect even the simplest restaurant to charge above-average prices. (*See Where to Stay page 377* for details on dining in hotels here.)
Da u'Batti
Vico Nuovo 17
Tel: 0185-269379
An intimate restaurant with a very pleasant veranda. A bounty of good seafood is on offer. Closed Mon and Dec–mid-Jan. €€€
Il Pitosforo
Molo Umberto 19
Tel: 0185-269020
Numerous VIPs and the international yachting

fraternity meet here to compare boats and bank balances. Ligurian specialities as well as international cooking. Reserve. Closed Sun and Jan–Feb. €€€€

San Remo

This destination is popular during the February San Remo Song Contest and in summer.
Il Bagatto
Via Matteotti 145
Tel: 0184-531925
The emphasis here is on Ligurian dishes, both meat and fish-based. Lovely setting in the old *palazzo* Borea d'Olmo. Extensive, well-chosen wine list. Reservations advised. Closed Sun and July. €€€

Paolo e Barbara
Via Roma 47
Tel: 0184-531653
Elegant, small Michelin-starred restaurant in the heart of town. Booking essential. Closed Wed and Thur; 19–30 Dec, 23–9 Jan, 22 June–7 July. €€€€

Vernazza

Gambero Rosso
Piazza Marconi 7
Tel: 0187-812265
Vernazza is the most popular of the scenic Cinque Terre coastal villages, and Gambero Rosso, a small *osteria* by the port, tends to be full at lunchtime but quiet in the evening. Closed Mon (except Aug) and mid-Dec–Feb. €€€

VENICE

The following restaurants are listed according to the area *(sestriere)* in which they are located. However, the official geography of Venice is fairly complex and the best way of working out where a restaurant is located is often to just call up beforehand and ask which main church or square is nearest.

One disadvantage of Venetian life is that most foodstuffs are imported and restaurants are consequently poor value compared to the mainland. In the grandest eateries, you are often also paying for the service and the atmosphere rather than for top-class cuisine. However, on the plus side, many Venetian restaurants are famed for the stunning views they offer.

Castello

L'Aciugheta
Campo San Filoppo e Giacomo
Tel: 041-522 4292
Excellent, good value *bacaro* but also has a proper menu featuring a variety of dishes from Adriatic fish to truffles and oysters. Also popular for its

fine Friuli wines. Closed Mon. €–€€
Al Covo
Campiello della Pescaria 3968
Tel: 041-522 3812
Set close to the Arsenale ferry stop, this enthusiastically run restaurant serves fish fresh from the lagoon, wild duck (in season) and wonderful desserts; it also has a great wine list. Lunch is less expensive than dinner. Closed Wed and Thur. €€€€

Dorsoduro

Ai Gondolieri
Fondamente de l'Ospedaleto 366
Tel: 041-528 6396
Close to the Guggenheim museum, this popular restaurant serves up exceptional risottos. Must book. Closed Tues. €€€€
Antico Pignolo
Calle dei Specchieri 451, San Marco
Tel: 041-522 8123
Classical Venetian ambience in this highly regarded restaurant. Venetian and traditional specialities include fresh fish. Exceptional wine list and attentive service in four spacious dining salons

where well-spaced tables ensure your privacy. €€€€
(Antica Trattoria) La Furatola
Calle Lunga San Barnaba 2870, Dorsoduro 30123
Tel: 041-520 8594
Unpretentious place where local foodies go for fish dishes. Closed Mon lunch and Thur, Jan and Aug. €€€
Cantinone Gia Schiavi
Fondamente Nani, Dorsoduro 992
Tel: 041-523 0034
On Rio di San Trovaso, this canal-side wine bar is extremely popular with locals. Do as the Venetians do and enjoy *cichetti*, typical bar snacks, with a glass of wine. It is especially atmospheric at the cocktail hour, from 7–8pm. Closed at 9.30pm and Sun dinner. €–€€€
Taverna San Trovaso
Fondamenta Priuli 1016
Tel: 041-520 3703
This cheap and cheerful inn serves decent food in a lovely spot by the canal, near the gondola repair yard. Closed Mon. €€

San Marco

Al Graspo de Ua
Calle dei Bombaseri 5094/a
Tel: 041-520 0150

Located close to the Rialto Bridge, this fish restaurant is centuries-old and an absolute delight for those seeking local colour and traditional Venetian fare, leavened by classic Italian dishes. Closed Mon and part of Jan. €€€–€€€€
Al Volto
Calle Cavalli
San Marco 4081
Tel: 041-522 8945
This is Venice's oldest *enoteca* (wine bar) where you can choose between several thousand different wines. Extremely popular. Closed Sun. €
Antico Martini
Campo San Fantin 1983
Tel: 041-522 4121
Set near the Fenice opera house, this place serves Venetian and international cuisine. It was popular with such celebrities as Igor Stravinsky and Laurence Olivier. Serves Venetian and international cuisine. Reservations advised. Closed Tues and Wed lunch. €€€
Caffè Quadri
Procuratie Vecchie
Piazza San Marco 120
Tel: 041-522 2105
Situated in the most prestigious area of Venice,

this fine restaurant is awash with Murano glass and sumptuous furnishings. It is also renowned for its innovative and classical Italian cuisine. Prices are predictably high, but acceptable by Venetian standards. Reservations essential. Closed Mon Nov–Mar. €€€€

Canova
Luna Hotel Baglioni
Calle Larga dell'Ascensione 1243
Tel: 041-528 9840
Exquisite dishes served in the gracious surroundings of the Canova restaurant of the Baglioni Hotel. An extensive menu includes Venetian specialities as well as international cuisine, all prepared with seasonal ingredients. Excellent service and very extensive wine menu. Must book. €€€€

Harry's Bar
Calle Vallaresso, San Marco 1323
Tel: 041-528 5777
For many people, Harry's Bar is a symbol of gastronomic Venice. Although prices are high, standards are also impressive and if you can't afford a full meal here, you could consider coming for a

cocktail instead. This bar and restaurant, which was once a favourite haunt of the writer Hemingway, is now patronised mainly by very wealthy Venetians, expatriates, and American tourists. Expect good home-made pastas at exorbitant prices, with a small discount for paying in cash. Reserve. €€€€

San Polo

Da Pinto
Campo delle Beccarie,
San Polo 367
Tel: 041-522 4599
This is a rough-and-ready *bacaro (see below)* in the market area in the middle of the Rialto district. It's a good place to begin a wine crawl and great for authentic Venetian snacks known as *cicchetti* – the seafood variety are particularly tasty. Open 7.30am–2.30pm and 6–8.30pm. Closed Mon. €

Osteria Da Fiore
Calle del Scaleter 2202/a
Tel: 041-721308
This is a small but chic gastronomic restaurant near Campo San Polo; many consider it the city's

best. It has one Michelin star and its good food, wine and elegant ambience attract Venetian celebrities. Must book. Closed Sun and Mon. €€€€

Trattoria alla Madonna
Calle della Madonna, San Polo 594
Tel: 041-522 3824
This is a popular fish and seafood restaurant near the Rialto. The place is large and, owing to its good-value food (by Venetian standards), always crowded, but there's still a good atmosphere. Service, however, can be a little brusque. Reservations advised. Closed Wed and part of Aug. €€€–€€€€

"Bacari"

Venice's **San Polo** district is home to a number of cheap and cheerful *bacari* (singular: *bacaro*), wine bars that also serve simple but good snacks. Most close early (usually by 9.30pm) and they normally keep rather odd hours, so telephone first to check opening times if possible. Most *bacari* are hidden away in the warren of alleys around the Rialto district.
Recommended places are:

Da Pinto; Da Mori (Calle de' Do Mori); and Do Spade (Calle de' Do Spade). The addresses are usually meaningless: to reach your destination, you're best advised to go to the Rialto Bridge and then ask a friendly local for directions from there.

Cannaregio

Vini da Gigio
Fondamenta San Felice 3628/a
Tel: 041-528 5140
This cosy, atmospheric inn has a canalside setting and good food, featuring both meat and fish. Reserve. Closed Mon and part of Jan and Aug. €€

Santa Croce

Antica Bessetta
Salizada de Cà' Zusto 1395
Tel: 041-721687
This authentic family-run *trattoria*, one of the city's oldest, is set somewhat off the beaten track, near San Giacomo dell'Orio. It serves regional cuisine and is fairly good value despite recent price rises. Closed Tues and Wed lunch. €€€–€€€€

THE VENETO

The Veneto has a distinguished culinary tradition. At Christmas, Verona produces *pandoro*, a distant cousin to *panettone* and just as delicious. Seafood is also on the menu, with specialities from the Adriatic including squid, mussels, mackerel, brill, bass and mullet. The region is also the biggest producer of poultry in Italy, so chicken is generally good here; salami is also recommended. Local pasta includes *bigoli*, wholewheat spaghetti, often served with *salsa*, a sauce made with anchovies and garlic. As for wine, you can explore the vineyards that produce Soave, sparkling Prosecco and full-bodied Bardolino and Merlot.

The Island of Burano

Trattoria Da Romano
Piazza Galuppi 221
Tel: 041-730030
Set on the colourful island of Burano, this is a popular, artistic *trattoria*, over-looking the sea, offering an artistic ambience, casual welcome and straightforward cuisine. Catch *motonave* No. 12 back to central Venice. Closed Tues and Dec. €€

Padua (Padova)

Dotto di Campagna
Via Randaccio 4, Località Torre (Ponte di Brenta)
Tel: 049-625469
This rustic restaurant is set 6 km (4 miles) northeast of town but it's worth the trip,

to taste authentic Veneto cuisine. Try the gnocchi, roast meats, *pasta e fagioli* (pasta and beans) and *baccalà* (salt cod). Reserve. Closed Sun dinner, Mon and Aug. €€–€€€

Verona

Expect above-average prices in this chic, perenially popular city. Many restaurants here are great, matching unusual cuisine with atmospheric settings and lovely Veneto wines such as Bardolino.

Bottega Del Vino
Via Scudo di Francia 3
Tel: 045-800 4535
Set in the historic heart of town, just off Piazza delle Erbe, this traditional Veronese inn (*osteria*) was

a haunt of the Futurist painters such as Boccioni. It is still frequented by an intellectual and artistic set, as well as by those who simply appreciate Veronese and classic Italian cooking Closed Tues except July and Aug. €€€

Locanda di Castelvecchio
Corso Castelvecchio 21/A
Tel: 045-803 0097
This elegant restaurant on a beautiful corner of the old town still has the ambience of an old *osteria*. Friendly

PRICE CATEGORIES

The price of a three-course meal for one (not including wine):
€ = under €25
€€ = €25–45
€€€ = €45–70
€€€€ = more than €70

service, exquisite Veronic cuisine. Closed Tues and Wed lunch. €€

12 Apostoli
Vicolo Corticella San Marco 3
Tel: 045-596999
Just off Piazza delle Erbe, this atmospheric family-run restaurant is one of the best places to eat in Italy. It produces Veronese and classic Italian cuisine,
including rabbit tagliatelle and squid risotto. Reserve. Closed Sun dinner, Mon and mid-June–5 July. €€€–€€€€

Il Desco
Via Dietro San Sebastiano 7
Tel: 045-595358
Located in a lovely old *palazzo*, this is a very elegant, highly acclaimed restaurant (two Michelin
stars), one of Italy's best. Elia Rizzo combines rare and expensive ingredients with the more traditional. Must book. Closed Sun, Mon and festivals. €€€€

Vicenza

Antico Ristorante Agli Schioppi
Contrà del Castello 26
Tel: 0444-543701
Located in the historic heart of the city, this rustic yet elegant restaurant housed in a *palazzo* specialises in traditional cuisine from the Veneto. Outside dining available in the summer. Closed Sat dinner, Sun, 1–6 Jan and 20 July–15 Aug. €€–€€€

TRENTINO-ALTO ADIGE

The regions of Trentino and Alto Adige offer mountain food with an Italian or Austrian twist. Wholesome dishes prevail, from hearty pork and beef sausages to polenta and pulse-filled soups. By Lake Garda and Trentino's lakes and mountain streams, fish dishes include Alpine trout poached in white wine.

In Alto Adige, Austrian influences are strong, with foods including smoked meats, sauerkraut, red-cabbage goulash, dumplings, gnocchi and apple strudel all popular. Check *Where to Stay*, pages 382–3, for entries on such excellent castle-restaurants as Castel Rundegg.

Bolzano (Bozen)

Laurin
Parkhotel Laurin, Via Laurin 4
Tel: 0471-311000
Liberty-style, very pleasant restaurant. The Mediterranean cooking of chef Luca Verdolini is highly innovative. Very good wine list and an attractive bar. Closed Sun lunch. €€–€€€

Pinzolo

Mezzosoldo
Spiazzo Rendena, Near Pinzolo, Trentino
Tel: 0465-801067
This cosy inn is in the mountainous Val Rendena area south of Pinzolo, within acceptable driving distance of the ski resort of
Madonna di Campiglio. (You can always stay in the inn overnight, if you can't face the drive back.) The reason for making the journey is simple: great home-cooking. The Lorenzi family pick the ingredients, including herbs and mushrooms, themselves. Meals begin with 10 (light) starters, including *radicchio dell'orso*, an edible root only exposed by avalanches. Closed part of May and Oct. €€–€€€

Trento

Chiesa
Parco San Marco 64
Tel: 0461-238766
Set on one floor of a 17th-century cloistered palace, this elegant restaurant
serves very refined food. Closed Sun. €€–€€€

Lo Scrigno del Duomo
Piazza del Duomo 29
Tel: 0461-220030
Elegant, minimalist restaurant set in an old *palazzo*. The restaurant (which holds a Michelin star) is noted for its regional cuisine, while the *enoteca* (wine bar) serves snacks and a wide choice of wines. Booking advised. Closed Mon. €€€–€€€€

Osteria a Le Due Spade
Via Don Rizzi 11 (corner Via Verdi)
Tel: 0461-234343
This 16th-century *osteria* is a temple to gastronomy specialising in the rich flavours of Trentino. It holds one Michelin star – so booking essential. €€€€

FRIULI-VENEZIA GIULIA

The cuisine of Friuli-Venezia Giulia, like the region, is often described as "not really Italian", which is hardly surprising given that the frontiers touch both the former Yugoslavia and Austria. Expect a lot of goulash, boiled pork and Viennese sausages. As a general rule, the cuisine of the hinterland is more frugal, while Venetian culinary influences prevail on the coast, with seafood generally good in Trieste. As for Friuli wines, the Italians have long recognised them as being among the great regional wines but the rest of the world has been slower to catch on.

Trieste

Al Bagatto
Via Venezian 2 (corner of Via Cadorna)
Tel: 040-301771
Flavoursome seafood and fish served in small but gracious surroundings. Very popular; booking advised. Closed Sun. €€–€€

All Faro
Scala Sforzi 2
Tel: 040-410092
A 10-minute drive out of town, on the road to Friuli, this restaurant is at the foot of the Vittoria lighthouse facing the Gulf of Trieste. From the beautiful terrace there are fabulous views and some excellent seafood dishes
and wines to sample. Under the skilful eye of Franco Eichberger, who recently took over the running of this establish-ment, this restaurant is now one of the best places in the area. Closed Sun and Mon. €€

Antica Trattoria Suban
Via Comici 2
Tel: 040-54368
Run by the same family for generations, this restaurant is probably the most traditional of Trieste's eating places. Friendly and simple in style, it serves good regional cuisine. Summer bower. Reserve. Closed Mon lunch, Tues and part of Jan and Aug. €€€

Udine

Alla Vedova
Via Tavagnacco 9
Tel: 0432-470291
This is a very old Friulian restaurant, with outdoor tables in summer. Good traditional cooking. Reserve. Closed Sun dinner and Mon. €€–€€

Là di Moret
Viale Tricesimo 276
Tel: 0432-545096
Welcoming, family-run restaurant in the Là di Moret Hotel. The traditional cooking is based on classical and Friulian influences. Closed Sun dinner and Mon lunch and 2 weeks in July/Aug. €€–€€

EMILIA-ROMAGNA

Although it is the gastronomic capital of Italy, Bologna also has its fair share of traditional taverns serving simple hearty cuisine. The city is famous for pasta of every description, although perhaps most famously for spaghetti bolognese, and for velvety sauces, salami and cold meats. Food is good across the region and each major town has its own specialities, from Parmesan and Parma ham in Parma to *aceto balsamico*, Italy's best vinegar, in Modena. Emilian wines include Trebbiano, Cabernet Sauvignon and Lambrusco.

Bologna

Buca San Petronio
Via de'Musei 4
Tel: 051-224589
Excellent-value restaurant set in a *palazzo* in the historical centre. Traditional, regional cooking and fresh pasta. Outdoor dining in summer. Closed Wed dinner (except during holidays/festivals) and Aug. €–€€

Caffè Commercianti
Strada Maggiore 23/c
Tel: 051-266539
Well-known watering hole for the litterati and intelligentsia of Bologna. Serves the best martini in town. €–€€

Cantina Bentivoglio
Via Mascarella 4b
Tel: 051-265416
Set in the cellars of a *palazzo*, this restaurant attracts a young crowd. Emilian specialities and live music. Closed Mon. €€

Da Bertino
Via delle Lame 55
Tel: 051-522230
This is a lively Emilian *trattoria*, with good cooking. Closed Sun and Mon dinner on alternate months, Sat dinner in July, and 5 Aug–4 Sept. €€

La Pernice e La Gallina
Via dell'Abbadia 4
Tel: 051-269922
Highly acclaimed restaurant in the historic centre of Bologna. Traditional and innovative cuisine are skilfully blended to produce gourmet delights. Closed Sun and Mon lunch, and part of Aug. €€€–€€€€

Le Stanze
Via di Borgo San Pietro 1
Tel: 051-228767
Housed in a 16th-century former chapel, this is the place where the smart set go to be seen. Closed Sat lunch. €€

Pappagallo
Piazza della Mercanzia 3c
Tel: 051-231200
Very popular restaurant not only for its location, near the two towers, but also for its Bolognese specialities. Good fish dishes. Closed

Sun, Sat in June and July, and part of Aug. €€€

Trattoria Battibecco
Via Battibecco 4
Tel: 051-223298
This elegant one-star Michelin restaurant is the place to sample the rich flavours of Bolognese cuisine. Must book. Closed Sat lunch, Sun and holidays. €€€€

Ferrara

La Romantica
Via Ripagrande 36
Tel: 0532-765975
Set in the heart of the medieval quarter, this well-established restaurant serves classic Italian cuisine with a few Jewish *Ferrarese* dishes. Closed Sun dinner, Wed, and part of July and Aug. €€–€€€

Modena

Oreste
Piazza Roma 31
Tel: 059-243324
This traditional restaurant has a pleasant "retro" atmosphere. Specialities are meat and home-made pasta. Closed Sun dinner and Wed, part of July and Christmas/New Year. €€

Fini
Rua Frati Minori 54
Tel: 059-223314
This is a smart yet homely Michelin-starred restaurant,

offering traditional regional cuisine. Try the *bolliti* (boiled meat) and cured meats for which Fini is renowned. Reserve. Closed Mon, 2 weeks in Aug and Christmas/New Year. €€€–€€€€

Parma

The home of Parma ham and Parmesan cheese is a centre of gastronomic excellence. It is pretty difficult to eat out badly in town, but prices often reflect this.

Ravenna

Antica Trattoria Al Gallo 1909
Via Maggiore 87
Tel: 0544-213775
This elegant Liberty-style restaurant has been run by the same family for almost a century. Al Gallo serves good regional food, which changes according to the seasons; good vegetarian options. Closed Sun dinner, Mon, Tues, Easter and 20 Dec–10 Jan. €€–€€€

San Marino

Righi-La Taverna
Piazza della Libertà 10
Tel: 0549-991196
Good rustic food. Closed Wed in winter, and first 2 weeks in Jan. €€–€€€

FLORENCE

Florence has a reputation for its proliferation of rather nasty fast-food joints and fake "tourist menu" places. Certainly, many restaurants are only too ready to produce indifferent food to indiscriminating tourists they will never see again. However, many restaurants are as good as any you will find in Italy, even if their prices are high. That said, the city still has a selection of simple inns where you can eat well on a reasonable

budget. In the Florentine hills, there are some stunning gastronomic restaurants set in gorgeous palaces or villas.

Alle Murate
Via Ghibellina 52r
Tel: 055-240618
Intimate restaurant which is very fashionable, especially with young Florentines. The atmosphere is relaxed and the excellent cuisine covers creative Tuscan as well as international dishes. Must book. Dinner only. Closed Mon 7–28 Dec. €€€€

Cibrèo-Cibreino
Via del Verrocchio 8r (restaurant)
Via dei Macci 122r (trattoria)
Tel: 055-234 1100
Cibrèo is a universally respected Tuscan restaurant that operates a double-pricing system. Those who are unfamiliar with the system book in the expensive restaurant, where they can expect delicious food. Those in the know eat virtually the same things in the adjoining, more modest-looking *trattoria* for a fraction of the price. Best to reserve.

Closed Sun, Mon, 26 July–6 Sept and Christmas/New Year. €€ *(trattoria)*; €€€€ (restaurant)

Del Fagioli
Corso Tintori 47r
Tel: 055-244285
Traditional Florentine

PRICE CATEGORIES

The price of a three-course meal for one (not including wine):
€ = under €25
€€ = €25–45
€€€ = €45–70
€€€€ = more than €70

TRANSPORT

ACCOMMODATION

EATING OUT

ACTIVITIES

A – Z

LANGUAGE

cuisine is on offer in this typical, family-run *trattoria*. Fresh fish is served on Fridays. Good value. Reservations advised. Closed Sat, Sun and Aug. **€€**

Enoteca Pinchiorri
Via Ghibellina 87
Tel: 055-242777
With three Michelin stars, this is one of the city's, and Italy's, most prestigious restaurants, set on the ground floor of a 17th-century palace, with a delightful courtyard for dining in the open air. The culinary highlights

include a superb, updated version of *nouvelle* French and Tuscan cuisine, with dinner treated as a work of art; there is also an impressive wine collection (almost 60,000 bottles). Reserve. Closed Sun and Mon, Tues and Wed lunch, Aug and Dec–Jan. **€€€€**

La Baraonda
Via Ghibellina 67r
Tel: 055-234 1171
Located in the historic Santa Croce quarter, this very pleasant *trattoria* is rustic and atmospheric. Tuscan cuisine and good

fish dishes are on offer, as well as excellent hand-made pasta. Reserve. Closed Sun and 9–31 Aug. **€€€**

La Loggia
Piazzale Michelangelo 1
Tel: 055-234 2832
Set outside the historic centre, part way up the hill on a grand square, where a copy of Michelangelo's *David* reigns supreme, La Loggia restaurant has a bewitching view down over the bowl of Florence. Serves international and Italian delicacies. Good service. Closed Mon. **€€€–€€€€**

Omero
Via Pian de' Giullari 11r, Località Arcetri (5 km/3 miles from Florence)
Tel: 055-220053
Set on a hill above the panoramic square of Piazzale Michelangelo, this is a gentrified rustic *trattoria* with outside tables in summer. The splendid view is matched by the Tuscan cuisine, prepared with excellent ingredients. Tasty dishes include ravioli stuffed with ricotta and herbs, grilled meats, steaks and pigeon. Reserve. Closed Tues and Aug. **€€€**

TUSCANY

Tuscan cooking is essentially *cucina povera*, peasant food, albeit delicious enough to make you want to cast off any pretence at urban sophistication. This being the case, it is wise to eat the food in its natural habitat, in unpretentious yet atmospheric country-style inns.

Arezzo

Antica Osteria l'Agania
Via Mazzini 10
Tel: 0575-295381
Very pleasant, family-style restaurant specialising in good, simple local cuisine. Excellent value. Closed Mon except June–Sept. **€–€€**

Colle di Val d'Elsa

Ristorante Il Cardinale
Relais della Rovere,
Via Piemonte 10
Tel: 0577-924696
Fax: 0577-924489
www.chiantiturismo.it
The Relais della Rovere began life in the 11th-century as an abbey but it was promoted to a cardinal's residence during the 15th century. The gentrified rustic restaurant, Il Cardinale, occupies the ancient wine cellars of the estate. The menu, which is essentially Tuscan, is matched by

excellent regional wines. The charm of the setting may well tempt you to stay the night. Closed 15 Jan–Feb. **€€–€€€**

Cortona

Il Falconiere
Località San Martino a Bocena (4 km/2½ miles north of Cortona)
Tel: 0575-612679
In a lovely setting in the hills, this elegant Relais hotel makes you feel as though time stands still. Good, imaginative cuisine includes both fish and meat dishes and service is excellent (one Michelin star). There is a lovely panoramic terrace. Must book. Closed Mon and Tues lunch (except Mar–Oct). **€€€€**

Gaiole in Chianti

Badia a Coltibuono
(5 km/3 miles outside Gaiole)
Tel/fax: 0577-749424
www.chiantinet.it/ristbadia
Situated in Chianti country, outside the wine-producing village of Gaiole, this estate was founded by Vallombrosan monks *circa* 1000. The rustic-style restaurant makes good use of local produce. From May to October, guests can visit the wine cellars, gardens and cloisters. It's slightly twee, so it might not be to everybody's

taste. Closed Mon (except May–Oct); 10 Jan–10 Mar. **€€€**

Lucca

Da Giulio
Via delle Conce 47
Tel: 0583-55948
Good plain food, such as minestrone and bean soups. Closed Sun (except third Sunday in month), Mon and Aug. **€**

La Buca di Sant'Antonio
Via della Cervia 1/3
Tel: 0583-55881
This traditional *osteria* (inn) is arguably the best in town for reliable rustic cooking. Closed Sun dinner, Mon, 12–19 Jan and 11–19 July. **€€**

Montalcino

Osteria di Porta Cassero
9 Via della Liberta
Tel: 0577-846116
This popular *trattoria* is run by ex-barber Piero and his family. Hand made pasta and local food are on offer. Closed Wed. **€€**

Taverna Il Grappola Blu
Via Scale di Moglio (off Via Mazzini)
Tel: 0577-847150
This intimate, well-run inn is the best in the quaint medieval village of Montalcino, 40 km (25 miles) south of Siena. The atmosphere is rustic but the cuisine is above average, and service is

friendly but correct. Typical dishes include filling soups, rabbit dishes and pasta with *funghi porcini* (ceps). The Taverna has an excellent wine list – wines produced by Fabio Pellegrini of La Cerbaia estate are particularly recommended. Closed Fri. **€€–€€**

Montepulciano

Caffè Poliziano
27/9 Via Voltaia del Corso
Tel: 0578-758615
Café/bar open every day. Listen out for the opera recitals on Saturday. Closed Sun. **€€**

La Grotta
San Biagio
Tel: 0578-757479
Fifteen years ago David Mazzuoli and his sister converted this 15th century post house next to San Biagio into a restaurant. The atmosphere is discreet and stylish and the menu features lots of local dishes. Try the asparagus with pecorino sauce or pigeon ravioli with saffron. Closed Wed. **€€€**

Pienza

Latte di Luna
24 Via San Carlo
Tel: 0578-748606
This family trattoria is run by the sweet and smiling Roberto Bartolucci. It takes its name from the dancing

light cast by moonstone which is found in the valleys around Pienza. Prized clients are rewarded with a chunk of selinite to take home with them. Find a table in the piazza and be sure to try the excellent home-made semi-freddo ice cream. Closed Tues. €€

Il Prato
Viale S Caterina
Tel: 0578-749924
Opened by local chef and restaurateur Riccardo Valenti in a converted hay loft, Il Prato offers traditional food in a classy ambience. Valenti is fastidious about selecting fresh, high-quality ingredients so the dish of the house, pasta al tartufo, comes with different truffles according to the season. For a taste of local cheese try the insalata di pecorino di Pienza. The al fresco dining area offers great views of the valley. Closed Tues. €€

Pisa

Il Campano
Via Cavalca 44
Tel: 050-580585
Set in a quiet spot by the marketplace, this restaurant dating back to

medieval times specialises in fish, seafood and pasta. In summer its terrace is a pleasant setting for dining al fresco. Good wine list. Closed Wed. €

Sergio
Lungarno Pacinotti 1
Tel: 050-580580
This famous restaurant offers elegant décor in a medieval setting and sound regional food. Reservation advised. Closed Sun, Jan and Aug. €€€

San Gimignano.

Dorando
2 Vicolo del'Oro
Tel: 0577-941862
Dorando is an intimate restaurant located off the Piazza Duomo. Marcello Bisogni and the chef Duccio Ferri spent a lot of time researching Etruscan, Roman and Medieval cuisine before opening. Marcello's enthusiasm and dedication to the authenticity of his menu is humbling. Dorando offers food from both the noble and popular Tuscan traditions. €€

La Collegiata
Localita Strada 27, San Gimignano
Tel: 0577-943201
Located in the former chapel of this spectacular

palazzo, it is worth eating here just to marvel at the service. Waiters whisper in cabals, forming strategies to bring a dish to your table. All this under the orchestration of Maitre D' Salvatore Roccoro, whose four-stage wine service is an oenic performance art. Fortunately the food lives up to the setting and delivery, order the ice cream and be amazed by the spun-sugar moulded shells which cradle each flavour. €€€

Siena

Da Guido
Vicolo del Pettinaio 7
Tel: 0577-280042
Set in a 15th-century building, this is an elegant restaurant in the gentrified-rustic style that Tuscans have perfected. Good service and traditional regional cooking including Etruscan-style pici (Tuscan spaghetti) and Florentine steak. Closed Wed and Jan. €€–€€€

Tullio Ai Tre Cristi
Vicolo Provenzano 1/7
Tel: 0577-280608
Managed for 40 years by the same family, this trattoria's specialities include pasta and soups.

Try the pici, a variant on home-made Tuscan spaghetti. Lovely frescoed walls. Closed Tues. €€–€€€

Sinalunga

Locanda dell'Amorosa
Restaurant Le Coccole
Tel: 0577-679282
www.amorosa.it
This fine restaurant is part of an enchanting medieval hotel complex long famed for its gastronomic excellence. Booking advised. Closed early Jan–early Mar. €€€€

Locanda La Bandita
Via Bandita 72, Località La Bandita (north of Sinalunga)
Tel: 0577-623447
The family-run La Bandita is set in an 18th-century farmhouse in the countryside near Bettolle, a village east of Sinalunga. (On the Florence–Rome motorway, take the Val di Chiana exit, and La Bandita is 1 km (¾ mile) from there, signposted along country lanes.) Highlights include homemade pasta, subtle antipasti and unusual Tuscan-inspired desserts. The restaurant is called Walter Redaelli. Reserve. Closed Tues and Feb. €€–€€€

UMBRIA AND THE MARCHES

What Umbria does best on the food front is unpretentious home cooking. Specialities of the region include pork, cured meats, carpaccio of funghi porcini and warm, nourishing soups. Umbria is also black-truffle (tartufo nero) country, with the prized tuber added to anything, from humble scrambled eggs upwards. Since black truffles are less prestigious than the white Piedmontese truffles, the Umbrians feel they can use them more liberally. The cuisine of the Marches celebrates all manner of seafood and fish soups, plus salami, lasagne with truffles, and roast meats.

Perugia

Il Falchetto
Via Bartolo 20
Tel: 075-573 1775
Il Falchetto serves authentic, unpretentious local cuisine using the best ingredients. Closed Mon and part of Jan/Feb. €–€€

Ancona

Passetto
Piazza IV Novembre 1
Tel: 071-33214
This is an elegant spot, serving traditional seafood cuisine. Lovely sea views from the terrace. Reservation recommended. Closed Sun dinner, Mon and part of Aug. €€€

Assisi

San Francesco
Via S. Francesco 52
Tel: 075-812329
This is the place for Umbrian dishes served in front of a fine fireplace, with views over the basilica. Umbrian dishes include carpaccio of funghi porcini, lentil-based dishes, wild herbs and lamb, ricotta cheese from Norcia and wines from Montefalco. Closed Wed and 1–15 July. €€–€€€

Foligno

Villa Roncalli
Via Roma 25
Tel: 0742-391091
Local specialities feature

strongly on the menu in this lovely old Patrician villa, which is a restaurant with rooms. Dine alfresco in the summer with splendid panoramic views. Reservations advised. Closed Mon and 5–30 Aug. €€–€€€

Orvieto

I Sette Consoli
Piazza Sant'Angelo 1a

PRICE CATEGORIES

The price of a three-course meal for one (not including wine):
€ = under €25
€€ = €25–45
€€€ = €45–70
€€€€ = more than €70

Tel: 0763-343911
Refined, excellent interpretations of local cuisine are on offer here. Dishes include *crostini* with ricotta cheese, stuffed rabbit, *baccalà* (salt cod) marinated in apple vinegar, and bean soup with fennel. Reservations essential. Closed Wed and Sun dinner Nov–Mar. **€€–€€€**

La Grotta
Via Lucca Signorelli 5
Tel: 0763-341348
Set just off the Piazza Del Duomo, this restaurant is particularly recommended for its roast meats. Closed Tues. **€–€€**

Spello

Il Molino
Piazza Matteotti 6/7
Tel: 0742-651305
The restaurant is housed in a converted 14th-century mill. Typical dishes include lamb and *funghi porcini*, with meats often roasted on the spit in front of diners. Closed Tues and 7–22 Jan. **€€**

Spoleto

Il Tartufo
Piazza Garibaldi 24
Tel: 0743-40236
The recently renovated Il Tartufo serves traditional cuisine in a quiet, dignified setting. The dining room has a 4th-century Roman floor. Typical dishes include *baccalà* and asparagus, rich soups, pork dishes and pear soufflé. Truffles are the main ingredient. Must book. Closed Sun dinner, Mon, 10 Feb–10 Mar and July. **€€–€€€**

Todi

Umbria
Via San Bonaventura 13
Tel: 075-894 2737
This restaurant is set in an building, with a terrace overlooking the hills. Good local food. Closed Tues and Christmas–9 Jan. **€€–€€€**

ABRUZZO AND MOLISE

Abruzzo has far greater culinary riches than the rather deprived Molise region. Mutton, lamb and kid represent the most important meats here, with lamb generally roasted or grilled. Adriatic fish is also in abundance, as is salami from the mountains and garden produce from the hinterland. Peppers, potatoes, figs and grapes are also specialities. Molise produces good pasta, served with simple chilli or tomato sauce.

Campobasso

Vecchia Trattoria da Tonino
Corso Vittorio Emanuele 8
Tel: 0874-415 2000
This lovely old *trattoria* in the heart of Campobasso has a welcoming, family atmosphere. It has a Michelin star for its modern, creative cuisine. Booking essential. Closed Sun and Mon Sept–June, Sat and Sun July–Aug, and 20–30 July. **€€–€€€**

Chieti

Venturini
Via Cesare de Lollis 10
Tel: 0871-330663
This restaurant, set in a former convent, has a traditional atmosphere and a nice terrace. Specialities include roast game and fish dishes. Closed Tues and part of July. **€€–€€€**

Guardiagrele

La Grotta di Raselli
Via Comino 146
Tel: 0871-808292
The chef Franco Spadaccini was born in England, but returned to Italy to inspire the kitchens of this fine local restaurant. **€€**

L'Aquila

La Grotta di Aligi
Viale Rendina 2
Tel: 0862-65260
This well-established restaurant is very popular with celebrities as well as locals. It features exceptionally good local cuisine, stylish décor and attentive service. Closed Sun. **€€–€€€**

Tre Marie
Via Tre Marie 3
Tel: 0862-413191
This old-fashioned restaurant has a homely atmosphere and offers good traditional local cuisine. Reservations recommended. Closed Sun dinner, Mon (except Aug) and 24–31 Dec. **€€**

Villa Dragonetti
Via Oberdan 4, Paganica
Tel: 0862-680222
Paulo Bazattelli restored this beautiful Liberty-style villa in 1992. It is now an elegant restaurant with hundreds of 17th-century frescos decorating the walls and ceilings. For a place of such style, the restaurant is a ridiculously economical place to dine. **€€**

Rocca Calascio

Il Rifugio
Loc. Rocca Calascio
Tel: 338-805 9430
www.roccacalascio.it
The Salvati's charming family-run *trattoria* is located in the highest village in the Appenines. Enjoy local cheeses, salami, grilled vegetables and wild boar ragù not forgetting the local pasta, *chitarra*. **€**

Teramo

Duomo
Via Stazio 9
Tel: 0861-241774
This modern restaurant, close to the Duomo, serves traditional local food. Reserve. Closed Mon, Sun dinner and 7–27 Jan. **€€**

NAPLES

Naples is the original home of the pizza – you should not leave without sampling this at least once during a visit. Don't be deterred by the pizza chains back home – these are far superior. The simple, inexpensive *pizzerie* are often the best, so don't turn your nose up at a place simply because of its scruffy exterior. The pizza crust tends to be thin and crispy here, with a tastier yet more limited filling than many people are used to abroad. Apart from pizza places, the city offers a wide range of restaurants and, given Naples' location, seafood figures heavily on any menu, as do *mozzarella di bufala*, tomato sauce and pasta.

Caruso
Grand Hotel Vesuvio,
Via Partenope 45
Tel: 081-7640 0044
Dedicated to the great tenor, Caruso, who was a guest of the hotel, this is a very stylish and elegant restaurant. Specialities include both Neapolitan and national Italian cuisine. The views across the Bay of Naples and the Castel dell'Ovo are breathtaking. Must book. Closed Mon and 5–25 Aug. **€€€€**

Ciro a Santa Brigida
Via Santa Brigida 73
Tel: 081-552 4072
In the old heart of Naples, this well-established restaurant has the reputation of being among the best places in town to

sample the authentic Neopolitan pizza. The full menu also offers good meat and fish dishes. Closed Sun (except Dec) and 7–25 Aug. €–€€

Da Michele
Via Cesare Sersale 1–5
Tel: 081-553 9204
This popular *pizzeria* off Corso Umberto serves classic pizza margherita and tasty fishy pizza marinara. Open late. Closed Sun and Aug. €

Di Matteo
Via Tribunali 94
Tel: 081-455262
This is the place for authentic rustic wood-fired pizzas. Closed Sun and Aug. No credit cards. €

Don Salvatore
Strada Mergellina 4a
Tel: 081-681817
This lively modern restaurant/pizzeria is very

popular – both for its food and location. Specialities include the buffet of *antipasti* and delicious fresh fish. A large bay window opens onto the seafront and port giving excellent views. Closed Wed. €€–€€€

Giuseppone a Mare
Via Ferdinando Russo 13
Tel: 081-575 6002
Set at Posillipo, right on the seafront, so expect great seafood. Closed Sun dinner, Mon, 18 Aug–4 Sept and 24–25 Dec. €€€

La Cantina di Triunfo
Riviera di Chiaia 64
Tel: 081-668101
Traditional Neapolitan dishes are served here and the menu varies according to the days of the week and what ingredients are in season. A brief menu is based on

finds at the market on that day. Dinner only. Closed Sun, August and public hols. €€–€€€

La Cantinella
Via Cuma 42
Tel: 081-764 8684
Set on the seafront, this is an elegant yet modish seafood restaurant, with a telephone on every table (so you can close that business deal while eating your sea bass). Must book. Closed Sun June–Sept, part of Aug and 24–25 Dec. €€€€

La Chiacchierata
Piazzetta Matilde Serao 37
Tel: 081-411465
This tiny family-run *trattoria* is one of the best places to have a meal in the historic centre. Neapolitan specialities feature, such as tender *polpette* (octopus) and hearty soups

made with flageolet beans, broccoli and leek. Reservation recommended. Lunch only (except Fri). Closed Sat and Sun June–Sept, and Aug. €€€

La Fazenda
Via Marechiaro 58/a
Tel: 081-575 7420
La Fazenda overlooks the Gulf of Naples and Capri and serves fine Mediterranean food. In summer, you can dine outside. Closed Sun dinner, Monday lunch and 15 Aug–1 Sept. €€€

Sbrescia Antonio
Rampe Sant'Antonio a Posillipo 109
Tel: 081-669140
Set on a steep street, this restaurant offers a fresh seafood menu and a beautiful view of the Gulf. Reservation recommended. Closed Mon and part of Aug. €€€

CAMPANIA COAST AND ISLANDS

Thanks to the rich volcanic soil, the fruit, vegetables and herbs grown in Campania are among the best in the country. Also expect good seafood from sea bass to squid and swordfish.

Amalfi

Da Gemma
Salita Fra' Gerardo Sasso 9
Tel: 0898-71345
Next to the Duomo, this stylish *trattoria* offers good, traditional cooking, especially seafood. If you have space, try the curious dessert from Salerno. Tables on the street in summer. Reservations recommended. Closed Wed and Jan. €€€

Capri

Given the number of foreigners pouring onto the island in summer, some of the cuisine is neutral "international style", which some restaurateurs think their cruise-liner day-trippers will be expecting. However, if you scratch the surface, you will find true

Campanian cuisine flourishing on this island. Value for money is probably not as good in Capri as elsewhere in Italy, but the fabulous views and ample opportunities for people-watching go a long way towards compensating for the price you have to pay.

Canzone del Mare
Via Marina Piccola 93
Tel: 081-837 0104
Founded by the singer Gracie Fields, who settled here at the height of her popularity, the atmosphere is reminiscent of the 1950s and the restaurant's customers read like a celebrities' Who's Who. The location remains as stunning as ever, set beside a swimming pool surrounded by gardens with views of the Faraglioni; and the food is good. Open lunch only Easter–Oct, plus dinner in Aug. €€€€

La Capannina
Via de Botteghe 12/14
Tel: 081-837 0732
This chic restaurant serves classic, traditional seafood, as well as regional and international cuisine. Reservations recom-

mended. Closed Wed (except June–Sept) and 10 Nov–10 Mar. €€€–€€€€

La Pigna
Via do Palazzo 30
Tel: 081-837 0280
This elegant restaurant is the perfect place for a romantic dinner, especially on the terrace, with its view over the Gulf of Napes. The ambience brings together international and local influences, and the Neapolitan cuisine is served with flair. Closed Mon and Feb. €€–€€€

Le Grottelle
Via Arco Naturale 13
Tel: 081-837 5719
There is a unique view of the Arco Naturale, which overlooks the Gulf of Salerno, in this rustic-style restaurant and pizzeria housed in a natural grotto. Dishes include home-reared rabbit and barbecued fish. Closed Thur except summer, and late Oct–mid-Mar. €€€–€€€€

Ischia

Da "Peppina" di Renato
Via Montecorvo 42, Località Forio

Tel: 081-998312
Furnished with old barrels, this enticing *trattoria* offers local cuisine, such as *pasta mischiata* (pasta with beans, lentils or chickpeas) and home-made *crostate* (tarts) and cakes. Must book. Dinner only. Closed Wed, except June–Sept, and Nov–Mar. €€–€€€

Il Melograno
Via Giovanni Mazzella 110
Tel: 081-998450
Located in Forio on the west side of the island, Il Melograno is noted as much for its gastronomy (one Michelin star) as its picturesque setting among olive groves. Creative fish cuisine is the speciality of the house. Must book. Closed 7 Jan–15 Mar, Mon Oct–Jan, Tues and Wed lunch Nov–Jan. €€€€

PRICE CATEGORIES

The price of a three-course meal for one (not including wine):
€ = under €25
€€ = €25–45
€€€ = €45–70
€€€€ = more than €70

Paestum

Nettuno
Via Principi di Piemonte 2,
Zona Archeologica
Tel: 0828-811028
This place offers good views of the temples and some fine Italian classic cooking. Reservations recommended. Closed 12–26 Nov; lunch only, except Fri and Sat July and Aug. €€–€€€

Positano

Chez Black
Via del Brigantino 19/21
Tel: 089-875036
A popular restaurant and pizzeria overlooking the beach at Spiaggia Grande. Fish is the speciality, and the mixed seafood grill is justly famous. For a less expensive option try perhaps *spaghetti alla Black*, cooked in squid ink. Excellent selection of wines. Closed 7 Jan–7 Feb. €€€

La Buca di Bacco
Via Rampa Teglia 4
Tel: 089-875699
In a beautiful location overlooking the sea, this hotel has a large veranda where the renowned restaurant serves good, regional food. Closed Nov–Mar €€€–€€€€

Salerno

Al Cenacolo
Piazza Alfano 1, 4/6
Tel: 089-238818
Good fish and pasta, and tasty desserts. This is probably Salerno's best restaurant. Closed Sun dinner, Mon, part of Aug and Christmas/New Year. €€€

Sorrento

Don Alfonso 1890
Corso Sant'Agata 11,
Sant'Agata sui due Golfi
(9 km/5½ miles from Sorrento)
Tel: 081-878 0026
This is a shrine to gastronomy and widely considered to be the best in the whole of southern Italy. The two Michelin-starred restaurant features fresh, seasonal dishes, exquisitely executed and served in gracious surroundings. Reservations essential. Closed Mon and Tues lunch June–Sept, Mon and Tues in alternate months. €€€€

La Fenice
Via degli Aranci 11
Tel: 081-878 1652
This restaurant/*pizzeria* has a pleasing décor and a nice welcoming atmosphere. Seafood and delicious *antipasti* are the specialities here, on a menu that has something for all budgets. Closed Mon, except Aug. €€–€€€

PUGLIA

The heel of the boot of Italy has a rich agricultural heritage, with a healthy cuisine based on pasta, lamb, seafood and vegetables. The most common form of pasta here is *orecchiette* ("little ears"), served with a variety of delicious sauces. Herbs also play a major role in this region's cooking, and olives, olive oil, almonds, aubergines, figs and watermelons are significant ingredients in many dishes.

Alberobello

Il Poeta Contadino
Via Indipendenza 21
Tel: 080-432 1917
For fans of fine Italian dining. Located in an old stable refurnished in Liberty style, this family run restaurant serves high-class regional cuisine. Don't miss the basil with ice cream dessert. The wine cellar is an ancient well, chilling to perfect temperature a top-drawer wine list. €€

Bari

Ai Due Ghiottoni
Via Putignani 11
Tel: 080-523 2240
This is a smart restaurant specialising in Puglian dishes with great food and a superb wine list. Closed Sun. €€–€€€

Murat
Via Lombardi 13
Tel: 080-521 6551
The elegant Murat restaurant of the renowned Palace Hotel offers an interesting choice of regional dishes, a good selection of cheeses and moderately priced set menus. Another draw is the panoramic view. Closed Aug. €€€

Barletta

Il Brigantino
Litoranea di Levante
Tel: 0883-533345
Il Brigantino is a large, elegant restaurant offering traditional cuisine, especially fish, efficient service and sea views from the terrace. Closed Jan. €€€

Brindisi

La Lanterna
Via Tarantini 14
Tel: 0831-564026
Set between the Colonno and the cathedral, La Lanterna is housed in a 15th-century *palazzo* and specialises in inventive twists on regional cuisine, with lots of new recipes. Closed Sat lunch, Sun and Aug. €€

Foggia

In Fiera – Cicolella
Viale Fortore, corner of Via Bari
Tel: 0881-632166
This elegant restaurant/*pizzeria* belongs to the Hotel Cicolella and specialises in Puglian and Mediterranean dishes. This is a good place to try the local delicacy, *orecchiette* (ear-shaped) pasta. Closed Mon and Tues and 7–24 Nov. €€–€€€

Lecce

Picton
Via Idomeneo 14
Tel: 0832-332383
In a baroque *palazzo*, this elegant restaurant specialises in local cuisine with an emphasis on inventive, light, seasonal dishes. Closed Mon and part of June and Nov. €€–€€€

Manfredonia

Coppola Rossa
Via dei Celestini 13
Tel: 0884-582522
Coppola Rossa is a friendly *trattoria* offering good local fish and home-made desserts. Closed Sun dinner, Mon, Christmas–10 Jan. €–€€

Taranto

Ponte Vecchio
Piazza Fontana 61
Tel: 0994-706374
Stylish seafood and fish restaurant where lobster and clams are specialities. Lovely terrace for alfresco dining. Closed Tues. €€

Trani

Il Melograno
Via Bovio 189
Tel: 0883-486966
A welcoming, family-run restaurant in the centre of town. Fish is the speciality but local seasonal dishes and fresh ingredients also feature. Closed Wed and Jan. €€–€€€

Palazzo Giardino Broquier
Via Beltrani 17
Tel: 0883-506842
In the heart of the city, this acclaimed restaurant has stylish surroundings in a former *palazzo* matching its excellent food. Summer dining in the very pretty garden. Must book. Closed Tues and 10–26 Nov. €€–€€€

TRANSPORT

BASILICATA

The food in Basilicata is a vegetarian's delight, with baked aubergines, pepper stew, and salads of bitter wild onions all popular.

Matera

Il Casino del Diavolo
Via la Martella
Tel: 0835-261986

Matera's speciality is bread made from durum-wheat baked in wood-fired ovens – several of which you will find around town. In this family-run restaurant you can eat traditional peasant dishes made with the local bread. To follow try the *mantecato di panna* – forest fruit ice cream dessert. **€€**

La Botteghe
Piazza San Pietro Barisano 22
Tel: 0835-344072
Regional dishes served here include roast meat, excellent cheese and homemade *orchiette* pasta. The evocative and homely atmosphere attracts locals and visitors alike. **€**

Maratea

I Lecci
Santavenere Hotel,
Via Santavenere
From seafood to pasta, chef Vincenzo Pinto makes sure everything here is prepared to the highest standard. Not cheap, but good value. **€€€**

ACCOMMODATION

CALABRIA

The food in Calabria is richer than Basilicata, with plenty of home-made pasta, focaccia and spicy dishes of swordfish, anchovies, tuna and cuttlefish.

Cosenza

L'Arco Vecchio
Piazza Archi di Ciaccio 21
Tel: 0984-72564
This renowned restaurant

in the old town serves local fare. In summer dine al fresco. Must book. Closed Sun and 10–18 Aug. **€–€€**
Da Giocondo
Via Pave 53
Tel: 0984-29810
Reliable restaurant in the old town. Don't miss the pickled mushrooms, the local cheeses (from the Sila), and the *maccheroni* in kid sauce. Delicious

local honey-based desserts. Closed Sun dinner and Aug. **€€**

Reggio di Calabria

Baylik
Vico Leone 3
Tel: 0965-48624
Lying close to the port, this restaurant offers the freshest fish. It's possible to dine till midnight on the

catch of the day and the swordfish accompanied with pumpkin flowers is highly recommended. Closed Thurs and part of Aug. **€€**
Hotel Ristorante il Gabbiano
Punta Alice, Ciro Marina
Tel: 0962-31338
Family beach hotel with a good restaurant serving pasta, fish and seafood. **€**

EATING OUT

SICILY

Sicilian food is rich in all areas, and the island's historic influences are perpetuated in its food. The Arab legacy has given Sicilians a sweet and spicy cuisine, and Spanish rule brought a more refined style of cooking. Typical dishes include *pasta con le sarde* (pasta with sardines), *pasta alla norma* (with aubergines), fish couscous, stuffed aubergines, deep-fried rice balls and chickpea fritters.

The Mediterranean provides lobsters, tuna, swordfish and octopus, while the volcanic soil provides a great range of fruit and vegetables.

Sicily produces some excellent wines; those produced by Corvo, Donnafugata or Regaleali are recommended.

Palermo

Charleston le Terrazze
Viale Regina Elena, Mondello
(11 km/7 miles from Palermo)

Tel: 091-450171
Located on the pier at Palermo's fashionable seaside resort, Mondello, this stylish restaurant attracts a chic clientele in summer. The menu features fish and seafood dishes served in the attractive Liberty-style dining room. Closed Wed (except May–Oct) and 10 Jan–10 Feb. **€€€–€€€€**
Santandrea
Piazza Sant'Andrea 4
Tel: 091-334999
Located just behind the Vucciria market, this well-regarded restaurant treats customers to the freshest produce, imaginatively presented. Specialities include fresh sardines with spaghetti and chocolate tart. Closed Tues, Wed lunch, Jan, and Sun and Mon in July–Aug. **€€–€€€**

Catania

La Siciliana
Viale Marco Polo 52/a
Tel: 095-376400

This is a classic, elegant restaurant, with a long family tradition of cooks. Specialities include *pasta all norma* and rice with cuttlefish. Reserve. Closed Sun dinner and Mon. **€€€**
Osteria I Tre Bicchieri
Via San Giuseppe al Duomo 31
Tel: 095-312294
This elegant restaurant is among the best in Sicily. There is an *enoteca* (wine bar), and the vaulted dining room serves excellent Mediterranean dishes. Fish and seafood feature strongly, but carnivores will also be happy. Dinner only. Closed Aug. **€€€–€€€€**

Siracusa

Archimede
Via Gemellaro 8
Tel: 0931-69701
Arguably the most authentic *trattoria* and *pizzeria* in the lovely quarter of Ortygia. The tasty fish dishes are rivalled by mouth-watering, mostly vegetarian, *antipasti*

and Sicilian pasta dishes. Book. Closed Sun. **€€**

Taormina

Al Duomo
Vico Ebrei 11
Tel: 0942-625656
Stylish restaurant which offers excellent dining. Try the Sicilian specialities menu. Must book. Closed Mon and Jan and Nov. **€€€**
La Giara
Vico la Floresta 1
Tel: 0942-23360
This restaurant/piano bar offers good food and fabulous views. Reserve. Dinner only. Closed Mon (except July–Sept) and Feb, Mar, Nov (except Fri and Sat); **€€€–€€€€**

PRICE CATEGORIES

The price of a three-course meal for one (not including wine):
€ = under €25
€€ = €25–45
€€€ = €45–70
€€€€ = more than €70

ACTIVITIES

A – Z

LANGUAGE

A CTIVITIES

THE ARTS, NIGHTLIFE, FESTIVALS, OUTDOOR ACTIVITIES, SPORT AND SHOPPING

THE ARTS

Italy has such a long recorded history that the biggest problem facing the traveller interested in culture is how to choose between the nation's countless attractions. All main centres, most provincial cities and many small towns have fine museums. Theatres, galleries and concert halls also offer something for every interest.

Regeneration and Restoration

The Jubilee effect: The wraps have finally come off many of the country's monuments after years of restoration. The whole country, but especially the capital, has felt the winds of change, largely thanks to the impetus given by Holy Year (2000), and the Pope's insistence that the event be commemorated by restoration of the city's churches.

However, the influence and political commitment of Rome's former mayor, Francesco Rutelli, a dedicated environmentalist, has also been considerable. Under his administration, attempts have been made to pedestrianise historic areas, such as Piazza del Popolo and a route linking the Trevi Fountain and the Pantheon.

Parts of the south are also improving greatly in terms of regeneration, renovation and even cultural life, but much depends on the political will of the local administration. As soon as a major city in the south has a good (ie uncorrupt and entrepreneurial) administration, investment in culture swiftly follows. This has been the case in Catania, Palermo and Naples, for example.

Opera and Concerts

Classical music- and opera-lovers will feel very much at home in Italy. Opera, for instance, is not at all a minority taste here, as it is in so many other countries, and magnificent concerts can be enjoyed all year round.

Rome

The city's most important music venue is the **Auditorium Parco della Musica** (www.auditorium.com). Designed by Genoan architect Renzo Piano, it features its own set of Roman ruins, three indoor halls and an outdoor amphitheatre, and hosts concerts that range from classical to electronica.

Opera, ballets and concerts are also held at the **Teatro dell'Opera**, Via Firenze 72 (which relocates to the Baths of Carcalla in high summer), www.operaroma.it. Concerts are also held in various churches, smaller auditoriums and outdoor venues during the summer-long festival called **Estate Romana**.

Florence

The most important musical event in Florence is the international music and arts festival, **Maggio Musicale Fiorentino**, which takes place in May and June at the Teatro Comunale, the principal opera house and concert hall.

Open-air concerts are held in the **Boboli Gardens** and in the cloisters of the **Badia Fiesolana** on July and August evenings. Another younger, but important, summer festival is **Estate Fiesolana**, which runs from June until August. This event fills the ancient Roman theatre in Fiesole and several churches in Florence with opera, concerts, theatre, ballet and films.

Milan

Milan's hallowed Teatro alla Scala has undergone a complete renovation. The programme is available at the La Scala website, where you can also buy tickets (www.teatroallascala.org). Reservations open two months before the date of the performances. Most sell out on the first day. Any tickets unsold one month before the performance are available at the La Scala box office, located in the Duomo metro station opposite the ATM point (which provides information on the public transport service in Milan). The ticket office is open noon–6pm daily. For information call 02-7200 3744 between 9am and 6pm. Expect to be on hold for some time.

Turin

In Turin, classical music is at its peak from late August until the end of September, when **Settembre Musica** takes over the city. This is an international music festival and features the cream of national and international performers.

Venice

Venice's renowned **La Fenice** opera house (www.teatrolafenice.it) was razed to the ground by a mysterious fire in 1996. It rose from the ashes and officially reopened in November 2004 with a celebratory performance of Verdi's La Traviata.

Verona

Verona's annual open-air opera season runs from June to August. Performances are held at the **Fondazione Arena di Verona** at Piazza Brà 28. For bookings tel:

045-8005151, fax: 045-8011566 or book online at www.arena.it. The marvellous open-air acoustics make it a memorable occasion. Classics like *Madama Butterfly* and Verdi's *Aida* are performed.

Naples
Naples is blessed with the largest opera house in Italy – **San Carlo** – a place with fine acoustics that draws performers and audiences throughout the year. The San Carlo opera house's season runs from January to mid-July. Tel: 081-797 2331. In the **Teatro delle Palme** (Via Vetriera 12, tel: 081-418134), a classical music season runs from January to April. Pick up a free copy of *Qui Napoli* from the tourist office to find out what's on when in the city.

Palermo
Here, opera is also performed in a grandiose setting. Bari's opera house may have been burnt down in a suspicious fire, but Palermo's **Teatro Massimo** (Piazza Giuseppe Verdi; guided tours Mon–Fri 9am–1pm, tel: 091-605 3515, www.teatromassimo.it) opera house has been finely restored after languishing in a state of abandonment for over 20 years. Ask the tourist office for a copy of its *Agenda* magazine, an up-to-date listing of events throughout the city (in English and Italian) or visit www.palermotourism.com.

Theatres
If your Italian is fluent enough for you to enjoy a play in the vernacular, make enquiries at the relevant city's tourist office (*see pages 417–419*) or check listings sections of local newspapers for information on performances.

In **Rome**, the principal theatres are: **Teatro Sistina**, Via Sistina 129, tel: 06-420 0711, www.ilsistina.com; **Teatro Valle**, Via del Teatro Valle 21, tel: 06-6880 3794, www.teatrovalle.it; and **Teatro Argentina**, Largo Argentina 52, tel: 06-684 000 345, www.teatrodiroma.net.

Two theatre companies put on plays in English: the **Miracle Players**, tel: 06-7039 3427, www.miracleplayers.org, summer only; and the **English Theatre of Rome**, tel: 06-444 1375.

In **Milan**, you can go to the **Piccolo Teatro**, Via Rovello 2, and its offshoot, **Teatro Studio**, Via Rivoli 6, as well as the new **Nuovo Piccolo Teatro** next door (booking number for all three theatres: 02-7733 3222; or visit www.piccoloteatro.org).

In **Florence**, you can take in an Italian production at **Teatro**

Comunale, Corso Italia 16, tel: 055-277 9350; at **Teatro della Pergola**, Via della Pergola 12/32, tel: 055-247 9652; or at **Teatro Verdi**, Via Ghibellina 101, tel: 055-212320 or 055-239 6242.

In **Naples**, there are two notable theatres: the **Mercadante Piazza Municipio**, tel: 081-552 4214, a small but beautiful theatre rebuilt in the 1940s; and the **Bellini**, Via Conte di Ruvo, tel: 081-549 1266.

NIGHTLIFE

In recent years, **Milan and Florence** have been the main centres of hip Italian nightlife: Milan for its rock and discos and Florence for its clubs. In the south, **Naples** and **Catania** have the liveliest nightlife. In Naples, which is famed for its stylish clubs, nightlife is concentrated in the newly revitalised historic centre and the Pozzuoli area by the port as well as Posillipo and Mergellina.

In **Palermo**, nightlife was, until recently, fairly non-existent, concentrated only around the chic summer resort of Mondello. Now, however, although Mondello is still thriving, the historic centre of Palermo is coming to life again. Small bars and cafés remain open at night, and such exciting ventures as Lo Spasimo cultural centre – a former monastic complex where concerts, exhibitions and other events draw visitors of all ages – are helping to regenerate the area.

In **Rome**, jazz and blues have long been fashionable, but now a taste for the Latin beat has emerged, with Brazilian dance music popular, as well as techno and house music. Roman nightlife has been rejuvenated with the success of the Jubilee Year and the growing popularity of the Testaccio area. The traditional heart of Roman nightlife, Trastevere, remains lively, although mainly for bars and restaurants.

Venice, by contrast, is less of a city for nightlife. Although there are piano bars, the casino and the odd folk club, most people prefer sitting in cafés and walking through the beautiful, labyrinthine streets here. Those desperate to go clubbing tend to drive at breakneck speed to the **Lido di Jesolo** coastal resort, a world away from sleepy Venice in atmosphere.

In **Turin** the best nightlife from a visitor's point of view lies in the seductive 19th-century cafés. The most famous are **Baratti E Milano**

in Piazza Castello and **Caffè Torino** on Piazza San Carlo.

Below is a list of the current hotspots. Trust advice on the ground as the scene is always changing.

Rome
To find out what's on in Rome, check in *La Repubblica* and *Il Corriere della Sera* newspapers, or the weekly *Roma C'e*, a useful listings booklet that comes out every Wednesday and has a section in English. Also *Wanted in Rome,* a fortnightly magazine in English.

Nightspots
Campo de' Fiori
On summer nights, this lovely, rambling square and its surrounding medieval streets become a lively and popular rendezvous point. An all-time classic on the square is the **Vineria**, at no. 15, but any other bar will do just as well to indulge in some memorable people-watching.

The Pantheon
Just east of Piazza Navona is the Pantheon district, which is extremely lively and beautifully illuminated at night. Apart from the sheer romance of this locality, the fine *gelaterie* (ice-cream parlours), especially the **Cremeria Monteforte** at Via della Rotonda 22, are another great draw.

Piazza Navona
This elegant Renaissance square becomes a good place for a night-time amble. Try the legendary *tartufo* ice from **I Tre Scalini** at no. 30.

Trastevere
Situated on the other side of the Tiber, Trastevere is an intimate and atmospheric part of town, though it is becoming quite touristy. Even so, its alleyways and tiny squares are lined with family-run inns and restaurants, and convivial bars. **Freni e Frizione** (Via del Politeana 4–6) is ever-popular.

Testaccio
This district, and above all its leafy and winding thoroughfare, Via di Monte Testaccio, is dotted with nightclubs and bars.

Music Clubs, Cabaret & Cinema
Alibi
Via di Monte Testaccio 40–47
Tel: 06-574 3448
A social and cultural centre with various activities on offer, such as gay discos on Tuesdays. Other nights are open to all and themed; Rome's oldest gay venue.

Roman Bars and Cafés

Many Romans prefer going on café-crawls to hitting the latest club. Many of the following open until late, and the clientele varies according to the time of day.

Antico Caffè della Pace
Via della Pace 3/7
Classic ivy-swathed café that also serves good *aperitivi* and *digestivi*.

Bar Navona
Piazza Navona 67
Familiar Roman spot on one of Rome's loveliest squares.

Bar San Calisto
Piazza San Calisto 4
Gritty and rough-hewn, but no less classic. It serves cheap coffee, beer, alcohol and ice cream.

L'Oasi della Birra
Piazza Testaccio 41
The place for beer and grappa in the fun Testaccio district.

Rosati
Piazza del Popolo 4/5
A historic bar that affords great views over the elegant Piazza del Popolo.

Tazza D'Oro
Via degli Orfani 84
Bustling bar and coffee roastery that sells the city's best coffee. No seating.

Alien
Via Velletri 13–19
Tel: 06-841 2212
One of Rome's biggest clubs. Amazing lighting and special effects.

Big Mama
Vicolo San Francesco a Ripa 18
Tel: 06-581 2551
Bastion of Rome's jazz and blues scene, this cosy Trastevere club offers live music most nights by Italian and international acts.

Black Out Rock Club
Via Saturnia 18
Tel: 06-7049 6791
The place for indie, punk and rock music, with some performances by British and US bands.

Caffè Latino
Via de Monte Testaccio 96
Tel: 06-5728 8556
Live Latin American music on most nights feeds the current Roman craze. Later, DJs play funk, acid jazz and Latin American sounds, and, on some nights, there are film screenings and cabaret.

Casa del Jazz
Viale di Porta Ardeatina 55
Tel: 06-704731
This state-funded jazz club, founded by Rome's mayor, jazz aficionado Walter Veltroni, attracts big names and also has a stylish café and restaurant.

Jackie O'
Via Boncompagni 11
Tel: 06-4288 5457
Very glamorous club with restaurant and piano bar – be prepared to queue. It pays to don your finest gear and emulate the Romans' style of *la bella figura*.

Joia
Via Galvani 20
Tel: 06-574 0802
This stylish club boasts a dance area with cosy banquette seating, an intimate restaurant and a large terrace for alfresco dancing in the summer months.

Nuovo Olimpia
Via in Lucina 16g
Tel: 06-686 1068
On a side street off Via del Corso, this cinema always dedicates at least one screen to a film in "VO" (original version). Wednesday is the day to catch a film in Rome: ticket prices are reduced in most cinemas.

Supperclub
Via de' Nari 14
Tel: 06-6830 1011
Exclusive haunt of Rome's well-heeled crowd, who come for the great DJs and the first-class cocktails, this bar-club-restaurant also hosts themed club events.

Milan

Given the eclectic nature of Milanese nightlife, it is tricky to categorise places – sometimes the same place peforms several functions. Nightlife of the hot, youthful variety is centred on the Navigli district, the canal quarter. You should just be able to turn up in the evening and see what is on offer. However, if you like to plan ahead, check what's on in the ViviMilano insert in Wednesday's Corriere della Sera or visit www.hellomilano.it. More refined nightlife, especially in the form of bars and low-key clubs, takes place in the Brera area. Outside these areas, Milan can be oddly quiet at night. If there are no taxis in the ranks, call: 02-8383, 02-6767, 02-8585 or 02-5251.

Absolut Ice Bar
Piazza Gerusalemme 12
Tel: 02-8907 8531
www.townhouse.it/icebar
Cloaks and boots are provided, but dress up warm as temperature inside is –5°C (23°F). Walls, bars, glasses and floors are all in ice. Open daily 6pm–midnight, it serves just vodka and fruit juice, with Swedish foods. Booking is advisable. €15 gives you admission and one drink, and 25 minutes inside – probably just about all that you can stand anyway.

Alcatraz
Via Valtellina 25
Tel: 02-6901 6352
One of the trendy mega clubs, with two dance floors, three bars, two performance areas and a pub.

Bar Daila Café
Via San Vicenzo 15
Tel: 02-5811 2288
This friendly jazz café has live music on Thursday and Friday evenings. (Happy hour is between 6 and 8pm; open until 2am but closed Sunday.)

Bar Giamaica/Jamaica
Via Brera 32
Tel: 02-876723
This bar in the Brera has no special gimmicks and doesn't look anything special, but it is a piece of Milanese history – a traditional meeting place for artists, intellectuals and celebs. Despite its fame, it's a calm place for drinking cocktails or sampling Italian regional dishes. Open in the day.

Blue Note
Via Borsieri 37
Tel: 02-6901 6888
This is Europe's only franchisee of the legendary New York jazz club, featuring some of the biggest names around. Restaurant, bar and Sunday brunch (increasingly popular in Milan). Open daily.

Blueshouse
Via Sant'Uguzzone 26
Live music on most nights, with tribute bands honouring legendary names such as Led Zeppelin and The Rolling Stones. At other times bands play blues, rock and even folk.

Café Cavalieri
Corso Genova 26
Tel: 02-832 3557
This is a great place for an *aperitivo* from 6–9pm, accompanied by plates of cured ham and seafood. There is always a warm welcome from the owner. Open daily 7am–2am.

Café L'Atlantique
Viale Umbria 42
Tel: 190-111 111
www.cafeatlantique.com
Reopened in October 2006, this disco and restaurant offers hip-hop and house music in luxurious surroundings and is currently one of the top nightspots in Milan.

Café Teatro Nobel
Via Asciano Sforza 81
Tel: 02-8951 1746
Shows, jazz and cabaret in the lively Navigli canal quarter. Take the metro to Porta Genova, then walk.

El Brellin
Vicolo dei Lavandai,
Via Alzaia Naviglio Grande 14
Tel: 02-5810 1351
This sophisticated Navigli piano bar
and restaurant is set in a quaint
converted wash-house. Only
Milanese dishes are served.
Open Mon–Sat 12.30–2.30pm and
7pm–2am, Sun noon–3pm.

Gasoline Club
Via Bonnet 11/a
Tel: 02-2901 3245
www.lustminute.org
Near Corso Como, a disco popular
with models on Friday nights, young,
informal atmosphere, gay-friendly.
Last Fri of every month, "Lust
Minute", from 11pm, international
DJs, electronic music, hard/soul/
tech-house, techno, progressive
trance. Closed Thur–Sun.

Gattopardo Café
Via Piero della Francesca 47
Tel: 02-3453 7699
www.ilgattopardocafe.com
Open Tues–Sun. Disco located in an
ex-church, with bar in the position
of the altar, dancing in the nave
amongst marble columns and
evocative lighting. R&B, mainstream,
house music. Strict entrance
selection.

Hollywood Rythmoteque
Corso Como 15
Tel: 02-6559 8996
One of the top nightspots in
Milan. The crowd is high-energy.
Be prepared to queue. Open
Tues–Sun 11pm–4am. Especially
popular with the glitterati on
Sundays. R&B night on Tuesday.

La Salumeria della Musica
Via Pasinetti 2
Tel: 02-5680 7350
Cabaret and live music in this
former factory, now transformed
into a buzzing club. Just like a
real salumeria, hams and
sausages dangle over the bar.
Closed Sunday.

Le Scimmie
Via Asciano Sforza 49
Tel: 02-8940 2874
An established, reputable jazz
and blues club in the Navigli area.
You can also dine on Italian or
French cuisine. Closed Tues.

Lime Light (previously C-Side,
previously Propaganda)
Via Castelbarco 11–13
Tel: 02-5831 0682
Open Wed 11pm–5am, Fri 11.45pm–
3.30am, Sat midnight–3.30am.
Large disco, popular with students.
Wednesday evening is "the university
evening".

Pasticceria Ricci
Piazza della Repubblica 27
Pastries are served during the day,

but at night it's a gay club and one of
the trendiest bars in Milan.

Pitbull Café
Corso Como 11
More mature locale, with chic white
interior and soft lighting. Music
ranges from soft rock to disco. Well-
stocked bar, though the aperitivo
spread is modest: couscous,
peanuts, bruschetta and the like.

Plastic
Viale Umbria 120 (MM3 Lodi)
Tel: 02-733996
www.clubplastic.biz
Open Thur–Sun. Disco,
transgression, avant-garde music,
one of Milan's favourite venues.
Fri and Sat house-electronic music.

Rolling Stone
Corso XXII Marzo 32
Tel: 02-733172
www.rollingstone.it
For live music, Rolling Stone is
Milan's temple of rock during the
week (dancing on Fridays and
Saturdays; dinner nightclub on
Tuesday).

Shocking Club
Via Bastioni di Porta Nuova 12
Tel: 02-8645 4630
This smart club is favoured by
models and showbiz types.
Wednesday night is "shocking"
night. Open 10.30pm–4am.
Closed Mon.

Sio Café
Via P. & A. Pirelli 6
Tel: 02-6611 8087
A venue in the up-and-coming Bicocca
area, with a summer garden. Fresh,
lively, brand-new. Closed Mon; Tues
university happy hour; Wed live jazz;
Thur "More Fashion Night" DJ set;
Fri "Hotel Viagra no. 1", DJ set with
live sax, violin, percussion, €10–15;
Sat "Show Time", DJ set, €10–15;
Sun "Crazy Ugly", happy hour and
dancing all evening.

Florence

Classic Cafés

Caffè Gilli
Piazza della Repubblica 39r
Tel: 055-213896
This historic café, an institution on
the piazza, is also an excellent
patisserie. Stand at the bar where
prices are far lower than at tables.

Caffè Rivoire
Piazza della Signoria 5r
Still one of the best places to be
seen in Florence. Closed Mon.

Caffè Strozzi
Piazza Strozzi
This is a low-key meeting place,
popular for evening aperitivi.

Vivoli
Via Isola delle Stinche 7r
Vivoli is universally acknowledged

as the city's best ice-cream parlour,
so expect queues in summer.
Closed Mon.

Fashionable Bars

Most trendy bars lie in the more
bohemian Oltrarno, on the far side
of the river, Florence's answer to
the Parisian Left Bank. At night,
lively quarters include the vaguely
alternative Santo Spirito area and
the bohemian-chic Santa Croce.
However, good Florentine bars and
clubs are dotted throughout the city,
and even in the Tuscan countryside.

Dolce Vita
Piazza del Carmine 5
Tel: 055-284595
This glamorous spot is the place
to go for cocktails, live music and
general hanging out. Open daily
5.30pm–11.30am.

Roses
Via del Parione 26r
Tel: 055-287090
This was Florence's first sushi bar.
Good for cocktails and long drinks.

Salamanca
Via Ghibellina 80r
Tel: 055-234 5452
Spanish restaurant and bar, open
until 2am. Live music, including
flamenco every Monday and Latin
singer-songwriters on Thursday.

Clubs

Given the number of special events
in Florentine clubs, it pays to check
times carefully; places only start to
fill up very late, after young
Florentines have had their fill of
hanging out in pizzerie and gelaterie.

Escopazzo Garden
Lungarno Colombo, Bellariva
Tel: 0556-76912
This eclectic Latin club has regular
themed nights, from Cuban to
Caribbean music. After midnight,
however, you are more likely to be
dancing to mainstream sounds.

Maramao
Via de Macci 79r
Tel: 055-244341
Sample the famous dolce vita in this
club, currently one of the hippest in
town. Closed Mon and May–Sept.
Open 11pm–3am.

Meccanò
Parco della Cascine
Viale degli Olmi 1
Tel: 055-331371
Set in the Cascine park, Meccanò is
the best-known Florentine club and
appeals to a wide age group. It is
home to La Piccionaia restaurant,
where dinner is accompanied by a
floor show. The club is the place to
spot visiting VIPs and Florentine
poseurs. Even the armchairs are
fashioned by the French designer

TRANSPORT
ACCOMMODATION
EATING OUT
ACTIVITIES
A – Z
LANGUAGE

Clubs in Naples

The following are among the most stylish or fashionable places for dancing in Naples, but the city is not known for cutting-edge clubs and avant-garde music. Most places tend to play a similar mix of classics from the 1970s and '80s to rap, house or the current chart hits, and are closed on Monday.

Chez Moi
Via del Parco Margherita 20
Tel: 081-407526
Similar in approach to **My Way**, another trendy club in the Chiaia area, with different nights (unofficially) for different crowds.
Kiss-Kiss
Via Sgambati 47
Tel: 081-546 6566

Located in the Vomero district, this large club has a restaurant and attracts a student clientele.
La Mela
Via dei Mille 40b, Chiaia
Tel: 081-413881/410270
This is a smart, trendy place. However, allegations of Mafia involvement stem from the occasional shootings, after which the place is closed for a while. Whatever its associations, many locals miss it when it's gone.
Dug Out
Mergellina
Tel: 081-662183
This club is hewn out of soft tufa rock, a cavern in a courtyard, echoing its name. Check what the night's theme is prior to going.

Has jazz sessions from 10.30pm. Entrance fee includes first drink.
Sannakura Club
Via Santa Chiara 10
Tel: 339-284 9423
This club specialises in rap and hip-hop sounds.
Slovenly R 'n' R Bar
Vico San Geronimo 24 (next to Via Benedetto Croce)
Tel: 335-611 5857
Live rock with an international flavour in an underground cellar.
Velvet Club
Via Cisterna dell'Olio 11
This club buzzes from 11pm until 6am. Different sounds range from pop to techno, hip-hop, rock and more.
Vinarium
Via Cappella Vecchia 7
Tel: 081-764 4114
This centrally located, classic wine bar is particularly popular with trendy professionals over the age of 30. The ambience is smart/casual, with a relaxing feel in spite of the relatively formal surroundings. A quick stroll away, Via Carlo Poerio is bursting with bars, pubs and wine bars.
Vineria
Via Palladino 8
This atmospheric wine bar was once a student haunt, but now attracts a wider cross-section. The atmosphere is defined as "intellectual yet homely", a mood enhanced by low lighting and wood-and-marble fixtures and fittings. Closed Mon.
Virgilio Sports Club
Via Tito Lucresio Caro 6
Tel: 081-575 5262
The name is a bit misleading, even if there is a sports club here too, since this is now a music bar for twenty- and thirtysomethings. However, in true Neapolitan style, different sets of people have their favourite nights, with Thursday a typical night for *per bene* (well-bred) over-30s. There are sea views from the terrace.

Philippe Starck. Open 11pm–4am Tues–Sat in summer, Thur–Sat in winter.
Space Electronic
Via Palazzuolo 37
Tel: 055-293082
This established club is an old favourite with the younger crowd.
Universale
Via Pisana 77r
Tel: 055-221122
This former cinema has been transformed into a huge venue, where you can eat, drink, dance and watch shows and concerts. A very versatile club. Open 8.30pm–3am. Closed Mon, Tues and June–Sept.

Naples

Neapolitan nightlife is concentrated in the chaotic but characteristic historic centre, the area stretching towards the sea, and the Pozzuoli district by the port. The Borgo Marinaro area, which used to be patronised by pensioners, is now popular with all ages, although the bars and *trattorie* are just the same as they were 30 years ago.

Classic Cafés, Wine Bars and Live Music

The top chic places change all the time, so pick up a copy of the latest *Qui Napoli* listings magazine in both English and Italian. There is a selection of venues on the official Naples website www.inaples.it. If you speak Italian visit www.napolinapoli.com. As well as classic cafés, such as the legendary Gambrinus, Naples has a decent range of bars, including several atmospheric wine bars. Bear in mind that most places here close on Monday.

A Ret' A' Palm
Piazza Santa Maria La Nova
Called "Behind the Palms" in Neapolitan dialect, this wine bar and inn *(osteria)* is set in a *palazzo* run by the Austrian-Neapolitan Alan Wurtzburger. This unpretentious place has an excellent wine list and good bar snacks at very reasonable prices. The music includes live performances every Wednesday by the musician-owner himself.
Caffè Gambrinus
Via Chiaia 1–2, Piazza Plebiscito
Tel: 081-414133/417582
This is the city's most famous bar, an elegant place adorned with gilt-and-plaster reliefs. The terrace is a good spot for watching the world go by, sipping *aperitivi* or downing a sweet coffee. Open from early morning until about 10 or 11pm.
Chez Moi
Via di Parco Margherita 20
Tel: 081-407526
Located in the upmarket Chiaia area, this well-established music bar caters for all ages, depending on the night (call ahead first).
Chiatamon
Via Chiatamone
This is an informal and fashionable bar overlooking the seafront of Via Caracciolo. Music and dancing is courtesy of DJs on most weekends.
Murat Live Club
Via Bellini 8
Tel: 081-544 5919
The emphasis here is on live music and especially jazz, including modern and contemporary. The action usually starts around 10pm. Located in the San Carlo Arena district.
Otto Jazz Club
Piazzetta Cariata 23
Tel: 081-552 4373

FESTIVALS

The year is packed with special events, some linked to festivals of the Catholic Church, others to the changing seasons, especially the harvest, and to local produce. There are also historical re-enactments connected to jousting or costumed cavalcades. Locals often consider their home festival the best, no matter how tiny; however, as far as outsiders are concerned, the festive set pieces in Tuscany, Venice and Sicily probably provide the biggest spectacle. These are some of the highlights of the festival calendar.

Carnevale. This period of festivities preceding Lent (February and March) is celebrated in unrivalled style in Venice. Apart from Venice, there are other excellent carnivals in Viareggio on the Tuscan Coast, and in Acireale and Sciacca in Sicily.

Easter involves major celebrations in Italy, especially in Sicily. The most dramatic and passion-filled festivals are the Mysteries (I Misteri) at Trapani, the Easter Devils at Prizzi and the Albanian festivities outside Palermo.

The Scoppio del Carro, or Explosion of the Carriage, takes place in Florence on Easter Sunday. A mechanical dove swoops through the cathedral and ignites a golden carriage filled with fireworks. The event symbolises the Resurrection. This is an event the Florentines themselves follow with great enthusiasm, so the centre of the city is always packed.

The Festival dei Due Mondi di Spoleto, in late June–early July, at Spoleto, in Umbria, offers theatre, concerts, ballet and exhibitions. Although the future of the festival has been under threat for many years, last-minute administrative solutions have always been found.

Biennale. This is a major exhibition of international modern art, held in Venice every June–October in odd-numbered years. The sites are not just in the Biennale pavilions and gardens, but also in unusual and striking buildings dotted throughout the city, including the old Arsenale.

Gioco del Calcio (also known as Calcio in Costume) is another Florentine event, held on 19, 24 and 28 June. This is a type of football played by men wearing 16th-century costumes.

The Palio horse race is held on 2 July and 16 August in Siena's Piazza del Campo. The bareback riders, who take part in a two-hour procession before the race, wear 15th-century costumes. This is the highlight of Siena's festive calendar, so book accommodation well in advance. You may find it difficult to see in the crowds, but the atmosphere is usually wonderful.

The Festa del Redentore is held in Venice, on the night of the third Saturday of July. A bridge of boats is built across the Giudecca Canal to the Redentore, the church that was built in gratitude for deliverance from the Plague in 1567. People row out to picnic on the water to watch the wonderful firework displays launched from Giudecca island.

The Festa di Noantri is a Roman

tradition, celebrated in the second half of July. This street festival, involving music, fireworks and food, is centred on Trastevere, one of the oldest quarters of Rome.

The International Film Festival is held at the Lido in Venice at the end of August each year. Recently, the new administration decided to focus less on Hollywood blockbusters and more on art-house and European films. However, since the Venetians like a celebrity-driven event, the changes have been minor. The new Rome Film Festival takes place in October.

In Tuscany, the city of Arezzo hosts the Giostra del Saracino on the last Sunday in August and the first Sunday in September. This medieval jousting match echoes the events of the Crusades.

A major food festival, Salone del Gusto, is held in October on alternate years in Turin, sponsored by the Slow Food Movement.

All Saints' Day, 1 November, is a holiday marked throughout the country.

7 December is the festival day of Milan's patron saint, Sant Ambrogio, and also the opening day of the season at La Scala.

In the run-up to Christmas there are Christmas fairs and, in Naples, the famous presepi (crib) festival.

OUTDOOR ACTIVITIES

National and Regional Parks

Italy has some stunningly beautiful national parks (see below). The regions of Abruzzo, Piedmont, Trentino and Alto Adige are just a few of the many areas that should be able to supply information on parks in their territory. A useful website for all parks is www.parks.it.

The Dolomites

The Dolomites have some of the most spectacular natural landscape in italy, and can be explored on skis or along marked hiking trails. For information contact the Trentino information service in London (tel/fax: 020-8879 1405), which will be able to supply brochures on parks, refuges, hiking, lakes, activities and accommodation. You can also check the English-language Trentino website: www.trentino.to.

Etna, Catania, Sicily

An intriguing and well-organised park, centred on the active volcano of Mount

Etna. Many excursions explore this strange area, which encompasses fertile areas from ancient eruptions and the volcanic moonscapes of the most recent lava flows. Contact the Catania tourist office (AAPIT Provincia di Catania & Acireale, Largo Paisiello 51, Catania, 95100 Italy; tel: 095-730 6211, fax: 095-316407) for free maps, brochures and descriptions of trips to the top or around the base, or contact Gruppo Guide Alpine Etna Sud, Via Etnea 49, Nicolosi, tel: 095-791 4755. Access is currently restricted due to continued volcanic activity. Visit the Mount Etna Regional Park website: www.parcoetna.it.

Parco Nazionale del Gran Paradiso

Home of the last steinbocks in Italy, this Alpine park is the oldest in the country and covers 720 sq. km (278 sq. miles). Spreading over parts of Valle d'Aosta and Piedmont, it has refuges and trekking facilities. For details contact the tourist boards of Piedmont, Via Magenta 12, 10128 Torino, tel: 011-43211, fax: 011-432 2440, www.regione.piemonte.it, and

Hiking in the Alps

If you want to go hiking in the mountains, pick up a map of the network of walking paths, with more than 80 overnight areas with shelters. Paths are marked with numerous red signs and distinctive small flags. Every stage calls for 5 to 7 hours of hiking time at an average of around 1,000 metres (3,300 ft) in altitude.

At the overnight rest areas (known as rifugi, or refuges) there are shelters with double-decker bunks, essential services and a kitchen. While many are in idyllic but fairly isolated spots, others are situated near hamlets or resorts, where it is possible to buy food, phone home, rest for a day, visit rural museums, chat with the local inhabitants and, last but not least, eat a good meal at an inn.

An itinerary can last a month, a week or a day. A lot of regions provide lists of recommended guides, members of the reputable Italian CAI association. From the Maritime Alps in the west to Lake Maggiore, on a route stretching for 650 km (400 miles) that spans five provinces, the hiker crosses many splendid parks, such as the Gran Paradiso, the Orsiera-Rocciavrè, the Alta Val Pesio and the Argentera. All national park areas are open to the public between July and September.

Valle d'Aosta, at Piazza Chanoux 3, 11100 Aosta, tel: 0165-236627, fax: 0165-34657, www.regione.vda.it/turismo or www.aostavalley.com/regione/index.

Parco Naturale dello Sciliar

This park is in the Alto Adige (South Tyrol) region and overlooks the vast plateaux of the Swiss Alps, with jagged rock faces, steep peaks and impressive ledges. Wildlife includes chamois, marmots and golden eagles. The park was established by the authorities of Bolzano (Bozen) – call the tourist office there on 0471-307001 or visit www.bolzano-bozen.it.

Parco Nazionale dell'Abruzzo

This park extends from the southern section of the Abruzzan Apennines and includes limestone and a Dolomitic landscape. King of the beasts here is the brown bear – some of the last of the species in Italy live in remote splendour in one of the highest sections of the Apennines. Other wildlife includes the Apennine wolf, the white-backed woodpecker and the Orsini's viper, which is less poisonous than the majority of other Italian vipers. Tel: 0863-910715 or visit www.parcoabruzzo.it for information.

Parco Nazionale della Maremma

This wonderful Tuscan park is a mixture of meadows, pine forests, sandy shores and swampland along the Tuscan Coast. Wildlife includes wild boar, porcupines, peregrine falcons and the pond tortoise. There are countless trails and opportunities to go riding. However, you will need to check itineraries and facilities before you arrive with the Grosseto tourist office in Tuscany. Visit www.parco-maremma.it for information. For all park reserves visit www.parks.it.

Parco Nazionale dello Stelvio

Italy's biggest park, at 1,350 sq. km (520 sq. miles), is situated close to Switzerland and is rich in forests and animal life. The mountains are beautiful, and there are plenty of hotels near by (open all year). For information tel: 0342-901654 (Lombardy) or 0463-985190 (Trentino), or visit www.stelviopark.it.

SPORT

Spectator Sports

Football (Soccer)

The national sport in Italy is football. Almost every city and village has a team and the most important national championship is the "Serie A" (First Division), the winner of which is eligible to play in a kind of European championship, the "Champions' League", against other top European teams.

The "Serie A" championship runs from September to May, and each of the 20 teams has to play the other teams twice. Traditionally, the most successful Italian team is Juventus FC from Turin, followed by Milan AC and Internazionale ("Inter") from Milan, but in recent years, other teams have had significant victories, including sides from Verona, Parma, Florence and Rome.

From September until late May, Rome's two teams, Roma and Lazio, play nearly every Sunday at the Stadio Olimpico. The cheapest tickets are about €20 and can be purchased at the Stadium's box office or one of the many Roma or Lazio stores around the city. (To get to the stadium take metro line A to Flaminio, then tram 225 to Piazza Mancini and follow the crowds. Or take metro line A to Ottaviano and then bus 32 up to the stadium.)

If you want to see a game, check the newspaper listings, but it is generally difficult to get tickets for an important match. Prices vary according to the importance of the team, the game, and the location of the seat you want. Unlike some European countries, matches here tend to be safe, family affairs.

Milan matches: You can book a football visit to Milan with certain UK tour operators, including Liaisons Abroad. You can also do a tour of Milan's San Siro football stadium (for details contact the Milan tourist office, see page 418). Contact the club for tickets to matches: AC Milan administrative office, Via Turati 3; tel: 02-62281. Curiously, you can also buy tickets at any branch of the Cariplo bank.

Other Sports

Almost every other sport is enjoyed in Italy, including basketball, golf, water polo, horse racing, rugby union, rowing and sailing. In addition, you can ski in the Alps, Dolomites and the Apennines.

May is an important month for sport in Italy. The Giro d'Italia cycle race is a major event on the cycling circuit, but it has recently been damaged by drug allegations. Also in May, there is the Italian Open tennis tournament, held at the Foro Italico in Rome. Equestrian sports followers also enjoy their major competition of the year in May, which takes place in Rome's Villa Borghese gardens.

Motor Racing

In Italy citizens typically support Ferrari and, consequently, the German champion, Michael Schumacher, who raced for them until recently. There is always a large crowd at the circuits in Imola (where the San Marino Grand Prix is held) and Monza (Italian Grand Prix). Although the car industry is centred on Turin, motor racing is based in the regions of Lombardy and Emilia Romagna.

Buying Tickets

For tickets for any sporting event, consult the local tourist office or, alternatively, buy the pink Gazzetta dello Sport newspaper, which should give you the low-down on what's on when and how to book.

SHOPPING

Shopping is an Italian passion, not just because the natives are natural consumers, in love with the latest designs, but also because it's often viewed here as an art, involving the search for the beautifully crafted object, the right coffee cups, or the right garment in the right shade and fabric. Italians are expert at marketing their designer labels around the world, so much so that Milan now rivals Paris as Europe's fashion capital. In addition, since most Italians also attach great importance to finding the right foodstuffs, you are likely to find good quality just about everywhere, even in the simplest street market.

Shopping Areas

Rome

The best shopping district is around the bottom of the Spanish Steps, the heart of Rome's design world, with the elegant **Via Condotti** lined with the most exclusive fashion boutiques (Gucci, Ferragamo, Prada, Armani and Bulgari). Other fashionable streets run parallel to Via Condotti, such as **Via Borgognona** (with the shops of Dolce & Gabbana and Hogan); **Via delle Carrozze** or **Via Frattina** (for ceramics, lingerie and costume jewellery); **Via Vittoria** (where the boutique of Laura Biagiotti can be found) and **Via della Croce**. Make sure you check out the new Fendi megastore in **Largo Goldoni** off Via Condotti. Most of these streets are closed to traffic.

For antiques, go window-shopping along **Via del Babuino** (do not miss the Giorgio Armani boutique there), along **Via Margutta** (the place for even more antiques) or **Via dei Coronari** (even more antiques in the streets leading to Piazza Navona).

Another fine shopping section is along the Via del Corso between Piazza del Popolo and Largo Chigi, where **Via del Tritone** begins.

Less expensive and more popular shopping streets include **Via Nazionale**, near the railway station, which is good for everyday clothes shops; this is also where Fiorucci (sportswear and shoes) has his main outlet, and **Via Cola di Rienzo**, a busy shopping thoroughfare in the Prati district.

"The other face of fashion" is represented by the open markets, such as the one in Via Sannio, which sells new and second-hand clothes, and, of course, the famous one at Porta Portese, open only on Sunday, from sunrise–2pm, where you can find almost everything. Via del Governo Vecchio near Piazza Navona is the place for inexpensive jewellery and vintage clothing bargains.

Milan

Milan is home to the major fashion houses and is a consumer paradise during the twice-yearly showing of the new collections. This city, more than

Rome, is Italy's principal centre for international fashion.

For those with expensive tastes, the most chic shopping streets are: Via Montenapoleone, Via della Spiga and Via Sant' Andrea, an area known as the "Quadrilatero" or "Golden Triangle" within walking distance of the Duomo and La Scala. These elegant streets are home to such fashion icons as Krizia, Giò Moretti, Trussardi, Kenzo, Sanlorenzo, Giorgio Armani and Ferragamo, as well as Versace, Gucci, Ermenegildo Zegna, Comme des Garçons, Valentino, Dolce & Gabbana, Hermès, Chanel, Moschino, Prada, Ferre and Fendi.

The **Brera district** is also a smart and discreet shopping location, with a good selection of clothing and antiques. Pick up a shopping guide from the Milan tourist office.

Florence

The whole centre of Florence could be considered a huge marketplace, crowded as it is with tourists and well-dressed locals. Handicrafts are fast disappearing, leaving the place to smart clothing shops. The most fashionable streets are still **Via dei Calzaiuoli**, **Via Roma** and **Via de' Tornabuoni**, home to the famous Ferragamo fashion house – visit its shoe museum in Palazzo Spini-Feroni – as well as **Via della Vigna Nuova** and **Via degli Strozzi** for the likes of Neuber, Principe and Diavolo Rosa.

Ponte Vecchio is famous the world over for gold and silver jewellery and antique shops, but prices can be extortionate. To buy gold or jewellery, you will probably get a better price and range in Arezzo, or in Verona, in the Veneto.

The area near the church of **Santa Croce** is full of top-quality leather goods, while for other handicrafts check out the city's two open markets, sprawling **San Lorenzo** and covered **Mercato Nuovo**, near Piazza della Signoria.

The **Oltrarno area**, over the Ponte Vecchio bridge, is home to what remains of Florence's renowned craft industries, from picture restorers to makers of marbled paper. Request a list from the Florence tourist office (see page 418).

Just 27 km (17 miles) away, at **The Mall**, you can snap up designer labels at up to 80 percent off the original price. The Mall is at Via Europa 8, Leccio Reggello; tel: 55-865 7775; www.outlet-firenze.com. Call for details of shuttle bus pick-ups from hotels in Florence or take the train to Rignano sull'Arno and taxi to Leccio.

Shopping in the Ghetto

Rome's artistic community has fallen for the Ghetto's quiet charm, transforming a shady side street, Via Della Reginella, into an artistic quarter. While Piazza Navona and Campo de' Fiori have turned themselves over to Irish theme pubs and your-name-on-a-grain-of-rice artists, the Ghetto is holding on to its old traditions.
Il Museo del Louvre: Via della Reginella 28. Giuseppe Casetti's antiquarian bookshop and gallery sets the trend for the new arts community in the ghetto.
Roberto Arzu: Via della Reginella 5–6. Arzu's sculptures take their inspiration from ancient Rome and Rennaissance masterpieces.
Salvatore Savoca: Via della Reginella 25. Savoca's iconic oils on canvas are created in the upstairs studio and exhibited in the gallery below. Much loved by high stylists.
Tonino Carcione: Via della Reginella 13. If you are looking for period restored furniture, this workshop offers a great selection.

Venice

The most exclusive shopping area in Venice is the **Via XXII Marzo** and the streets around **St Mark's Square**. Try the Rialto Bridge and San Polo for local shopping. A market is held on the **Lido** on Tuesday morning.

Bargains in this city include shoes, clothes, gifts and fur coats. However, few tourists leave without a supply of at least one Venetian craft, such as hand-blown Murano glassware, or colourful carnival masks. The full range of Italian designer goods are on sale in Venice, but prices tend to be higher than on the mainland.

Naples

Naples is the capital of Italian fakes, so look out for cheap copies of designer goods on the streets or in markets. However, the city also has its own designer shops and crafts, such as Christmas cribs and their accompanying tiny figurines (a local art form) and Capodimonte porcelain.

The best shopping area is around **Piazza Amedeo** to **Piazza Trieste e Trento**. **Via dei Mille** and **Via Filangieri** are home to numerous famous-name designer shops. Mariella, one of Italy's most famous and expensive menswear outlets, is located near by, in **Via Riviera di Chiaia**. A less expensive street is the **Via Roma**, quite near to the San Carlo opera house.

Size Chart

Women's dresses:

Italian	UK	US
38	8	6
40	10	8
42	12	10
44	14	12

Men's shirts:

Italian	UK	US
36	14	14
38	15	15
41	16	16
43	17	17

Women's shoes:

Italian	UK	US
37	4	6
38	5	7½
39	6	8½
40	7	9

Men's shoes:

Italian	UK	US
40	6½	7½
41	7	8
42	8	8½
43	9	9½

A – Z

A HANDY SUMMARY OF PRACTICAL INFORMATION, ARRANGED ALPHABETICALLY

Age Restrictions

Cigarettes and alcohol cannot be sold to under-16s. Anyone over age 14 can ride a 50cc moped, but 14–18s can only do so once they have passed a practical test and have obtained a provisional driving licence.

Business

If you are in Italy for business, it may be worth visiting your embassy's commercial section for trade publications and databases of buyers, sellers and distributors. See www.deliciousitaly.com for information on business services in Italy.

Business Hours

Shops are open 9am–12.30pm and 3.30pm or 4pm–7.30 or 8pm. In areas serving tourists, hours are generally longer than these: in Taormina, Venice and popular towns in Tuscany, many shops remain open on Sunday, while elsewhere almost everything is closed on that day. Shops often also close on Monday (sometimes in the morning only) and some shut on Saturday.

Climate

Italy experiences marked regional variations, ranging from the more temperate north to the typically Mediterranean south, which is drier and sunnier, especially on Sicily and Sardinia. Summers tend to be hot and dry along mainland coastal areas, with mild winters, but the mountains are cool in summer and snowy in winter, especially in the Alps and Apennines. Cities in the north can get considerable snow, while Ancona, Pescara and the eastern Apennines are subject to blizzards. Much of the north, including Milan and Bologna, has a true Continental climate, while south of Florence the climate becomes more Mediterranean. Florence itself typically enjoys hot, dry summers, but is often struck by thunderstorms. Beyond Rome, winters tend to be mild, but can be freezing further north, especially across the foggy plains of Lombardy and Emilia Romagna, or in river cities such as Florence and Verona. Even if the Po Valley is swathed in fog in winter, it can be stifling in summer. Italy's east coast is not as wet as the west coast, but is usually colder in winter. As for

temperature, there is considerable variation between north and south, especially in winter. In January, Milan might be a snowy –2°C (28°F), with Turin a freezing –12°C (10°F), and Palermo a cloudy but mild 17°C (63°F). Winter lows can occasionally reach –14°C (7°F) in the Po Valley, or –5°C (23°F) in Florence, while in the south, summer highs of 46°C (115°F) have been recorded in Catania (Sicily) and Alghero (Sardinia).

Crime & Security

Throughout Italy, Jubilee Year (2000) sparked an increased police presence and therefore greater security for visitors. Rome, in particular, has benefited from increased police presence. As for the north, Venice is generally the safest city in Italy. Milan now has a heavy police presence at Stazione Centrale, the main train station and traditionally one of the most crime-prone areas in the city. Semi-official vigilante groups of Guardian Angels also act discreetly in dodgy areas of the city. Crime campaigns, increased civic pride, and the greater number of bars and restaurants in southern cities have also helped reduce crime.

CLIMATE CHART

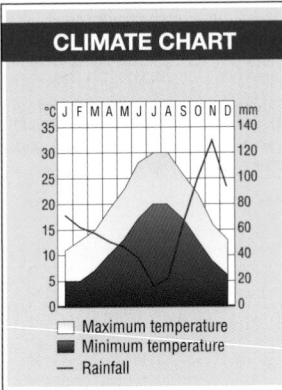

°C / J F M A M J J A S O N D / mm
35 / 140
30 / 120
25 / 100
20 / 80
15 / 60
10 / 40
5 / 20
0 / 0

☐ Maximum temperature
■ Minimum temperature
— Rainfall

Although violent crime is rare, many offences in the north have recently tended to be gang- or drug-related, with an increase in crimes committed by or on immigrants or refugees. With rising numbers of people entering Italy, the harassment of foreigners (essentially from former Yugoslavia, Eastern Europe, Albania or Africa) is on the increase in a country that is traditionally unused to dealing with incomers.

The main problem for tourists is petty crime – pickpocketing, bag-snatching and theft from cars; it is wise to have insurance cover against this and to take basic, sensible precautions against theft. Always lock your car and never leave luggage, cameras or other valuables inside. This applies particularly in major cities, and in the south. If walking, especially at night, in the tiny alleys of the historic city centres of, for example, Bari, Genoa or Palermo, try to blend in and avoid wearing flashy jewellery.

If you are the victim of a crime (or suffer a loss) and wish to claim against your insurance, it is essential to make a report at the nearest police station and get documentation to support your claim. If you need a policeman, dial **113** (**112** for the *carabinieri*, a national police force).

Customs & Entry

Used personal effects may be imported and exported into Italy without formality. Importing narcotics, weapons and pirated materials is forbidden. Alcoholic drinks, tobacco and perfume may be imported in limited quantities, depending on your nationality.

Goods on which duty has already been paid in another EU country may be freely imported, provided the amount falls within what might be reasonably described as "for

personal use", for example for a wedding or family party.

However, the recommended allowances for each person over 18 years of age are as follows:
• 10 litres spirits or strong liqueurs over 22 percent vol.
• 20 litres fortified wine
• 90 litres wine (of which no more than 60 litres may be sparkling)
• 200 cigars
• 400 cigarillos
• 3,200 cigarettes
• 110 litres beer
• 3 kilos tobacco
If you are any in doubt about what you can bring back, check with your local customs office. In the **UK**, contact HM Revenue & Customs, Dorset House, Stamford Street, London SE1 9NG (tel: 0845-010 9000) or log on to www.hmrc.gov.uk

For **US** citizens, the duty-free allowance is: 200 cigarettes, 50 cigars or 3 lb tobacco, 1 US quart of alcoholic beverages and duty-free gifts worth up to $100.

Visas and Passports

EU citizens do not need a visa or a passport to enter Italy: an identification card valid for foreign travel is sufficient.

Visitors from the following countries need a passport but are exempt from needing a visa providing they do not stay for more than three months: Australia, Austria, Barbados, Canada, Iceland, Jamaica, Japan, Kenya, South Korea, Kuwait, Malaysia, Maldives, Malta, Mexico, Monaco, New Zealand, Nigeria, Norway, Paraguay, Singapore, Switzerland, Trinidad and Tobago, United States, Uruguay and Venezuela (up to 60 days). Other nationalities should contact their nearest Italian consulate for information on entry regulations.

You are supposed to register with the police within three days of arriving in Italy. In fact, this procedure will be taken care of by your hotel, whatever the level of accommodation. If you are not staying in a hotel, theoretically you should contact the local police station, but virtually no one does.

Travelling with Pets

Pets must be vaccinated against rabies, and you should obtain an official document stating that your animal is healthy no more than one month before you arrive in Italy.

D isabled Travellers

Many of Italy's older cities are not easily navigable by disabled travellers: cobblestones, narrow

Emergency Numbers

General Emergency Assistance and police: 113 (24-hour service)
Caribinieri (**Police**): 112
Fire Brigade: 115
Medical assistance, ambulance: 118
Breakdown service: 803116
Route information; motorway tolls; weather forecasts: 1518
Train information: 892021
International operator assistance: 170

pavements and cramped lifts can make getting around tricky. The Rome-based company CO.IN offers information on disabled facilities in restaurants, shops and stations; tel: 800-271027 (toll-free, Italy only); www.coinsociale.it. CO.IN can also organise guided tours with transport equipped for disabled passengers; tel: 06-7128 9676. Roma Per Tutti is a useful information line for disabled travellers to Rome; tel: 06-5717 7094.

Transport in Italy's larger cities is gradually becoming more accessible, with increasing numbers of buses and trams now wheelchair-accessible. For train travel check the Trentalia website www.trenitalia.it; the wheelchair symbol denotes accessible trains. Call the relevant station to arrange assistance 24 hours prior to departure.

Accessible Italy is a non-profit organisation which organises accommodation and tours for people with disabilities; tel: 39-378-941111; www.accessibleitaly.com.

E lectricity

220 volts – you will need an adaptor to operate British three-pin appliances and a transformer to use 100–120 volt appliances.

Embassies & Consulates

The following consulates and embassies are all based in Rome, but employees there can put you in touch with other consulates (eg in Milan or Venice), should one of those be more convenient. Generally, appointments are necessary, so always ring before visiting. (Remember to dial the Rome code, even if calling from within Rome.)
Australia: tel: 06-852721 (emergencies, toll-free: 800-877-790)
Canada: tel: 06-445981 (24-hour emergency service)
France: tel: 06-6880 6437
Germany: tel: 06-492131

Ireland: tel: 06-697 9121
New Zealand: tel: 06-441 7171
UK: tel: 06-4220 0001
US: tel: 06-46741

G ay & Lesbian Travellers

Gay life in Italy is becoming more
mainstream, helped by increasing
numbers of dedicated club nights
and festivals such as Rome's
summer-long Gay Village. Attitudes
are generally more tolerant in the
north: Bologna is regarded as Italy's
gay capital, and Milan, Turin and
Rome all have a lively gay scene.
The Bologna-based Arcigay network
can advise gay and lesbian travellers;
tel: 051-649 3055; www.arcigay.it.

H ealth

To receive free treatment in cases of
illness, accident or childbirth, EU
citizens should obtain a European
Health Insurance Card (EHIC) before
leaving home. However, this will not
entitle you to repatriation in the
event of serious illness. Citizens of
non-EU countries must pay for
medical assistance and medicine.
Health insurance is recommended,
and you should keep receipts for
medical expenses if you want to
claim. Most hospitals have a 24-hour
emergency department (Pronto
Soccorso) but a stay in an Italian
hospital can be a grim experience,
particularly in the south.

For minor complaints, seek out a
farmacia (signs have a green cross).
Normal opening hours are 9am–1pm
and 4–7.30 or 8pm, but outside
these hours the address of the
nearest farmacia on duty is posted in
the window.

I nternet

Most hotels will allow you to plug a
modem into their phone system; 4-
and 5-star hotels should have built-in
dataports and/or wireless facilities.
All Italian cities now have their fair
share of internet cafés, usually
located near tourist sites or near the
train station. In Rome, EasyEverything
in Piazza Barberini 2 has 250
computer terminals, scanning and
photo facilities and low rates;
www.easyeverything.com.

L ost Property

Ask about lost items at the local lost
property office (ufficio oggetti
smarriti). Items lost on public
transport are generally directed to
the transport authority's own lost
property office. In Rome, items found

on the city's buses, trams and
metros are sent to Via Bettoni 1;
tel: 06-581040.

M edia

The Italian press is concentrated
in Milan and Rome. The biggest
papers are La Repubblica and Il
Corriere della Sera, which publish
regional editions. Il Mattino is the
main newspaper for Naples, while
Il Giornale della Sicilia and La Sicilia
are widely read in Sicily. However, Il
Corriere dello Sport, the pink sports
paper, is probably the one you will
notice most.

It is worth buying the local
newspaper for entertainment listings
and bus and ferry timetables. Most
major cities publish weekly listings
magazines: Roma C'e, which has a
section in English at the back, is a
guide to everything going on in Rome
and is available from newsstands
every Wednesday. La Repubblica also
publishes Trovaroma, a what's-on
section, every Thursday. Listings
magazines for Milan include the
monthly Milano Mese.

Television stations include RAI (the
national network with three channels,
which is due to be privatised), the
Vatican network, plus various
privately owned national channels,
and over 450 local commercial
stations. Many European channels
and the US channel CNN are available
by cable.

Money Matters

The currency in Italy is the euro (€),
which is available in 500, 200, 100,
50, 20, 10 and 5 euro notes, and 2
euro, 1 euro, 50 cent, 20 cent, 10
cent, 5 cent, 2 cent and 1 cent coins.
There are 100 cents to one euro.

Italy is a society that prefers cash
to credit cards, except for large
purchases, or, for instance, hotel
bills. In the case of modest
restaurants and smaller shops, it is
usual to pay in cash. Check
beforehand if there is any doubt.
Most shopkeepers and restaurateurs
will not change money, so it is best
to change a limited amount at the
airport when you arrive, especially if
it is the weekend, when banks are
closed. Try to avoid changing money
in hotels, where the commission
tends to be higher than in banks.

Travellers' cheques are still
recommended in Italy, as they can be
replaced if stolen or lost. Note,
however, that commission will be
charged for changing them.

Banks are generally open
8.30am–1.30pm and for one hour in

the afternoon (usually between 3pm
and 4pm). Unfortunately, most
banks are notoriously inefficient,
and currency conversion can easily
turn into a tedious saga, so use
cashpoints where possible. You can
also change money at airports and
main railway stations.

Cash Machines & Credit Cards

Given the long queues for money-
changing in Italy, it is simplest to
get cash from cashpoint machines,
which are widely available. Most
Switch cards work in Italian
machines, with your normal PIN
number, as do credit cards, though
you may sometimes have to look for
particular "Bancomats" (cashpoint
machines) that take your card.

In cities, many restaurants, hotels,
shops and stores will take major
credit cards (Visa, American Express,
MasterCard and Carte Blanche), but
in rural areas, especially, you may be
able to pay only in cash.

P ostal Services

Some post offices open 8am–1.30pm
only, but many towns have a main
post office that is open throughout
the day. The post office can provide
such services as raccomandata
(registered post), espresso (express
post) and telegrams. Stamps can
also be bought at tobacconists
(tabacchi).

You can receive mail addressed
to Posta Restante, from the Fermo
Posta window of the main post
office in every town, picking it up
personally with identification.
However, internet cafés are now a
more popular way for travellers to
keep in touch.

Public Holidays

January New Year's Day (1),
Epiphany (6)
March/April Easter Day, Easter
Monday
April Liberation Day (25)
May Labour Day (1)
August Assumption of the Blessed
Virgin Mary (15)
November All Saints' Day (1)
December Immaculate Conception of
the Blessed Virgin Mary (8), Christmas
Day (25), St Stephen's Day (26)

In addition to these national
holidays, almost all cities have
a holiday to celebrate their own
patron saint, for example St Mark,
25 April (Venice); St John the Baptist,
24 June (Turin, Genoa and Florence);
SS Peter and Paul, 29 June (Rome);
St Rosalia, 15 July (Palermo);
St Gennaro, 19 September (Naples);

St Petronius, 4 October (Bologna); St Ambrose, 7 December (Milan).

R eligion

Roman Catholic Mass is celebrated every day and several times on Sundays in Italian. Some non-Catholic churches hold services in English; in Rome, you can find services in English at the Church of England All Saints, Via del Babuino 153b and at the Scottish Presbyterian St Andrew's, Via XX Settembre 7. The Jewish Synagogue is at Lungotevere Cenci 9. The city's mosque is in Via della Moschea. Ask at the local tourist office about places of worship in the area.

S tudents

In the UK, the Italian Cultural Institute can provide advice on courses in Italy, particularly language-based; tel: 020-7235 1461; www.icilondon.esteri.it. In the US, try the American Institute for Foreign Study; tel: 866-906 2437; www.aifs.org and www.studyabroad-italy.com.

If you are intending to study in an Italian university, you will need to get your certificates translated and validated by the Italian consulate in your own country before making your application at the *ufficio stranieri* (foreign department) of the university of your choice in Italy; www.study-in-italy.it offers useful advice.

T elephones

Public telephones are widespread, particularly in major cities – Rome even introduced a new-style telephone box for Holy (Jubilee) Year 2000. Most accept phonecards *(carte telefoniche* or *schede telefoniche)*, available from tobacconists or post offices; few telephones accept coins. From post offices and some bars you can call *scatti* (ring first, pay later).

You can also make calls using a British BT chargecard or one of the cards issued by AT&T, Sprint, NCI and other North American long-distance telephone companies. This allows more flexibility by charging the calls to your home address.

The cheapest time for long-distance calls is between 10pm and 8am Monday to Saturday, and all day Sunday.

For directory enquiries dial 12. For international enquiries call 176, and to make a reverse-charge (collect) call, dial 170.

Italy has an extremely high ownership of mobile phones, and in

Area Codes

When dialling numbers either inside or outside your area in Italy, dialling must always be preceded by the area code, including the zero. Area codes of some of the main cities are:

Bologna	051
Florence	055
Genoa	010
Milan	02
Naples	081
Palermo	091
Pisa	050
Rome	06
Turin	011
Venice	041

To call abroad from Italy, dial 00, followed by:

Australia	61
Canada	1
Ireland	353
New Zealand	64
UK	44
US	1

Then dial the number, omitting the initial "0" if there is one.

the major cities, such as Rome, Milan, Venice and Florence, it is possible to hire one.

British, Australian and New Zealand mobile phones can generally be used in Italy, but US non-tri-band mobiles are on a different frequency and do not generally work as well. The main mobile phone networks in Italy are TIM, Vodaphone and Wind; all three have numerous branches throughout the country.

Time Zone

Italy follows Central European Time (GMT plus 1 hour, EST plus 6 hours: add one hour in summer).

Tipping

It is customary to tip various people for their services, especially in restaurants and hotels. Most restaurants continue to impose an outdated cover and bread charge *(coperto* and *pane)* of around €5, although it has "officially" been eliminated in most cities. Often, in addition, a 10 percent service charge *(servizio)* is added to the bill. If the menu says that service is included, a small extra tip is discretionary. If service is not included, it is usual to leave 12 to 15 percent of the bill. Gondoliers need not be tipped, but water-taxi drivers may expect a small tip. For taxis, round the fare up to the nearest euro.

Tourist Information
Regions and Provinces

Administratively, most of Italy is divided into regions *(regioni)* such as Tuscany and Sicily, then into provinces *(provincie)*. Certain regions, such as Sardinia and Sicily, are autonomous.

Every major town has an **Azienda Provinciale per il Turismo (APT)**, possibly with subsidiary IAT offices. As well as helpful information, main APT offices should offer a free city map, a hotel list and information about museums. The tourist offices in the main cities are listed below.

As another source of information, major cities have a **Touring Club Italiano** (TCI) office, which provides free information about points of interest. Telephone numbers are listed in the local telephone book. The club also produces some good maps and food and wine guides.

Italian State Tourist Board

The Italian State Tourist Board, known as ENIT (Ente Nazionale per il Turismo), provides general tourist information. ENIT's headquarters are in Via Marghera 2/6, Rome (tel: 06-497 1222).

In the UK, ENIT, 1 Princes Street, London W1B 2AY; tel: 020-7408 1254; fax: 020-7493 6695, www.enit.it.

In the US, ENIT, Suite 1565, 630 Fifth Avenue, New York, NY 10111; tel: 212-245 4822/212-245 5618; fax: 212-586 9249, www.italiantourism.com. There are also offices in Chicago, Los Angeles and Canada.

Key Italian Tourist Offices

Arezzo: APT Arezzo, Piazza Risorgimento 116; tel: 0575-377678; fax: 0575-20839; www.apt.arezzo.it.
Assisi: APT Assisi, Piazza del Comune 12; tel: 075-812450; www.bellaumbria.net/assisi.
Bergamo: APT del Bergamasco, Viale V. Emanuele 20; tel: 035-213185/210620; fax: 035-230184; www.apt.bergamo.it.
Bologna: APT Bologna, Via De' Castagnoli 3; tel: 051-218756/7; www.provincia.bologna.it. APT Bologna, Piazza Maggiore 1e, Palazzo del Podestà, Bologna; tel: 051-246541; fax: 051-6393171; www.comune.bologna.it.
Bolzano (Bozen): APT Bolzano, Piazza Walther 8, Alto Adige; tel: 0471-307000; fax: 0471-980128; www.sudtirol.com/bolzano.
Capri: APT Capri, Piazza Umberto I; tel: 081-8370686; www.capri.it.

Top Three Tourist Destinations

Rome

APT Rome (main office): Via Parigi 5; tel: 06-488991; Mon–Sat 9am–7pm. There is also a multi-lingual **tourist call centre** (tel: 06-8205 9127) that operates daily 9am–7.30pm. **Termini station** (opposite platform 4): tel: 06-4890 6300; daily 8am–9pm. **Fiumicino airport** (International Departures, Terminal C): daily 8.15am–7pm.

There are several other tourist info points around town, all daily 9.30am–7.30pm. **Piazza dei Cinquecento** (opposite Termini station); **Piazza Pia** (in front of Castel Sant'Angelo); **Piazza del Tempio della Pace** (on Via dei Fori Imperiali); **Piazza Sonnino** (in Trastevere); **Piazza delle Cinque Lune** (near Piazza Navona).

The privately run tourist office **Enjoy Rome**, near the station, is staffed by helpful English-speakers, offers a free tourist information and accommodation booking service and organises walking tours of the city. Via Marghera 8a; tel: 06-445 1843; www.enjoyrome.com.

The toll-free number 060606 is a reliable tourist information line run by the city council.

Florence

APT Florence: Via Manzoni 16; tel: 055-23320; fax: 055-234 6286; apt@firenzeturismo.it; info@firenzeturismo.it; www.firenzeturismo.it.

APT Firenze & Provincia (Florence & Province): Via Cavour 1 (just north of the Duomo); weekdays 8.30am–6.30pm; tel: 055-290832; fax: 055-276 0383; infoturismo@provincia.fi.it.

APT Airport (Vespucci/Peretola): tel: 055-315874.

APT Fiesole (in the hills above Florence): Via Portigiana 3–5; tel: 055-598720; fax: 055-598822.

Firenze Comune (Florence Council, tourism section): tel: 800-055055;

fax: 055-238 1226; weekdays 8.30am–5.30pm, weekends 8.30am–1.45pm. www.comune.fi.it.

Venice

Head office: APT Venice, Castello 5050; tel: 041-529 8711; fax: 041-523 0399; www.turismovenezia.it

Santa Lucia train station: tel: 041-529 8727; 8am–7pm (little literature available, but the staff are helpful).

Lido di Venezia (on the island of the Lido): Gran Viale S.M. Elisabetta 6/A; tel: 041-529 8700; only open from the beginning of June to the end of September.

Marco Polo airport: 041-541 5887; daily 9.30am–7pm.

San Marco: 71F Piazza San Marco; tel: 041-529 8711; 9am–3.30pm, later in summer.

Hoteliers freephone number for bookings in Venice: tel: 800-843 006 (calls from within Italy only).

Catania: AAPIT Provincia di Catania and Acireale, Via Cimarosa 10–12; tel: 095-730 6211/730 6222; fax: 095-730 6233; www.apt.catania.it.

Elba: APT Elba, Calata Italia 26, Portoferraio; tel: 0565-914671; fax: 0565-914672; www.aptelba.it.

Genoa: Aeroporto C. Colombo; tel: 010-601 5247; Stazione Principe, Piazza Acqua Verde; tel: 010-246 2633; www.apt. genova.it. Ferry Terminal; tel: 010-246 3686.

The Lakes
• Lake Como (Lago di Como)
APT Bellagio: Piazza Mazzini, Bellagio, Lombardy; tel: 031-950204.
IAT Como: Piazza Cavour 17, Como; tel: 031-269712.
APT del Comasco (Como area): tel: 031-330 0111; fax: 031-261152; lakecomo@tin.it; www.lakecomo.org.
• Lake Garda (Lago di Garda)
Main APT Lake Garda: Via Roma 8 Gardone Riviera; tel: 0365-290411; fax: 0365-290025; www.lagodigarda.it.
APT Desenzano, Via Porto Vecchio 34, Desenzano; tel: 030-914 1510.
APT Riva del Garda: Giardini di Porta Orientale 8, Riva, Trentino; tel: 0464-554444.
APT Sirmione: Viale Marconi 2, Sirmione, Lombardy; tel: 030-916114/916245.
Navigation on Lake Garda: tel: 030-914 9511; freephone: 800-551801.
• Lake Iseo (Lago d'Iseo)
APT Iseo: Lungolago Marconi 2, Iseo, Lombardy; tel: 030-980209.

Navigation on Lake Iseo: tel: 035-971483; freephone: 800-551801.
• Lake Maggiore (Lago Maggiore):
Navigation on Lake Maggiore: tel: 0322-233 2000; freephone: 800-551801.
Stresa: Piazza Marconi 16 (near the Navigazione Lago Maggiore ticket office); tel: 0323-30150; fax: 0323-31308.
Verbania: Corso Zanitello 6/8; tel: 0323-503249; fax: 0323-556669; www.lagomaggiore.it.

Milan
APT Milano: Via Marconi 1 (by the Duomo); tel: 02-7252 4301; fax: 02-7252 4250
IAT Milano: Via Marconi 1 (by the Duomo); tel: switchboard: 02-7252 4300; fax: 02-7252 4350.
IAT Stazione Centrale (tourist office in Milan's central railway station): tel: 02-7252 4360/7252 4301; www.milanoinfotourist.com.

Naples
APT: Palazzo Reale, Piazza Plebiscito; tel: 081-252 5711; fax: 081-418619; www.inaples.it.
EPT Napoli: Piazza Del Gesù Nuovo; tel: 081-552 3328; e-mail: ept@netgroup.it; Mon–Sat 9am–8pm; Sun 9am–3pm.
Stazione Centrale (Naples's main train station): tel: 081-206666.

Orvieto: APT Orvieto, Piazza Duomo 24, Orvieto; tel: 07633-41772;

fax: 07633-44433; info@iat.orvieto.tr.it.
Padua: Padua APT, Riviera dei Mugnai 8; tel: 049-876 7911; fax: 049-650794; www.padovanet.it.
Palermo: Palermo APT, Piazza Castelnuovo 35; tel: 091-586122/583847; fax: 091-586338; www.aapit.pa.it.
Perugia: APT Perugia, Piazza Matteotti 18, Loggia dei Lanari; tel: 07557-36458; www.tourism. comune.perugia.it.
Pisa APT: Via Pietro Nenni 24; tel: 050-929777; fax: 050-929764; www.pisa.turismo.toscana.it.
Rimini APT: Piazzale F. Fellini 3; tel: 0541-56902; fax: 0541-56598; www.riminiturismo.it.
San Gimignano: Piazza Duomo 1; tel: 0577-940008; fax: 0577-940903; www.sangimignano.com.
Siena: APT Siena, Piazza del Campo 56; tel: 0577-280551; fax: 0577-281041; daily 9am–7pm; e-mail: aptsiena@turismo.toscana.it; www.terresiena.it.
Siena Hotels Promotion: Piazza Madre Teresa di Calcutta 5; reservation on: 0577-288084; fax: 0577-280290; hotel information, email: info@hotelsiena.com.
Sorrento: APT Sorrento, Via Luigi De Maio 35, Sorrento; tel: 081-807 4033; fax: 081-877 3397; www.sorrentotourism.it.
Taormina: APT Taormina, Piazza S. Caterina, tel: 0942-23243; fax: 0942-24941; www.gate2taormina.it.

Trentino: Via Romagnosi 11, Trento; tel: 0461-839000; fax: 0461-260245; www.trentino.to (information in English).

Trento: APT Trento, Via Manci 2, Trento; tel: 0461-216000; fax: 0461-216060; www.apt.trento.it.

Turin APT: Piazza Castelli 161, Torino; tel: 011-535181/535901; fax: 011-530070; www.turismotorino.org.

Urbino APT: Piazza Duca Federico 35, Urbino; tel: 0722-2613; fax: 0722-2441; www.comune.urbino.ps.it/turismo.

Verona: Verona APT, Via degli Alpini 9; tel: 045-806 8680; fax: 045-800 3638; e-mail: iatverona@provincia.vr.it; www.tourism.verona.it.

Arena di Verona (for booking opera tickets in the Verona Arena): Piazza Brà 28, Verona; tel: 045-8005151; www.arena.it; Ticket Office, Via Dietro Anfiteatro 6/b, Verona.

Vicenza APT: Piazza Matteotto 5, Vicenza; tel: 0444-320854; Piazza Duomo 5; tel: 0444-544122; www.ascom.vi.it/aptvicenza.

W ebsites

General Sites
Database on all Italian museums: www.museionline.com
Piazze d'Italia: www.mediasoft.it/piazze
Visit different squares in Italy, including virtual tours.
National Parks
www.parks.it

Rome
Official site of the Rome municipality: www.comune.roma.it
Information on the Vatican museums: www.vatican.va
Cultural information and special events: www.whatsoninrome.com
English-speaking guided tours and walks: www.enjoyrome.com
Museum and cultural listings and news on Rome and Italy (plus classifieds): www.wantedinrome.com
Information on currrent exhibitions: www.romaturismo.it
Rome transport information: www.atac.roma.it

The North
Venice
Venice water transport (ACTV Venezia): www.actv.it
Clear site in English and Italian.
Biennale art festival:
www.labiennale.org
The City of Venice:
www.comune.venezia.it
Official site of Comune di Venezia.
La Fenice opera house:
www.teatrolafenice.it
Saving Venice (Salviamo Venezia): www.savevenice.org
Venice Carnival (Carnevale di Venezia): www.carnivalofvenice.com
British-led organisation that funds restoration projects to save the city: www.veniceinperil.org

Veneto
Padua (Padova) APT:
www.turismopadova.it
Arena di Verona: www.arena.it
Verona tourist office (APT Verona): www.tourism.verona.it
Consorzio di Verona:
www.veronatuttintorno.it
Consortium promoting Verona's churches, hotels and restaurants.
Verona general information:
www.turismoverona.it

Milan
La Scala:
www.teatroallascala.org
Milan general information:
www.milanoinfotourist.com

The Lakes
Lake Garda:
www.lagodigarda.it
Trentino:
www.trentino.to
Information on the Trentino area of Lake Garda.
Turin general information:
www.turismotorino.org

Central Italy
Emilia Romagna
APT site: www.emiliaromagnaturismo.it

Pisa
Pisa general information:
www.pisa.turismo.toscana.it

Florence
General information plus hotels and restaurants:
www.firenzeturismo.it
The Uffizi Gallery:
info@uffizi.firenze.it
E-mail address for booking a precise time slot in which to visit the gallery.
Agriturismo in Tuscany:
www.agriturismo.regione.toscana.it
Official site giving information on rural farm stays in this popular area.
Tuscany: general information: www.turismo.toscana.it

Umbria
Umbria general information:
www.umbria2000.it
www.umbriaonline.com
Umbria jazz festival:
www.umbria jazz.com
Perugia city: www.comune.perugia.it
Perugia province:
www.bellaumbria.net/perugia

Abruzzo
Abruzzo national park headquarters: www.parcoabruzzo.it

Abruzzo general information:
www.terradabruzzo.com

The South, SIcily and Sardinia
Naples
Naples hotels: www.napleshotels.na-it
For details of cumulative card for several museums:
www.napoliartecard.com
Campania
Guide to the island of Capri:
www.caprinet.it
Online magazine on the Campania coast:
www.giracostiera.com

Puglia (Apulia) and Calabria
The city of Bari, capital of Puglia:
www.barionline.cjb.net
General information.
Calabria's official site:
www.it/eng/Regioni/calabria
General Caabrian site:
www.madeincalabria.com

Weights & Measures

The metric system is used for all weights and measures. For a quick conversion: 2.5 cm is approximately 1 inch, 1 metre is about a yard, 100 g is just under 4 oz and 1 kg is 2 lb 2 oz. Distance is quoted in kilometres. One kilometre equals five-eighths of a mile, so 80 km is 50 miles.

What to Wear

Although the Italians are known for their sense of style, this does not mean that one should always dress formally in Italy. However, when sightseeing, both men and women are advised to cover their shoulders and avoid wearing shorts (or short skirts in the case of women), as some churches bar visitors who are deemed unsuitably dressed. Unless you are visiting mountain areas, the moderate climate makes heavy clothing unnecessary in summer. A light jacket should be adequate for summer evenings. In winter (November–March), the climate can be cold and wet throughout Italy.

Women Travellers

The difficulties encountered by women travelling in Italy are often overstated, but women – especially young blondes – usually have to put up with much male attention. Though often annoying, it is rarely dangerous, but take particular care in Genoa, Bari, Naples, Palermo and Catania. Ignoring whistles and questions is the best way to discourage unwanted attention.

TRANSPORT
ACCOMMODATION
EATING OUT
ACTIVITIES
A – Z
LANGUAGE

L ANGUAGE

UNDERSTANDING THE LANGUAGE

Basic Communication

Yes/No *Sì/No*
Thank you *Grazie*
Many thanks *Grazie mille/tante grazie/molte grazie*
You're welcome *Prego*
All right/OK/that's fine
Va bene
Please *Per favore/Per cortesia*
Excuse me (to get attention) *Scusi* (singular), *Scusate* (plural)
Excuse me (to get through a crowd) *Permesso*
Excuse me (to attract attention, eg of a waiter) *Senta!*
Excuse me (sorry) *Mi scusi* (singular), *Scusatemi* (plural)
Wait a minute! (informal) *Aspetta!* (formal) *Aspetti!*
Could you help me? (formal) *Potrebbe aiutarmi?*
Certainly *Ma certo*
Can I help you? (formal) *Posso aiutarLa?*
Can you show me...? (formal) *Può indicarmi...?*
Can you help me? (formal) *Può aiutarmi, per cortesia?*
I'm sorry *Mi dispiace*

I don't understand *Non capisco*
Do you speak English/French/ German? *Parla inglese/francese/ tedesco?*
Could you speak more slowly, please? *Può parlare più lentamente, per favore?*
Could you repeat that please? (formal) *Può ripetere, per piacere?*
slowly/quietly *piano*
here/there *qui/là*
What? *Cosa?*
When/why/where? *Quando/perchè/dove?*
Where is the lavatory? *Dov'è il bagno?*

Greetings

Hello (good day) *Buon giorno*
Hello/hi/goodbye (familiar) *Ciao*
Good afternoon/evening *Buona sera*
Goodnight *Buona notte*
Goodbye *Arrivederci*
Pleased to meet you (formal) *Piacere di conoscerLa*
I am English/American/Canadian *Sono inglese/americano/canadese*
Irish/Scottish/Welsh *irlandese/scozzese/gallese*

Do you speak English? *Parla inglese?*
I'm here on holiday *Sono qui in vacanza*
How are you (formal/informal)? *Come sta/come stai?*
Fine thanks *Bene, grazie*
See you later *A più tardi*
See you soon *A presto*
Take care (formal) *Stia bene,* (informal) *Stammi bene*

Telephone Calls

the area code *il prefisso telefonico*
I'd like to make a reverse charges call *Vorrei fare una telefonata a carico del destinatario*
May I use your telephone, please? *Posso usare il telefono?*
Hello (on the telephone) *Pronto*
My name's *Mi chiamo/Sono*
Could I speak to...? *Posso parlare con...?*
Sorry, he/she isn't in *Mi dispiace, è fuori*
Can he call you back? *Può richiamarLa?*
I'll try again later *Riproverò più tardi*
Can I leave a message? *Posso lasciare un messaggio?*
Please tell him I called *Gli dica, per favore, che ho telefonato*
Can you speak up please? (formal) *Può parlare più forte, per favore?*

In the Hotel

Do you have any vacant rooms? *Avete camere libere?*
I have a reservation *Ho fatto una prenotazione*
I'd like... *Vorrei...*
a single/double room (with double bed) *una camera singola/doppia (con letto matrimoniale)*
a room with twin beds *una camera a due letti*

Pronunciation and Grammar Tips

Italian speakers claim that pronunciation is easy: you pronounce it as it is written. This is roughly true, but there are a few rules to bear in mind: *c* before *e* or *i* is pronounced "ch", eg *ciao, mi dispiace, la coincidenza*. *Ch* before *i* or *e* is pronounced as "k", eg *la chiesa*. Likewise, *sci* or *sce* is pronounced as in "sheep" or "shed" respectively. *Gn* in Italian is rather like the sound in "onion", while *gl* is softened to resemble the sound in "bullion".

Nouns are either masculine (*il*, plural *i*) or feminine (*la*, plural *le*). Plurals of nouns are most often formed by changing an *o* to an *i* and an *a* to an *e*, eg *il panino, i panini; la chiesa, le chiese*.

Words are generally stressed on the penultimate syllable unless an accent indicates otherwise.

Italian has formal and informal words for "You". In the singular, *Tu* is informal while *Lei* is more polite. It is best to use the formal form unless invited to do otherwise.

Days and Dates

morning/afternoon/evening *la mattina, il pomeriggio, la sera*
yesterday/today/tomorrow *ieri/oggi/domani*
the day after tomorrow *dopodomani*
now/early/late *adesso/presto/ritardo*
Monday *lunedì*
Tuesday *martedì*
Wednesday *mercoledì*
Thursday *giovedì*
Friday *venerdì*
Saturday *sabato*
Sunday *domenica*

a room with a bath/shower *una camera con bagno/doccia*
for one night *per una notte*
for two nights *per due notti*
Could you show me another room please? *Potrebbe mostrarmi un'altra camera?*
How much is it? *Quanto costa?*
on the first floor *al primo piano*
Is breakfast included? *È compresa la prima colazione?*
Is everything included? *È tutto compreso?*
half/full board *mezza pensione/pensione completa*
It's expensive *È caro*
Do you have a room with a balcony/view of the sea?
C'è una camera con balcone/con vista sul mare?
Can I see the room? *Posso vedere la camera?*
I'll take it *La prendo*
big/small *grande/piccola*
What time does the hotel close? *A che ora chiude l'albergo?*
What time is breakfast? *A che ora è la prima colazione?*
Please give me a call at... *Mi può chiamare alle...*
Come in! *Avanti!*
Can I have the bill, please? *Posso avere il conto, per favore?*
dining room *la sala da pranzo*
key *la chiave*
lift *l'ascensore*
towel *l'asciugamano*

Eating Out

Bar Snacks and Drinks

I'd like... *Vorrei...*
coffee *un caffè* (espresso: small, strong and black)
un cappuccino (with hot, frothy milk)
un caffè latte (milky coffee)
un caffè lungo (weak)
uno corretto (laced with alcohol – usually brandy or grappa)
tea *un tè*
lemon tea *un tè al limone*

herbal tea *una tisana*
hot chocolate *una cioccolata calda*
orange/lemon juice (bottled) *un succo d'arancia/di limone*
fresh orange/lemon juice *una spremuta di arancia/di limone*
orangeade *un'aranciata*
water (mineral) *acqua (minerale)*
fizzy/still mineral water *acqua minerale gasata/naturale*
a glass of mineral water *un bicchiere di minerale*
with/without ice *con/senza ghiaccio*
red/white wine *vino rosso/bianco*
beer (draught) *una birra (alla spina)*
milk *latte*
a (half) litre *un (mezzo) litro*
bottle *una bottiglia*
ice cream *un gelato*
sandwich *un tramezzino*
Anything else? *Desidera qualcos'altro?*
Cheers *Salute*

In a Restaurant

I'd like to book a table *Vorrei riservare un tavolo*
Have you got a table for... *Avete un tavolo per...*
I have a reservation *Ho fatto una prenotazione*
lunch/supper *il pranzo/la cena*
I'm a vegetarian *Sono vegetariano/a*
Is there a vegetarian dish? *C'è un piatto vegetariano?*
May we have the menu? *Ci dà il menu, per favore?*
wine list *la lista dei vini*
What would you like? *Che cosa prende?*
What would you recommend? *Che cosa ci raccomanda?*
What would you like to drink? *Che cosa desidera da bere?*
a carafe of red/white wine *una caraffa di vino rosso/bianco*
fixed-price menu *il menu a prezzo fisso*
the dish of the day *il piatto del giorno*
VAT (sales tax) *IVA*
cover charge *il coperto/pane e coperto*
That's enough; no more, thanks *Basta (così)*
The bill, please *Il conto per favore*
Is service included? *Il servizio è incluso?*
Where is the toilet? *Dov'è il bagno?*
I've enjoyed the meal *Mi è piaciuto molto*

Menu Decoder

Antipasti (Hors d'œuvres)

caponata mixed aubergine, olives and tomatoes
insalata caprese tomato and mozzarella salad
insalata di mare seafood salad

insalata mista/verde **mixed/green salad**
melanzane alla parmigiana **fried or baked aubergine** (with parmesan cheese and tomato)
mortadella/salame **salami**
pancetta **bacon**
peperonata **vegetable stew** (made with peppers, onions, tomatoes and sometimes aubergines)

Primi (First Courses)

Typical first courses include soup, risotto, gnocchi or numerous varieties of pasta in a wide range of sauces. Risotto and gnocchi are more common in the north than in central Italy.
il brodetto **fish soup**
il brodo **consommé**
gli gnocchi **potato dumplings**
la minestra **soup**
pasta e fagioli **pasta and bean soup**
il prosciutto (cotto/crudo) **ham**
i tartufi **truffles**
la zuppa **soup**

Secondi (Main Courses)

Main courses are typically fish-, seafood- or meat-based, with accompaniments (*contorni*) that vary greatly from region to region across Italy.

La Carne (Meat)

arrosto **roast meat**
ai ferri **grilled**
al forno **baked**
al girarrosto **spit-roasted**
alla griglia **grilled**
stufato **braised, stewed**
ben cotto **well done** (steak, etc.)
al puntino **medium** (steak, etc.)
al sangue **rare** (steak, etc.)
l'agnello **lamb**
la bistecca **steak**
il capriolo/cervo **venison**
il cinghiale **wild boar**
il coniglio **rabbit**
il controfiletto **sirloin steak**
le cotolette **cutlets**

Numbers

1	*uno*	**16**	*sedici*
2	*due*	**17**	*diciassette*
3	*tre*	**18**	*diciotto*
4	*quattro*	**19**	*diciannove*
5	*cinque*	**20**	*venti*
6	*sei*	**30**	*trenta*
7	*sette*	**40**	*quaranta*
8	*otto*	**50**	*cinquanta*
9	*nove*	**60**	*sessanta*
10	*dieci*	**70**	*settanta*
11	*undici*	**80**	*ottanta*
12	*dodici*	**90**	*novanta*
13	*tredici*	**100**	*cento*
14	*quattordici*	**200**	*duecento*
15	*quindici*	**1,000**	*mille*

il fagiano **pheasant**
il fegato **liver**
il filetto **fillet**
il maiale **pork**
il manzo **beef**
l'ossobuco **shin of veal**
il pollo **chicken**
le polpette **meatballs**
la salsiccia **sausage**
il saltimbocca (alla romana)
veal escalopes with ham
le scaloppine **escalopes**
lo stufato **stew**
il sugo **sauce**
il tacchino **turkey**
la trippa **tripe**
il vitello **veal**

Frutti di Mare (Seafood)

surgelati **frozen**
alla griglia **grilled**
fritto **fried**
ripieno **stuffed**
al vapore **steamed**
le acciughe **anchovies**
l'aragosta **lobster**
il baccalà **dried salted cod**
il branzino **sea bass**
i calamari **squid**
i calamaretti **baby squid**
i crostacei **shellfish**
le cozze **mussels**
il fritto misto **mixed fried fish**
i gamberi **prawns**
i gamberetti **shrimps**
il granchio **crab**
il merluzzo **cod**
le ostriche **oysters**
il pesce **fish**
il pesce spada **swordfish**
il polipo **octopus**
il risotto di mare **seafood risotto**
le sarde **sardines**
la sogliola **sole**
la trota **trout**
il tonno **tuna**
le vongole **clams**

I Legumi/La Verdura (Vegetables)

gli asparagi **asparagus**
le carote **carrots**
la cipolla **onion**
i fagioli **beans**
i fagiolini **French (green) beans**

il finocchio **fennel**
i funghi **mushrooms**
l'insalata mista **mixed salad**
l'insalata verde **green salad**
la melanzana **aubergine**
le patate **potatoes**
le patatine fritte **chips/French fries**
i peperoni **peppers**
i pomodori **tomatoes**
il radicchio **red, bitter lettuce**
i ravanelli **radishes**
la rughetta **rocket**
gli spinaci **spinach**
la verdura **green vegetables**
gli zucchini **courgettes**

I Dolci (Desserts)

al carrello **(desserts) from the trolley**
un semifreddo **semi-frozen dessert (many types)**
la cassata **Sicilian ice cream with candied peel**
le frittelle **fritters**
un gelato (di lampone/limone) **(raspberry/lemon) ice cream**
una granita **water ice**
una macedonia di frutta **fruit salad**
il tartufo (nero) **(chocolate) ice cream dessert**
il tiramisù **cold, creamy cheese and coffee dessert**
la torta **cake/tart**
lo zabaglione **sweet dessert made with eggs and Marsala wine**
la zuppa inglese **trifle**

La Frutta (Fruit)

le albicocche **apricots**
le arance **oranges**
le banane **bananas**
il cocomero **watermelon**
le ciliegie **cherries**
i fichi **figs**
le fragole **strawberries**
i lamponi **raspberries**
la mela **apple**
il melone **melon**
la pesca **peach**
la pera **pear**
il pompelmo **grapefruit**
l'uva **grapes**

Basic Foods

l'aceto **vinegar**
l'aglio **garlic**

il burro **butter**
il formaggio **cheese**
la frittata **omelette**
i grissini **bread sticks**
l'olio **oil**
la marmellata **jam**
il pane **bread**
il pane integrale **wholemeal bread**
il parmigiano **parmesan cheese**
il pepe **pepper**
il riso **rice**
il sale **salt**
la senape **mustard**
le uova **eggs**
lo zucchero **sugar**

Sightseeing

Si può visitare…? **Can one visit…?**
Suonare il campanello **ring the bell**
aperto/a **open**
chiuso/a **closed**
chiuso per la festa/ferie/restauro **closed for the festival/holidays/restoration**
Is it possible to see the church? È possibile visitare la chiesa?
We have come a long way just to see… Siamo venuti da lontano proprio per visitare…

At the Shops

What time do you open/close? A che ora apre/chiude?
Closed for the holidays Chiuso per ferie
Pull/push Tirare/spingere
Entrance/exit Entrata/uscita
Can I help you? Posso aiutarLa?
What would you like? Che cosa desidera?
I'm just looking Stò soltanto guardando
How much does it cost? Quant'è, per favore?
How much is this? Quanto viene?
Do you take credit cards? Accettate carte di credito?
I'd like… Vorrei…
this one/that one questo/quello
Have you got…? Avete…?
We haven't got (any)… Non (ne) abbiamo…
Can I try it on? Posso provare?
the size (for clothes) la taglia
What size do you take? Qual'è la sua taglia?
the size (for shoes) il numero
Is there/do you have…? C'è…?
Yes, of course Sì, certo
That's too expensive È troppo caro
cheap economico
It's too small/big È troppo piccolo/grande
I (don't) like it (Non) mi piace
I'll take/leave it Lo prendo/lascio
Anything else? Altro?
Give me some of those Mi dia alcuni di quelli lì

Tourist Signs

abbazia (Badia) **abbey**
basilica **church**
belvedere **viewpoint**
castello **castle**
centro storico **historic centre**
chiesa **church**
duomo/Cattedrale **cathedral**
fiume **river**
giardino **garden**
lago **lake**
monastero **monastery**

monumenti **monuments**
museo **museum**
parco **park**
pinacoteca **art gallery**
ponte **bridge**
ruderi **ruins**
scavi **archaeological site**
spiaggia **beach**
tempio **temple**
torre **tower**
ufficio turistico **tourist office**

Road Signs

alt **stop**
autostrada **motorway**
avanti **go/walk**
casello **toll gate**
dare la precedenza **give way**
deviazione **diversion**
divieto di passaggio/senso vietato
no entry
divieto di sosta/sosta vietata
no parking
entrata **entrance**
galleria **tunnel**
incrocio **crossroads**
limite di velocità **speed limit**
parcheggio **parking**
pedaggio **toll road**
pericolo **danger**
rallentare **slow down**
rimozione forzata **parked cars will
be towed away**
semaforo **traffic lights**
senso unico **one-way street**
sentiero **footpath**
solo uscita **no entry**
strada chiusa **road closed**
strada interrotta **road blocked**
strada senza uscita/vicolo cieco
dead end
tangenziale **ring road/bypass**
uscita **exit**
vietato il sorpasso **no overtaking**
vietato il transito **no thoroughfare**

a (half) kilo *un (mezzo) chilo*
100/200 grams *un etto/due etti*
more/less *più/meno*
with/without *con/senza*
a little *un pochino*
That's enough/No more *Basta così*

Types of Shop

antique dealer *l'antiquario*
bakery/cake shop *la
panetteria/pasticceria*
bank *la banca*
bookshop *la libreria*
boutique *il negozio di moda*
bureau de change *il cambio*
butcher *la macelleria*
chemist *la farmacia*
delicatessen *la salumeria*
department store *il grande
magazzino*
dry cleaner *la tintoria*
fishmonger *la pescheria*
florist *il fioraio*
food shop *l'alimentari*
greengrocer *il fruttivendolo*
grocer *l'alimentari*
hairdresser *il parrucchiere*
ice-cream parlour *la gelateria*
jeweller *il gioielliere*
post office *l'ufficio postale*
shoe shop *il negozio di scarpe*
supermarket *il supermercato*
tobacconist *il tabaccaio*

Travelling

Transport

airport *l'aeroporto*
arrivals/departures *arrivi/partenze*
boat *la barca*
bus *l'autobus/il pullman*
bus station *l'autostazione*
car *la macchina*
ferry *il traghetto*
ferry terminal *la stazione marittima*
first/second class *la prima/seconda
classe*
flight *il volo*
left-luggage office *il deposito bagagli*
motorway *l'autostrada*
no smoking *vietato fumare*
platform *il binario*
railway station *la stazione (ferroviaria)*
return/single ticket *un biglietto di
andata e ritorno/di andata sola*
sleeping car *la carrozza letti/il
vagone letto*
smokers/non-smokers *fumatori/
non-fumatori*
stop *la fermata*
taxi *il taxi*
ticket office *la biglietteria*
train *il treno*

At the Airport

**Where's the office of British
Airways/Alitalia?** *Dov'è l'ufficio
della British Airways/dell'Alitalia?*
I'd like to book a flight to Venice
Vorrei prenotare un volo per Venezia
When is the next flight to...? *Quando
parte il prossimo aereo per...?*
My suitcase has got lost *La mia
valigia è andata persa*
The flight has been delayed *Il volo
è rimandato*
The flight has been cancelled *Il volo
è stato cancellato*

At the Station

Can you help me please? *Mi può
aiutare, per favore?*
Where can I buy tickets? *Dove
posso fare i biglietti?*
at the ticket office/at the counter
alla biglietteria/allo sportello
When does the train leave/arrive?
A che ora parte/arriva il treno?
Can I book a seat? *Posso prenotare
un posto?*
Are there any seats available?
Ci sono ancora posti liberi?
Is this seat free/taken? *É libero/
occupato questo posto?*
You'll have to pay a supplement
Deve pagare un supplemento
Do I have to change? *Devo
cambiare?*
You need to change in Rome
Bisogna cambiare a Roma
**Which platform does the train leave
from?** *Da quale binario parte il treno?*
The train leaves from platform one
Il treno parte dal binario uno

**When is the next train/bus for
Naples?** *Quando parte il prossimo
treno/pullman per Napoli?*
When does the bus leave for Siena?
Quando parte l'autobus per Siena?
How long will it take to get there?
Quanto tempo ci vuole per arrivare?
Is this the right stop? *È la fermata
giusta?*
The train is late *Il treno è in ritardo*
Can you tell me where to get off?
Mi può dire dove devo scendere?

Directions

right/left *a destra/a sinistra*
first left/second right *la prima a
sinistra/la seconda a destra*
Turn to the right/left *Gira a
destra/sinistra*
Go straight on *Va sempre diritto*
up/down *su/giù*
traffic lights *il semaforo*
junction *l'incrocio, il bivio*
Where is...? *Dov'è...?*
Where are...? *Dove sono...?*
**Where is the nearest bank/
petrol station/bus stop/
hotel/garage?** *Dov'è la banca/il
benzinaio/la fermata di autobus/
l'albergo/l'officina più vicino/a?*
How do I get there? *Come si può
andare/faccio per arrivare a...?*
How long does it take to get to...?
*Quanto tempo ci vuole per
andare a...?*

On the Road

Where can I rent a car? *Dove posso
noleggiare una macchina?*
**Is comprehensive insurance
included?** *È completamente
assicurata?*
Is it insured for another driver?
È assicurata per un altro guidatore?
driving licence *la patente (di guida)*
petrol *la benzina*
petrol station/garage *la stazione
di servizio*
Fill it up *Faccia il pieno*
lead free/unleaded/diesel *senza
piombo/benzina verde/diesel*

Emergencies

Help! *Aiuto!*
Stop! *Fermate!*
I've had an accident *Ho avuto
un incidente*
Call a doctor *Per favore, chiami
un medico*
**Call an ambulance/the police/
the fire brigade** *Chiami
un'ambulanza/la Polizia/
i Carabinieri/i pompieri*
Where is the nearest hospital?
Dov'è l'ospedale più vicino?
I would like to report a theft
Voglio denunciare un furto

FURTHER READING

General

Bitter Almonds, by Mary Taylor Simeti and Maria Grammatico. Poignant memoir of a much-fêted Sicilian chef and former nun, and a collection of her recipes.
The Dark Heart of Italy, by Tobias Jones. A provocative portrait of Italy highlighting the interplay between politics, society and crime.
The Italians, by Luigi Barzini. Originally published in the sixties, this is still worthwhile reading for the frankness of Barzini's portrait of his fellow countrymen.
La Bella Figura – A Field Guide to the Italian Mind, by Beppe Severgnini. A wry look at the paradoxes of the Italian psyche.
Cosa Nostra: A History of the Sicilian Mafia, by John Dickie. Favourably reviewed by critics.
Mafia Women, by Clare Longrigg. A courageous investigation into the changing role of women in Cosa Nostra. Compulsive reading.
The Prince, by Niccolò Machiavelli. A new translation by Peter Bondanella of Machiavelli's classic treatise on power in the Renaissance.
Slow Food: The Case for Taste, by Carlo Petrini. A book with a powerful message to challenge our attitude to eating and shopping.
Venice for Pleasure, by J.G. Links. A guide to the city – not practical, but beautifully written by a man who is passionate about his subject.

Art and Architecture

The Architecture of the Italian Renaissance, by Peter Murray. Originally published in 1967, this volume remains the classic guide to art and architecture of the Renaissance period.
Brunelleschi's Dome: The Story of the Great Cathedral in Florence, by Ross King. This book celebrates one of the greatest architectural feats ever accomplished – the dome of Santa Maria del Fiore cathedral – and its creator.
Fellini on Fellini, by Federico Fellini. A collection of essays, letters and interviews charting the film director's controversial life and work.

Italian Architecture from Michelangelo to Borromini, by Andrew Hopkins. Tracking the artistic period from the High Renaissance through Mannerism to baroque, this helps explain the background to the artistic patrimony of Florence and other Italian cities.
The Italian Painters of the Renaissance, by Bernard Berenson. Hard to find, the essays in this book provide a good guide to a number of important figures in Italian art, including Caravaggio and Giotto.
The Stones of Florence and Venice Observed, by Mary McCarthy. A travel companion which is an accessible introduction to art history.

Culture and History

The Civilisation of the Renaissance in Italy, by Jacob Burckhardt. Published in 1860, this was a defining work in the study of the Italian Renaissance. It remains an illuminating account of the myriad of developments of the era.
Florence: The Biography of a City, by Christopher Hibbert. This book weaves together the history and culture of Florence, with excellent photographs and illustrations.
The Ghetto of Venice, by Roberta Curiel. A history of the city's Jewish community.
History of Sicily, by M.I. Finley and Dennis Mack Smith. The best overall Sicilian history.
The Merchant of Prato, by Iris Origo. An intimate and accessible account of the life of a 14th-century Italian merchant, which Origo has pieced together from a huge cache of letters and documents unearthed in 1870.
The Oxford Illustrated History of Italy, by George Holmes. An extensive, though concise, insight into Italy's colourful past for those who want a deeper understanding of the country as a whole.
The Rise and Fall of the House of Medici, by Christopher Hibbert. By an author who has written extensively on Florence, this book provides a witty insight into the dynasty which ruled Florence and are responsible for gathering much of the art to be found there today.

Other Insight Guides

The books and maps published by Insight Guides include comprehensive coverage of Italy. **Insight Guides** to Northern Italy, Southern Italy, Tuscany, Sardinia and Sicily. Insight's highly successful **City Guide** series includes Rome, Florence & Siena and Venice. Insight **Pocket Guides** are itinerary-based guides with full-colour pull-out maps. Titles in the series include Bologna, Milan, and Sardinia. Also available:
Insight Smart Guides cover Rome and Venice in an easily portable and convenient format in handy A–Z sections.
Insight Fleximaps to Florence, Milan, Italian Lakes, Rome, Sicily, Tuscany.

Send Us Your Thoughts

We do our best to ensure the information in our books is as accurate and up-to-date as possible. The books are updated on a regular basis using local contacts, who painstakingly add, amend and correct as required. However, some details (such as telephone numbers and opening times) are liable to change, and we are ultimately reliant on our readers to put us in the picture.

We welcome your feedback, especially your experience of using the book "on the road". Maybe we recommended a hotel that you liked (or another that you didn't), or you came across a great bar or new attraction we missed.

We will acknowledge all contributions, and we'll offer an Insight Guide to the best letters received.

Please write to us at:
**Insight Guides
PO Box 7910
London SE1 1WE
United Kingdom**
Or email us at:
insight@apaguide.co.uk

ART & PHOTO CREDITS

PICTURE SPREADS

INSIGHT GUIDE
ITALY

Cartographic Editor Zoë Goodwin

Production Linton Donaldson

Design Consultants
Klaus Geisler, Graham Mitchener

Picture Research Hilary Genin

INDEX

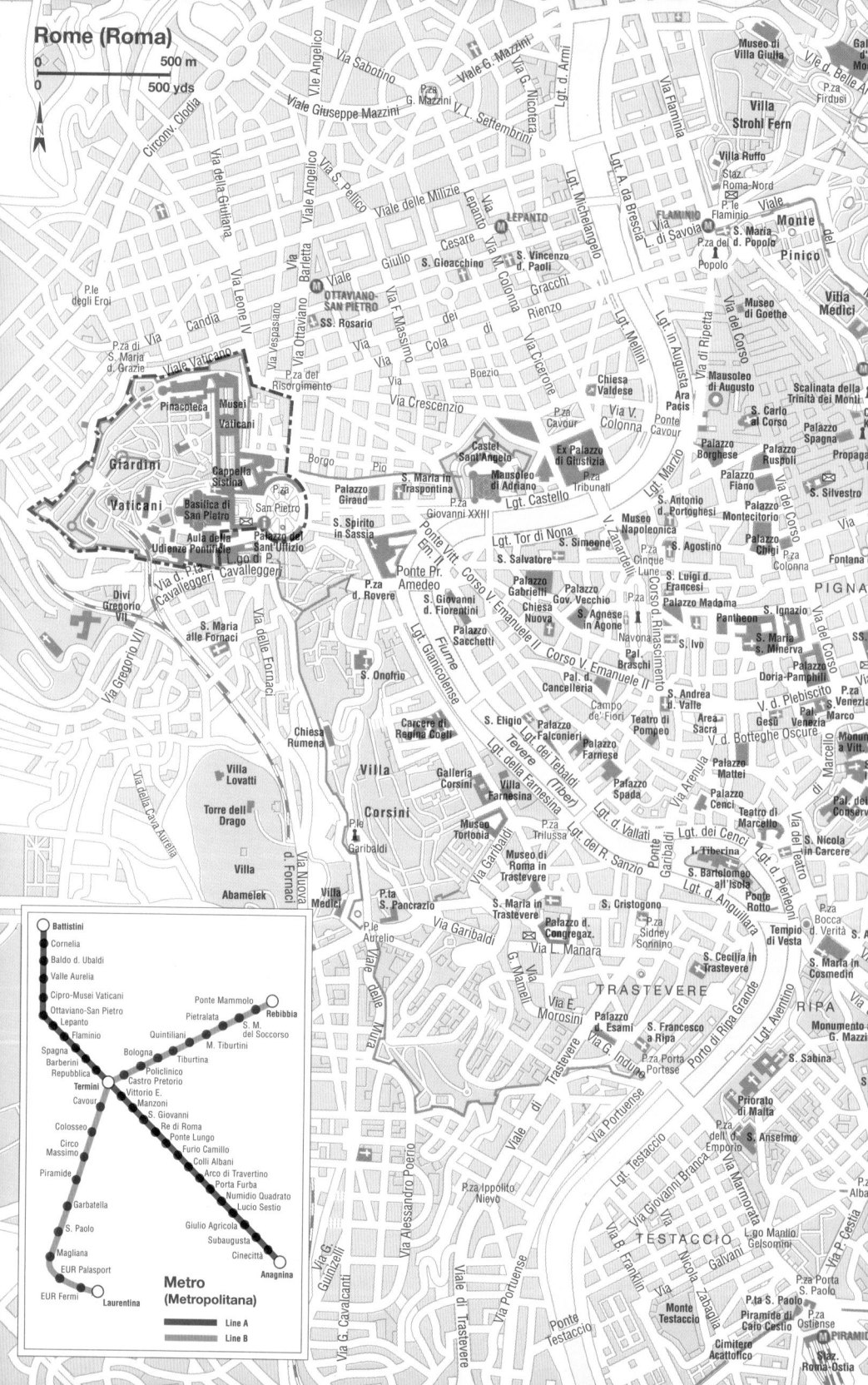

Rome (Roma)

0   500 m
0   500 yds

N

Via Sabotino
Viale G. Mazzini
Via G. Mazzini
Viale Giuseppe Mazzini
V. L. Settembrini
Via L. Nicotera
Via d. Armi
Via Flaminia

Museo di Villa Giulia
Viale d. Belle A.
P.za Firdusi
Gal. d' Mor

Villa Strohl Fern

Villa Ruffo
Staz. Roma-Nord
Via Flaminio

FLAMINIO
Viale
P.za del d. Popolo
Popolo

Monte Pinico

Villa Medici

Via Angelico
Via S. Pellico
Viale delle Milizie
Cesare
Giulio
S. Gioacchino
S. Vincenzo d. Paoli
Via Col. Colonna
Gracchi
Rienzo
Via Michelangelo
Lgt. A. da Brescia
Lgt. Michelangelo
L. di Savoia
P.za del d. Popolo

Via Leone IV
Viale Vaticano
Pinacoteca
Musei Vaticani
Cappella Sistina
Giardini
Vaticani
Basilica di San Pietro
Aula della Udienze Pontificie
Palazzo del Sant'Uffizio

Museo di Goethe
S. Maria d. Grazie
P.za di S. Maria d. Grazie

Mausoleo di Augusto
Scalinata della Trinità dei Monti
S. Carlo al Corso
Palazzo Spagna
Propaga

Palazzo Borghese
Palazzo Ruspoli
S. Silvestro

PIGNA

TRASTEVERE

RIPA

TESTACCIO

Metro (Metropolitana)

Battistini
Cornelia
Baldo d. Ubaldi
Valle Aurelia
Cipro-Musei Vaticani
Ottaviano-San Pietro
Lepanto
Flaminio
Spagna
Barberini
Repubblica
Termini
Cavour
Colosseo
Circo Massimo
Piramide
Garbatella
S. Paolo
Magliana
EUR Palasport
EUR Fermi
Laurentina

Ponte Mammolo
Pietralata
Rebibbia
Quintiliani
S. M. del Soccorso
M. Tiburtini
Bologna
Tiburtina
Policlinico
Castro Pretorio
Vittorio E.
Manzoni
S. Giovanni
Re di Roma
Ponte Lungo
Furio Camillo
Colli Albani
Arco di Travertino
Porta Furba
Numidio Quadrato
Lucio Sestio
Giulio Agricola
Subaugusta
Cinecittà
Anagnina

Line A
Line B